# The Structure of Russian History

# The Structure of
# Russian History

## INTERPRETIVE ESSAYS

EDITED BY
## Michael Cherniavsky    *State University of New York at Albany*
*Columbia University*

RANDOM HOUSE  NEW YORK

Library of Congress Catalog Card Number: 73-98271

Manufactured in the United States of America. Printed and Bound by Kingsport Press, Inc.,
Kingsport, Tenn.

Designed by Andrew Zutis

First Edition
9876543

# Contents

## Aspects of Imperial Nineteenth-Century Russia

# Introduction

HE PURPOSE OF this collection is to present, in convenient form, some of the most recent Western interpretive scholarship on the significant problems of Russian history.

There are many articles in the field of Russian history that are descriptive, that tell us new facts, recount a story, and describe the course of events. Quite a few are of high quality and extremely useful to the scholar and the student. But the criterion of selection for this volume was interpretation, with the focus on problematics. Though limited by considerations of space, the articles do touch at least on the main issues of Russian historiography: testing the older interpretations, finding new patterns and solutions, and rearranging well-known facts.

In "Russia's Byzantine Heritage," Professor Dmitri Obolensky takes up a very old problem, encrusted with clichés and prejudices, and shows the methodological and substantive mistakes committed in dealing with this major fact of early Russian history as well as the direction that the study of this subject should take. As the other side of the same coin, Professor Ihor Ševčenko demonstrates with extraordinary erudition and finesse the substantive content of this heritage in the realm of political theory for later mediaeval Russian history. And, to complete the Byzantine strand, the essay "Moscow the Third Rome" by the late Dimitri Strémooukhoff reexamines the origin and the significance of that notorious epithet, sweeping away the traditional exaggerations and placing it within a proper and limited historical context.

The problem of the Mongol conquest of Russia and the ensuing two and a half centuries of the "Mongol Yoke" is even more loaded with bias, preconceptions, and traditional misrepresentations than that of the Byzantine heritage. Michel Roublev's study breaks through this wall of abstractions and suggests both an extremely convincing and highly provocative answer to the question "Just what were the cost and the significance of the Mongol domination for mediaeval Russia?" My essay "Khan or Basileus" tries to determine the ideological consequences of the Mongol period and to suggest how they tie in with or affect Russian mediaeval political theory, studied in its Byzantine aspects by the other scholars represented here.

Father Georges Florovsky's "Old Russian Culture" is a tour de force, an original synthesis of the first seven centuries of Russian history, while my article on the Old Believers is an attempt, from a quite different point of view, to re-examine the confrontation of mediaeval Russia, the Russian people, with the emerging secular state in the course of the seventeenth century. This secular state, the absolutist gentry monarchy of the eighteenth century, presents us with one of the most curious historiographic abortions—the idea of "Westerniza-tion." This is not the place to discuss the origins and history of the extraordinary semantic fallacy that made the word "west," signifying direction, become "the West," a place—one that is a total abstraction, moving around in time and from place to place according to the political and cultural prejudices of a particular observer. The articles of Marc Raeff and Henry L. Roberts break up this abstraction, "Westernization," endow it with substance, and indicate the proper methodology for using such a concept historically. And Raeff's study on the education of the Russian gentry—the ruling class—demonstrates the concept of "Westernization" in its concreteness, with all the modifications and limitations that the historical record of daily life brings to great and dangerous generaliza-tions. And, again as the other side of the same coin, the economic studies of Arcadius Kahan describe, for the first time, the actual cost of this new culture, the amazingly small number of those who could afford and absorb it, and, by implication, the unique tension within a ruling class that, in its mass, was too poor to afford the advantages of its exclusive privileges.

The studies on the nineteenth and early twentieth centuries collected here fall into two groups. One of them is made up of the articles of Leopold H. Haimson, which show in convincing detail, and also for the first time I believe, the political, social, and psychological processes of Russia's prerevolutionary period. The other group is made up of Professor Alexander Gershenkron's article on Russian economic development, the articles on bureaucracy and on Russian literature by Sidney Monas, and the study of Russian art by Alain Besançon. All of the studies are broad and sweeping, based as they are on the well-known history of modern Russia; and all of them, individually and collectively, demonstrate brilliantly the tensions and connections between the history of a complex society and its style and culture.

These articles were not chosen with the idea of "originality at all costs." The scholars published here disagree with one another on many issues, and no attempt has been made to provide complete coverage—to discuss all the impor-tant problems in Russian history. Yet one must note that virtually all the articles do offer a new and original interpretation and that, despite all disagreements, there is a unity—a questing and sceptical spirit—in the volume. Considering that all but three of these studies are by American scholars and that the oldest of them dates back only to 1950, their range and scope are quite astonishing for they span the millennium from reinterpretations of ancient Russian culture to a new con-ception of the origins of the Russian Revolution.

As a whole, this collection, then, represents classic "revisionism," a new, vigorous, and, hopefully, continuing reinterpretation of Russian history by scholars no longer satisfied with the framework provided by the great Kliuch-evsky a century ago (a framework that has dominated Western scholarship in the field of Russian history ever since). These scholars are asking new questions of old evidence and are getting new answers, always aware that many historical problems remain for us to work on, that the answers change, and that, in this sense, the structure of Russian history will never be completed. If it is the chief task of the historian to ask questions and pose problems rather than to settle them, these essays represent historical scholarship of the highest order.

MICHAEL CHERNIAVSKY

# Aspects of Mediaeval Russia

# Russia's Byzantine Heritage

DMITRI OBOLENSKY

The title of this essay might seem to suffer from the measure of ambiguity attached to the term "heritage." A heritage, bequeathed in the past, might still be possessed by its recipient; or it might have subsequently been lost or abandoned. "Russia's Byzantine heritage" might thus mean either a quasi-permanent, and still existing, ingredient of Russian civilization, or a set of influences formerly exerted upon Russia by Byzantium which can no longer be detected at the present time. In theory this distinction is somewhat artificial, for on the plane of history no important element in a country's past is ever completely lost, and, if we assume that the "Byzantine heritage" was once an essential factor of Russian culture and if no trace of this heritage were apparent in that culture today, we could not for this reason deny *a priori* that the influence of Byzantium continues to condition the historical background of present-day Russia. In practice, however, the distinction has its importance; and it is implicit in the contrast between two methods by which the problem of "Russia's Byzantine heritage" is sometimes approached today. There are those who, starting from the present, try and work back to the past: there is much in contemporary Russia that seems unfamiliar and puzzling to the modern Western observer—ideas, institutions, and methods of government that seem to run counter to the basic trends of his own culture; and so, wishing to understand the origin and meaning of these strange phantoms, he is tempted to single out those which appear to him most striking and to trace them back as far as possible into Russia's past history. Our observer could scarcely fail to remark that a strong dose of Byzantine influence is a feature that distinguishes the medieval history of Russia from that of western Europe; and if, furthermore, his reading of East Roman history will have suggested to him some traits of similarity between the institutions of Byzantium and those of Soviet Russia, he will be inclined to conclude that the similarity is a proof of historical filiation. The other method implies a reverse process, from the past towards the present: a study of the culture and

FROM Dmitri Obolensky, "Russia's Byzantine Heritage," *Oxford Slavonic Papers*, I (1950), 37–63. Based on two lectures delivered at Oxford in February 1949. Reprinted by permission of the author and the Clarendon Press, Oxford.

institutions of the Byzantine Empire leads to an analysis of the precise character of the influence of Byzantine civilization on medieval Russia; the most important features of this influence are then singled out, and an attempt is made to trace them down the centuries in order to discover how long they remained an effective ingredient of Russian culture.

It seems to me that both these methods are unsatisfactory. The first is based on an essentially unhistorical approach which comes near to begging the whole question and generally results in biased and spurious judgments of value passed on both medieval Russia and Byzantium. The second method conceals dangers of a more subtle kind: if one concentrates mainly upon those aspects of medieval Russian culture which are regarded as a by-product of Byzantium, abstracting them from the wider context of Russian history, there often results a certain lack of proportion, facts of secondary importance being given undue prominence and vice versa. This approach, moreover, is particularly open to the danger, from which historians are never totally immune, of confusing a derivation with an explanation, of forgetting that any set of circumstances or events can never be fully understood except in the whole context of its own development, and of falling a prey to what Marc Bloch has called *l'idole des origines.*[1]

An historically valid approach to the problem of Russia's Byzantine heritage would thus exclude both an endeavour to "read back" any features of contemporary Russian culture to a hypothetical Byzantine prototype and an attempt to isolate the Byzantine features of Russian medieval culture from the whole context of Russian history in order to follow their development and fortune down the ages. It is only, I would suggest, within a wider framework and as part of a larger picture that the problem of Russia's Byzantine heritage can successfully be studied by the historian. Such a wider framework would include not only the history of Russia, of the Byzantine Empire, and of their mutual relations in the field of culture; Russia's connections with the European and Asiatic worlds that surrounded and affected her during different periods of her history should also form part of the picture.

An attempt to approach the problem from all these angles would far exceed the scope of an essay, whose aim can be no more than to suggest a few general topics for reflection. These topics might be expressed in the form of questions: how far can Russian history be adequately studied with special reference to the history and culture of the Byzantine Empire? What would be the implications of such a study from the wider field of view of European history? And these two questions bring a third one in their wake, which, however briefly and inadequately, must be answered in conclusion: what is the specific nature of Russia's Byzantine heritage?

I believe that today, at least in those countries where scholarship is free from the control of the State, we are witnessing a reaction against the nationalistic interpretation of history. It can no longer be reasonably claimed that the history of any single nation of the modern European world can successfully be studied in isolation from the history of other countries. Those who would wish to apply the modern notion of the autarchic sovereign state to the writing of history may paint a flattering and idealized picture of their own nation's past, but it would be a picture bearing but little resemblance to reality. Professor Toynbee has convincingly argued that the national state is not "an intelligible field of historical study" and has illustrated this thesis with special reference to the history of England. In his opinion, the history of an individual nation becomes fully intelligible only if studied as part of a larger whole, a Society or a Civilization. In the case of English history this civilization is Western Christendom.[2]

Now it seems to me that to illustrate the truth of Professor Toynbee's thesis, Russian history is an equally good test case, and that the results, if we apply here this method of investigation, would be no less revealing. If we survey the course of Russian history the following episodes might be taken to represent its main chapters: (1) the conversion of the Russians from Slavonic paganism to Byzantine Christianity, which began on a large scale in the late tenth century; (2) the Mongol yoke which lay on most of Russia from 1240 to 1480; (3) the growth of the religious nationalism of the sixteenth-century Moscow autocrats, exemplified in the formula "Moscow the Third Rome"; (4) the ecclesiastical schism of the Old Believers in the seventh decade of the seventeenth century; (5) the Westernizing reforms of Peter the Great in the first quarter of the eighteenth century; (6) the liberal reforms of Alexander II in the seventh decade of the nineteenth century; (7) the Bolshevik Revolution of 1917.

It should not be difficult to show that each of these chapters illustrates Russia's close dependence on the outside world; for none of them is fully intelligible unless we view it against the background of one or several civilizations more extensive than Russia herself. (i) The conversion of the Russians to Christianity was an event which united the scattered tribes of the Eastern Slavs into a single state, linked to Byzantium by a common religion, and made that state a member of the Christian community of nations. (ii) The period of Mongol domination is generally regarded—and with some justification—as that of Russia's "withdrawal into the wilderness." Yet Russia was then a dependency of a Turko-Mongol Empire which was affiliated to the cultural centres of central Asia, and the Golden Horde has left its mark on Russian history; nor was Russia's isolation from Europe in the fourteenth and fifteenth centuries as complete as is commonly supposed: western and south-western Russia were then part of a Lithuanian-Polish State, closely associated with western Europe by religion and culture; the cities of north-western Russia were commercially linked with Germany through the Hanseatic League; while Muscovy itself, the most segregated part of Russia, was in those centuries opened to a fresh flow of cultural influences from Byzantium and the south Slavonic countries. (iii) The great imperial dream of the sixteenth century and the attribution by Russian clerics to the Tsars of Muscovy of religious pre-eminence throughout the world were partly due, no doubt, to factors of Russia's own history: national consciousness and pride were intensified by the territorial expansion of Muscovy in the late fifteenth and early sixteenth centuries and by the liberation from the Tatar yoke in 1480. But the new Russian imperialism was also powerfully stimulated by the growth of diplomatic relations with the powers of central and northern Europe and by the claim of the Muscovite rulers, consciously formulated in the late fifteenth century, to those remaining lands of their ancestral "patrimony" which formed part of the Lithuanian-Polish State. And it is significant that the stimulus which created and justified the doctrine of "Moscow the Third Rome" came from outside: Byzantium had fallen to the Turks—a just punishment for tampering with the purity of the Orthodox faith and signing with the Latins the detestable Union of Florence; the First Rome had long ago lapsed into heresy; the Second Rome, Constantinople, was in the hands of the infidels: the Imperial mantle should now fall by every right on Moscow, the Third Rome; "and a fourth there will not be." So argued the official panegyrists of Holy Russia in the sixteenth century. It is surely remarkable that this extreme glorification of Russian religious nationalism was, in one of its aspects, a by-product of an event of world-wide importance—the fall of Byzantium—and that the formula which sustained it was, it would seem, derived from political ideas current in fourteenth-century Bulgaria.[3] Finally, the doctrine of the divinely ordained and universal Monarchy, which gave religious sanction to the theory of "Moscow the Third Rome" and political significance to Ivan the Terrible's Imperial coronation in 1547, can be traced back in direct line of ascent to the Byzantine theory of the Christian Empire, adapted from the political philosophy of Hellenism in the fourth century of our era.

(iv) The great religious schism of the seventeenth century, due to the revolt of the "Old Believers" against the liturgical reforms of the Patriarch Nikon, was in one sense the result of Russian national exclusiveness: the Old Believers on the stake and in the Tsar's torture chambers were convinced that they were dying and suffering for the ideal of Holy Russia, where alone the true faith shone as brightly as the sun. This, indeed, would seem to be the very essence of religious separativeness, of deliberate cultural isolation; yet in this case also the stimulus came from outside: the Old Believers fought desperately, and unsuccessfully, against foreign influences in Russian life. Nikon, the servant of Antichrist, would impose on his Church the Scriptural texts and liturgical practice of the contemporary Greeks; he had declared himself: "I am a Russian . . . but my faith and religion are Greek."[4] And the Old Believers preferred to rend the Russian Church in two rather than accept these foreign innovations. (v) The reforms of Peter the Great were patently a response to the impact of outside forces, pressing on Russia from the West; their purpose was to transform Russia's military machinery, social structure, and economic life in accordance with Western institutions and with the help of Western technology. (vi) Alexander II's reforms, particularly the emancipation of the serfs, were both a product of Western liberalism and a consequence of the Crimean War; they, too, aimed at giving Russia the efficient machinery of a progressive Western State. (vii) Finally, the Bolshevik Revolution and the Soviet régime to which it gave birth were at least in part the product of forces which arose and developed outside Russia: the two corner-stones of the Soviet State—Marxism and technology— were borrowed by Russia from the West.

These seven examples, taken from the main chapters of Russian history, show quite clearly that at no time was Russia a self-contained unit and that we cannot understand her history in terms of cultural self-sufficiency. "We have," to quote Professor Toynbee, "to think in terms of the whole and not of the parts; to see the chapters of the story as events in the life of the society and not of some particular member; and to follow the fortunes of the members, not separately but concurrently, as variations on a single theme or as contributions to an orchestra which are significant as a harmony but have no meaning as so many separate series of notes. In so far as we succeed in studying history from this point of view, we find that order arises out of chaos in our minds and that we begin to understand what was not intelligible before."[5]

Can we discover a larger "whole," a civilization of which Russia is a part and from whose standpoint her history will become intelligible?

Our survey of the main chapters of Russian history will have suggested that at different periods of her history Russia was more or less closely connected with Asia, western Europe, and Byzantium. Her relations with Asia were maintained through the nomadic or semi-nomadic empires which successive waves of invaders from the dawn of Slavonic history to the fourteenth century of the Christian era established in the Pontic steppes. Some of them—especially the Khazars in the eighth century, the Cumans in the twelfth, and the Golden Horde in the fourteenth—entered into close relations with the Eastern Slavs and undoubtedly affected their destiny. And at least twice in her history Russia seemed on the verge of becoming an Oriental Empire, with her face and policy turned towards the East: the first occasion was in the tenth century, when the Viking rulers of Russia made an attempt to gain control of the Caspian and Caucasus regions and when Vladimir of Kiev, before deciding to accept Christianity in the name of his people, hesitated for a moment before the beckoning hand of Islam; the second opportunity occurred in the middle of the sixteenth century, when Ivan IV of Moscow captured the Tatar strongholds of Kazan and Astrakhan: this double event, which marked the final victory of the agriculturist and town-dweller over the Eurasian horseman of the steppe, brought about the incorporation of large regions of Islamic culture into the new Russian Empire, signified the Tsar's assumption of the political heritage of the Tatar Khan, and started Russia's career of expansion towards Siberia and the Pacific. Yet the importance of Russia's connections with Asia should not be exaggerated. The recent "Eurasian" school of Russian historians, while holding that the whole territory of the Soviet Union forms a sub-continent separate from both Europe and Asia, has nevertheless laid the main emphasis on the Asiatic, "Turanian," affinities of Russian civilization.[6] It is very doubtful whether much evidence could be found to support this interpretation. The Tatars have often enough been held responsible for all the sins of Russia, though historians are still divided on the question of the extent of the influence exerted by the Golden Horde on Russian culture. On the whole, it does not seem that this influence was very considerable. And we must not in any case forget that Russia's conversion to Christianity separated her from Asia by a moral and

cultural gulf which not even the thousand-year-long intercourse with her subsequent Asiatic rulers and subjects was able to bridge. It is not to the East that
we must look in our search for Russia's parent civilization.

Does "the West"—the Christian and post-Christian countries of western
and central Europe—provide a more satisfactory alternative? In our survey
of the seven main chapters of Russian history, the last three, covering the
period from the beginning of the eighteenth century to the present day, were
concerned with the direct effect of Western techniques, institutions, and ideas
upon Russia. This in itself suggests that Russia's process of "Westernization,"
which has progressed at an increasing tempo during the past three centuries,
has been a more important and vital factor in her cultural history than her
connections with Asia. Nor has she been a mere recipient: since the time of
Peter the Great Russia has formed an inseparable part of the European state
system; for more than a century she has powerfully contributed to European
culture, in literature and music, in science and scholarship, and in recent years
she has re-exported to the West, in a new and to some extent characteristically
Russian form, the creed and practice of Marxist Socialism.

Yet we may hesitate to place modern Russia unreservedly within the pale of
that "Western" civilization which originated in the Western territories of the
Roman Empire, the ecclesiastical orbit of the Papacy and the political domains
of the Carolingian State, and gradually extended its influence over the greater
part of the inhabited globe. Resistance and hostility to all forms of Western
Christianity are ingrained in a large proportion of Russians, particularly sometimes in those who have ceased to concern themselves greatly about religion.
Most educated Russians have long been conscious of a dichotomy in their
cultural inheritance; as early as the beginning of the seventeenth century an
acute Russian observer remarked: "we are turning our backs to one another:
some of us look to the East, others to the West."[7] Among the historical and
philosophical problems debated by Russian thinkers in the nineteenth century
none was so constantly advanced and led to such passionate searchings of heart
as the question of Russia's status and destiny: was she part of Europe or a
separate world *sui generis*; should she look to the "West" or the "East?" And
the ambiguity in Russia's relations with the West is forcibly apparent at the
present time, when a political creed, a social programme, and an industrial
technology, all of which are Western in origin, are used from a Russian base of
operations to criticize and assail the very foundations of contemporary Western
society. It is also significant that the Westernization of Russia in the eighteenth
and nineteenth centuries created a cultural dichotomy, a drawback from which
Muscovy, for all its social disunity, had not appreciably suffered. The influence
of Polish education and manners in the seventeenth century, Peter the Great's
cultural reforms, the assimilation of French literature and German philosophy by the intelligentsia, the impact on Russia of the Industrial Revolution,
the spread of Socialism and Marxism, these were practically limited in their
effects to the upper class and educated minority. The life and outlook of the
peasants—the overwhelming majority of the population—remained, at least

until the twentieth century, untouched by these alien importations. In the Russian villages life was lived as it had been for centuries past. The faith and toil of the humble folk, their strong belief in God, their veneration of the holy man, the monk, and the pilgrim, the annual cycle of work and prayer, their legends, costumes, and folk-songs, these had not altered very much since the dawn of Russian history. It may be said, in fact, that in the eighteenth and nineteenth centuries Russia was living under a dual dispensation: the ruling minority —Westernized nobles, technicians, and the intelligentsia—educated in a cosmopolitan spirit, frequently out of touch with the native culture and even with the faith of their fathers, proselytes of the modern West; and, on the other hand, the mass of the peasants who continued to live in strict accordance with the rules and ethos inherited from their remote ancestors. It would thus seem impossible to regard Russia as an offshoot or a part of modern "Western" Civilization; for even during the last two centuries, when Western influences in Russia were at their strongest, some important aspects of her life and history cannot be explained in terms of this civilization.

It will be noticed that our attempt to discover a larger cultural unit in whose terms Russian history may become intelligible has so far been reduced to a search for a culture which has exerted a sufficiently profound and lasting influence on Russia to deserve to be considered as Russia's parent civilization. This method of investigation will prove helpful if we shift our attention once more to the medieval chapters of Russian history. There can be no doubt that the influence of Byzantium on Russian history and culture was far more profound and permanent than that of the Turko-Mongol hordes and more homogeneous than that of the modern West. Russia owes her religion and the greater part of her medieval culture to the Byzantine Empire, both directly, through her connections with Constantinople in the ninth and tenth centuries, and indirectly, through the Slavo-Byzantine schools of the tenth-century Bulgaria. Much has been written of late on the remarkable and precocious culture of Kievan Russia, but there is still scope for an essay which would fully reveal the extent to which it was indebted to the civilization of East Rome.[8] The eleventh and twelfth centuries, I would suggest, might prove particularly suited to such an investigation: Byzantine civilization was then in its prime, its attractive power still at its height; Russia was a young and growing nation, with no heavy burden of inherited traditions, no very rigid view of herself or her neighbours: such conditions breed tolerance and favour intercourse and could reveal, from behind the often obstructive screen of later importations, some salient features of her original culture. Such an essay might well be devoted to an illustration of Mr. Sumner's comprehensive formula: "Byzantium brought to Russia five gifts: her religion, her law, her view of the world, her art and writing."[9] The spread of Byzantine Christianity to Russia in the tenth century, the growth of the young Russian Church under the leadership of Constantinople, and the first flowering of Russian monasticism in the eleventh and twelfth centuries; the introduction into Russia of Byzantine law—which was an extension of Roman law—and its fusion, and sometimes clash, with the customary law of the Eastern

Slavs; the radiation of Byzantine art of the Macedonian and Comnenian periods to Russia, where it achieved some of its greatest works and informed the first native schools of architecture and painting; the adoption by the Russians, mainly through Bulgaria, of the Slavonic alphabet and vernacular literature, a gift from Byzantium which enabled them at the dawn of their Christian life to produce works of literature which rank high in the history of their culture; and finally, the question of how far the Russians in the Kiev period assimilated "the thought-world of East Rome"[10]—an important but difficult question, where generalizations and hasty conclusions are especially dangerous: these are some of the problems that would be faced in such a study.

A much-needed essay could also be written on the second and more imperfectly known phase of Russia's relations with Byzantium, the period between 1250 and 1450. And here two awkward questions arise: did Russia really "relapse into barbarism"[11] for two centuries after the Tatar invasion? and how far did the Mongol yoke seal her off from the civilizing influence of the Byzantine world? It is not easy to answer these questions precisely, but it may be suggested that the political catastrophe of the Mongol invasion did not break the continuity in Russian culture nor substantially interrupt the flow of Balkan influence into Russia: the latter, indeed, grew particularly strong in the fourteenth and fifteenth centuries; the new literary trends and the theory and practice of contemplative monasticism, two of the most characteristic features of those centuries of Russian history, were imported from Byzantium, Mount Athos, and the Balkan countries; while, in the field of art, the remarkable school of painting of Novgorod in this period was profoundly influenced by the last great phase of Byzantine art, in the age of the Palaeologi.[12]

It will be observed that the influence exerted by Byzantine civilization on Russia between the tenth and the fifteenth centuries was markedly different in character and scope from the impact of western Europe after the middle of the seventeenth century; the latter, we have seen, split Russian society into two and created a gulf between the ruling and educated minority on the one hand and the peasantry on the other; Byzantine influence, which spread to Russia through the medium of Christianity and the channel of the upper class, was often slow in filtering down to the other sections of society; but filter down it did, and over the course of the Middle Ages it pervaded in varying degrees the whole of Russian society from the prince to the peasant, leaving practically no aspect of Russian life untouched.[13]

We may thus conclude that Russia's civilization was the Byzantine culture of East Rome, in whose terms Russian history remains intelligible at least until the middle of the fifteenth century. Leaving aside for the moment the task of defining and describing this civilization, we must consider how far, after the fifteenth century, Russia's parent civilization remains the "intelligible field" for the study of Russian history. There can be no doubt that a strong influence of Byzantine culture can be observed in all sections and classes of Russian society, at least until the second half of the seventeenth century. Two examples may suffice to illustrate this fact. In the early sixteenth century an authoritative spokesman of the Russian Church wrote: "by nature the Tsar is like all other men; but in authority he is like the Highest God";[14] this definition of the functions of the sacred and universal Autocrat, so characteristic of the Byzantine conception of imperial sovereignty, reads like a sentence from the pen of Constantine Porphyrogenitus or Eusebius of Caesarea. And in the second half of the seventeenth century the Archpriest Avvakum, who suffered death on the stake for refusing to accept the practice of making the sign of the cross with three as against two fingers, and reciting the triple as against the double Alleluia, and who exhorted his numerous followers to sacrifice their lives rather than accept the reforms of Nikon, signified his faith in the following words: "I hold to this even unto death, as I have received it. . . . It has been laid down before us: let it lie thus unto the ages of ages."[15] Thus did a Russian parish priest, in his heroic refusal to countenance the slightest deviation from the sacred wholeness of the liturgical practice, echo the words of the Byzantine Patriarch Photius, who wrote eight centuries previously: "even the smallest neglect of the traditions leads to the complete contempt for dogma."[16]

But, for all this persistence of Byzantine traditions, there was already much in late fifteenth- and sixteenth-century Muscovy that indicated a parting of the ways. It is often argued that, after the fall of the Byzantine Empire and the marriage of Ivan III with Zoë Palaeologa in 1472, Russia consciously took over the political heritage of Byzantium and that the theory of "Moscow the Third Rome," erected in the following century as an ideological superstructure on these events, represented the final triumph of Byzantine influence in Russia. Yet it is difficult to accept this conventional picture of a sixteenth-century Russia, Byzantinized afresh, absorbing and continuing the cultural and political traditions of East Rome. Of course, there can be no doubt that Russian Tsarism welcomed the theory that the seat of Imperial sovereignty had migrated to Moscow after the fall of Constantinople: the Tsar's adoption of Byzantine titles, heraldry, and ceremonial can be regarded as a visible symbol of this claim. But the political implications of the doctrine of "Moscow the Third Rome" do not seem to have been taken very seriously by the Tsars of that time.[17] All the attempts made by the diplomatists of the Catholic West to entice the sixteenth-century Tsars into an alliance against the Turks were ignored in Moscow, and while Pope and Holy Roman Emperor, and the Greeks themselves, were dangling before their eyes the glittering prospect of a victorious entry into Constantinople and the dream of an Orthodox Empire uniting the power of the Third Rome with the historical inheritance of the Second, the Muscovite rulers turned a deaf ear to those blandishments, and, sheltering behind the modest but authentic title of "Sovereign of All Russia," merely claimed the inheritance of the Russian lands formerly possessed by their Kievan predecessors. Here, it may be suggested, is an early example of Russia's conscious turning away from the historical heritage of Byzantium: here, in the wake of the *Realpolitik* of Ivan III and Basil III and Ivan IV, the Christian universalism of East Rome was transformed and distorted within the more narrow framework of Muscovite nationalism. The really significant fact is that the beginning of Russia's turning away from her Byzantine heritage in the late fifteenth century coincided with the growth of her connections with the West; Ivan III's marriage with Zoë was a harbinger of these connections: for the niece of the last Byzantine Emperor came to Russia from Italy accompanied by a papal legate, and the marriage had been arranged in Rome; the relations then established between Russia and Renaissance Italy were paralleled by the growing Western influences in Novgorod in the late fifteenth century, which soon spread to Moscow.[18] The policy of the Muscovite rulers of that time, of Ivan III, Basil III, and even Ivan IV, has been compared to that of their Western contemporaries, a Louis XI, a Henry VII, or a Ferdinand of Spain; and it is perhaps true to say that in their autocratic policy which relied on a growing national sentiment and on the increasing need for a strong centralized state making for order, and in the means by which they pursued it—the struggle with the great nobles—they resemble more closely the contemporary monarchs of western Europe than the former emperors of East Rome.

We must not, of course, exaggerate the importance of these early connections between Muscovy and the West: until the middle of the seventeenth century soldiers and technicians, rather than ideas and institutions, formed the bulk of the Western exports to Russia. Moreover, between 1450 and 1650, with her Byzantine traditions on the wane and Western influences only slowly filtering in, Russia was developing into a world *sui generis* and fast expanding into a Eurasian Empire. Her culture, however, in these two centuries of the late Muscovite period, was still a fairly homogeneous whole and would, I believe, be still partly intelligible in terms of her Byzantine heritage. Yet in her history this was a period of transition: for when Russia, at the close of the fifteenth century, began to emerge from her "Middle Ages," she started to drift away from her Byzantine inheritance and to fall gradually into step with the political, diplomatic, and economic life of western and central Europe.

The rest of the story is better known and needs no emphasis here, save perhaps in one respect. The wholesale and spectacular policy of Westernization carried out by Peter the Great has often obscured the fact that he was merely continuing on a vaster scale and in a more drastic manner a process which had been gaining momentum from the second half of the seventeenth century. About 1650 the manners, literature, and learning of the Muscovites began to be strongly affected by the influence of Poland and of the latinized culture of the Ukraine.[19] The cultural dualism which these Western influences created in the Russian society was aggravated by the schism of the Old Believers, which alienated the various streams of popular spirituality and devotion from a now partly secularized ecclesiastical hierarchy; and both these rifts—the cultural and the religious—anticipated and prepared the profounder gulf between the ruling classes and the peasantry brought about by the Westernizing and secularizing reforms of Peter the Great.

I have already suggested that from the early eighteenth century onwards Russia was living, as it were, under a dual dispensation. The upper strata of society had exchanged the Byzantine traditions of Muscovy for the education and ethos of the modern West, while the peasantry still clung to the old way of life. Yet elements of the Byzantine tradition survived in all classes of Russian society; thus a notable section of the Russian nineteenth-century intelligentsia, the Slavophiles, for example, regarded the Orthodox tradition derived from Byzantium as their surest bulwark against the encroaching rationalism and materialism of Western "bourgeois" culture. Above all, the continuing strength of the Byzantine inheritance in modern Russia has asserted itself again and again in the form of the Orthodox Christian faith to which much of the peasantry and a section of the educated classes have remained profoundly loyal; and there is no conclusive evidence to suggest that the recent attempts of their rulers to destroy or subvert this religious allegiance have met with any notable or lasting success. Especially, perhaps, the vitality of the Byzantine heritage in Russia is manifested in the liturgy which retains a powerful hold on the mind and emotions of all those, both educated and untutored, who have not succumbed to atheism or religious indifference, and which is one of the greatest and original creations of Byzantine genius.

This dichotomy in the Russian culture of the eighteenth and nineteenth centuries shows that Byzantium, Russia's parent civilization, cannot be regarded as the "intelligible field" for the study of Russian history in this period. We have likewise examined, and rejected, the possibility that western Europe might fulfil that purpose in respect of these centuries. Can any other cultural unit be found to take up the role relinquished by Byzantium?

To answer this question we must attempt a brief definition of Byzantine civilization in terms of space and time. A compound of the Roman, Hellenistic, and Christian traditions, it can be described in terms of the geographical area over which its influence was once predominant. Originally limited to the territories of the East Roman Empire, above all to the Balkans and Asia Minor, Byzantine civilization made a thrust northward into Russia shortly before most of Asia Minor was lost to Islam. The Balkans and Russia remained its main strongholds during the remaining part of the Middle Ages. Today the area occupied by "the heirs of Byzantium" is basically the same, with the addition of the territories won for Orthodox Christianity by Russia's eastward expansion; it comprises the European lands inhabited by the Serbs, the Albanians, the Greeks, the Bulgarians, the Rumanians, and the Russians. The history of these six peoples reveals a striking similarity which to some extent overshadows their ethnic and linguistic differences; they are united by a common membership of the Eastern Orthodox Church and by the powerful influence exerted by Byzantium on their medieval culture; moreover, they were all subjected for several centuries to the rule of Asiatic empires—the Balkans to the Ottoman, Russia to the Mongol—and on emerging from their political servitude succumbed, gradually in the case of Russia, more rapidly in the case of the Balkans, to the influence of west European ideas and institutions.

It is less easy to define the limits of Byzantine civilization in time. Its beginning can be plausibly dated from the first half of the fourth century, for Professor Baynes has cogently argued that the distinctive elements of this civilization were first brought together into the melting pot in the age of Constantine.[20]

The difficulty of discovering a corresponding *terminus ad quem* became apparent
when we considered the case of Russia, where elements of Byzantine culture
have survived in various forms to the present day. It seems, however, that these
elements are too isolated from the other forms of social life to allow us to extend
the effective hegemony of Byzantine civilization in Russia beyond the beginning
of the eighteenth century. In the Balkans Byzantine civilization survived longer
and, strange though it may seem, this was due to the Turkish conquest. No more
than the Mongol rule in Russia did the *Pax Ottomanica* in the Balkans undermine the Byzantine culture of the subject peoples. In a book bearing the suggestive title of *Byzance après Byzance*,[21] the late Professor Iorga has shown the
extent to which the Byzantine inheritance was kept alive among the Christian
subjects of the Ottoman Empire; the Orthodox Church, the preciously guarded
symbol of their former greatness, presided over by the Patriarch of Constantinople, who was recognized by the Sultan as the spiritual overlord and temporal
chief of all his Christian subjects[22] and was thus able at last to vindicate his
ancient title of "Oecumenical"; the political inheritance of the former East
Roman Basileis, taken over partly by the Sultans themselves, partly by the
Rumanian princes of the sixteenth and seventeenth centuries who steeped themselves in the imperial tradition of Byzantium to a greater extent than their Russian
contemporaries, the Muscovite Tsars; the preservation of Greek literature and
Byzantine learning, fostered in the Danubian courts of the Rumanian *Domni*
and the schools of the Phanariot Greeks in Constantinople—this survival of
Byzantium under the Ottoman rule is a further example of the astonishing
vitality and continuity of its civilization. It was not until the late eighteenth
century that the East Roman heritage began to decline in the Balkans, undermined by Western influences of the Age of Enlightenment, and in the early
nineteenth century, under the impact of the ideas of the French Revolution and
modern nationalism, occurred what Iorga has called "the death of Byzantium."
Yet even then, Byzantine memories continued to influence the new Balkan
statesmen, and the appeal of Orthodox Chistianity has remained as strong
among the peoples of these countries as it has in Russia.

Our attempt to determine the limits of Byzantine civilization in space and
time has thus led us to conclude that Russia and the Balkan Orthodox countries,
which share a common inheritance from Byzantium and whose history, despite
many local differences, is similar in several important respects, can be regarded
as part of one larger cultural area. It is this area that would appear to constitute
the wider "whole," the "intelligible field" against the background of which
Russian history should be studied. The name "Byzantine civilization" is clearly
inadequate to describe this field over the whole course of medieval and modern
history, for, as we saw, the term is not applicable to Russia beyond the late
seventeenth century, or to the Balkans after the early nineteenth, in view of the
more complex and heterogeneous culture of these countries in modern times.

As a term to describe this area I would suggest "Eastern Europe." At first
sight it has certain disadvantages: the Balkans, from a geographical point of
view, are in south-eastern rather than in eastern Europe; but this argument

could be met by observing that the Iberian Peninsula, though geographically in south-western Europe, is generally included in the European "West"; the criterion in both cases is cultural rather than geographical. It might also seem unjustifiable to exclude from eastern Europe a country like Poland, which in certain periods of her history has played a prominent role in the destinies of Russia and of the Balkans; yet Poland, since the dawn of her Christian history, has derived her civilization from the Western, and particularly the Latin, world, and her cultural associations with both Russia and the Balkans have been far less intimate; indeed, there would seem to be a strong case for including Poland in central, rather than in eastern, Europe.[23]

More serious objections could be raised against the attempt to group the modern histories of Russia and the Balkans within a single unit, at least after the beginning of the eighteenth century, when Byzantine civilization, still paramount in the Balkans, had already ceased to be the "intelligible field" of Russian history. Indeed, in spite of the close relations between Muscovy and the Balkan Slavs[24] and of Russia's championship, since Peter the Great, of the cause of the Balkan Orthodox peoples, the two regions would seem to have followed divergent lines in their recent political history. Their cultural backgrounds, moreover, are far from identical, for apart from the ethnic and linguistic differences that divide the Russians from the Greeks and both from the Rumanians, the two regions have not always been subjected to the influence of the same foreign cultures. But any distinction between a "North-Eastern" and a "South-Eastern" Europe, however legitimate, must not obscure the essential fact that, in so far as their culture has been decisively moulded by the influence of Orthodox Christianity and Byzantine civilization and the history of their peoples has, since the Middle Ages, followed a similar pattern (subjection to an Asiatic yoke, followed by political emancipation and increasing Westernization), these two sub-areas constitute a single cultural unit, which may be conveniently termed Eastern Europe.[25]

There is, I would suggest, a further advantage in the term "Eastern Europe," and this brings me to my next point: how far can we really speak of a Byzantine, or East European, world essentially different in culture and historical inheritance from the Christian countries of the Latin and Germanic West? What was, and is, the exact nature of this relationship? Questions such as these only emphasize how inadequate our knowledge still is of the relations and interdependence between different regions of Europe, particularly in the Middle Ages. If our discovery and assessment of Russia's parent civilization have any meaning, this must imply that her cultural inheritance was different in some degree from that of the countries of western and central Europe whose historical fountainhead was Rome. It is indeed the fashion today to emphasize the distinction between the cultures of Byzantium and the West, to stress the contrasts between the medieval histories of eastern and western Europe. I do not wish to deny or minimize these differences, yet there seems to be a real danger of interpreting the division between East and West in too rigid and absolute a sense. In the first place, we must not imagine that the Roman and the

Byzantine spheres of influence were ever separated by a rigid geographical frontier: the medieval history of the Balkan Slavs and the fate of the Ukraine between the fourteenth and eighteenth centuries provide examples of a close interrelation between Byzantine and Western cultures; while medieval Venice was, in many respects, a Byzantine enclave in a Latin world. It is also frequently argued that the Schism of 1054, which divided Christendom into a Western and an Eastern section, for ever separated them by the barrier of an *odium theologicum*; and that this Schism was itself only a formal recognition of a gradually increasing rift between Byzantium and the West which began with the very birth of Byzantine civilization. But is this an adequate picture and the whole story? For all the theological disputes between Rome and Constantinople, the rivalry of conflicting jurisdictions, the differences of language, customs, and traditions, in spite even of Charlemagne's coronation as Emperor of the Romans, there is surely no convincing evidence to suggest that, at least until 1054, the majority of the churchmen and statesmen of East and West were not conscious of belonging to one Christian society. Would it not be truer to say that at least on two occasions, at Chalcedon in 451 and at the Festival of Orthodoxy in Constantinople in 843, the Byzantine Church triumphantly asserted against the claims of Asiatic creeds—Monophysitism and Iconoclasm—its basic heritage, Roman, Hellenistic and, as it proved, European? The often bitter contentions between the First and the Second Rome are more suggestive of a fraternal rivalry for the supreme position in Christendom than of a struggle between two alien civilizations. But we can perhaps go even farther, and ask ourselves whether the consciousness of a united Christendom did not survive the very Schism of 1054. The episcopate of East Rome might have detested what they regarded as Latin innovations in the fields of dogma, ritual and ecclesiastical discipline; though its most enlightened members could still urge their flocks to feelings of charity towards their Western brethren in Christ: some forty years after the Schism the Greek Archbishop of Bulgaria, Theophylact, severely criticized his colleagues for unjustly slandering the customs of the Latin Church.[26] And the simple folk of Byzantium, how would the Schism have appeared to them? When the Roman legates laid the Papal Bull of excommunication upon the altar of St. Sophia, could they think that the Church of Christ was being rent in twain for at least nine centuries to come? There had been schisms and excommunications before; the schisms had been healed, the excommunications lifted; was not the Universal Church the very body of Christ? And was not Rome, for all the unorthodox teaching and claims of its pontiffs, a sacred and venerable city, a revered centre of pilgrimage containing the tomb of St. Peter, prince of the Apostles? Anna Comnena is sometimes cited as proof of the hatred and contempt entertained by the East Romans for the Latin West; and she certainly says many bitter things about the ruffians of the First Crusade who caused so much trouble to her father, the Emperor Alexius. But if you reread the *Alexiad* you will probably be struck by the great difference in the tones she adopts when referring to the Crusaders and to the Bogomil heretics: these inspire her with horror and loathing; the former, for all their undesirable qualities, are still fellow-Christians. Of course, mutual antipathy and distrust between East and West increased during the twelfth century, and for this the Crusades were largely responsible. But can the picture of two mutually exclusive civilizations be reconciled with the Western influences we find in Byzantine society in the reign of Manuel Comnenus, and with the strongly pro-Latin sympathies of the Emperor, the court, and the aristocracy in the second half of the twelfth century?[27]

As one reads afresh the history of the later Roman Empire in the East one wonders sometimes whether historians have not exaggerated the significance of the events of 1054. If, in the process of gradual estrangement between Byzantium and the West, we sought for an event that seems to mark a real turning-point, we could point perhaps with better reason to the climax of the Fourth Crusade; and we would probably conclude that it was then that the folk of Byzantium, disgusted at the desecration of their hallowed City by men who called themselves Christians, finally turned away from their society and hardened their hearts to the West. If so, is not 1204 rather than 1054 the real date of the schism in the body of Christendom? Yet on further scrutiny and in the long run the first of the dates may well prove to have as little magical significance as the second. One of the many gaps which still remain in our knowledge of later Byzantine history relates to the problem of the precise nature and scope of the relations between Byzantium and western Europe, especially Italy, in the fourteenth and fifteenth centuries. But there is no doubt that, at least in the fields of learning and art, there was close and constant interpenetration. And if we asked ourselves the question: were the relations between Byzantium and the West in the age of the Palaeologi any less close than they had been under the Comnenian of the Macedonian dynasties—what would our answer be?

If it be in the negative, the picture we shall have of Byzantium and the medieval West will be of two different but closely interwoven halves of one Graeco-Roman Christian and European civilization. Neither half, on this reading, was in any real sense a self-contained unit or a fully "intelligible field of historical study" at least until the late fifteenth century: and if we were inclined to doubt the truth of this interpretation, we have only to think how much will remain unintelligible in the medieval history of western and central Europe unless we consider the Byzantine contributions to its culture: Anglo-Saxon scholarship of the eighth century, the Carolingian art of the ninth, Otto III's restoration of the Roman Empire, the growth of the Norman kingdom of Sicily, the cultural aftermath of the Crusades, the Italian Renaissance, these and other important events of European history cannot be understood without reference to eastern Europe. The Basilica of St. Mark in Venice, the art of Duccio and El Greco, are these not eloquent signs of how much the Western world owes to the genius of Byzantium?

If from Byzantium we turn to medieval Russia and to her relations with the West, what shall we find—mutual hostility or interpenetration? It would be easy, but hardly necessary, to show that Russia's distrust of and hostility towards the West on the political and religious planes originate in the distant past.

Since the thirteenth century she has had to face and repel at least six major invasions from the West, three of which came near to destroying her national existence. It would seem natural to conclude that since the dawn of her history Russia has regarded the West as the hereditary foe, whose weapons are to be borrowed the better to resist its encroachments, and tempting to assume that she inherited this attitude from Byzantium. But the facts of early Russian history lend little support to either of these assumptions. Recent research has revealed the extent to which Russia in the eleventh and twelfth centuries shared in the common life of Europe: trade relations with Germany, the continued immigration of Scandinavians, intermarriages between members of the Russian dynasty and those of the principal reigning families of Europe, cultural connections with Bohemia and Poland, ecclesiastical contacts with Rome—these facts of Russian history in the pre-Mongol period do not suggest any segregation from or hostility towards the nations of the West.[28] Nor did the Schism of 1054 substantially affect Russia's relations with the West, until the thirteenth century. It is true that her clergy sometimes issued warnings against the doctrinal errors of the Latins, and that anti-Roman polemical literature began to circulate in Russia in the late eleventh and twelfth centuries. But there is a story that is better evidence of the Russians' friendly attitude to the Westerners at that time. In 1087 some Italian merchants from Bari, sailing home from Antioch, put in at the harbour of Myra, a city in Lycia on the south coast of Asia Minor. By a mixture of cunning and violence they succeeded in carrying off the relics of St. Nicholas from the basilica of the city and sailed home in triumph with this inestimable treasure. In Bari they were treated as heroes, and two years after the perpetration of this robbery the Pope instituted a new feast in the Western Church—commemorating the "translation of the relics of St. Nicholas to Bari," annually celebrated on the 9th of May. It is scarcely surprising that this feast does not occur in the calendar of the Byzantine Church: for the East Romans had every reason to regard themselves as the innocent victims of an act of brigandage. But the Russians had no such inhibitions. St. Nicholas belonged to the common heritage of Christendom; the transfer of his relics to Italy was clearly the work of Divine Providence; Bari was in any case a safer place than Myra, as Asia Minor was devastated by the Turks. It was a cause for rejoicing that one of the greatest saints of Christendom should now, by his posthumous presence, extend his special favour to the West: and so the Russian Church in its turn instituted the annual feast of "the translation of the holy relics of our father among the saints, Nicholas, the Worker of Miracles, from Myra to the city of Bari."[29] The Russian liturgical hymns of this feast, composed at the very end of the eleventh century, eloquently express the spirit of united Christendom: "the day has come of brilliant triumph, the city of Bari rejoices, and with it the whole universe exults in hymns and spiritual canticles. . . . Like a star thy relics have gone from the East to the West . . . and the city of Bari has received divine grace by thy presence. . . . If now the country of Myra is silent, the whole world, enlightened by the holy worker of miracles, invokes him with songs of praise."[30] So conscious were the Russians, half a century after the Schism, of the universal nature of the Christian Church; so little did they feel cut off from Western civilization.

We can now perhaps make a distinction in the history of Russia's relations with the West, which I believe to be important. Two different phases in these relations may be detected: the modern phase, which is commonly associated with Peter the Great, but really began in the late fifteenth century, when Russia borrowed from the West first the rudiments of technology and then, on an increasing scale, literary and philosophical trends, social ideas, and political institutions; these borrowings, as we saw, only affected a small section of the Russian people, at least until the present generation; and the early phase, corresponding to the eleventh and twelfth centuries, when the Russians were conscious of an organic link between themselves and Western Christendom. Sir John Marriott has written: "Russia is not, and has never been, a member of the European family":[31] the first of these statements may seem justified in part by contemporary events; the second is, I submit, a serious misrepresentation. The two phases in the history of Russia's association with the West are separated by two and a half centuries of Mongol yoke, which, by virtually severing the relations between Muscovy and western Europe, was an important cause of their long estrangement. And another turning-point in Russia's relations with the West occurred simultaneously: in the same years of the thirteenth century, when the Tatars, after their devastation and conquest of central Russia, were establishing their rule in the Ukraine, the Prince of Novgorod, Alexander Nevsky, fought back the armed offensives of the Swedes and the Crusading Orders of the Livonian and Teutonic Knights against the Russian Baltic frontier lands. It was now for the first time that the West faced Russia no longer as an associate, but as a hostile force carrying eastwards its double threat of territorial conquest and militant Catholicism.

The use of the term "Eastern Europe" to describe the area over which Byzantine civilization held sway in the Middle Ages has at least the merit of emphasizing the underlying unity of the history of European Christendom. And if it be objected that this unity was broken by the incorporation of Russia and the Balkans into Asiatic empires, and that these regions were for many centuries lost to Europe, it may be said in reply that not only was the Byzantine heritage in these countries preserved intact under alien yoke, but that the Orthodox peoples of Russia and the Balkans remained Europeans at least in so far as they successfully defended their Christian civilization against their Islamic overlords, and, by bearing the full brunt of the Asiatic conquest, made possible the cultural and material progress of their fellow-Christians in the West.

A closer integration of the history of eastern Europe into our text-books of European history—especially in regard to the Middle Ages—is, I would suggest, a matter of great importance. Unconsciously influenced perhaps by the legacy of Gibbon's contempt of Byzantium, or by the picture of Slavonic barbarism painted by some German nineteenth-century historians, are we not sometimes apt to regard western and central Europe—France, England, Germany, and Italy—as the true centres of European civilization, the primary objects of a medievalist's study? On this reading, the countries east of the Carpathians and south of the Danube seem to play the part of an appendage, or at least of an isolated and self-contained unit, in either case admitted only grudgingly and sparingly into our manuals of European history. There can be no doubt that the writing of history has suffered from this one-sided presentation. Nor are the dangers of cultural parochialism limited to the sphere of the technical historian. In the countries of the West the general public is beginning to appreciate how much our common European inheritance has been obscured, and the international life of modern Europe perverted, by the fact that history has so often during the past century been written from a nationalistic point of view. But the tendency to an egocentric reading of history may conceal dangers of a more subtle kind: the view entertained by present leaders of the Western world that in resisting aggressive totalitarianism they are defending the true values of European civilization has much to commend it; yet it may be asked whether this view would not acquire greater force and conviction if it were rid of two widespread assumptions: the notion that Western culture is identical with European civilization *tout court*, and the belief that there is something perennial and almost predetermined in the present schism in the body of Europe.

The theme of this essay was expressed in the form of three questions. Two of them we have now attempted to answer. We have examined the basic trends of Russian history in terms of Byzantine civilization and found that, at least until the end of the fifteenth century and to a more limited but still notable extent until the late seventeenth, this approach provided us with a guiding thread which made our subject "intelligible." From the eighteenth century, however, Russia's Byzantine heritage, overlaid with influences from the contemporary West, ceased to be the primary source of Russian culture, and the "intelligible field" of Russian history in this period should be widened to include the greater part of Europe. In any case the realm of Byzantine civilization, which in geographico-cultural terms can, both in medieval and modern times, be largely described as eastern Europe, was never a self-contained unit, but should be regarded as an integral part of European Christendom. We must now, in conclusion, consider briefly our third question—the specific character of Russia's Byzantine heritage.

"Russia's Byzantine heritage" is the title of a chapter in Professor Toynbee's book *Civilization on Trial*.[32] The author stresses the continuity in Russian history and argues that, for all the sweeping changes introduced by Peter the Great and Lenin, the Russia of today still preserves some salient features of her Byzantine past. It is well that we should be reminded of this continuity, which underlies the changing pattern of revolution and reform, and has preserved, even in the Russia of Stalin, something at least of the thought-world of Byzantium. Yet I believe that not all students of Russian history will be able to accept Professor Toynbee's view as to the nature of Russia's Byzantine inheritance. In his opinion the rulers of Soviet Russia have inherited from Byzantium a state of mind and an institution: the conviction that they are chosen to inherit the earth and are hence always in the right; and the structure of the totalitarian State. I shall not here discuss in detail the origin of this outlook and this institution, both of which undoubtedly exist in the Soviet Union today. But Professor Toynbee's thesis is so relevant to our present subject that I feel impelled to cite some of my reasons for believing that, at least without serious qualifications, it is likely to mislead.

A totalitarian state, for Professor Toynbee, is one "that has established its control over every side of the life of its subjects"; the proof of the totalitarian nature of the Byzantine polity lies in the fact that its emperors succeeded in making the Orthodox Church of the Empire "virtually a department of the medieval East Roman state"; this enslavement of the spiritual by the temporal he calls "Caesaro-papism." Caesaro-papism, in his view, had the disastrous effect of stunting and crushing Byzantine civilization and transmitted to medieval Russia the seeds of totalitarianism; cultivated in the political laboratory of the rulers of Muscovy, these seeds were later brought to full fruition under the Soviet régime. Professor Toynbee has argued his conception of Byzantine "Caesaro-papism" at considerable length in the fourth volume of his *Study of History*;[33] the problem is clearly of the greatest importance, for the view we take of the relationship between Church and State in Byzantium will inevitably colour some of our basic notions of east European history, both in the Middle Ages and in more recent times.

It would be impossible, within the span of two paragraphs, to attempt a detailed criticism of Professor Toynbee's thesis. But I venture to suggest that neither of these formulae—Caesaro-papism or totalitarianism—is an adequate description of the complex relations that existed in Byzantium between the Emperor and the Church. It is true that: (1) in the Byzantine society the Emperor occupied a supreme and sacrosanct position; (2) the canons and rules of the Church required his sanction before they became effective; (3) he could generally in the last resort depose a recalcitrant patriarch; (4) some emperors claimed the authority of defining ecclesiastical dogma; and (5) the freedom of the Church frequently suffered from their heavy-handed patronage. But each of these statements has its own significant counterpart: (1) the conception of the Emperor as "the living law" and of his sovereignty as the earthly reflection of Divine wisdom and power, borrowed by Eusebius from the Hellenistic pagan philosophers, was accepted in Byzantium, but it was gradually infused with a Christian interpretation, so that the notion of the Emperor as vicegerent of God, without losing any of its original force, shades off—through the idea of his duty as Defender of the Faith—into the obligation generally assumed after the sixth century by the Emperor at his coronation to preserve untainted the Orthodox faith, and, later, to "remain the faithful and true servant and son of Holy Church."[34] (2) The canons of the Church were drawn up and issued by the ecclesiastical Councils: the Basileus only sanctioned and enforced them. (3) On the occasions of conflict with the Church authorities, the emperors often seemed victorious on the surface; but usually in the end, and increasingly so from the ninth century onwards, the Church would vindicate its inner freedom and its right to impose the moral law on the Emperor. Professor Toynbee himself admits that "every famous Western champion of the rights of the Church has his counterpart and peer in Orthodox Christendom."[35] (4) The Imperial claims to define dogma, occasionally asserted, were in general regarded by the Church as an intolerable abuse and, in the long run, successfully resisted; and (5) it is significant that these attempts, due not so much to the emperors' desire to enslave the Church as to their wish to enforce compromise solutions with a view to preserving peace and unity within the State or securing military aid from the West, were always in the end defeated by the refusal of the Church to tamper with the purity of the Orthodox faith. The antithesis between these two sets of propositions constitutes perhaps the crucial problem in any study of the relations between Church and State in Byzantium. And it may be suggested that the solution of this still obscure question might be approached by an attempt to transcend both Professor Toynbee's interpretation of Byzantine Caesaro-papism and, at the opposite extreme, the recent assertion that "the religious history of Byzantium could be represented as a conflict between the Church and the State, a conflict from which the Church emerged unquestionably the victor."[36] Any true solution of this problem, I would suggest, must rest on three essential and often neglected facts: firstly, in spite of the interpenetration of the spiritual and temporal spheres in Byzantine society, there always existed in the mind of the Church an unbridgeable gulf between the competence of the State and the sanctifying and saving functions of the Church; secondly, the Emperor's sovereignty was limited—intrinsically, by its subordination to Divine Law and the duties of "philanthropy" incumbent upon him, and extrinsically, by the spiritual authority of the East Roman bishop and the moral authority of the ascetic holy man;[37] and thirdly, whilst the attitude of the Church to the Christian Empire remained substantially the same, the attitude of the State to the Church appears to have undergone a significant change, from the heavy-handed intervention of the early Byzantine emperors in ecclesiastical affairs, through the bitter struggles of the Iconoclast period, to the ninth-century settlement, expressed in Basil I's *Epanagoge*: "as the Commonwealth consists of parts and members, by analogy with an individual man, the greatest and most necessary parts are the Emperor and the Patriarch. Wherefore agreement in all things and harmony ($\sigma\upsilon\mu\phi\omega\nu\iota\alpha$) between the Imperium and the Sacerdotium bring peace and prosperity to the souls and the bodies of the subjects."[38] "Parallelism" and "symphony" between Church and State—are these formulae not a more faithful reflection of the Byzantine mind than Caesaro-papism or totalitarianism?

And in medieval Russia it was the same: here too, in spite of local differences, Church and State remained bound by the same twofold relationship which is implicit in the Byzantine *Epanagoge*:[39] parallelism and virtual equality on the one hand, indissoluble of purpose on the other. Sometimes, as in the thirteenth and fourteenth centuries when the secular power was weak and decentralized, the Church assumed a preponderance in public affairs; sometimes, as in the sixteenth century, the State, in the person of the all-powerful monarch, would impinge upon the sphere of ecclesiastical jurisdiction. But generally speaking, after each of these oscillations the pendulum would swing back and in the end the balance would be restored in accordance with the Byzantine theory. The most autocratic Tsars of Muscovy cannot be described as totalitarian rulers; for they, too, like the Byzantine Basileis, were forced to respect the doctrinal suprem- acy and moral authority of the Church. The seeds of Russian totalitarianism were sown by Peter the Great. It was he who first began to enforce the State's claim to be recognized as the source of all authority in the realm, the ultimate object of men's loyalty. Inevitably this led to the curtailment of the Church's freedom and to its partial secularization. For two centuries between 1721 and 1917 something akin to Caesaro-papism could be found in Russia. But it is significant that this partial subjection of the Russian Church to the imperial power was brought about by Peter's imitation of Western Lutheran models, and that to carry out his reforms he was forced to try and break down that Byzantine relationship between Church and State that was Russia's medieval legacy from East Rome.[40]

Professor Toynbee's other thesis—his claim that the Soviet Russians have in- herited Byzantium's intolerance of the West—also, I would suggest, requires considerable qualification. There is, of course, a measure of truth in this com- parison. It would be hard to deny the resemblance between the messianic *credo* of the Russian Communist party and the sublime belief of the Byzantines in their Universal Empire, destined to unite all the Christians of the earth under the sacred sceptre of the Basileus. Both attitudes reflect something of a mixture of faith and politics. Both are strongly intolerant of rivals and opponents. The Bolshevik party has often reserved its fiercest hatred not so much for the capital- ists of the West as for the other Socialist parties who, with programmes different from its own, are deviationists and traitors to the Cause. The Byzantines were so deeply repelled by the theological innovations of the Latin West that a few months before the fall of the Empire a high dignitary could publicly declare that he would "rather behold in Constantinople the turban of the Mahomet than the Pope's tiara or a cardinal's hat."[41] And when Constantinople fell to the Turks in 1453 and, as it seemed to men of that time, the Imperial legacy of Byzantium was proudly assumed by the autocrats of Russia, it was Moscow, the Third Rome, that became the unique repository of the Orthodox faith and its guardian against the heretical West. It would be difficult to resist the impression that there is at least something in common between the religious messianism of the Second and Third Rome and the fanatical belief of the Russian Communist in the exclusive truth of the Marxist Gospel, immortally enshrined in the collected works of Marx, Engels, Lenin, and Stalin. Yet this simile, in my opinion, should not be pushed too far: it may give us some insight into the psychological background of contemporary Russia; if taken as a full explanation, it may become a real obstacle to our understanding of both Russia and Byzantium. Historical con- tinuity, like most other facts, is subject to the laws of change, development, and decline. From Byzantine universalism to Russian religious nationalism, and from the latter to the doctrine of world revolution, the change is very great; some, indeed, may be tempted to regard it as a gradual debasement. There is, surely, at least one important difference between the intolerance of Byzantium and that of the Kremlin. The latter brand has, at least so far, expressed itself in hatred and violence: all means can legitimately be employed in pursuit of the final goal. That was not so in Byzantium: hatred of the West could sometimes be found there, no doubt, but it was not a hatred of Western culture or of the Western way of life, but rather a bitter resentment against the barbarians of the Fourth Crusade, who, under the pretext of securing their advance to the East, had stormed and looted the Imperial capital. Byzantine intolerance was never actively aggressive: rather was it due to the pride felt by the East Romans in their own achievement: for centuries they had passionately and successfully defended their way of life against the barbarians hammering at the gate, and the purity of their Christian faith against all attempts to tamper with Orthodoxy. The Byzantines were deeply attached to their religion: there could be no compromise in matters of faith; and some of them were doubtless sincere in preferring to see their capital under the heel of the Turk than their Church forced to subscribe to the unacceptable doctrines of the Papacy. It has been well said that "Byzantine intolerance is in its essence an affair of the spirit."[42] It is, I think, important that we should remind ourselves of this difference between Communist Moscow and Christian Byzantium.

It may even be doubted whether any historical connection can really be found between the "intolerance" of Byzantium and that of the contemporary Russian Marxists. It is fashionable today to trace the roots of the Soviet leaders' hostility towards the West back to the distant past, through the anti-Western feelings of a section of the nineteenth-century intelligentsia to Muscovite "messianism" and thence to Byzantine Orthodoxy. But the historian may feel justifiably doubtful of the validity of a method which, as I have suggested, results only too often in a process of "reading back" the origin of modern Russian ideas and institutions to a hypothetical or imaginary Byzantine past. It cannot be the purpose of this essay to discover the origins of the present Soviet attitude towards the West. But one final question may be asked in this connection: was not that criticism of modern "European" culture, which we find in the writings of several prominent Russian thinkers of the nineteenth century, itself largely a Western, rather than a Russian, product?

If neither totalitarianism nor a messianic intolerance of the West forms part of Russia's Byzantine heritage, can another formula be found to express the true nature of this inheritance? We have in the course of this essay gained a glimpse at several fields in which Byzantine civilization exerted a deep and lasting influence upon Russia. But there is one feature of this heritage which, I would suggest, informs and epitomizes the rest. This feature is best revealed in Russian history of the Kievan period. Then, as we saw, with her doors wide open to the influence of Byzantium, Russia was also closely linked with central and western Europe, by trade, culture, and diplomacy, above all by the consciousness of belonging to one world of Christendom, where, for the most part, there was still no Hellene nor Latin, but a common culture and a common faith. It is significant that Russia entered the European family of nations through her conversion to Christianity, for which she is indebted to Byzantium. The heritage of East Rome was not, as it is sometimes suggested, Russia's "mark of the beast" that isolated her from medieval Europe: it was the main channel through which she became a European nation. Byzantium was not a wall, erected between Russia and the West: she was Russia's gateway to Europe.

## NOTES

1. Marc Bloch, "Apologie pour l'histoire ou métier d'historien," *Cahier des Annales*, no. 3 (Paris, 1949), pp. 5–9.

2. Arnold J. Toynbee, *A Study of History* (2nd ed., London, Oxford University Press, 1948), i. 17–26.

3. Cf. M. de Taube, "A propos de 'Moscou, troisième Rome,'" *Russie et Chrétienté*, nos. 3–4 (Paris, 1948), pp. 17–24.

4. William Palmer, *The Patriarch and the Tsar*, ii. (London, 1873), 175.

5. Toynbee, *op. cit.*, i. 23.

6. On the "Eurasians," see the provocative article by D. S. Mirsky, "The Eurasian Movement" (*Slavonic Review*, vol. vi, no. 17 (1927), pp. 311–19) and the more balanced account by B. Ishboldin, "The Eurasian Movement" (*Russian Review*, vol. v, no. 2 (1946), pp. 64–73).

7. Ivan Timofeev, in S. F. Platonov, *Drevnerusskiya skazaniya i povesti o smutnom vremeni XVII veka, kak istoricheski istochnik* (2nd ed., St. Petersburg, 1913), p. 206.

8. For the culture of Kievan Russia and its Byzantine foundations see: André Mazon, "Byzance et la Russie," *Revue d'histoire de la philosophie et d'histoire générale de la civilisation* fasc. 19 (Lille, 1937), pp. 261–77; G. P. Fedotov, *The Russian Religious Mind: Kievan Christianity* (Cambridge, Mass., 1946); B. D. Grekov, *The Culture of Kiev Rūs* (Moscow, 1947) (in English); G. Vernadsky, *Kievan Russia* (New Haven, 1948); A. Meyendorff and N. H. Baynes, "The Byzantine Inheritance in Russia," in *Byzantium*, ed. by N. H. Baynes and H. St. L. B. Moss (Oxford, 1948), pp. 369–91, and the bibliography on pp. 417–21.

9. B. H. Sumner, *Survey of Russian History* (2nd ed., London, 1947), p. 178.

10. The expression is borrowed from Professor Norman Baynes, whose two lectures, *The Hellenistic Civilization and East Rome* (London, Oxford University Press, 1946) and *The Thought-world of East Rome* (ibid., 1947), form an admirable introduction to the study of medieval Russian culture.

11. The expression "relapse into barbarism" is used by Professor Toynbee to describe the consequences of the shift of Russia's political centre from Kiev to the upper Volga region, an event which he dates in the last quarter of the eleventh century, i.e. some 150 years prior to the Mongol conquest (*A Study of History*, vi. 309). Apart from the fact that he antedates this shift by at least half a century, it is scarcely justifiable to speak of a "relapse into barbarism" in the north-eastern region of pre-Mongol Russia. The whole of this area was closely connected with the Southern civilization of Kiev, and the twelfth- and early thirteenth-century architecture of the Suzdal' and Vladimir region remains one of the finest achievements in the history of Russian art. Cf. Vernadsky, *Kievan Russia*, pp. 259–61; N. Voronin, "Kul'tura Vladimiro-Suzdal'skoy zemli XI–XIII vekov," *Istoricheski Zhurnal*, vol. iv (Moscow, 1944), pp. 35–43; *Pamyatniki Vladimiro-Suzdal'skogo zodchestva XI–XIII vekov* (Moscow, 1945); D. R. Buxton, *Russian Mediaeval Architecture* (Cambridge, 1934), pp. 24–7.

12. For an account of Russian thirteenth-century literature see V. M. Istrin, *Ocherk istorii drevnerusskoy literatury domoskovskogo perioda* (Petrograd, 1922), pp. 199–248; for the Balkan influences on Russian fourteenth- and fifteenth-century literature see N. K. Gudzy, *History of Early Russian Literature*, trans. by S. W. Jones (New York, 1949), pp. 232–43; cf. P. Kovalevsky, *Manuel d'histoire russe* (Paris, 1948), pp. 94–102, for an attempt to justify the term "Russian Renaissance of the fourteenth century." For the spiritual tradition of medieval Russia see N. Zernov, *St. Sergius—Builder of Russia* (London, n.d.). For the Novgorod painting of the fourteenth and fifteenth centuries see N. P. Kondakov, *The Russian Icon*, trans. by E. H. Minns (Oxford, 1927), pp. 71–100; L. Réau, *L'Art russe des origines à Pierre le Grand* (Paris, 1921), pp. 136–95; C. Diehl, *Manuel d'art byzantin*, vol. ii (Paris, 1926), pp. 836–40, 870–2.

13. Professor Vernadsky, on the contrary, suggests a sociological parallel between the Kievan and the "Imperial" periods of Russian history; he compares the rift which the reforms of Peter the Great helped to create between the Westernized upper classes and the conservative peasantry to the cleavage caused by Russia's conversion to Christianity between the Christian and the pagan sections of the community; both processes, he maintains, "affected first the upper classes of society and accentuated the cultural cleavage between the élite and the masses" (*Kievan Russia*, pp. 241–2). It is true that in Russia the eleventh and twelfth centuries were to some extent a period of "cultural dualism," but the comparison should not be pressed too far. The cleavage created in Russian society by the increasing Westernization after the middle of the seventeenth century proved deep and permanent, at least until the present century. Christianity, on the other hand, "gradually enveloped more and more of the various social strata," as Vernadsky himself admits. Nor was the distinction between Christianity and paganism in medieval Russia a distinction between the upper classes and "the masses," even in the Kievan period: the former retained something of the pagan ethos at least as late as the end of the twelfth century, as is evident in the *Lay of Igor's Campaign*; and, on the other hand, Christianity seems to have spread fairly rapidly among the peasantry soon after Vladimir's conversion, partly, no doubt, owing to the Slavonic liturgy and translation of the Scriptures.

14. Joseph, Abbot of Volokolamsk: *Prosvetitel'* (4th ed., Kazan, 1904), p. 547.

15. Avvakum, *Zhitie*, ed. by N. K. Gudzy (Moscow, 1934), pp. 138–9; cf. *The life of the Archpriest Avvakum by himself*, trans. by Jane Harrison and Hope Mirrlees (London, 1924), p. 132; *La Vie de l'Archiprêtre Avvakum, écrite par lui-même*, traduite par Pierre Pascal (Paris, 1938), p. 185.

16. Photius, Ep. 13, Migne, *Patrologia Gracca*, vol. cii, col. 724 D; quoted in Baynes, *The Thought-world of East Rome*, p. 10.

17. D. Likhachev goes as far as to claim (*Kul'tura Rusi epokhi obrazovaniya russkogo natsional'nogo gosudarstva* (Moscow, 1946), p. 32, that in no extant official Russian document, or even diplomatic correspondence, of the fifteenth or sixteenth centuries, is Moscow described as the heir of Byzantium. This is something of an exaggeration: in the Paschal Tables compiled by the Metropolitan Zosima in 1492 Ivan III, the Grand Prince of Moscow, is described as "the new Emperor Constantine of the new City of Constantine—Moscow" (see M. D'yakanov, *Vlast' moskovskikh gosudarey* (St. Petersburg, 1889), pp. 64–6). However, the political implications of the doctrine of "Moscow the Third Rome" seem to have been ignored by the Russian statesmen of the time: cf. N. Chaev, "'Moskva—Treti Rim' v politicheskoy praktike moskovskogo pravitel'stva XVI veka," *Istoricheskie Zapiski*, vol. xvii (Moscow, 1945), pp. 3–23.

18. The relation between the growth of Western influence and the decline of Byzantine traditions in the fifteenth- and sixteenth-century Muscovy is discussed by Fr. Georges Florovsky in *Puti russkago bogosloviya* (Paris, 1937), pp. 11–29.

19. L. R. Lewitter, "Poland, the Ukraine and Russia in the 17th century," *Slavonic Review*, vol. xxvii, no. 68 (Dec. 1948), pp. 157–71; no. 69 (May 1949), pp. 414–29.

20. N. H. Baynes, *The Byzantine Empire* (Home University Library, London, 1939), pp. 7–10; *Byzantium*, pp. xv–xx.

21. N. Iorga, *Byzance après Byzance* (Bucharest, 1935).

22. With the temporary exception of the Serbs, who preserved an independent ecclesiastical organization until 1459, and again between 1557 and 1766.

23. Professor O. Halecki's book *The Limits and Divisions of European History* (London and New York, 1950) deals with several problems touched upon in this essay, particularly with the relationship between western and eastern Europe. The author argues convincingly that "Eastern Europe . . . is no less European than Western Europe" (p. 121), but his definition of Eastern Europe is far from clear. He suggests two different methods of dividing Europe into geographico-cultural areas. The first method is based on a twofold division between a "Western" and an "Eastern" Europe, the latter including Poland, Hungary, Rumania, the Balkans, and the land of the Eastern Slavs in "those periods of their past which are definitely European" (p. 110): these would consist of Kievan Russia of the eleventh and twelfth centuries and of the West Russian lands of the Ukraine and White Russia which were incorporated in the fourteenth century into the Grand Duchy of Lithuania. The second method involves a fourfold distinction between Western, "West-Central." "East-Central," and Eastern Europe. "East-Central" Europe is taken to consist of Czechoslovakia, Hungary, Poland, Finland, Rumania, and the Balkan peninsula; Eastern Europe, in this classification, should be equated either with

the Ukraine and White Russia (but only when they are liberated from the political control of Soviet Russia) or with Great Russia, "if and when Russia is considered part of Europe" (p. 137). Both these methods of classification result in the exclusion from Europe of Muscovy, the Russian Empire, and the Soviet Union, and in a complete cultural separation between these successive epiphanies of a Eurasian Empire on the one hand and the essentially "European" regions of the Ukraine and White Russia on the other.

Professor Halecki's interpretation of Russian history is undoubtedly the weakest part of his valuable book. In the first place, his attempts to justify the exclusion of Muscovite and Imperial Russia from European civilization (pp. 92–9) are far from convincing, and he himself seems to experience some doubts as to the validity of his thesis when applied to the eighteenth and nineteenth centuries. Moreover, the opposition between a "European" Ukraine and a Great Russian "Moscovia," so favoured by modern Ukrainian historians and now by Professor Halecki, rests on several historical misinterpretations which have often been pointed out by leading Russian historians. It is astonishing to find the opposite view, which includes the history of the Ukraine and of White Russia in the general course of Russian history, summarily dismissed by the author as a theory held only by "some Russian scholars" (p. 137). To try and trace the frontier of Europe along an imaginary border-line between the Ukraine and White Russia on the one hand and Muscovite Great Russia on the other is to do violence to historical facts. Finally, it is surely inconsistent to claim, as Professor Halecki does, that while Russia was permanently "cut off from Europe" by the Mongol conquest (p. 93), the Christian nations of the Balkans, similarly placed outside Europe by the Turkish invasion, were "reunited with Europe" after their liberation from the Ottoman yoke (p. 120). In fact, the Ottoman rule in the Balkans lasted twice as long and was considerably more effective than the Mongol domination of Russia. In both cases, as I have suggested, the Christians of eastern Europe preserved their faith, their Byzantine heritage, and their essentially European culture under the Asiatic yoke; and their political liberation was accompanied and followed by an influx of influence from Western Europe.

24. M. N. Tikhomirov, "Istoricheskie svyazi russkogo naroda s yuzhnymi slavyanami s drevneyshikh vremen do poloviny XVII veka," *Slavyanski Sbornik* (Moscow, 1947), pp. 125–201.

25. The problem of defining the notion of eastern Europe has led to some controversy, in which Czech and Polish historians have played a leading role. See: J. Bidlo, "L'Europe orientale et le domaine de son histoire," *Le Monde Slave* (Paris, 1935), tome iv, pp. 1–20, 204–33; "Ce qu'est l'histoire de l'Orient européen, quelle en est l'importance et quelles furent ses étapes," *Bulletin d'Information des sciences historiques en Europe Orientale* (Warsaw, 1934), tome vi, pp. 11–73; M. Handelsman, "Quelques remarques sur la définition de l'histoire de l'Europe orientale," ibid., pp. 74–81; O. Halecki, "Qu'est-ce que l'Europe orientale?," ibid., pp. 82–93; G. Vernadsky, *Kievan Russia*, pp. 9–12; and other articles by Halecki cited in his book *The Limits and Divisions of European History*, p. 205.

26. Theophylact, Archbishop of Ochrida, *Liber de iis quorum Latini incusantur*: Migne, *Patrologia Graeca*, vol. cxxvi, cols. 221–49. Cf. B. Leib, *Rome, Kiev et Byzance à la fin du XIᵉ siècle* (Paris, 1924), pp. 41–50.

27. Cf. N. Iorga, *Relations entre l'Orient et l'Occident* (Paris, 1923), pp. 168–81; C. Diehl, *La Société Byzantine à l'époque des Comnènes* (Paris, 1929), pp. 75–90.

28. Cf. F. Dvornik, "The Kiev State and its Relations with Western Europe," *Transactions of the Royal Historical Society*, vol. xxix (1947), pp. 27–46; *The Making of Central and Eastern Europe* (London, 1949), pp. 236–61; Vernadsky, *Kievan Russia*, pp. 317–47.

29. For the "Translation of the Relics of St. Nicholas" see Leib, *Rome, Kiev et Byzance à la fin du XIᵉ siècle*, pp. 51–74. For the possible role played by Russian Varangians in south Italy as intermediaries between Bari and Russia, see Vernadsky, *op. cit.*, pp. 345–6.

30. *Menologion der orthodox-katholischen Kirche des Morgenlandes,* ed. Rev. A. v. Maltzew, ii (Berlin, 1901), 281–2. Cf. Leib, *op. cit.*, pp. 70–2.

31. Sir J. A. R. Marriott, *Anglo-Russian Relations, 1689–1943* (2nd ed., London, 1944), p. 1.

32. Arnold J. Toynbee, *Civilization on Trial* (London, Oxford University Press, 1948), pp. 164–83 (first published in *Horizon*, August 1947).

33. Arnold J. Toynbee, *A Study of History*, iv. 320–408, 592–623.

34. Codinus, *De Officiis,* cap. 17 (ed. Bonn), p. 87. Cf. L. Bréhier, *Les Institutions de l'Empire Byzantin* (Paris, 1949), pp. 9–10.

35. Toynbee, *op. cit.*, iv. 594.

36. Henri Grégoire, in *Byzantium* (ed. Baynes and Moss), p. 130.

37. On this point I am indebted to Fr. Gervase Mathew's course of lectures on "Church and State in the Byzantine Empire," delivered at Oxford in the autumn of 1949.

38. *Epanagoge*, tit. iii, cap. 8. Ed. Zachariae von Lingenthal, *Collectio librorum juris graeco-romani ineditorum* (Leipzig, 1852), p. 68.

39. For the influence of the *Epanagoge* in Russia see V. Sokol'ski, "O kharaktere i znachenii Epanagogi," *Vizantiiski Vremennik* (St. Petersburg, 1894), i. 17–54; G. Vernadsky, "Die kirchlich-politische Lehre der Epanagoge und ihr Einfluss auf das russische Leben im XVII. Jahrhundert," *Byzantinisch-Neugriechische Jahrbücher* (Athens, 1928), vi. 119–42.

40. In two footnotes in his *Study of History* (iii. 283, n. 2, and iv. 398, n. 2) Professor Toynbee admits the Western origin of Peter's ecclesiastical reform ("Peter borrowed his 'totalitarian state,' 'Caesaro-papism' and all, from the contemporary West''), but in his *Civilization on Trial* this essential fact is ignored.

41. The Byzantine historian Ducas (*Historia Byzantina*. cap. 37, ed. Bonn., p. 264) attributes these words to Lucas Notaras, the emperor's chief minister during the last days of the Empire.

42. Henri Grégoire, in *Byzantium* (ed. Baynes and Moss), p. 132.

# The Mongol Tribute According to the Wills and Agreements of the Russian Princes

## MICHEL ROUBLEV

The influence of the Mongol conquest on Russia has already been examined in a number of studies. However, the role played in the economic life of Russia by the tribute imposed by the Khan and appropriated with a certain regularity for almost two centuries has drawn but little attention. The present paper constitutes an attempt at an evaluation of the amounts paid to the Khan by the Russian princes and an examination of the distribution among the various Russian principalities of the lump sum owed to the conquerors as well as of the variations of the tribute during the two centuries of Mongol domination.

The Mongol tribute was collected from the end of the thirteenth century by the Russian princes, acting as delegates of the Khan. The total sum paid to the Horde is designated in the sources by the term *vykhod*, sometimes used as a synonym of the more general term *dan'* (tribute). The *tamga*, or urban tax, and the *iam*, or appropriation destined for the maintenance of the Mongol couriers, were collected irregularly; and it may be supposed that they were confused little by little with the principal tribute paid en bloc to the Horde, first by the Prince of Vladimir, then by the Prince of Moscow.

### The Amount of the *Vykhod*: Estimates

The various Russian chronicles furnish only fragmentary indications concerning the tribute paid to the Mongols, and they do not mention its amount. Nor are further indications found in Chinese and Mongol sources.[1] A number of historians have, nevertheless, attempted to evaluate it. Of these various attempts, that of George Vernadsky merits particular attention, as much for its ingenuity as for the importance of the monograph in which it is included and which constitutes one of the few studies in American historiography of the Mongol period of Russian history.[2]

FROM Michel Roublev, "Le Tribut aux Mongols d'après les Testaments et Accords des Princes Russes," *Cahiers du monde russe et soviétique*, VII (1966), pp. 487–530. Reprinted by permission of the author.

Vernadsky's argument can be summarized in the following manner: in 1384, Khan Tokhtamysh, after pillaging Moscow, once again imposes the tribute on Russia and sets it at one half ruble (one *poltina*) per farm (*derevnia*).[3] But in a letter sent in 1409 by Edigey to Vasily I, the Khan specifies that to his knowledge the Grand Prince of Moscow appropriated one ruble per two *sokhi* for the tribute.[4] From this Vernadsky derives the equation one *derevnia* equals one *sokha*. A charter granted by Novgorod to Vasily II for the collection of "the black tax" (*chernyj bor*) defines the *sokha* as a fiscal unit equal to "two horses and one horse attached sideways;"[5] on the other hand, Vernadsky takes the following definition from a chronicle: "Three *obzhi* constitute one *sokha*. An *obzha* is one man laboring with a horse. And when a man works with three horses and the help of two laborers, this is a *sokha*."[6] The comparison of these two texts leads Vernadsky to consider that in the fifteenth century a *sokha* constituted a unit of taxation of at least three men. This would correspond, women, children, and dependents included, to a group of about twenty persons.

The author then attempts to establish the total number of *sokhi* in Northeast Russia in order to evaluate the amount of the tribute. He mentions the Mongol administrative division into tens (*desiatki*), hundreds (*sotni*), thousands (*tysiachi*), and tens of thousands (*t'my*) and postulates that each of these units constituted a military and financial entity that had to furnish a certain number of recruits and a certain amount of money; the number of recruits to be supplied for the army would then be based on this division, as it was in Mongolia: the *desiatok* would furnish ten men, the *sto*, one hundred, and so forth. However, at the time of their invasion in 1237, the Mongols required "a tithe on everything: men, princes, horses, one-tenth of everything."[7] The quota of recruits thus reaches 10 percent of the male population, or 5 percent of the total population. From this Vernadsky deduces that the *desiatok* included 200 people; the *sto*, 2,000; the *tysiacha*, 20,000; and the *t'ma*, 200,000. Thus a *sokha* which constituted a group of about twenty people, would be the tenth part of the *desiatok*, and the *t'ma* would include 10,000 *sokhi*. At the rate of one half ruble per *sokha*, this would be equivalent to a tribute of 5,000 rubles per *t'ma*.

The number of *t'my* in Russia remains to be established. A list of them has been restored from a Lithuanian chronicle and a letter sent in 1540 by Sigismond I of Poland to the Khan of the Crimea, Sahib Giray. These documents attest to a total of 29 *t'my*, excluding Novgorod and Pskov. Vernadsky reaches the conclusion that the annual tribute paid to the Mongols amounted to 145,000 rubles, with Novgorod adding another 25,000 rubles to this amount.

This long exposition demonstrates precisely to what point the sources used to evaluate the Russian population are variegated and nonconducive to a precise estimate. Any construction such as the one that has just been summarized necessarily rests upon a number of rather dubious postulates, and the conclusion reached can at best be merely hypothetical. In the present case, there is no reason to believe that each of the administrative units established by the Mongols had to furnish a corresponding quota of recruits. Vernadsky himself leaves room for doubt when he writes: "As in Mongolia, the quota of soldiers to be furnished by the district *must have been* based on each of the numerical divisions,"[8] and even quotes one of his previous articles in which he concludes that the number of inhabitants of each district corresponded to the number of taxable inhabitants, so that the *t'ma* only included ten thousand persons;[9] however, the thesis that he finally decides to adopt remains unsupported.

To consider another weak point of the argument, the *derevnia-sokha* equation is based on only one document. But it is generally admitted that the *derevnia* is an agglomeration of several homes, including a variable number of *sokhi* which is certainly greater than one.[10] Finally, the demand for the payment of a tithe "in men, in princes, and in horses" was put forth by the Mongols only in 1237, as the chronicle points out, on the eve of their offensive against the principality of Riazan'; and there is no possibility of establishing whether it was applied to all of Russia after the conquest.

These uncertainties are enough by themselves to make us doubt Vernadsky's conclusions about the size of the tribute; one is led to reject them completely if the weight of silver supposedly paid in each year is calculated. If we consider, as Vernadsky himself does,[11] that the ruble weighed 92 grams of silver, the tribute would reach some 15.6 tons of this metal! This figure can even be increased to seventeen tons if we refer to Spassky, according to whom the *poltina*, or half ruble of Novgorod, weighing 100 grams of silver, constitutes the original Moscow ruble.[12] We would therefore have expected to find Vernadsky postulating the existence of large-scale commerce which drained silver from Central Europe to Moscow; however, no such postulation can be found. Although commercial problems are examined in a number of pages,[13] the fact that the rural population had to furnish the bulk of the tax is emphasized.[14] No indication is given of the source of such important quantities of silver.

Calculation of the *vykhod* has also been attempted from various sources by a number of Soviet historians. P. P. Smirnov, for example, arrives at the annual figure of 5,000 rubles around 1410, and 7,000 rubles around 1434;[15] K. Basilevich comes to the same conclusion while noting a reduction in the tribute toward the end of the fourteenth century.[16] Finally, in an article that we were unable to consult, P. N. Pavlov concludes that in the middle of the fourteenth century the tribute reached 10,000 rubles, of which 4,000 were paid by Tver' and Nizhny-Novgorod.[17]

Part of the archives of the princes of Moscow, containing a number of documents that date back to the middle of the fourteenth century, have been preserved, including wills of the grand princes and agreements passed with the appanaged princes of several Russian principalities.[18] These are the sources that we shall put to use in an attempt to estimate the *vykhod* and analyze the methods of its imposition.

Many references to the *vykhod* can be found in the above documents, but its total amount is hardly ever mentioned, most of the charters merely stipulating that the tribute must be paid to the Prince of Moscow in accordance with previous customs. However, a number of texts explicitly mention what might be considered the amount of the tribute paid to the Mongols at the end of the fourteenth and in the fifteenth century. We have deemed it necessary to group the documents for the sake of analysis on a geographic basis, leaving their chronological examination for the end of our study. Given that the political history of Russia in this period has already been the object of numerous studies, we shall refer the reader to the latter without analyzing the political circumstances that surrounded the composition of each of the studied documents.

## The Principality of Serpukhov

It is for the principality of Serpukhov that we have the most data both as to the total amount of the *vykhod* and its distribution among the various cities. However, the first explicit document is dated 1389, that is, almost a half-century after the formation of the principality; it is therefore necessary to dwell briefly upon its history and determine its territorial limits at a time when we can evaluate the importance of its contribution to the collected tax for the Mongols.

The principality of Serpukhov originates in the apportionment carried out among the sons of Ivan I Kalita at his death in 1341.[19] We possess two slightly different texts of the will, both drawn up in about 1339.[20] Following the description of the possessions left to the two elder sons of Ivan I, Semen and Ivan, the will enumerates the regions bequeathed to the third son of the Grand Prince:

I give this to my son Andrey: Lopastna, Seversk, Narunizhskoe, Serpukhov, Nivna, Temna, Golichichi, Shchitov, Peremyshl', Rastovets, Tukhachev. And these villages (*sela*): Talezhskoe, Serpukhovskoe, Kolbasinskoe, Narskoe, Peremysh'skoe, Bitiagovskoe, Trufonovskoe, Iasinovskoe, Kolomninskoe, Nogatinskoe.[21]

The second version of the will adds two supplementary villages—Varvarskoe and Melovskoe.[22] If we pinpoint these localities on the map, the possessions of Prince Andrey Ivanovich are seen to occupy essentially an arc-shaped zone south and southwest of Moscow, delimited by a line running through Borovsk, Serpukhov and Kashira, whose width is approximately represented by the distance from Serpukhov to the present city of Podol'sk.[23] The legacy also includes a number of villages situated outside of this zone, such as Trufonovskoe near Kaluga, Kolomninskoe at 10 kilometers from Moscow, and the 2 villages named in the second version, Varvarskoe and Melovskoe in the region of Iurev, some 120 kilometers northeast of Moscow.[24] To complete this territorial gift, Ivan I granted Andrey a number of rights that are later to be transmitted to the descendants of the Prince of Serpukhov:

My sons will divide the *tamga* and the other urban districts;[25] they will do the same with the *myty*,[26] each one taking for himself those of his district (*uezd*). And the honey tax of the city administered by [the hundred of] Vasil'tsevo[27] will be divided among my sons. And each one will take the beekeepers and the tax-paying men (*obrochniki*) whom I have bought, each according to his list. . . . The men recorded in the census will be governed by my sons in common and all as one man will protect them. And as for my people bought with the great charter, my sons will divide them.[28]

The next document, affording information as to the situation of the Prince of Serpukhov, is an agreement concluded with his brothers, Grand Prince Semen and Prince Ivan (the future Ivan II) in 1350–1351, a few years after the death of Ivan I.[29] The agreement stipulates that the two brothers must serve the Grand Prince at his will, obey him, and refuse asylum to the Boyars revolting against him. The Grand Prince binds himself to respect the apportionment made by his father, but in recognition of his "seniority" his brothers must cede half of the *tamga* to him (they are to divide the other half between themselves) and the entirety of a number of other prestations destined to remain henceforth the appanage of "the eldest." This clause is followed by the concession to the two younger brothers of four villages: Mikhalevskoe, Mikul'skoe, Nikiforovskoe, and Parfenevskoe. The agreement does not specify to whom each village goes, but if we refer to the will of Ivan II drawn up in 1358, we see that the first village on the list is bequeathed to his son Ivan, whereas the second falls to the widow of his predecessor, Semen.[30] We can conclude from this that these villages had been granted to Ivan II in 1350–1351, whereas Nikiforovskoe and Parfenevskoe went to Andrey of Serpukhov.[31] The reign of the first prince of Serpukhov thus ended with a slight increase in his territorial possessions, but his share in the revenues of Moscow was diminished.

Andrey of Serpukhov died in 1353, bequeathing his possessions to his son Vladimir. Andrey's brother, Ivan II, assumed the title of Grand Prince in that same year, after the death of Semen. The possessions of Vladimir Andreevich were considerably increased by the will of Ivan II, drawn up in about 1358.[32]

I grant my patrimony, Moscow, to my sons, Prince Dmitry[33] and Prince Ivan. And to my nephew, Vladimir of Moscow, one-third of the revenue of the representative of the prince (*namestnik*) and a third of the *tamga* and of the *myty* and of the customs, of all that belongs to the city. The honey tax of Vasil'tsevo and the beekeepers bought by my father . . . will be divided in three parts. And the three princes will protect in common the men counted in the census.

Vladimir thus regained the third of the *tamga* and other incomes that his father had to cede to Grand Prince Semen in recognition of the latter's rank. The patrimony of the Prince of Serpukhov receives formal and universal recognition for the first time in this document; concerning the territory of the principality, the testament specifies: "My nephew, Prince Vladimir, will govern the district (*uezd*) of his father."[34] Nevertheless, Ivan II proceeds to a slight modification, made necessary by circumstances:

And as for the lands belonging to Riazan' which I have obtained on this side of the Oka, I give Prince Vladimir Novyj Gorodok on the estuary of the Porotlia in replacement for Lopastnia; and the other exchanged lands of Riazan' will be divided equally and without transgression among my sons, Prince Dmitry and Prince Ivan.[35]

We know that in 1353 the princes of Riazan' had recovered Lopastnia[36] and that at the time of the signing of the peace they had given in exchange to Moscow a number of their possessions north of the Oka, such as Novyj Gorodok, Borovsk, Luzha, and Vereia.[37] Finally, Vladimir of Serpukhov also receives a part of the inheritance left by Ivan I, his grandfather, to his widow, Ul'iana; upon her death, her possessions were to be divided equitably, "in four parts, without transgression" among Vladimir, Princes Dmitry and Ivan, and the widow of Ivan II.

Henceforth, in most of the documents concerning the Prince of Serpukhov, his possessions are enumerated according to the four categories established by the will of Ivan II: (a) one-third of the revenues of Moscow, which were apparently granted to the first prince of Serpukhov, Andrey Ivanovich;[38] (b) the territorial possessions acquired by Andrey, which are sometimes designated by the term *uezd* (district) or *udel* (appanage, share); (c) the portion of the possessions of Princess Ul'iana, widow of Ivan I, which fell to the princes of Serpukhov; (d) the successive territorial increases obtained by Vladimir as a result of political circumstances. This classification will be most useful for the analysis of the taxes paid to the princes of Moscow for the Mongol tribute.

The agreement of 1367 between Vladimir of Serpukhov and Grand Prince Dmitry Ivanovich (Donskoy)[39] does not offer us any new details about the territorial limits of the principality, despite the meticulous statement of the rights and duties of the contractors, which leads us to believe that Vladimir's possessions had not changed since 1358: they are alternately defined as patrimony (*otchina*) or appange (*udel*), and this is done indiscriminately.[40] The agreement does, however, contain the first reference to the Mongol tribute and to the manner of its payment: "You will give the yoke (*tiagost'*) and the rents (*protor*) due the Horde to [me] your older brother for your appanage (*udel*) according to the ancient scroll."[41]

The second agreement between the two princes is dated 1374–1375 and has reached us in a copy in very bad condition.[42] We shall retain from this document the designation of the possessions of Serpukhov (*votchina* and *udel*) and an intact clause of the text in which Vladimir receives from Dmitry as an appanage the cities of Galich and Dmitrov and their rural districts,[43] north and northeast of Moscow.

A third and last agreement between Vladimir of Serpukhov and Grand Prince Dmitry is dated 1389.[44] An interesting detail about this text is found in a description of the archives of the Posol'sky Prikaz (the Bureau of Foreign Affairs of the Princes of Moscow); after a description of the charter, the archivist noted: "and on the charter it is written: agreement with Prince Vladimir dated from the winter in which the Grand Prince took Galich and Dmitrov from his brother for himself."[45] The document defines once again in detail the possessions of the Prince of Serpukhov that are to be respected by the Grand Prince of Moscow and his descendants:

... That which your father, Prince Andrey, has granted you; one-third of the city of Moscow and the depots [*stany*] and one-third of all customs, and the appanage [*udel*] which your father has granted you, and that which my father, Grand Prince Ivan, has given you, Gorodets in replacement for Lopastnia;[46] and you then addressed a petition to me through my Father Aleksey, metropolitan of all Russia, and I granted you Luzha and Borovsk, and that which you have obtained from the appanage of Princess Ul'iana.[47]

The agreement of 1389 is the first text affording details of the amount of tribute owed to the Mongols. We have seen that the tribute was mentioned in

1367 in general terms, without any figures being given. The details of the clause that we are examining here are no doubt explained by the events of 1382, that is, the destruction of Moscow by Khan Tokhtamysh, who sowed terror throughout the country and tightened his hold on the Grand Prince of Moscow. The chronicler reports the very words of the Khan:

> I govern my own territories (*ulus*) and every Russian prince of my territory lives on his patrimony according to previous custom, and while he serves me I pledge him justice; and the prince of my *ulus*, Dmitry of Moscow, lied to me, and I frightened him, and he serves me with justice, and I grant him his patrimony according to previous custom.[48]

And the chronicler adds:

> In that same year a tribute (*dan'*) was levied on the whole principality of Moscow, one *poltina* per village; gold was then also given to the Horde.[49]

We see then that Dmitry had to pay the Horde a heavy tribute in exchange for confirmation in his duties, and the agreement with the Prince of Serpukhov sets the latter's share:

> You will give me the yoke (*tiagost'*) and the rents (*protor*) to the Horde . . . on your appanage (*udel*) and on the appanage of Princess Ul'iana, on your third, 320 rubles of [the] 5,000 rubles. And if something is added to it or deducted from it, [you will pay] differently according to the calculation. And we will appropriate the Moslem debt and the taxes and the Russian debt according to the same calculation.[50]

The "Moslem debt" refers to amounts owed to the Horde for former incomplete payments; the "Russian debt" refers to a sum borrowed by Dmitry from Constantinople in 1377.[51]

The agreement contains two more passages relating to the tribute:

> And when I must send my tax collectors (*dan'shchiki*) into the city [of Moscow] and the depots, you will send yours together with mine. And as for the tribute that I ceded to you in Rastovets and Peremyshl', we will send our tax collectors together, as it was in the time of our grandfather, the Grand Prince. And whatever our tax collectors collect in the city and the depots and the distilleries (*varia*) will go to my treasury, and you will give it to me in the *vykhod*. And you will send your tax collector to Kozlov Brod, this I concede to you. And whatever he collects will go to my treasury as the tribute (*dan'*) of the city. And if God delivers us from the Horde, I shall have two parts and you, the third.[52]

This paragraph should be compared with a passage from the agreement of 1374–1375 which we have not analyzed and which casts a certain light on the method of collection of the tribute. This agreement included the following clause: "And as for that which formerly . . . myshyl', in Rastovets, in Kozlov Brod was ceded to me, you, Sire, will not send your tax collectors into those places."[53] The comparison of these passages permits us to specify certain details about the method of collection of the tribute. Let us first note that a concession granted in the first document is abolished in the second because of previous custom dating from Ivan I. The dispatch of tax collectors together into the lands granted in appanage was without any doubt the current practice and was a method of assuring that all of the appropriated sums would arrive at the Grand Prince's treasury. This explains why no document defines the amounts owed by the

Prince of Serpukhov, since the collection of taxes remained strictly controlled by the Grand Prince. The methods of collection were no doubt set by a document that has not been preserved, to which the first agreement between Vladimir and Dmitry Donskoy, concluded in 1367, refers.[54] The agreement of 1374–1375 introduces the first modification of this custom by stipulating that the collection would be made, at least in the three localities cited, without any control from Moscow; finally, the text of 1389 reestablishes the former practice for Rastovets and Peremyshl', whereas collection for Kozlov Brod remains under the sole control of the Prince of Serpukhov.

It is clear that the amount appropriated for the first two cities had been the same in the past, and that is why the contractors found it useless to specify that the sum would be paid to the treasury of the Grand Prince. The precision employed in this context for the possessions of the Prince of Serpukhov leads us to assume that in this case the payments had not been carried out regularly. As for Kozlov Brod, which was, no doubt, a relatively recent acquisition of Vladimir Andreevich,[55] Dmitry finds it necessary to specify that the appropriated sums must be sent to his treasury for the payment of the *vykhod*, which leads us to suppose that this contribution was not considered automatic.

A supplementary indication makes it possible to affirm that the payment of the Mongol tribute to Moscow by the Prince of Serpukhov was to be carried out according to traditional norms; the last clause of the agreement concerning the tribute stipulates: "And if I must collect the tribute from my great Boyars . . . then you must do the same from yours . . . and you will give [it] to me, and this aside from that sum of 320 rubles. . . ."[56] We see then that the 320 rubles demanded of Vladimir make up his ordinary total contribution; the sums appropriated from new acquisitions, such as Luzha and Borovsk, were also part of it.

Two new texts will permit us to define more precisely the distribution of the tribute paid by the Prince of Serpukhov to Moscow; these are the two agreements concluded between Vladimir Andreevich and Grand Prince Vasily I, son of Dmitry Donskoy, one in 1390, the other in 1401–1402.[57]

The document of 1390 defines the territorial possessions of Serpukhov in the following way:

We will safeguard you, and we will not infringe upon what was granted you by your father, our father, the Grand Prince, who ceded to you one-third of Moscow and your *otchina* Serpukhov and the other places . . . which you obtained in exchange for Lopastna, Gorodets, Borovsk, Luzha, and the *uezd* of Princess Ul'iana, as our father divided it with you, a third of Mushkova Gora after the death of the princess and one-third of Dobriatinsk, and one-third of the men counted in the census, as it was in the time of the Grand Prince, and all that I have given you as *udel*—Volok with its *volosti*, and these *volosti* are Izdetemle and Voinichi and Rzhev with its *volosti*.[58]

Reading the document in its entirety leads us to the conclusion that the terminology used to characterize the various possessions is quite precise. Thus, all of the clauses stipulating administrative independence, or the immunity of the possessions of Vladimir Andreevich, always specify that the area concerned is the *udel i otchina* or the *otchina i udel*.[59] One might claim that this is a matter of a set judicial expression the meaning of which is imprecise and which is being used by the writer of the agreement in a way that does not permit a differentiated analysis. We have just seen that this is not the case in defining the possessions of Vladimir. Two further passages of the text are convincing in this respect.

1. The Grand Prince's possessions are also designated by the pair *udel i otchina*, but in one sentence this formula is modified in such a way that it cannot be considered a conventional expression: Vladimir Andreevich is forbidden to send his tax collectors into or to buy villages in "our *udely*, and in the *otchina*, in the grand principality."[60] The plural *udely*, which denotes here the totality of possessions acquired by the Grand Prince outside of Moscow (which is his *otchina*, or patrimony), indicates that the term *udel* has here a definite meaning.

2. Finally, the use of the term *otchina* in connection with the Prince of Serpukhov is explained in another passage. From the chronicle we know that immediately after the accession of Vasily I to power, Vladimir of Serpukhov left for the capital of his principality, whence he traveled to Torzhok, on the border of the territory controlled by Novgorod,[61] because of a conflict around the two territories of Galich and Dmitrov, which had been regained by Dmitry Donskoy and bequeathed to his sons;[62] the trip to Torzhok must have permitted Vladimir to summon the forces of Novgorod against the Grand Prince. In the agreement of 1390, which puts an end to this conflict, there is a reference to this double trip:

> You will give us the yoke (*tiagost'*) of the Horde and the expenditures of the messengers of Kolomna [incurred] while you were in your *otchina* according to calculations. And you do not owe us the expenses of the messengers of Vladimir while you traveled outside of your *otchina*.[63]

Thus *otchina* has a clearly defined meaning here: it refers to Serpukhov and, by extension, to the territories that Vladimir had received from his father.

An exception to this general principle must, however, be mentioned at this point. The situation of Rastovets, Peremyshl', and Kozlov Brod, which are part of the *otchina*, is a peculiar one because of the very fact that in the past it had been the object of various transactions. Moreover, that of the first two localities is again modified by a special clause stating that the collectors of the tribute would not be sent there together by the two princes. It is unquestionably because of these peculiar circumstances that the three cities are again mentioned explicitly in the clause of the agreement that touches upon the payment of the tribute:

> And you will give, brother, to me, to the Grand Prince, 320 rubles out of the 5,000 rubles for your *otchina*. And you will take from Rastovets and from Permeyshl' and from Kozlov Brod out of this same money. And for Volok you will give me 170 rubles out of the 5,000 rubles. And if something is added to it or deducted from it, this will be according to calculations. And if God destroys the Horde[64] and if I shall not have to give . . . scovite and from your *otchina* and from the *udel*, whatever you take will be yours.[65]

If we compare the two passages of the agreement that we have just cited, the one that defines the territorial possessions of the Prince of Serpukhov and the one that specifies the amount to be paid in tribute, the following conclusions may be reached:

1. The *otchina* comprises one-third of the revenues of Moscow, Serpukhov, and "the other places" (that is, the possessions bequeathed to Vladimir by his father, including Rastovets, Peremyshl', and Kozlov Brod), as well as Novyj Gorodok (Gorodets), Borovsk, Luzha, and Princess Ul'iana's part of the inheritance.[66] The Prince of Serpukhov must pay Moscow 320 rubles for this territory, the same sum as in 1389.[67]

2. A part of the possessions held as *udel*, that is, newly granted by Vasily I, the region of Volok (this refers to Volok Lamsky or Volokolamsk) owes a supplementary amount of 170 rubles and can in no case be considered part of the old possessions of Serpukhov, which pay according to a traditional scale.[68]

3. Finally, the city of Rzhev, which was also granted as an *udel* by Vasily I, is not mentioned in the enumeration of the taxable areas. We know from the chronicle that Rzhev, situated on the border between the Muscovite and Lithuanian possessions, had long been an apple of discord among Moscow, Tver', and Lithuania. Vladimir Andreevich, acting on behalf of Moscow, had driven the Lithuanians from Rzhev in 1368,[69] but the city was again taken by the latter. A new attempt by Vladimir in 1376 ended in failure.[70] Moreover, the granting of Rzhev in the agreement was precarious, the document foreseeing that "if for some reason Rzhev were taken from you, I would give you Iaropolch and Medushi in place of Rzhev. And [in that case] we will fight together for Rzhev. And if we regain Rzhev, Rzhev will be yours; and our *volosti*, ours."[71] The silence of the text with regard to the tribute that had to be paid for Rzhev by the Prince of Serpukhov leads us to conclude that this locality did not have to pay a tribute, and that this was the case for the districts that Vasily I promised to grant should Rzhev be taken by the enemy.

The second and last agreement between Vladimir of Serpukhov and Vasily I is dated 1401–1402.[72] As one of the clauses attests ("and we will live according to our first charter as agreed and according to the present charter, as will our children"),[73] the two princes had before their eyes the text of the preceding agreement, to which the new treaty brought territorial modifications due to political circumstances.

Let us first examine the terms used to characterize the possessions of Moscow and of Serpukhov. Although we have concluded that in the agreement of 1390 the terms *udel* and *otchina* had a very precise meaning, that is not the case here. The document, referring again to Volok and Rzhev, states that they had been granted as *udel*;[74] but all of the Grand Prince's new territorial concessions to the line of Serpukhov princes are called *udel* and *votchina*.[75] Moreover, one may think that this treaty was drawn up simultaneously with the will of Vladimir of Serpukhov,[76] which we shall examine later, since a special clause assures the rights of the heirs of Vladimir in the case of his death: the Grand Prince and his descendants are obligated to respect "their third of Moscow, and their *votchiny*, and the places which I have granted as *udel* and *votchina*."[77] The terms that interest us here keep their precise meaning when defining the old possessions of the line of Serpukhov, but they seem more vague when applied to the territories recently granted to Vladimir. This peculiarity is explained when we consider that the treaty constitutes only a supplementary agreement, an appended one, which completes the one concluded in 1390. In fact, when the definition of the amount owed to Moscow for the Mongol tribute is in question, there is no reference found to the *votchina* of Serpukhov; only the new territories granted to Vladimir are considered.

Let us pass to the territorial clauses. Vladimir gives back to the Grand Prince of Moscow Volok, Rzhev, and their districts, which had been granted to him as *udel*, and receives in exchange, conferred as *udel* and *votchina*:

In exchange for Volok, Gorodets[78] with the *volosti,* and the *volosti* of Gorodets: Belgorod'e and Iurevets, and the village (*sloboda*) of Koriakovo, and Cherniakova and the *tamga* of Unzha, and all of the revenues and customs of Gorodets and of its *volosti*. . . . And in exchange for Rzhev, I yield Uglich with its revenues and customs and the village (*selo*) of Zolotorosskoe. . . . And to this I add . . . Kozelsk and Gogol, and Aleksin and Peresvetova and Lisin.[79]

These territories are situated in three different regions: (a) Gorodets and its dependencies are located on the Volga 350 kilometers northwest of Moscow and upstream from Nizhny-Novgorod; possession of this territory is considered precarious, for the agreement stipulates that if it is lost, the Grand Prince will grant the district of Toshna to Vladimir;[80] (b) Uglich is situated on the Volga, some 200 kilometers north of Moscow; (c) the group of cities "added" to these two territories are located south and southeast of Moscow, in the area of the traditional appanage of Serpukhov-Borovsk. As with Gorodets, possession of Kozelsk is unsure; in case of its being lost, the Grand Prince considers replacing it with the districts of Rozhalovo and Bozhenok.

The clause of the agreement concerning the Mongol tribute affords some important data:

And I shall give you, Sire, 105 rubles out of [the] 7,000 rubles for Uglich, and for Gorodets and the *volosti* which you added to Gorodets I shall give you 160 rubles out of [the] 1,500 rubles. And whatever will be added to this or subtracted from it, I will give differently according to calculations. And I will give you, Sire, whatever remains of the old debt of 3,500 rubles for Nizhny-Novgorod, according to the *vykhod*, according to calculations. And if God destroys the Horde, Sire, I shall have the tribute of my *votchina* and of my *udel* and I will not have to give it to you, Sire, to the Grand Prince.[81]

We see that the sum of 320 rubles mentioned in the document of 1390 as owed for the *otchina* of the Prince of Serpukhov is not mentioned here, and that the clause concerns only the newly granted lands. We can immediately notice that the sums are collected for very definite territories and that their amount does not depend on the prince collecting them: Vladimir paid 170 rubles for Volok while it was in his possession; he must henceforth pay 105 rubles for Uglich and 160 rubles for Gorodets. At the same time, we find once again, as in the case of Rzhev, cities and districts that are not mentioned, and it appears difficult to explain this gap as an omission of the copyist: Kozelsk, Gogol, Aleksin,

Peresvetova, and Lisin, newly granted to the Prince of Serpukhov, do not owe any payment, and they are thus implicitly attached to the hereditary territory of the principality, which pays a lump sum of 320 rubles to the treasury of the Grand Prince.

Vladimir Andreevich's will,[82] drawn up in about 1401–1402, permits us to draw precise conclusions about the amount of the *vykhod*, the method of its payment to the Prince of Moscow, and its distribution throughout the principality. It contains a detailed description of all the possessions of the principality that were divided among the five sons of Vladimir Andreevich and his widow.

The will is not specific about the terms used to characterize the possessions of Vladimir's sons. Each one's share is uniformly designated by the term *udel*, with the exception of one sentence in which the term *votchina* also appears.[83] The distinction here is easily established: each of the sons receives an appanage with hereditary ownership (*votchina*); however, to the extent that the will defines the amount each one must pay to make up the lump sum of the tribute owed by the principality, it is normal that the text should mention the areas in question as parts or shares (*udely*) of the total inheritance.

Vladimir's detailed description of the principality enables us to observe the enlargement of his territory. Dozens of villages and rural districts are mentioned for the first time as belonging to the principality of Serpukhov without the slightest reference to the method or date of their acquisition. A list of these possessions can easily be established and compared to that of the territories of Serpukhov which we have already been able to enumerate on the basis of the agreements previously concluded with the princes of Moscow. This multiplication of villages and districts acquired either through purchases or through marriage contracts, or quite simply resulting from an internal colonization of the principality due to a demographic expansion, concerns us here only to the extent that it enables us to illustrate a general principle that we have already been able to observe: the traditional territory of the principality of Serpukhov pays a fixed amount to the Prince of Moscow, and this amount does not increase in proportion to the growth of the principality. The clause of the will clearly stipulates: "And when the tribute of the Grand Prince goes to the Horde, out of [the] 5,000 rubles my children and my princess and their *udel* owe 320 rubles, except for Gorodets and Uglich."[84] This is the same amount that we have already seen mentioned in the agreement of 1389[85] and again in 1390.[86] It no doubt refers to a traditional payment set by "the ancient scroll" mentioned in the agreement of 1367.[87]

The detailed paragraph of Vladimir's will that concerns the apportionment of the tribute throughout the principality is interesting from more than one point of view. First of all, it affords details as to the total amount of the tribute. The preceding agreement concerned, among others, "the old debt of 3,500 rubles for Nizhny-Novgorod" as well as the sum owed for Gorodets, which amounted to "160 rubles out of [the] 1,500 rubles."[88] In the same context, the will specifies "and my sons, Prince Semen and Prince Iaroslav, will collect a tribute for Gorodets and the districts of Gorodets for the *vykhod* of Novgorod; out of [the]

1,500 rubles they will collect 160 rubles according to our agreement."[89] The region of Nizhny-Novgorod thus pays a special tribute of 1,500 rubles that is clearly distinguished from the ordinary tribute; nevertheless, the comparison of the two texts does not permit us to conclude that this tribute was paid regularly to the Horde, for "the old debt" is not a multiple of the (annual?) *vykhod* of 1,500.

Secondly, the clause concerning the tribute is a characteristic example of an error in calculation, which brings out the complexity of the problem. After having mentioned the traditional sum of 320 rubles owed to Moscow by the principality, Vladimir indicates to his heirs the partition of this tribute, fixing the amount that each must pay for his *udel*. Then, the total we obtain by addition amounts to 328.5 rubles! This does not trouble the scribe in any way. Specifying again that Uglich must pay Moscow 105 rubles, as was stipulated before, the paragraph ends: "Thus my children and my princess will appropriate the tribute for their *udely* and for Gorodets and for the districts of Gorodets and for Uglich, 585 rubles,"[90] which reestablishes quite exactly the total obtained by adding the traditional 320 rubles to the sums owed by Gorodets and Uglich.

Finally, this paragraph demonstrates that the distribution of the tribute within each principality depends entirely on the local prince and is by no means dictated by the Grand Prince of Moscow. Let us consider, for example, the case of Kozelsk, Gogol, Aleksin, Peresvetova, and Lisin. These towns are granted to Serpukhov in 1401–1402 by the Prince of Moscow and are not under the obligation of any payment to Moscow (that is, to the Horde). Vladimir Andreevich then bequeaths them to his older son, Ivan, whose share includes Serpuhkov and its districts as well as certain rights in Moscow and a large number of Muscovite villages; in the clause of the will that concerns the tribute, the amount which Ivan must collect is defined thus: "and my son, Prince Ivan, will collect 48.5 rubles as the tribute for Serpukhov and for his entire *udel*."[91] It thus seems indisputable that certain territories are free from any tribute in the eyes of the princes of Moscow. Once granted to princes holding appanages, they become taxable at their discretion and the amounts collected there are fixed arbitrarily by their inheritors. This may be clearly deduced by comparing the amounts owed by Vladimir's heirs and the importance of the territories that fell to them. To take only two examples, Vladimir's widow is to pay 88 rubles out of the total 320 for her *udel*, which essentially comprises Luzha and its districts as well as several Muscovite villages; one of Vladimir's sons, Iaroslav, pays 76 rubles for his share, which includes the town of Iaroslavl', two Muscovite villages, and one pond; in contrast, Ivan, the eldest, heir to Serpukhov—the center of the principality and without any doubt the richest city of the territory—to numerous Muscovite villages, and to the five towns granted to Vladimir by Vasily I, only owes 48.5 rubles. Here we see the illustration of a general principle which, as will be seen, also applies to Moscow's payments to the Horde: the tribute imposed on each principality is a traditionally fixed sum paid en bloc to Moscow, but its collection inside each principality is determined by political criteria. The richest areas are not necessarily taxed the highest; on the contrary, this is so for the peripheral zones, granted to princes of lesser importance. This clearly demon-strates that it is impossible to postulate, as Vernadsky tried to do, a uniform and proportional levy of the tribute throughout all of Russia. The cases in which such a type of *vykhod* was paid out are exceptions to the general rule, due to particular political circumstances.

Vladimir's will also contains a number of other valuable indications:

1. It appears that inside each appanage, the tribute is apportioned into smaller and smaller units down to that of the village (*selo*). This may be deduced from the following passage: "And in Uglich I grant my princess the village of Bogoroditskoe with all of its new hamlets (*derevni*) and its lakes and its forest; and my sons, Prince Andrey and Prince Vasily, will not interfere in this village . . . my princess will judge this village and will have [its] tribute."[92]

2. The amount collected from each village or region could vary according to circumstances and only the lump sum owed by the *udel* was pre-set without entering into details. This may be seen in the passage concerning Gorodets, which Vladimir divides between his two sons, Semen and Iaroslav:

> The city and the *stany*[93] will be divided in two parts by my sons, with all the customs. . . . My son Prince Semen will have the *stany* on this side of the Volga, below Gorodets, as well as Belgorod. And my son Prince Iaroslav will have the *stany* on the other side of the Volga, above Gorodets, as well as Iurevets. My sons will divide the *stany* equally between themselves. And he who has the most in the *stany* (*budet bole v stanekh*), the other will have to yield to him. And if Belgorod is more than Iurevets and Cherniakova, my son Prince Semen will add from Koriakova to his brother, Prince Iaroslav. And if Iurevets and Cherniakova are greater than Belgorod, it will be the reverse in the same manner.[94]

Although the terms *dan'* and *vykhod* do not appear in this passage, it seems evident that it concerns the collection of the tribute; otherwise the details that follow the clause about the division equally between the princes would be unnecessary.

3. Finally, let us again note that after having been divided among the various appanages bequeathed by Vladimir to his heirs, the tribute still continues to be paid en bloc to Moscow;

> And when the Grand Prince has to pay the tribute to the Horde, my children and my princess will collect the tribute, each one for his *udel* according to the calculations written in the present charter; and after each has collected the tribute for his *udel*, he will send his Boyar with his money together to the treasury of the Grand Prince, and they will deposit the money together.[95]

The lack of complementary documents forces us to conclude this analysis of the taxes paid by the principality of Serpukhov-Borovsk to the Grand Prince of Moscow as part of the tribute to the Horde. The other agreements and wills that we possess concerning this principality contain practically no data about the tribute. The agreement concluded in 1433 between Vasily II of Moscow and the Prince of Serpukhov, Vasily Iaroslavich, stipulates only that the latter must pay for his "*otchina* according to the division, as the *vykhod* and the *iam* had previously been paid."[96] The will of Vladimir Andreevich's widow is dated 1433;[97] six years earlier an epidemic had decimated the Serpukhov dynasty, leaving as sole heir of the principality Vladimir's grandson, Vasily Iaroslavich, whose grandmother must have administered the principality during his minority.[98] It seems that the regency was not a very effective one; the princess addresses a plea to the Grand Prince begging him to restore to her creditors some money that she had borrowed to pay "280 rubles for the *otchina* of my grandson, Prince Vasily, and 500 rubles for Luzha."[99]

An agreement concluded between Vasily II and Vasily Iaroslavich of Serpukhov in 1477 modifies the structure of the principality. The Prince of Moscow was not able to secure for Serpukhov possession of the territories granted in 1401–1402 (Uglich, Gorodets, Kozelsk, Gogol, Aleksin, Peresvetova, Lisin); as compensation, Vasily Iaroslavich receives "Dmitrov and its districts, and the taxes and the villages, and all the customs as *udel* and as *votchina*, with all that belonged to Dmitrov [when it was] mine, the Grand Prince's, and I also grant you, brother, the district of Vyshgorod, Sukhodol' and Krasnoe Selo."[100] The paragraph specifying the payment of the tribute does not cite a precise amount: "And you must give me, Brother, the Grand Prince, for your *otchina* according to what was previously given for the *vykhod* and the *iam*. In the same manner, Brother, for Dmitrov, your *otchina*, you must give to me, to the Grand Prince, and to my children, for the *vykhod* and the *iam* according to the first imposition (*oklad*), according to calculations."[101] Moreover, although the concession of Dmitrov is mentioned when the specification of the payment of the tribute is in question, this is not the case for Sukhodol' and Krasnoe Selo. This omission can only be explained by postulating that this region, like others that we have already encountered, does not pay a tribute. This hypothesis is confirmed by a second agreement concluded by the two princes in 1450–1454.[102] The concession of Dmitrov and its dependencies is annulled, but the Grand Prince takes it upon himself to maintain and preserve the *udel* of the Prince of Serpukhov, whose possessions, among which are Sukhodol' and Krasnoe Selo, are enumerated. In this context the charter specifies: "And you will take the tribute of Sukhodol' and Krasnoe Selo for yourself, and you do not have to give me the tribute of Sukhodol' and Krasnoe Selo in the *vykhod*."[103] The agreement does not indicate any precise figure for the *vykhod*.

This concluded the series of texts that we possess concerning the principality of Serpukhov. Thus, the only charters affording details about the amount of the *vykhod* and the method of its distribution and collection are those that cover the period of 1389–1402.

## The Principality of Moscow

The two wills of the princes of Moscow whose analysis can contribute to the elucidation of our subject were drawn up at an interval of more than a century. The first, that of Dmitry Donskoy (second version), is dated 1389,[104] that is, during the same period as the agreement with Serpukhov; the second, drawn up by Ivan III in 1504,[105] can be used only for a general comparison, the enumerated territories being divided in such a way as to render impossible any estimate of the tribute paid by each one.

Given that the detailed examination of Dmitry Donskoy's will necessitates numerous comparisons between its various clauses, we have deemed it necessary to give a translation of the most important passages. The paragraphs have been numbered for convenient reference.

(1) I entrust my *otchina*, Moscow, to my children, Prince Vasily,[106] Prince Iury, Prince Andrey, Prince Petr. My brother, Prince Vladimir (of Serpukhov) will administer his third, which his father, Prince Andrey, granted him. To my son Prince Vasily, I grant, because of his seniority, half of the two portions of the city and of the *stany* of my *udel*, and half to my three sons, and half of the customs of the city.

There follows an enumeration of other rights in the region of Moscow divided among the heirs.

(2) I give my son, Prince Vasily, Kolomna with all of its districts and its commercial taxes (*tamga i myty*) and its beehives and its villages and all of its customs. And the districts of Kolomna are: Meshcherka, Ramenka, Pesochna, Brasheva with the small village (*sel'tso*) of Gvozdnoia, and Ivani, Gzhel', the hamlets of Levichin, Skulnev, Makovets, Kanets, Kochema, Komarev and its shore, Gorodna, Pokhriane, Ust-Merskoe. Of the villages of Moscow, I give my son Prince Vasily the *pochinok* (newly cleared land) of Mitin, Malakhovskoe, Konstantinovskoe, the hamlets (*derevni*) of Zhyroshkiny, Ostrovskoe, Orininskoe, Kopotenskoe, Khvostovskoe, the large meadow near the city and beyond the river. Of the villages of Iurev I give my son Prince Vasily my acquisition of Krasnoe Selo and Elezarovskoe and Provatov and the village of Vasilevskoe at Rostov.

(3) I give my son, Prince Iury, Zvenigorod with all its districts and commercial taxes and its beehives and villages and all its customs. The districts of Zvenigorod are: Skirmenovo, with Belmi, Trostna, Negucha, Surozhyk, Zamoshskaia *sloboda* (hamlet of colonization), Iureva *sloboda*, the borough (*gorodok*) of Ruzha, Rostovtsi, Kremchina, Fominskoe, Ugozh, Sukhodol' with Ysteia and Istervaia, Vyshegorod, Plesn, Dmitrieva *slobodka*. Of the villages of Moscow I give my son, Prince Iury, Mikhalevskoe, Domantovskoe, and the meadow of Khodinsk. Of the villages of Iurev I give him: my acquisition, the village of Kuzmydem'ianskoe, to which I add the *pochinok* of Krasnoe Selo beyond the Vezka, and the village of Bogoroditskoe at Rostov.

(4) I give my son, Prince Andrey, Mozhaisk with all its district and commercial taxes and its beehives and its villages and all its customs and the districts controlled by itineraries (*ot'ezdnye volosti*). The districts of Mozhaisk are: Ismeia, Chislov, Boian, Berestov, Porotva, Kolocha, Tushkov, Vyshnee, Glinskoe, Pnevichi with Zagor'e, Bolonsk. I add to Mozhaisk, Korzhan and the Moishin Hill. The districts controlled by itinerary are: Vereia, Rud, Gorodoshevichi, Gremichi, Zaberga, Sushov, and the village of Repinskoe. . . . Koluga and Roshcha also [go] to my son, Prince Andrey . . . and Tov and Medyn [taken] from Smolensk. Of the villages of Moscow I give him Naprudskoe and Lutsinskoe on the Iauza with its mill, Deuninskoe, Khvostovskoe at Peremyshl', the meadow of Borovsk. . . . Of the villages of Iurev I give him Aleksinskoe on the Peksha.

(5) I give my son, Prince Petr, Dmitrov with all its districts and villages and all its customs and commercial taxes and beehives. The districts of Dmitrov are: Vyshegorod, Berendeva *sloboda*, Lutosna . . . Inobash. Of the districts of Moscow, I give Prince Petr, Mushkova Gora, Izhvo, Ramenka, the *slobodka* of Prince Ivan, Vori, Korzenevo, Rogozh, Zagar'e, Vokhna, Selna, Gusletsia, the borough of Sherna. Of the villages of Moscow I give Prince Petr, Novoe Selo . . .

Sulishin. Of the villages of Iurev I give him my acquisition the village of Bogoroditskoe on the Bogonia.

(6) I give my son, Prince Ivan, Rameneitse with its beekeepers and all that depend from it, and the village of Zverkovskoe and the *pochinok* of Sokhonsk, which were taken from Prince Vladimir. I also give Sokhna to my son, Prince Ivan. In this *udel* my son, Prince Ivan, is free; he will give [of it] to those of his brothers who will be good to him.

(7) I grant my son, Prince Vasily, my *otchina*, the grand principality (*velikoe kniazhenie*).

(8) I grant my son, Prince Iury, the acquisition of his grandfather, Galich, will all its districts and villages and all its customs, as well as the villages that depended on Kostroma: Mikul'skoe and Borisovskoe.

(9) I grant my son, Prince Andrey, his grandfather's acquisition, Beloozero, with all its districts and Vol'sky and Shagot'ia and Miloliubsky. . . .

(10) I grant my son, Prince Petr, his grandfather's acquisition, Uglich, and all that depends from it, as well as Toshna and Siama.

(11) I give my princess out of the grand principality, in the land of my son, Prince Vasily: out of Pereiaslavl'—Iulka, and out of Kostroma—Iledam with Komelaia; and in the land of Prince Iury, out of Galich—Sol; in the land of Prince Andrey, out of Beloozero—Vol'skoe with Shagotia and Miloliubsky. . . . Of the villages of Vladimir I give my princess the village of Andreevskoe, and of the villages of Pereiaslavl'—the village of Dobroe and all that depends from it. And out of the *udel* of my son, Prince Vasily—Kanev, Pesochna, and the villages— Malinskoe, Lystsevo. Out of Prince Iury's *udel*—Iureva *sloboda*, Sukhodol' with Ysteia and Istervaia, and the village of Andreevskoe and Kamenskoe. And out of Prince Andrey's *udel*— Vereia and Chislov and the village Lutsinskoe on the Iauza with its mill. Out of Prince Petr's *udel*—Izhvo and Siama. And concerning the districts and villages that I have given my princess from the *udel* of my son, Prince Vasily, and from that of Prince Iury, [and] from that of Prince Petr, if God thinks of [calls to him] my princess, the districts and villages in the *udel* of each one will be his.

(12) I give my princess my acquisition of Skirmenovskaia *slobodka* with Shepkov, Smoliane with the *pochinok* of Mitiaevsky and with the beehives and the beekeepers of Vyshegorod, Kropivna with its beekeepers and those of Ismeiskoe[107] . . . and of Gorodoshevichi and of Ruza, Zheleskova *sloboda* with its beehives and the village of Ivan—Khorobry, Iskonskaia *slobodka*, Kuzovskaia *slobodka*. . . Lokhno, a purchase of my princess, will be hers. And in Kolomna, my acquisition, the *pochinok* of Samoiletsev with its hamlets, the *pochinok* of Savelevsky, the village of Mikul'skoe, Babyshevo, Oslebiatevskoe. . . . Her village of Repenskoe and whatever she has added to it by purchase remain hers. Of the villages of Moscow I give my princess: Semtsinskoe with the mill of Khodinsk, the village Ostaf'evskoe and Ilmovskoe. I give her out of the villages of Iurev: my purchase, the village of Petrovskoe, and Frolovskoe, and Elockh. Kholkhol and Zaiachkov belong to my princess.

(13) When my children have to collect the tribute (*dan'*) for their *otchina*, which I have granted them, my son Prince Vasily will take from his *udel*—from Kolomna and from all the districts of Kolomna—342 rubles, and my princess will give him 47 rubles of this sum for Pesochna and 22 rubles for Kanev. Prince Iury will take from Zvenigorod and from all the districts of Zvenigorod 272 rubles; and my princess will give him 50 rubles of this sum for Iureva *sloboda* and 45 rubles for Sukhodol', and 9 rubles for Smoliany and 9 rubles for Skirmenovskaia *slobodka*. Prince Andrey will take from Mozhaisk and from all the districts of Mozhaisk 167 rubles and [he will take] from the places controlled by itineraries 68 rubles; and my princess will give him 22.5 rubles of this sum for Vereia, and 7.5 rubles for Chislov, and 22 rubles for Zaiachkov, 6.5 rubles for Iskonskaia *slobodka*, 6.5 rubles for Kropivna. Prince Petr will take 111 rubles from his *udel* and my princess will give him 30 rubles of this sum for Izhvo. Prince Ivan will give 5 rubles to Prince Vasily for Sokhna, and for Rameneitse he will give Prince Petr 5 rubles. They will take this for [the] 1,000 rubles; and if it is more or less, so it shall be different according to the same calculations. And if God destroys the Horde, my children will not have to give the *vykhod* to the Horde, and each son will keep for himself the *dan'* which he will collect from his *udel*.[108]

In the analysis of Donskoy's will, at which we now arrive, it is our purpose to examine: (a) the terminology used to characterize the possessions of the heirs; (b) the territories for which each son is indebted for a tribute to the eldest, Vasily; (c) the possessions of the widow and the amounts owed for these lands.

Let us first note that although the list of Moscow's possessions divided by Dmitry among his heirs is quite long, it is not exhaustive. In fact, if we compare paragraphs (1) and (2)—describing Vasily's legacy—to the beginning of paragraph (11), we see that Donskoy's widow receives two villages "in the land of Vasily," one depending on the city of Pereiaslavl' and the other on Kostroma. But Pereiaslavl' and Kostroma are not explicitly mentioned in the legacy made to Vasily, and they are no doubt included in the territories defined in the general paragraph (7). This leads to a methodological difficulty in the sense that it will be impossible for us to draw conclusions from the omissions of the text until the former can be explained in each particular case.

The term *otchina* appears in two different contexts and has two distinct meanings. Moscow is Dmitry's *otchina*, that is, his hereditary patrimony, which he bequeaths to his eldest son, Vasily—paragraph (1). Following the enumeration of the main territories bequeathed to his heirs, Dmitry "grants" his "*otchina*, the grand principality," to Vasily—paragraph (7)—*otchina* here meaning at the same time the possessions traditionally dependent on Moscow and the duties of the Grand Prince. Finally, the term appears one last time at the beginning of paragraph (13), and in this particular case it designates exactly the same territory as the term *udel*.

We do not find any terminological precision concerning the territories granted to each son—paragraphs (2) to (6). At the beginning, each legacy mentions an important city, enumerates the districts that depend on it, then the villages that depend on Moscow, Iurev, and in two cases—paragraphs (2) and (3)—Rostov. A new enumeration of the divided territories occupies paragraphs (8) to (10); once again, no precise term is used for these legacies, which have, nevertheless, a special status that explains their donation in separate clauses: they are lands acquired by Ivan II. When we pass to paragraph (13), which deals with the tribute to the Horde, we are immediately struck by the definition of the territory of each prince from which the tribute must be collected: for Vasily, "his *udel*—Kolomna and all the districts of Kolomna"; for Iury, "Zvenigorod and all the districts of Zvenigorod"; for Andrey, "Mozhaisk and all the districts of Mozhaisk"; for Petr, "his *udel*." It may thus be concluded that the *udel* of each prince, as it is defined in this paragraph, constitutes not the territories that were bequeathed to him by Donskoy in their entirety, but the principal city and the rural districts delimited in paragraphs (2) to (6). We will find confirmation of this hypothesis in the examination of the distribution of the tribute paid by Donskoy's widow. The only exception to this rule involves paragraph (6), in which all of Ivan's possessions are called his *udel*.

By comparing paragraphs (11), (12), and (13), we can specify the distribution of the tribute throughout the territory left by Donskoy to his descendants. Each son must pay the tribute for only a part of his legacy, defined in paragraph (13).

It is only in the case of Petr that the tax is collected for his entire appanage, no details being given. It would be possible to oppose to this conclusion the argument according to which a literal interpretation of paragraph (13) should not be adopted. If we were to invoke the lack of detail in the documents under examination, we could not fail to conclude that each of Donskoy's sons had to collect the tribute for his entire appanage and that the definition of taxable territories in paragraph (13) is not a precise one; from this point of view, Kolomna, Zvenigorod, and Mozhaisk would be but convenient abbreviations designating Donskoy's sons' appanages in their entirety; and it would be for the whole of each appanage that the tribute would be collected. Such an interpretation might appear authentic if we consider that certain of the documents analyzed above are sometimes imprecise. In the case at hand, it cannot be a satisfying one for the following reason: in addition to the "global" dues owed by each of the princes, paragraph (13) defines quite precisely the payment that must be paid to them by Donskoy's widow and by his youngest son, Ivan; these amounts are to be paid for territories belonging to the latter two but situated within the other princely appanages. In almost every case it is possible to locate the village or the region granted to Donskoy's widow and to Ivan for which the amount of the tribute is specified. Pesochna and Kanev, for which Vasily is to receive 69 rubles, are 2 rural districts of Kolomna—see paragraph (2); Iureva *sloboda*, Sukhodol', Smoliany, and Skirmenovskaia *slobodka*, for which Iury is to receive 113 rubles, are all part of the region of Zvenigorod—see paragraph (3);[109] the 84 rubles that Prince Andrey receives from his mother are due for Vereia and Chislov, both dependent on Mozhaisk—see paragraph (4)—and for 5 other possessions: Zaiachkov, controlled by Mozhaisk,[110] Kholokhl,[111] Zheleskovy (which we were not able to locate), Iskonskaia *sloboda* in the region of Ruza-Mozhaisk,[112] and Kropivna in the region of Tarussa-Vereia,[113] that is, also dependent on Mozhaisk; a total of 30 rubles must be paid to Petr for Izhvo, a district of Dmitrov that was granted to his mother;[114] finally, Prince Ivan must pay a total of 5 rubles to Vasily for Sokhna, southwest of Moscow,[115] and 5 rubles to Petr for Rameneitse.[116]

In every case but the last—and there the matter is explained by the circumstances that the gift of Rameneitse to Ivan was likely to remove the village definitively from Moscow's authority, since its possessor had but a slight chance to accede to the throne—the territories granted to Donskoy's widow and to his young son, and which had to pay a tribute to the other sons of the Grand Prince, are all located in the sections of their appanages defined in paragraph (13); that is, in the regions of Kolomna, Zvenigorod, Mozhaisk, and Dmitrov. The paragraph in question must thus be considered precise; we deduce from it that *the other parts of each of the appanages were not indebted for any tribute to the Mongols.*

This may also be demonstrated in another way. Paragraph (11) clearly distinguishes between the lands granted to the widow "in the lands of" her sons and the territories that she received in the *udel* of her sons, and we therefore find two distinct enumerations. The first refers to the territories belonging to

Vasily, Iury, and Andrey by virtue of paragraphs (7) to (9), the distinctive
character of which has already been noted:[117] the "grand principality," that is,
the villages of Moscow as well as those of Pereiaslavl', Kostroma, and Vladimir
(bequeathed to Vasily), of Galich (to Iury), of Beloozero (to Andrey), and of
Uglich (to Petr). Not only are these regions not listed in paragraph (13) as
paying tribute, but none of the possessions that are included in them and that
are granted to Donskoy's widow—see the first part of paragraph (11)—are
mentioned as taxable. As for the territories included in Petr's *udel*, the district
of Izhov (dependent on Dmitrov) is taxable, whereas that of Siama (dependent
on Uglich)—see paragraph (10)—is not. This, then, would support the conclusion
we have reached. The second enumeration of paragraph (11), that of the possessions of Donskoy's widow in the *udely* of her sons, which should therefore
be integrally found in paragraph (13), also reveals an anomaly. Not all the
territories included there are later enumerated with their dues; thus, the villages
of Malinskoe and Lystsevo, located in Vasily's territory,[118] the villages of
Andreevskoe and Kamenskoe in Iury's territory,[119] the village of Luchinskoe
on the Iauza in Andrey's territory,[120] and the district of Siama in Petr's territory[121] all belong to Donskoy's widow; and all are situated inside the regions
that must pay a tribute en bloc to Grand Prince Vasily, but are not themselves
individually taxed. It may thus be seen again, as in the case of the principality of
Serpukhov, that not only is the tribute collected for only part of the territories
divided by Dmitry among his sons, but also that the distribution of the tribute
varies inside these regions; certain villages or properties are completely exempt.
This conclusion is confirmed by an analysis of paragraph (12): the lands belonging to Donskoy's widow, which are enumerated therein, all come from purchases
made by the legatee or by the widow herself. The paragraph does not mention
the *udel* or *udely* in which these places are located, and we know only that they
are included in the *udely* of Iury and Andrey because they are listed with their
dues in paragraph (13). The possessions enumerated in paragraph (12), which
owe a tribute by virtue of the subsequent paragraph, are all in the region of
Zvenigorod and Mozhaisk, whereas other villages of the same region, and
villages of Kolomna, Moscow and Iurev, owe nothing to the prince governing
these territories, in this case Vasily.

The examination of paragraph (13) and its comparison to paragraphs (11) and
(12) have led us to conclude that the only regions owing a tribute to the Horde
according to Donskoy's will are those of Kolomna, Zvenigorod, Mozhaisk, and
Dmitrov. The implication of this fact is evident: the other territories bequeathed
as appanages, such as Galich, Beloozero, and Uglich, pay no tribute. But another
area, the most important of all, is not mentioned in paragraph (13). Grand Prince
Vasily must pay a tribute only for Kolomna and its districts and not for what is
defined in paragraph (7) as the *otchina* of Donskoy, the "grand principality."
By making the same comparison as before between the beginning of paragraph
(11) and paragraph (12), we also find, in confirmation of this, that Donskoy's
widow does not have to pay her oldest son anything as tribute for her possessions
in the region of Pereiaslavl', Kostroma, Vladimir, Iurev, and Moscow. Within

the vast "grand principality," which will soon become the heart of Russia, there is *an enclave, centered around Moscow, which pays no tribute to the Horde.*

Let us proceed still further. Analysis of the documents concerning the principality of Serpukhov has shown that the first texts affording precise data as to the total amount of the tribute were written at the same time as Donskoy's will. The agreement of 1389 mentions the payment of 320 rubles by Serpukhov out of a total of 5,000;[122] the agreement of 1390 stipulates that Serpukhov must pay 320 rubles, and Volok 170 rubles, again out of a total of 5,000;[123] and the two documents of 1401 and 1402 mention lump sums of 7,000, 5,000, and 1,500 rubles.[124] Serpukhov and Volok are part of the same fiscal zone, taxable at the rate of 5,000 rubles; Uglich is included in a zone (which might encompass the first zone or might be a completely different one) taxed at 7,000 rubles; and Gorodets is located in the taxation zone of Nizhny-Novgorod, which must pay a tribute of 1,500 rubles. On the other hand, as specified by paragraph (13) of Donskoy's will, *the calculation of the tribute for the central territories of Russia is based on only 1,000 rubles.* Not only is the distribution of the tribute within Moscow's possessions unequal, numerous regions being totally exempt, but the total that these territories must pay is completely out of proportion to their political and economic importance. This is, no doubt, the essential motive for the struggle led by the Russian princes to obtain from the Horde the title of Grand Prince, the *iarlyk* (charter) of the Khan. The recipient would profit not only from the exclusive right to centralize the tribute paid by all the Russian principalities (with all of the financial advantages implied by such a centralization), but he would also be allowed to pay only a small part of the total sum collected from Russia.

The inequality of the distribution of the tribute within the Muscovite possessions becomes evident if we evaluate the fraction of the tribute paid by Donskoy's widow out of the total owed by her sons. It is not possible to estimate, without having recourse to the archeological data, the relative importance of each of the districts or villages enumerated in paragraphs (2) to (5) of the will; and such an examination would go beyond the frame of our subject. We can, however, evaluate approximately the relative importance of Donskoy's widow's possessions within each *udel* and compare this to the tribute she must pay each of her sons. This may be done by comparing the total number of districts in each *udel* to the number of districts belonging to Donskoy's widow; moreover, these districts are considered to be of identical economic importance; this method is evidently not very precise, but it affords an order of magnitude.

Thus, the Grand Prince's widow receives 2 districts of Kolomna or 14.3 percent out of a total of 14 districts—see paragraph (2)—and she must pay Vasily a sum of 69 rubles, that is 20.2 percent, of the total 342 rubles due for Kolomna. In the *udel* of Zvenigorod, she received 3 districts and 1 village,[125] or 20 percent of a total of 15 districts; and she pays Iury a tribute of 113 rubles, or 41.5 percent of the 272 owed by the *udel*. In the *udel* of Mozhaisk, she receives 2 districts, or 11.8 percent of a total of 17;[126] and she must pay Andrey 84 rubles, or 37.7 percent of the 235 owed by his *udel*. Finally, she receives only

1 taxable district of Dmitrov[127] (6.6 percent) out of a total of 15 districts and pays 30 rubles (27 percent) out of a total of 111. According to the calculation included in paragraph (13), Kolomna, Zvenigorod, Mozhaisk, and Dmitrov must pay a total tribute of 960 rubles, of which Donskoy's widow, despite the relatively small extent of her possessions, owes 296, or 30.8 percent. It is apparent, then, that, as in the case of the principality of Serpukhov, the distribution of the tribute is not proportionate to the importance of the territory, but is rather determined by political considerations. It is considered normal that Donskoy's widow should administer on her sons' behalf the lands granted to her that are part of their appanages and that must return to them upon her death, as stipulated at the end of paragraph (13), she herself being satisfied with a small part of the collected revenues; this is how we can explain the disparity between the extent of her possessions and the dues she must pay.

Lastly, in the case of the will of Vladimir Andreevich of Serpukhov, redrawn up some ten years later, the calculation of the *vykhod* established in paragraph (13) reveals an evident inaccuracy. There it is stipulated that the *udely* will pay respectively 342 rubles (Kolomna), 272 (Zvenigorod), 235 (Mozhaisk and all of its dependencies), and 111 rubles (Dmitrov), this list being followed by the stipulation: "They will take this for [the] 1,000 rubles, and if it is more or less, so it will be differently according to the same calculations" (end of paragraph [13]). But the addition of the 4 figures gives us a total of only 960 rubles. It might once again be a matter of a simple error, but the fact that it was able to creep into an account that seeks to be so precise, in which the debts of certain villages belonging to Donskoy's widow are calculated to the half ruble, cannot fail to surprise us. We have already found a similar error in the detailed paragraph of the Prince of Serpukhov's will.[128] After the conclusions to which we have just come, it seems possible to advance an explanation.

In both cases, we are presented with divergent totals, the stipulated theoretical total unmistakably different from that obtained by the addition of the various partial figures. The total theoretically owed by the lands of Serpukhov is 320 rubles, paid as part of the 5,000 rubles of the Russian tribute; but in fact, the principality of Serpukhov must collect 328.5 rubles for its lands in 1401–1402. As for Moscow, the total amount theoretically is 1,000 rubles, whereas the amount actually collected in 1389 reaches only 960 rubles. Serpukhov thus pays 2.6 percent more than the *vykhod* it owes to Moscow, whereas the latter pays a total amount which is 4 percent less than that which it should pay, the difference being of the same order of magnitude. If we reject the possibility of a gross error in calculation this can be explained by supposing that not only is the internal distribution within each principality left to the discretion of the prince controlling the territory in question but also that the distribution of the total Russian *vykhod* among the different principalities may be subject to variations; in other words, the total tribute set at 5,000 rubles by the Mongols is not subject to modification by the Grand Prince, whereas its internal partition (here, 320 rubles for Serpukhov and 1,000 rubles for Moscow) may be slightly modified. Thus, the Prince of Moscow would again manage to reduce his share in the total tribute at the expense of the Prince of Serpukhov: while paying 40 rubles less for the grand principality, he retrieves 8.5 rubles from a prince who would have to pay, according to "the ancient scroll," only 6.4 percent of the Russian *vykhod*. This explains the meaning of the expressions that follow, in the agreements and wills, the statement of the amount of the *vykhod*:

. . . and if it is greater or smaller, you will pay differently according to the calculations . . .

. . . and if it is more or less, so it will be differently according to the same calculation . . .

. . . and whatever is added to it or subtracted from it, I will give differently according to the calculation . . .[129]

. . . and if the tribute is greater or smaller, they will collect the tribute according to the same calculations. . . .[130]

Unfortunately, none of the other agreements or wills preserved enable us to gain precise comparative data for the other principalities.

The only other document affording facts about the tribute paid by Moscow, the will of Ivan III, is dated 1504, or twenty-four years after the battle on the Ugra, which for many historians marks the end of Mongol domination.[131] Having become the heart of an immense state, Moscow had gained by this time much larger areas than those controlled by Dmitry Donskoy at the end of the fourteenth century. The passage of the will that concerns the tribute stipulates:

My children, Iury and his brothers, will give my son Vasily[132] from their *udely* for the *vykhody* of the Horde and for the Crimea and for Astrakhan and for Kazan' and for the Tsarevich *gorodok* and for the other kings and petty kings who will live on the lands of my son, Vasily, and for the Mongol messengers who will come to Moscow and to Tver' and to old Riazan' and to Perevitsk . . . and for the Mongol expenses (*protory*), towards [the] 1,000 rubles. My son Iury will give 82 rubles less 1 *grivna* for his entire *udel* and for Kashin. And my son Dmitry will give 58 rubles, 1 *poltina*, and 7 *den'gi* for his entire *udel* and for Zuptsov and for Opok. And my son Semen will give 65 rubles less 10 *den'gi* for his entire *udel*. And my son Andrey will give 40 rubles, 1 *poltina*, and 3.5 *den'gi* for his entire *udel* and for Staritsa and the lands of Kholm and Novyj Gorodok and Oleshin and Sinie and the other districts of Tver' which were given to him. And my son Vasily will give for the same 1,000 rubles, 717.5 rubles and 2.5 *den'gi* for Moscow and for the entire grand principality, the lands of Moscow, and for Tver', and all the lands of Tver' that were given to him and for old Riazan' and for Perevitsk. And Fedor, the son of my brother Boris, will give my son Vasily 37.5 rubles towards the same 1,000 rubles for his *otchina* and for Kolp and for Buigorod. And if the Mongol expenses are more or less than this, my son Vasily and my children, Iury and his brothers, and my nephew Fedor will give according to calculations.[133]

Because the distribution of the possessions of Moscow among the heirs of Ivan III is so complex, we shall not analyze it here,[134] but even a cursory glance shows that the amount of the *vykhod* collected for each region is appreciably diminished.[135] Let us note that each prince owed an amount which he distributed throughout his entire *udel*, and not only over a fraction of his appanage, as was the case at the end of the fourteenth century, a fact that already considerably reduces the tax due by each city or region. To take but one example, the region of Zvenigorod, for which Dmitry's will set a payment of 272 rubles,[136] is now part of a much larger area bequeathed to Iury Ivanovich, including, among others, the cities of Dmitrov, Kashin, and Ruza.[137] In 1504 this whole appanage owed no more than a sum slightly below 82 rubles.[138]

Moreover, as the first sentence of the above text shows, the will merely assigns to each of Ivan's sons his share in the various expenses entailed by relations with the remains of the Horde, the "petty kings" whose attachment Moscow buys with gifts. Nevertheless, it must be noted that the lump sum that had to be collected by Ivan's sons is still 1,000 rubles, the same as that set by the will of 1389. With Moscow's seizure of all the Russian principalities and the gradual disappearance of the Mongol menace, the sum of 1,000 rubles constituted at the beginning of the sixteenth century the total tribute collected, as though, while increasing its territory, the principality of Moscow had succeeded in maintaining the principle according to which the Grand Prince owed for his possessions only the set amount that his predecessors had traditionally paid.

The last texts that may be used for estimating the tribute to the Horde concern three regions which have already been mentioned, either in the will of Dmitry Donskoy or in the series of documents concerning the principality of Serpukhov. We refer here to the will of Prince Iury Dmitrievich of Galich (1433), two agreements between Ivan III and Andrey Vasil'evich of Uglich (1481 to 1486), and two other agreements concluded between Ivan III and Boris Vasil'evich of Volok at the same time.

## The Principality of Galich

The tribute paid by this territory changed significantly during the period that separated the drawing up of Dmitry Donskoy's will (1389) from that of his son Iury's will.[139] An agreement concluded in 1428 between Vasily II and Iury stipulates the payment of the tribute in the following manner:

> I must give you the tribute (dan') and the iam from the votchina, from Galich and its districts, as I previously gave it to your father, the Grand Prince. You have granted me the tribute and iam for Zvenigorod and the districts of Zvenigorod for four years. And after four years have passed, I will give you the tribute and the iam, as I formerly gave them to your father, the Grand Prince.[140]

The agreement does not mention the amount of the tribute, but it does, however, give two important details. The example of Zvenigorod shows that the Grand Prince retains the power to grant an exemption from the tribute for a certain number of years. It is impossible to state precisely whether this exemption corresponds to a single tax-collection, that is, whether the tribute was collected only once every four years at the most or whether Vasily II thus conceded an exemption to his uncle for the amount of four annual tributes; in the latter case, this could reach a considerable sum.[141] It is also not known whether such an exemption was made with the agreement of the Horde, that is, whether the Grand Prince could deduct the amount thus conceded from the total amount paid to the Khan or whether he had to balance his accounts by collecting this deficit from other principalities or paying it from his own treasury. As for Galich, we see that this region had paid a tribute since the reign of Vasily I, the father of Vasily II, although it is not mentioned in Donskoy's will, which transferred it to Iury.[142] We thus find one more example of the extension of the tribute to territories that had not been originally subject to it when they were directly dependent on Moscow. In the next document, the amounts owed for Zvenigorod and Galich are specified again.

The period 1428–1433, which separates the conclusion of the above agreement from the composition of Iury Dmitrievich's will, is marked by an intense struggle between the two princes to win the favor of the Horde: both visited the Khan and asked for his arbitration; and it was only by concluding a series of agreements with the other appanaged princes that Vasily II succeeded, no doubt in exchange for a considerable sum, in being confirmed by the Mongols in his duties as Grand Prince;[143] but his confirmation did not end the conflict. Iury drew up his will upon his return from the Horde, while he was preparing to march on Moscow in order to drive his nephew from the throne.

Iury Dmitrievich's will divides his possessions among his three sons; but the methods of payment of the tribute are not given with as much detail as in the case of Donskoy's heirs:

> When my sons have to pay the Grand Prince the tribute (*dan'*) for their *otchina*, for Zvenigorod and Galich, Zvenigorod owes 511 rubles out of the *vykhod* of 7,000; and my children will distribute this in their *udely* according to the tax which I have imposed on each district. . . . Galich owes 525 rubles out of the *vykhod* of 7,000.[144]

The description of the districts of Zvenigorod corresponds exactly to that of Donskoy's will; that is, the region considered here is the same as in 1389. However, the sum owed for the *vykhod* changes from 272 to 511 rubles. The fact that the total mentioned is 7,000 rubles should not be surprising. We have already seen that the region of Moscow is privileged and that the tribute that it had to pay the Mongols did not exceed 1,000 rubles. With the formation of the principality of Zvenigorod and Galich, Zvenigorod loses its privileged status and is integrated into the area paying a *vykhod* of 7,000, which considerably increases the amount for which it is indebted.

As for the territory of Galich, which had not been taxed in Donskoy's will (his widow, who received a part of it—Sol'—did not have to pay anything to Iury Dmitrievich), henceforth it owed a sum of 525 rubles, a new example of a territory exempt from the tribute when it depended directly on Moscow, and subject to it when it was transferred to a prince holding an appanage.

Iury Dmitrievich's will also brings to light a new fact. The territory of Dmitrov, which had been bequeathed to Petr Dmitrievich in 1389, was then taxed for the Horde at a sum of 111 rubles.[145] But since Petr died without heirs, Dmitrov was granted by the Khan to Iury Dmitrievich,[146] who was to divide it among his sons. In the clause of the will concerning the tribute, although Zvenigorod and Galich are mentioned together with regard to the amounts to be collected (despite the partition of Zvenigorod among Iury's three sons), Dmitrov is not mentioned at all. We could assume that the region did not have to be mentioned in a clause concerning dues owed to the Grand Prince, for Iury had received his *iarlyk* directly from the Horde. But Petr's former *udel* is divided among Iury's three sons in the will, and if the area in question were to be taxed at all, even if the sum were to be paid directly to the Horde, it would have been normal to mention this in order to avoid any conflict among the heirs. The very fact that Dmitrov is not mentioned, whereas Zvenigorod and Galich are, tends to show that at that time this *udel* ceased to be subject to the *vykhod*, perhaps in exchange for an increase in the tribute collected from the two others.

After taking power in Moscow in 1433 and driving his nephew, Vasily II, from the throne, Iury Dmitrievich did not succeed in maintaining ground in the face of aristocratic opposition. He then concluded an agreement with the Grand Prince in which he abandoned all claims to Moscow. The document[147] does not mention the amount of the tribute; it merely stipulates the restitution of Dmitrov to the Grand Prince with the *iarlyk* of the Khan, which Iury had received; from then on the tribute would be paid for Zvenigorod and Galich "according to the old custom as I gave it to your father, the Grand Prince."[148] An interesting indication is found there, however: "As for what I paid the Horde for my *otchina*, for Zvenigorod and for Galich, two *vykhody* . . . I will settle the account with you";[149] here we have one of the rare examples of payments still owed for the account of the tribute, but there is nothing to indicate the frequency of payment of the *vykhod*.

## The Principality of Uglich

Two agreements passed between Ivan III and his brother Andrey Vasil'evich—one in 1481, the other in 1486—have been preserved. The agreement of 1481,[150] in the same manner as other documents of the same type that we have examined, defines the possessions of Prince Andrey in stereotyped formulas. There is the one-third of the revenues of Moscow, which Andrey is to enjoy every second year, as well as "what our father, the Grand Prince, granted you, the cities of Uglich, Bezhitsky Verkh, Zvenigorod with its districts and villages, and that which I, Grand Prince, have given you as *votchina* and *udel*, Mozhaisk with its districts and villages"; there follows a long enumeration of villages and properties in the regions of Rostov, Pereiaslavl', Iur'ev, and Moscow. This essentially refers, therefore, to territories that had belonged to different princes in 1389 and were reunited here in the hands of a single appanage prince. If we refer to Donskoy's will, it can be noted that in 1389 Zvenigorod and Mozhaisk paid 272 and 167 rubles respectively for the tribute.[151] The agreement of 1481 contains the following clause: "You must give me 100 rubles and 30 *altyn* and 3 *den'gi* out of 1,000 rubles for the vy*khod*[152] until we take a census [of our territories] according to our father's will."[153] Not only had the tribute to the Horde decreased considerably since 1389–1402, but the lump sum quoted in the agreement had once more dropped to 1,000 rubles, although it concerned territories that were not dependencies of Moscow, whereas the totals mentioned at the end of the fourteenth and at the beginning of the fifteenth centuries reached 5,000 and 7,000 rubles.

One last agreement between Ivan III and Andrey Vasil'evich of Uglich,[154] dated 1486, constitutes a faithful copy of the agreement of 1481 with regard to the delimitation of the prince's territory.[155] The clause concerning the *vykhod* differs, however, from that of the preceding agreement: "You will give us 105.5 rubles and 7.5 *altyn* out of 1,000 rubles for the *vykhod* of your entire *votchina*[156] until we take a census [of our territories] according to our father's will."[157] The formula "according to our father's will" concerns not the amount of the tribute, but the census. The agreement of 1486 therefore constitutes a further example of the variability of the tribute collected for the same territory; the lump sum mentioned in both cases being 1,000 rubles, the *vykhod* owed by the Prince of Uglich increased by 4.81 rubles, or 4.7 percent, in 5 years.

It is impossible to follow the latter evolution of the tribute paid by the principality, for with the death of Andrey Vasil'evich in 1492, his appanage was annexed to the lands of Moscow. Ivan III divided it among his sons: Mozhaisk going to Vasily, Zvenigorod to Iury, Uglich to Dmitry, and Bezhitsky Verkh to Semen.[158] Since each [of these territories] was included in a larger *udel*, the amount that each owed for the tribute cannot be calculated.


## The Principality of Volok

Two agreements concluded between Ivan III and Boris Vasil'evich of Volok, also dated 1481 and 1486, have come down to us.[159] As with the two documents concerning Uglich, the territorial clauses of the two agreements are identical;[160] however, the paragraphs concerning the *vykhod* are also identical in this case;[161] the Prince of Volok must pay a sum of 61,30 rubles out of a total of 1,000 rubles to the Grand Prince. The distinction from Uglich's case is thus evident here: agreements drawn up at the same time for different territories stipulate an increase in the *vykhod* paid to the Grand Prince; here there is a fixed tribute. This clearly illustrates the arbitrary nature of the distribution of the tribute among the principalities at the end of the fifteenth century.

With regard to the principality of Volok, the evolution of the tribute may be followed until 1504. After the death of Boris Vasil'evich in 1494, the principality fell to his eldest son, Fedor, whose dues are mentioned in the will of Ivan III. Having received the cities of Kolp and Buigorod from the Grand Prince in 1497 in exchange for several possessions situated in the vicinity of Tver',[162] in 1504 Fedor owes "37.5 rubles for his *otchina* and for Kolp and Buigorod."[163] The decrease of the *vykhod* is clear in this case. The appanage that owed slightly more than 61 rubles in 1481 and 1486 pays only 37.5 rubles 18 years later (a reduction by more than 61 percent), and this despite the fact that this territory does not profit from the special status that Moscow's possessions enjoy.

## Conclusions

The various sums mentioned in the texts that we have analyzed can be reassembled in the form of a table showing the variation of the *vykhod* paid by certain regions from the end of the fourteenth to the beginning of the sixteenth centuries. Considering the restricted number of texts we are using and their geographical distribution, this table can give only general indications, which lead to a number of possible hypotheses.

Each column corresponds to one of the documents that have been analysed. We have indicated at the top the principalities from which the corresponding text originates, the date which the latter bears, and its page number in *DDG*. The word "Moscow" inserted in the last column indicates that the corresponding area is annexed to the Moscow principality and transferred by Ivan III to Grand Prince Vasily. In the same column, the sign (/) is used when the corresponding area is part of a much vaster appanage, for which the total sum due is indicated.

Summing up the various parts of our analysis, we arrive at the following conclusions:

1. The total *vykhod* paid periodically to the Horde reached at least 5,000 rubles in 1389–1390; it rose to 7,000 rubles in 1401 and remained at this level until 1433.[164] From 1481 onward, the expense incurred by Russia in her relations with the Mongols did not exceed 1,000 rubles. This reduction corresponded to the end of Mongol domination in 1480.
2. At the end of the fourteenth century, Moscow's possessions paid a total sum of only 1,000 rubles, despite their economic and political importance. There is no trace of payments made by the city of Moscow (at least the part of the urban revenues controlled by the Grand Prince) or by the territories directly controlled by its prince.[165]
3. When a region was granted as an appanage, it had to pay a tribute to the Grand Prince for the *vykhod*, even if it had not been previously taxed (such as Uglich in 1401). Conversely, the Prince of Moscow could grant exemptions from the tribute for a certain number of years (see the cases of Zvenigorod and Dmitrov).
4. The portion of the tribute assigned by the Grand Prince to each appanage was fixed from the end of the fourteenth century onward, according to an immutable scale that does not take into account territorial increase or the enrichment of the appanage in question: 320 rubles were owed by the *udel* of Serpukhov both in 1389 and 1402, despite the Prince's new acquisitions.
5. Within the appanages, as within the possessions of Moscow, the apportionment of the tribute was determined by the prince holding the appanage; certain regions could be exempted while others were heavily taxed. The amount collected does not seem to have depended directly upon the relative economic

**Table I**

| Regions | Moscow-1389 DDG, p. 35 | Serpukhov-1389 DDG, p. 31 | Serpukhov-1389 DDG, p. 38 | Serpukhov-1401–2 DDG, p. 44 | Serpukhov-1401–2 DDG, p. 49 | Galich-1433 DDG, p. 74 | Uglich-1481 DDG, p. 254 | Volok-1481 DDG, p. 270 | Uglich-1486 DDG, p. 325 | Volok-1486 DDG, p. 318 | Moscow-1504 DDG, p. 362 |
|---|---|---|---|---|---|---|---|---|---|---|---|
| Kolomna | 342 | | | | | | | | | | Moscow |
| Zvenigorod | 272 | | | | | 511 | | | | | ( )81.900 |
| Mozhaisk | 235 | | | | | | 100,915 | | 105,725 | | Moscow |
| Uglich | | | | 105 | 105.0 | | | | | | ( )58.535 |
| Dmitrov | 111 | | | | | | | | | | divided |
| Galich | | | | | | 525 | | | | | Moscow |
| Serpukhov | | | | | 48.5 | | | | | | Moscow |
| Borovsk | | | | | 33.0 | | | | | | |
| Luzha | | 320 | | | 88.0 | | | | | | |
| Peremyshl' | | | 320 | 320 | 41.0 | | | | | | |
| Rastovets | | | | | 76.0 | | | | | | |
| Iaroslavl' | | | | | 42.0 | | | | | | Moscow |
| Radonezh | | | | | | | | | | | Moscow |
| Nizhny-Novgorod | | | | | 1,500.0 | | | | | | |
| Gorodets | | | | 160 | 160.0 | | | | | | |
| Rzhev | | | | | | | | | | | Moscow |
| Volok | | | 170 | | | | | 61.305 | | 61.305 | ( )58.5350 |
| Vyshgorod | | | | | | | | | | | ( )40.5155 |
| Ruza | | | | | | | | | | | |
| Total *vykhod* mentioned | 1,000 | 5,000 | 5,000 | 7,000 | 7,000 | 7,000 | 1,000 | 1,000 | 1,000 | 1,000 | 1,000 |

importance of the taxed region: the central zone of the appanage paid less than the periphery, and the minor heirs were disfavored.

6. The tribute traditionally paid by each region varied slightly, this variation being revealed by an examination of the local distribution (as with Moscow and Serpukhov). It did not affect the lump sum, always indicated in round numbers, and it might have been the result of transactions between the Grand Prince and the princes of the appanages.

7. At the end of the fifteenth century, with the reduction of the tribute to 1,000 rubles, the quota set by Moscow for the appanages that still remained independent was no longer immutable, as was the case at the beginning of the century. The *vykhod* was determined by agreements passed between Moscow and the appanage princes; and it remained fixed in some (principality of Volok), while varying in others (principality of Uglich).

These conclusions leave two important questions open, which cannot be answered with precision on the basis of our sources.

1. These documents offer no indication of the amount of the *vykhod* during the period 1237–1389, the most severe period of Mongol domination. The Mongols took a census of the territories conquered, in 1246 (southern Russia), 1255–1256 (Suzdal'), 1257–1259 (Novgorod). And they took another census in 1273.[166] The chronicles give very few details on this subject and do not specify whether it was a census of the inhabitants or the establishment of a cadastre, although the former hypothesis is the more probable one.[167] It may be assumed that taxation during this period (the second half of the thirteenth and almost all of the fourteenth centuries), during which the Mongols relentlessly exerted pressure on the Russian princes (pressure that diminished only slightly after the Russian victory of Kulikovo in 1380), must have been even more severe than during the fifteenth century and must have burdened, with no exception whatever, the men included in the census by the conquerors. This leads us to a second implication, which goes beyond the scope of the present article.

2. The frequency with which the *vykhod* was paid to the Horde can't be determined. That is to say, the weight of the Mongol yoke on the economic life of Russia cannot be estimated with any degree of precision. But let us note that the exemption granted to the Prince of Zvenigorod for four years in 1428[168] indicated regular payments. This same deduction can be made on the basis of the will of the regent of Serpukhov (1433): after six years of regency, she had borrowed a sum of 780 rubles or more than twice the sum owed by the principality per payment.[169]

But even if it is admitted that the tribute was not paid to the Horde with perfect regularity, it may be assumed that every four to six years a considerable sum left the treasury of the Grand Prince of Moscow. The total amount of silver in metal thus extracted from Russia during the fourteenth and fifteenth centuries must have been very important, without, however, attaining the amounts calculated by Vernadsky; and one can only speculate as to the origin of this treasure. In the absence of large-scale commerce whose profits would have been gradually drained by the princes of Moscow, only the presence of silver mines in Russian territory could explain the payment of a Mongol tribute of such importance.

The existence of mines of precious metal was generally accepted by historians on the basis of two sources, one Russian, the other foreign, both referring to the reign of Ivan I, Kalita. The chronicle of Novgorod notes that in 1332 Ivan required that "the silver coming from beyond the Kama" (*zakamskoe serebro*) be delivered to him.[170] It is on the basis of this passage that one of the greatest economic historians of Russia assumed the existence of silver mines in this region and of the formation of a reserve of precious metal belonging to Novgorod.[171] This hypothesis has not been completely abandoned today, since it is still found in a work as important as that of Liashchenko.[172] It is true that it seems to be confirmed by a description of Russia attributed to the Arab geographer, Ibn Batuta. Referring to the Russians in Kalita's time the text states: "They possess silver mines, and *sauma*, that is, silver ingots used for the sale and purchase of merchandise in this region, are imported from their country."[173]

Numismatists are unanimous today in rejecting this hypothesis,[174] thus confirming later descriptions (Herberstein, Ermolay Erazm) which note the absence of silver mines in Russia before the seventeenth century.[175]

Whatever the case may be, it remains difficult to explain the mechanism by which the amount of the *vykhod* came to be collected regularly by the Prince of Moscow. Nothing in the generally accepted image of Russia, an essentially agricultural country with only limited commercial ties, can afford a solution to this enigma. The detailed passage of Donskoy's will concerning the tribute even includes two localities designated by the term *slobodki*, or hamlets of colonization of very small size, which pay a tribute of 9 and 6.5 rubles, or a quantity of 900 and 650 grams of silver metal!

Russia's economic structure appears to be one of the fundamental problems of medieval Russian history. The indications assembled here seem to show the existence of a developed monetary economy. For all that, should we accept the thesis, recently proposed by a Soviet historian,[176] that Russia of the fifteenth and sixteenth centuries must have had a flourishing merchant economy, destroyed by the reforms of Ivan the Terrible? The texts presented here cannot by themselves afford any answer to this question. A reexamination of all the documents relating to this period of Russian history would without any doubt be most fruitful in this context

## NOTES

1. See B. Spuler, *Die Goldene Horde. Die Mongolen in Russland 1223–1502* (Leipzig, 1943).

2. G. Vernadsky, *The Mongols and Russia* (New Haven, 1953). The arguments examined here are scattered throughout section 8 of Chapter III, which is titled "The Mongol Administration in Russia" (pp. 214–232).

3. This detail is found in a large number of chronicles; see, for example, *Polnoe Sobrainie Russkikh Letopisei* (henceforth abbreviated to *PSRL*), XXVIII 85 and 248. (Moscow, Leningrad, 1963).

4. *PSRL*, XI (St. Petersburg, 1897), 210.

5. *Gramoty Velikogo Novgoroda i Pskova* No. 21 (Moscow, 1950), p. 39.

6. *PSRL*, XII (St. Petersburg, 1901), 184.

7. *Novgorodskaia pervaia letopis' starshego i mladshego izvodov* (Moscow, Leningrad, 1950), pp. 74 and 287.

8. Vernadsky, *op. cit.*, p. 216 (the italics are ours).

9. *Ibid.*, note 285; the article cited, which examines the origins of the *Servi Regales*, was published in *Speculum*, No. 26 (1951), pp. 255–264.

10. Cf. two important studies on Russian agriculture during the Mongol period, a study by S. B. Veselovsky, *Selo i derevnia v. Severo-Vostochnoi Rusi XIV-XV vv.* (Moscow, Leningrad, 1936), pp. 26–30, and an article by G. E. Kochin, "Razvitie zemledelia na Rusi," published in the collection *Voprosy ekonomii i klassovykh otnoshenii v russkom gosudarstve XII-XVII vekov* (Moscow, Leningrad, 1960), pp. 264 ff. Veselovsky established that the average *derevnia* consisted of one to three hearths, whereas Kochin stresses that no clear difference can be determined between the agglomeration designated by the term *derevnia* and the *selo*, or village. In the majority of cases, the *derevnia* thus seems to have been occupied by several families.

11. Vernadsky, *op. cit.*, p. 231, note 353.

12. I. G. Spassky, *Russkaia monetnaia sistema*, 3rd ed. (Leningrad, 1962), p. 67.

13. Vernadsky, *op. cit.*, pp. 342–344.

14. *Ibid.*, p. 341.

15. P. P. Smirnov, "Obrazovanie russkogo gosudarstva v XIV–XV vv," *Voprosy Istorii*, Nos. 2–3 (1946), p. 72, note 3.

16. K. Bazilevich, "K voprosu istoricheskikh usloviiakh obrazovaniia russkogo gosudarstva," *Voprosy Istorii*, No. 7 (1946), p. 32.

17. P. N. Pavlov, "K voprosu o russkoi dani v Zolotuiu Ordu," *Uchenye Zapiski Krasnoiarskogo Gosudarstvennogo Pedagogicheskogo Instituta*, t. 3, Seriia Istorii i Filosofii, II (Krasnoiarsk, 1958), 112. Unfortunately, we have not been able to consult this article and give its conclusion from A. L. Khoroshkevich, *Torgovlia velikogo Novgoroda v XIV–XV vekakh* (Moscow, 1963), p. 297.

18. Published in various collections before the Revolution, these documents have been newly edited by L. V. Cherepnin; we have used this edition, *Dukhovnye i dogovornye gramoty velikikh i udel'nykh kniazei XIV–XV vv.* (Moscow, Leningrad, 1950), designated by the abbreviation *DDG*.

19. *DDG*, No. 1, pp. 7–11.

20. The reasoning as to the dates of composition of all these texts may be found in L. V. Cherepnin, *Russkie feodal'nye arkhivy*, Vol. 1 (Moscow, Leningrad, 1948). Kalita's testament is examined on pages 12–20.

21. *DDG*, pp. 7–8.

22. *Ibid.*, p. 10.

23. A partial identification of the localities listed in the testament has been attempted by the editors of *Pamiatniki russkogo prava* (abbreviated to *PRP*), 3 (Moscow, 1955), 312–313 in their commentary to the document, which is also included in this collection. We have also used the geographical index of *DDG*, A. N. Nasonov's *Russkaja zemlia i obrazovanie territorii drevnerusskogo gosudarstva* (Moscow, 1951), as well as two works by M. N. Tikhomirov, *Srednevekovaia Moskva v XIV–XV vv.* (Moscow, 1957) and *Rossiia v XVI stoletii* (Moscow, 1962).

24. This dispersion is only an apparent one, since all the *volosti* (rural districts) as well as the majority of the villages given to Andrey are included in the area defined above (Narunizhskoe, which we have not been able to situate, remains a case in doubt).

25. Of Moscow; Cf. Cherepnin, *op. cit.*, p. 43.

26. Both the *tamga* and *myty* are commercial taxes.

27. According to the commentator of *PRP* (Vol. 3, p. 318), this is a territorial and administrative unit that includes the Grand Prince's beekeepers.

28. *DDG*, p. 8.

29. *Ibid.*, pp. 11–13.

30. *Ibid.*, p. 15.

31. Nikiforovskoe could be in the Ruza area, west of Moscow (see *DDG*, the geographical index at page 546); the second village could not be identified.

32. *DDG*, pp. 15–19.

33. The future Dmitry Donskoy.

34. *DDG*, p. 15.

35. *Ibid.*

36. *PSRL*, X (St. Petersburg, 1885), 227.

37. *Ocherki istorii SSSR, period feodalizma, chast' vtoraia (XIV–XV vv.)* (Moscow, 1953), p. 134; Cf. *DDG*, p. 29.

38. This can be seen from the 1389 agreement between Vladimir Andreevich and Dmitry Donskoy (*DDG*, p. 31).

39. *DDG*, pp. 19–21.

40. *Ibid.*, p. 20.

41. *Ibid.*

42. *Ibid.*, pp. 23–24.

43. *Ibid.*, p. 23.

44. *Ibid.*, pp. 30–33.

45. Passages from this description are given in *DDG*; the above sentence is on page 461. Donskoy's testament grants these towns to the two sons of the Grand Prince; see also page 33.

46. This is no doubt Novyi Gorodok, at the confluence of the Porotlia and the Oka, which was granted in 1358 (see above, p. 33) and not Gorodets on the Volga, which only passes later into the hands of the Serpukhov princes.

47. *DDG*, p. 31; Luzha and Borovsk are slightly to the west of the area controlled by the prince of Serpukhov, some sixty miles southwest of Moscow.

48. *PSRL*, XL, 84.

49. *Ibid.*, p. 85.

50. *DDG*, p. 31. The words in brackets have been added for a clear translation of the text in accordance with our interpretation. Thus, we have translated "of *the* 5,000 rubles," whereas some historians interpret this passage as meaning "*out of* 5,000 rubles," which gives a lesser degree of precision to the clause; in the latter case the 5,000 rubles are only a unit for convenient computation, and the total *vykhod* is a multiple of this number. This interpretation is also Vernadsky's (*op. cit.*, pp. 230–231), for whom "clearly [?] none of the sums (mentioned in the wills and provisions) was the total of the *vykhod*." The sum of 5,000 would then be the quota due for each *t'ma* (*ibid.*, p. 231, note 354). If this were so, it would be impossible to explain the figure of 7,000 rubles, which, as will be seen, appears in the same context. For a second inner contradiction in Vernadsky's thesis, see below, p. 51, note 130.

51. *PSRL*, VIII, 32, cited in Cherepnin, *op. cit.*, p. 43, note 127.

52. *DDG*, p. 31.

53. *Ibid.*, p. 23; the dots represent passages missing in the text.

54. See above, p. 34.

55. This locality is listed for the first time in the agreement of 1374–1375; we have not been able to find it on the map, but its position in the list of possessions found in the will left by Vladimir Andreevich in 1401–1402 (cf. *DDG*, p. 47) leads us to assume that it is an important village of the Luzha region.

56. *DDG*, p. 32.

57. *Ibid.*, pp. 37–39 and 43–45.

58. *Ibid.*, p. 37.

59. *Ibid.*, pp. 38–39.

60. *DDG*, p. 38.

61. *PSRL*, XI, 121.

62. Cf. Cherepnin, *op. cit.*, p. 63, and above, p. 34.

63. *DDG*, p. 38.

64. A part of the text is missing here.

65. *DDG*, p. 38.

66. Borovsk and Luzha are not, strictly speaking, part of Vladimir's inheritance, since he had received them from Dmitry Donskoy by the agreement of 1389 (see p. 34); however, if we examine this document, in which Vladimir's possessions are defined by the term of *udel*, which bears here the general meaning of "part," we find that these two localities are grouped together with Vladimir's hereditary possessions inasmuch as payment of the sum of 320 rubles is concerned. Mushkova Gora was part of Princess Ul'iana's possessions, as defined by the

testament of Ivan I (*DDG*, p. 8); as to the third of the revenues from Dobriatinskoe, it had been granted to Vladimir's father by an agreement concluded with Semen in 1350–1351 (*DDG*, p. 11) and is therefore part of Vladimir's *otchina*.

67. See above, p. 36.

68. This may be the "ancient scroll" mentioned in the 1367 agreement; see p. 36.

69. *PSRL*, XI, 10.

70. *Ibid.*, p. 25.

71. *DDG*, p. 38.

72. *Ibid.*, pp. 43–45.

73. *Ibid.*, p. 45.

74. *Ibid.*, p. 43.

75. A synonym for *otchina*.

76. Cf. Cherepnin, *op. cit.*, pp. 72–73.

77. *DDG*, pp. 43–45.

78. Gorodets-Radilov, on the Volga.

79. *DDG*, p. 43.

80. *Ibid.*, p. 44.

81. *Ibid.*

82. *DDG*, pp. 45–51.

83. *Ibid.*, p. 45.

84. *Ibid.*, p. 49.

85. See above, p. 36.

86. See above, p. 36.

87. See above, p. 36.

88. See above, p. 36.

89. *DDG*, p. 49. The italics are ours.

90. *Ibid.* A tentative explanation for this apparent mistake can be found below (p. 50).

91. *DDG*, p. 49.

92. *DDG*, p. 48.

93. The original meaning of this term is "way stations"; it is used here to designate an administrative division of the appanage.

94. *DDG*, p. 47.

95. *Ibid.*, p. 48.

96. *Ibid.*, p. 71.

97. *DDG*, pp. 71–73.

98. Cf. Cherepnin, *op. cit.*, p. 156.

99. *DDG*, p. 73.

100. *Ibid.*, p. 130.

101. *Ibid.*, p. 131.

102. *Ibid.*, pp. 168–175.

103. *Ibid.*, p. 170.

104. Cf. Cherepnin, *op. cit.*, p. 59.

105. *Ibid.*, pp. 220–221.

106. Vasily I, Grand Prince of Moscow from 1389 to 1425.

107. A passage of approximately 15 letters is missing here.

108. *DDG*, pp. 33–36.

109. Smoliany is an exception, since it isn't mentioned in paragraph (3); however, Iury's testament of 1433 shows that Smoliany is part of the area of Vyshgorod, one of the districts of Zvenigorod; cf. *DDG*, p. 74; see also paragraph (12), in which Smoliany is listed together with the Vyshgorod beehives.

110. *DDG*, p. 13.

111. Its localization remains uncertain; according to Tikhomirov (*Rossiia...*, *op. cit.*, p. 119), it is found in the area of Maloiaroslavets, some twenty miles south of Borovsk; according to Zimin and Poliak (*PRP*, Vol. 3, p. 321), the name is that of a district controlled by Staritsa on the upper Volga (it is similar to that of the river Kholokhna or Khol'khol'nia, a tributary of the upper Volga; cf. Nasonov, *op. cit.*, p. 253). Whatever the case, it is not one of the villages depending from Moscow; and the first alternative, that is in the Mozhaisk area, is the most probable one.

112. Cf. *PRP*, Vol. 3, p. 321.

113. *Ibid.*; see also *DDG*, p. 540.

114. *PRP*, Vol. 3, p. 320; *DDG*, p. 74; Izhov is seen to be a dependency of Dmitrov and not of Moscow, as could have been assumed on the basis of the enumeration in paragraph (5). The Moscow districts granted to Petr are therefore by the same act made dependent on Dmitrov.

115. The village will be later added to the district of Vereia (cf. *PRP*, Vol. 3, p. 320); after its grant to Ivan, its ties with Moscow weaken, since it is later granted to Iury's son (cf. *DDG*, p. 108).

116. This could be a village situated eight miles from Moscow, also later granted to Iury's son; cf. *DDG*, p. 108.

117. See above, p. 46.

118. In the Kolomna area; cf. *DDG*, pp. 542–543.

119. In the Zvenigorod area; cf. *DDG*, pp. 15 and 526.

120. In the Moscow area; cf. *DDG*, p. 542.

121. In the Uglich area; see above, p. 45.

122. See above, p. 36.

123. See above, p. 37.

124. See above, pp. 40–41.

125. The latter, Smoliany, is of so little consequence that it is not even mentioned in the description of the Zvenigorod *udel* included in paragraph (3).

126. The five other villages of the *udel*, for which relatively important sums are due, are of so little consequence that they are not mentioned in the description of the Mozhaisk *udel* in paragraph (4) and must therefore be considered as constituting a small fraction of one or several districts.

127. The second district, Siama, is a dependency of Uglich and is not taxable.

128. See above, p. 41.

129. See above, pp. 35, 37, 39 and 45.

130. Will of Vladimir Andreevich of Serpukhov, *DDG*, p. 49. The systematic repetition of this clause is left unexplained by Vernadsky and conflicts with his hypothesis, according to which the 5,000 rubles mentioned in the agreements are merely a unit of calculation (see above, p. 35, note 50). If the *vykhod* were equal to *n* times 5,000 (*n* being the number of *t'my*— 29 according to Vernadsky), it would always be greater than 5,000 rubles; however, the above clause takes into consideration the possibility of a *vykhod* smaller than this amount.

131. Cf. L. V. Cherepnin, *Obrazovanie russkogo tsentralizovannogo gosudarstva v XIV–XV vv.* (Moscow, 1960), pp. 874–887. The section dealing with the political events of 1480 bears the heading: "Russia's Liberation from the Mongol Yoke."

132. Vasily III.

133. *DDG*, p. 362.

134. The amounts due by each of Ivan's sons may be calculated as follows. It has been established that a modification of the monetary system comes into effect in the second half of the fifteenth century. The ruble is then divided into 200 *den'gi* and includes 2 *poltiny* of 100 *den'gi* each and 10 *grivny* of 20 *den'gi* each. In addition to this, 1 *altyn* = 6 *den'gi* (Cf. E. I. Kamentseva and N. V. Ustiugov, *Russkaia metrologiia* [Moscow, 1965], pp. 63–64). The sums listed in the will of Ivan III may thus be calculated in rubles and fractions of rubles; they reach 81.9 rubles for Iury, 58.535 rubles for Dmitry, 64.95 rubles for Semen, 40.5175 for Andrey, 717.5125 for Vasily, and 37.5 for Fedor. The total obtained is 1,000.915 rubles, which differs only very slightly from the theoretical total amount quoted in the charter.

135. The case of Fedor Borisovich of Volok will be examined below (see p. 55), since other documents concerning this principality make it possible to compare the amount of the *vykhod* paid in at various dates. The table found in the last part of the present article shows the approximate decrease of the *vykhod* paid by the various territories listed in the will of Ivan III.

136. See above, p. 45.

137. *DDG*, p. 359.

138. Depreciation of the ruble in the second half of the fifteenth century reduced its silver value to 80 grams (Kamentseva and Ustiugov, *op. cit.*, p. 64), i.e. a decrease of approximately 20 percent, which reduces even more the real value of the *vykhod* paid in 1504.

139. For a description of the relations between Iury Dmitrievich and his father's successors on the Moscow throne (his brother Vasily I and his nephew Vasily II), see the analysis of Cherepnin, *Russkie feodal'nye arkhivy. . . , op. cit.*, pp. 100–102.

140. *DDG*, p. 66.

141. We have seen (p. 45) that Zvenigorod and its districts paid a tribute of 272 rubles in 1389.

142. This could have been embodied in an agreement that has not been preserved.

143. Cf. Cherepnin, *Russkie feodal'nye arkhivy . . ., op. cit.,* pp. 103–108.

144. *DDG,* p. 74.

145. See above, p. 45.

146. Cf. L. V. Cherepnin, *Russkie feodal'nye arkhivy . . ., op. cit.,* p. 103.

147. *DDG,* pp. 75–78.

148. *Ibid.,* p. 76.

149. *Ibid.,* p. 77.

150. *Ibid.,* pp. 252–268.

151. See above, p. 45. Since no data is available on this point, we assume that Andrey Vasil'evich only received Mozhaisk and its districts on this occasion, without the *ot'ezdnye volosti,* for which sixty-eight rubles more had to be paid.

152. This is equal to 100.915 rubles.

153. *DDG,* p. 254.

154. *Ibid.,* pp. 322–328.

155. For the comparison of the corresponding paragraphs, see *DDG,* pp. 253 and 324.

156. That is, 105.725 rubles.

157. *DDG,* p. 325.

158. *Ibid.,* pp. 354–361.

159. *Ibid.,* pp. 268–275, 315–322.

160. The corresponding paragraphs are on pages 269 and 317 of *DDG.*

161. *DDG,* pp. 270 and 318.

162. *Ibid.,* pp. 341–344.

163. See above, p. 51.

164. It is assumed here that the 1,000 rubles paid by Moscow in 1389 are included in the 5,000 and that this sum as well as the 1,500 paid for Nizhny-Novgorod in 1401 are part of the 7,000 mentioned at that date. If this is not so, the *vykhod* would reach 6,000 and 9,500 rubles, respectively.

165. This conclusion is based on the fact that these regions are omitted in Donskoy's will. Direct proof may also be adduced. The testament of Ivan II (1358) contains the following clause: "If, as a consequence of our sins, the Horde were to attack Kolomna, or the territories of Lopastnia, or the territories exchanged with Riazan', and if because of our sins one of these territories were to be captured, my children . . . will share among themselves in its place tax-free lands (*bezpennye*)"; *DDG,* pp. 15–16.

166. The best analysis of this subject is that given by N. D. Chechulin in his article "Nachalo v Rossi perepisei i khodi do kontsa XVI veka," *Bibliograf,* No. 2 (St. Petersburg, 1889), pp. 41–61.

167. *Ibid.,* p. 43.

168. See above, p. 52.

169. See above, p. 51.

170. *Novgorodskaia pervaia letopis' . . ., op. cit.,* p. 344.

171. N. I. Aristov, *Promyshlennost' Drevnei Rusi* (St. Petersburg, 1886), pp. 127–128.

172. P. I. Liashchenko, *Istoriia narodnogo khoziaistva SSSR,* Vol. 1 (Moscow, 1956), p. 199.

173. Smirnov, *op. cit.,* p. 72.

174. See the study by V. L. Ianin, "Numizmatika i problemy tovarnodenezhnogo obrashcheniia v drevnei Rusi," *Voprosy Istorii,* No. 8 (1955), p. 140.

175. These sources may be found in A. L. Khoroshkevich, *Torgovlia velikogo Novgoroda v XIV–XV vv.* (Moscow, 1963), pp. 269–270.

176. D. P. Makovskii, *Razvitie tovarno-denezhnykh otnoshenii v sel'skom khoziaistve russkogo gosudarstva v XVI v.* (Smolensk, 1963).

# Khan or Basileus: An Aspect of Russian Mediaeval Political Theory

## MICHAEL CHERNIAVSKY

Every historian interested in Russia has to deal with one of the most vivid and fundamental facts of Russian history: the Tatar Yoke, when the larger portion of Russia was conquered in the thirteenth century, and remained for over two centuries, *de jure* at least, a province of an Asiatic empire. Completely within the area conquered by the Tatars or Mongols was northeast Russia, the foundation of the later Muscovite tsardom and of Imperial Russia. The historians of Russia generally interpret the Mongol conquest and yoke as a *diabolus ex machina*, an external factor, which interrupted or distorted the natural, internal logic of Russian historical development. As such the Tatar Yoke was mainly significant for its implications in later Russian history; the chief historiographic quest was to find out in what way and to what extent it actually interrupted or distorted Russian history. Underlying this procedure was, of course, the particular view each historian had of the pattern and logic of Russian history as a whole.[1] A corollary of this view of the historiography for Russia's thirteenth, fourteenth, and fifteenth centuries is a relative paucity of works on the Tatar state and Tatar-Russian relations;[2] a corollary, because there seems to have prevailed a vague desire to get rid of, to by-pass, the whole problem as quickly as possible, and to get back to the "natural course" of Russian history no matter how badly it had become distorted by the long interruption.

The concern of the present paper is to deal with only one aspect of the general problem of the Tatar Yoke and the changes in Russian society and life induced by it. What consequences did it have for Russia's image of her ruler, the Grand Prince and later Tsar of Russia? To answer this one must start by asking what was the mediaeval Russian image of the ruler? What models of rulership were available?

The traditional and largely correct interpretation has been that, for mediaeval Russia, the supreme image of absolute power and rule was the Byzantine emperor, the *basileus*, the "tsar." From the moment of St. Vladimir's baptism

FROM Michael Cherniavsky, "Khan or Basileus: An Aspect of Russian Mediaeval Political Theory," *Journal of the History of Ideas*, 20 (October–December 1959), 459–476. Reprinted by permission of the publisher.

the Russian state entered the Universal Christian Empire, living under one holy emperor, the image of God on earth, the source of orthodoxy and law and thus of salvation. During the ensuing centuries, whatever the political realities might be, Russians acknowledged the legitimacy of at least the spiritual or eschatological sovereignty of the basileus.[3] The dialectic of this acknowledgment was finally completed after the fall of Constantinople and the death of the last Roman Emperor on its walls, when Moscow (the Third Rome) and its orthodox ruler acquired, in Russian eyes, the prerogatives of the former Empire.[4]

Though the basileus determined the image of rulership for mediaeval Russia, this did not necessarily mean that the Russians also acknowledged his sovereignty over them; on the contrary, time and again, Russian princes usurped the privileges of the emperor. In Kievan Russia, princes were sometimes portrayed as Byzantine patricians or despots, hierarchic members of the universal Christian society, and sometimes portrayed in the garb and with the regalia of the emperors themselves.[5] The coins of Kievan Russia, patterned on Byzantine money, show the Russian prince in the place of the basileus.[6] Finally, in the liturgy of the eleventh and twelfth centuries the name of the Russian prince frequently replaces that of the emperor in the diptychs—the commemoration lists—where the priest prays for and glorifies the ruler and all Christendom.[7] But this very usurpation of the formal and basic attributes of rulership—regalia, coinage, liturgy—is in itself the best proof of the power emanating from the image of the basileus. Recognition and usurpation created, within the image of the ruler, a tension which found its expression in the inconsistency of the Russian view itself.

The same inconsistency appears perhaps even more crudely when the Russian acknowledgment could be exploited after 1453, when there no longer was a Byzantine-Roman emperor, while the vacant throne which remained "for as long as the world lasted" demanded a basileus.[8]

The steps which the Russian Grand Prince took toward this throne were slow and hesitant. Far more frequently than in the Kievan period do the prayer-books contain a prayer for the emperor when in fact there was no emperor; and only with the coronation of Ivan IV as Tsar, in 1547, does the confusion in the diptychs cease.[9] Titulature shows the same ambivalence. It is true, Dimitrii Donskoi is called tsar in praise for his victory over the Tatars at Kulikovo in 1380, but the title refers to his tsarlike qualities and achievements rather than to his actual status.[10] The fall from Grace of the Byzantine Empire at the Council of Florence and its final fall in 1453 does not result in a consistent adoption of the imperial title on the part of the Grand Prince. Only with the reign of Basil III (1505–1533) do Russian "schoolmen," writing for internal consumption, begin to call the Grand Prince "tsar" with any regularity;[11] and, again, only by the coronation of 1547 was the Russian ruler established, universally and formally, as tsar. Even this coronation, however, presents us with problems. The first imperial coronation[12] was anticipated with what seems to be typical ambiguity, when Grand Prince Ivan III, in 1498 crowned his grandson Dimitrii as co-ruler and Grand Prince. A glance at the coronation ceremony shows that it was a copy of the Byzantine coronation ritual for a caesar only, a junior co-emperor.[13] This implies that Ivan III, as Grand Prince, performed the rôle of the senior emperor, the augustus, the basileus.

What all this amounts to is that Russian reception of the basileus image oscillated between the need to acknowledge and the desire to usurp this very image. The process of assimilating this image, of identifying the Russian ruler with the basileus took a long time.[14] So much so that for over a century the throne of the ideal "universal empire" remained vacant before the Russian Grand Prince was crowned as tsar and autocrat.

If the central, supreme image of rulership for the Russians was the basileus, what was the significance for Russian political theory of the fact that after 1240 another concrete image of rulership was available—that of the *khan*, who ruled over a vast empire of which northeastern Russia was only a province? What modifications, nuances or distortions in the Russian ruler-image were induced by this fact?

From the beginning of the Mongol or Tatar period in Russia, the Tatar ruler was always referred to in the chronicles as "tsar."[15] Russian pet names for the Tatars are hardly polite,[16] but even when used as epithets for the ruler, the khan,[17] they are used in conjunction with the title of tsar. This is to say that the Russians assigned to their conquerer and his heirs the title which, both before and after the Tatar Yoke, was reserved for only one ruler—the universal Christian emperor.[18] Some proof that the Russians used this title deliberately and with full awareness of its implications lies in the careful distinctions they drew between the various titles: the khan of Chingizide blood, was always tsar; his heir and co-ruler was referred to as "tsesar," i.e., the caesar or junior emperor. Members of the khan's family were "tsarevichi."[19] But Mamai and Edigei, powerful *de facto* rulers of the Golden Horde in the 1380s and the 1410s respectively, but not of the blood, were called only princes; Mamai particularly was considered to be a usurper of the tsar's authority over Russia.[20] Iconographic sources are as consistent as the chronicles about the imperial status of the khan. In all images, including miniatures showing Russian victories over the Tatars, the khan is always shown wearing a radiate crown, contrasted with the grand prince in his cap.[21]

That the title "tsar" as applied to the khan carried definite connotations of legitimacy, is revealed by the chronicles in other ways as well. In 1245–6 prince Michael of Chernigov travelled to the Horde. Upon arrival, before being admitted to Khan Batu, he was required to perform a purification ritual, passing between lines of fires and stone idols. He was informed that the khan ordered him to go through the ceremony but the prince was stubborn; according to the chronicle, however, he prefaced his final refusal with the words: "I bow to you, oh Tsar, for God has given you the tsardom and the glory of this world. . . ."[22] He will submit himself to the khan, the "Tsar," but not to the pagan gods; for this Michael gladly suffered martyrdom. The Pauline note of all power being from God and thus legitimate was also sounded in the summons of Batu to Grand Prince Alexander Nevski, the defender and the "sun" of Russia, recorded in the Grand Princely chronicle: "God has subjected to me many tongues. Do you alone wish not to submit yourself to my power; yet if you wish to preserve your land, then come to me and witness the glory of my reign (*tsarstviia*)."[23] As "Tsar" the khan was the ruler ordained by God and he acquired the ideological weight of Christian conceptions of the ruler. "Fear God and honor the prince. And whosoever opposed the ruler will be subject to Divine justice, because he opposed the command of God" states a thirteenth-century tractate;[24] to attack the prince is to defy God, and this sentiment is echoed in one of the earliest Russian epics in which the epic hero, Ilia Muromets, knows that one is not allowed to, that one cannot actually kill the Tatar "tsar."[25]

There was a fundamental difference, however, between the basileus and the khan. The one was the orthodox Christian emperor ruling over all men insofar as the world was a Christian society; the other was a pagan or, even worse, from the fourteenth century on, a Moslem infidel. What effect did this difference have for the Russian image of the khan? In 1393 patriarch Antonios of Constantinople wrote his famous letter to Grand Prince Basil I in which he outlined the whole doctrine of Byzantine imperial ideology. The occasion for this letter was the disrespect supposedly shown by Basil to the patriarch and the emperor; among other things, the patriarch wrote: "people say that you do not allow the metropolitan to mention the divine name of the emperor in the diptypchs, that is, you want to do something which is quite impossible and you say: 'yes, we have the church, but we have no emperor and do not wish to know him.'"[26] The letter belongs properly to the history of Russo-Byzantine relations, of Russian ambivalence towards the imperial idea, and as such does not concern us here. But it raises an interesting question: what of the imperial name in the liturgy while Russia was part of the Tatar state? The sources are extremely sparse, but except for the personal missal of the Greek metropolitan Cyprian[27] (1374–1406) there is no mention of the emperor during the thirteenth and fourteenth centuries in any case.[28] If we consider, however, that the liturgy of the Kievan period frequently omitted the emperor in the diptychs, Basil's defiance seems to be the flogging of a very dead horse, unless it was in response to an attempt by the Greek metropolitan to re-introduce the basileus into the liturgy. Could this long omission lasting two centuries have been affected, then, by the existence of the khan? The Russian mediaevalist Grekov gives a very definite answer: "The public prayer of the clergy for the khans inculcated in the masses the idea of the necessity of submission to Tatar power."[29] The khan's name does not actually appear in any of the missals and service books, but there is impressive evidence to support Grekov.

This evidence is contained in a number of *iarlyks* or charters given by various Tatar khans to the Russian church in the person of the metropolitan of all Russia.[30] The contents of these charters are virtually identical: all of them are immunity grants, exempting the metropolitan and the entire clergy with all their possessions from all civil duties and taxes. The khans based this immunity on the tradition established by the law code of Chingiz-khan himself,[31] and it was granted against the officials of the khan and against all Russian officials and princes, including the Grand Prince himself.[32] The Russian church was placed under the immediate jurisdiction of the khan-tsar, retaining a universal rather than a national-territorial character under a ruler of many states and peoples. In return for all these privileges the church had but one duty—to pray for the khan: "That they may pray to God in peace . . . and pray to God for Us and Our House (*plemiia*) from generation to generation."[33] And, as if anticipating possible reservations, charter after charter warns: "If any clergyman prays with mental reservations, he commits a mortal sin."[34]

Even though the service books of the liturgy are silent on this question, it is difficult to escape the conclusion that in practice the prayer for the khan did replace the memorial for the basileus. The fact that this did not enter into the missals is comprehensible, considering that the ruler for whom one prayed was an infidel, a "godless one." As such he could not be entered into the official cult, he could not become part of the commemoration of all Christians, but he could, and did, occupy the traditional rôle of the ruler who is from God, appointed by God and therefore prayed for to God. It is not necessary here to argue the need for consistency on the part of the Russians, nor to impose on them the need for a clear choice between the basileus or the khan. In fact, such a clear-cut choice would be impossible and ideological astigmatism could and did occur. What did exist was yet another kind of tension, an atmosphere where the image of the khan overlapped that of the basileus, vaguely fused with the latter; exactly because it did not replace the latter, the image of the khan could borrow the attributes of the image of the basileus and could become identified in the popular and in the official mind with it. All this is to say that, through the encounter of political reality and ideological tradition, the khan as "tsar" acquired, in the liturgy as in titulature, the attributes of the universal and unique emperor.

One more area with implications and possibilities of image-making remains— that of numismatic iconography. Russian coinage of the Kievan period, patterned on Byzantine models, appears to have ceased towards the middle of the twelfth century.[35] For the next 250 years or so Russian princes did not mint any coins. The minting of coins was resumed sometime between the sixties and the eighties of the fourteenth century, in Moscow.[36] A purely economic cause for the resumption of coinage is not very convincing.[37] Of political causes, three are suggested: desire on the part of the Tatars for another concrete acknowledgment by the Russians of Tatar sovereignty; desire on the part of Dimitrii Donskoi, the Grand Prince, in the 1360s and 1370s to express nascent Russian nationalism which culminated with the battle of Kulikovo in 1380; and (for those who suggest the 1380s as the starting date) desire to celebrate the new national consciousness won on the field of Kulikovo.[38] The evidence which we shall now examine appears to support the first of the political causes. Briefly, Russian coinage from the reign of Dimitrii Donskoi till 1480, the formal end of the Tatar Yoke, falls into two periods: the first consisting of the reigns of Dimitrii, Vasilii I, and the early years of Vasilii II;[39] and the second, of about 50 years, made up of the greater part of Vasilii II's reign and of the first twenty years of Ivan III's. The coinage of the first period shows a consistent pattern: on the obverse of the coins is the name of the reigning Grand Prince and one of a limited number of symbols, usually animals or birds; on the reverse there is, in Arabic, the name of the reigning khan, sometimes accompanied by the slogan: "May he live long"; sometimes by a profiled head which was, in all probability, a portrait of the khan.[40] Only infrequently, on the coins of this first period is there found, on the reverse, an inscription which is just a scribble designed to imitate Arabic lettering —at best an attempt to copy Arabic by someone who did not know the language.[41] The second period presents us with coins in which the meaningless copy of an Arabic inscription is the rule rather than the exception;[42] in addition, a number of coins of Basil II carry, on the reverse, instead of the name of the khan in Arabic, the inscription in Russian: "Grand Prince Vasilii of all Russia."[43]

What significance can be attached to the evidence of Russian coins? In 1383, at the beginning of the great struggle between Tamerlane and the ruler of the Golden Horde of the Tatars, Kahn Tokhtamysh, one of Tamerlane's grievances was the minting of coins with Tokhtamysh's name in Khwarezm which Tamerlane considered to be part of his own empire.[44] In 1399, during the course of negotiations between the Golden Horde (led by prince Edigei) and Lithuania (under Grand Prince Vitovt), the Russian chronicle tells us that ". . . Vitovt desired that in all the Horde, there should be on the money of the Horde his mark, his sign (or image)," while Edigei demanded that: "In all your principality, on your Lithuanian coins there should be my Horde mark."[45] There is little doubt then, that the Tatars, the Lithuanians, and, considering the origin of the chronicle, the Russians, recognized the inscription of a ruler's name on a coin as a sign of sovereignty.[46] The existence of the coins with the distorted Arabic inscription has given rise to the argument that it was placed on the coins for purely economic reasons, in order to present Oriental merchants with familiar-looking objects. The argument for "familiarity," however, does not really negate the political content of the coinage. It is clear that the name of the Khan on the early Russian coinage signified his sovereignty over Russia. With the civil war of the 1430s and 1440s in Moscow, nationalist, anti-Tatar slogans began to be used;[47] this, at the same time that Tatar power declined perceptibly. Coupled with the decline of Byzantine prestige and influence due to the Union of Florence and the finality of 1453, this situation led to an ever-greater disregard for the khan's privileges and to attempts to indicate a new and independent status on the coins of Basil II and Ivan III.

That this was the pattern of Russian thought during the century and yet that the coins symbolized the sovereignty of the khan was most clearly expressed after 1480. After this formal liberation from the Tatar Yoke by Ivan III a new coin type appeared in Muscovite Russia. The coins can actually be dated rather accurately and remarkably from 1480, i.e., from the very same year of the liberation.[48] On the obverse they display a crowned horseman, spearing a dragon or a snake, with the inscription—"Grand Prince Ivan Vasilievich"; on the reverse, in Arabic, is the name "Iban," with a Russian inscription around it—"Sovereign of all Russia."[49] The iconography of these striking coins has been interpreted in terms of requirements of eastern trade with Kazan and other Tatar states, the need for familiar looking coins; as with the imitation Arabic coins, this is irrelevant for our argument. What is relevant is the implicit recognition of coin-iconography as symbol of sovereignty, and the explicit pronouncement not so much of the independence of the Russian Grand Prince from the khan, as the replacement of the khan by the Grand Prince of all Russia.

One final consideration remains. The sources indicate quite clearly that the consent of the khan and the participation of his representative were necessary and customary for the coronation of Russian Grand Princes during the Tatar period.[50] Thus, part of the ritual involved the formal and ceremonial recognition of the suzerainty of the khan. Moreover, the testament (1339) of the founder of the Moscow dynasty, Ivan I Kalita, mentions for the first time the "golden cap" which, from the early sixteenth century on became known as the cap of Monomachos.[51] The consensus of scholarly opinions seems to be that the cap or crown of Monomachos is not of Byzantine origin but is Central Asiatic, perhaps a gift from khan Uzbek to Grand Prince Ivan I.[52] What became with the centuries the main regalia of the Russian state was originally, in this case, an expression of the sovereign position of the Tatar khan.

My purpose has not been to document the obvious—that for over two centuries the Tatar Golden Horde and its ruler exercised more or less effective political control over Russia. The evidence I have adduced presupposes the political realities of the Tatar Yoke. The Grand Prince of Moscow had to be crowned with the participation of the Tatar envoy, no matter what the Russian ideological rationale may have been. The church necessarily depended on the supreme political power for its rights and possessions, and, in the realm of political realities was so much aware of this, that as late as 1500 it used the khan's *iarlyks* in order to defend itself against the expropriations of the Russian ruler.[53] No matter what Russian ideologists would have liked to think, the image of the Russian prince was limited by the political situation, by the need to pay tribute and acknowledge suzerainty. My present purpose, rather, is to demonstrate the consequences of the political realities in the realm of ideas. What these consequences were during the Tatar Yoke itself, has been shown: the image of the Tatar khan as tsar, replacing or merging with the image of the basileus in respect to the prerogatives—coronation, liturgy, titulature, iconography. With the fall of Constantinople the Russian ruler begins to emerge as the Christian tsar, in the image of the basileus. What did the image of the Tatar khan signify for the Russian Grand Prince and tsar after 1480, after the lifting of the Yoke?

That the khan's image could not be dismissed casually, that the political realities created a strong tradition of Tatar sovereignty,[54] can be seen from a rather dramatic piece of evidence: the immediate reaction of Ivan III, in 1480, to the invasion of khan Akhmet was apparently a desire to abandon Moscow and retire with his family and treasure to the north. To forestall this, to induce the Grand Prince to fight, archbishop Vassian of Rostov wrote his famous "Epistle to the Ugra [River]." The letter begins: "To the pious and Christ-loving, noble and God-crowned, confirmed by God, in piety shining to the ends of the universe, certainly the most glorious among tsars, the Glorious Sovereign Grand Prince Ivan Vasilievich. . . ."[55] Such is the image of the Russian ruler that

Vassian tries to create; it is in this rôle of a God-crowned tsar, a basileus, that Ivan III ought to face the enemies of his state and faith. The Grand Prince is the shepherd of the flock of Christ, and the archbishop points out the responsibility assumed by past leaders of the flock, the great Grand Princes of Russia who fought for the Christian people. He tries to anticipate any possible arguments on the part of the advisers of Ivan III: "And if some will argue that you are under the oath of your ancestors not to raise your hand against the tsar; listen God-loving tsar! If an oath is made because of necessity, we are allowed to forgive the breaking of it and to bless for it, the metropolitan and we, the whole God-loving synod, [the oath being] not to a tsar but to a brigand and savage and fighter against God. . . . And who of the prophets of the prophecies or who of the apostles or saints have taught you to obey this God-shamed and most evil so-called tsar, you, the great Christian tsar of the Russian lands?"[56] The archbishop is trying here to destroy the image of the khan-tsar by raising the image of the tsar-basileus; only one tsar is possible, the orthodox Christian one, and the other is an impostor. Yet in order to fight this impostor it is necessary, Vassian felt, to raise the Grand Prince to the rôle of tsar himself. What Vassian was trying to do was to solve an ideological problem. Ivan III's reluctance to face the khan in battle was caused by political and military fears, not by his awe before his sovereign. Yet, politically and militarily, the Tatars remained a most serious danger for Russia not only during the 15th but also during the 16th century.[57] Vassian's problem, the ideological problem, was not just to defeat the Tatars in battle—it was to destroy the image of the khan as tsar. The fall of Constantinople, by making available, suddenly and immediately, a whole new world of the "Byzantine heritage" for Russian political theology, forced the issue and, at the same time, provided a solution: the basileus versus the khan. That this solution was at least partially adopted, can be seen in the case of the cap of Monomachos. The fourteenth-century Tatar crown was drawn into the legend of Russia's Byzantine heritage in the early sixteenth century;[58] in accordance with the Vassian solution, with the birth of the Russian tsar-basileus, the Tatar period should come to an end, the continuity should be broken.

The thesis that the continuity was not broken was the great contribution of the "Eurasian" school of Russian historians in the 1920s, and particularly of the distinguished mediaevalist, Professor George Vernadsky. But if Russia became heir to the empire of Chingiz Khan,[59] it remains to be seen in what sense this was true. What does seem clear is that, for Russians of the sixteenth century, the title of "tsar" was firmly connected with the image of the khan; more so than with that of the basileus. A Russian diplomatic note of 1556 to Poland and Lithuania justified Ivan IV's title not only through the Byzantine heritage but also through his possession of Kazan and Astrakhan, and "the throne of Kazan and Astrakhan has been a tsar's see from their origins."[60] The seventeenth-century writer Gregory Kotoshikhin explained that: "Grand Prince Ivan Vasilievich of Moscow, the Proud . . . went to war against the tsardoms of Kazan and Astrakhan and Siberia; and with God's will he captured the tsars of these tsardoms, together with their states and lands. . . . And from that time on he became

Grand Prince over the Moscow State and over the conquered tsardoms and over former principalities, [he became] tsar and Grand Prince Ivan Vasilievich of all Russia, in this way did tsardom originate in Russia."[61] The titulature of the Russian tsar confirmed the special rôle of the Tatar successor states: "Great Sovereign, Tsar and Grand Prince of all Russia, of Vladimir, of Moscow, of Novgorod, Tsar of Kazan, Tsar of Astrakhan, Sovereign of Pskov, Grand Prince of Smolensk, Tver'. . . ."[62] It is significant that the coronation of Ivan IV as tsar took place shortly before his campaign against Kazan, in 1547, and while Kazan had been fought, defeated and controlled already by Ivan III and Vasilii III, Ivan IV had himself crowned tsar before setting out on a campaign not just to defeat but to conquer Kazan, the first tsardom to belong to the Russian state. During Ivan IV's reign, Tatar Chingizide princes retain a particularly high status,[63] and the recognition of the very high ranking of Chingizide blood remained alive at the Russian court throughout the nineteenth century.[64]

Professor Vernadsky ends his monumental work with the statement that autocracy was part of the price Russia had to pay for survival under the Tatars and in the period immediately following.[65] Autocracy as such, however, is not a very rigid or definite form of government. The autocracy of the basileus was, after all, rule under Law, the rule of the Christian emperor. Russian autocracy was most clearly expressed by what was in effect, Basil III's belief about his subjects: "All are slaves (Vse kholopy)."[66] If this does not derive from the image of the basileus, it may well derive from the image of the khan.

Psychologically, the exaltation of one's own conqueror is quite understandable.[67] If Russia was to be subject, let her be subject to a great ruler, a legitimate tsar. The consequence of this, of course, is the exaltation of the Russian prince who could successfully oppose the tsar. This note is already quite clear after the victory of Dimitrii Donksoi at Kulikovo in 1380. Contrasted with the power and glory of the Tatars is the power and glory of the leader of all Russia, who in reality was only the Grand Prince of Moscow.[68] This note, too, is sounded and proclaimed in 1480 by the new coinage of Ivan III where the name "Ivan" replaces the name of the khan. What takes place is not so much the liberation of Russia as a change of dynasty, the conquest of Russia from its former legitimate ruler by the new legitimate tsar, the Grand Prince of Moscow. The Arabic "Ivan" on the coin may have been addressed, for economic reasons, to the eastern subjects of the Horde; but to them, or to the Russians, it also meant that in addition to the Russian Grand Prince on the obverse there was a new khan, still, traditionally, on the reverse side.

I am not prepared, of course, to argue that ideas determine material conditions and reality; but evoked by those conditions, ideas have a logic and life of their own and carry their consequences into reality. That the idea of conquest, of the Russian ruler as the khan existed, implicitly at least, is suggested by the slogan of Basil III's time mentioned above. It was made quite explicit by Ivan IV the Terrible, when official mythology departed from the traditional Kievan origin, from the emphasis on St. Vladimir, and created the fantastic descent of the Russian rulers from Prus, the brother of Augustus.[69] Ivan IV himself pointedly disclaimed any Russian blood in his veins.[70] It is doubtful whether the conquest idea expressed through the Roman descent ever gained much currency. The image of the khan in that context, however, did receive an expression, both sickly and fantastic though it was, when Ivan IV "abandoned" the state, divided Russia into two parts, taking one himself under a guise of great humility, and giving the other, the greater and traditional part a ruler, a Grand Prince, in the person of a Tatar tsarevich from Kasimov, Simeon.[71] The irony was not in the division, or in the use of a Tatar prince, but in the reversal of rôles. For it was the traditional, orthodox Christian Russia that got the Chingizide prince, and the new absolutist secular Russia that got the God-crowned tsar.

Speculations on the Asiatic-barbaric element in Russian history have been innumerable in the course of the last two centuries, yet I should like to add one more. Barbarism, of course, is not the issue; Western history has shown sufficiently that barbarism can be attained without an Asiatic image or myth. If the image of the basileus stood for the orthodox and pious ruler, leading his Christian people toward salvation, then the image of the khan, perhaps, was preserved in the idea of the Russian ruler as the conqueror of Russia and of its people, responsible to no one. If the basileus signified the holy tsar, the "most gentle" (tishaishii) tsar in spiritual union with his flock, then the khan, perhaps, stood for the absolutist secularized state, arbitrary through its separation from the subjects.[72] The two images were not really synthesized; both existed separately, if in a state of tension which the first Russian Tsar, Ivan IV, exemplified so tragically: killing by day and praying by night.


*NOTES*

1. An excellent summary of the opinions of the great historians is given in V. D. Grekov and A. I. Iakubovskii, *Zolotaia Orda i ee padenie* [*The Golden Horde and Its Fall*] (Moscow, 1950), 247–61. Three views are in evidence: that the Tatar conquest meant a general barbarization (Karamzin, Bestuzhev-Riumin, Platonov in the sense of isolation, as well as the Byzantinists Diakonov and Savva); that the Tatars contributed to the political and administrative unification (Kliuchevsky, Kostomarov, the jurist Sergeevich and the Marxist Pokrovsky); finally, that the Yoke was of little importance (Soloviev, Rozhkov, and, in particular, the great Russian historian of the 20th century, Presniakov).

2. The first serious study was the collection of sources on the Golden Horde including its Russian relations edited by Baron V. G. Tizengausen, *Sbornik materialov otnosiashchikhsia k istorii Zolotoi Ordy* [*Collection of Sources Referring to the History of the Golden Horde*], I (St. Petersburg, 1884), II (Leningrad, 1941). B. Spuler's *Die Goldene Horde* (Leipzig, 1943) does not concentrate on Tartar-Russian relations primarily; the three major works known to me are all very recent: A. N. Nasonov, *Mongoly i Rus'* [*The Mongols and Russia*] (Moscow, 1940); Grekov and Iakubovskii, *op. cit.*; and G. Vernadsky, *The Mongols and Russia* (New Haven, 1953).

3. The problem of determining in detail just what image the Russians had of the emperor and how much of it they accepted at different times is a very complex one. Much of Byzantine political theology was unknown to the Russians or, if known, incomprehensible. The letter of the Emperor John Cantacuzene in 1347 to Grand Prince Simeon the Proud, quoting the latter, probably expressed the general and rather vague Russian view of the rôle of the emperor: "Yes, as you wrote, the Empire of the Romans and the most holy great Church of God are the sources of all piety and the school of sanctity and lawgiving." F. Miklosich and I. Müller, *Acta patriarchatus Constantinopolitani* (Vienna, 1860), I, 263. Despite all the attempts at ideo-

logical rebellion, Basil II, as late as 1451–2, after the Union of Florence, which marked the apostasy of the Byzantines, and on the eve of the empire's fall, acknowledged in detail the supremacy of the emperor implied in Simeon's statement. Cf. letter of Basil II to Emperor Constantine XI, *Russkaia Istoricheskaia Biblioteka* (St. Petersburg, 1880), VI, no. 71, p. 575. On the general problem of Russian relations with and views of Byzantium, see F. Ternovskii, *Izucheniie vizantiiskoi istorii i eiia tendentsioznoe prilozhenie v drevnei Rusi* [*The Study of Byzantine History and Its Tendential Application in Ancient Russia*] (Kiev, 1875); M. A. Diakonov, *Vlast' Moskovskikh Gosudarei* [*The Power of the Muscovite Sovereigns*] (St. Petersburg, 1889); V. Val'denberg, *Drevnerusskie ucheniia o predelakh tsarskoi vlasti* [*Old-Russian Teachings on the Limits of Tsarist Power*] (Petrograd, 1916); A. A. Vasiliev, "Was Old Russia a Vassal State of Byzantium?" *Speculum,* VII (1932), 350–360; C. Chernousov, "K voprosu o vlianii vizantiiskogo prava na drevneishee russkoe" ["On the Problem of the Influence of Byzantine Law on the Earliest Russian"], *Vizantiiskoe Obozrenie* (Iurev, 1916), II, 303–322; I. Ševčenko, "A Neglected Byzantine Source of Muscovite Political Ideology," *Harvard Slavic Studies II* (1954), 141–181.

4. The amount of literature on this subject is considerable and repetitive. See H. Schaeder, *Moscau das Dritte Rom* (Hamburg, 1929); V. Malinin, *Starets Eleasorova monastyria Filofei i ego poslaniia* [*The Elder of the Eleazar Monastery, Philotheus and his Epistles*] (Kiev, 1901); I. Ševčenko, "Intellectual Repercussions of the Council of Florence," *Church History,* XXIV (1955), 291–323; M. Cherniavsky, "The Reception of the Council of Florence in Moscow," *ibid.,* 347–359.

5. See N. P. Kondakov, *Izobrazhenie Russkoi kniazheskoi sem'i v miniaturakh XI veka* [*The Representation of a Russian Princely Family in Miniatures of the 11th Century*] (St. Petersburg, 1906); Kondakov, *Russkie Klady* [*Russian Treasure-Troves*] (St. Petersburg, 1896), I, 61 f.; *Russkie drevnosti v pamiatnikakh iskustva* [*Russian Antiquities in Monuments of Art*], ed. I. A. Tolstoi and N. P. Kondakov, vol. III, fig. 166, vol. IV, 35 f.; A. Grabar, "Les fresques des escaliers à Sainte-Sophie de Kiev et l'iconographie impériale byzantine," *Seminarium Kondakovianum,* VII (1935), 103–119.

6. A. V. Oreshnikov, *Denezhnyie znaki domongol'skoi Rusi* [*Moneys of Pre-Mongol Russia*], Trudy Gos. Istor. muzeia (Moscow, 1936); see also Oreshnikov, *Russkie Monety do 1547 goda* [*Russian Coins till 1547*], Imp. Ross. Ist. Muzei, Opisanie Pamiatnikov I (St. Petersburg, 1910), 1–5, pl. I., hereafter referred to as *Monety.*

7. Diakonov, *op. cit.,* 24, note 2, argues, on the basis of three pre-Tatar missals, that the name of the emperor was usually omitted from the liturgy; cf. also A. Gorskii and K. Nevostruev, *Opisanie slavianskikh rukopisei Moskovskoi sinodal'noi biblioteki* [*Description of Manuscripts of the Moscow Synodal Library*] (Moscow, 1894), III: 1, p. 2 f., p. 250 f. Considering the later history of the diptychs, however, this argument from silence is not very convincing. On diptychs in Eastern liturgy, see I. M. Hanssens, *Institutiones Liturgicae de Ritibus Orientalibus* (Rome, 1932), III, 1340–1, 1354–5.

8. The monk Philotheos, ideologue of Moscow the Third Rome, expressed this idea most clearly; cf. Malinin, *op. cit.,* Appendix, 50 f. *et passim.* For the Byzantine conception of the emperor, see O. Treitinger, *Die Oströmische Kaiser- und Reichsidee* (Jena, 1938). The Russians never acknowledged the imperial rôle or position of the Western emperors, awarding to them the subordinate rôle of caesar (tsesar); cf. D. I. Prozorovskii, "O znachenii tsarskogo titula do priniatiia russkimi gosudariami titula Imperatorskogo" ["On the Meaning of the Title of 'Tsar' till the Adoption by Russian Sovereigns of the Title of 'Emperor'"], *Izvestiia Imp. Russkogo Arkheologicheskago Obshchestva,* VIII (1877), 449 f.

9. In a service book of 1457, for example, twice the prince is mentioned instead of the emperor, and then twice again the emperor is referred to: Gorskii and Nevostruev, III: 2, no. 501, pp. 266–7, 273–4, in *Chteniia v Obshchestve Istorii i Drevnostei Rossiiskikh* (1917), 4. While a missal of ca. 1500 enjoins the priest to "memorialize . . . our princes and not the tsar, for there is no tsardom here in our Russia" (*Izvestiia Imp. Arkheologicheskogo Obshchestva,* V, 138), a service book of about the same date speaks only of the tsar (Gorskii and Nevostruev, III: 1, 48). The emperor is memorialized in prayer books of 1462 (Gorskii and Nevostruev, III: 1, 46), 1481 (Gorskii and Nevostruev, III: 1, 199) and in a number of codices of the late 15th and early 16th centuries (Gorskii and Nevostruev, III: 1, 66; II: 2, 182; I. Sreznevskii, *Svedeniia i zametki o maloizvestnykh i neizvestnykh pamiatnikakh* [*Studies and Notes Concerning Unknown and Little Known Sources*], no. LXXIX, in *Sbornik otdeleniia russkago iazyka i slovesnosti Imp. Akademii Nauk,* XX: 4, 558). On the other hand, the prince is mentioned in a number of service books (Gorskii and Nevostruev, III: 1, 37; III: 1, 53; III: 2, 259; III: 1, 45,

where both prince and tsar are mentioned; *Pamiatniki Drevnei Pismennosti*, III, 1880, Protokol zasedaniia Komiteta, April 4, 1880) and even in one missal of 1551 or later, i.e., after the coronation of Ivan IV as tsar (Gorskii and Nevostruev, III: 1, 60). It is probable, however, that, by the middle of the 16th century, the distinction between "tsar" and prince ("kniaz'") was slowly obliterated; see, for example, the Minea of 1567 where the emperor is called prince, in Kh. Loparev, *Opisanie Rukopisei Imp. Ob. Liubitelei drevnei Pismennosti* [*Description of Manuscripts of the Imperial Society of Lovers of Ancient Literature*] (St. Petersburg, 1892), 45 *et passim*.

10. Cf. *Polnoe Sobranie Russkikh Letopisei*, VI, app. "B" 90 f.; S. Shambinago, "Povesti o Mamaevom poboishche" ["Tales of Mamai's Battle"], *Sb. otd. russ. iaz. i slov.*, LXXXI, no. 7. Hereafter, P.S.R.L. refers to the first work.

11. Cf. Prozorovskii, *op. cit.*

12. Compare Ivan's coronation rite (E. V. Barsov, *Drevne-russkie pamiatniki sviashchennago venchaniia tsarei no tsarstvo* [*Old-Russian Sources for the Sacred Coronation of the Tsars*], *Chteniia*, 1883; I, 42–90) with Constantine Porphyrogenitus, *Le Livres des Cérémonies*, ed. A. Vogt (Paris, 1939), II, 1 f., and Codinus Curopalates, *De Officialibus Palatii Constantinopolitani*, ed. I Bekker, C.S.H.B., XIV (Bonn, 1839), 86 f. Cf. Val'denberg, *op. cit.*, 275 f.; G. Olšr, "Chiesa e Stato nell'incoronazione degli ultimi Rurikidi," *Orientalia Christiana Periodica*, XVI (1950), 290 f. suggests that the coronation rite included the ceremony of unction; however, the statement about unction in the chronicle was probably added after the coronation of Michael Romanov in 1613 (cf. "Tsarstvennaia Kniga" ["The Imperial Book"], *P.S.R.L.*, XIII, 452, note 1).

13. Olšr, *op. cit.*, 285 f., argues that the coronation *ordo* for Dimitrii differs significantly from the Byzantine imperial coronation, and explains it by the greater religiosity of the Russians who therefore assigned a greater rôle to the clergy than was done in Constantinople. The coronation *ordo* of Dimitrii, however, is a translation of a Serbian manuscript of the 14th century, which in turn was a translation of the Byzantine coronation *ordo* for a caesar or junior emperor. Cf. Barsov, *op. cit.*, for the coronation of Dimitrii, 33 f.; for the Serbian and Byzantine rites, 25 f.

14. The title "By the Grace of God" was introduced by Basil II still within the "Byzantine" period, in 1449, in his diplomatic documents (*Dukhovnye i Dogovornye Gramoty Velikikh i Udel'nykh Kniazei XIV–XVII vv.* [*Testaments and Treaties of Grand and Appanage Princes of the 14th–16th Centuries*], ed. L. V. Cherepnin [Moscow, 1950], 160, 163, hereafter referred to as *Gramoty*). The title "tsar" appears in diplomatic documents (*Pamiatniki Diplomaticheskikh Snoshenii Drevnei Rossii s Derzhavami Inostrannymi* (St. Petersburg, 1851), I, 46, 47, 59–61, 87, 96, 98, 114), but, for internal consumption, the title of "Tsar" is used to signify spiritual qualities (c.f Paschalia for the year 7000, *Russkaia Istoricheskaia Biblioteka*, VI, no. 118, 795 f.). Despite Ivan's marriage (1472) to the Byzantine heiress, Sophia Paleologus, which is supposed to have influenced Russian political thought profoundly (cf. G. Olšr, "Gli ultimi Rurikidi e le basi ideologiche della sovranita dello stato russo," *Orientalia Christiana Periodica*, XII [1946], 322–73), Byzantine court ranks were introduced very gradually, beginning with 1495; V. Prokhorov, *Khristianskie i russkie drevnosti i arkheologia* (*Christian and Early Russian Antiquities and Archeology*) (St. Petersburg, 1872), 36 f. The problem of the new Russian seal with the two-headed imperial eagle on it is a very complex one. There is no doubt that the eagle stood for the state symbol of the empire (cf. A. V. Soloviev, "Les emblèmes héraldiques de Byzance et les Slaves." *Seminarium Kondakovianum*, VII [1935], 149 f.). A. V. Oreshnikov argues that Ivan III began to use the double-headed eagle in 1472, immediately after his marriage with Sophia ("Materialy k russkoi numizmatike do-tsarskogo perioda" ["Sources for Russian Numismatics of the Pre-Tsar Period"], *Trudy Moskovskogo Numizmaticheskago Obshchestva*, II [1901], 12), but the first known use of the new seal dates from July 1497; *Gramoty*, no. 85, p. 341.

15. It is curious that despite the long associations with the steppe nomads the Sophia chronicler did not recognize "khan" as a title but thought it part of the name of the Tatar leaders; *P.S.R.L.*, V, 175 *et passim*.

16. *P.S.R.L.*, XXV, 126–7, 143, *et passim*. However, the Russians with great impartiality and good logic assigned the same epithets to Germans, Catholics in general, and Lithuanians (*ibid.*, 150, 193, *et passim*). On the popular view of the Tatars see I. U. Budovnitz, "Ideinaia osnova rannikh narodnykh skazanii o tatarskom ige" ["The Ideological Basis of Early Popular Tales about the Tatar Yoke"], *Trudy Otdela Drevnerusskoi Literatury Akademii Nauk*, XIV (1958), 169–175.

17. *P.S.R.L.*, XXV, 136. See, however, the very interesting study of R. Jakobson where he shows that the epithet "dog" (sobaka) was not really a denigrating one but derived from Tatar tribe names (O. Jansen, "Sobaka Kalin Tsar," *Slavia*, XVII [1939–40], 82–89). (Jakobson wrote under the pseudonym of O. Jansen.)

18. For the Russian attitude toward the title of "tsar" see Prozorovskii, *op. cit.* For the general European view of the title and its significance, see E. Stengel, "Kaisertitel und Suveränitätsidee," *Deutsches Archiv*, III, 1939, 1–57.

19. *P.S.R.L.*, XXV, 151, 152, 155, 238.

20. "I razgordeesia okannyi Mamai i mnia sia iako tsaria . . . ," *P.S.R.L.*, XXV, 201.

21. See the miniatures of the Nikon Chronicle, A. V. Artsikhovskii, *Drevnerusskie miniatiury kak istoricheskii istochnik* [*Old-Russian Miniatures as a Historical Source*] (Moscow, 1944), 53, 129, 144, 180; for discussion of regalia in general, see *ibid.*, 111 f. For representations of Russian princely caps, see, e.g., icon of SS Boris and Gleb, P. Mouratow, *L'Ancienne Peinture Russe* (Prague, 1925), fig. 33. For Russian conception of a crown, see, e.g., the crown of King Solomon in 15th-century fresco in the cathedral of the Assumption in Moscow, *ibid.*, fig. 41; the crown of the Byzantine emperor in the fresco of 1500–2 in the Ferapont Monastery, *Istoriia Russkogo Isskustva* [*History of Russian Art*], ed. I. Grabar, A. N. SSSR (Moscow, 1955), III, 511. An interesting ideological problem is raised by a fresco of 1508 in the cathedral of the Annunciation, Moscow, showing Grand Prince St. Vladimir in a princely cap, while Iaroslav the Wise is wearing a tsar's crown, *ibid.*, 545. How closely the crown was identified with tsardom can be seen in a miniature from the *Tsarstvennaia Kniga*, 1560–70s, showing the coronation of Ivan IV. The young tsar is shown in the radiate crown, just like the khans and the emperors (*ibid.*, 601). The point is, of course, that Ivan IV was crowned with the "Cap of Monomakhos" and Russian regalia did not include a radiate crown.

22. *P.S.R.L.*, XXV, 138.

23. *P.S.R.L.*, XXV, 139; this corresponds closely with the usual Mongol imperial diplomatic correspondence; cf. P. Pelliot, *Les Mongols et la Papauté* (Paris, 1923).

24. "Slovo sviatykh Otsov, kako zhiti krestianom" ["The Sayings of the Holy Fathers, On How Should Christians Live" ], *Zhurnal Ministerstva Narodnago Prosveshcheniia* (1854), no. 12; also see Sreznevskii, *op. cit.*, 307; "Izbornik Sviatoslava," *Obshchestvo Liubitelei Drevnei Pismennosti*, LV (1880), 95–6. For the legal consequences of this view, see "Merilo Pravednoe," *Arkhiv istoriko-iuridicheskikh svedenii o Rossii* [*An Archive of Historico-Juridical Information About Russia*] I: 3, 33.

25. Jakobson, *op. cit.*, 95. Cf. *supra*, n. 17.

26. *Acta patriarchatus*, I, 190.

27. Gorskii and Nevostruev, III: 1, no. 344, p. 14.

28. I exclude the 15th century here because of the extreme difficulty in dating the MSS. accurately, i.e., in the first or second halves of the century. For the diptychs, see Diakonov, *op. cit.*, 24, note 2; Gorskii and Nevostruev, III; 1, no. 347, p. 29; no. 371, p. 130; no. 431, pp. 555–564, here the word "tsar" is replaced, throughout, by the words "Grand Prince"; no. 350, p. 46 where the fifth offering is for the "tsars, princes and all laics" but in the remembrances and prayers only princes are mentioned. Compare this with Serbian missals of the early 15th century, when, under the Turks, Stephan (1389–1427) is called despot and tsar (no. 373, p. 154; no. 374, p. 168).

29. Grekov and Iakubovskii, 223. The statement does go too far in its definitiveness considering the lack of proof.

30. The best edition is by M. D. Priselkov, *Khanskie Iarlyki Russkim Mitropolitam* [*The Khans' Charters to Russian Metropolitans*] (Petrograd, 1916).

31. Priselkov, 83, 92, 96.

32. *Iarlyk* of khan Tuliak, *ibid.*, 91–2, redaction "a."

33. *Ibid.*, 92, 93, *et passim*.

34. *Ibid.*, 58, 97.

35. Oreshnikov, *Denezhnye znaki*, 76 f.; G. B. Fedorov, "Den'gi Moskovskogo Kniazhestva vremeni Dimitriia Donskogo i Vasiliia I" ["Coins of the Moscow Principality During the Reigns of Dimitrii Donskoi and Basil I"], *Materialy i Issledovaniia po Arkheologii SSSR*, Akademiia Nauk, Moscow, XII (1949), 145 (hereafter referred to as Fedorov).

36. Fedorov, 156 f.; V. L. Ianin and S. A. Ianina, "Nachal'nyi period Riazanskoi monetnoi chekanki" ["The Beginning of Riazan' Coin-Minting"], *Numizmaticheskii Sbornik*, Moscow, I (1955), 116 f.

37. In order to be able to pay the tribute. Cf. A. A. Il'in, *Klassifikatsia russkikh udel'nykh*

*monet* [*The Classification of Russian Appanage Coins*] (M.L., 1940), 32, in Fedorov, 157. The Russians, however, had been paying tribute for over a century by this time.

38. For the literature on this problem, see Fedorov, 158–9, Ianin, *op. cit.*, 121 f.

39. This periodization is suggested not only by the great changes in the political situation in the 1430s, which are mentioned below, but also by the virtual impossibility of distinguishing between most coins of Basil I and Basil II. The dating suggested is based on the premise that there is a regular pattern of diminution of weight of the coins throughout the reigns of Basils I and II.

40. *Monety*, nos. 320, 321, 367, 329, 749, 327; Fedorov, pl. 1, 16; pl. 2, 23, 27, 28.

41. *Monety*, nos. 325, 336; Fedorov, pl. 2, 21.

42. *Monety*, nos. 374, 375–8, 383.

43. Fedorov, pl. 2, 19, 22.

44. Vernadsky, 269.

45. The Nikon Chronicle, *P.S.R.L.*, XI, 173.

46. It is interesting to note that this acknowledgment of sovereignty is not found on the Russian Grand Princely seals. I would argue that this was because the seals were personal ones, not state seals, and perhaps deliberately so. The Grand Princely seals up to the time of Ivan III were personal in the sense that each had on it the image of the personal saint of the prince. Ivan III introduced a new seal, with a state symbol of the double-headed eagle, only after the liberation from Tatar sovereignty (cf. *Gramoty*, 567 f.).

47. *P.S.R.L.*, VI, 172 f.; XXV, 263 f.; cf. N. M. Karamsin, *Istoriia Gosudarstva Rossiiskogo* [*History of the Russian State*] (St. Petersburg, 1892), V, 160 f.

48. Fedorov, "Moskovskie Den'gi Ivana III i Vasiliia III" ["Moscovite Coins of Ivan III and Basil III"], *Kratkie Soobshcheniia, I.I.M.K.*, XXX (1949), 71–2.

49. *Ibid.*, 72. *Monety*, no. 495.

50. *Troitskaia Letopis'* [*The Trinity Chronicle*], ed. M. D. Priselkov, Akademiia Nauk (1950), 434; *P.S.R.L.*, V, 264; *P.S.R.L.*, XXV, 211. Moreover, with the death of the reigning khan, a new confirmation was necessary for the Russian prince (*P.S.R.L.*, XXV, 181); see description of miniature showing the coronation of Basil I, Artsikhovskii, *op. cit.*, 130.

51. *Gramoty*, 8.

52. For the Byzantine origin of the cap, see Kondakov, *Russkie Klady*, I, 75 f.; for the opposite view, see Vernadsky, 386, and the summary of the literature on the problem by K. V. Basilevich, "Imushchestvo Moskovskikh kniazei v XIX–XVI vv" ["The Property of the Moscow Princes During the 14th–16th Centuries"], *Trudy Gosudarstvennogo Istoricheskogo Muzeia* (Moscow, 1926), III, 20–21.

53. Cf. A. S. Pavlov, "Istoricheskii ocherk sekuliarizatsii tserkovnykh zemel' v Rossii" ["A Historical Sketch of the Secularization of Church Lands in Russia"], *Zapiski Imp. Novorossiiskogo Universiteta*, VII (1871), 41 f.; V. Zhmakin, *Mitropolit Daniil i ego Sochineniia* [*The Metropolitan Daniel and his Writings*] (Moscow, 1881), 196 f.

54. Cf. D. Likhachev, "K voprosu o teorii Russkogo gosudarstva v kontse XV i v XVI vv." ["On the Problem of the Theory of the Russian State at the End of the 15th and During the 16th Centuries"], *Istoricheskii Zhurnal*, 1944, no. 7–8, pp. 31–39. This tradition accounted, in part, for the late date of the official liberation considering the decline of Tatar power.

55. *P.S.R.L.*, VI, 225.

56. *Ibid.*, 228.

57. Cf. K. V. Basilevich, *Vneshniia Politika Russkogo Tsentralizovannogo Gosudarstva* [*The Foreign Policy of the Russian Centralized State*] (Moscow, 1952), 36 ff.

58. Baron S. Herberstein, *Zapiski o moskovitskikh delakh* [*Memoirs of Muscovite Affairs*], A. I. Malein, trans. (St. Petersburg, 1908), p. 32, cited in Vernadsky, 386.

59. I. R. (prince E. Trubetskoi) *Nasledie Chingiskhana* [*The Heritage of Chenghis Khan*] (Berlin, 1925), 27 f. *et passim*.

60. *Sbornik Russkogo Istoricheskogo Obshchestva*, LIX, 437; 452. For a most striking illustration of this, see Ivan's letter to the patriarch of Constantinople in 1557, asking for confirmation of his imperial coronation and status on the part of the Greek orthodox patriarchate and clergy, *Sobornaia gramota dukhovenstva Pravoslavnoi vostochnoi tserkvi* [*The Synodal Letter of the Clergy of the Orthodox Eastern Church*], ed. M. Obolensky (Moscow, 1850), 32–33.

61. G. Kotoshikhin, *O. Rossii v tsarstvovanie Alekseia Mikhailovicha* [*On Russia in the Reign of Alexis Mikhailovich*] (St. Petersburg, 1884), 1; cf. Vernadsky, 387.

62. *Pamiatniki Diplomaticheskikh Snoshenii*, I, 500–1.

63. See, for example, the description of a banquet at the court of Ivan IV, in 1557, by the English merchant Anthony Jenkinson. Jenkinson wrote that the highest place next to the Terrible tsar was occupied by the ten-year-old captive heir to the throne of Kazan' (*Izvestiia anglichan O Rossii vo vtoroi polovine XVI v* [*English Memoirs on Russia in the Second Half of the 16th Century*], ed. and trans. S. M. Seredonin, *Chteniia*, 1884: 4, p. 32). Also see analysis of *Gosudarev Rodoslovets* of 1555 in N. P. Likhachev, *Razriadnye d'iaki XVI veka* [*The Clerks of the Razriad in the 16th Century*] (St. Petersburg, 1888), 415–6 *et passim*.

64. See Prince P. Dolgorukov, *Rossiiskaia Rodoslovnaia Kniga* [*The Book of Russian Genealogy*] (St. Petersburg, 1857), vol. I, for the numerous Central Asiatic families, such as the princes Chingiz, who received from the emperor Nicholas I the status of imperial princes.

65. Vernadsky, 290.

66. Cf. Herberstein, *op. cit.*, 74.

67. For the most vivid expression of this phenomenon one has only to think of the English attitude towards William the Conqueror.

68. Cf. A. V. Soloviev, "Avtor 'Zadonshchiny' i ego politicheskie ideii" ["The Author of the 'Zadonshchina' and his Political Ideas"], *T.O.D.R.L.*, XIV, 196 f.

69. *Skazanie o kniaziakh vladimirskikh* [*The Tale About the Princes of Vladimir*], ed. R. P. Dmitrieva, ANSSR (M.-L., 1955), 162 f.

70. See, for example, Giles Fletcher, *O Gosudarstve Russkom* [*Of the Russian Commonwealth*], trans. O. M. Bodianskii (St. Petersburg, 1905), 19.

71. On the division of Russia into the *Oprichnina* of Ivan IV and the *Zemshchina* and its meaning, see V. O. Kliuchevsky, *Kurs Russkoi Istorii* [*Lectures on Russian History*] (Moscow, 1937), II, 199 f. and his *Boiarskaia Duma* [*The Boyar Council*] (Moscow, 1883), 334 f.

72. Carrying this speculation further, one might argue that the ideal of the orthodox ruler of the orthodox people was the one retained by the masses (cf. my study "Holy Russia: A Study in the History of an Idea," *American Hist. Review*, LXIII [1958], no. 3, 617–637), while the government of imperial Russia relied upon the practice of the conquering khan.

# A Neglected Byzantine Source of Muscovite Political Ideology

## IHOR ŠEVČENKO

*Poèty naši prozrevali značenie vysšee monarxa, slyša, čto on neminuemo dolžen, nakonec, sdelat'sja ves' odna ljubov', i takim obrazom stanet vidno vsem, počemu gosudar' est' obraz Božij, kak èto priznaet, pokuda čut'em, vsja zemlja naša. . . .*
*Tam tol'ko iscelitsja vpolne narod gde postignet monarx vysšee značenie svoe—byt' obrazom Togo na zemle, kotoryj Sam est' ljubov'.*

N. V. GOGOL'

It has long been a commonplace of historical writing that the Byzantine ideas on the character of imperial power influenced the political thought of the Kievan State and later, considerably more, the ideology of Muscovite Russia.[1] It is much more difficult to show—especially for the earlier period—precisely what this influence was, through what channels it passed, what the Byzantine literary models were which found their way into the works of the Kievan and Muscovite periods, and, finally, at just what time. The chief obstacle is the vastness of the Byzantine and Slavic fields, but a recent article has shown what stimulating results may be produced by collaboration between a Byzantine and a Russian historian. The findings, or rather the rediscoveries, made there will provide a point of departure for some remarks on the fate of quotations from a Byzantine political theorist of sorts in Kievan and Muscovite literature.

E. H. Kantorowicz, assisted by M. Cherniavsky, has shown[2] that a passage of the Laurentius Chronicle (*sub anno* 1175, where the murder of Prince Andrej Bogoljubskij is described), which asserts in substance that "though an Emperor in body be like all other, yet in power he is like God," has its exact counterpart in a Greek sentence, commonly attributed to Philo the Jew. Here are the texts:

est'stvom bo zemnym podoben est' vsjakomu čelovĕku cĕsar', vlastiju že sana jako Bog. Vĕšča bo velikyi Zlatoustec' tĕmže protivjatsja volosti, protivjatsja zakonu Božiju.[3]

τῇ μὲν οὐσίᾳ τοῦ σώματος, ἴσος παντὸς ἀνθρώπου ὁ βασιλεύς, τῇ δὲ ἐξουσίᾳ τοῦ ἀξιώματος ὅμοιός ἐστι τῷ ἐπὶ πάντων Θεῷ.[4]

FROM Ihor Ševčenko, "A Neglected Byzantine Source of Muscovite Political Ideology." Reprinted by permission of the publishers from Horace G. Lunt, editor, *Harvard Slavic Studies*, Volume II (Cambridge, Mass.: Harvard University Press), Copyright, 1954, by the President and Fellows of Harvard College.

The complete correspondence between the two maxims is beyond doubt. What remains to be seen is how this piece of Greek wisdom spread into the Suzdal' Principality—where this passage was written—and exactly where it originated.

The Philo fragment reproduced in the text of the Chronicle is quoted by Kantorowicz from a collection of maxims gathered from earlier works of this type by an eleventh century Byzantine monk, Antonius.[5] This kind of collection went under the name of Μέλισσα, the *Bee*. Antonius was not the only compiler of a *Bee*: at least three other recensions of the Byzantine Μέλισσα have come down to us.[6] One of them (not that of Antonius) was translated into Church Slavonic. What is more important, the translation was made in Kievan Rus'.[7] Although by their very nature these anthologies fluctuated in their arrangement and contents, a great number of maxims are common to all of them. Accordingly, the Kievan *Bee* (*Pčela*) contains the sentence on the Divine nature of the Emperor's office:

Plot'skym sušč'stvom raven est' vsěm čelověkom čěsar', vlastiju že sanovnoju podoben est' Bogu vyšnemu. Ne imat' bo na zemli vyš'šago sebe, *etc.*[8]

This Kievan *Pčela*, then, or some collection containing excerpts from it,[9] is the immediate source of the passage in the Laurentius Chronicle and such other chronicles as either share its source for the part comprising the year 1175[10] or have inserted the excursus on the murder of Andrej Bogoljubskij into their otherwise different narrative.[11] In the chronicles the saying was not copied verbatim. *Plot'skym* has been replaced by *zemnym*, possibly under the influence of *na zemli* of the following sentence, and *podoben est'* is connected with man instead of God. This gives the impression of a quotation from memory, and perhaps indicates that at least certain parts of the *Pčela* had become familiar to learned scribes of Rus' by the time the excursus on Andrej Bogoljubskij was composed. The original form of the *Pčela* quotation in the excursus must have been closer to its immediate source than is the text of the Laurentius Chronicle. Towards the end of this passage, the Hypatian Chronicle reads *vlastiju že sana vyš'ši jako Bog*, "By the power of his office he is higher than God," which remains a blasphemy in spite of the editors' efforts to save the situation by putting a comma after *vyš'ši*. In view of the *Bogu vyšnemu* of the *Pčela*, something like *vlastiju že sana jako Bog vyšnii* has to be postulated for the original text of the excursus.

The story of Andrej Bogoljubskij's murder, perpetrated in 1175, seems to have been incorporated into a historical work which was sponsored by Bogoljubskij himself and which was completed two years after his death.[12] In any case, it presents such a wealth of detail that it must have been written very soon after the event. M. N. Speranskij, in his lengthy considerations on the date of the translation of the *Pčela*, proposed either the late twelfth or the thirteenth century.[13] A more precise dating is now possible, as the passage of the excursus furnishes the year 1175 or 1177 as the *terminus ante quem* for the appearance of the Church Slavonic *Pčela* in Vladimir on the Klaz'ma. How much earlier than 1177 the Μέλισσα was translated must remain a matter of conjecture. If the supposition that the author of the excursus quoted from memory is true, the translation may have been in use for quite some time before that date.[14]

It is known that towards the end of the twelfth century—ca. 1193, if one adopts the opinion of M. D. Priselkov[15]—another quotation from the *Pčela* was introduced, this time with an indication of the source, into a historical work compiled in Vladimir. This work, among others, has been incorporated into the *Letopisec Perejaslavlja Suzdal'skogo* which notes under the year 1186: *jakože v Bčele glagolet': bran' slavna luče mira skudna, s lživym že mirom živušče veliju pakost' zemljam tvorjat'*.[16] The fact that this *Letopisec* is the only one to give the source of its quotation correctly, while all the other chronicles reproducing the same recension (*svod*) give the vague *jakože prorok glagolet'*, should be well kept in mind. This one instance should suffice to prove the *Letopisec's* high value not only for the reconstruction of the *Letopis' Perejaslavlja Suzdal'skogo* (= *Radziwill Letopis'* in modern terminology[17]), but also for ascertaining the original form of the recension (of 1193?) from which a part of the Laurentius Chronicle is derived.

The saying on the divine character of the emperor's office is attributed by the *Pčela* not to Philo, but to "Agipitos."[18] This is by no means an innovation of the Church Slavonic text. While no edition of the Μέλισσα is yet available, it is known that at least the MSS representing its so-called "long" recension make Agapetus the author of the maxim.[19] I do not know on what authority, except that of editions of Antonius, it found its way into Mangey's and Richter's collections of Philo's fragments[20] and even into a recent treatise on Philo's political theory.[21] It must be said in Antonius' defense, that he transmits the maxim anonymously. A cursory survey of his edition by Gesner[22] shows that the *lemma* "Philonis" there stands in the margin of the Latin translation of the saying: rather flimsy grounds for determining the authorship of the Greek text. The maxim of the Μέλισσα and Antonius figures verbatim as chapter 21 in Deacon Agapetus' Ἔκθεσις κεφαλαίων παραινετικῶν.[23] Of course, this is not the only chapter of his *speculum principis* which entered into gnomic collections under the guise of Philo. Thus, to quote some examples, all the three "unidentified" passages of Harris' edition of Philonic fragments[24] coincide in full with the three respective chapters of Agapetus, two of which are also given as Philonic by the Μέλισσα.[25]

It would be idle to adduce detailed arguments proving that these "Philo" fragments also found in Agapetus are spurious and refuting an imaginary objection that they might be genuine Philonic passages taken over both by Agapetus, who concealed his borrowing, and, e.g., the Μέλισσα, which preserved the name of the author correctly. Not that Agapetus excelled in originality; many a source of his sometimes platitudinous precepts, sources ranging from Isocrates to St. Basil, has been identified.[26] But he had the ambition to be a brilliant writer and to improve upon his sources by turning his sentences into what he believed to be little jewels sparkling with punlike *paromoea*, assonances, and parallel constructions. All the "Philonic" sentences which reappear as Agapetus' chapters display the very mannerisms peculiar to the whole of his work. This is particularly true of chapter 21, which is the most interesting to us. Moreover, it is striking that the boundaries of the suspect "Philo" fragments should in all cases exactly coincide with those of Agapetus' chapters and that we should precisely discover the "unidentified" Philo fragments in Agapetus, while no correspondence between him and some authentic saying of Philo can be established. Finally, at least the "Philo" fragment θεὸς οὐδενὸς δεῖται (Harris, p. 104 = Agapetus 63), sometimes attributed to Hippocrates, is definitely of gnomic origin and cannot be Philonic in its "Agapetian" form. [27]

Thus Agapetus, not Philo, made its first modest appearance in Rus' towards the third quarter of the twelfth century at the latest. This point is worth stressing, for the "Hortatory Chapters" of this sixth-century Byzantine author were to stay there for well over five hundred years. The 72 chapters of this *opusculum*, rather loosely connected by an acrostic announcing that the humble Deacon (of the Great Church of Constantinople) Agapetus dedicated his work to the Very Pious Emperor Justinian,[28] could serve a fairly wide range of purposes. Those interested in extolling the ruler's position could find in Agapetus an ample supply of *dicta* on the divine nature of the emperor's office. But as the ruler, wielding godlike power, was, like all mortals, but dust that perisheth, he was reminded by the Deacon of the various duties he had towards his subjects and Him Who had placed him above all men. Agapetus' chapter 21, which epitomizes the twofold nature of the whole *opusculum*, runs as follows:

Τῇ μὲν οὐσίᾳ τοῦ σώματος, ἴσος παντὶ ἀνθρώπῳ ὁ βασιλεύς, τῇ ἐξουσίᾳ δὲ τοῦ ἀξιώματος, ὅμοιός ἐστι τῷ ἐπὶ πάντων Θεῷ, οὐκ ἔχει γὰρ ἐπὶ γῆς τὸν αὐτοῦ ὑψηλότερον. χρὴ τοίνυν αὐτὸν καὶ ὡς Θεὸν μὴ ὀργίζεσθαι, καὶ ὡς θνητὸν μὴ ἐπαίρεσθαι. εἰ εἰκόνι θεικῇ τετίμηται, ἀλλὰ καὶ κόνει χοικῇ συμπέπλεκται, δι' ἧς ἐκδιδάσκεται τὴν πρὸς πάντας ἰσότητα.

Though an emperor in body be like all other, yet in power of his office he is like God, Master of all men. For in earth, he has no peer. Therefore as God, be he never chafed or angry; as man, be he never proud. For though he be like God in face, yet for all that he is but dust which thing teaches him to be equal to every man.[29]

The good ruler had to lend a willing ear to good counsels and shun flatterers. But foremost among his duties was that of charity towards the poor, and, we might almost add, that of liberality towards impecunious divines like Agapetus himself. Some of the emperor's virtues praised in the Hortatory Chapters could well adorn a man of less exalted rank. As will be seen, the authors of Kievan and Muscovite Rus' extracted now this and now that of Agapetus' precepts according to the main tenor of their writings and to the interests of the epoch into which these writings fall.

Some of Agapetus' chapters appeared once more on Kievan soil in the twelfth century, again through the intermediary of another work. The Greek text of the *Barlaam and Joasaph* novel contains two lengthy interpolations on the king's duties, both of which make liberal use either of Agapetus directly or, less probably, some source common to Agapetus and to them.[30] Both of these interpolations went into the Slavonic version of the novel and many sentences of Agapetus, transmitted anonymously, thus became available to Kievan and later to Muscovite *knižniki*. Curiously enough, most of these "Agapetus" passages of the *Barlaam and Joasaph* seem never to have been used in writings of the Kievan Rus'. It is true that these excerpts stressed God's greatness and the ruler's humility and moderation rather than his splendor as God's imitator on earth.

This, however, does not provide an adequate explanation for the neglect of the Kievan writers to take advantage of the presence of a ready set of political maxims and to adopt some of them to local needs. "Agapetus" passages like *se bo ustav istin'nago carstva, eže carstvovati vozder'žatisja sladostej*: "This is the (chief) precept of a true Rulership, that the Ruler should abstain from voluptuous passions" (cf. Agapetus, ch. 18),[31] or *i pravda uže ispravisja emu* (i.e., the king) *jakože věn'cem cělomudrija obolčenu i bagrjaniceju pravdy odějanъ* (read, *odějanu*): "And truth (justice?) was attained by him, who was adorned with the wreath of chastity and arrayed with the purple robe of justice" (cf. Agapetus, ch. 17),[32] or, finally, *těmže blagopristupen budi moljaščimsja i otverzaj uši obniščavšim, da obrašteši božie uxo otversto*: "Therefore, be thou accessible to those who entreat thee and open your ears to the Poor, so that you may find God's ear open" (cf. Agapetus, ch. 8),[33] were to be used by political writers of sixteenth-century Moscow, already able to quote from a full Slavonic translation of Agapetus. The rudimentary political theory of Kievan Rus' did not stress the exalted position of the prince, and it was many years before Agapetus' hour would come.

At least one twelfth-century author, however, utilized one of the Agapetus passages transmitted by the *Barlaam and Joasaph* novel. This was no less a figure than Cyril of Turov. Since M. I. Suxomlinov, it has been known that Cyril had made use of *Barlaam and Joasaph* in his *Address* to Vasilij, Abbot of the Kievan Monastery of the Caves.[34] There, Cyril paraphrased and adapted the simile—which he had found in *Barlaam and Joasaph*—on the otherwise good but pagan ruler, converted to the true faith by his wise councilor who showed him two poor people living in happiness, that is, having preferred eternal salvation to earthly pleasures.[35] What has not been seen up to the present time is the dependence of Cyril's *Address* on another part of *Barlaam and Joasaph* as well, the interpolation outlining the duties of a ruler, which is found towards the end of the work. Of course, he applies the "Agapetus" passage to the ideal monk rather than to the ideal king when he writes: *nъ sut'* (sc. the monks) *cělomudriem obolčeni i pravdoju pojasani, směreniem' ukrašeni*; "but they are clad in chastity and girdled with truth, adorned with humility."[36] For all that, his dependence on the *Barlaam and Joasaph* "Agapetus" passage, *jakože věn'cem cělomudrija obolčenu i bagrjaniceju pravdy odějanu*: "who were adorned with the wreath of chastity and arrayed with the purple robe of justice," is unmistakable. In practice this means that Cyril of Turov used the full text of *Barlaam and Joasaph*.

The *Pčela*, which soon began a life of its own, absorbing elements of local literature, served in turn as an ideal source for compilers of specialized collections. Among them was an anthology of legal texts, called *Měrilo pravednoe*. It consists of two parts written simultaneously and complementing each other. The first one, a kind of introduction, is didactic and moralistic in character, although juridical in tendency; the second is an outright selection of juridical texts, some of them Byzantine. As none of the elements which found their way into the *Měrilo* is later than the eighties of the thirteenth century, and as the oldest known manuscript of this work dates from the fourteenth, it is fair to assume that this compilation was put together towards the very end of the thirteenth century and to reckon it among the products of Kievan literature.[37] The didactic part of the *Měrilo* contains a chapter entitled *ot bčely izbrano o knjažen'i*, "Selections from the Bee on Dominion," in which the compiler, omitting the author's name, has placed the slightly mutilated sentence from Agapetus on the ruler's godlike power: *plot'ju roven est' vsěm čelověkom, a volost'ju sanovnoju podoben est' Bogu.*[38]

Nothing seems to be known of the fate of Agapetus quotations in fourteenth-century East Slavic literature, a period from which a relatively small number of monuments has come down to us. Among these few, texts whose authors we might expect to turn to Agapetus for inspiration are extremely scarce.[39]

The fifteenth century is characterized by the consolidation of Muscovite predominance in Russia and by the first deliberate Russian (not exclusively Muscovite) attempts to transform Russian princes into the counterparts of Byzantine Emperors and, later, to claim the Byzantine heritage for themselves and their lands. It was at that time that panegyrists first coined hybrid epithets, calling their rulers *velikij knjaz'* (grand prince) and *bogověnčannyj car'* (Emperor Crowned by God = $\theta\varepsilon\acute{o}\sigma\tau\varepsilon\pi\tau\sigma\varsigma \ \beta\alpha\sigma\iota\lambda\varepsilon\acute{u}\varsigma$) in the same breath, thus anticipating the developments lying a hundred years ahead. Following in the steps of time-honored Byzantine tradition, although possibly imitating South Slavic models,[40] the eulogists compared the subjects of their praise to Moses—a standing device of Byzantine imperial oratory since Constantine the Great—to Constantine himself—no novelty even for Rus' literature—or to other Byzantine emperors, like Leo the Wise. It is not surprising, then, that the full text of Agapetus' precepts should appear on Russian soil in a century which saw the beginnings of Russian "Imperial" ideology.

This text is transmitted anonymously in MS 202 of the former Synodal Library in Moscow, a manuscript containing (with one sure exception) various texts of East Slavic recension. Its title is *Poučenie blagago cěsarstva, se že i k boljarom i k episkopom i ko igumenom, lěpo est' i čern'cem*, "Admonition on Good Rulership, Also Addressed to Magnates, Bishops and Abbots, and Becoming to Monks."[41] In the mind of the author of the title, Agapetus' chapters (the Slavic text has only 67 of them) were works of wide application. The readers followed the scribe's advice. Indeed, we shall see the *opusculum* used by an abbot, generously quoted by a metropolitan, and, finally, published under the auspices of another abbot. As for magnates, the first tsar of Muscovy was among its users.

The manuscript dates surely from the fifteenth century, since a note on the inner side of its back cover refers to "my lord, the abbot Ioachim of Pesnoššk." This abbot is mentioned elsewhere under the year 1468. Unfortunately, under present circumstances, no idea can be formed on this translation and we are reduced to the *incipit* given in the description of the manuscript by Gorskij and Nevostruev,[42] and to a few excerpts made from two fifteenth-century manuscripts by V. Malinin.[43] Nor can we say where the translation originated. It may have been made in Russia proper by a local *knižnik* anxious to add a useful piece to the Muscovite propaganda library or perhaps ordered to do so by Zoe

Palaeologina, who may have brought Agapetus in her baggage. It also may have come, among the many translations from Greek imported in the late fourteenth and the fifteenth centuries, from the South Slavic lands, for instance from Bulgaria, where the writers of Tsar John Alexander's court (fourteenth century) were well acquainted with the Byzantine political jargon.

All we have to go by in trying to assess the influence of Agapetus in fifteenth-century Russia are the writings of contemporary ecclesiastical publicists, who were the chief mouthpieces of the new but still fluid ideology. Here, the results are disappointing. Of the two principal Muscovite political pamphlets of the period, the first one including a *Poxvala blagověrnomu velikomu knjazju Vasil'ju Vasil'eviču vseja Rusi,* "Eulogy to the Grand Prince Vasilij Vasil'evič of All Rus'," was compiled in 1461 by an anonymous author—believed, on quite insufficient grounds, to have been Pachomius the Serb.[44] Its Byzantine elements boil down to a stress on the divine character of the ruler's office, expressed by an assiduous and repetitious use of epithets like *bogoukrašennyj,* "adorned by God," *bogověnčannyj,* "God-crowned," *bogom naučennyj,* "taught by God." These epithets are connected with the name of Prince Vasilij II, called tsar in some passages of the treatise. All this may have been learned from the Bulgarians. The most important contribution of the treatise, a first hint at the *translatio imperii,* the transfer of the ideal rule over the Christian world from Constantinople, now sullied by the Turkish conquest and moral surrender of the Papists, to Moscow, the upholder of the Pure Faith, cannot have been directly inspired by Byzantine sources.

Slightly less frustrating is the second pamphlet, the "Letter of Vas'jan (Rylo), Archbishop of Rostov . . . to Ivan Vasil'evič . . ."[45] written on the eve of the momentous, though bloodless, Russo-Tartar encounter on the Ugra (1480), which was to put an end even to the nominal dependence of the Muscovite Rus' on the Golden Horde. The purpose of Vassian's (d. 1481) appeal was to push the apparently inhibited Ivan III over the brink—to Liberty. The bishop who took his task seriously, set about it with reference books at his side. One of these books was the *Pčela,* especially its ninth chapter on "Power and Rulership," *o vlasti i knjaženii,* from which Vassian got his heartening and appropriate quotation from "Democrat the Philosopher," i.e. Democritus, to wit: "It is becoming to a prince to show wisdom whenever the moment requires it, to display strength, manliness and courage when facing the enemy," and so on.[46] The Agapetus quotation of the *Pčela* was about two folios away from the one chosen by Vassian. In all likelihood, Vassian did read it in the process of scanning chapter nine for fitting material to be used in his work extolling Ivan III as a ruler. Yet he has not quoted Agapetus, and it seems that his was a deliberate omission.

One of the psychological reasons of Ivan III's hesitation may be inferred from Vassian's text. Was not the word of the Holy Writ "Fear God. Honor the Emperor (in Slavic: *car')"* (= I Peter 2:17), the cornerstone of the contemporary —and past—political thinking of Rus'? But in 1480, when the Byzantine tsar was no more, the only tsar, ordained by God, and therefore unassailable, was the *car' ordyn'skij,* the Khan of the Golden Horde, and Moscow princes were the first to preach the doctrine that one should not oppose the powers that be. Vassian's course, therefore, was to present the Tartar pagan tsar as a usurper, and Ivan, the heir to St. Vladimir's tradition, as the more legitimate, because Christian, tsar of the two. This, however, was easier proved than felt. The Agapetus quotation, insisting on a "tsar's" equality with God, could produce an adverse psychological effect and was out of place in a treatise virtually inciting to rebellion. The needs of the hour remain the ultimate reason for the rejection of acceptance of an "Ideal."[47]

Viewing the historical developments from the dubious vantage point of our time, we incline to take it for granted that Moscow, the victor in the struggle for supremacy over "All Russia," should have been the only power interested in furthering Byzantine autocratic political ideas. In the fifteenth century, however, this matter of predominance was by no means considered a foregone conclusion, at least in some quarters. Tver', whose princes had been the first to call themselves *velikij knjaz' vseja Rusi*, Grand Prince of All Rus',[48] was not subdued until 1485. Until that date she could wishfully hope to wring the supremacy from her traditional rival. It is not surprising, therefore, to find a glorification *alla maniera bizantina* of a fifteenth-century prince of Tver', Boris Aleksandrovič (d. 1461). It was written by Thomas (Foma) the Monk, the Tver' member of the Russian delegation to the Florentine Council, about 1453, several years earlier than the Muscovite praise of Vasilij II.[49] What is striking is the degree of similarity between the Tver' and the Muscovite eulogies. It starts with the title of both texts and the event they describe—the "Praises" are connected with a relation of what happened at the Council of Florence—but it does not stop there. Boris Aleksandrovič is treated like a Byzantine emperor. He is a prince, well known and admired in far away lands, and praised by the Emperor of Constantinople himself. He receives the various imperial epithets, is called *car'*, compared with Moses, Leo the Wise, Constantine, and represented as a rightful successor of Vladimir and Jaroslav.[50] This identity of claims in itself pointed to an inevitable showdown. As earlier in the Balkans, so now in Russia, whoever accepted the imperial game, had to bear its merciless consequences. There is no place for two at the top of the pyramid.

Similar as Thomas's text is to its Muscovite counterpart, it is livelier, and, what is of interest here, it offers three short passages which may be considered as probably indirect reminiscences of Agapetus. When Bosir is called "earthly eye" (as a counterpart to the "heavenly all-encompassing eye," a Byzantine paraphrase of God), *i iže byti emu zemnomu oku*, one is reminded of Agapetus chapter 46, "as the eye is ensconced in the body, so is the God-sent ruler installed on earth," a phrase which we shall encounter again. The characteristic of the prince as "accessible to all," *vsim dobroprestupen* (read, *-pristupen*), already familiar from the discussion of the *Barlaam and Joasaph* novel, has a parallel in Agapetus, chapter 8 "thou art accessible ($\epsilon\dot{v}\pi\rho\acute{o}\sigma\iota\tau os$) to those who entreat thee." Finally, Thomas's reference to the purple garb of piety (or virtue) adorning Boris, *i čestnoju bagrjaniceju ego ukrašaema vidjašči*[51] is close to Agapetus' chapter 81, also mentioned in connection with *Barlaam and Joasaph*, "crowned with chastity, arrayed with the purple robe of justice." Of course, these parallels are not cogent. Yet, as they occur in a cluster and are slightly less banal than the usual Byzantine clichés on similar topics, they had to be mentioned here. The provisional conclusion, then, is that although both an excerpt from and the full text of Agapetus were available in translation to some of the fifteenth-century Russian *literati*, little if any use was made of his "Hortatory Chapters" in the gestation period of the Russian Imperial ideology. The situation changes radically at the very beginning of the sixteenth century.

Joseph Volockij, Abbot of Volokolamsk (d. 1515), is generally considered as the author of the first important theoretical work of Muscovite Rus'. This work, in which the previous views on the princely power had been systematized, was to make a profound impact upon the political thought of the following two generations. Joseph's work is a collection of sixteen pamphlets (*slova*), composed at various dates and published under the title of *Prosvětitel'*, "Illuminator," after the year 1507. The pamphlets inveigh against the Sect of "Judaisers" of whom Joseph was the principal adversary. In good Byzantine tradition, the prince (Ivan III, d. 1505) was exhorted by Joseph to lend the secular arm to the work of extirpating the heresy and told that the persecution of heretics was among the chief duties of a good ruler, whereas failure to uphold the true faith would make him into a tyrant (*mučitel'*). This line of thought provided Joseph with an opportunity to state his views on the prince's office. A pregnant summary of these views is given in *slovo* 16, at the very end of the "Illuminator," a place which attests that we are presented with Joseph's later thought. The passage on the Divine character of the ruler's functions as opposed to his human nature is found there in the form familiar to us through the *Pčela* and the chronicles, and has become a stock phrase invariably quoted in modern historical works.[51a] We already know that it comes from Agapetus chapter 21. But where did Joseph read it? To obtain a sure answer to this question, it suffices to go beyond the classical phrase of Joseph and to analyse the whole group of statements on the princely power inserted at the end of *slovo* 16:

1. Vas bo Bog v' sebe město posadi na prestolě svoem.

Cf., e.g., Agap. 1: ἔδωκέ σοι τὸ σκῆπτρον τῆς ἐπιγείου δυναστείας, and Agap. 45: νεύματι Θεοῦ τὴν δυναστείαν παραλαβών. Cf. also Agap. 30.

These parallelisms alone are too general to be conclusive.

2. Sego radi podobaet carem že i knjazem vsjako tščanie o blagočestii iměti i suščyx pod nimi ot trevolnenija spasati duševnago i tělesnago.

A clear hint at Ivan III's duty to suppress the "Judaisers."

3. Solncu ubo dělo est', eže světiti suščix na zemli; carju že svoe est', eže peščisja o vsěx suščix iže pod nim.

= Agap. 51: ἡλίου μὲν ἔργον ἐστί, τὸ καταλάμπειν ταῖς ἀκτῖσι τὴν κτίσιν, ἄνακτος δὲ ἀρετή, τὸ ἐλεεῖν τοῖς δεομένοις.[52]

A simple translation of Agapetus, with *světiti* ruling the accusative, after the model of the Greek, and the substitution of *suščix iže pod nim,* "subjects," for Agapetus' "Those who entreat him" at the end.

4. Skipetr cěsarstvija priim ot Boga, bljudi kako ugodiši davšemu ti togo,

= Agap. 61: σκῆπτρον βασιλείας παρὰ Θεοῦ δεξάμενος, σκέπτου πῶς ἀρέσεις τῷ ταύτην σοι δεδωκότι.[53]

Coincidence literal.

5. i netokmo o sebě otvět dasi k Bogu,

A bridge.

6. no eže inii zlo tvorjat, ty slovo otdasi Bogu, volju ž dav im.

= Agap. 30: ὧν γὰρ ἂν ἐκεῖνοι κακῶς διαπράξωνται, λόγον ὑφέξει Θεῷ ὁ τὴν ἰσχὺν αὐτοῖς δεδωκώς.[54]

7. Car' ubo estestvom podoben est' vsěm čelověkom, vlastiju že podoben est' vyšnemu Bogu.[55]

This is practically a translation of Agapetus 21.

Joseph came to speak once more on the ruler's duties in his letter to a prince, the "Orthodox X, Who Had Asked Him for a Useful Admonition."[56] There Joseph declared that he had taken the liberty of writing down some sayings from the Holy Scriptures for the edification of the addressee. The sense in which Joseph understood the expression "Holy Scriptures" must have been quite broad, since his quotations included St. John Chrysostom, whom he mentioned, and Agapetus, whom he did not name. Here is the passage:

Poistině, iže veliku vlast' priem, datelju oblasti dolžen est' po silě podobitisja: ničemže tako moščno Bogu podobitisja, jakože milostiju.[57]

= Agap. 37: ὁ μεγάλης ἐξουσίας ἐπιλαβόμενος τὸν δοτῆρα τῆς ἐξουσίας μιμείσθω κατὰ δύναμιν. . . . ἐν τούτῳ δὲ μάλιστα τὸν Θεὸν μιμήσεται, ἐν τῷ μηδὲν ἡγεῖσθαι τοῦ ἐλεεῖν προτιμώτερον.

Only the beginning and the end of Agapetus' chapter were used by Joseph. While Vasilij III was compared with God in *Prosvětitel',* the middle of Agapetus' chapter 37, "For if the emperor represent God, Lord of all things and by His liberality has the governance of everything" was omitted in the letter. A prince is not a tsar. Besides, in the "Illuminator," Sanin's purpose was to underscore the ruler's glory and might, in order to spur him into action against the heretics. In the letter, a didactic work, in spite of its mock deference, Joseph rather browbeat the addressee into mercifulness—and chastity.

Thus Joseph of Volokolamsk is the first author so far known who used the full Slavic translation of Agapetus for his outline of "imperial" ideology.[58] True enough, his *Prosvětitel'* exerted a profound influence throughout the whole of the sixteenth century.[59] But as one of the most suggestive passages of this work is based on Agapetus, it will be seen that the similarity between Joseph's and his successors' opinions is partly due to the use of this common source. Joseph is only the first in a series of sixteenth-century writers who turned to the Deacon of Constantinople for ready formulas by which to articulate their views.

As the immediate roots of the State ideology of the *Roi Soleil* are to be sought under his father Louis XIII, so is the prefiguration of some of Ivan the Terrible's conceptions to be found in the writings of the time of his father Vasilij III (d. 1533) and of the regency. Next to the letters of Philotheus of Pskov, the most important ideological text of the period immediately preceding Ivan the Terrible's sole rule is the anonymous account of the birth of Vasilij's son, Ivan IV, the God-sent (*ot Boga darovana*), an account coupled with a posthumous eulogy of Vasilij III. The inclusion of almost the whole of this otherwise unpublished work into the *Kniga Stepennaja*,[60] a collection of legitimistic biographies of rulers and saints composed under the supervision of the metropolitan Macarius between 1560 and 1563, gave it official endorsement. The anonymous work could have been written at any time between 1533 and 1563, but its double contents seem to indicate that it was composed shortly after Vasilij's death, under the regency.

The treatise is strongly redolent of the lamp, and the lamp's oil is Byzantine. One may attribute its Greek clichés and bizarre composita to South Slavic influence,[61] and the puns on Ivan's "joyful" name[62] to the consultation of a Slavic reference work, giving the vernacular meanings of Hebrew names.[63] When, however, the author admits that he draws upon a source,[64] when his tone becomes suddenly "universal"—the birth of Ivan the Terrible "filled the Orthodox in all corners of the universe with joy"[65]—when he asserts that Vasilij III was loved by everyone and worshipped by people from near and far, to wit by inhabitants of Sinai and Palestine, Italy and Antioch,[66]—a perspective which suits the Byzantine picture perfectly, but is perfect nonsense for Muscovy—we know he is copying a eulogy of Byzantine origin.[67] But he also has another source, Agapetus,[68] whom he adapts rather skillfully, toning down the Byzantine's references to the ruler's earthly nature and presenting as Vasilij's actual achievements those virtues which Agapetus postulated for an ideal emperor. It may be argued that this adaptation had already been performed by the hypothetical Byzantine panegyrist whom the Muscovite Anonymus copied. The question is difficult to decide. An analysis of Agapetus' passages, however, seems to indicate that the changes are due to the anonymous author himself. The texts are as follows:

1. I sego radi vsegda carskoe ego (*sc.* Vasilij III) serdce i um bdja i mudr'stvuja, okormljaja vsěx opasně vo blagozakonii, bezzakonii že potoki krěpce otganjaja, da ne pogrjaznet karabl' velikago ego deržavstva v volnax nepravdy.

= Agap. 2: ὡς κυβερνήτης ἀγρυπνεῖ διὰ παντὸς ὁ τοῦ βασιλέως πολυόμματος νοῦς, διακατέχων ἀσφαλῶς τῆς εὐνομίας τοὺς οἴακας, καὶ ἀπωθούμενος ἰσχυρῶς τῆς ἀνομίας τοὺς ῥύακας, ἵνα τὸ σκάφος τῆς παγκοσμίου πολιτείας μὴ περιπίπτῃ κύμασιν ἀδικίας.[69]

The adaptation is successful. Only the "many-eyed mind" of Agapetus' Emperor was evidently too much for the Anonymus who replaced it with "heart and mind." What is more significant, the "universal empire" (παγκόσμιος πολιτεία) of the original was cut down to Muscovite proportions and rendered by "great rule," or "state." This detail speaks for a Russian adaptation rather than for a plagiarism from the supposed Byzantine eulogy already containing

Agapetus. A Byzantine using Agapetus' text would have no reason to balk at a familiar reference to universal monarchy, a cornerstone of Byzantine political thinking. Official Moscow was reluctant to raise open claims to universality. True enough, Philotheus of Pskov, the mouthpiece of the doctrine of Moscow the third Rome, wrote to Vasilij III, about 1510, *edin ty vo vsei podnebesnoi xristianom car'*,[70] "Thou art the only Emperor unto the Christians under the vault of Heaven," but his was the voice of a quisling free-lance publicist. In a well known reply to Possevino, Ivan the Terrible declared that he did not aspire to temporal rule over the whole world: *zděšnjago gosudarstva vseě vselennye ne xotim.*[71] By his adaptation of Agapetus, the Anonymus seems to have reflected the authoritative line more faithfully.

The use of Agapetus by the Anonymus does not stop with chapter two. His text continues as follows:

2. Takova bjaše mnogopopečitel'-naja ego careva duša; po podobiju zercala vsegda isčiščaetsja i božestvennymi lučami vynu oblistaema i vešč'mi razsuženija ottudu naučaetsja,

= Agap. 9: τὴν πολυμέριμνον τοῦ βασιλέως ψυχὴν κατόπτρου δίκην ἀποσμήχεσθαι χρή, ἵνα ταῖς θείαις αὐγαῖς ἀεὶ καταστράπτηται, καὶ τῶν πραγμάτων τὰς κρίσεις ἐκεῖθεν διδάσκηται.[72]

3. Jako že něgdě pišet,

The device of announcing a quotation at this place is astute, as it creates the impression that everything but what follows is the author's own invention.

4. Iže ubo suščestvom tělesnym raven est' čelověkom car', vlastiju že dostojnago ego veličestva priličen vyšnemu, iže nado vsěmi, Bogu: ne imat' bo vysočajša sebe na zemli.

Agap 21. (For Greek text and translation, see page 83, above.)

5. Ne prestupim (*read* nepristupim) ubo čelověki vysoty radi zem'nago carstvija, blagopim (*read* blagopristupim) že byvaet polučenija radi gornjago carstvija.

= Agap. 8: ἀπρόσιτος μὲν ὑπάρχεις ἀνθρώποις διὰ τὸ ὕψος τῆς κάτω βασιλείας, εὐπρόσιτος δὲ γίνῃ τοῖς δεομένοις διὰ τὸ κράτος τῆς ἄνω ἐξουσίας.[73]

Only the first part of Agapetus 21, the glorification of the emperor, has been taken over. Its second part, exhorting to humility, has been skillfully replaced by the beginning of Agapetus 8. The over-all effect is more stress on the ruler's lofty station. The text continues:

6. Jako že oko tělesi vodruzisja, sice i car' v miřě ustroisja ot Boga darovannym emu pospěšeniem k poleznym, da promyšljaet ubo o čelověcěx i sam vo blagix da prebyvaet, vo zlyx že da ne pretykaetsja.[74]

= Agap. 46: ὥσπερ ὀφθαλμὸς ἐμπέφυκε σώματι, οὕτω βασιλεὺς τῷ κόσμῳ ἐνήρμοσται, ὑπὸ τοῦ Θεοῦ δεδομένος εἰς συνεργίαν τῶν συμφερόντων. χρὴ οὖν αὐτὸν ὡς οἰκείων μελῶν, οὕτω πάντων ἀνθρώπων προνοεῖν, ἵνα προκόπτωσιν ἐν καλοῖς καὶ μὴ προσκόπτωσιν ἐν κακοῖς.[75]

7 Po istině ubo car' naricašesja, iže carstvuja (*read* carstvujaj) nad strast'mi i slastem odolěvati mogij, iže cělomudrija ven'cem ven'čannyj i porfiroju pravdy obolčenyj.[76]

= Agap. 18: βασιλέα σε κατὰ ἀλήθειαν ὁρίζομαι, ὡς βασιλεύειν καὶ κρατεῖν τῶν ἡδονῶν δυνάμενον καὶ τὸν στέφανον τῆς σωφροσύνης ἀναδησάμενον, καὶ πορφύραν τῆς δικαιοσύνης ἀμφιασάμενον.[77]

After this quotation, familiar to us from the earlier discussion of *Barlaam and Joasaph*, Cyril of Turov and Thomas the Monk, the author winds up saying "Such was also the pious Tsar of Tsars, Grand Prince Vasilij'."

Towards the middle of the sixteenth century, another Byzantine manual on the ruler's duties and prerogatives became fashionable with the *literati* of Muscovy. The authorship of these "Hortatory Chapters" is attributed—wrongly—to the ninth-century emperor Basil I. (According to the acrostic, Basil addressed his admonitions to his son, Leo VI.[78]) The author—probably Photius himself[79]—who hints at his sources except for Agapetus, imitates and paraphrases him at length, in some instances closely following the wording of his model. Through Pseudo-Basil, ch. 51, a part of Agapetus' chapter 8 found its way into such venerable texts as the Coronation Ritual of Ivan IV, in which approximately one-half of the "Metropolitan's Admonition to the Great Prince," probably written by the learned Metropolitan Macarius, consists of literal excerpts from Pseudo-Basil's little work.[80] From there, Agapetus 8 wandered from one Ritual to another, and can be read, for instance, in the Metropolitan's "Admonition" prepared for the coronation of Peter II (d. 1730).[81] However as the dependence of the Russian coronation ritual on Pseudo-Basil is a known fact, it shall not be discussed here.

Ivan IV may have quoted Pseudo-Basil in his Testament.[82] It is possible that the chief polemical writing attributed to Ivan, his first reply to Prince A. Kurbskij, a lengthy work so teeming with erudite quotations that the historian Ključevskij dubbed it *učennaja kaša*, a learned medley, contains reminiscences from Agapetus. First, two passages reminiscent of Agapetus 21:

1. ašče bo i perfiru nošu, no obače vem se, jako po vsemu nemoščiju, podobno vsem čelovekom obložen esm' po estestvu.[83]

ašče ubo perfiru nosim, zlatom i biserom ukrašenu, no obače tlenny esmi čelovečeskoju nemoščju obloženy.[84]

At first sight, it seems strange that the tsar, elsewhere so bent upon asserting his divine rights to rule, should treat this passage in the same way in which his adversaries were to treat it later. The equality with God is replaced by the "purple," and even this distinction is referred to in a concessive clause. Was this twist necessitated by the general line of the argument? Ivan had to invoke his human weakness in order to prove that his sins did not make an apostate of the True Faith out of him, as Kurbskij contended. In fact, by this contention, the prince required Ivan to show superhuman qualities, this being a heretical demand.[85] Further Agapetus reminiscences are:

2. Podovlastnyx že svoix blagix blagaja podavaem zlym že zlaja prinositca nakazanija.[86]

Cf. Agap. 28: $\kappa a \grave{\iota}$ $\tau o \grave{\upsilon} s$ $\tau \grave{a}$ $\kappa \acute{a} \lambda \lambda \iota \sigma \tau a$ $\pi o \iota o \hat{\upsilon} \nu \tau a s$ $\pi \rho o \tau \acute{\iota} \mu a$, $\kappa a \grave{\iota}$ $\tau o \hat{\iota} s$ $\tau \grave{a}$ $\chi \epsilon \acute{\iota} \rho \iota \sigma \tau a$ $\delta \rho \hat{\omega} \sigma \iota \nu$ $\epsilon \pi \iota \tau \acute{\iota} \mu a$.[87]

3. I vsegda ubo carem podobaet obozritel'nym byti, ovogda krotčajšim, ovogda že jarym.[88]

Cf. Agap. 48: $\gamma \acute{\iota} \nu o \upsilon$ $\tau o \hat{\iota} s$ $\dot{\upsilon} \pi \eta \kappa \acute{o} o \iota s$, $\epsilon \dot{\upsilon} \sigma \epsilon - \beta \acute{\epsilon} \sigma \tau a \tau \epsilon$ $\beta a \sigma \iota \lambda \epsilon \hat{\upsilon}$, $\kappa a \grave{\iota}$ $\phi o \beta \epsilon \rho \grave{o} s$ $\delta \iota \grave{a}$ $\tau \grave{\eta} \nu$ $\dot{\upsilon} \pi \epsilon \rho o \chi \grave{\eta} \nu$ $\tau \hat{\eta} s$ $\dot{\epsilon} \xi o \upsilon \sigma \acute{\iota} a s$, $\kappa a \grave{\iota}$ $\pi o \theta \epsilon \iota \nu \grave{o} s$ $\delta \iota \grave{a}$ $\tau \grave{\eta} \nu$ $\pi a \rho o \chi \grave{\eta} \nu$ $\tau \hat{\eta} s$ $\epsilon \dot{\upsilon} \pi o \iota \acute{\iota} a s$.[89]

The following passage goes back not immediately to Agapetus' chapter 30[90] but to Joseph Sanin's "Illuminator," which had excerpted from it:

4. *Ivan IV*: i ne tokmo o svoix, no podvlast-nyx dati mi otvet, ašče čto moim nesmo-treniem pogrešitca.[91]

*Sanin*: i netokmo o sebě otvet dasi k Bogu, no eže inii zlo tvorjat, ty slovo otdasi Bogu, volju ž dav im.[92]

There is nothing extraordinary in the fact that Muscovite adherents of the theocratic imperial ideology should have drawn upon a Byzantine author who had dedicated his treatise on Rulership to a Justinian. Ivan the Terrible, how-ever, like his counterparts in seventeenth-century France, had to assert himself against the anti-autocratic party of the nobility. Not only blood, but ink was spilled profusely in this struggle. What were the ideological arguments of Ivan's opponents, what the authorities invoked by them? The question is worth in-vestigating.

Some of autocracy's adversaries like Kurbskij, were manoeuvered into exile and treason. But among those who defied the tyrant at home, the figure of Metro-politan Philip (Kolyčev) (1566–1568) towers above all the others. He fought the establishment of the *opričnina*, first tried to admonish Ivan, the "divider of the Kingdom," in private, then publicly upbraided him for his murders. For this, he was deposed, and as the story goes, strangled by Maljuta Skuratov (1569). The Russian Church made Philip a saint.

One of the two recensions of the Vita of Philip,[93] possibly written by a con-temporary and an eye-witness to the events,[94] preserves three speeches allegedly delivered by the metropolitan. Up to the present, they have been considered our most important source for the reconstruction of the ideas prevalent among the Russian ecclesiastical circles opposed to Ivan IV's system of values. If this opin-ion is upheld—and I think it should be modified—then these ecclesiastics had hardly an idea of their own. The first speech put in Philip's mouth was an in-auguration address, supposedly delivered after his consecration. Be it said in advance that five-sixths of it is but a cento from various chapters of Agapetus. The compiler's originality is limited to choosing appropriate quotations and in-troducing slight changes into others. Here is the text of the address.

1. O blagočestivyj car', Bogom sotvorennoe sokrovišče blagoj very, poskol'ku bol'šej spodobilsja ty blagodati, postol'ku i dolžen Emu vozdat'. Bog prosit ot nas blagotvorenij, ne odnoj liš blagoj besedy, no i prinošenija blagix del.

= Agap. 5: ἴσθι, ὦ εὐσεβείας θεόπευκτον ἄγαλμα, ὅτι ὅσῳ μεγάλων ἠξιώθης παρὰ Θεοῦ δωρεῶν, τοσούτῳ μείζονος ἀμοιβῆς ὀφειλέτης ὑπάρχεις αὐτῷ. . . . εὐχαριστίαν δὲ ζητεῖ παρ' ἡμῶν, οὐ τὴν διὰ ῥημάτων ἀγαθῶν προφορὰν ἀλλὰ τὴν διὰ πραγ-μάτων εὐσεβῶν προσφοράν.[95]

2. Postavlennyj nad ljud'mi vysoty radi zemnogo tvoego carstvija, (krotok budi deržavy radi gornija vlasti = K.). Otverzaj uši tvoi k niščete stražduščej, da i sam obrjaščeš slux Božij k tvoim prošenijam, ibo kakovy my byvaem k našim klevretam, takovym obrjaščem k sebe i svoego Vladyku.

= Agap. 8: ἀπρόσιτος μὲν ὑπάρχεις ἀν-θρώποις διὰ τὸ ὕψος τῆς κάτω βασιλείας, εὐπρόσιτος δὲ γίνῃ τοῖς δεομένοις διὰ τὸ κράτος τῆς ἄνω ἐξουσίας. καὶ ἀνοίγεις τὰ ὦτα τοῖς ὑπὸ πενίας πολιορκουμένοις, ἵνα εὕρῃς τὴν τοῦ Θεοῦ ἀκοὴν ἀνεῳγμένην. οἷοι γὰρ ἂν τοῖς ἡμετέροις γενώμεθα συνδούλοις, τοιοῦτον περὶ ἡμᾶς εὑρήσομεν τὸν δεσπότην.[96]

The changes introduced by the Vita of Philip are small but noteworthy. They tone down the glorification of the emperor, and amplify the restraining notes present in Agapetus' text, a procedure of which the later treatment of Agapetus 21 will be a perfect example. Here ἀπρόσιτος ὑπάρχεις, "Thou art aloof," has been changed into the neutral "Thou art put over men," and "accessible," strengthened into *krotok*, "humble," a word Agapetus would not dare to use with respect to the emperor. The metropolitan's speech continues as follows:

3. Kak vsegda bodrstvuet kormčij, tak i    = Agap. 2.[97]
carskij mnogoočityj um dolžen tverdo soder-
žat' pravila dobrago zakona, izsuščaja potoki
bezzakonija, da ne pogrjaznet v volnax
nepravdy korabel' vsemirnyja žizni.

The "many-eyed" mind of the emperor, which seemed disconcerting to the eulogist of Vasilij III, did not trouble the compiler of Philip's Vita. But παγκόσμιος πολιτεία, the "universal empire," fitted the Muscovite aspirations in the second half of the sixteenth century no better than it did in the first. In the rendering of the Vita, "all world life," πολιτεία was taken to mean "life," since this was one of the acceptations of the Byzantine word. The error, however, was made by the Slavic translator of Agapetus, not the compiler. What follows in Philip's address is the admonition to choose right counselors and not to lend an ear to flattery (*laskatel'stva*). It seems that finally we have found an original allusion to the situation then prevailing at the court of Ivan IV. Kurbskij's contemporary diatribe against the Tsar's "flatterers" (*laskateli*), comes immediately to mind.[98] One scholar sees in this passage of the Vita a thinly veiled hint at the *opričnina*.[99] He may be right, only that the hint is not of Russian making. It is a literal translation of Agapetus' chapter 22:

4. Prinimaj xotjaščix sovetovat' tebe blagoe, a ne domogajuščixsja tol'ko laskatel'stv; ibo, odni radejut voistinu o pol'ze, drugie že zabotjatsja tol'ko o ugoždenii vlasti.
= Agap. 22: ἀποδέχου τοὺς τὰ χρηστὰ συμβουλεύειν ἐθέλοντας, ἀλλὰ μὴ τοὺς κολακεύειν ἑκάστοτε σπεύδοντας. οἱ μὲν γὰρ τὸ συμφέρον συνορῶσιν ἐν ἀληθείᾳ, οἱ δὲ πρὸς τὰ δοκοῦντα τοῖς κρατοῦσιν ἀφορῶσι.[100]

5. Pače vsjakoj slavy carstvija zemnogo ukrašaet carja venec blagočestija.
= Agap. 15: ὑπὲρ πάντα τῆς βασιλείας τὰ ἔνδοξα, τῆς εὐσεβείας τὸ στέμμα τὸν βασιλέα κοσμεῖ.[101]

6. (Ratnym pokazuet vlast', pokorlivym že čelověkoljubije, i pobĕždajušče onĕx siloju oružija, nevooružennoju ljuboviju ot svoix pobĕždaetsja. = K.)
= Agap. 20: . . . τοῖς πολεμίοις μὲν δεικνύει τὴν ἐξουσίαν, τοῖς ὑπηκόοις δὲ νέμει φιλανθρωπίαν, καὶ νικῶσα ἐκείνους τῇ δυνάμει τῶν ὅπλων, τῇ ἀόπλῳ ἀγάπῃ τῶν οἰκείων ἡττᾶται.[102]

7. Ne vozbranjat' sogrešajuščim est' tol'ko grex, ibo esli kto i živet zakonno, no prilepljaetsja k bezzakonnym, tot byvaet osužden ot Boga, kak součastnik v zlyx delax.[103]
= Agap. 28: ἴσον τῷ πλημμελεῖν τὸ μὴ κωλύειν τοὺς πλημμελοῦντας λογίζου. κἂν γάρ τις πολιτεύηται μὲν ἐνθέσμως, ἀνέχηται δὲ τῶν βιούντων ἀθέσμως, συνεργὸς τῶν κακῶν παρὰ Θεῷ κρίνεται.[104]

After this passage, which sounds so genuine in the mouth of an adversary of the *opričnina*, Philip's speech closes with a few lines exhorting the tsar to uphold the true faith and to keep it free from heresy.

Another part of the Vita in which Philip's "own" words are related, is a secret dialogue between the prince of the Church and the temporal ruler, supposed to have taken place towards the beginning of Philip's pontificate. In the dialogue, the metropolitan is made to proceed systematically and to start right away with Agapetus' chapter 1:

8. O deržavnyj, imeja na sebe san prevyše vsjakoj česti, počti Gospoda davšago tebe sie dostoinstvo, ibo skipetr zemnoj est' tol'ko podobie nebesnago, daby naučil ty čelovekov xranit' pravdu.

= Agap. 1: τιμῆς ἁπάσης ὑπέρτερον ἔχων ἀξίωμα, βασιλεῦ, τίμα ὑπὲρ ἅπαντας τὸν τούτου σε ἀξιώσαντα Θεόν, ὅτι καὶ καθ' ὁμοίωσιν τῆς ἐπουρανίου βασιλείας ἔδωκέ σοι τὸ σκῆπτρον τῆς ἐπιγείου δυναστείας, ἵνα τοὺς ἀνθρώπους διδάξῃς τὴν τοῦ δικαίου φυλακήν.[105]

Philip, however, does not stop with this borrowing from Agapetus. He goes on:

9. Zemnogo obladanie bogatstva rečnym vodam upodobljaetsja i malo-po-malu iždivaetsja; soxranjaetsja tol'ko odno nebesnoe sokrovišče pravdy.

= Agap. 7: τῶν ἐπιγείων χρημάτων ὁ ἄστατος πλοῦτος τῶν ποταμίων ῥευμάτων μιμεῖται τὸν δρόμον, πρὸς ὀλίγον μὲν ἐπιρρέων . . . μετ' ὀλίγον δὲ παραρρέων . . . μόνος δὲ τῆς εὐποιίας ὁ θησαυρὸς μόνιμός ἐστι.[106]

10. Esli i vysok ty sanom, no estestvom telesnym podoben vsjakomu čeloveku (ašče ubo, carju, i obrazom Božim počten esi, no persti zemnoj priložen esi. = M.).

Compare Agapetus 21, p. 83 above.

This was the familiar Agapetus chapter 21, with its "moderating" second part duly recorded and its first deifying clause provided, as it were, with a minus sign. By this device, a statement exalting the ruler's power has been turned into its opposite. It has been seen that Ivan the Terrible found it expedient to give this quotation the same twist in his polemics against Kurbskij. Incidentally, the comparison between *obložen* (*oboženy*), used by Ivan IV in the passage reminiscent of Agapetus 21, and *priložen* of the Slavic translation of Agap. 21 inserted into the Vita of Philip, should remove all doubt as to the "Agapetian" origin of Ivan's passage, quoted by the tsar from memory. The metropolitan continued:

11. Tot po istine možet nazyvat'sja vlastelinom, kto obladaet sam soboju, ne rabotaet strastjam.

= Agap. 18.[107]

Finally, the tsar succeeded in breaking this chain of quotations and giving a retort, whereupon there ensued between the two a lively and interesting altercation on the metropolitan's right to intercede for the tsar's oppressed subjects. But even this part of the dialogue contains two gems from Agapetus:

12. Esli odin iz služitelej korablja vpadaet v iskušenie, ne bol'šuju delaet on bedu plavajuščim, no esli sam kormčij, to vsemu korablju nanosit oibel.' gnpo

= Agap. 10: ὅταν μὲν ὁ ναύτης σφαλῇ, μικρὰν φέρει τοῖς συμπλέουσι βλάβην, ὅταν δὲ αὐτὸς ὁ κυβερνήτης, παντὸς ἐργάζεται τοῦ πλοίου ἀπώλειαν.[108]

13. (bogatstvo bo otxodit i deržava mimo grjadet = K.) bezsmertno tol'ko odno žitie po Boge.[109]

= Agap. 15: . . . ὁ γὰρ πλοῦτος ἀπέρχεται καὶ ἡ δόξα μετέρχεται, τὸ δὲ κλέος τῆς ἐνθέου πολιτείας ἀθανάτοις αἰῶσι συμπαρεκτείνεται.[110]

The last speech attributed to Philip by the compiler of his Vita was delivered in the solemn setting of the Dormition Cathedral of the Kremlin in 1568. There the clash occurred which brought the tension between Philip and Ivan into the open and was followed by the metropolitan's deposition. The pontiff first refused to bless the tsar. Then he bitterly reproached him for spilling blood at the instigation of "flatterers," that is, Ivan's new creatures, who had replaced the council of magnates. A part of the reprimand was couched in terms avowedly borrowed from a "God-inspired chronicler"—this was the rank to which Agapetus had been promoted. *Istinu skazal bogoduxnovennyj letopisec*, Philip is made to say,

14. (otvraščajsja laskovcev lestnyx sloves; vrany xititel'nyja iskopyvajut tělesnyja očesa, sii že duševnyja oslěpljajut mysli, ne popuščajušče viděti istiny. Ovii bo xvaljat suščaja xuly dostojnaja, druzii že xuljat mnogaždy xvaly dostojnaja. = K.)[111]

= Agap. 12: ἀποστρέφου τῶν κολάκων τοὺς ἀπατηλοὺς λόγους, ὥσπερ τῶν κοράκων τοὺς ἁρπακτικοὺς τρόπους. οἱ μὲν γὰρ τοὺς τοῦ σώματος ἐξορύττουσιν ὀφθαλμοὺς, οἱ δὲ τοὺς τῆς ψυχῆς ἐξαμβλύνουσι λογισμοὺς, μὴ συγχωροῦντες ὁρᾶν τὴν τῶν πραγμάτων ἀλήθειαν. ἢ γὰρ ἐπαινοῦσι ἔσθ᾽ ὅτε τὰ ψόγου ἄξια, ἢ ψέγουσι πολλάκις τὰ ἐπαίνων κρείττονα.[112]

One other phrase of the metropolitan's reprimand is an echo of the second part of Agapetus chapter 21: *ili zabyl, čto i sam ty pričasten persti zemnoj i proščenija grexov trebueš?*[113] "Hast thou forgotten that thou too art (by nature) a participant in the earthly dust, and needest thy sins absolved?" This echo, insignificant but unmistakable, will perhaps help to elucidate the question of the authenticity of Philip's speech. It may be asked whether the quotations from Agapetus put into Philip's mouth are entirely the product of a late sixteenth-century Muscovite scholar's zeal for copying, or whether some of them were uttered by the real metropolitan, for instance, at the moment of the clash in the Dormition Cathedral. At first, it seems more than improbable that Philip should have found nothing better to say on that occasion than to repeat the wisdom of the "God-inspired chronicler." Scholars, although unaware of the source of Philip's speeches, have expressed doubts as to their authenticity, preferring to see in them the reflection of opinions held by the anti-autocratic ecclesiastical circles of the late sixteenth century.[114] The present writer, all his insistence upon the cento character of Philip's words notwithstanding, is inclined to believe that Agapetus' chapter 21 was really echoed by the walls of the Dormition Cathedral during the scene of 1568.

Philip's Vita is not the only account of what occurred in the Cathedral. J. Taube and E. Cruse related the pontiff's speech in their lampoon on Ivan IV which appeared in 1572, four years after the event.[115] It is safe to assume that Agapetus was not a *livre de chevet* with these international adventurers and cheats. And yet they make Philip say to the tsar: "Think that although God has put you high in this world, you nevertheless are a mortal man."[116] If it stood alone, this phrase would be commonplace enough. But, according to the Vita, the metropolitan quoted chapter 21, as well as another passage from Agapetus. Therefore Taube's and Cruse's version is to be evaluated as an echo of the same chapter. It is difficult to deny that very soon after the event of 1568 a tradition existed of Philip's having used the God-Man antithesis inspired by Agapetus to upbraid Ivan IV. This tradition may have had a foundation in fact.

It appears now that the adversaries of Ivan's absolutism used Agapetus to an even greater extent than did the apologists and theoreticians of the Muscovite imperial claims. This fact, if considered solely from the point of view of this author's usefulness for the "liberal" party, poses no problem. In Agapetus' work, praise is entwined with humble admonitions, the latter perhaps prevailing. This has even prompted the rather incongruous theory that the Deacon's chapters were but a veiled criticism of Justinian's reign.[117] The "liberals" had only to strengthen the admonitions and to weaken the praise. Such was, in fact, their procedure. A basic problem arises as soon as we turn to the political struggle of that time.

It has been recently maintained, on general grounds, that in sixteenth-century Muscovy the anti-autocratic party had no ideology of its own to distinguish it from the supporters of the Tsar's absolute rule.[118] It should be added that this weakness may have partly contributed to the "liberals'" defeat. The extensive use of Agapetus by the anonymous eulogist of Vasilij III and by Ivan IV on one hand and by Philip or the compiler of his Vita on the other, explains the common traits in the ideological proclamations of both hostile camps, and provides a textual, and therefore cogent, argument converging with the recent thesis.

The first attempts to create a politically—and spiritually—independent center in the North in defiance of Kiev fall in Andrej Bogoljubskij's time. This development culminated in Ivan the Terrible's Moscow, where it received the articulate ideological form which was to endure until the twenties of the eighteenth century. Whatever the construction of late fourteenth- to sixteenth-century propaganda may have been, it is as plausible to maintain that the line of this development goes from twelfth-century Suzdal' to sixteenth-century Muscovy. It is hardly a coincidence that Agapetus should have entered Russian literature at both these historical junctures. No less significant is the vogue for Agapetus' chapter 21, whose boldness is by no means representative of the Byzantine standard doctrine of the emperor as the imitator of Christ.

Our investigation might well have ended at this point. But it is tempting to follow the somewhat different fate of Agapetus in sixteenth- and seventeenth-century Ukraine.

On the eve of the Union of Brest, in 1592, the Orthodox Stauropegiac Fraternity of Lwów (L'viv) petitioned Tsar Fëdor Ivanovič and some influential court personages for assistance in the construction of a Church in that city. The letter to the tsar may or may not have been written by the metropolitan of Tьrnovo, Dionysius, Constantinople's exarch in "Great and Little Russia," but the approval of its final form certainly lay with the Fraternity. As the following passages prove, L'viv must have been aware that the correct approach in attempting to get money out of the heir to Ivan IV was to show that it knew what was, ideologically, the order of the day in Moscow:

1. Česti vsjakoja prevyše imja (*read* imějaj) dostojanie carju, počitaeši bo pače vsex sie tebě darovavšago Boga, jako i po podobiju nebesnago carstvija, dade tebě skipetr zemnago vlastitel'-stva, da jakože nebesnyj car' Bog na nebesi, sice i ty tixoobrazně čelověky milueši na zemli i učiši six bljusti pravednaja . . .

This is almost word for word Agapetus chapter 1 (for Greek text, see above, page 88), only that the admonition has been changed into a statement of fact, a technique which will be repeated later, and, what is more important, the tsar is here likened to God not in power, but in love. Centuries later, Gogol' will follow the same line of thought. The letter continues:

2. . . . mnogobodrstvujuščim umnym carskim tvoim okom . . .

—this is the "vigilant and many-eyed mind" of the emperor which caused trouble to almost every Slavic excerptor of Agapetus—

. . . krěpko upravljaja ix na blagyjanažiti.

(Compare Agap. 2; for text see page 90, above.)

3. Neprikosnoven bo esi čelověkom vysokosti radi dol'njago carstvija, blagopristupen že moljaščimsja byvaeši vosprijatija radi gornjago i otverzaeši sluxi blagoprijatně iže v niščetě mnogobedstvujuščim, da obrjaščeši Božij slux tebě priklonennyj. I jako ubo milostiv ko pros-jaščim milosti byvaeši, takova i sebe moljaščus' Vladyku milostiva obrětaeši.

This is almost word for word Agapetus 8 (for text, see p. 91, above), with its general tenor applied to Fëdor; a most appropriate choice in a petition asking for a subsidy.

Agapetus 21 follows a few lines later, with significant modifications:

4. Suščestvom ubo tělese raven esi čelověkom, o carju, dostojaniem že prevosxodiši vsjačeski: i jako blagonaučen ne gněvaešis', i jako tlěnen, ne voznosišis'.[119]

τῇ μὲν οὐσίᾳ τοῦ σώματος, ἴσος παντὶ ἀνθρώπῳ ὁ βασιλεύς, τῇ ἐξουσίᾳ δὲ τοῦ ἀξιώματος ὅμοιός ἐστι τῷ ἐπὶ πάντων Θεῷ. οὐκ ἔχει γὰρ ἐπὶ γῆς τὸν αὐτοῦ ὑψηλότερον. χρὴ τοίνυν αὐτὸν καὶ ὡς Θεὸν μὴ ὀργίζεσθαι καὶ ὡς θνητὸν μὴ ἐπαίρεσθαι.

The changes are worth discussing. Agapetus' "He is like unto God high above" has been omitted altogether; the words "Thou excellest all" seem to correspond to "He hath not his higher on earth" of the Greek; instead of "as God, he should not show anger," the Fraternity text reads "well instructed, Thou showest not anger."[120] The passage on the ruler's transient nature, which the eulogist of Vasilij III has omitted, is included here. All these omissions and modifications occur not in a polemical anti-autocratic treatise but in an address intended to please the Tsar of Moscow. Here all may be in the nuances; but what is expressed is a different conception of the supreme ruler's office. No further conclusions are possible as long as the authorship of the Fraternity's missive remains in doubt. Although the changes may reflect the view of a high dignitary of the Patriarchate of Constantinople, they certainly did not contradict the opinions of the Ukrainian intellectuals of that time. They knew not only their Latin and their Polish, but also their Greek quite well and could have found the less extravagant forms of the Byzantine imperial doctrine more acceptable.

And yet, the first Slavic edition of Agapetus appeared in the Ukraine in the printing press of the Kievan Laura in 1628.[121] Unfortunately, no details can be given on this translation, as the pamphlet is not accessible in the West. It has been asserted that the translation was done by Peter Mogila (Mohyla), the later archimandrite of the Laura and metropolitan of Kiev, directly from the Greek in 1627.[122] The title of the 1628 edition announces that it is destined for "all those who righteously seek to rule over their passions." The intention is moralistic, not political. The archimandrite of the Laura, if he is the translator of Agapetus, is to be put on the same plane with Canon Thomas Paynell, who, approximately a hundred years earlier, declared in the preface to his English translation of Agapetus: "I saie it is a booke of great wysedome and learnying, conteyning all these preceptes, by the whiche not only a prince but all other estates may learne to do iustyce."[123] The closest parallel to the Muscovite interest in Agapetus is not to be sought in the near seventeenth-century Ukraine, but in the faraway seventeenth-century France. About the very time when the "Hortatory Chapters" were being translated in Kiev, the youthful Louis XIII improved his Latin by translating Agapetus into French under the guidance of his preceptor David Rivault, the same man whom he commissioned to publish the French version of the Chapters of Pseudo-Basil[124] which had so decisively influenced the Russian coronation ritual. In this context, the counterpart of the Metropolitan of Moscow, Philip, is not the Metropolitan of Kiev, Mohyla, but the Catholic Bishop Bossuet who said to the Dauphin "vous êtes des Dieux, c'est à dire vous avez dans vôtre autorité . . . un caractère Divin . . . mais, ô Dieux de boue et de poussière,"[125] amalgamating Ps. 81:6 with the second part of Agapetus 21. What all this means for the French State theory under Louis XIV is outside the scope of this article.

Muscovite autocracy was a native creation, although the garb it donned was of foreign making. Muscovite imperial ideology did not come into being because some *literati* chanced upon Agapetus' little work. Ideologies, more or less prefabricated, are found when they are needed. But there is a certain range of choice in the search for a ready ideological mold into which the still inarticulate tendencies can be forced. Its selection is a matter of importance. The mold, once chosen, predetermines the form and the modes of expression of certain desires and beliefs to which a political system corresponds. To some extent, this mold is a guaranty of the system's durability, since it determines the way of thinking even of its opponents. In Muscovy, the choice fell upon Agapetus with the chapters of Pseudo-Basil ranking next. By our standards, these texts were rather second-rate compendia. Even the Byzantines would agree that they had better literature to offer on the subject of government and its ideological basis.

Whatever Agapetus' value was, he not only affected political thinking in Muscovy, but often proved almost a substitute for such thinking. Original

Muscovite speculation on matters politic, if existent, will have to be sought outside the conventionally quoted Russian passages, unless one wants to discover this speculation in their modifications of Agapetus' text. One more feature, perhaps reflecting a general quality of the human mind, has become apparent: the tenacity with which the same texts of Agapetus were used to express opposed views, or even any views at all. Herein lies the power, and the threat, of catechisms. It is as important to bring this point out as to have identified the source of a series of passages from Kievan and Muscovite literature.[126]

## *NOTES*

1. The literature on the subject is too vast to be adduced here in detail. The most recent publications in English which may serve as bibliographical introduction are the two following: William K. Medlin, Moscow and East Rome (= *Études d'histoire économique, politique et sociale,* I) (Geneva, 1952)—not always reliable—and D. Stremooukhoff, "Moscow the Third Rome: Sources of the Doctrine," *Speculum,* XXVIII (1953), 84–101. Also the well-written book by H. Schaeder, *Moskau das Dritte Rom* (Hamburg, 1929) contains a long list of works consulted by the author.

2. E. H. Kantorowicz, "Deus per Naturam, Deus per Gratiam," *The Harvard Theological Review,* XLV (1952), 269, n. 55.

3. *Polnoe Sobranie Russkix Letopisej* I, 2nd ed. (1927), p. 370. The "message" of John Chrysostom seems to consist, for the author of the excursus, of Rom. 13:2. Some modern scholars have connected it with the preceding words and referred to a passage in Chrysostom's III Homily on Rom. 13:1. This attempt barred the way to the correct identification of the source of the excursus. Cf. H. Schaeder, *Moskau das Dritte Rom,* p. 46, n. 1, taken over by Medlin, *Moscow and the East Rome,* p. 57, n. 2.

4. Antonius called Melissa, p. ex. in Migne, *Patr. Graeca,* CXXXVI, col. 1012B: "By the essence of his body, an emperor is like any man. Yet in power of his office, he is like God, ruler of the All."

5. That there never was an Antonius, Melissa by name, has been known at least since Coxe; cf. R. Dressler, "Questiones criticae ad Maximi et Antonii Gnomologias spectantes ...," *Jahns Jahrbuecher ... Supplementband,* V (1864), 311–314.

6. M. N. Speranskij, *Perevodnye sborniki izrečenij v slavjano-russkoj pis'mennosti. Issledovanie i teksty* (Moscow, 1904) [also in *Čtenija v imp. obšč. istorii i drev. rossijskix pri Mosk. Univ.,* CXCIX (1901); CCXII (1905); CCXIII (1905)], p. 155 ff., and especially p. 216 ff. Speranskij's somewhat long-winded argument is well summarized in an otherwise disappointing book by S. A. Ščeglova "Pčela po rukopisjam kievskix bibliotek," in *Pamjatniki drevnej pis'mennosti i iskusstva,* CLXXV (1910), 13 ff.

7. M. N. Speranskij, *Perevodnye sborniki ...,* p. 305 ff.; 329.

8. V. Semenov, "Drevnjaja russkaja Pčela po pergamennomu spisku," *Sbornik Otd. Russ. Jaz. i Slov. Imp. Akad. Nauk,* LIV, 4 (1893), 111.

9. Perhaps similar to the later *Měrilo pravednoe,* see below.

10. These are in the first place the Radziwill Chronicle, the *Akademičeskij Spisok* and the *Letopisec Perejaslavlja Suzdal'skogo.* The readings of the first two may be conveniently reconstructed from the apparatus of the 1927 edition of the Laurentius Chronicle, cf. above note 3; for the *Letopisec Perejaslavlja Suzdal'skogo,* cf. the ed. by K. M. Obolenskij (Moscow, 1851), p. 84.

11. The Hypatian Chronicle, ed. of the Archaeographical Commission (1871), p. 402.

12. On this point, cf. D. S. Lixačev, *Russkie letopisi* (Moscow-Leningrad, 1947), p. 429, who sums up the results obtained by M. D. Priselkov, "Lavrent'evskaja letopis' (istorija teksta)," *Učenye zapiski Leningr. Gos. Univ.,* no. 32 (1939).

13. M. N. Speranskij, *Perevodnye sborniki,* p. 305 ff.; cf. p. 315.

14. M. V. Šaxmatov, *Opyty po istorii drevne-russkix političeskix idej* I. *Učenija russkix letopisej domongol'skogo perioda o gosudarstvennoj vlasti* (Prague, 1927), appendix, has collected parallels between a series of passages from Rus' chronicles and chapter nine of the *Pčela, O*

*vlasti i knjaženii*, "On Power and Rulership." The few quite convincing parallels in Šaxmatov's list date from 1175 and later years.

15. M. D. Priselkov, *Učenye zapiski Leningr. Gos. Univ.*, no. 32 (1939).
16. K. M. Obolenskij, *Letopisec Perejaslavlja Suzdal'skago* (Moscow, 1851), p. 99.
17. Cf. Lixačev, *Russkie Letopisi*, p. 434 and 436.
18. M. V. Šaxmatov (*Opyty*, p. 160, n. on p. 162 and p. 561) quotes this passage from the *Pčela* and compares it with the Laurentius Chronicle. It is not clear whether he realizes who "Agipitos" was. It is noteworthy that although both Medlin, *op. cit.*, pp. 23–24 and V. Val'denberg, *Drevnerusskie učenija o predelax carskoj vlasti* (Petrograd, 1916), pp. 59–61 give long extracts from Agapetus, neither of the authors establishes the connection between the Deacon of Constantinople and the writings discussed in the present article.
19. M. N. Speranskij, *Perevodnye sborniki*, p. 237.
20. Thomas Mangey, Φίλωνος τοῦ Ἰουδαίου τὰ εὑρισκόμενα ἅπαντα... II (1742), p. 673, in the chapter "ex Antonio." Richter, *Philonis ... opera*, V (1828), p. 235 copies Mangey.
21. E. R. Goodenough, *The Politics of Philo Judaeus* (New Haven, 1938), pp. 99–100, with conclusions on Philo's ideas drawn from the passage in question and a reproach directed against J. Rendel Harris for having omitted it from his collection of Philo's fragments.
22. On the three editions by K. Gesner, cf. R. Dressler, *Questiones criticae*, p. 315 ff. I was able to use only the last one, of 1609. The Migne text is a reprint from Gesner.
23. Most conveniently accessible in Migne, *PG*, LXXXVI, 1, col. 1163–1186. In all subsequent quotations from Agapetus, the Migne text will be used.
24. J. Rendel Harris, *Fragments of Philo Judaeus* (1886), pp. 104–105: "τοιοῦτος γίνου" = Agap. 23; "ὁ μὲν θεὸς οὐδενὸς δεῖται" = Agap. 63; "πλέον ἀγάπα". = Agap. 50. [I see, after the completion of the present article, that K. Praechter, *Byzantinische Zeitschrift*, XVII (1908), 153, n. 2 has already identified a number of "Philonic" fragments of Antonius as borrowed from Agapetus.]
25. M. N. Speranskij, *Perevodnye sborniki*, pp. 232, 235.
26. K. Krumbacher, *Geschichte der byz. Literatur* (2nd ed., 1897), p. 457; K. Praechter, *Byzantinische Zeitschrift*, II (1893), 455–458. Of course K. Emminger, *Studien zu den griechischen Fürstenspiegeln*, II, III (Munich, 1913), p. 49, n. 60 may be right in assuming that Agapetus took the royal road to erudition and found all his many sources in one florilegium which he had at his disposal. But it is also possible to think of several florilegia as Agapetus' sources. One of them may have been John Stobaeus (fifth century), who, among others, quoted the Neopythagorean theorists on kingship, Ecphantos, Diotogenes and Sthenidas. Compare Louis Delatte, *Les Traités de la royauté d'Ecphante, Diotogène et Sthénidas* (Liége-Paris, 1942), p. 36, 3 ff. with Agap. ch. 11; 13; 41; p. 39, 18 ff. with Agap. ch. 18; 68; p. 42, 7 ff. with Agap. ch. 20; 62; p. 46, 4 ff. with Agap. ch. 45.
27. This has already been seen by J. F. Boissonade, *Anecdota Graeca* I (1829), p. 45, who gives a list of authors where this "Philo" fragment is found. Cf. *ibidem*, p. 127.
28. The acrostic runs: "τῷ θειοτάτῳ καὶ εὐσεβεστάτῳ βασιλεῖ ἡμῶν Ἰουστινιανῷ Ἀγαπητὸς ὁ ἐλάχιστος διάκονος."
29. This and all the other English renderings of Agapetus subsequently given in this article are based on the translation from Latin made by Canon Thomas Paynell sometime between 1532 and 1534. Cf. *Dict. of National Biography*, XLIV (1895), s.v. Paynell, Thomas. The Houghton Library, Harvard University, possesses a copy of the 1546 edition of Paynell's translation.
30. Cf. K. Praechter, "Der Roman Barlaam und Joasaph in seinem Verhältnis zu Agapets Königsspiegel," *Byzantinische Zeitschrift*, II (1893), 444–460. Praechter believes in a common source rather than in a direct use of Agapetus, since the Deacon's stylistic embellishments are never taken over literally in the interpolations. This is hardly a decisive argument. In his Κεφάλαια, Pseudo-Basil, who depends heavily on Agapetus, almost never copies him verbatim.
31. The Slavic *Barlaam and Joasaph*, facsimile ed. of the *Obščestvo Ljubitelej Drevnej Pis'mennosti*, LXXXVIII (1887), 449. For the Greek original of the passage, cf., e.g., J. F. Boissonade, *Anecdota Graeca* IV (1832), 309; cf. Agap. 18: "βασιλέα σε κατὰ ἀλήθειαν ὁρίζομαι ὡς βασιλεύειν καὶ κρατεῖν τῶν ἡδονῶν δυνάμενον."
32. The Slavic *Barlaam and Joasaph*, *ibidem*, p. 449; cf. Boissonade, *ibidem*, p. 310; cf. Agap. 18: "καὶ τὸν στέφανον τῆς σωφροσύνης ἀναδησάμενον καὶ τὴν πορφύραν τῆς δικαιοσύνης ἀμφιασάμενον."
33. The Slavic *Barlaam and Joasaph*, *ibidem*, p. 485; cf. Boissonade, *ibidem*, p. 333; cf. Agap. 8: "εὐπρόσιτος δὲ γίνῃ τοῖς δεομένοις διὰ τὸ κράτος τῆς ἄνω ἐξουσίας, καὶ ἀνοίγεις τὰ ὦτα τοῖς ὑπὸ πενίας πολιορκουμένοις, ἵνα εὕρῃς τὴν τοῦ θεοῦ ἀκοὴν ἀνεῳγμένην."

34. Ed. K. Kalajdovič, *Pamjatniki rossijskoj slovesnosti XII veka* (Moscow, 1821), pp. 117-125.

35. M. I. Suxomlinov, *O sočinenijax Kirilla Turovskogo* (1858), conveniently reprinted in "Issledovanija po drevnej russkoj literature," *Sbornik Otd. Russ. Jaz. i Slov. Imp. Akad. Nauk,* LXXXV (1908), 273-349; for dependence of Cyril on *Barlaam and Joasaph,* cf. pp. 325-331.

36. Ed. K. Kalajdovič, *Pamjatniki,* p. 123.

37. The results obtained by M. N. Speranskij, *Perevodnye sborniki,* pp. 316-320 have been summarized here.

38. Speranskij, *Perevodnye sborniki,* appendix, p. 55.

39. Such is the short eulogy of Ivan Kalita, *Zapis' s poxvaloju vel. kn. Ioannu Kalite,* dating from 1339. Publ. by I Sreznevskij, "Svedenija i zametki o maloizvestnyx i neizvestnyx pamjatnikax," in *Priloženie k XXXIV tomu Zapisok Imp. Akad. Nauk* (1879), no. 86, pp. 145-148. Most of the quotations of the Eulogy come from Ezekiel and the Psalter. As for Byzantine references, Kalita is compared to Constantine and Justinian (on account of his piety), and, curiously enough, to Manuel Comnenus (on account of his love for books: *mnogim knigam napisanym ego poveleniem revnuja pravovernomu cěsarju greč'skomu Manuilu*).

40. A good example of such models is the Praise of Tsar John Alexander of Bulgaria, written in 1337 ed. V. D. Stojanov "Bŭlgarski star rŭkopisen pametnik ot XIV vek," *Periodičesko spisanien a bulgarskoto kniževno društestvo v Sredec,* XXI (1887), 267-277. This interesting *Res Gestae*-like document contains many overbearing anti-Byzantine passages. But the elements of this better-than-thou attitude come from the foe. John Alexander is called *car' carem', bogom' izbrannyj* and *bogom' ven'čenyj*; he is compared to "Alexander of old" and Constantine.

41. A. Gorskij and K. Nevostruev, *Opisanie slavjanskix rukopisej moskovskoj sinodal'noj biblioteki,* II, 2 (1859), p. 622 = ms. no. 202, fols. 33-47.

42. *Česti vsjakyja prevyše imějaj san carju, česti* (read, *č'ti*) *pače vsego semu tja spodobivšago Boga.*

43. V. Malinin, *Starec Eleazarova monastyrja Filofej i ego poslanija* (Kiev, 1901), p. 548 and p. 85 of notes. The passages are: *nepriložen ubo esi čelověkom vysoty radi zemnago carstvia* (= Agap. 8), and the familiar *est'stvom ubo tělesnym točen vsjakomu čelověku car', vlastiju že sana podoben est' nad vsěmi Bogu, ne imat bo na zemli vyššago sebe. Podobaet' ubo emu jako smertnu ne v'znositisja i jako Bogu ne gněvatisja* (= Agap. 21). In note 2039 Malinin quotes the Laurentius Chronicle *sub anno* 1175 as a parallel to the Slavic Agap. 21. On principle, the present article could have been written by anyone since 1901.

44. ed. A. Popov, *Istoriko-literaturnyj obzor drevne-russkix polemičeskix sočinenij protiv latinjan* (Moscow, 1875), pp. 360-395. Pachomius the Serb is held to be the author of the *Poxvala* by A. Pavlov in his critical review of Popov's work, cf. *Otčet o XIX prisuždenii nagrad grafa Uvarova* (SPb., 1878), p. 285 ff. According to Pavlov the "imperial" ideas present in the *Poxvala* were unfamiliar to native writers of mid-fifteenth-century Russia. The Eulogy of Boris Aleksandrovič by Thomas the Monk, a text discovered after Pavlov had expressed his hypothesis, disposes of this kind of argument.

45. *Poslanie Vas'jana arxiepiskopa Rostovskago . . . Ivanu Vasil'eviču,* p. ex. in *Kniga Stepennaja, Poln. Sobr. Russ. Let.* XXI, 2 (1913), 557-564.

46. *Poln. Sobr. Russ. Let.* XXI, 2 (1913), 559. Cf. V. Semenov, *Drevnjaja russkaja Pčela,* p. 103. M. I. Suxomlinov had already realized that Vassian copied the *Pčela* when he quoted Democritus: "Zamečanija o sbornikax izvestnyx pod nazvaniem Pčel," in *Sbornik Otd. Russ. Jaz.,* LXXXV (1908), 494-509.

47. The "Demokrat" quotation in Vassian's letter has recently been discussed by I. M. Kudrjavcev, "Poslanie na Ugru Vassiana Rylo kak pamjatnik publicistiki XV v.," in *Trudy Otdela drevne-russkoj literatury Instituta russkoj literatury,* AN SSSR, VIII (1951), 158-186, cf. p. 174 f. Kudrjavcev thinks that the words of Democritus suited the situation of 1480 better than any other saying of chapter nine of the *Pčela.* This is a matter of opinion. What seems sure is that some of the sayings were not quotable in the circumstances of 1480. Agapetus chapter 21 was one of them.

48. M. D. D'jakonov, "Kto byl pervyj velikij knjaz' 'vseja Rusi'," *Bibliograf* V (1889), 11-17. (Mixail Jaroslavič of Tver', about 1315.)

49. N. P. Lixačev, ed., "Inoka Fomy slovo poxval'noe o blagověrnom velikom knjazě Borisě Aleksandroviče," *Pamjatniki dr. pis'm. i isskustva,* CLXVIII (1908).

50. Boris called *car':* N. P. Lixačev, *op. cit.,* p. 28; compared with Moses: *ibidem,* pp. 2, 13, 14; with Augustus and Justinian: *ibidem,* pp. 12, 16; with Leo the Wise: *ibidem,* p. 11;

called New Constantine or compared with him: *ibidem*, pp. 2, 12; successor of Vladimir and Jaroslav: *lbidem*, pp. 2, 16.

51. Cf. N. P. Lixačev, *op. cit.*, pp. 1, 2, 29.

51a. Cf., e.g., as two recent examples, I. U. Budovnic, *Russkaja publicistika XVI veka* (Moscow, 1947), p. 98, and W. K. Medlin, *Moscow and the Third Rome*, p. 89.

52. Agap. 51: "The function of the sun is to illuminate the world; the emperor's virtue is to be merciful and to help those who entreat him."

53. Agap. 61: "Having received from God the imperial sceptre, look Thou, endeavor Thyself to please the One who has given it to Thee."

54. Agap. 30: "For he that gave them power (to act) shall account before God for their evil deeds."

55. Quotations 1–7 in *Prosvětitel'*, (3rd ed., Kazan', 1896), p. 547.

56. ed. G. Kušelev-Bezborodko, *Pamjatniki starinnoj russkoj literatury* IV (SPb., 1862), 192–193. For a discussion of the letter, cf. I Xruščev, *Issledovanie o sočinenijax Josifa Sanina* (SPb., 1868), pp. 94–96. Xruščev's identification of the prince with a brother of Vasilij III is inconclusive. His dating of the letter (after 1505) depends on the identification and therefore cannot be more reliable than the latter.

57. Cf. G. Kušelev-Bezborodko, *op. cit.*, p. 192.
Agap. 37: "He that has obtained high power should imitate, as near as he may, the Giver thereof. . . . he will best imitate him by esteeming no thing more desirable than deeds of mercy."

58. This conclusion would not have been warranted, if we had to rely on the Agapetus passages in *Prosvětitel'* alone. There, they are embedded in an appeal which is announced as a quotation from the Emperor Constantine "*tako bo pišet' . . . car' velikii Konstjantin o carěx i o knjazex i o sudjax zemskix.*" As it is difficult to determine where this quotation ends, the suspicion might have arisen that Joseph found the Agapetus passages in his "Constantine" source. The independent use of Agapetus' chapter 37 in the letter to a Prince disposes of this doubt.
The most recent treatment of Joseph's doctrine, A. A. Zimin's "O političeskoj doktrine Iosifa Volockogo," *Trudy Otd. drevne-rus. lit.*, *AN SSSR*, IX (1953), 159–177, seems to take a stand against those who suspected that the Volokolamsk abbot's views were not an original product of Russian thought (p. 160). In his otherwise quite interesting article, Zimin dates the theory of theocratic kingship, propounded by Joseph, as 1507–1511, and presents it as the result of Joseph's own searchings. It is in such a context that the passage derived from Agapetus ch. 21 is adduced (p. 174 f.).

59. On Ivan IV's use of *Prosvětitel'*, cf. below, p. 93; Metropolitan Macarius transcribes some of Joseph's formulas in his *Admonition* to the newly crowned Tsar, inserted into the Coronation Ritual of 1547 (final version compiled about 1560; cf. M. V. Šaxmatov, "Gosudarstvenno-nacional'nyja idei Činovnyx knig venčanija na carstvo russkix gosudarej," *Zapiski russkago naučnago instituta v Belgrade*, I [1930], 245–278, cf. pp. 248–251); about 1560, *Stepennaja Kniga* respectfully mentions Joseph's testament (*Poln. Sobr. Russ. Let.* XXI, 2 [1913], p. 505) and *Prosvětitel'* (*ibidem*, p. 568). Cf. also the *Stoglav* of 1551, chapters 1 and 79.

60. *Poln. Sobr. Russ. Let.* XXI, 2 (1913), pp. 605–615.

61. P. 606: *ispravleniem blagočestija* = κατορθώμασι εὐσεβείας; p. 608: *pravoslavnyx ispolnenie* = τὸ τῶν ὀρθοδόξων πλήρωμα; p. 613: *skipetrokrestonosnyja*.

62. P. 606: Ivan is a *blagodatnoe imja*; cf. p. 609: *imja . . . Ivan . . . ego že . . . slyšanie veselit serdca*. Byzantines often indulged in puns resulting from their awareness that ᾽Ιωάννης = θεοῦ χάρις in Hebrew. A frequent Byzantine paraphrase of "John" is χαριτώνυμος. For other (fourteenth-century) examples cf., e.g., Ed. Kurtz, "Emendationsvorschläge zu den Gedichten des Manuel Philes," *Byzantinisch-Neugriechische Jahrbücher*, IV (1923), 75.

63. For an example, cf. *Reč' židovskago jazyka preložena na ruskuju . . .* ed. as Appendix in K. Kalajdovič's *Ioann eksarx bolgarskij* (Moscow, 1824), p. 193, where *Ioann* is translated by *blagodat'*.

64. P. 606: *o takovom carskom . . . roženii pisano bjaše někdě ot někoix mudroljubnyx trudopolož'nikov . . . zde že o* (v.l. *ot*) *six v male javleno* (v.l. *-na*) *sut'*.

65. P. 606: *vsi pravoslavnii vo vsex kon'cyx vselennyja radosti ispolnišasja*.

66. P. 611.

67. This is yet to be found. The present remarks aim only at speeding up the identification.

68. M. D'jakonov, *Vlast' moskovskix gosudarej* (SPb., 1889), p. 107, n. 2, thinks that the eulogist of Vasilij III and Ivan IV was inspired by Pseudo-Basil's Κεφάλαια. This is an error.

To clarify, it suffices to compare the treatment of Agapetus chapter 8 by Pseudo-Basil and the eulogist respectively.

69. Agap. 2: "Like the pilot of a ship, the emperor's many-eyed mind keeps a continuous watch, firmly handling the oars of equity and justice, and strongly repelling the vehement waves of iniquity, that the boat of this worldly commonwealth be not crushed by the waves of wickedness."

70. V. Malinin, *Starec Eleazarova monastyrja Filofej* (Kiev, 1901), appendix, p. 50. Cf. *ibidem*, p. 63: *edin pravoslavnyi velikii russkii car' vo vsei podnebesnoi.*

71. Cf., e.g., N. S. Čaev, "'Moskva-Tretij Rim' v političeskoj praktike mosk. pravitel'stva v XVI v.," *Istoričeskie Zapiski*, XVII (1945), 9, with indication of source.

72. Agap. 9: "The pensive soul of an emperor must be evermore as pure as the mirror so that it may continually send forth divine rays, and also that it may learn therefrom to acquire right judgment of things."

73. Agap. 8: "Because of the loftiness of thy earthly empire, Thou art inaccessible; and yet Thou speedily admit'st supplicants (to Thine presence) by reason of the heavenly Power."

74. The final passage corresponds to a hypothetical ἵνα πάντων ἀνθρώπων προνοῇ καὶ αὐτὸς προκόπτῃ ἐν καλοῖς καὶ μὴ προσκόπτῃ ἐν κακοῖς. The modification, however, must be attributed to the Anonymus, whose chief purpose was to speak of the ruler, not of his subjects.

75. Agap. 46: "As the eye is ensconced in the body, so is the God-Sent ruler installed in the world, to minister those things that may be profitable for man. Therefore he should provide for men as he would for his own limbs, that they may prosper in goodness and not stumble in doing evil."

76. Passages 1–7 in *Vkratce poxvala samoderž'cu Vasiliju, Poln. Sobr. Russ. Let.*, XXI, 2 (1913), 610. M. D'jakonov, *Vlast' moskovskix gosudarej* (1889), p. 107, who read the full MS text of the *Poxvala*, quotes a passage from it which did not enter into *Stepennaja Kniga: Bog ne trebuet ni ot kogože pomošči, car' že ot edinago Boga.* This is of course the beginning of Agapetus 63: "ὁ μὲν θεὸς οὐδενὸς δεῖται, ὁέ βασιλεὺς δ, μόνου θεοῦ." "God needeth nothing. An emperor hath only need of God."

77. Agap. 18: "For certain I affirm Thee to be an emperor, seeing Thou rulest over and subduest Thy voluptuous passions, and That thou art crowned with the diadem of chastity and arrayed with the purple robe of justice."

78. Best edition by K. Emminger, *Studien zu den griechischen Fürstenspiegeln*, III Βασιλείου κεφάλαια παραινετικά (Diss. Munich 1913), pp. 50–73, with excellent indications of sources. Most accessible text in Migne, *PG,* CVII, col. XXI–LVI.

79. The authorship of Photius, at first rejected since scholars were reluctant to attribute platitudes to their great colleague of the ninth century, now seems highly probable. Cf. K. Emminger, *op. cit.*, p. 49; I. Dujčev, "Au lendemain de la conversion du peuple bulgare. L'épître de Photius," *Mélanges de Science Religieuse*, VII (1951), 211–226; cf. p. 214. The only correct approach to solving this question is to compare Pseudo-Basil's *Chapters* with the second part of Photius' letter to Tsar Boris-Michael. The resemblance of the two texts is highly suggestive. Cf. p. ex., Photius § 41 with Pseudo-Basil, chapter 26; Photius § 109 with Pseudo-Basil, chapter 38.

80. First seen by X. Loparev, "O čine venčanija russkix carej," *Žurn. Min. Nar. Prosv.*, CCLIII (October 1887), 312–319. A Slavic translation of Pseudo-Basil was known in Muscovite Rus' since the fifteenth century at the latest. A. I. Sobolevskij, "Perevodnaja literatura moskovskoj Rusi," *Sbornik Otd. Russ. Jaz. Slov.*, LXXIV, 1 (1903), 20 mentions three fifteenth century MSS of Pseudo-Basil's *Glavy nakazatel'nyja.* The dated one is of 1457.

81. Text, e.g., in E. V. Barsov, "Drevne-russkie pamjatniki svjaščennago venčanija carej na carstvo," in *Čtenija v imp. obšč. istorii i drevn. Rossijskix* CXXIV (1893), 114 f.

82. X. Loparev, *art. cit.*, p. 319, n. 1. Cf. The Testament of 1572: *ašče kto množestvo zemli priobrjaščet i bogatstva a trilakotna groba ne možet izbežati* (p. ex. in D. S. Lixačev and others, *Poslanija Ivana Groznogo* [1951], p. 526 cf. p. 527) with Pseudo-Basil ch. 45: "εἰ τῆς γῆς ἀπάσης κατακρατῆσαι φιλονεικήσῃς, ἀλλ'οὐ πλέον τριπήχεως γῆς μετὰ θάνατον κληρονομήσεις." It is not sure, however, that Ivan quotes Pseudo-Basil, in whose passage there is no mention of a "grave". The motif of the inescapable "three-cubit-long grave" was known in Rus' literature, cf. a text of 1414: . . . *kamen' grobu Arilakotnago* (read, *trilakotnago*) *ne ubežiši* quoted from Sobolevskij by Schaeder, *Moskau das Dritte Rom*, p. 53, n. 7. Cf. also V. Semenov, *Drevnjaja russkaja Pčela*, p. 136. Filistion.

83. D. S. Lixačev, J. S. Lur'e, V. P. Adrianova-Peretc, eds., *Poslanija Ivana Groznogo*, (1951), p. 49 f.

84. *Ibidem*, p. 46. "Although I am wearing the purple robe, I know nevertheless that by nature I am perishable and weighed down with all human weakness."

85. *Ibidem*, p. 46; 14; 15.

86. *Ibidem*, p. 61.

87. Agap. 28: "Honor them that do good and punish them that do evil."

88. *Poslanija*, p. 20.

89. Agap. 48: "Be thou, o most pious Emperor, to Thy subjects, through the excellence of Thy power, terrible, and by Thy liberality, amiable."

90. "For he that gave them power (to act) shall give an account to God for their evil deeds."

91. *Poslanija.*, p. 50 f.

92. *Prosvětitel'* (3rd ed., Kazan', 1896), p. 547. Cf. above, p. 89.

93. Cf. V. Ključevskij, *Drevnerusskija žitija svjatyx kak istoričeskij istočnik* (Moscow, 1871), p. 311 and n. 2; G. P. Fedotov, *Svjatoj Filipp, mitropolit moskovskij* (Paris, 1928), *passim*. I have seen neither of the versions of Philip's Vita. I am therefore reduced to (a) a few excerpts made from one of them by N. M. Karamzin, *Istorija gosudarstva rossijskago*, IX, especially n. 178; (b) a few quotations in V. Malinin's *Starec Eleazarova monastyrja*, pp. 733–737; 743 f.; (c) a modern Russian paraphrase of the Vita, amounting to a translation, by A. N. Murav'ev "*Žitija svjatyx rossijskoj cerkvi. Janvar'*'" (SPb., 1857) (inaccessible to me); (d) a series of excerpts, apparently copied from Murav'ev, in G. P. Fedotov's work quoted in this note. In the present article, I am using Fedotov's excerpts and substituting for them Karamzin's ( = K.) and Malinin's ( = M.) original quotations whenever available.

94. Cf. Karamzin, *Istorija*, IX, n. 179: *ne ot inogo slyšax no sam viděx* V. Ključevskij, *Drevnerusskija žitija*, p. 311, n. 2 points out, however, that only one version of the Vita's first recension has this remark and that the text of the Vita contains several errors of fact. At another place in the Vita, the author says that he had gathered his material from *iněix dostověrno predajuščix o něm* (sc. Philip).

95. Agap. 5: "Know, O God-wrought embodiment of piety, that the greater the gifts awarded to Thee by God, the deeper Thou art in His debt. . . . God asks us for gratitude, not that expressed by gentle words, but that shown in offering Him good deeds."

96. Agap. 8: "Because of the loftiness of this earthly Empire, Thou art inaccessible; and yet Thou speedily admit'st suppliants (to thy presence) by reason of the Heavenly Power. Thou doest listen to those who suffer poverty, that God may in Thy necessity kindly hearken to Thee. For as we are to our fellow servants of God, so shall we find the Heavenly Ruler disposed toward us."

97. "Like the pilot of a ship, the emperor's many-eyed mind keeps a continuous watch, firmly handling the oars of equity and justice, and strongly repelling the vehement waves of iniquity, so that the boat of this world's commonwealth be not crushed by the waves of wickedness." For Greek text cf. above, p. 90.

98. The epithet occurs towards the end of the first letter of Kurbskij to Ivan IV. Text, e.g., in *Poslanija Ivana Groznogo* (1951), p. 536.

99. G. P. Fedotov, *op. cit.,* p. 181.

100. Agap. 22: "Accept and favor them that desire to give Thee good counsel, but not those that strive to flatter Thee on every occasion. The former truthfully consider what is advantageous; the latter look after what may please those in power."

101. Agap. 15: "Above all glorious ornaments of a Kingdom, the crown of piety does best ornate an emperor."

102. Agap. 20: ". . . he shows power to his enemies; but to his subjects, he shows humane kindness. Therefore, as he overcomes the enemies by strength of arms, so he is subdued by his subjects on account of his peaceful ( = "weaponless") love for them."

103. Passages 1–7 in G. P. Fedotov, *Svjatoj Filipp,* p. 179 f.

104. Agap. 28: "Not to chastise sinners is in itself a sin. For whosoever leads a lawful life, but suffers wicked livers, is before God held their accomplice."

105. Agap. 1: "Considering, O mighty emperor, that Thou hast the highest and most honorable dignity of all dignities, Thou shouldest above all honor God, Who has bestowed such honor upon Thee. For God, in likeness of His celestial empire has delivered to Thee the sceptre and governance of this world to teach men to keep justice."

106. Agap. 7: "The unsteadfast possession of earthly riches follows the course of flowing waters. For a short while, it floats to those who fancy themselves in their possession, but

shortly after they float by and enrich others. The only permanent acquisition is the treasure of good deeds."

107. For certain I affirm Thee to be an emperor seeing Thou rulest over and subduest Thy voluptuous passions. For text, cf. above, p. 91.

108. Agap. 10: "Whenever a sailor commits an error, he hurts but little those that sail with him. But if it is the pilot who goes off course, the whole ship goes to wrack."

109. Passages 8–13 in G. P. Fedotov, *Svjatoj Filipp*, pp. 142–144.

110. Agap. 15: . . . "for why, earthly riches and glory do soon vanish away, but the renown of godly life is immortal for all time to come."

111. Karamzin, *Istorija*, IX, n. 178; cf. G. P. Fedotov, *op. cit.*, p. 147.

112. Agap. 12: "Thou shalt withstand the enticing words of flatterers, as Thou wouldst eschew the ways of ravening crows. For crows peck out the corporal eyes. But flatterers blind the understanding of man's soul, since they will not suffer him to perceive the truth of things. For either they praise things that are worthy to be dispraised, or else dispraise things most worthy to be praised."

113. G. P. Fedotov, *Svjatoj Filipp*, p. 147.

114. G. P. Fedotov, *op. cit.*, p. 182; V. Leontovitsch, *Die Rechtsumwälzung unter Ivan dem Schrecklichen und die Ideologie der russischen Selbstherrschaft* (Stuttgart, 1947), p. 45.

115. Ed. G. Ewers and M. von Engelhardt, *Beiträge zur Kentniss Russlands und seiner Geschichte*, I [ = *Sammlung Russischer Geschichte*, X, 1] (Dorpat, 1816), 187–238.

116. Cf. Ewers and v. Engelhardt, *op. cit.*, p. 210: *Gedenck doch, ob Dich Gott in der Welt erhoehet, Du dennoch ein sterblicher Mensch bist.*

117. Emitted by A. Bellomo, *Agapeto diacono e la sua scheda regia* (Bari, 1906). (Cf. the destructive review by K. Prächter in *Byzantinische Zeitschrift*, XVII [1908], 152–164).

118. V. Leontovitsch, *Die Rechtsumwälzung*, pp. 44–51.

119. Passages 1–4 in *Akty . . . Zapadnoj Rossii*, IV (1851), 47 f. The petition contains one more familiar quotation, *car' ubo esi,iže věncem cělomudrija obložen i porfiroju pravdy oboločen* = Agap. ch. 18.

120. Unless one reads *Bogom naučen* for *blagonaučen*. Cf. *Bogom vrazumlevaem* in the fifteenth-century *Poxvala*, ed. A. Popov, *Istoriko-literaturnyj obzor*, p. 362.

121. *Ljubomudrejšago kyr Agapita diakona blažennejšemu i blagočestivejšemu carju Iustinianu, pače že vsěm pravedno xotjaščim nad stras'mi carstvovati,glavizny poučitel'ny.* Exact description of the print in F. Titov, "Materijaly dlja istoriji knyžnoji spravy na Vkrajini v XVI–XVIII vv.," *Ukr. Akad. Nauk, Zbirnyk ist.-fil. viddilu*, no. 17 (Kiev, 1924), p. 193 f. Cf. also, I. Karataev, *Xronologičeskaja rospis' slavjanskix knig napečatannyx kirillovskimi bukvami 1491–1730* (1861), p. 40. It should be noted that Pseudo-Basil's Chapters were also first printed in the Ukraine, namely in Ostroh, in 1607. The text, in Slavonic and in the vernacular, appeared as an appendix to two sermons of John Chrysostom. It bears the title: *Testament hreckaho cesarja Vasylija do syna svojeho L'va*. Cf. A. S. Arxangel'skij, *Obrazovanie i literatura v moskovskom gosudarstve konca XV–XVII vv.* (Kazan', 1901), p. 428.

122. S. Golubev, *Kievskij mitropolit Petr Mogila i ego spodvižniki* I (1883), p. 400.

123. English ed. of 1546; cf. above, note 29.

124. David Rivault, Sieur de Fleurance, *Remonstrances de Basile, Empereur des Romains, à Léon son cher fils* (2nd ed., Paris 1649). According to the title page, the translation was made *par l'exprés commandement du très-Auguste . . . Louis XIII.* The first edition appeared about 1613. The reëdition of 1649 was made in order to provide the young Louis XIV with a suitable textbook on government. Louis XIII's own translation of Agapetus appeared in Paris in 1612.

125. *Politique tirée des propres paroles de l'écriture sainte,* livre V, article IV, proposition I, *in fine.*

126. An investigation of seventeenth- and eighteenth-century Agapetian passages, although less important for the purposes of the present article, would be a worthwhile undertaking. With some authors, we could almost postulate the use of Agapetus. Ivan Timofeev, a staunch defender of absolute power, believed that no one but God could judge the Tsar's actions, and he made a clear distinction between a sovereign's person, capable of error, and the ever immaculate throne, "animate" and innocent of sin. ["Animate" (*oduševlen*) corresponds to ἔμψυχος of the Greek and hearkens back to related antique and Byzantine notions on the ruler as "Living Law."] It is not surprising, then, that in his *Vremennik*, written about 1617 and dealing with the Time of Troubles, Timofeev quoted a part of Agapetus, chapter 21: *ašče i čelovek car' be po estestvu, vlastiju dostoinstva privlečen est' Bogu, iže nado vsemi, ne imat' bo na zemli vysočajši sebe* [ = fol. 205$^v$ of the MS. cf. O. A. Deržavina, V. P. Adrianova-

Peretc, eds., *Vremennik Ivana Timofeeva* (Moscow-Leningrad, 1951), p. 107]. It is more unusual to find a cento from Agapetus in a work dedicated to Peter the Great. Its author is the Ukrainian "Cossack-Versifier" Semen Klymovs'kyj-Klymov, who submitted his poems "On the Impartial Administration of Justice by Those in Office" and "On Humility of the High" to Peter during the latter's sojourn in Khar'kov in 1724. The prose "Preface to the Pious Reader" contains Agapetus, chapters 2, 46, 51, 37, 1, 8, 21 in that order. Texts in V. I. Sreznevskij, *Klimovskij-Klimov, "Kazak-Stixotvorec," i dva ego sočinenija* (Khar'kov, 1905) [an offprint from *Sbornik Xar'kovskogo Ist.-Fil. Obščestva*, XVI]. Sreznevskij may go too far when he finds that Klymovs'kyj was "far from praising monarchs in general and the recipient of his poems in particular." Nevertheless, Klymovs'kyj, apparently wronged in the courts by a venal official of the Tsar, maintained a fairly independent attitude and arranged his Agapetian material (derived from the 1628 edition?) correspondingly. This is in line with the treatment of Agapetus by the Fraternity of L'viv. What is characteristic of the new situation is the fact that the first Tsar of Moscow to break with Byzantine traditions and to become Emperor of Russia, Western style, should be presented with sixth-century Byzantine arguments in the Ukraine from where the first strong wave of Western influences had reached Moscow less than a century earlier. I am indebted to Professor Čiževsky for drawing my attention to the texts of Timofeev and Klymovs'kyj.

[*Addendum*: I note with regret that V. Val'denberg's "Nastavlenie pisatelja VI v. Agapita v. russkoj pis'mennosti," *Vizantijskij Vremennik,* XXIV (1926), 27–34, has escaped my attention. At present I can only recommend that the reader consult Val'denberg's note].

# Moscow the Third Rome:
# Sources of the Doctrine

## DIMITRI STRÉMOOUKHOFF

Although the sixteenth-century Russian doctrine which proclaimed Moscow the "Third Rome" has become a subject of increasing interest to historians,[1] its origin and sources still remain—despite the meticulous research of M. D'jakonov, V. Malinin, and Mme H. Schaeder—to some extent obscure.[2] In the hope, therefore, that it may be of some use in elucidating a point of such importance to the grasp of both Muscovite ideology and Russian history, we have devoted this further study to the genesis of this doctrine.[3]

Before coming to the Muscovite conception, we should first make a rapid outline of the imperial doctrine which was adapted and transposed on the soil of Moscow. In searching for the idea of universal monarchy, probably of Iranian origin, we need go no further than the Hebrew prophets, in whose writings (particularly those of Daniel) it is expounded. Universal history up to the advent of the Messianic kingdom is shown by Daniel as a succession of four empires, represented either by the parts of the idol that appeared in Nebuchadnezzar's dream (Daniel, ii) or by the four animals (Daniel, vii), which tradition interprets as the Babylonian, Persian, Macedonian, and Roman empires. At times, this fourth empire of Daniel was regarded by the Christianity then developing within the boundaries of the Roman Empire as the kingdom of Antichrist (Apocalypse); at others, as the power by which the advent of Antichrist (II *Thessal.*, ii, 5) was being held back.[4] That the Roman empire should have been subject to interpretations so opposed as to its eschatological role, is an enduring and essential characteristic of the Christian apocalyptic.

After the union of Christianity and imperial Rome, consummated by Constantine the Great, the conception of a Roman-Christian empire is to stamp profoundly European history. In the West, the empire will be overthrown by the barbarians, and not restored until 800, when the coronation of Charlemagne will mark a deep rift in world-unity as it then existed. Embodied in this *renovatio imperii* will be found the idea of a *translatio potestatis imperii a Graecis in Germanos.*[5]

FROM Dimitri Strémooukhoff, "Moscow the Third Rome: Sources of the Doctrine," *Speculum* (January 1953), 84–101. Reprinted by permission of the Mediaeval Academy of America.

The Eastern Empire, which did not fall into barbarian hands, "continued to uphold, on the Bosphorus, the tradition of the Roman empire of which it rightly considered itself the legitimate successor."[6] These eastern possessors of the imperial power felt bound to confer upon their capital the eternal name of Rome. Professor F. Dölger has studied the subject of the "transfer" of the name Rome, to Constantinople, which, from the end of the fourth century, became the "New Rome."[7] The emperor became the *basileus* of the Romans and of all the Christians; Constantinople was to be considered as *urbs orbis* and *urbs aeterna*.

This Byzantine ideology, which, when assuming less markedly Roman forms, was stamped with a certain "messianism," seems to have blossomed out under the Macedonian dynasty, and at a moment coincident with the beginnings of a conversion to Christianity among the Slavs.[8] It is not surprising, therefore, that it should rapidly have penetrated the Slav world, more especially as the Byzantines must have looked on the doctrine as a particularly advantageous export.[9] It was spread either by the teaching and canonical acts of Greek ecclesiastics or by means of translations into Slav of Byzantine works (certain *novellae* of Justinian, St Andrew of Cesarea's commentaries on the Apocalypse, various imperial prophecies).[10]

If all this brought enormous prestige to the city which the Slavs called Tsar'grad, the universality of the Byzantine doctrine was not to be unresistingly adopted by a people eager for independence.

The opposition was particularly stubborn among the Balkan Slavs. Bulgaria and Serbia, in fact, endowed their sovereigns with the title of *tsar*, derived from Caesar and equivalent with *basileus*, set up their church as an independent patriarchy, and even dreamed of the conquest of Constantinople.[11] At Tirnovo in particular there flourished in the fourteenth century, during the reign of John-Alexander and under the patriarchy of Euthymius, a school of literature whose rhetoric abounds in pompous panegyrics.[12] To take an example which, for us, has a certain importance, the Bulgarian translator of the Chronicle of Manasses, in speaking of the fall of Rome in the fifth century, opposes this city not (as Manasses does) to Constantinople but to "our new Tsar'grad which grows, and strengthens herself"; the city he so designates would appear to be Tirnovo.[13]

The Russians became acquainted with the Byzantine doctrine both directly and through the agency of the Southern Slavs who adapted it to suit their own national aims. The Russian metropolitan was, in fact, attached to the patriarchy of Constantinople: with a few exceptions, the metropolitans were Greeks consecrated in the imperial city;[14] on the other hand, towards the end of the fourteenth century, and particularly in the fifteenth, the "second influence" of the Southern Slavs—having as its protagonists the Serbian and Bulgarian emigrants to Russia—may be seen to be taking shape.

In 1390 a Bulgarian called Cyprian succeeded in becoming the metropolitan of Moscow, where he introduced the literary style of Tirnovo.[15] It was at this moment, in 1393, that Anthony, the patriarch of Constantinople, addressed himself to the Grand Duke Vasili I. Disturbed by certain rumors, according to which the Grand Duke of Moscow had shown him a lack of respect, asserting even that "we have the Church, but we have not the Emperor," the patriarch stated the Byzantine conception of the part played by the emperor in the Christian world. He combatted the opinion of the Grand Duke, and gave as his own, "that it is impossible for Christians to have the Church without having the Emperor, because the Empire and the Church constitute one unity and one community." He then described the high position occupied by the Emperor in the Church, insisting upon the universality of the title, and the illegality of its being conferred upon the rulers of other nations.[16]

The question was, would Moscow remain faithful to the Byzantine teachings, or would she, urged by a desire for independence and the example of the Balkan Slavs, take this opportunity to build up the doctrine of a national state?[17] As we shall see, historical circumstances of an exceptional nature allow her to remain— in principle—faithful to the Byzantine doctrine of a unique empire, while at the same time putting it, as the Southern Slavs had tried to do, to her own uses.

In his letter the patriarch Anthony had made it clear that the esteem which the empire had enjoyed should not be weakened on account of the vicissitudes it had gone through, and that Christians should not turn away from any but a heretic mperor. These were the exact conclusions which the Muscovites, good pupils of the Greeks, were to draw from the events of the Council of Ferrara-Florence (1438–1439), where, in the hope of obtaining western aid against the Turks, the delegates of the Eastern Church had accepted the union with Rome. Moscow had been represented there by the Metropolitan Isidore, a Greek by origin and a conspicuous supporter of the union, also by Abraham, bishop of Suzdal', accompanied by several priests. When, on his return to Moscow, the Metro-politan Isidore proclaimed the union, he was dismissed from office by Vasili II, who remembered that the Greeks had always depicted the Latins as heretics.[18] Simon Suzdalec, one of the priests who had accompanied the bishop of Suzdal', has left a description of this Council which has been preserved in several versions. In these accounts it is asserted, firstly, that the Greeks, from motives of greed, had betrayed Orthodoxy, and, secondly, that, by dismissing the Metropolitan Isidore, the Grand Duke Vasili had become Orthodoxy's champion. This idea is set forth in the form of a panegyric, in which Vasili is put on the same level as Constantine the Great and Saint Vladimir: "Rejoice, pious Prince Vasili," cries the panegyrist, "supporter of the Orthodox faith and of all Russia, upholder of the Greek faith."[19] The "treason" of the Greeks provided reason enough for making the Russian church self-governing (autocephalous). Isidore once set aside, in 1441, the Russian bishops in 1448 elected, and enthroned as metro-politan a Russian, Jonas.[20] This decision was, in other ways, a fateful one, for, Jonas not being recognized at Kiev, the last weak bond uniting the Russian territories was loosened. Henceforward, there were to be two metropolitans, one at Kiev,[21] the other at Moscow, where the "Russian piety"[22] was set up against the rapidly waning prestige of the Greeks.

Before the relations between Moscow and Constantinople had had time to be defined,[23] the catastrophe of 1453 had put an end to the millenary empire. The fall of Byzantium plunged the whole world into a state of consternation. It was looked upon as a retribution. In the west, Pope Nicholas V saw in it a punishment for the rejection of the unity established at Florence; in Moscow, on the contrary, the Metropolitan Jonas in 1458 attributed it to this union: for as long as Constantinople had adhered to the true faith, she had resisted all invasions but, once having betrayed it and united herself with the Latins, she fell under the infidel's yoke.[24]

The fall of Constantinople, which had been thought of as the eternal city of Christianity, and the disappearance of the Empire, which was held to be the essential corollary of the Church, cast the souls and spirits of the eastern Christians into a profound despair. How could the Church continue to exist without the Empire? And what, now, would be Muscovy's place in history? These questions presented themselves at the moment when the grand duchy of Moscow gradually developed into a powerful state, became aware of itself as the last independent supporter of Orthodoxy.[25] Muscovite chronography, in the fifteenth century, abandoned its local character to become pan-Russian and developed the idea of Russian unity, tending thus to ascribe to Moscow a central place in history. In order to preserve the traditional structure of Christianity—which involved the Christian Empire—and to assign to Russia her place in history, three eventual solutions could be contemplated: to admit that the fall of Byzantium was not final, and that the imperial city would be freed by the Russians; to admit the supremacy of the Holy Roman Empire of the West; or, lastly, to set up Moscow herself as a definite empire, the successor to that of Byzantium.[26]

It was the first of these solutions which, safeguarding as it did the ancient conception of the world, appealed, on first thoughts, to the Muscovite spirit. We find it referred to in various versions of the Russian account of the taking of Constantinople by the Turks. The author, after having described the fall of the imperial city, adds: "If all the predictions of the time of Constantine the Great, such as were made by Methodius of Patara and Leo the Sage, if all the predictions concerning this great city have come to pass, then the ultimate prophecy will come to pass also, for it is said: 'the Russian tribes will battle against the Ishmaelites with the help of her erstwhile inhabitants, will conquer the city of the seven hills [Constantinople], and will reign there.'"[27] To understand this passage one must remember that in Byzantium, and especially in Russia, it was reckoned that the world would last seven thousand years.[28] The Byzantine calendar counted the years as from the creation of the world, and the year 7000 fell in 1492 of the Christian era; the end of the world was expected at that date. The Pseudo-Methodius planned his statement of history according to the millenaries; in the course of the seventh millenary the Ishmaelites were to take possession of the Greek Empire, but there would then arise an emperor who would liberate it, after which the Antichrist would appear, and the end of the world, which seems to have been coincident with the end of the seventh millenary, would take place.[29] Viewed in this light, the taking of Constantinople by the Turks would seem to have been as predicted, and nothing remained but to await the appearance of the liberating emperor, and, subsequently, in 1492, the end of the world.[30] Some ancient prophecies, attributed to Leo the Sage and to an inscription on Constantine's tomb, fit themselves easily into the prophetic scheme of the Pseudo-Methodius. These prophecies declare that Constantinople will be liberated by a ξανθὸν γένος and this fair-skinned tribe was often identified with the Russians.[31] The Muscovites, therefore, assigned to themselves the mission of liberating the imperial city. If its perennial character could thus be safeguarded, then the Muscovite scholars, under the influence of the Southern Slavs, could still confer upon their sovereign the title of tsar provided that he did not endow his empire with a definitely imperial status.[32] This conception could be further reinforced by the idea of the "Byzantine inheritance" consequent upon the marriage of Ivan III, in 1472, with the heiress of the Paleologues.[33]

Such building upon prophecies, however, seems to have corresponded very little with the practical aims of a Muscovite government preoccupied with the assembling of the Russian territories and the restoration of Saint Vladimir's heritage.[34] It was with reserve, therefore, that Moscow received the Western proposals that she should involve herself in the problems of the East.

At this moment, in Italy and in Germany, there were dreams of a new Crusade, in which it was hoped that Russia would take part. The diplomatic relations which linked Moscow with the West were not particularly easy ones. For the Western World, as the Soviet historian of diplomacy has noted, the only means of legitimizing the new state so as to introduce it into the European state system, was to confer a royal crown upon the sovereign of Moscow.[35] In 1489 the imperial envoy, Nicholas Poppel, offered to obtain the royal crown for Ivan III, but Ivan refused it, insisting that "he had never wanted to be made king by anyone, and that he did not wish it." In another reply to Emperor Frederick III he declared that his earliest ancestors had maintained friendly relations with those Roman emperors who had given Rome to the Pope, and had afterwards reigned at Byzantium.[36] Ivan III had already begun to call himself tsar, and Emperor Maximilian seems to recognize this title in the translated form of Kaiser.[37] Moscow, therefore, refused to accept the crown from the West, and, in that way, refused to recognize the Western Empire as the Christian Empire.[38] How far we are from the example of the Southern Slavs!

In the meantime the redoubtable year of 1492 arrives. The apocalyptic catastrophe does not take place. The Russians, therefore, are able to breathe more freely, even though the fear of the end of the world is not completely dispelled. They must continue to live, and in order to live like Christians it is necessary to establish a new paschal canon (the old one had ended in 1492) to disprove the claim, made by the Judaists, that the Christian prophecies had lied, and, finally, to elaborate a new historical doctrine about the Christian Empire.

It was now that they inclined towards the third of the possible solutions already mentioned: assigning to Moscow the role of the Christian Empire. We find the first outlines of this in a charter (1492) of Zosimius, metropolitan of Moscow. In this he gives the paschal canon for the beginning of the eighth millenary, which is then starting and in which he says: "we are awaiting the advent of the Lord, even although, according to the Holy Writ, the day and the hour of His coming cannot be established." He also gives here an abridged version of historical events: Constantine the Great founded the New Rome, Saint Vladimir baptized Russia, and now Ivan III is "the new Emperor Constantine of the new Constantinople-Moscow."[39] This, to our knowledge, is the first text in which Moscow is openly and officially proclaimed an imperial city. There remained only one more step to take: the "new Constantinople" had to become the "Third Rome."

Around the same date, a renewal of interest in theology was awakened in Novgorod, probably due to the appearance of the Judaist heresy.[40] The end of the world, in which the Christians had so firmly believed, not having occurred, the heretics adopted a new argument; the Christian prophecies, said the Judaists, had lied. The archbishop of Novgorod, Gennadius (Gonzov) headed the movement which opposed the heretics.[41] He decided to endow the Russian church with the complete Bible; certain books, missing in the Slav translation, were to be translated from the Vulgate. This was interpreted as a considerable victory for the Catholic influence.[42] Owing to this codification of the Bible, several new texts were put into circulation, and among them, the Apocalypse of Ezra, which, until then, had been practically unknown in Russia.[43] The fourth Ezra, translated from the Vulgate at a moment when apocalyptic problems were a matter of passionate concern, was certain to excite a strong interest. In one of his visions, Ezra had observed an eagle with twelve wings and three heads. These heads reign successively on earth. An angel explained to him that the eagle was the fourth animal of Daniel's visions (that is to say, the Roman empire), and that the heads symbolized three reigns (IV Ezra, xii, 23). What exegesis could be given to this passage? We know that it was translated from the Slav by Benjamin, a Dominican, assisted by Dimitri Malyj, who is sometimes identified with Dimitri Gerasimov. In the third head of the eagle of Ezra, Benjamin probably recognized the Holy Roman Empire of the German Nation.[44] But would this exegesis have been accepted by the Orthodox Dimitri Gerasimov? Would he not, rather, have thought of interpreting this head as Moscow, which, at this time, had adopted the two-headed eagle for her coat of arms? One has no means of confirming this; but would incline to suppose it, in view of the fact, that in the celebrated "Legend of the White Klobuk"—which is prefaced by a letter from Dimitri Gerasimov to Archbishop Gennadius—Russia is described as the "Third Rome."[45] In this letter, Dimitri Gerasimov tells of his discovery, in Rome, of the manuscript of this legend and sends its translation to the archbishop of Novgorod. It is not, however, generally accepted that Dimitri Gerasimov is the author of this legend, and even if we did accept this, there would be no way of confirming whether or not the legend had been interpolated at some later date.[46] Be this as it may, the fact that the form "Third Rome" occurs for the first time in a work which represents itself as being by one of the translators of Ezra should be born in mind.

The impetus given to theological thought by Archbishop Gennadius was to increase; Saint Joseph of Volokolamsk (Sanin) was to oppose the Judaistic heresy in his celebrated *Prosvetitel'* and, equally, to discard the basis on which the theocratic theory of the power of the Muscovite tsars had rested.[47] But it is a monk of Pskov who will assign to Moscow a role in universal history, and develop the formula "Moscow—New Constantinople," which we have already encountered in the preface to the paschal canon of the Metropolitan Zosima.

Philotheus, who was born early in the second half of the fifteenth century, and spent his whole life in the monastery of Eleazar at Pskov—of which, in the reign of Vasili III, he was probably the *hegumen*—is the author of several epistles setting forth both his views on the action of Providence in the lives of nations and of men.[48] Occasions for him to write were not lacking, for at this time the existence of his fellow citizens was much troubled. In 1510 Vasili III, having taken definite possession of the merchant city, abolished her ancient rights. One part of the population was transplanted to Moscow; the other remained at Pskov where they endured every kind of vexation from the first Muscovite governors. In the "Account of the Taking of Pskov," included in the first Chronicle of Pskov, the glorious city laments that a many-winged eagle, endowed with lion's claws has despoiled her of two Lebanon cedars.[49] A. N. Nasonov points out that this image derives from the prophet Ezekiel, who represented Nebuchadnezzar taking Jerusalem in the form of an eagle with big wings and many feathers (*Ezekiel*, xvii, 3).[50] The idea of applying the image to Moscow probably came the more readily on account of the two-headed eagle that had become the coat-of-arms of the Muscovite state.[51] It is possible that in the Chronicle Ezekiel's eagle was embellished with features borrowed from other prophetic visions; that of the fourth Ezra, who endowed his eagle with twelve wings, and of Daniel, who bestowed claws upon his animal (*Daniel*, vii, 19).

Another (and more anti-Muscovite) chronicle of Pskov goes so far as to see in Moscow the sixth king of the Apocalypse (*Apocalypse*, xvii, 10).[52] In interpreting this text, V. Malinin stresses—to our mind, very rightly—the fact that in 1510 the Pskovians, desolated by the fall of their city, were expecting the end of the world. This is confirmed by modern authorities on ancient Russian literature who also express the view that, owing to the sufferings of Pskov and Novgorod, an expectation of the end of the world had been renewed in these cities.[53] The academician Šaxmatov, on the contrary, reads into this passage no more than a parody of Philotheus.[54] His arguments, however, strike us as being weak, for it is difficult to see how an almost word-for-word quotation from the Apocalypse can contain the parody of a phrase of Philotheus. The conception of the Muscovite monarchy as one of the kingdoms preceding the advent of Antichrist[55] is, in itself, an idea which could easily have sprung up in the Pskov of 1510. The public misfortunes having quite naturally created an apocalyptic atmosphere, it was this atmosphere, probably, that confirmed Philotheus in his belief that the time was near.[56] One must not forget that in the Christian tradition the empire was regarded, sometimes as a bad, sometimes as a good thing. The Pskovians saw it as a misfortune; Philotheus will consider it as a benefit.

We have an epistle of Philotheus, dating precisely from this troubled period, in which he addresses his fellow citizens, consoling them in their distress and encouraging them to support their trials in a Christian spirit.[57] Certain passages

of this epistle lead us to suppose that they are directed at those who have mur-
mured against the sovereign; Philotheus maintains that thoughts, either of
ingratitude to God or antagonism to the tsar, are not permissible, for the heart
of the sovereign rests in the hands of God, of whom he is the servant.[58] In
another epistle, addressed to Vasili III in person, and dating, probably, from
about the same time or a little later, Philotheus writes in the hope of alleviating
the sufferings of his fellow-citizens,[59] and implores the tsar to remedy certain
ills common to all Russia. Here, also, he gives a preliminary outline of his
doctrine which, though it is scattered throughout the epistle, he finally sums up in
these words: "And if thou rulest thine empire rightly, thou wilt be the son of
light and a citizen of the heavenly Jerusalem, as I have written thee. And now, I
say unto thee: take care and take heed, pious tsar; all the empires of Christendom
are united (*snidošas*) in thine, for two Romes have fallen and the third exists
and there will not be a fourth; thy Christian empire, according to the great
theologian, will not pass to others, and, for the Church, the word of the blessed
David will be fulfilled: she is my place of eternal rest; I shall dwell there, for I
have desired it. And Saint Hyppolytus says: when we see Rome surrounded by
the Persian armies, and the Persians and the Scythians attack us, then we will
know, beyond all doubt, that this is the Antichrist."[60]

Before specifying Philotheus's sources, let us pause at another of his epistles,
written, probably, towards 1524.[61] He was then on corresponding terms with
Munexin, *d'jak* to the tsar at Pskov, a person of influence with whom Philotheus
had already interceded on behalf of the inhabitants of the city. Munexin, a man
of learning, had several correspondents, notably Dimitri Gerasimov, and a
certain Nicholas the Latin.[62] The latter is identified with Nicholas Bulow,
doctor to Vasili III. This "professor of medicine and astrology and of all
sciences" is a strange sixteenth-century Muscovite figure; a propagator of
Catholicism and of astrology, he was to be violently criticized by another
"humanist," the Greek Maxim. Nicholas had sent one of his writings to
Munexin, and this must have excited the interest of the learned *d'jak*, for he
communicated its contents to Philotheus. This action gave birth to the epistle
"Against the Astrologers and the Latins" with which Philotheus replied to
Munexin.[63] Judging from this refutation, Nicholas Bulow had supported two
theses; one was the astrological thesis, dear to the men of the Renaissance,
according to which the destinies of men and nations are ruled by the stars and
which led to the prediction of cosmic changes in 1524, being thus in conformance
with the astronomer Stoeffler, who had predicted a new deluge for this date.[64]
The second thesis, of minor importance in the writings of Nicholas, was favored
by Catholic polemicists who spread the following idea: if the Eastern Empire
fell, it was because it had divorced itself from the true faith; if that of the West
continued to exist, it was because it had remained faithful. Philotheus summarizes this thesis in the following manner: "The Latins say: our Roman Empire
remains indestructible; if we did not confess the true faith, the Lord would not
allow this."[65]

In the first part of his epistle, Philotheus develops an entire cosmology and refutes, with the aid of Holy Scripture, the astrological thesis. Then he proceeds to the second thesis. The Catholic argument that Rome remained free and independent was bound to make a profound impression upon the Russians, who held that Constantinople had fallen because it had betrayed the true faith in uniting with the Latins. Philotheus, therefore, found himself obliged to refute this argument, and his refutation, it must be admitted, is rather weak: doubtless, he says, the walls and columns of Rome are not in the power of the infidels, but the souls of the Latins have fallen into heresy, and, if Rome is immutable, it is because the Lord is "inscribed" in this empire.[66] Thus—and the explanation is hardly original[67]—the immutability of Rome is solely due to the fact that Christ was recorded in the census at Bethlehem. This explanation demands another, for, if it tells us why Rome has remained independent, it does not indicate where the true Christian Empire lies. Thus Philotheus in this epistle has to take up again his theory of Moscow the Third Rome, which he has already broached in his epistle to Vasili III. Although the epistle to Munexin must have been written nearly ten years, at least, after the formation of Philotheus' doctrine, his reaction against the Catholic point of view must have been earlier and may be considered —Novgorod and Pskov being rather open to Western influences—as one of the factors in the origin of his doctrine. Thus, this doctrine is elaborated, on the one hand, against the Pskovians, who saw in Moscow the kingdom of the Antichrist, and, on the other, against the Catholics, who believed the true Christian Empire to be conserved in the West.

Malinin, in emphasizing that the theory of Philotheus rests upon the prophecies of Daniel, adds: "It is difficult to say which are the commentaries known in Slavic translation that Philotheus used."[68] Nevertheless, he has made a considerable effort to clarify them; Mme Schaeder has followed up his research. We shall endeavor to throw some light on Philotheus' sources.

First of all, one can establish that Philotheus borrowed the formula of the unification of monarchies from the first Slav translation of the Pseudo-Methodius. In fact, in speaking of the unification of monarchies, which constitutes the thread of universal history, this translation uses the word *snidošesne* and this term we find again under the pen of Philotheus when he says that all the empires are reunited in that of Moscow.[69] But the Pseudo-Methodius in no way enables one to visualize an empire which will replace that of Byzantium, called, according to him, the last to the end of time. It is here that the creative work of Philotheus begins, unless the way was marked out for him by Dimitri Gerasimov.

It is generally admitted that it was under Bulgar influence, and especially that of the Bulgar translation of the chronicle of Manasses which calls Tirnovo "new Tsar'grad," that Philotheus named Moscow the Third Rome. P. Miljukov has formulated this hypothesis in the following way: in recognition of aid given the Southern Slavs by Moscow, the former bestowed upon it the title of "new Tsar'grad" and of "Third Rome"; thus the principal sources for the thought of Philotheus is to be found in the Bulgar translation of Manasses, which he would have used in writing the Russian Chronograph of 1512, a work of which he must have been the author.[70] We have admitted the influence of the Southern

Slavs upon the formation of the Muscovite ideology to have been considerable, but in that which concerns Philotheus, if we set aside the hypothesis of Šaxmatov on the Chronograph of 1512, this thesis seems to us erroneous for different reasons.[71] Philotheus had no need to be influenced by the Bulgar chronicle which names, not without ambiguity, Tirnovo "new Tsar'grad," since, as early as 1492, the Metropolitan Zosimius had officially awarded to Moscow the title "new Constantinople."[72] Also, Philotheus developed his theory, as he himself says, "according to the prophetic books."[73] The Bulgar chronicle could not be considered among these, and yet it is in them that one must search for the sources of Philotheus. It should be remembered here that the Apocalypse of Ezra is included in the Bible of Gennadius, translated by the work of the Dominican Benjamin, and of Dimitri Gerasimov, who was in communication by letter with Munexin. We have already suggested that this apocalyptic text had probably been commented on and may have influenced the "Account of the Taking of Pskov."[74] In any case, this text influenced Philotheus since he refers to it—on another occasion, it is true—in his epistle "On the Submission of Reason to Revelation."[75] From this, since the fourth beast of Daniel, the Roman Empire, is represented there as having three heads (considered as three more or less successive kingdoms), it is not difficult to interpret these three heads as Rome, Byzantium, and Russia, which thus becomes the Third Rome.[76]

The correctness of our interpretation would seem to be confirmed by a legend concerning the foundation of Moscow. This legend tells how, in 1206, the Grand Duke Daniel Ivanovič discovered in a swamp an enormous beast with three heads. A Greek sage explained to him that in this same place, a large city would be built, and it is there that Daniel Ivanovič laid the foundations of Moscow.[77] We are probably in the presence of a folklore interpretation of the vision of Ezra. Moreover, for J. Križanić, who was the first to study and combat the theory of the Third Rome in the seventeenth century, when it was still a living idea, the connection of this theory with the visions of Ezra seemed not at all doubtful. In fact, he writes: "I do not know what the patriarch Jeremiah was thinking of when he called Moscow the Third Rome. It would follow from that that the empire of Moscow is one of the three heads of the eagle (of Ezra), doomed to damnation and perdition." For him the three heads of the eagle of Ezra symbolize the Roman, Greek, and German empires, this last coming to an end with Charles V.[78]

To return to Philotheus. Why should he conceal his sources? His reasons are quite understandable: he could not, a pious monk and apologist for the Christian Empire, proclaim that Moscow is the third head of the fourth beast of Daniel. The theoreticians of the empire always based their work on the visions of Daniel, but they did not always acknowledge their sources or the identifications that they drew from them, because of the ambiguity of this notion of the last empire, which was sometimes considered as the Christian Empire and sometimes as that of the Antichrist. Philotheus, therefore, saw himself under the obligation of finding another apocalyptic image, one which would be less compromising, to justify his theory. Mme H. Schaeder has quite justly remarked that this image is his original work, of which we are able to follow the development.[79] In his epistle "Against the Astrologers and the Latins," Philotheus summarizes, rather awkwardly to be sure, the chapter (xii) of the Apocalypse about the woman dressed in the sun. The latter, according to the commentaries of Saint Andrew of Cesarea, which were very widespread in Russia, represents the Church.[80] In speaking of her flight into the desert, when she is pursued by the dragon which spits out water in order to submerge her (Apocalypse, xii, 15), Philotheus expresses himself thus: "the water signifies unbelief. You see, O chosen of God, that all the Christian empires are submerged by the infidels and the empire of our sovereign is the only one to exist by the grace of Christ."[81] It is probable that this text is an allegorical explanation of the flood which the Latin Nicholas foretold for 1524. This image is amplified, however, in his epistle to Ivan IV.[82] He here declares that the woman dressed in the sun—the Church—flees ancient Rome because the latter is fallen into heresy.[83] She also flees the new Rome—Constantinople—because at Florence the Greeks joined with the Latins."She flees into the third Rome which is the new great Russia, that is to say, the desert (*pustynja*), for it was empty (*pusta*) of the holy faith, the divine apostles not having preached there and it is only after all other countries that it has been enlightened by divine grace . . . , and now, alone, the Holy Catholic and Apostolic Church of the East shines more brightly than the sun in the universe, and only the great Orthodox Tsar of Russia, like Noah saved from the flood in the ark, directs the Church."[84] Such is the apocalyptic image which enables Philotheus to legitimize his conception of the removal of the Christian Empire to Moscow, and which justifies, in his eyes, the title which he gives to the tsar, that of "the only emperor (tsar) of the Christians in all the universe."[85]

V. Val'denberg emphasizes that Philotheus gives the name of the Third Rome not to Moscow but to all Russia.[86] Literally, he is not wrong, for it is the empire and not the city which, in Philotheus' eyes, merits this name. However, in his epistle to Munexin, he speaks of the church of the Assumption at Moscow, and in the epistle to Vasili III, of the church of the Assumption "of the Third Rome of your empire," which seems to imply an identification of Moscow with the Third Rome. The Byzantine and Roman empires were often designated by their capitals, (First Rome, Second Rome); it was natural to designate Russia by its capital and thus Moscow became the Third Rome.

Ivan III, as we have already seen, had begun officially to bear the title of tsar; in 1498 he had his grandson Dimitri crowned tsar, a ceremony to be revived with much greater pomp by Ivan IV in 1547. A little later, the Eastern Church recognized him as *basileus*.[87] The notion of empire thus became, as early as the end of the fifteenth century, one of the important factors in the history of the Grand Duchy of Moscow, which was becoming the great power of Eastern Europe.

The theory of the Third Rome, as Čajev has quite justly noted, in giving ideological form to, and justifying, the activity of the government, in view of the creation of a strong centralized state, was called upon to shape the Muscovite mind.[88] In the domain of internal politics, the centralization of power in the autocratic hands of the tsar influenced the whole social evolution of the Muscovite world. In the domain of external politics, the creation of the empire at Moscow led to the protection of Eastern Christians, to the colonization and Christianization of territories located to the East, and finally influenced Muscovite diplomats to an attitude marked by pride in their relations with the states of the West. The theocratic nature of the tsar's power enabled the sovereign to keep his hand upon ecclesiastical affairs. This did not prevent the Church from developing an apostolic tradition for itself, canonizing numerous saints; and at last, in 1589, its chief received the much-desired title of patriarch.[89] In architecture, literature, and even in the language the new political concepts were profoundly reflected.

Though it is not possible here to trace the development of the theory of the Third Rome, it should be added that, while in principle universalist, it exalted Russian piety and national sentiment, thus tending towards a national and religious particularism. This Muscovite particularism, foreign to Ukrainian Orthodox Christians and hostile to those of Greece,[90] no longer seemed to meet the exigencies of Russian politics in the second half of the seventeenth century.[91] For it was now a question of definitely winning over the Orthodox of Kiev (the old metropolitanate had entered into the obedience of Moscow in 1659); it was also a question of liberating the Christians of the East and this idea began to appear in the plans of the Muscovite government.[92]

The day that Patriarch Nikon (1605–1681) proclaimed himself Russian by birth but Greek by faith[93] the past of the Muscovite Church was condemned, and with it, Russian piety. The theory formulated by Philotheus seemed to lose its importance. Only the "Old Believers" remained faithful to it, and for them the Third Rome, like the two preceding, had fallen into heresy, this time the Nikonian heresy.[94] Nikon was for them the precursor of the Antichrist, whom they were to discover in Peter the Great. Thus, in the eyes of the "Old Believers" Moscow—the Third Rome—was transmuted from the Christian Empire into the Empire of Antichrist, and in this way they returned to the ideas of the Pskovians at the beginning of the sixteenth century, against which, as we have seen, Philotheus had reacted.

We shall briefly sketch here the place of the theory of Moscow the Third Rome in the ideology and national consciousness of the Muscovites in the sixteenth century. We possess several writings expressing this ideology. Some, different versions of the "Account of the Princes of Vladimir,"[95] develop the theme of empire in justifying its translation by genealogies and the transmission of certain relics; others insist on the purity of Russian orthodoxy, equally proved by the transmission of relics, such as the celebrated *white klobuk*. These accounts, these legends, have their importance in particular domains, but they do not succeed in connecting the idea of the empire with that of the purity of the faith, or in justifying the translation and restoration of the empire at Moscow by its attachment to the true faith. However, it is just this that seems to us most characteristic of the new Muscovite national consciousness. That is why we consider the theory definitively formulated by Philotheus to occupy a central place in Muscovite ideology: it forms the core of the opinions developed by the Muscovites about their fatherland and erects them into a doctrine. To justify in Russian eyes, by scriptural and historical arguments (or at least by arguments held to be scriptural and historical), the *translatio* of the empire to Moscow and its *renovatio*—such is the significance of the theory of Moscow the Third Rome.[96]

## NOTES

1. N. S. Čajev, "Moskva—tretij Rim v̇ političeskoj praktike moskovskogo pravitel'stva XVI-go veka," *Istoričeskie zapiski*, XVII (1945), 23; M. N. Tixomirov, *Istočnikovedenie istorii S.S.S.R.* (1940), I, 138.
M. Denissoff ("Aux origines de l'Eglise russe autocéphale," *Revue des Études Slaves,* Paris, 1947, fasc. 1–4) and I. U. Budovnic (*Russkaja Publicistika XVI-go v.,* 1947, pp. 100, 173, 289) also emphasize the importance of the doctrine of "Moscow—Third Rome." M. Budovnic is interested in it the more as he considers the Muscovite autocracy to be a "more progressive phenomenon" than the monarchy limited by feudal institutions. Cf. also J. Pirenne, *Les grands Courants de l'histoire* (Neuchâtel, 1944), II, 272.
2. D'jakonov, *Vlast' moskovskix gosudarej* (1889); V. Malinin, *Starec Eleazarova monastyrja Filofej i ego poslanija* (1901; with an edition of texts of Philotheus); H. Schaeder, *Moskau das dritte Rom* (Hamburg, 1929).
3. This question has interested me for a long time. I treated it in 1930 in a communication to the Société des Slavisants (cf. *Revue des Études Slaves,* x, 180). I wish to express here my cordial thanks to M. André Grabar, professor at the Collège de France, from whose friendly suggestions this study has greatly benefitted.
4. Bousset, *Der Antichrist* (Göttingen, 1895), pp. 77 ff.
5. F. Kampers, *Die deutsche Kaiseridee in Prophetie und Sage* (Munich, 1896); by the same author, *Vom Werdegange der abendländischen Kaisermystik* (Berlin, 1924); Hahn, *Das Kaisertum* (Leipzig, 1913); and J. Bryce, *The Holy Roman Empire* (London, 1913).
6. L. Bréhier, *Vie et Mort de Byzance* (Paris, 1947), p. 14; As to the pivotal Byzantine idea of "symphony" of Church and State as represented by the "diarchy" of the Patriarch and the Emperor see V. V. Sokol'skij, "O Xaraktere i značenii Epanogogi," *Vizantijskij vremennik,* I (1894), and G. Vernadskij, "Vizantijskie učenija o vlasti carja i patriarxa," *Recueil Kondakov* (1926).
7. F. Dölger, "Rom in der Gedankenwelt der Byzantiner," *Zeitschrift für Kirchengeschichte,* LVI (1937); cf. also H. Schaeder, *op. cit.,* pp. 9 ff., and O. Treitinger, *Die oströmische Kaiser- und Reichsidee* (Jena, 1938).
8. Byzantine "messianism" recognized, beside its "Roman" form, a "Hierosolymitan" form. Byzantines in fact called Constantinople "New Jerusalem" or "Second Jerusalem," Cf. A. Grabar, "L'art religieux et l'empire byzantin à l'époque des Macédoniens," in the *Annuaire de l'École Pratique des Hautes Études,* 1939–1940, p. 35, and the epistle of the patriarch Photius in *Pravoslavnyj palestinskij sbornik,* XXXI (1892), 231–235. The Russians knew this terminology and applied it also to their capital. The late Michel Gorlin held that "the theory of the third Rome was going to bind Moscow to Byzantium and Jerusalem would find itself set aside" (*Revue des Études Slaves,* XVIII, p. 62); but it does not seem that the name "third Rome" had definitively replaced that of "new Jerusalem," for we find the latter in the collection of verse of Alexandre Mezenec (Stremouxov) and in certain chronicles (Bezsonov, *Kaliki perexožie,* fasc. 6, p. IX, and I. Zabelin, *Istorija Goroda Moskvy,* 1905, p. 36).
It is probable, as R. Stupperich has pointed out ("Kiev, das zweite Jerusalem," *Zeitschrift für slavische Philologie,* XII, p. 352), that the name of Rome implied a political role and that of Jerusalem a more ecclesiastical role.
9. F. Dvornik, *Les Légendes de Constantin et de Méthode vues de Byzance* (Prague, 1933), p. 365. Cf. A Grabar, *art. cit.,* p. 24. It is true that the apostle of the Slavs named the Byzantine empire not the "Roman Empire" but the "Empire of Christ."
10. Migne, *P.G.,* CVI, col. 376, 381; *Velikie Minei četii,* 1883, 25–30 Sept., col. 1766–67; Istrin, *Otkrovenie Mefodija Patarskogo,* in *Čtenija,* 1897, II–IV; 1898, I.

11. K. Jireček, Dějiny národa bulharského (Praha, 1876), pp. 187 ff.; same author, *La Civilisation serbe au moyen âge* (1920), pp. 6 ff.; Émile Haumant, *La Formation de la Yougoslavie* (1930), pp. 52 ff.; and H. Schaeder, *op. cit.*, pp. 4 ff.

12. K. Radčenko, *Religioznoe i literaturnoe dviženie v. Bolgarii v epoxu pered tureckim zavoevaniem* (1898), pp. 21 f.; K. Jireček, *op. cit.*, pp. 270 ff.

13. *Kronike lui Constantin Manasses* (ed. Ivan Bogdan, Bucarest, 1922), p. 99. Cf. Jireček, *op. cit.*, p. 215, and Schaeder, *op. cit.*, pp. 14 and 51. Nearly the same phrase is to be found in the Russian Chronograph of 1512 (*P.S.R.L.*, XXII, 1, p. 258). However, the author of the Chronograph, by all the evidence, sets in opposition to Rome not Tirnovo or Moscow but rather Constantinople, as does the Greek Manasses. This is why he says not "our new Tsar'grad" but "our new Rome—Tsar'grad."

14. E. Golubinskij, *Istorija russkoj cerkvi* (1901), I, 1, pp. 289 ff. Cf. also D'jakonov, *op. cit.*, pp. 1 ff.

15. H. Schaeder, *op. cit.*, p. 3. Cf. Golubinskij, *op. cit.*, II, 1, pp. 297 ff., and A. S. Orlov, *Drevnjaja russkaja literatura XI–XVI v.* (1937), pp. 234 ff.

16. *Pamjatniki drevne-russkogo kanoničeskogo prava* (R.I.B., VI), t. 1², priloženie, pp. 269–271.

17. D. S. Lixačev finds the first criticism of the Byzantine concept in Russia in the writings of the Metropolitan Hilarion (*Nacional'noe samosoznanie v drevnej Rusi* (1945), pp. 24–25).

18. Cf. A. Pavlov, *Kritičeskie opyty po Istorii drevnejšej greko-russkoj polemiki protiv latinjan* (1878).

19. Malinin, *op. cit.* (texts), pp. 99–100; cf. pp. 76–128.

20. Golubinskij, *op. cit.*, II, 1, pp. 470 ff. Cf. Denissoff, *art. cit.*, p. 77 ff.

21. *Ibid.*, II, 3, p. 507. Cf. H. Schaeder, *op. cit.*, p. 28.

22. *Pamjatniki drevne-russkogo kan. prava*, p. 653. Cf. D'jakonov, *op. cit.*, p. 57, and Malinin, *op. cit.*, pp. 480 ff.

23. Vasili II and the Metropolitan Jonas explain the necessity of electing the metropolitan at Moscow and not at Constantinople by the dissension which divided the imperial city when there was no longer a patriarch of the ancient piety. (*Pamjatniki drevne-russkogo kan. prava*, pp. 557–558, 584–585).

24. *Ibid.*, p. 623, and Karamzin, *Istorija gosudarstva Rossijskogo* (1842), V, 212.

25. It cannot be denied that the principality of Tver, rival of Moscow, also played a role in the elaboration of the idea of unity and of the imperial idea. In the fourteenth century the monk Akindin had already written to Prince Michael of Tver, "you are tsar in your country" and in the fifteenth century another monk, Thomas, bestowed upon Prince Boris the title of tsar and compared him with Constantine. Cf. Val'denberg, *Drevne-russkie učenija o predelax carskoj vlasti* (1916), p. 140 ff. and Lixačev, *op. cit.*, pp. 92 and f. The formula of Akindin corresponds to the definition of French legists: "the king is *imperator in suo regno.*"

26. We had come to conclusions which, in broad outline, coincide with those of M. Denissoff (*art. cit.*, p. 76) before seeing his article.

27. I. Sreznevskij, *Povest' o Car'grade* (1855), and Jakovlev, *Skazanija o Car'grade* (1868), p. 114. In the lamentations on the taking of Constantinople, inserted at the end of the Chronograph of 1512, the author also expresses the hope that the infidels will be driven out and the Christian kingdoms re-established. He ends his lamentations with a paraphrase of Manasses (see above, n. 13), which paraphrase he applies to Russia, but taking care not to call it "new Tsar'grad."

28. The belief that the world would last six (or seven) thousand years is very ancient. The apocryphal epistle of Barnabus teaches that, just as the world has been created in six days, it would last six millenniums, a day being interpreted, according to Psalms, LXXXIX, 4–5, as a millennium. The Talmudists, certain heretics and certain Church Fathers shared this belief. If one includes *the millennium* (corresponding to the seventh day) in history, the end of the world might be foretold for the year seven thousand after creation. This is exactly what happened in Russia. Cf. P. Voltz, *Die Eschatologie der jüdischen Gemeinde im neuen testamentlichen Zeitalter* (Tübingen, 1934), pp. 135 ff., and Saxarov, *Esxatologičeskie sočinenija i skazanija v drevne-russkoj pis'mennosti*, 1879.

29. Istrin, *op. cit.* (study), pp. 20–21.

30. A complete prophetic chronology of apocalyptic occurrences is to be found in the paschal canons of 1460 to 1492.

31. Concerning these prophecies, see Sreznevskij, *op. cit.*; Istrin, *op. cit.* (study), pp. 273 ff.; Malinin, *op. cit.* (study), pp. 471–472; D'jakonov, *op. cit.*, pp. 62 ff. According to Mme

Schaeder (*op. cit.*, pp. 28 ff.) this prophecy is based upon Ezekiel, xxxviii, 2, after the *Septuagint*: υἱὲ ἀνθρώπου, στήρισον τὸ πρόσωπόν σου ἐπὶ Γὼγ καὶ τὴν γῆν τοῦ Μαγὼγ, ἄρχοντα Ῥώς, Μεσὸχ καὶ Θοβὲλ.

32. In a later report of the Council of Florence, written in 1461, to glorify Russia's autocephaly and attributed to Pacomus the Serbian (A. Pavlov, *op. cit.*, pp. 99, 101, 106; cf. H. Schaeder, *op. cit.*, p. 26); the emperor declares to the Pope that it is only due to his modesty and piety that Vasili II does not make use of the title of *tsar* (Malinin, *op. cit.*, texts, p. 117). It seems thus that the author tries to legitimize this title by the authority of a Byzantine emperor. So Pacomus the Serbian seems to be one of the first to call Vasili II *tsar*. (Cf. Pavlov, *op. cit.*, pp. 100–101 and Ždanov, *Russkij bylevoj Epos*, 1895, pp. 107 and ff.

33. Thus, for example, the Venetian Seigniory wrote that the Eastern Empire "wanting a male heir, returns to the duke of Moscow, in consequence of his illustrious marriage." (Pierling, *La Russie et l'Occident*, Paris, 1891.)

34. Lixačev, *op. cit.*, pp. 96 ff.

35. *Histoire de la diplomatie* published under the direction of V. Potemkin (Paris, I), p. 187. N. S. Čajev holds that diplomatic relations with the West exercised a certain influence on the formation of the theory of the Third Rome (*art. cit.*, p. 10).

36. *Pamjatniki diplomatičeskix snošenij* (1851) I, 11–12, 17.

37. *Pamjatniki diplomatičeskix snošenij*, I, 1502. Peter the Great used this text, the authenticity of which has, moreover, been called into doubt, to justify the title of emperor with which he replaced that of tsar. D. S. Lixačev (*op. cit.*, p. 102) points out that Ivan III begins to use the title of tsar in his diplomatic relations after definitively freeing himself from the yoke of the Tartars (1480) and not after his marriage with Sophie Paléologue. It is, nevertheless, true that he had already used it in 1473, that is, immediately after his marriage, in a treaty with the city of Pskov. (Solov'ev, *Istorija Rossii*, ed. Obšč. Pol'za, I, 1483.) Cf. Schaeder, *op. cit.*, p. 39, and Malinin, *op. cit.* (study), pp. 553 ff.

38. According to N. S. Čajev (*art. cit.*, p. 15) Muscovite diplomats fought to establish the equality of the tsar with the emperor of the Holy Roman Empire, whom they considered of greater rank than the kings. It is, however, evident that the Holy Roman Empire, not being Orthodox, could not in their eyes be the true Christian Empire.

39. *Pamjatniki drevne-russkogo kan. prava*, pp. 795–802. Cf. D'jakonov, *op. cit.*, p. 66.

40. For the heresy of the judaisers see the exposition by G. Vernadsky, "The Heresy of the Judaisers and Ivan III," SPECULUM, VIII, 4 (October, 1933), 436–454.

41. For Archbishop Gennadij see *Russkij biografičeskij slovar'*.

42. I. E. Evseev, "Gennadievskaja Biblija 1499g." *Trudy 15-go arxeologičeskogo s'ezda* (1916), II, 15–16.

43. Gorskij i Nevostruev, *Opisanie slavjanskix rukopisej Moskovskoj sinodal'noj biblioteki*, I, 43 ff., and Golubinskij, *op. cit.*, II, 2, p. 263. Cf. also A. I. Sobolevskij, *Perevodnaja literatura moskovskoj Rusi*, p. 254 (in Sbornik O. R. Iaz. i Sl., LXXIV, I), and Beneševič, "Iz istorii perevodnoj literatury v Novgorode v konce XV-go v." *ibid.*, CI, 3, p. 378.

44. A. Sedel'nikov ("K izučeniji slova kratka i dejatel'nosti dominikanca Venjamina," in *Izvestija* O. R. Iaz, i Sl., XXX, 205 ff.) has given definitive proofs in favor of the attribution to Benjamin of *Slovo kratko* (this text appeared in the *Čtenija* of Moscow, 1902, 2). In this treatise the author ascribes characteristics to the Roman Empire which makes it possible to establish that for him it represents the fourth beast in the visions of Daniel (cf. *Slovo kratko*, p. 58, and Daniel, vii, 19) and, in consequence, the eagle of Ezra. He further says that this empire already has partially disappeared and will finally disappear entirely, which is probably an exegesis of the reigns of the three heads of the eagle of Ezra. Under these conditions the third head would quite naturally be identified with the Holy Roman Empire of the German Nation. It should be noted, moreover, that at this time numerous prophecies concerning Emperor Frederick III existed (Kampers, *Die Kaiseridee*, pp. 139 ff.), which the Dominican Benjamin, who had perhaps come to Novgorod in the suite of the ambassador of Frederick III (Jevsejev, *art. cit.*, p. 15), must have been aware of.

45. *Pamjatniki starinnoj russkoj literatury*, I, 296 ff., and D. I. Kožaničkov, *Povest' o novgorodskom klobuke* (1861), p. 38.

46. The legend of the white *klobuk*, symbol of the purity of the faith, is set forth as the translation of a manuscript, given by a Roman librarian to Dimitri who, in 1492, communicated it to Archbishop Gennadij. Historians of Russian literature are considerably divided on the subject of the attribution of this legend to Dimitri (see the discussion of this question in Malinin, *op. cit.*, notes 1881 and 1889). Malinin admits that Dimitri Gerasimov is the author

of this legend and holds that he is the first to call Russia the Third Rome. (*Ibid.*, Study, p. 525.) Mme H. Schaeder, on the other hand, dates this legend of the end of the sixteenth century (*op. cit.*, pp. 81–82). A. Sedel'nikov ("Vasilij Kalika, Histoire et Légende," *Revue des Études Slaves*, VII, p. 234) chiefly studies the early history of this legend at Novgorod. The question would merit the trouble of being reviewed. It is therefore impossible to state, as M. Denissoff does, that the doctrine of the Third Rome was born before the sixteenth century (*art. cit.*, p. 86).

47. D'jakonov, *op. cit.*, pp. 91 ff.

48. Malinin, *op. cit.* (study), Chap. I.

49. *P.S.R.L.*, IV, V, p. 287, and A. Nasonov, *Pskovskie Letopisi*, 1941, I, p. 95. The text is in the *Svod* of 1547 which, according to A. N. Nasonov, must have been composed in the monastery of Philotheus. ("Iz istorii pskovskogo letopisanija," *Istoričeskie Zapiski*, XVIII (1946), 270.

50. A. N. Nasonov, *art. cit.*, p. 266.

51. A. Solov'ev, "Les emblêmes héraldiques de Byzance et des Slaves," *Seminarium Kondakovianum*, VII (1935).

52. *P.S.R.L.*, IV, V, p. 282. According to Nasonov (*art. cit.*, p. 267) this text was an extremely anti-Muscovite part of the *Svod* of 1567.

53. Malinin, *op. cit.* (study), p. 169, and *Istorija russkoj literatury* (ed. Akademii Nauk, 1945), II, 398 and 405.

54. Šaxmatov, "K voprosu o proisxoždenii xronografa," *Sbornik O. R. Iaz. i Sl.*, LXVI, 9, p. 112. Cf. Nasonov, *art cit.*, p. 267. Mme Schaeder considers it a "spätere verderbte Variazion der Lehre des Philotheus," *op. cit.*, p. 56.

55. It should be mentioned that the chronicler of Pskov refers to Moscow as the "Scythian island." The word "island" seems unexplainable; the adjective *Scythian*, on the other hand, can only be explained in the following manner: where the Pskovian *Svod* of 1547 sees Moscow under the features of the eagle of Ezekiel, that of 1567 seeks the apocalyptic etymology of the word Moscow with the help of Ezekiel, xxxviii, 2. (Cf. above, n. 31.) Polish scholars in the sixteenth century thought the Muscovites descendants of Mosoch and considered them Scythians. (Cf. J. Križanič, *Tolkovanie istoričeskix proročestv*, pp. 16 ff. in *Čtenija* of Moscow, 1891, 2). Under these circumstances, it is understandable that Philotheus should refer to a text of Saint Hippolytus where the Scythians are mentioned. (Cf. n. 60.) This quotation seeks perhaps to prove that the Muscovites are not the apocalyptic Scythians.

56. Malinin, *op. cit.* (study), pp. 441–442.

57. *Ibid*, pp. 166–170.

58. *Ibid.*, (texts), p. 16.

59. *Ibid.* (study), pp. 371–373.

60. *Ibid.* (texts), pp. 54–55. As Malinin has shown (*op. cit.* (study), pp. 434–435) the words attributed to the great theologian seem to be a reference to Daniel, ii, 44, and those attributed to David, to Psalms, cxxxii, 14. Malinin adds that the reference to Saint Hippolytus is hardly clear. (Cf. above n. 55.)

61. Malinin, *op. cit.* (study), pp. 266–269.

62. *Ibid.*, pp. 159, 268 ff. For Nicholas the Latin, who is quite identifiable with Nicholas Bulow, see *Russkij biografičeskij slovar'*, and Malinin, *op. cit.* (study), pp. 256 ff.

63. *Ibid.* (texts), p. 48, and (study), pp. 270 ff.

64. *Ibid.* (texts), p. 48; (study), p. 268; Golubinskij, *op. cit.*, II, 1, p. 690.

65. Malinin, *op. cit.*, p. 42. One can judge the weight of this argument by the following detail: In the sixteenth century the Catholics esteemed that God had delivered the Greeks to the Turks, relates Ivan Peresvetov. To this the Greeks answered: "We have an empire and a free emperor," making an allusion thus to Moscow (V. F. Ržiga, *I. S. Peresvetov*, p. 77 in *Čtenija* of Moscow, 1908, 1).

66. Malinin, *op. cit.* (texts), p. 43.

67. *Ibid.* (study), p. 352.

68. *Ibid.*, p. 525.

69. Cf. Istrin. *op. cit.* (texts), p. 89 cf. p. 17 and (study), p. 139; Malinin, *op. cit.* (texts), p. 45 cf. pp. 50–51, 54, 56.

70. P. Miljukov, *Očerki po Istorii russkoj kul'tury* (1930), III, pp. 52–55 cf. also Tixomirov, *op. cit.*, p. 139. This thesis, rests among others on the hypothesis of Šaxmatov, according to which Philotheus was the redactor of the Chronograph of 1512 which modifies that of 1442, attributed to the Serbian Pacomus. This Chronograph, as we already know, had been subject

to the influence of the Bulgarian translation of the Manasses. Philotheus, according to Šaxmatov, is supposed to have added the lamentations on the fall of Constantinople. Cf. Šaxmatov, *art cit.*, pp. 80 and 109; and Šaxmatov, "Putešestvie M. G. Munexina" in *Izvestija O. R. Iaz. i S.*, IV, I, p. 214. H. Schaeder, although rejecting this hypothesis of Šaxmatov, admits the influence upon Philotheus of Manasses. (*Op. cit.*, pp. 49–59.)

71. See notes 70 and 72.

72. The academician Šaxmatov, in attributing to Philotheus the Chronograph of 1512, based his conclusions primarily on the presence in this work of ideas common to both Philotheus and the Chronograph. To our mind, however, this community of ideas is very relative. The author of the Lamentations, which are inserted at the end of the Chronograph both looks forward to the liberation of the Balkan countries, and hopes for the reestablishment of the Christian Empire; Philotheus on the other hand, takes the view that the Christian Empire is already established at Moscow, and even goes so far as to say that Constantinople will not be restored. Furthermore the Chronograph speaks of St. Andrew the Apostle's journey to Kiev, an event in the validity of which Philotheus did not believe. These arguments against the hypothesis of Šaxmatov are favorable to those of H. Schaeder.

73. Malinin, *op. cit.* (text), p. 45.

74. See above.

75. Malinin (*op. cit.* [text], p. 34, and [study], pp. 244–245) writes the "third" Ezra, but the quotation used is from the fourth Ezra, iv, 5 and ff. This text, being followed by a reference to Mark, xiii, 32, it is probable that Philotheus quoted it in relation to eschatological questions.

76. H. Schaeder writes only: "dass ein viertes Rom nicht sein werde, mag durch die Dreizahl an sich gegeben sein, ist ausserdem durch Daniel VII, 8 und 24 und viertes Ezdra, XII, 22 präformiert." (*Op. cit.*, p. 56.)

77. Zabelin, *op. cit.*, pp. 28 ff. and S. Šambinago, "Povest" a načale Moskvy' in *Trudy otdela drevnerusskoj literatury*, III, 92, ff.

78. Križanič, *op. cit.*, p. 11, and by the same author *Russkoe gosudarstvo v polovine XVII-go v.* (1858), I, 354–356. Cf. Schaeder, *op. cit.*, p. 118. See n. 89.

79. H. Schaeder, *op. cit.*, p. 55.

80. *Velikie minei četii*, 25–30 Sept., col. 1743.

81. Malinin, *op. cit.* (text), p. 46.

82. We admit, though not without hesitation, that the fragment called "Epistle of Philotheus to the tsar Ivan Vasilevič" does, in fact, contain a passage capable of justifying its claim to this title and is addressed to Ivan IV. On the other hand, we are very skeptical about the whole writing, which Malinin considers as the integral text of this epistle (Malinin, *op. cit.*, (study), pp. 75 ff. and text pp. 57–66) for it is really an assemblage of quotations most of them identifiable (II Tim. iii, 1–3; the canons of a Concilium and of the Metropolitan Cyril II of Russia; *Jud.*, i, 5–7, II Peter, iii, 3–18) and which would be hard to imagine as an epistle to the sovereign.

83. Philotheus, according to an ancient tradition of the Orthodox polemists, accuses the Catholics, especially on account of the use of unleavened bread, of following the heresy of Apollinaris.

84. Malinin, *op. cit.* (text), p. 63. Malinin in accordance with certain manuscripts, reestablished the lesson "not having preached there."

85. *Ibid.*, p. 45, cf. p. 50. M. V. Šaxmatov, examining the doctrine of the crowning of the Moscow tsars, distinguishes in their power, that of the Russian and that of the Orthodox sovereign. Only the Orthodox power was entitled to claim universality (*Zapiski russkogo naučnogo Instituta v Belgrade*, 1, 257 and 264).

86. V. Val'denberg, *op. cit.*, pp. 267–268.

87. Kn. M. A. Obolenskij, *Sobornaja gramota duxovenstva pravoslavnoj vostočnoj cervki utverždajuščaja san carja* (1850).

88. N. S. Čajev, *art. cit.*, p. 23.

89. P. Miljukov, *op. cit.*, II, I, pp. 31 ff. D'jakonov, *op. cit.*, p. 91. The formula of the Philotheus "Russia–Third Rome," has found its place in the Statute of the Patriarchate of Moscow, signed by the Patriarch Jeremy II of Constantinople (*Sobranie gosudarstvennyx gramot i dogovorov*, II, 97).

90. For the discussions with the Greeks on the subject of Muscovite customs, see *Sočinenija Arsenija Suxanova* in *Čtenija* of Moscow, 1894; on the occasionally antimuscovite attitude of the upper clergy of Kiev, who wished to maintain their obedience to Constantinople, see V. Ejgorn, *O Snošenijax malorossijskogo duxovenstva s moskovskim pravitel'stvom*, pp. 35, 62, 78 in *Čtenija* of Moscow, 1893, II.

91. N. S. Čajev (*art. cit.*, p. 3) notes that the ecclesiastical reform of the seventeenth century was in accordance with Moscow's foreign policy.

92. *Putešestvie Antioxijskogo patriarxa Makarija*, p. 171 in the *Čtenija* of Moscow, 1898, IV. A little later, in 1686, Moscow for the first time joined a European coalition against the Turks. Cf. also Dr. Mošin, "Treći Rim i južni Slovene" in the *Rusko-jugoslavenski Almanah* (Belgrade, 1934), p. 59.

93. N. Kapterev, *Patriarx Nixon i car' Alexej Mixailovič*, I, 161.

94. Malinin (*op. cit.*), study, pp. 767–768, has reassembled some of the writings of the old-believers which are concerned with Moscow—the Third Rome.

95. About these legends see the already mentioned work of Ždanov.

96. N. S. Čajev also regards the theory of the Third Rome as being the foundation of Muscovite ideology. Cf. D'jakonov, *op. cit.*, pp. 67 ff., and *Istorija russkoj literatury*, izd. Akademii Nauk S.S.S.R., II, 1, p. 304.

This article was ready for publication in 1947; since then two articles discussing the importance of the doctrine of Philotheus have appeared. O. Ogloblin (*Moskovs'ka Teorija III Rimu*, Munich, 1951) states, from the Ukrainian point of view, that Philotheus' theory has become the official doctrine of Moscow. On the other hand, Maslennikov ("Ideologičeskaja Bor'ba v Pskovskoj Literature v period obrazovanija russkogo centralizovannogo gosudarstva" in *Trudy otdela drevne-russkoj literatury*, VIII), following Lixačev (*op. cit.*, pp. 100–104), denies it. We esteem also that it is exaggerated to qualify it "official." Its importance is more ideological than political; messianic and imperial, it is not really imperialistic. This theory includes renunciation of Constantinople—Maslennikov (*art. cit.*, p. 201) brings the same argumentation as mine in note 72; cf. also Kizevetter, "Rossija i Južnoe Slavjanstvo v XIV–XVII vv" in *Proslava na Osvoboditelnata Voina, 1877–78 g.* (Sofia, 1927)—and becomes even embarrassing in the seventeenth century, on account of its too outspoken particularism. On Byzantine influence in Russia see D. Obolenskij, "Russia's Byzantine Heritage" in *Oxford Slavonic Papers* (1950), I. On relations between church and state see W. K. Medlin, *Moscow and East Rome* (Geneva, 1952).

# The Problem of Old Russian Culture

## GEORGES FLOROVSKY

*Die wahre Kritik liegt im Verständnis.*
BACHOFEN, *Antiquarische Briefe*

### I. The Pattern of Interpretation

There was, in Russian historiography of the last century, an established pattern of interpretation, and, to some extent, it is still commonly used. It was traditional to divide the history of Russia into two parts, and to divide it sharply and rigidly: the Old and the New, Ancient and Modern. The time of Peter the Great was regarded as the Great Divide, as the decisive turning point in the total process. Of course, it was much more than a chronological demarcation. Passionate value judgments were implied therein. Kliuchevsky has rightly stated: "The whole philosophy of our history was often reduced to the appraisal of Peter's reform; by a certain scholarly foreshortening, the whole problem of the meaning of Russian history was condensed into one single question—about the deed of Peter and the relation of his new reformed Russia to the old."[1] The Old Russia was regarded and evaluated in the perspective of the New, in the light of "the Reform." In fact, this approach was itself an integral part of the Reform, and its most ponderous legacy. This pattern of interpretation was first invented by the pioneers of the Reform in order to justify the break, which was intended to be radical and definitive, and then it was maintained in its defense. The story of Old Russia had to be presented in such a way as to show that the Reform was inevitable, necessary, and just. "The Old" meant in this connection the obsolete, sterile and stagnant, primitive and backward. And "the New" was depicted, by contrast, in the brightest colors as a great achievement and a glorious promise. The whole history of Old Russia, before Peter, was usually treated as a kind of prehistory—a dark background against which the whole splendor of the new cultural awakening could be spectacularly presented; or as a protracted period of infancy and immaturity, in which the normal growth of the nation

FROM Georges Florovsky, "The Problem of Old Russian Culture," *Slavic Review*, XXI, No. 1 (March 1962), 1–15. Reprinted by permission of the American Association for the Advancement of Slavic Studies.

was inhibited and arrested; or else as a lengthy preparation for that messianic age which had finally descended upon Russia, under Peter and by his sovereign will, from abroad if not from above. "History," in the proper sense of the word, was supposed to have begun in Russia only with Peter. It was assumed that only at his time did Russia enter the stage of history and civilization—indeed as a belated newcomer, sorely delayed in development, and thereby destined to tarry for a long time in the humble position of a learner, in the commonwealth of cultured nations.

There were manifold variations on this basic theme in Russian historiography. For our immediate purpose it would suffice to quote but one of them. Sergius M. Soloviëv had the reputation of a sober historian, and he well deserved the praise. His monumental *History of Russia from the Oldest Times* is still the most reliable survey of the subject, well documented and skillfully arranged. It is highly significant that Soloviëv simply loses his temper when he comes to the times of Peter, to the Reform. About Peter he writes in a very special style, passionate, nervous, and pathetic, at once elevated, ornate, and excited. It is the style of heroic legend. Indeed, for Soloviëv, Peter was *the* hero of Russian history, probably the only hero, and the last one. "Only Christian faith and the nearness in time saves us—and still incompletely—from the cult of this demigod and from the mythical conceptions about the exploits of this Hercules." Peter was almost a supernatural being. "The period of heroes comes to its end with the coming of civilization."[2] Peter concludes the epic period of Russian history and opens the era of civilization for Russia. It means that for Soloviëv there was no civilization in Russia before Peter, even if there was an enormous dynamic potential —in the state of chaotic fermentation. The change under Peter was most radical: from epic to history—from prehistory to history proper. Only since Peter has Russia become an "historic" nation.

There is in this interpretation a striking discrepancy between the political and the cultural course of the process. The political history of Russia was continuous from the very beginning, through the Reform—in spite of its cataclysmic character—up to the present. Old Russia was just a stage in the formation of the definitive Russian Empire. The unity of Russian history is seen precisely in the history of the Russian state. On the other hand, there is a radical discontinuity in the history of Russian culture. The culture of Old Russia has been simply dismissed, and it is assumed that it had to be dismissed and discarded, and replaced by another. It was not a link in the continuous chain. There was rather no such continuous chain at all. The true Russian culture had to be created afresh; actually, it had to be imported. As Soloviëv phrased it himself, "It was the turn of the Russian people to serve a foreign principle."[3] The true history of Russian culture is, from this point of view, the history of Western culture in Russia. Old Russia was contrasted with the New as a "primitive society" with the "civilized." Many Russian historians of the last century were using these and similar phrases. Theodore I. Buslaev, one of the great founders of Russian historical philology, could not find in Old Russia any trace of genuine culture: no intellectual curiosity, no aesthetic vision, no literary skill. There was no dynamism, no advance whatever. In the same vein, A. N. Pypin would contend that actually there was almost no "chronology" in the history of Old Russian literature. For Buslaev the whole period of Russian history up to Peter could be characterized by two words: "primitivism" (*pervobytnost'*) and "stagnation" (*velikoe kosnenie russkago naroda*).[4] From this point of view, Old Russian culture was to be studied by archaeologists, not by historians. Indeed, it was under the guise of "Russian antiquities" that the history of Old Russian culture was studied in the last century. The term "culture" is often used in a wider sense to include "primitive cultures." In that sense one could also speak of Old Russian culture, but only in that sense. It was a field for antiquaries, not for historians.

The line of Russian cultural development was not merely bent but really broken. The old order had passed away. Old Russia was a dead world. It had to be admitted, however, that the Reform, as radically as it had been conceived from the beginning, was not accomplished at once. The old world was terribly shaken, but it did not disappear. Much of the old order survived, but only beneath the level of "civilization" in those strata of the nation which resisted the Reform and attempted an escape. But these strata were, in a sense, outside history, and it had to be hoped that finally, with the spread of "enlightenment," they would also be dragged in. What remained from the old order was no more than "survivals." As Pypin said, "The life of the small civilized class was surrounded by the element of old custom." All survivals were actually in the realm of customs and routine, in that realm which is denoted by the untranslatable Russian word, *byt*.[5] But *byt*, at its best, is no more than a dead mask of culture. The Reform had split the nation into two parts: the civilized elite and the masses. It was in the masses that relics of Old Russia had been preserved. It was assumed that in good time they would be completely discarded.

It has been commonly assumed that culture had to be autonomous, that is, secular. The whole history of European civilization was usually presented in this way—as a story of progressive emancipation of culture from the stiffening control of the established religion, or of the Church. This scheme of interpretation was derived partly from the philosophy of the Enlightenment, partly from Positivism. It has been faithfully applied to Russian history also. By this criterion the whole history of Old Russia was summarily discredited in advance. Indeed, the major charge that has been raised against Old Russia is that its life was dominated by religion, enslaved in the dogmatic and ritual forms. There was little room in this old structure for criticism and free search. Very often "culture" was simply identified with "criticism." There was little understanding of its organic aspect. Only critical trends, within the established structure, could have had, from this point of view, any cultural significance. Accordingly, it was among the dissenters or non-conformists of various types that signs or tokens of potential cultural awakening were looked for, just as it was the fashion at one time to discover forerunners of modern times in the heretical and rebellious groups in the Middle Ages. Peter's Reform itself was warmly appraised as a deed of liberation from the control of religion. The concept of a "religious culture" was for the historians of the last century at least a paradox, and for most an obsolete dream and an ominous threat.

The vision of the contemporary historian has been drastically enlarged in recent decades. The fiction of "unchanging Russia," ever the same for several centuries, in which many historians of older generations were still able to believe, has crumbled. One is bound to distinguish ages and stages. "Old Russia" appears to be an artificial and unhistorical concept. One must speak rather of various local cultures—of Ancient Kiev, of Novgorod, Tver, Moscow, and the like, and of Western Russia. These local cultures were, of course, interrelated and ultimately integrated into one great national culture. But first of all they must be understood in their distinctive characters. Some regional studies in the field of Old Russian culture were initiated already in the last century, and a number of provocative observations were accumulated. But much has been left undone. On the other hand, there was in these regional studies a tendency to overstress local distinctions. In any case, it is still too early to attempt a synthetic description of Old Russia as a whole. Obviously, there were deep internal tensions within the realm of Old Russian culture. The cultures of all societies are more or less stratified: there are always different levels, and high culture is always kept and promoted by a minority, the leading and creative elite. The problem is much more intricate and complex than was admitted by the historians of earlier generations.

The time has come when the story of Old Russia must be carefully revised and probably rewritten. This time it must be written as a history in its own right, and not just as a preamble to the history of New Russia. Of course, historical interpretation is inevitably retrospective—that is the very heart of the historical method. It was inevitable to look back at Old Russia. What was wrong in the traditional pattern was not the retrospection itself but the unfortunate selection of the observation point—and also the lack of congeniality with the subject of study.

The term "culture" is ambiguous; it is currently used in more than one sense. On the one hand, "culture" is a descriptive term. It denotes the structure of a particular society or of a particular group. Culture in this sense includes at once a certain set of aims and concerns and a complex of established habits. There is always an element of normative routine in any given culture, but culture is maintained only by exercise, by an active pursuit of certain goals. On the other hand, culture is a system of values. Of course, these values are produced and accumulated in the creative process of history in a particular environment and setting, and in this respect they are inevitably situation-conditioned. And yet they always tend to obtain a quasi-independent existence, that is, they become independent of that original historical context in which they came into being. Cultural values always claim universal recognition. Though they are rooted in their native soil, cultural values can be transplanted. This transfer of cultural systems is one of the major events of history. Cultures and societies are not identical. Societies may collapse and even disappear completely, but their cultures do not always perish with them. The most conspicuous example is ancient Greece. One can speak of its permanence in the life of other societies. Great creations of thought, charity, art, and letters may retain their intrinsic validity, even if there is nobody to appreciate them or if they are vigorously disavowed and repudiated in a particular group and at a particular time. There is always some prospect of recovery and revival. True values are perennial.

There are two different tasks for the historian of culture, although it is difficult to separate them in practice. On the one hand, there is a descriptive task. One has to establish an accurate inventory of those cultural values which are accepted and circulated in a given society at particular stages of its historical life. One must also find out in what particular manner they functioned in this society, and whether they were really living values and not just an external garb or a conventional decorative frame. It may happen that some of the accepted values are discredited in a particular society at a given date and cease to function. It may also happen that society itself degenerates and loses its cultural vitality. It may prosper; it may decay. And the historian must accurately record all the stages of the process. On the other hand, there is the task of interpretation. The complex of values can be studied as such. Thus we speak, for instance, of classical civilization. The fall of the classical world did not discredit classical civilization. One may speak at the same time of the corruption of imperial Rome and of the immortal glory of Roman law.

Let us return now to the problem of Old Russian culture. It may be true that Old Russia was not successful in her cultural endeavor, that her cultural effort resulted ultimately in a deadlock. Indeed, historians are never permitted to idealize the subject of their studies. Yet the historic collapse of Old Russia, accelerated by the intervention of new forces, does not by itself prove the inconsistency of that culture to which Russia was pledged and addicted. This culture must be examined in its inner structure, apart from its historic fate. These two different lines of research, in which different methods must be used, were unfortunately often confused by the historians.

## II. The Ways of Old Russia

Old Russia stood in a very definite cultural succession. She was in no sense isolated in the cultural world. She entered the commonwealth of civilized nations when she was christened by the Byzantine. She received then, together with the Christian faith, an impressive cultural dowry—a complex of cultural values, habits, and concerns. The Byzantine inheritance of ancient Kiev was conspicuous. The city itself was an important cultural center, a rival of Constantinople, an adornment of the empire. It was not the only center: Novgorod in any case must be mentioned. The literary production of the Kievan period was intense and diverse. Russian art was also taking shape. Behind the documents of the time we cannot fail to discern cultural activity, cultural forces. We discern groups and individuals eagerly committed to various cultural tasks. The movement of ideas has already begun.

The Kievan achievement must be regarded in a wider perspective. It was an integral part of the incipient Slavic culture. V. Jagić once suggested that in the tenth century there was a chance that Slavic civilization might have developed as a third cultural power, competing with the Latin and the Greek. The Bulgarian literature of the Simeonic age was already so rich and comprehensive as to stand comparison with the Byzantine.[6] Indeed, it was the same Byzantine literature, but already indigenized. This cultural promise was curtailed and frustrated. The great cultural impetus was checked. Yet the promise was real, and the actual achievement was by no means negligible. Of course, this incipient Slavic civilization was deeply rooted in the Byzantine tradition, just as Western culture was rooted in the traditions of the classical world. But it was more than a repetition or an imitation. It was an indigenous response to the cultural challenge. And it was mainly from Bulgaria that a rich supply of literary monuments was transferred to Kiev and other centers. Cultural taste and skill were formed. Cultural interests were aroused. Kievan Russia was not isolated from the rest of the Slavic world, as it was not separated from Byzantium and the West, or from the East. Kievan Russia was able to respond conscientiously to the cultural challenge. The ground was already prepared.

At this point certain doubts may be reasonably raised. First of all, the promise was actually frustrated, even if the measure of this frustration and lack of success should not be exaggerated. Was this due only to adverse conditions— the Germano-Latin pressure on the Western Slavs, the defeat of Bulgaria by the Greeks, the Mongolian conquest of Russia? Or was there an inherent weakness, a constitutional disease, that arrested the development both in Old Russia and in the Balkans? The adversity of external conditions was bound to have at least a psychological impact on the whole cultural situation, but further questions may be asked, and indeed have been asked, by modern scholars. Was the Byzantine inheritance a healthy one? Was the task undertaken by the Slavs sound and reasonable? Was their attempt to create a new national culture a sound enterprise? Or was it doomed to failure by its inner inconsistency? The questions were sharply put, and answers were often negative.

It was inevitable that in the beginning the cultural elite should have been small, and the outreach of its activity rather limited. It was development at a normal pace. But was the Byzantine civilization really "received" in Old Russia? Golubinsky, for one, bluntly denied the fact. St. Vladimir wanted to transplant culture to his land, but his effort failed completely. Culture was brought in and offered but not taken, and, as Golubinsky added, "almost immediately after its introduction it disappeared without leaving any trace." Until Peter's time there was no civilization in Russia. There was no more than plain literacy, that is, the skill to read and to copy texts. Literacy, not literature, was the upper limit of Old Russia, according to Golubinsky. "Literacy, not culture—in these words is summarized all our history for the vast period from Vladimir to Peter the Great." Before Peter, Russians were, on the whole, quite indifferent to culture and enlightenment—*prosveshchenie* was Golubinsky's own term. Those few contradictory instances which he had to acknowledge, Golubinsky would hastily dismiss as incomprehensible riddles.[7] No contemporary historian would dare to endorse these sweeping generalizations of Golubinsky. But under some other guise they are still repeated. It must be noted that Golubinsky in no sense held the Greeks responsible for the Slavic failure. He never contested the value of Byzantine civilization. He only felt that probably the Byzantine offered too much at once, and also expected too much from the newly baptized nations. The fault was with the Russians themselves. Some others, however, would shift the blame to Byzantium. According to Jagić, the greatest misfortune of the Slavs was that they had to be reared in the school of senility: a young and vigorous nation was to be brought up on the decrepit culture of a moribund world that had already lost its vitality and creative power. Jagić was quite enthusiastic about the work of the Slavic Apostles. He had only praise for their endeavor to stimulate indigenous culture among the Slavs. But he had no appreciation for Byzantine civilization. This attitude was typical of his generation, and also of the next. The failure was then inevitable: one cannot build on a rotten foundation. There was no genuine vitality in the Old Slavic civilization, because there no longer was living water in the Byzantine springs. Seemingly there was a promise, but actually there was no hope.

The charge has been repeated recently in a new form. Quite recently the late Professor George Fedotov suggested that the cause of Old Russian backwardness, and indeed the tragedy of Russian culture at large, was precisely the attempt at indigenization. He had serious doubts about the benefits of the use of the Slavic vernacular. Having received the Bible and a vast amount of various religious writings in their own language, the Slavs had no incentive to learn Greek, for translations once made were sufficient for immediate practical needs. They were enclosed, therefore, within the narrow limits of an exclusively religious literature. They were never initiated into the great classical tradition of Hellenic antiquity. If only our ancestors had learned Greek, speculated Professor Fedotov, they could have read Homer, could have philosophized with Plato, could have reached finally the very springs of Greek inspiration. They would have possessed a golden key to classical treasures. But this never happened. Instead they received but *one* Book. While in Paris, a poor and dirty city as it was in the twelfth century, the Schoolmen were already discussing high matters, in the golden and beautiful Kiev there were but monks engaged in writing chronicles and lives of saints.[8] In other words, the weakness and backwardness of Old Russia depended upon that narrow foundation, exclusively religious, on which its culture had been built. The charge is by no means new. The lack of classical tradition was often emphasized as one of the peculiar and distinctive features of Old Russian culture. Fedotov's imaginary picture is pathetic, but is his argument fair and sound? The West seems to have had the golden key of Latin. How many in the West, however, were using that key for the purpose of which Fedotov speaks? And was the Latin known at that time sufficient for the task? Classical values were transmitted rather indirectly through Christian literature. Platonism was accessible through Augustine, Pseudo-Dionysius, Origen, and Gregory of Nyssa. It could be no less readily discovered in Byzantine ecclesiastical sources. The Christian Hellenism of Byzantium neither impresses nor attracts Fedotov. He has a twisted picture of Byzantium: Byzantine Christianity appears to him to be a "religion of fear," of *phobos*; human values were suppressed in it.[9] Anyhow, Fedotov contended that Kievan Russia never accepted this grim version of Christianity and developed its own conception: humanitarian and kenotic. And, in fact, that picture of Kievan Russia which Professor Fedotov himself has given us in his impressive book, *The Russian Religious Mind*, is bright and moving. Kievan Christianity, in his appraisal, has perennial value: "that of a standard, a golden measure, a royal way," in his own phrase. Indeed, we are given to understand that its attainments were so high because the Russians did not follow either the Byzantines or the Bulgarians, because they created their own Christian vision and way. In any case, it appears that Kievan Russia was vigorous and creative—at least in one field. What is more significant, basic human values were firmly established, high ethical standards acknowledged, and personal initiative disclosed and encouraged. There was strong human impetus in the Kievan culture. One has to assume, as was indeed Fedotov's own contention, that cultural growth and advance were impeded at a later stage. The absence of the classical tradition probably was not so tragic and fatal.

There is an increasing tendency in modern historiography to idealize the Russian beginnings. The Kievan period is depicted as a kind of golden age, a golden legend of Russia. Dark times came later—after the Mongolian conquest. There was a visible decline in literary production, and there were no outstanding personalities in this field. A closer scrutiny of extant sources, however, corrects this first impression. Writers of that time, from the twelfth century to the fifteenth, are aware of problems with which they are wrestling—the problems of the artistic craft: problems of style and representation, problems of psychological analysis. There were in Russia at that time not only scribes and *nachetchiks*, but true writers. There were not only skillful craftsmen but real masters in art. The recent studies of D. S. Likhachev are very suggestive, especially his analysis of the problem of man in the literature and art of Old Russia.[10] Behind the stylistic devices used by the artists one can detect their spiritual vision, and this vision was the fruit of reasoning and contemplation. The new wave of the "South Slavic" impact did not mean just a transfer of new literary documents, mainly translations, of spiritual and hagiographical content. It was a wave of inspiration, a deep spiritual movement, stemming from the great Hesychast tradition, revived at that time both in Byzantium and in the restored Bulgarian kingdom. Both writers, chroniclers and hagiographers, and painters, including the iconographers, were fully aware of the problem that they had to wrestle with—the presentation of human personality. It may be true that their concept of personality and character was different from the modern view, and probably at this point their insight was deeper. They did not depict fixed characters; they saw men in process obsessed and confronted with problems, in the state of decision and indecision. One may speak almost of their "existentialist" approach to the problem of man. One may contend that psychology based on the concept of temptation, inner struggle with the passions, conversion and decision, was a deeper psychology than that which would deal with the fixed character. In any case, it is more dynamic and less in danger of falling into schematism of characteristic types. In the great Russian art of the fourteenth and fifteenth centuries one discovers not only a high level of artistic mastery but also deep insights into the mystery of man. And this art was not only produced at that time but appreciated. Obviously, there was both a demand for this high art and an understanding of it, in circles which could not have been very narrow. It would not be an exaggeration to assume that the aesthetic culture of that time was refined and profound. It was still a religious culture, but artistic methods were adequate to the problem of revealing and interpreting the ultimate mysteries of human existence in all its unruly and flexible complexity. The challenge probably came from outside—from Byzantium once more—but the response was spontaneous and creative. There was more than dependence or imitation. There was real response.[11]

One may be tempted to regard precisely this "dark" period, the period of intensive political and internecine strife, as the climax of Old Russian culture. Indeed, Russian art definitely declined in the fifteenth and especially in the sixteenth century and lost its originality and daring. The literary culture, however, was preserved on a high level till the Time of Troubles, and even later. The ideological content of literature became more comprehensive in the sixteenth century. There was an enormous synthetic effort in various fields of culture at that time. Strangely enough, it seems that precisely that synthetic effort, powerful and dynamic as it was, was the most conspicuous sign and symptom of decline, or at least of an internal crisis. The cultural inheritance of Moscow was rich and comprehensive enough to suggest the idea of systematization. The great national state, aware and conscious of its vocation or destiny, needed a culture of great style. But this culture had to be built up as a system. It was an ambitious and attractive task. The plan "to gather together all books available in Russia," which was undertaken under Metropolitan Macary in the middle of the sixteenth century, was probably a naïve and simplistic expression of a deeper conception. The plan itself was deeply rooted in the awakened consciousness of national greatness. But the vision was intrinsically static, and there was in it more than just a reflection of political ambition. There was a deeper urge for "establishment." The overarching idea was that of order. The danger to culture implied therein was probably felt in certain quarters. It has been usual to emphasize the importance of the conflict between the "possessors" and "nonpossessors" in the late decades of the fifteenth and the early decades of the sixteenth century. At one time the sympathy of the historian was rather on the side of St. Nilus of Sora and the Trans-Volga Elders. It seems that now the sympathy has been shifted to the other side. In any case, St. Joseph has won. And the idea of an established order was his greatest commitment. Indeed, he himself never speculated on the themes of culture. Nor, probably, did St. Nilus. But there is undoubtedly deep truth in the suggestion that it was in the tradition of St. Nilus that the only promise of cultural advance was available. Cultures are never built as systems, by orders or on purpose. They are born out of the spirit of creative initiative, out of intimate vision, out of spiritual commitment, and are only maintained in freedom. It may be contended that Moscow missed its opportunity for cultural progress when it yielded to the temptation of building its culture on the social order of the day—*po sotsial'nomu zakazu*, as it were. The cultural capital of Moscow was not so meager and limited as has been often assumed. Even its technical equipment should not be minimized. The root of the cultural trouble and failure was in the pattern. One may use the word "utopia" in this connection. And one may specify this utopia as theocratic. But actually it was a kind of politico-cultural utopia, not in full conformity with the higher aspirations of the Christian man. Of course, the Christian conception is intrinsically bifocal: The community—the Church—is the form of Christian existence, but human personality is a supreme value. Man is a political being; but culture is built by creative individuals, and there is always the danger when it is oversystematized that it may degenerate into a routine. The weakness of the Moscow culture was not so much in the poverty of the content as in the failure of spirit.

The most disquieting question in the history of Old Russian culture is this: What was the reason for what can be described as its intellectual silence? There was a great art, and there was also an intensive creative activity in the political and social field, including ideological speculation. But surely nothing original and outstanding had been produced in the realm of ideas, theological or secular. It was easier to answer this question when it was assumed that Old Russia was simply primitive, slumbering and stagnant. But now we know that in many other respects Old Russia was able to attain a high level. Still one may be tempted by easy answers. It may be suggested, and actually has been suggested more than once, that the "Russian soul" was, by its inner constitution, rather speculative or intuitive than inquisitive, and that therefore the language of art was the only congenial idiom of self-expression. It may be suggested, on the other hand, that the "Russian soul" approached the mystery of Christian faith by way of charity and compassion and was therefore indifferent to the subtleties of theological speculation. It does not help very much if we try to collect scattered data indicating that a certain amount of philosophical information was available to people of Old Russia. A solid amount of patristic writings was indeed in circulation, but there is no proof that theological interest had been awakened. All easy formulas are but evasions. And the riddle remains. Moreover, all speculations that operate with the precarious concept of the "Russian soul" are utterly unsafe. Even if "national souls" do exist, they are made, shaped, and formed in history. For that reason they cannot serve as a principle of interpretation. Again, the character of the "Russian soul" has been so diversely described and defined as to require a thorough re-examination. It has been usual to emphasize the irrational aspect of Russian mentality and its constant lack of form. There is enough evidence to the contrary. With adequate reason it has been contended that the "Russian soul" had always a strong feeling and understanding for order and form, and this specific insight was the root of its great aesthetic achievements.[12] In its extreme expression it led to ritualism, to the worship of external forms.

Kliuchevsky had much to say about the thrill of rite and habit when he attempted to explain the genesis of the great Russian *raskol*.[13] And the same striving after orderliness has created in Russia what we call *byt*. Of course, it may be claimed that underneath the *byt* there was always chaos. Finally, we are left with an antinomy, with an unresolved paradox.

In the total perspective of Russian historical development the paradox is even more spectacular. In the later period, after the Reform, Russians have appeared to be probably one of the most intellectual nations in Europe, inwardly troubled by all "damned problems" of religion and metaphysics. Exercise in philosophy, of various shapes and shades, and commitment to theory and speculation were the distinctive mark of the Russian mind in the last two centuries. This striking phenomenon was usually explained by Western influence, direct and indirect. It was suggested that dormant curiosity had been awakened by the challenge of Western thought. One should ask at this point why this intellectual curiosity was not awakened by the challenge of Byzantine civilization, which was renowned and notorious for its unquenchable commitment to speculation, in a measure offensive for the sober taste and mind of the West. Byzantium was not only dogmatic, but ever searching and rather unquiet in its heart. Indeed, Byzantium knew the mystery of harmony and cosmic order. But it also knew the thrill of search and the "clouds of unknowing." But Byzantine challenge did not awaken the alleged Russian soul.

The tragedy of Old Russia, which led to its inner split and impasse, was not a tragedy of primitivism or ignorance, as has been contended more than once. It was a tragedy of cultural aberration. The charge of Golubinsky and of Fedotov is valid to some extent, but they were unable to phrase it properly. One may suggest that Byzantium had offered too much at once—an enormous richness of cultural material, which simply could not be absorbed at once. The charm of perfection was tempting: should not the whole harmony be transplanted? The heritage was too heavy, and too perfect, and it was thrilling in its harmony, in its accomplishment. Art also requires training, but in this case training is probably more formal—the acquisition of technical skill. In the realm of the mind, training is indissolubly bound with the essence of the task. In this realm questions are no less important than answers, and unresolved problems, the "perennial questions," are the real stimulus and token of mental advance. Old Russia seems to have been charmed by the perfection, completeness, and harmony of Byzantine civilization, and paralyzed by this charm. Once more it must be stressed that Russian Byzantium was not just a servile repetition but a new and peculiar version of Byzantine culture, in which one can discern a true creative power. Some years ago I inscribed the chapter of my book, *The Ways of Russian Theology*, dealing with Old Russia: "The Crisis of Russian Byzantinism," and have re-phrased it in the text: "The crisis of Byzantine culture in the Russian spirit."[14] The phrase was misunderstood by the critics and reviewers, or rather was not understood at all. I am willing to assume full responsibility for the vagueness: I should have explained my thought in a more explicit way. What I wanted to say then I am bound to repeat now. The crisis consisted in that the Byzantine achievement had been accepted, but Byzantine inquisitiveness had not. For that reason the achievement itself could not be kept alive.

The crisis became conspicuous in Moscow in the seventeenth century, in that great age of changes, shifts, and troubles in the Russian state and society. It was an age of great cultural confusion. Certain elements of Byzantine achievement were strongly challenged, including the traditional "symphony" of state and church. Moscow was moving hesitantly toward an increasing secularization of its political order. The impact of Western mentality was growing, first in the form of the new Kievan learning, which itself was an unfortunate hybrid of Polish and quasi-Byzantine factors. The spread of this pseudomorphic culture was felt at Moscow more as a shock or offense than as a challenge, and provoked only resistance along with blind imitation. There was a search, but it was a search for ready solutions. Probably it was a blind alley. And then came the Reform.

The ultimate tragedy was that the Reform itself was promoted in the same old manner. There was again the thrill of accomplishment or achievement. The spirit of the Reform was intrinsically utilitarian. There was again a charm—a charm of Western achievement, of Western habits and forms. Curiosity was aroused, but was it a sound and sober intellectual curiosity? The new civilization was accepted in its ready form, into which the life of the nation could not be fitted. There was an effect of astonishment, but no real awakening. The new culture was much less organic than the old one, and therefore even less spontaneous and creative. It is instructive that it was possible to present the whole history of Russian literature, including its ideological content, as a story of Western influence, as a story of consecutive waves of imported ideas and forms. Was the cultural initiative really awakened? One may have very grave doubts. It is not surprising that a paradoxical resistance to culture as such has been one of the vigorous trends in the new culture; though it was to some extent provoked also by the thought of a Westerner, Rousseau, it was deeply rooted in the psychology of "reformed" Russians. Was not the way of simplicity higher than the way of culture? Technical culture has indeed been transplanted. But did Reform promote any disinterested concern for higher culture? Was it a real advance in comparison with the culture of Old Russia? During the whole modern period complaints were loudly voiced on this theme: there was no genuine *will for culture*, although admiration and even respect for culture were rather widespread. The root of the trouble was still the same: Culture was still regarded as an order, as an achievement, as a system. For that reason one could propagate the acceptance of foreign forms; they were finished and ready to hand. Indeed, there was sometimes much vigor and also much obstinacy in this endeavor of adaptation, and it could instill vitality into the products. The thrill of the modern Russian culture is in its scattered explosions—the deeds of individuals. But there was no general culture. Moreover, the larger part of the nation was not yet involved in the process, and was much more outside the culture, and thus outside history, than it had been in the days of Old Russia. This was the sharpest objection against the new order in comparison with the old, as Kliuchevsky has so eloquently phrased it.

So much can be said about the old "society." Did this "unsuccess," to use the term of Wladimir Weidlé,[15] discredit that system of cultural values to which Old Russia was pledged and committed? Did this system crumble also? It is not for the historian to answer this question. It is a question for the philosopher. But the historian must insist that there are perennial achievements in the inventory of Old Russian culture. The greatness of the Old Russian religious art is in our day widely acknowledged, with understanding or simply by fashion. The vigor and freshness and the profundity of the Russian religious quest, although it seems to be often disguised by ritual formalism, is also increasingly recognized. There were profound human values in this old culture, as detached, as archaic, as exotic as it may appear to those trained in the Western ways. And it becomes more and more evident that Old Russian culture did, from its very inception, belong to the wider circle—to the circle of that civilization which had been built, on the composite basis of ancient classical culture, under the creative impact, and often under direct guidance and deep inspiration, of Christian faith and mission.

Old Russia, indeed, left a precious legacy, at least in the realm of art. At this point its "culture" survived its "paternal society," and must be studied as a perennial treasure in its own right.

## NOTES

1. V. O. Kliuchevsky, *Kurs russkoi istorii*, Part IV, lecture 68, in Sochineniia, IV (Moscow, 1958), 201.

2. S. M. Soloviev, *Istoriia Rossii s drevneishikh vremen*, XIV, chap. ii (St. Petersburg, n.d.: "Obshchestvennaia Pol'za"), Book III, cols. 1057–58: "Obshchestvo iunoe, kipiashchee neustroennymi silami, proizvelo ispolina, kak iunaia zemlia v dopotopnoe vremia proizvodila gromadnyia sushchestva, skelety kotorykh privodiat v izumlenie nash melkii rod. . . . Devstvennaia strana predstavliala takoe obshirnoe poprishche dlia bogatyrei vsiakago roda"; cf. XXII, chap. v, Book V, col. 542: "Kto-to sil'nyi, neobyknovennyi iavilsia, proshel, ostavil neizgladimye sledy, porazil voobrazhenie, ovladel pamiat'iu naroda. Vsiudu dlia liudei chutkikh, ispolnennykh sily, slyshalis' slova: 'Idi za mnoi, vremia nastupilo'!" It must be noted, however, that in his *Public Lectures on Peter the Great* (1872) Soloviëv seems to be more cautious and reserved on this point. "Great men" should not be isolated from their environment, from the nation, and should not be regarded as miraculous or supernatural beings: they are children of their age and embody the hidden urges of the nation. Soloviëv then stresses the inevitability of historical development, the rhythm of history, the necessary stages of the process. Yet the general scheme of interpretation is still the same. There are two stages, or ages, of national life: in the first the life of the nation is dominated and guided by "feeling"—the period of youth, of strong passions and movements, the time of fire. And yet it is the time of immaturity, as vigorous as the energy may be. The nation must come of age, or perish. In the second stage its life is ruled by reason, or by thought. Everything is subjected to doubt. There are dangers in these awakenings, in the transition from superstition to unbelief. Nevertheless, it is a step forward. Western Europe passed into the mature age, the age of thought, at the time of the Renaissance. Russia did the same two centuries later. In fact, only at this point of transition does real history begin, although it is possible only on the basis of what had been accumulated or created in the age of feeling. There is, in Soloviëv's vision of history, a peculiar blending of Hegelianism and the motives of the Enlightenment: belief in general laws of history and worship of knowledge and critical thinking. See "Publichnye chteniia o Petre Velikom," *Sochineniia Sergeia Mikhailovicha Solovieva* (St. Petersburg, 1882), pp. 88 ff.

3. Soloviëv, *op. cit.*, Book III, col. 1057: "Ochered' porabotat' chuzhomu nachalu."

4. F. I. Buslaev, "Obshchiia poniatiia o russkoi ikonopisi" (1886), *Sochineniia*, I (St. Petersburg, 1908), pp. 3–4, 21, 29, 32.

5. A. N. Pypin, "Do-Petrovskoe predanie v XVIII-m veke," *Vestnik Evropy*, July, 1886, pp. 330 ff.; cf. N. Trubytsin, *O narodnoi poezii v obshchestvennom i literaturnom obikhode pervoi treti XIX veka* (St. Petersburg, 1912), chap. i, pp. 1–3.

6. V. Jagič, *Historija Književnosti Naroda Hrvatskoga i Srbskoga*, Vol. I.: *Staro doba* (Zagreb, 1867), pp. 52, 66.

7. E. Golubinsky, *Istoriia russkoi tserkvi*, I/1 (2nd ed.; Moscow, 1901), pp. 701 ff., 720.

8. G. P. Fedotov, "Tragediia intelligentsii" (1927), in *Novyi grad: Sbornik statei* (New York, 1952), pp. 19–22.

9. George P. Fedotov, *The Russian Religious Mind: Kievan Christianity* (Cambridge, Mass.: Harvard University Press, 1946), pp. 21–41.

10. D. S. Likhachev, *Chelovek v literature drevnei Rusi* (Moscow-Leningrad, 1958); *Nekotorye zadachi izucheniia vtorogo iuzhnoslavianskogo vliianiia v Rossii* (Moscow, 1958).

11. This theme must be elaborated in detail with reference to the modern study. It is enough to mention the recent works of Igor Grabar, V. N. Lazareff, M. Alpatov, etc.

12. See the penetrating essay of V. Shchepkin, "L'Ame du Peuple Russe dans l'Art Russe," in *Le Monde Slave*, May and June, 1928; the Russian text in *Volia Rossii*, VIII–IX, X–XI, XII.

13. Kliuchevsky, *Kurs* . . . , Vol. III, lectures 54 and 55; cf. "Zapadnoe vliianie v Rossi XVII veka: Istoriko-psikhologicheskii ocherk" (1897), in *Ocherki i Rechi*, 1912.

14. *Пути русскаго богословгя* (Paris, 1937), pp. 1–2.

15. Wladimir Weidlé, *Russia: Absent and Present* (New York, 1952), pp. 15 ff.

# The Old Believers and the New Religion

## MICHAEL CHERNIAVSKY

For nearly two hundred years the history of the *Raskol*,[1] the Russian Church schism of the seventeenth century, was a secret one. To be sure, the Old Believers wrote, and in enormous quantities, but they wrote—by hand—secret manuscripts, copied secretly and circulated secretly. And, except for official condemnations of schismatic teachings and the publication of laws directed against the *raskol'niki*, more or less serious historical investigation started only in the last years of the reign of Emperor Nicholas I and was confined to printed but highly restricted memoranda passed around in the Ministry of Internal Affairs.[2] Even the nature and the chronology of early *Raskol* historiography raise questions about the nature of the schism. Why was the history of the *Raskol* secret for such a long time? Why were the Old Believers persecuted by the government for so long? Was it all, as the government maintained, because they were ignorant, illiterate, superstitious, fanatical, and disobedient toward the Church?

With the death of Nicholas the persecution of the Old Believers slackened, and the historiography of the schism emerged into the open. In the last century an enormous amount has been published on the *Raskol*—its meaning, early history, and development—and in most of this work the motivation and presuppositions are unequivocal.

First, there is the official Orthodox position, represented largely by professors at the various imperial theological academies.[3] The historians of this "school" did excellent work in publishing the source material;[4] their explanation of the schism and the schismatics was simple: the rejection of the Nikonian church reform in the seventeenth century was a reflection of popular (and clerical) ignorance and obscurantism, the mistaking of ritual for substance. Rejecting all progress and change, the schismatics had rejected and continued to reject legitimate authority—of the church hierarchy, on which their souls depended, and of the state as well, inasmuch as it supported the official church—sinking ever deeper into a fanaticism of either total and irreverent individualism and

FROM Michael Cherniavsky, "The Old Believers and the New Religion," *Slavic Review*, XXV, No. 1 (March 1966), 1–39. Reprinted by permission of the American Association for the Advancement of Slavic Studies.

sectarianism or of hopeless internal theological and ritualistic contradictions.[5] The Old Believers were impelled by a superstitious religiosity, though this basic motivation carried political overtones to the extent that the *raskol'niki* disobeyed the authorities who tried to rescue them from perdition. There is little one need say about these nineteenth-century Orthodox professors. They were convinced that the Old Believers were heretics or, at best, schismatics for rejecting the authority and legitimacy of the Church hierarchy; they published a great deal of source material, and we should not expect anything else.

Simultaneously with the Orthodox view emerged a liberal, populist position. Led by Shchapov, a whole group of historians suggested a more comprehensive explanation of the schism which produced the Old Believers.[6] The *Raskol*, as they saw it, was only superficially a religious split. Religious issues provided the opportunity for the expression of social and political protest: social, against the ever-increasing importations from the West—clothes, customs, institutions; political, against the central fact of seventeenth-century Russian history—the legalization in 1649 of the complete enserfment of the peasants. These historians observed that, after the first few years, the schismatics were exclusively of lower-class origin—peasants and some of the poorer townspeople—but that, rather than being the ignorant and dark element of Russia, they contained and continued to contain a much higher percentage of literate people than the Orthodox population. Hence, the Old Believers represented general popular opinion and its desire to preserve, if nothing more, popular customs and institutions against the encroachment of the centralizing and bureaucratizing state.[7] The conception of the *Raskol* as social protest is shared, of course, by Soviet historians, though initially few interested themselves in this problem. But in the last fifteen years, under the impetus of the enthusiasm and erudition of V. I. Malyshev, Old Believer studies have acquired a new prominence.[8] The chief concerns of Soviet scholars have been with the social structure and ideology of the Old Believers and with the writings of the Old Believer church fathers—Avvakum, Epifanii, Lazar', Feodor—as secular literature.[9]

Within this historiographic context, recent American scholarship sounds a curious note. No special work on the schism as such has been written, but all the recent (or recently revised) general histories of Russia, of course, mention the *Raskol*, presenting it as the expression of Muscovite traditionalism, attention to form rather than substance, ignorance, inertia—the antithesis to the Western Reformation and its search for change.[10]

What does it mean to speak of the Russian masses in the seventeenth century as tradition-bound? Compared with whom? Traditions are not immutable, and each age has its own. In the West as well as in the East, all Christian reform movements offered a return to the past (whatever the real motives of the movements may have been). The problem always has been which of the many pasts to defend. Why is it more "intelligent" to use three fingers in crossing oneself than two? Despite patronizing references to the "strange practices" of the Old Believers, all religious practices, or perhaps none, have "scholarly foundation"; in matters of ritual and theology a source can always be found to support one's position, and the Old Believers could and did point to many very ancient icons showing the two-fingered sign of the cross.[11] True, as Florinsky has stated, there seems to have been little "principle or dogma" involved, but the issue of a double or triple "hallelujah" is equal in importance to the *filioque* clause and the leavened-unleavened bread controversies which, supposedly, have divided the Roman and Greek churches, until today. These categories then—traditionalism, the "perfectly correct form," even national self-awareness[12]—are abstractions which explain nothing and which, in turn, create other abstractions—the Reformation, Orthodoxy, "scholarly foundations" of ritual.

From the contributions of populist and Soviet scholars, we can derive four general observations without going into the details of the arguments. A very significant number of Russians embraced the schism—from the start, probably as many as 20 percent were Old Believers.[13] The *Raskol* was most widespread in the areas where the power of the central government was less effective than elsewhere for a variety of reasons—lack of serfdom, distance, political considerations. Hence northern Russia, the Urals, Siberia, the Cossack lands, and large sections of the western frontier were overwhelmingly schismatic.[14] Old Believers were severely, and often brutally, persecuted from the beginning of the schism until the middle of the nineteenth century.[15] And the *Raskol* began in a century of profound social upheaval and tension. It is hard to find a decade of the seventeenth century which is not marked by rebellions and unrest of peasants or Cossacks, townspeople or *strel'tsy*.[16]

Paralleling these are the triumph of the gentry service class after the Time of Troubles, the *Ulozhenie* (Law Code) of 1649, which legalized serfdom, the state-church controversy of Tsar Alexis and Patriarch Nikon, and the beginning of the Petrine reforms.

In other words, the *Raskol* assumed huge dimensions; it was most prevalent where government authority could be most easily resisted or disregarded. It was considered a serious and major problem by the government. And there were more than enough concrete political and social reasons to account for its origins and spread. This is not to argue that the other factors in the schism—cultural tradition, theology, ritual—did not exist. Like all heterodox or schismatic movements, the *Raskol* developed and expressed its ideology in the language of religion. This language is not ours today and hence offers difficulties of interpretation. The issue is not that the Old Believers (or the Russians, or medieval man in general) necessarily thought in a manner so different from ours about politics, economics, social problems, or their life in general but that they used a particular and comprehensive vocabulary to express their thoughts.[17] And this theological or religious language, like all language, possessed a logic of its own. And, indeed, in the course of their history the Old Believers (like the Protestants in the West) could be forced into rather radical theological views because theological terms, no matter why used, evoked theological consequences.[18] Still, this language can be analyzed, its origins suggested, and its meaning understood in its proper context.

The Old Believers wrote about many things—details of ritual, dogma, way of life—but at all times one of their chief concerns was with authority, government, or, symbolically, the tsar. For, in the final analysis, it was the tsar, wielding absolute power over both state and church, who cut them off from the rest of society, approved their being excommunicated and even anathematized, forced them to be so different, distinct from others, and persecuted them with such violence. This strand of Old Believer thought, regarding the state and the tsar but expressed in theological terms—what one may call the political theology of the *Raskol*—is our theme. Our first concern, then, is with the language in which the concrete social and political problems involving imperial power were couched. Where did the Old Believers find the terms they used, what was the logic of their thought, what were the consequences of this thought, and by whom was it understood?

The obvious starting point is the religious reforms in the middle of the seventeenth century which provoked the schism—but without losing sight of the fact that correction of texts and changes in ritual began in Russia before Nikon became patriarch in 1652. In the fourteenth century, when Hesychast influence transmitted the Neoplatonic concern with words and meanings, Russia was probably flooded by corrected texts from the South Slavic lands;[19] in the fifteenth century a Grand Prince, Ivan III, and a Metropolitan of Russia, Gerontii, clashed violently on points of ritual;[20] and in 1551 Ivan IV (the Terrible) called together the so-called *Stoglav* Council to legislate reforms of morals and ritual.[21] Finally, as N. F. Kapterev showed some seventy years ago, a systematic program to correct liturgical texts began, probably under Patriarch Filaret in the 1620s, and at the latest under Patriarch Iosif in the 1640s; consequently, Nikon and the higher clergy in general were the executors of reforms initiated and guided by the tsar, that is, the secular government.[22]

The reform movement, in fact, was by no means monolithic, and one can distinguish three strands of reform thought and action. There were what one may call purely administrative reforms—legislation effected by the state, culminating in the article of the *Ulozhenie* which established the *Monastyrskii Prikaz* (Department of Monasteries) and which, in effect, abolished separate ecclesiastical jurisdiction and much of ecclesiastical economic power.[23] This strand necessarily overlapped with the administrative-intellectual reform—correction or emendation of texts and ritual out of desire for accuracy and uniformity. This reform can be identified with Greek and South Russian scholars subsidized and supported by Tsar Alexis and by his chamberlain (*postel'nichii*), the boyar F. Rtishchev, who paid for much of the research and founded a school for theological and linguistic studies.[24] Then there were the "Zealots of Piety" (*Revniteli blagochestiia*), a group of priests under the leadership of the archpriest Stepan Vonifatiev, confessor to Tsar Alexis.[25] The concern of these priests was the moral, spiritual reform. This does not mean that they were not involved with the administrative and intellectual reforms, as in the case of the famous issue of *edinoglasie*,[26] but their main efforts were directed toward improvement of public morality, toward a religious revival. Their chief vehicle, one which was dormant in Russian ecclesiastical practice, was the public sermon. In fact, the clerics of this group owed much of their power and influence to their effectiveness as preachers in the various churches of Moscow.[27] The members of this group were, in effect, the founding fathers of the *Raskol*—reformers who were closely associated with Nikon before he became patriarch but who opposed his later reforms to the point of schism. Hence, even on a purely religious plane it is not possible to contrast "reform" and "tradition." All the parties involved, ecclesiastical and lay, were for reform of some kind or other.[28]

Now a summary of the ecclesiastical controversy:[29] In the first two years of his patriarchate, 1652–54, Nikon decreed changes in ritual—the sign of the cross, the number and manner of prostrations, the hallelujah glorification—and published new service books. He was opposed by the majority of the white clergy and many of the prelates. In a series of councils between 1654 and 1656 Nikon forced through acceptance of his reforms and condemnation of his priestly opponents who would not submit.[30] By 1656 these were, apparently, very few in number—a small group of the Moscow preachers led by the archpriest Avvakum. They were severely punished and exiled, in the line of hierarchic discipline, but in the last two years of his tenure Nikon appears to have lost interest in the whole reform issue.[31] After the abdication—or removal—of Nikon in 1658 the obstreperous priests took heart. They were allowed to return to Moscow, where they continued to argue against the ritual and textual changes and to plead with the Tsar to abolish the work of the deposed patriarch. So far, then, no issue of schism; at most, an ecclesiastical controversy and a problem of discipline—priests enjoined to obey their hierarchic superiors and the Russian Tsar. The explanation for this mildness on the part of Church and state authorities is probably in the fact that both the prelates and the Tsar were too much involved with the problem of the patriarchate—Nikon's attempts to regain his see and to involve the whole Orthodox world in this issue—to bother with a few disobedient and popular priests. As late as 1666 a council of Russian bishops offered, in effect, a compromise—it confirmed the Nikonian reforms but without condemning the earlier practices and texts and, in return, asked the Avvakumians (for so they may be called by this date) to refrain from insisting that the new practices and texts were heretical. Avvakum and his colleagues rejected the compromise, and the Patriarchal Council of 1666–67, led by the patriarchs of Antioch and Alexandria, settled the issue; the old practices and texts were proclaimed heretical, and those refusing to obey the council were anathematized.[32] The council also insisted on secular punishment. Avvakum and his companions Feodor, Lazar', and Epifanii (all three with their tongues cut out) were imprisoned in the far north, at Pustozersk. In 1682 they were burned at the stake.[33]

The schism, instituted in 1667, seems at first to have been between the Russian Church on the one side and four Russian clerics on the other.[34] Yet by the 1680s Old Believers were spreading over much of Russia. At some points and in some ways, then, the thought of the *Raskol* fathers must have intersected with other ideological strands within Russian society. What were the thoughts of these lonely clerics?[35] From the beginning, of course, they were able to attack the

Nikonian changes at their most vulnerable point—their scholarly foundation. The deacon Feodor pointed out that the six editions of the missal published by Nikon all differed from one another.[36] With the best will in the world and despite the help of the monasteries of Mt. Athos, the scholars employed by Nikon could not obtain and properly date and collate all the necessary materials, and the results of their work were inevitably inconsistent. Hence, what shocked and outraged Avvakum and his followers was the arbitrariness of Nikon's despotism in matters of faith. The changes were inconsistent, confusing, wrong; yet the Patriarch threw in his whole enormous police power to enforce them against the opposition of the lower clergy. Was it all the personal whim of Nikon? Avvakum thought so at the beginning,[37] but then found that the explanation could not suffice. The issue was whether the Nikonian reforms were necessary, and what they signified.

Inasmuch as both the Nikonians and the anti-Nikonians stood for reform to some degree, the justification for their positions had to be found in the past. For the anti-Nikonian priests, with their emphasis on the moral and the spiritual, true religious reform touched only the inner man. The past these men drew upon was the individual past, for all men really knew or could be reminded of what was good. The Nikonian reform, though, raised quite different issues. It lies outside our scope to search for the original reasons for textual and ritual emendations, but there is little evidence to support the hypothesis that the reforms were motivated by foreign policy ambitions of the Russian government.[38] A more simple explanation may be merely the presence in Moscow of Ukrainian theologians, well trained as philologists. Concern with texts, translations, collation, and nuances was their profession, in defending Orthodoxy from Catholicism in the Ukraine. And turning their critical apparatus on Muscovite texts, they could point out many problems. Neither the problems nor the Nikonian reforms involved any principle or dogma. Both Nikon and Tsar Alexis probably thought of them, in the beginning, as at best desirable rather than vital. But then, how were these changes to be proven necessary, and how were they to be justified? The first principle used for justification was authority; the patriarch had the right to legislate changes in texts and rituals, and this right was confirmed by the council of 1654; the duty of his flock, and that included priests, was to obey (it was the use of this principle with all its implications of arbitrary decisions that provoked the violent hatred for the person of Nikon). At the same time, there was the legitimate appeal to the past—to the furthest past of Russian Christianity, which was Greek Orthodoxy. That past, however, was ambiguous. Necessarily, Nikon turned from the dead past to the living—the Eastern patriarchs of his own day. Here came the most revealing aspect of the Nikonian reforms, for the answer from Constantinople was that the new practices conformed to the Greek practices but that no issue of dogma was involved; so that, in effect, there was no reason to forbid the traditional Russian usages.[39]

The internal logic of Nikon's legislative reforms rendered this answer unacceptable, however, exactly because the reforms were legislative. Tsar Alexis had been able to issue his new Law Code in 1649 with the rationale that the old laws were either inadequate or no longer relevant. Nikon, and the Tsar, legislating on ritual and sacred texts, could not use this rationale. The only justification possible for religious changes was that the old ritual and the old texts were wrong; and, if wrong, they had to be condemned and forbidden. For this reason the Russian prelates had to anathematize the two-fingered sign of the cross in 1656, and the Patriarchal Council of 1666–67, in supporting Nikonian reforms, had to go on all the way and deny the legitimacy of the *Stoglav* Council of Ivan the Terrible, which, too, had legislated on ritual and usage.[40] The issue, then, was the legitimation of Church legislation parallel to that of the secular civil legislation of 1649. But, given the nature of the necessary justification for religious changes, this issue of legislation resulted not only in a reaffirmation of the ideal Christian past but also in a condemnation of the Russian historical past.

The fathers of the *Raskol* accepted the challenge with eagerness. Time and again they posed the confrontation: if one is to impute heresy, one must make one's choice either for the Russian past, the saints, and the Holy Council presided over by the pious and Orthodox tsar, Ivan IV, or for the despotic Nikon.[41] And thus they evoked the obscure doctrine of "Moscow the Third Rome"[42]— meaning to them that in the process of *translatio imperii* Moscow was the spiritual capital of Christianity and that her unique and exclusive orthodoxy was historically proven and divinely confirmed. And, as the Third Rome was also the last, this meant that Muscovite Orthodoxy was the only currency of the economy of salvation. If Moscow were to fall from grace, betray the faith as had the first two Romes, it would mean not only the fall of Moscow as a state, as divine punishment, but the end of the whole world; a fourth Rome there could not be, and Moscow's fall would signify the end of the possibility of salvation for all men, and the coming of the last days. Both the utility and the danger of this doctrine are obvious. On the one hand, it allowed the Old Believers to dismiss the authority of the Eastern patriarchs, representatives of the Second, and fallen, Rome. On the other hand, the issue was imbued with enormous tension and urgency; one could not afford a mistake, even a temporary one, for the stakes were ultimate and the penalty irreversible.

The framework of Moscow the Third Rome, of the confrontation of Ivan the Terrible with Nikon, made the argument a historical one, over the meaning of the Russian past and the significance of the Russian present. The historical focus allowed and encouraged the expression of prejudices—dislike for the Greeks coming for alms, for the learned Ukrainians corrupted by "Latinity," and for the presence of Western foreigners of all sorts in Moscow, with their heretical religions and strange customs; all these stirred noisy argument on Russia and its religion. But within the religious controversy there seems to have been very little religion. For the Nikonians the issue was one of authority, of discipline, of the right to legislate, and how little the substance of the reforms mattered to the arrogant and obstinate Patriarch can be seen from his lack of interest in them after his first abdication in 1658. If Nikon was inconstant, the anti-Nikonians were inconsistent. For them, too, the issue seems to have been authority, the right of legislation. And the Third Rome doctrine made them peculiarly vulnerable in this respect. For what they denied to Nikon and Tsar Alexis—the right to legislate on ritual—they gladly granted to Metropolitan Makarii, Tsar Ivan IV, and the council of 1551.

The problem does not end here, however, for it is clear that the Nikonians, too, accepted the doctrine of the Third Rome. Nikon used the authority of the Greeks as long as he found it useful, but after 1658 his denunciation of their corruption and heresy more than matched that of Avvakum.[43] True, the Greeks became Nikon's political enemies in his struggle with Tsar Alexis, but to express his enmity he used a Third Rome, anti-Greek vocabulary which was, apparently, becoming commonplace. And Alexis' view of the Greeks (and hence, of Russian Orthodoxy) was best shown at the council of 1666–67. There the Tsar learned (as did everyone else) that the patriarchs who condemned Nikon, confirmed Nikon's reforms, and anathematized the Old Believers were—both Macarios of Antioch and Paisios of Alexandria—deposed and no longer patriarchs.[44] Although the Tsar spent much effort to have them restored to their sees, in his contempt for the Greeks—and even for the Russian prelates—he did not see fit to question the decisions of a council conducted under such dubious chairmanship. The issue, therefore, was not whether one rejected or accepted Moscow as the Third Rome, but what the Third Rome meant. Nikon and Alexis could afford to drop the Greek patriarchs, or anyone else, precisely because Moscow was the Third Rome; for, then, anything that the tsar and the patriarch of the Third Rome did was, by definition, orthodox and legitimate.

At a more profound level, then, the controversy was not really historical but theological. It was equally possible to argue that, because Moscow was the essence of Orthodoxy, all its actions and changes were legitimate, as to contend that, because Moscow was Orthodoxy, nothing might be changed. But the theology was political in its implications. This is best illustrated by the fact that, for both Nikonians and Avvakumians, the final and supreme authority in matters of faith, of ritual, of the Church was the tsar. At the center of the Third Rome doctrine, and at the center of Russian seventeenth-century political theory, stood the theocratic Russian tsar. In the eyes of the monk Filofei, who first formulated the Third Rome ideology, it was the Russian ruler who preserved Orthodoxy in Russia and hence in the whole world, and the burden of the Third Rome, of keeping the faith, rested on his shoulders.[45] The seventeenth century, the reign of Alexis in particular, was the apogee of the theocratic ideal.[46] Elected by God, Crowned by God, Most Pious and Orthodox, the Most Gentle Tsar ruled Russia as autocrat, but his life was conducted, down to the smallest detail, to correspond to the religious ideal.[47] Certainly Alexis lived up to this ceremonial ideal as successfully as had Ivan the Terrible, the pious tsar of the *Stoglav* Council. The controversy thus becomes still more puzzling—why and how resist the Most Gentle Tsar, how deny him the right to do what his pious and saintly predecessors had done legitimately?

The answer I would like to suggest is that the theocratic tsar began to ring a little false in the ears of the *raskol'niki*, that something different and new was beginning to show through the theocracy. What that something was can be illustrated by the first law of the *Ulozhenie* of 1649, which established a new category of crimes, political crimes.[48] The law itself only gave form to a conception which had arisen in the early seventeenth century, conveyed by the sacramental phrase *slovo i delo gosudarevo* (word and deed concerning the sovereign).[49] In other words, we have here a symbolic indication of the early secular state, for which the sacramental phrase was *crime d'état*, as for the full-blown secular state it was, and is, *raison d'état*.[50]

The tenuous nature of my illustration should warn us, however, that the process described here was very complex and subtle. Secularization, that is, the justification of this world *by* this world, showed through but little and was not, of course, recognized as such, and the theocratic ideology persisted for a long time. Men went on using the old formulas as their content slowly evaporated or changed. So, while Nikon acted, and could only act, with the support of the Tsar, the *Raskol* fathers deluged the "Most Pious, Most Orthodox and Most Gentle" Tsar with their appeals to defend the Orthodoxy of his saintly ancestors, to save the faith and make salvation possible. To these appeals no answer came, and the council of 1666–67 left little room for hope. What could one make of all this? The logic of schismatic thought is extremely simple, deceptively simple, for it does not convey the enormous painfulness of the whole issue, the shock of the logically necessary deductions, and their revolutionary significance for the Old Believers.

There was only one general conclusion possible: if Moscow, the Third Rome, had instituted religious changes which required the condemnation of itself in its own past, then Moscow had accepted heresy—and the end was at hand. The end was not something vague or ambiguous. It was the apocalypse, described in greatest detail by St. John of Patmos and St. Cyril of Jerusalem. The end of the world was preceded by the second coming of Christ, who, in turn, was preceded by the Antichrist. To repeat, this conclusion was emotionally so monstrous that even Avvakum could not come to it easily; he struggled hard to postpone the ultimate confrontation. The Cyrillian interpretations gave him some leeway: Antichrist was a person, but there was also the spirit of Antichrist, manifest whenever apostasy took place. Apostasy on a mass scale certainly presaged the physical Antichrist but still left room for hope that the process could be stopped and even reversed.[51] Nevertheless, the spirit of Antichrist needed some material instrument through which to work, and the candidate for such an instrument was not hard to find—a patriarch of the Third Rome who was a manifest heretic.[52]

Nikon as the precursor of Antichrist was shocking enough, although sheer hatred for the person of the Patriarch may have made the idea less painful. But this explanation was not sufficient, first, because Antichrist himself was an imperial, not an ecclesiastical figure and, second, because Nikon was not acting on his own authority. Behind him was the figure of the pious and Orthodox Tsar, traditionally responsible for Orthodoxy and salvation. This is to say that, as apostates, Nikon, Alexis, and the bishops who obeyed them all signified the spirit of Antichrist. But, as holders of supreme power, Nikon and particularly Alexis had a greater responsibility.[53] They were not just part of the general spirit of the times but were guiding the work of Antichrist; they were, in a sense, a part of Antichrist, or at least of the apocalyptic vision—being cast interchangeably as precursor, as Antichrist himself, or as the Beast of the Apocalypse.

Tsar Alexis as a precursor, or symbolically one of the two "horns," of Antichrist was far more painful to accept; nothing could more surely mean the end of the world than the Orthodox Tsar as a horn of Antichrist.[54] But it made sense, particularly after 1658, when Nikon was gone and the reforms were nonetheless maintained. Still, Nikon, too, had done his work, and therefore both Tsar and Patriarch, the former as Antichrist, the latter as the Beast of the Apocalypse, appear in an illustrated apocalypse (Figure 1).[55] It is certainly hard to prove that the portrait is that of Alexis (not to mention Nikon).[56] But in comparing the imperial crowned figure of the miniature with the official portrait of Tsar Alexis (Figure 2) and, particularly, with that of his father, Tsar Michael (Figure 3)— and confusion of these two in official portraiture would be natural enough— the resemblance is suggestive.[57] Equally suggestive is an eighteenth-century miniature showing the "rulers and judges" bowing before the spirit of Satan (Figure 4),[58] especially when compared with an early portrait of Alexis (Figure 5).[59] And any doubts about the identification are completely removed by a nineteenth-century miniature, drawing upon an old iconographic tradition, which shows the unholy trinity—Alexis, Nikon, and Arsenii Sukhanov (a scholar much involved on the work of the textual reforms)[60]—as the serpent, the beast, and the false prophet of the Apocalypse (Figure 6).[61] The human number and the number of the beast—666—rules over both the complementary images.

If Tsar Alexis was the precursor of Antichrist, he could not have become that overnight. In fact, as deacon Feodor, one of the four Pustozersk fathers heard, Alexis was from the start—that is, 1645, when he inherited the throne—a horn of Antichrist.[62] In other words, the conclusion had to be drawn that the apostasy of the Tsar was not an accident, temporary and random, but part of an irrevocable divine and satanic process. If so, when was Antichrist himself to come? The Old Believer position on the dating of the apocalypse was established by the mid-1650s, at the very beginning of the schism, and subsequent events confirmed it by giving substance to the date of 1666.[63] Cabalistically this worked out quite nicely in at least two computations, given that 666 was the number of Antichrist.[64] Substantively, the council of 1666–67 acted as the final proof, although most of those waiting for the apocalypse—Avvakum among them—still could not face the logical conclusion that the end of the world was really at hand. It may have been the enormous vitality of the archpriest that prevented him from accepting the idea of the total end; and while he spared few curse words when describing Nikon and even Alexis, he preferred to emphasize that only the spirit of Antichrist was present—that is, the apostasy which was not final as long as men were willing to hold out against it. Yet this reluctance of Avvakum to face the apocalypse may have led him to ideas which hint at the political underpinnings of apocalyptic theology. For, in order not to accept Antichrist, Avvakum in effect attacked the theocratic nature and role of the Russian tsar. By this stage he was furious with Nikon's exaltation of the "most pious, most gentle, most autocratic sovereign."[65] Nikon was praising the Tsar above all the saints, and called Alexis *sviatoi tsar'* (holy tsar).[66] Though Avvakum argued that Nikon was confusing the person of the tsar with the imperial office, the very image of the theocratic tsar was inevitably based on this confusion.[67] But even the office of the tsar was not exempt from Avvakum's arguments: the tsar had no right to "possess the Church and change dogma"; his task was only to protect the faithful, "not teach [them] how to hold the faith."[68] In other words, if Alexis was not responsible for the faith of the Third Rome, then his heresy was not so decisive. Thus Avvakum seems to have abandoned the "traditionalist," conservative position on the level of political theology, just as he had on the level of pure theology. Obviously, there were inconsistencies within his view, as when

FIGURE 1

FIGURE 2

he denied Alexis the imperial rights which he defended for the Tsar's ancestors; but then, Ivan the Terrible was dead and gone and no longer a problem. Alexis was alive and pressing, and in desperation Avvakum pleaded with him: "After all, we are not taking away from you your empire . . . but are defending our faith."[69]Despite the various inconsistencies, however, toward both Church and state, the Old Believer, Avvakumian positions appear far more consistently revolutionary and "reformist" than they have been generally thought.

The *Raskol* fathers were driven by their circumstances to explore the logic of their own views. But if they were understood and followed by others, as they were, it meant that their language and their logic were also understood and accepted. One reason for this understanding was the apocalyptic mood of the mid-seventeenth century. Parenthetically, one might note that apocalyptic thought, the expectation of the end, does not seem to arise at moments of great and apparently cataclysmic threats to Russian (nor probably any other) society —the Mongol conquest, the Time of Troubles with its Polish intervention—but

rather at a time when society is undergoing an internal crisis of basic transformation and change.[70] In the seventeenth century we can date this mood at least as early as May 1644, when the government's Printing Office published the so-called *Book of Cyril*, a collection of South Slavic and Ukrainian apocalyptic writings. The volume sold over 500 copies in one month—an incredible sale for the time.[71] The book, and others like it printed a little later, obviously met intense popular demand. Probably, however, the apocalyptic strand of thought was present as early as the 1630s. It is associated with the name of Kapiton, a hermit renowned for his asceticism, founder of a hermitage near Tot'ma, in the north, in 1630.[72] Very little is known of his theology, but his name is linked with the earliest—pre-Old Belief—cases of self-immolation, and *Kapitonovshchina* was a movement of flight from the world, the expectation of an immediate apocalypse.[73] In fact, it was from the hermit Mikhail, a follower of Kapiton, that deacon Feodor learned that Tsar Alexis was "not a tsar but a horn of Antichrist."[74] By the 1640s, then, there was a certain mood or ideology of insecurity, of rejection, in which men associated the evil they were rejecting, or fleeing from, with the Tsar. And the ideology of the early *Raskol* intersected with, if it did not draw upon, this mood.

The apocalyptic outlook was not restricted to the *Kapitonovshchina* runaways, hermits, and dissatisfied lower clergy. This is not the place to discuss the great controversy between Patriarch Nikon and Tsar Alexis; on the face of it, Nikon's drive for power and his motivations in general were quite different from those of Avvakum.[75] But after the break came, in 1658, Nikon began to sound very much like Avvakum. We have already noted that the disgraced Patriarch accepted and used, in his defense, the doctrine of the Third Rome. But Nikon went much further than this, for he attacked the theocratic role of the "most pious, most gentle" Tsar. "How did you acquire the insolence to inquire about us [prelates] and to judge us?" wrote Nikon to Alexis.[76] In his insistence that the priesthood was above secular authority, Nikon denied the Tsar any role in the Church

**FIGURE 4**

**FIGURE 5**

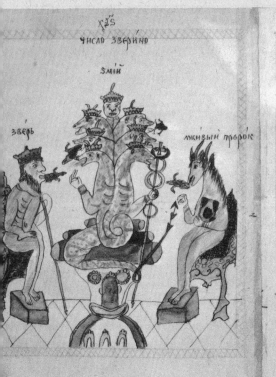

## FIGURE 6

except as an obedient executor.[77] His greatest fury he directed at the *Ulozhenie*—
the Law Code of 1649—which established the *Monastyrskii Prikaz* and generally
presumed to legislate on the Church. The compiler of the Code, Prince N.
Odoevskii, pretended to refer to the old sacred laws of the apostles, the Church
fathers, and the Byzantine emperors; but, in fact, he was making up new laws,
"like a new Luther"! And these laws were suggested to him by his teacher, the
Antichrist.[78] So, Nikon, too, ended up denying Alexis the rights he allowed to
Ivan the Terrible or to the Byzantine emperors. He could draw only one conclusion from the situation as he saw it—the reign of Antichrist had come. In
accord with St. John the Divine, Nikon wrote, he envisaged the Antichrist as
spiritual rather than incarnate; the power of the Antichrist would be manifested
by the fact that "lay authority, stepping over divine commandments, will take
possession of the Church,"[79] and this, obviously, had come to pass. In other
words, Nikon's logic paralleled that of Kapiton and Avvakum within a general
apocalyptic mood. The end of the world was near, and the responsibility for this
cataclysm lay with the Tsar, whose power was spreading out into new areas or
was no longer legitimate in areas where it had once prevailed. Hence, the apocalypse as political theology focused pretty exclusively on Antichrist; few men
seem to have been interested in what was theologically to follow—the second

coming of Christ. The Russian Church, beginning with the successor of Nikon, Iosaf, and on through the great prelates of Petrine Russia—Dimitrii of Rostov, Stepan Iavorskii, Feofan Prokopovich—hammered away at the fact that the second coming was a mystery and that men were forbidden to try to anticipate God's will concerning it. But no one was trying to anticipate the second coming, and an Old Believer "Booklet about Antichrist" of 1707 cunningly pointed out that the proscription against guessing the date applied to the coming of Christ only; the coming of Antichrist was not a mystery and obviously belonged to a different theology.[80]

It is clear that the political theology of Avvakum and his friends interacted with a tradition that was both older and broader than the immediate religious controversy in which these men were involved. Still, so far we have been discussing a general mood and an ecclesiastical controversy. At what point and in what way did it all become a schism, the *Raskol* proper? It is not possible, for lack of evidence, to trace the spread of the *Raskol* in time, place, and numbers. But three major events took place during the lifetime of the *Raskol* fathers, and these events can serve to illustrate at least what it was that was spreading so rapidly over large parts of the Russian state. First, there is the case of the Solovetskii Monastery, one of the holiest places of Russia, situated on an island in the Arctic Ocean, rich, remote (and hence accustomed to independence)—the monastery, like so many of the white clergy, refused to accept the Nikonian reforms.[81] The monks went much further, however, than the majority of the opposition; they embarked upon outright rebellion, and closed the monastery to imperial authority. Their arguments were not new; like Avvakum, they did not admit any disloyalty to the Tsar, but professed a greater loyalty to their faith and their salvation, which were being threatened.[82] Still, they refused to obey the Tsar, ceased to pray for him, and endured a siege of eight years (1668–76) before the monastery fell and the monks and laymen within it were massacred. The significance of this drama is heightened by the second of our events—the great rebellion of Stepan Razin, 1670–71. The rebellion followed what had been the classical pattern since the Time of Troubles, at the beginning of the century—it was started and organized by Cossacks, then spread to the peasants. The organized, Cossack phase of the rebellion was over within a year, though the government was badly shaken by the massive nature of the revolt. There seems to be no evidence that the Razin uprising included Old Believer elements or ideology, though Razin himself, in previous years, had twice visited the Solovetskii Monastery as a pilgrim.[83] But the reverse was certainly not the case. Whether to exonerate themselves or to say things which their interlocutors expected and welcomed, the captives taken after the fall of the monastery all testified to the leading role of outsiders—followers of Kapiton, runaways, Don Cossacks—in the monastery.[84] Certainly the government believed that the main impetus for resistance in the monastery was provided by former members of Razin's scattered armies.[85]

It is not possible to prove conclusively a connection between the Razin uprising and that of the Solovetskii Monastery; the significance of this conjunction lies in the fact that the Moscow government firmly believed in such a connection and that it even acted accordingly. It is at least difficult to see as pure coincidence the fact that the year of the outbreak of the Razin rebellion, 1670, marked new and brutally severe measures toward Avvakum and his fellow prisoners of Pustozersk.[86] But if one may have doubts about the intersection of Old Belief and *Razinovschina*, none can exist regarding the third event in this series—the *strel'tsy* uprising of 1682. True, this uprising did not occur within the life span proper of Avvakum and his colleagues—they were executed in April, while the *strel'tsy* rose in May of 1682—but the dates are close enough, and the *strel'tsy* did not know, when they marched on the Kremlin, that Avvakum was dead. The many political and economic grievances of the *strel'tsy* had been complicated by the delicate palace situation of the two young co-tsars (Peter I, ten years old, and his half brother, Ivan V, sixteen and half-witted) being edged out by their older sister, Sophia.[87] In any event, the "Petition" of the *strel'tsy* was an Old Belief tract, drawn up by the *Raskol* priest Nikita Dobrynin "Pustosviat" (the Bigot), who was in close touch with Pustozersk. All the economic and political grievances were submerged in the religious language of the "Petition." The *strel'tsy* pleaded for tolerance: What was wrong in using two fingers to make the sign of the cross? Should one mutilate and burn men for this? Moscow, after all, was the Third Rome, and its faith should not be determined by renegade Eastern patriarchs.[88] At the debate which took place in the imperial palace, however, the plea for toleration quickly turned into a demand for religious restoration. If the reforms were suggested by renegades, they were heretical, and, as Tsarevna Sophia pointed out in a burst of anger, the *strel'tsy* were accusing of heresy not only Nikon but her father, Tsar Alexis, as well.[89]

The soldiers were pacified by a mixture of force and concessions, and they repudiated Nikita, who was executed on Red Square. But again the government showed its awareness of the intersection of *Raskol* ideology with popular discontent; and again one wonders whether the execution of the Pustozersk prisoners at a time of great *strel'tsy* unrest, just before the outbreak in May, was purely a coincidence. Shortly afterwards the government demonstrated its conviction that the theology of the *Raskol* was primarily a political one; a law of 1684 made adherence to the schism a secular, state crime with the punishment of death for the nonrepentant schismatic.[90] And the government had reason: Beginning with the insurrection of 1682, every popular uprising in Russia—the continued *strel'tsy* troubles, the Cossack rebellions under Peter I (Azov, Astrakhan, Bulavin's uprising), and the climax of the great uprising of Pugachev under Catherine II—was fought under the banner of the Old Belief; the restoration of old ritual, icons, and books was inextricably connected with the program of massacring the aristocracy and abolishing serfdom. Thus, the early 1680s mark the beginning of the real *Raskol*, the mass movement within the Russian state, which came with the death of the first generation, the ideologues of Old Belief who still had hopes for ecclesiastical victory; the first uprising with *Raskol* slogans and program; and the initiation of relentless government persecution of the *Raskol* as a crime against the state.

As a mass movement with complex motivations, the *Raskol* soon lost its theological unity, for in the realm of theology the choices and possibilities were virtually unlimited, as they always are when men are suddenly bound only by the limits of their individual reason. In the sphere of the politics of apocalypse which concerns us here, however, three choices were possible. One was the belief that the end was here and now; the last days had come and Antichrist was present, in person. The second was the conception of the spiritual Antichrist, manifest in general apostasy and corruption, focused in the government as the source of all power, but diffused over all of Russian society and the world at large. These were legitimate theological alternatives. The third choice was expressed in a curious synthesis of the first two: the idea of an incarnate Antichrist ruling on earth, but without the theological consequence of this fact, that is, the end of the world and the second coming within forty-two months (Antichrist's reign was supposed to last three and a half years). The escape from this impasse lay in the positing of an Antichrist who, though corporeal, was a body corporate—that is, the person of Antichrist was the Russian imperial dynasty. So long, then, as the dynasty went on reigning, the world continued, though corrupted, as in the eyes of those who believed in the spirit of Antichrist only; but the source of all corruption was a flesh-and-blood entity—each successive Russian ruler, who was the physical Antichrist while he ruled.

How one chose one's apocalyptic politics and what the choice meant can be seen most easily in the case of the most extreme choice. If Antichrist was here on earth, in person, there was only one way to escape him, and that was by death. It is significant that suicide as a solution appeared (and the first reported instances of collective self-immolation occurred) within *Kapitonovshchina*, before the *Raskol* fathers took a position on the question. The logic was clear: Believers fled Antichrist, hiding in the forests, but if he reached out for them, if he sent his servants —officials, soldiers, tax collectors, census takers—then they died, preferably by the cleansing fire, before salvation was endangered by contact with, or submission to, Antichrist. The *Raskol* fathers were not in agreement about this solution, but Avvakum, for one, acknowledged its legitimacy as a last resort in the struggle against the Antichrist.[91] Beginning some time before 1664 and reaching its climax in the reign of Peter I, the wave of self-immolation carried away whole communities, and the total number of suicides ran into tens of thousands (on a small scale the practice continued at least until 1860).[92] Our knowledge of the motives for the mass suicides necessarily comes from government reports, and the government, for once, felt confused and unsure as its traditional and reliable means of persuasion—the whip and Siberia—proved singularly irrelevant. But we know the general setting for the self-immolations: in every case, a peasant group or community of Old Believers; in every case, an impending government intervention of some sort, either rumored or real. And in at least one case, in 1756, we know the motives, stated by the leader of the suicides just before they set fire to the chapel in which they had barricaded themselves: *Za mnogimi nyne narodnymi tiagostiami, nikakoi chelovek v mire spasti sebia ni kak ne mozhet, a kogda de sozhgutsia, to de spasenie poluchit' mogut*

(Because of the many present burdens on the people, no man in the world can save himself by any means; but if they burn themselves, then they can obtain salvation).[93] The theological conclusion is based on concrete secular conditions. The argument is powerful and touching—life, the purpose of which was to allow men to gain salvation, had become so difficult and burdensome that it no longer provided even the possibility of salvation.

In the world of the immanent Antichrist the other side of the coin of despair was outright rebellion. The shift to this other side is suggested by the fact that in nearly all cases of mass suicide there was active resistance to the police or soldiers sent by the government. The theocratic ideology continued to survive for a long time; hence the many rebels during the reign of Peter I fought him as the Antichrist but also argued that he was an impostor, not the real and legitimate tsar. Yet, as in the case of the suicides, underlying the correct theology were nontheological motivations: *Chto nam tsar'? Takaia ikh mat' kak i nasha . . . Vot, poidem na Moskvu . . . tak, kak s Sten'koi s nami uzhe ne sdelaiut* (What about the tsar? They [tsars] have mothers just as we do. . . This time, when we march on Moscow . . . they will not manage to do to us what they did to Sten'ka [Razin]), argued the Cossacks in 1686.[94] In other words, the Cossacks were rejecting the world in which they lived, with its political (and other) values, including the conception of the unique and exalted Most Gentle Tsar; for them too, in that world, there was no "salvation."

Not very many men, of course, were driven to accept the extreme solution—killing oneself or the world around one—and the extreme political theology that corresponded to it. The surprising thing is how many did accept it. For the great majority of the Old Believers the apocalyptic choice and the problems it involved can be illustrated by the case of the Vyg *Pustyn'* (Hermitage).[95] Situated on the Vyg, between St. Petersburg and Arkhangel'sk, this very early Old Believer community helped Peter I to develop the vital northern route, built ships, found and worked iron mines, and, given effective protection by the Emperor, enjoyed virtually complete autonomy. Under the Empress Anna, in the 1730s, however, the community was twice denounced and a government investigation followed,[96] in the course of which the old hidden debate came out into the open: Was one living in a world filled with the spirit, and only the spirit, of Antichrist, or was the Antichrist present and visible, to be identified by all? The charge against the community, however, was that the Old Believers had not been and were not offering any prayers for the ruler, refusing to perform the most traditional and obvious duty of a subject. The crime was a political one, and so was the debate, in effect. The Denisov brothers, founders and leaders of the community, argued that Antichrist was a spirit, manifested in all cases of apostasy and heresy; hence the problem did not lie with the ruler. They did not defend Peter the Great's lapse from Orthodoxy (nor that of Catherine I, Peter II, or Anna), but they argued that even apostolic law required prayers for "alien," pagan rulers and that Peter, after all, was a descendant of God-loving and pious ancestors. Under him the Old Believers (that is, the Vyg community) were free from persecution and even prospered greatly.[97] When in

1738, on pain of destruction, the prosperous community had to decide, the leadership and a small majority voted to pray for the ruler; that is, they voted for a spiritual and invisible Antichrist, ever-present, dangerous, corruptive, and pervasive, but not identical with political authority.

A large minority refused to go along and left the Vyg, starting a new splinter sect—the *Filippovtsy*, named after their spokesman, the elder Filipp.[98] Their choice was the third, the synthesis. They were not prepared to die nor to rise in rebellion; but for them Antichrist was incarnate in the person of the Russian ruler. The theology of their politics was best formulated in the 1780s by Evfimii, founder of the sect of *Stranniki* (Pilgrims, Wanderers), or *Beguny* (Fugitives):[99] Peter I was the material Antichrist, the real and the last Antichrist; his successors were but extensions of the physical Antichrist in time. Evfimii simply extended the forty-two months of Antichrist's reign indefinitely, but maintained that nothing would change, no hope was justified.[100] The Beast of the Apocalypse, in fact, was imperial power as such; the "icon" (or image) of the Beast was all civil authority; its body, spiritual authority.[101] Here is the crux of the matter—was government as such the Beast of the Apocalypse?

To repeat, the *Raskol* splintered away into dozens of sects separated by the finest and pettiest theological distinctions. Overarching all of them, however, was one great distinction: the spiritual or the material Antichrist, praying or not praying for the ruler. The nature of the choice was indicated by the Vyg community; it had prospered, and the world, though dangerous, was bearable if not pleasant. The majority of the Old Believers did not prosper. And so, while a theological debate on the prayer went on endlessly, the merchants, as Evfimii himself suggested, prayed for the ruler (however reluctantly); the peasants did not.[102]

The politics of apocalypse reached their climax in the first four decades of the eighteenth century. But here a caution about the sources is in order. The Old Believers wrote enormously; in particular, hundreds, if not thousands, of illustrated apocalypses, handwritten, have come down to us. But if they wrote or said anything explicitly political, in the eighteenth century the risks they ran were monstrous—the whip and Siberia could be counted a stroke of luck. So Old Believer literature is strongly dichotomous. On the one side is the enormous mass of tracts—repetitive, cautious, hinting but not really saying very much, sometimes daring and then pulling back.[103] On the other side is the smaller number of things said or written by men who could keep silent no longer, who frequently were looking for martyrdom. Even the government of Peter I was disturbed by this phenomenon; a law of 1722 tried to prove that self-willed martyrdom, a result of criminal and traitorous acts, was not true martyrdom and could not bring glory and salvation. Moreover, it argued, "sufferers who insult and dishonor their judge, even if he is unrighteous, are not following in the footsteps of Christ. And, if one does not follow Christ, how can one be legitimately martyred and hope for a heavenly crown?" Men who did this were suicides and blasphemers.[104] Yet these were the men, "extremists" though they were, that are now our best sources, conveying both the drama and the flavor of apocalyptic politics.

Grigorii Talitskii was a Moscow scribe, copying books and manuscripts for sale. Some time before 1700 he became obsessed with the problem of Antichrist. He set down his conclusions in two treatises: "Concerning the Coming of Antichrist into the World, and the Time from the Creation of the World to Its End" and "The Gates," which proved, with elaborate calculations, that Peter I, as the eighth tsar of the apocalypse, was the Antichrist and that the last days had come. Talitskii enjoined the people not to obey Peter or pay taxes. He made copies of his writings and sold them widely and, apparently, quite openly. One of his customers was Ignatii, bishop of Tambov, who wept as he listened to the scribe's exhortations, kissed him, and gave him five rubles. Finally Talitskii decided to give away his treatises free and tried to have the texts engraved on boards with the purpose of printing many copies. At this point, on June 28, 1700, he was denounced and taken to the Preobrazhenskii Prikaz—the political or state police office.[105] There, questioned and tortured, Talitskii readily admitted all that he had done, planned, and thought.[106] He named eighteen people among those who had aided, listened to, or agreed with him, including Bishop Ignatii and Prince Ivan Khovanskii, scion of a family with strong *strel'tsy* and hence *Raskol* connections. All were found guilty by the Prikaz and repented, except for Talitskii and his friend, an icon painter named Ivan Savin. Talitskii, Savin, and three priests in the group were condemned to death, the others to the whip, branding, and Siberia. Talitskii and Savin, unrepentant, were condemned to *kopchenie*—being smoked to death like bacon. In the course of this ordeal Talitskii gave way; he was taken down and confessed that all he had said and written was a lie. Hearing this, Savin, too, asked to be taken down and also confessed, meanwhile reproaching Talitskii for having lied to him and misled him. The record breaks off at this point, but, according to Old Believer traditon, both men earned the milder death at the stake. There is no evidence in his case that Talitskii, or anyone else involved, was an Old Believer.[107]

Vasilii Levin was of the very poor provincial service gentry. From the peasants on his small estate during his childhood he had heard talk of Antichrist, of the last days, and of Peter I as Antichrist (according to his testimony); two of the villagers had been burned at the stake in Moscow for belonging to the *Raskol*. In 1701, very unwillingly, Levin enrolled in the dragoons and became a captain by 1711. By 1715 he was determined to leave the military service, to flee Antichrist; but his request for retirement in order to enter a monastery was denied, as Peter had forbidden this kind of transfer. In 1719, pretending insanity and paralysis, Levin managed to get his release. By this time he had become friendly with the father confessor of Prince Menshikov himself, the priest Lebedka; the two men discovered that they thought alike—that all piety and orthodoxy were gone, that Peter was the Antichrist, the proof of which was that he had killed his own son.[108] Among other things, Levin heard while in St. Petersburg that ships had brought in branding irons from abroad and that only those who were willing to be branded would receive any bread, that Peter had drilled three companies of troops on the surface of the waters of a river, and that Peter had transformed water into blood. Most of Levin's informants were soldiers or corporals in the guard regiments. In 1721 Levin decided to go to an obscure monastery close to his home—Zhadovskaia Pustyn'—and there preach the existence of Antichrist. On December 6, 1721, Levin was attending mass in church; as the priest came forth with the cross to bless the parishioners, Levin shouted: "Listen, Orthodox Christians, listen! Soon there will be the end of the world! The Sovereign has collected the entire people of Moscow and will destroy it there." Pointing to his palm, he went on: "Right here, on this spot, the Tsar will brand them, and they will believe in him then." The end came for Levin in 1722 when, already a monk, he was preaching his repertoire to a country fair from the roof of a house. On his testimony—Levin implicated everybody—the inhabitants of an entire monastery were shipped in irons to Moscow. After five torture sessions Levin admitted that he had implicated some people, his family for instance, hoping that they would want to share his martyrdom; he stuck to everything else he said and declared that he would speak no more. He was condemned to death by torture, but when the execution began, he recanted, as did Talitskii, and was beheaded a week later.[109]

In 1733 Akinfii Sysoev was caught giving alms to Old Believers who had been arrested and were on their way to jail. When he was searched, a notebook in his handwriting, containing a great deal of cabalistic information, was found. According to his calculations (slightly outdated) there was to have been (and had been) great news and commotion in the world in 1731. Desolation and rebellion were to have come in 1732; the sun and moon would change places, portents would appear in the sky. In 1733 and 1734 all the world would recognize Christ again. In 1735–36 one quarter of the world would perish. In 1737 the false Christ would come, and then, in 1738–39, Christ himself would come to judge all men. Under torture Sysoev said that Peter was the first Beast of the Apocalypse and then for a time refused to say more despite all the skilled persuasion of the Secret Chancellery (successor of the Preobrazhenskii Prikaz). Finally, he asked for a copy of the Book of Revelation and read his exegesis to his curious and most peculiar audience: the seven heads of the Beast of the Apocalypse were Ivan the Terrible, his son Feodor, Tsar Michael, Tsar Alexis, Ivan V, Peter I, and Peter II.[110] Sysoev even had an explanation for the ten crowned horns on the seven heads: these were the ten oligarchs, *Vremenshchiki*, who tried to rule after Peter II by imposing a limited monarchy on the new empress, Anna. (One might argue that, for the so-called constitutional crisis of 1730 and the oligarchic constitution of the ten aristocrats and Petrine executives, apocalyptic politics provide as good an explanation as *Realpolitik*.) Sysoev thought that all the heretical Church reforms were introduced by Peter I, simultaneously with the laws on beards and foreign clothing. Further confirmation of Peter as the Beast of the Apocalypse was that the Beast had the feet of a bear and the mouth of a lion. An acute observation, this—for Peter was pigeon-toed, and his mouth was grim enough. The Empress Anna was identified easily by reading Revelation, Chapter 17, about the great whore sitting upon the waters. Sysoev died in prison, after three torture sessions, including one by fire.[111]

These are three cases among many,[112] but they are representative enough to convey some features of the apocalyptic atmosphere in early eighteenth-century Russia. One of the striking aspects of this atmosphere is the intermingling or identity of Old Believer and non-Old Believer ideology. Talitskii had no *Raskol* connections at all; Levin had known Old Believers in his childhood but took his vows in a monastery of the official Church; Sysoev gave alms to Old Believer prisoners, but except for the fact that his case is to be found in the *Raskol* section of the archives, there is no evidence that he was an Old Believer himself, and he denied having any questionable associations. Yet all three men expressed the pure *Raskol* political theology. And at least the first two had been able to express it to an astonishingly wide public, literally shouting it from the roof tops, for a long time with impunity. Only after years of active preaching were they denounced, and one must assume that their audience shared their views or sympathized with them.[113] (An interesting feature of these audiences, by the way, is the very great number of lower clergy—priests, monks—involved in such cases; the tradition of priestly participation in the schism was being carried on and indeed spread at a time when, with the abolition of the patriarchate and the establishment of the Holy Synod under a lay procurator, the Church had become a bureaucratic department of the government.)[114] The thought of these ideological rebels displayed a truly scholastic consistency; every event, every feature (even Peter's feet and mouth), every portent were fitted into the apocalyptic scheme and explained thereby. Hence the fanatic strength of conviction, the nonviolent but total opposition to the government, the acceptance, and even seeking, of martyrdom—all broken, if at all, only by unspeakable tortures.

To an enormous degree the apocalyptic vision, before 1725 and after, was focused on Peter I. But it would be incorrect to assume that Peter forced the Old Believers to a new conception, that his actions and policies, independent of his predecessors, evoked the image of Antichrist. The *strel'tsy*, the Cossacks, Talitskii, Levin, and many others whose cases fill the records of the Preobrazhenskii Prikaz thought of Peter as Antichrist *before* 1700, before Petrine policies and reforms could really be identified and rejected. Still, the world which the Old Believers tried to explain was dominated by him far more than by Nikon, Alexis, or anyone else because, as we shall see, he defined that world more bluntly and more violently than anyone else. There is at least one vivid iconographic testimony to this—the illuminated Apocalypse 156 of the Museum Collection in the State Historical Museum, done shortly after 1725.[115] In this case there is no need to speculate about the possible identifications. The illustration for the verse reading that Antichrist will be born of the tribe of Dan shows Antichrist with the face of Peter I, dressed in the uniform of the Preobrazhenskii Regiment (Figure 7). The baby Antichrist, sitting on the arm of his mother, Antichrist's wife, is a small double of his father.[116] Again, Antichrist supervising the building of the new temple in Jerusalem is Peter in his usual

FIGURE 7

FIGURE 8

uniform; except for one companion and the demons, the people in the miniature are dressed in traditional Russian clothes (Figure 8).[117] (There is a complete resemblance between this Peter-Antichrist and the Peter of the numerous secular paintings which show the Emperor, with outstretched arm, supervising the building of St. Petersburg.) Every one of the dozens of miniatures in this manuscript hammers away at the same point, that the world of Peter is the world of Antichrist: the demons are dressed in Petrine army uniforms; the woman sitting upon the waters is portrayed in the garb of a Russian empress of the early eighteenth century; the text describing the time of Antichrist as one of war and trouble is illustrated by a battle scene between Cossacks and Petrine demon-soldiers; the prophecy that the army of Antichrist would come and devastate the land is illumined by the Russian guards regiments, and so on.[118] Again there is the consistency of explanation, the daring (in view of the risk), and the profound conviction that Peter and everything Petrine embodied Antichrist, material and immediate.

If Peter was Antichrist (or even only the Beast of the Apocalypse, the eighth tsar-Antichrist of the Third Rome),[119] how did one know this, or, rather, how did one substantiate one's conviction within the closed circle of apocalyptic logic? Levin indicated some of the portents and some events, such as the execution of Tsarevich Alexis, and Sysoev anachronistically attributed the Nikonian reforms to Peter; but while we can hardly expect historical accuracy from the sources, it is worthwhile to fill in, in greater detail, the *Raskol* image of Peter. A virtually universal premise among the Old Believers and the discontented, a tribute to the strength of the theocratic ideal, was that Peter I was illegitimate.[120] Some expressed the theologically correct position that, inasmuch as Peter was born in 1672, after Alexis' apostasy, he was by definition not the legitimate and true tsar.[121] Most thought of him as a changeling, brought into the palace after the birth of a daughter to the wife of Alexis, or substituted for the real Peter during the latter's travels abroad; the man on the Russian throne was a non-Orthodox foreigner, a German. But whatever the variations on the theme, Peter was not a true tsar,[122] for the Antichrist could not be of true imperial birth.[123]

His name, too, gave him away. His original name was Augustus, according to one tradition, but he was then given the name of Peter, signifying "stone" to reveal the nature of his reign.[124] The name "Peter" had a higher rationale, according to Evfimii, for it was part of the tension Simon-Peter ~ Simon Magus, and hence Simon-Peter, in this case, was the proper name of Antichrist.[125] Peter himself named his new capital St. Petersburg, Evfimii pointed out, saying that he was as holy as St. Peter the Apostle.[126] His titles were even more revealing. In 1721 he usurped the title of the patriarchal office, which he himself had abolished, by calling himself *otets otechestva* (father of his country).[127] In the same year he all but openly declared himself by taking on the new title of *imperator*, which was a slight disguise; but if analyzed and spelled out as *inperator*, it revealed the number—666—which was the mark of Antichrist.[128] Thus, with Peter's two titles—*blagochestivyi gosudar'* (the pious sovereign) and *imperator*—he bore two horns, the horns of Antichrist.[129] Constantly empha-sizing the dualism of Peter—the proper and the terrible title, the imperial and the patriarchal title, the acting out of more than the one proper role—the Old Believers saw one of the chief symbols of the state, the two-headed eagle of the Russian coat of arms, as a reflection of these two horns and accused Peter of taking it from the satanic Pope of Rome.[130] Not all Old Believer sources at-tributed to Peter the two-headed eagle (adopted at the end of the fifteenth century by Ivan III), but in the general tradition it was a symbol of Antichrist,[131] and the Antichrist-Emperor was made to carry it together with the patriarchal staff (Figure 9).[132]

All these aspects of Peter-Antichrist illustrate the peculiarly dialectic nature of apocalyptic thought. The point about Antichrist was that he was a mirror image of Christ; hence, once the premise that he was present had been accepted, he was to be identified by his Christlike features. The same qualities which identi-fied the Most Gentle Tsar, the Christlike (Byzantine) Emperor, the saintly prince, the theocratic ruler in general, also, and for that very reason, identified the Antichrist, when the aim of political theology had been changed. This logic was applied to the issue of imperial anointment as well. Peter, it was asserted, had been anointed all over his body, "in the Jewish manner," and therefore was given the title which distinguished Antichrist—*pomazannik*, the anointed one.[133] The "Booklet about Antichrist" of 1707 pointed out that Peter, prince of this world, whose title was *obderzhatel' vsego mira* (possessor of the whole world) and who was the false Christ, was called Christ (*khristos*), and by whom? By the archbishop Stefan Iavorskii, who should have called him, correctly, "Antichrist."[134] Actual anointment with oil at the coronation was adopted only in the seventeenth century, at the coronation of Michael, and hence was something of an innovation;[135] and the perfectly correct appellation—the anointed one (*pomazannik* in Russian, *khristos* in Greek)—began to be used, interestingly enough, only with Peter.[136] There was room, therefore, for con-fusion and misunderstanding of terms. But Old Believer causality and method-ology remain quite clear: that Peter was Antichrist was not deduced from evidence but revealed as a premise, and the more Christomimetic Peter was, the more the premise was confirmed; and again, the same consistent utilization of every fact—anointment, Russian translation, Greek original word—for every fact was revealing for those who had eyes to see and ears to hear.[137] A fas-cinating and final illustration of this kind of reasoning: Peter, according to Old Believer tradition, instituted a governing Synod of the Russian Church made up of twelve prelates, so that he, presiding over it, would be the thirteenth, that is, Christ, thus again revealing his true nature as Antichrist. In other words, Peter was accused of doing something which every Christian ruler from Con-stantine the Great had done—imitating Christ—and the irony of this accusation is that the Old Believers had to tamper with facts in order to make this charge—the Synod of the Russian Church had only eleven members.[138]

Peter the Antichrist meant doom for the whole world and threatened the souls of all men. But this doom was also prefigured, over and over, in the daily

FIGURE 9

policy conducted by the ruler-Antichrist, which made life more and more intolerable. One aspect of this policy, of course, was the extraordinary brutality
Peter displayed.[139] In broader terms, Petrine policy was conveyed, rather
effectively, by an epithet applied to Peter—*tsar' voin*, the warrior tsar.[140] The
coming of Antichrist meant war and destruction, and therefore it was fitting
that Peter's whole reign was virtually one long war. Death and destruction as
features of the reign of Antichrist, however, are still a theological conception
fully justified by sacred texts. The Old Believers went a good bit further, into
the sphere of apocalyptic sociology. What did the reign of Antichrist mean,
concretely, to those living under his rule? The answer was given by Satan or
Antichrist himself, in response to an imaginary plea for justice: "Your passport,

please, your soul tax for this year, and any other back taxes [first], inasmuch as you live on my land."[141] In this instance the theological language becomes quite transparent. Certainly the Old Believers took advantage of the term *podushnaia podat'* (soul tax), with all its obvious levels of meaning; and the passport, a consequence of the census which the new individualized tax required but which carried all the implications of the Augustan census, was also pregnant with apocalyptic meaning.[142] (This is what Levin was trying to convey with his image of the brand of Antichrist.) But under all this was the simple fact that one had to pay more money and that the government knew who one was and could collect more efficiently.

The apocalyptic word-play and the reality behind it allowed the radical Evfimii to construct a striking image of apocalyptic society and state. Before the census, this display of state control, men were free, he argued; now counted —stamped with the seal of Antichrist—they belonged to Antichrist. The social evil of Peter-Antichrist was that he divided men, introducing the idea of *svoe*, "one's own"—the idea of property—which was the ultimate evil. Peter, in fact, introduced three evil passions among men: avarice, self-love, and voluptuousness.[143] That is to say, Peter created a social order or society such as we know, which was so unacceptable to Evfimii that he saw in it the origin of all social evils. Hence to his earlier description of Antichrist as having an icon (image) and a body, he added a third component: Antichrist was made up of image, body, and corpses; the government was the image or visage, spiritual authority was the body of Antichrist, and the people were the corpses.[144]

Though all such arguments were based, to some degree, on the Revelation of St. John, the connection was rather tenuous. Political theology, in effect, allowed, as always, a reversal of causality—it was not the Antichrist of Revelation who determined the features of Peter I, but Peter I who determined the features and behavior of Antichrist. And Peter contributed to at least one rather curious aspect of Antichrist. From the beginning, as we have seen, one of the features of Antichrist for the Old Believers was that he united in himself both spiritual and temporal authority. Lazar', the companion of Avvakum, had written that Antichrist reigned in Rome because "the spiritual man, the pope, has usurped imperial divine power."[145] The formulation is a bit strange, yet recognizable; "spiritual" rather than "ecclesiastical" or "clerical" could hardly be accidental and, repeated time and again, seems designed to evoke a particular association.[146] The most obvious is the famous Pauline formula—the spiritual man judges all and is judged by none—designed to describe the free man under God, and utilized historically to buttress papal claims to universal judicial supremacy. It is most likely that, from Nikon's claims for the supremacy of the ecclesiastical over the temporal, the Old Believers knew about the papal use of the formula, but their translation of St. Paul involved much more than a traditional condemnation of the Roman papacy: The Antichrist, not the spiritual man, "subjects all [men] to his judgment but will not himself be subject to the judgment of any man" (*vsekh sudy svoemu podverzhet, a sam nikomu podsudnym byt' ne pokhoshchet*).[147] I am not able to suggest any clues to either the origins or the implications of this extraordinary conception. Perhaps, with all the associations of the Last Judgment, at which Christ is the Judge Ordinary of all men, it relates to the final and ultimate accusation raised by the Old Believers against Peter the Great. The basic issue, argued their "Petition, or History of Peter the Great," was that Peter made himself god; he was the god on earth (*zemnoi bog*), the mirror image and total antithesis of the God in Heaven.[148]

So far we have dealt, in some detail, with the very complex, yet steady reaction by the Old Believers to the many and also complex changes, most of them non-religious, that took place in Russian society and the state during the first decades of the *Raskol*. These details have been arranged in the rather procrustean, overarching scheme of political theology with its climactic conception of the Russian ruler as Antichrist and god on earth. Rather than attempt to trace more closely the various social and political changes and relate them to the details of Old Believer thought, I would like to suggest an equally overarching conception which sums up these many changes and describes them in the language of political theology.

The obvious focus for these issues of political theologies is the Petrine paradox. Whatever the Old Believers were opposing was, clearly, concentrated in Peter I, expressed by Peter I, hated in Peter I. Yet one of Peter's early laws (1702) proclaimed the principle of religious toleration as the law of the Russian state.[149] Admittedly, religious tolerance was not practiced widely, and there were legal limitations to the profession of Old Belief: Old Believers could live openly and practice their faith by registering as Old Believers and paying double taxes;[150] they had no right to preach their doctrines;[151] they could not be elected or appointed to any public office.[152] Still, in comparison with the law of 1684, Peter's religious legislation was truly enlightened, as the leader of the Vyg community, Andrei Denisov, emphasized in arguing that one should pray for Peter. But then we must repeat the question, why was Peter seen as the enemy above all others, as god on earth? The reign of Peter I was also the time of the worst persecutions, of horrible and endless torture and investigation. And Peter, who passed laws on religious tolerance, pointed up this paradox in a law in which he fulminated against "treasonable and *Raskol* inventions" (*vorovskie i raskol'nich'i vymyshleniia*), equating treason and Old Belief in heinousness.[153]

The contradiction is compounded if we consider Peter's personal religiosity, significant enough in the context of absolutism. One need only think of the All Holy Drunken Council (*Vsesviateishii Pianyi Sobor*), established by Peter and headed by the Prince-Pope, Nikita Zotov, personal servant and court jester of Peter. At the frequent meetings of this "Council," which included every prominent man in the government, all conceivable and inconceivable blasphemies were performed; and though Peter himself held only the rank of deacon, he was obviously the leader in them.[154] Yet Peter's views on religion were not limited to his drunken mock council. Golikov, in his *Anecdotes*, tells us what happened when Peter heard that the historian and statesman V. N. Tatishchev was engaging in free-thinking, castigating greedy and ignorant clergy and superstition in general. The Tsar called out to him at a court assembly: "'How dare you weaken a string which forms the harmony of the whole tone? And, on top of this, you did not speak with sufficient respect about some of the sacred writings . . . I will teach you . . .' And the Emperor hit Tatishchev with his cane: 'Don't tempt believing souls . . . don't introduce free-thinking, which is fatal to good order; I did not train you and teach you so that you should end up an enemy to society and to the Tsar!'"[155]

The paradox, on the face of it, remains unresolved. Religious tolerance and the double tax, appeals against suicide and the equating of the *Raskol* with treason, blasphemy and the conception that religion was the weft of the social fabric—what in all this was the unifying principle for Peter, and what was it for the Old Believers, convinced that Peter was Antichrist? The answer clearly lies not in the religious sphere but in the nature of the Petrine state and society—a state and society which can be characterized, sketchily and only symbolically, by some of Peter's laws (not necessarily representative of the whole mass of Petrine legislation but suggestive of the essence of the Petrine state): In 1698 Peter ordered all members of the ruling class—aristocracy, office holders (*d'iaki*), service gentry—to shave off their beards.[156] A law of 1700 ordered the same people, as well as all the registered townspeople—merchants, artisans—to wear "Hungarian"-style clothes, with precise specifications provided by the government.[157] A law of 1714 forbade the sale of Russian-style clothes and boots on pain of the whip and hard labor in Siberia.[158] A law of 1715 pointed out that Russian boots were soled with nails and metal strips; the punishment for selling these items was hard labor in Siberia.[159] Another law of 1715 imposed fines for not confessing and attending communion at least once a year.[160] The Ecclesiastical Code (*Dukhovnyi Reglament*) of 1721 required reports from parish priests on those who did not confess yearly.[161] A law of 1722 transferred to lay courts cases of nonperformance of "Christian duties," including confession and communion.[162] The law of July 3, 1722, set out the particular holidays on which church attendance was obligatory (they were about evenly divided between Christian and imperial holidays).[163] The law of May 17, 1722, required priests to report to the authorities secrets heard at confession, if they involved either crimes planned for the future or crimes for which the confessant did not repent.[164] A law of 1717 forbade the writing of letters behind closed doors (except for teachers in church schools) and punished those who did not report such secret letter-writing as offenders against His Majesty's honor, even though "they did not know what was being written, but only that someone was writing behind locked doors."[165]

The law of Alexis on political crime, in 1649, was a hint; proclaimed half a century later, these all-embracing laws reveal the essence of the absolutist secular state. The material foundations of such a state cannot be dealt with here; suffice it to say that secular absolutism means mobilization of the resources of a society on a larger scale than previously, the reordering of the social structure (for example, the gentry) to achieve this mobilization, the control of society for the purposes of efficient exploitation and of eliminating the opposition created by this mobilization and this social restructuring, and, finally, the exercise of far greater power than before because the centralized state possessed far more power than it had ever had. The ideology built on such foundations was based on two related conceptions: the state as a perfectly self-sufficient, self-contained entity, and the state as the measure of all things. Everything necessary for man's existence was to be found within the state, and, at the same time, reasons of state, the interests of the state, were the ultimate standard for judging all actions and motives. The ruler of the secular absolutist state filled with his own person the full ideological gamut from "the First Servant of the State" to "l'Etat c'est moi," serving an abstraction which only he had the right to define.

These are all certainly secular conceptions; yet it is possible to revert to the language of the Old Believers and translate them, without much difficulty, into theological terms. Theologically, secular absolutism meant the translation of the heaven above to the state on earth. Formerly the existence of the state was justified by its role within the economy of salvation; the purpose of life and thus of political society lay outside of life and political society, and the state existed in order to help men achieve salvation above. The secular state had to justify its existence by offering men salvation—the good life—here on earth, within its own boundaries, for it acknowledged nothing of independent value beyond or above these boundaries. Hence, the multiple role of the ruler, which so disturbed the Old Believers, for the old dichotomy of Christ's functions—king and priest, ruling men and saving men—became meaningless when salvation was achieved through ruling. And hence the all-embracing nature of the claims of secular absolutism (including prohibition of letter-writing behind locked doors)—now all of men's actions and thoughts involved salvation, for the old distinctions between spirit and body, God and Caesar, were no longer relevant; it was the state, or ruler, who alone dispensed salvation.

The real nature of the crime of the *Raskol* now becomes evident. As religious eccentrics the Old Believers could be tolerated (though taken advantage of and exploited) as long as they registered and paid the taxes—in other words, belonged. But their real and ultimate crime was exactly their refusal to register, to pay taxes, to participate, and hence to accept the society of Antichrist. This is what Levin meant when he warned his audience that by accepting the "brand of Antichrist"—census, registration, participation—they would "*believe* in him." And this is why there was the mad intensity of persecution, without any legislation to justify it in fact, for the crime of rejecting the state is the ultimate crime and yet by its very nature it eludes laws designed to define the state. The Old Believers were "outside," denying the reality of the new salvation, and this the state could not forgive.[166]

Levin's suggestive phrase should be taken seriously. It signified that the new theology was the rationalization of a new religion—the religion of the secular state. The reforms of absolutism were many, varied, and overwhelmingly secular in nature. Yet one can illustrate their religious overtones by one example: The issues of beards (or shaving) and of "foreign" style clothes were discussed and debated in Muscovite Russia from the early years of the sixteenth century.[167]

They were the subject of ecclesiastical injunctions, prescriptions, and insistence, but until Peter I they were not the subject of legislation. What do the Petrine laws on clothes, beards, habits, and customs mean? They are, theologically, the definitions of the new priesthood required by the new religion; whereas canon laws had previously prescribed priestly and episcopal raiments in minute detail, departure from which implied heresy, now such details prescribed the appearance of clerks, service gentry, aristocracy, and particularly the new *ecclesia armata*, the army.[168]

Iconographic evidence on this new priesthood and its symbol, the Emperor, is overwhelming in quantity, but the illustrations provided by the opposite side, the Old Believers, are more dramatic and also indicate how great was *Raskol* awareness of the issue. One drawing held by the Leningrad Museum of the History of Religion and Atheism—unfortunately, not of sufficient definition to reproduce here—depicts the Nikonian church. The altar is surrounded by Nikonian symbols—the "Latin" four-pointed cross, the "new" spelling of the name of Jesus (*Iisus*), the episcopal staff; and, standing to the right of the altar, is a new priest—booted, sworded, clean-shaven—an officer of a guards regiment.[169]

Figures 10–12 are from a manuscript entitled "On the Two-Fingered Sign of the Cross" (*O Dvoeperstii*). The manuscript, of the late nineteenth or even early twentieth century, is aesthetically crude and yet powerful in its total commitment to the now traditional and rigid identification of the evil in this world. Figure 10 illustrates the apocalyptic text of martyrs about to be executed by the evil tsar who forbids them to worship Christ, and the tsar is a rather good portrait of Alexander II.[170] In Figure 11, overlooked by the sun of the Apocalypse, the prophet Ezekiel is about to die again at the hands of the servant of Antichrist, dressed in the uniform of a general serving as aide (*general-ad'utant*) to Alexander II and hence having the right to the initial of the Emperor on his epaulets.[171] Figure 12 illustrates the two churches, of Christ and of Antichrist, with the latter borne on the shoulders of his priests, carefully arrayed in the uniform of nineteenth-century Russian gendarmes; one of them carries the big gendarme sword, the *palash*, in his right hand.[172]

Finally, there are the illustrations of an apocalypse of the nineteenth century, done in an aesthetic genre which suggests a cartoon series entitled either "The Adventures of St. John" or "The Adventures of Antichrist." One of the miniatures shows the dramatic moment when, with the breaking of the second seal, the red horseman of the Apocalypse rides forth—the horseman who will destroy peace and law on earth and spread destruction with his sword (Figure 13).[173] What we see as the destroyer of peace and order is a gendarme, the embodiment of imperial law and order, waving his large sword, shooting off a revolver (the smoke rings indicate this), and smoking a big cigar.[174]

In the eyes of the Old Believers the new priesthood served Antichrist, and within the secular state it served the new god, the ruler, whether it was the Emperor Peter I, who was also Petr Alekseevich, most pious and gentle tsar,[175] or the Empress Anna (daughter of Ivan V but duchess of Courland and a woman),

FIGURE 10

**FIGURE 11**

**FIGURE 12**

who was incongruous as a theocratic tsar. This does not mean that the old religion of the state and the old theocratic imagery were abandoned. The new religion was, as usual, a syncretism of old political theologies, and the sermons of the eighteenth century are filled with images of the Emperor as Christ, as David, as Moses, as Constantine, [176] as well as the newly added images of the ruler as Hercules, Apollo, Astraea, and Minerva.[177] Theologically, one can argue that the secular absolute ruler meant in general the shift from the ruler as the image of Christ to the ruler as the image of God the Father. This made sense, for the Christomimesis of the theocratic ruler involved a model and a standard which were above the ruler and outside his realm; or, to put it in another way, the ruler who judged all was judged by at least one, Christ. To be God the Father was to be the lawgiver, the Creator, and this was the constant theme in the panegyrics to Peter I.[178] "Our father, Peter the Great! You have led us from nonexistence to existence.... The drops of sweat of your labors were our aromatic myrrh," wrote P. N. Krekshin, and though the sweat imagery was borrowed from the Christlike Byzantine emperors, it was applied to the labor of creation.[179]

**FIGURE 13**

To create from nothing, denying the past, being the fatherless Peter I, the Great, rather than the Tsar Petr Alekseevich, son of Alexis, was certainly a mark of divinity. For those who lived within the self-contained universe created by the secular ruler, he was the god, and this is what the priests of Peter, his officers and servants, called him—*zemnoi bog*, the god on earth.[180] The Old Believers knew the famous verse of Lomonosov, *On bog tvoi, bog tvoi/ O Rossiia . . .* (He is your god, your god/ O Russia . . .), and threw it back into the faces of the new priests: "You call him the God of Russia!"[181] If here the Old Believers and the new religion seem to have shared a common political theology, it is only because the new religion continued to use the old theological language, although the meaning of the terms and the context had changed; and in all their writings the Old Believers showed their awareness of this fact and their bitter outrage over it.

Why the outrage? Again, the answer can be given in theological terms. The Old Believers were of the lower classes and represented the ideology and aspirations of the Russian masses. The new dispensation, the good life here on earth, offered them nothing; it was a caricature of the old salvation. Yet, as I have tried to show, even the old dispensation, socially at least, no longer worked, for in the seventeenth century men increasingly doubted the efficacy of theocracy. So, for the Old Believers, ever growing in numbers, there was no way out. Rejecting the new salvation which offered them no salvation, they lived in a state of permanent apocalypse.

Obviously these forms of the secular absolutist state and the Old Believer reaction to it were, in many ways, peculiarly Russian; uniquely so in the inability of the secular state to provide salvation for the great masses and hence in the permanence and ideological violence of the reaction, symbolized by the *Raskol*. Yet some Russian aspects of the transition from the theocratic central-ized state to the secular absolutist state seem to carry outside the Russian bor-ders. It is surely not pure coincidence that the Spanish Inquisition reached its heights not during the Middle Ages but during the secularization of the Spanish state in the seventeenth century; that the rigid laws of Religious Conformity were imposed in England, in the seventeenth century, by a secular-minded government; that the German Reformation, completed politically by the Thirty Years' War, produced the curious theological principle *Cuius regio, eius religio;* and that the revocation of the Edict of Nantes took place at the end of the seven-teenth century under Louis XIV, whose secular concern was expressed in the slogan engraved on some of his medallions, again expressing a curious theology: *Un roi, une foie, une loi.*

If this is so, wherever the secular state was being constructed, sympathy might well be found for the cry of the Old Believers which symbolized their real protest: All power is Antichrist because *u nei vsia chelovetsy v pokorstve sostoiatsa* (all men are in subservience to it).[182]

# NOTES

1. *Raskol* means schism. Until 1905 the official name for all the sectarians who did not acknowledge the official church was *raskol'niki* (schismatics). The term *staroobriadsty* (Old Ritualists or Old Believers) was used only by the liberals. After 1905 the official, legal appellation, too, became *Staroobriadsty*. In this paper, to avoid monotonous repetition, I use the terms *Raskol*, "schism," and "Old Belief" interchangeably.

2. They were sometimes obtained through underground channels and printed abroad. See the collection put out by V. Kel'siev, *Sbornik Pravitel'stvennykh Svedenii o Raskol'nikakh* (4 vols.; London, 1860–62). Even some of the laws concerning the Old Believers were, in effect, secret and cannot be found in the *Polnoe Sobranie Zakonov* (hereafter referred to as *PSZ*); see *Sobranie Postanovlenii po chasti raskola*, printed by the Ministry of Internal Affairs (St. Petersburg, 1875), editorial note. See also F. Sakharov, *Literatura, istoriia i oblicheniia russkogo raskola* (3 vols.; Tambov, 1887–1900), *passim*.

3. See the numerous works of N. Subbotin, N. Nil'skii, V. Belolikov, and E. V. Barsov, particularly their studies in *Khristianskoe chtenie, Tserkovnyi vestnik, Pravoslavnoe obozrenie, Trudy Imperatorskoi Kievskoi dukhovnoi akademii*, and *Bratskoe slovo*.

4. See, for example, the basic collection by N. Subbotin, *Materialy dlia istorii raskola za pervoe vremia ego sushchestvovaniia* (9 vols.; Moscow, 1874–90), hereafter cited as Subbotin; E. V. Barsov, *Novye materialy dlia istorii staroobriadchestva, XVII–XVIII vv.* (Moscow, 1890) and his "Akty otnosiashchiesia k istorii raskola v XVIII stoletii," *Chteniia v Obshchestve istorii i drevnostei rossiiskikh*, No. 2, 1889, pp. 1–87; and the sources published in *Bratskoe slovo* (edited by Subbotin) in 1884, 1888, 1890, and 1891.

5. A prime example of this dilemma was the Old Believer position on the priesthood. Not wishing any change, let alone reform, the Old Believers found themselves in an impossible situation: as the first generation of *Raskol* priests died off and no bishop joined the schism, where were they to get new priests? If from the Nikonian church, then the whole schism would be rendered meaningless. And if they did without any priests, then they had either to give up all the sacraments or end up (as many did) with the Protestant logic of each man his own priest.

6. See A. Shchapov, *Russkii raskol staroobriadchestva* (Kazan, 1859) and *Zemstvo i raskol* (St. Petersburg, 1862); and the many works of A. S. Prugavin, V. V. Andreev, V. G. Druzhinin, and I. Iuzov (I. I. Kablits).

7. Shchapov, *Zemstvo i raskol*, pp. 59 ff.

8. Malyshev began his hunt for Old Believer documents some thirty years ago. Since 1947 every volume of the *Trudy Otdela Drevnerusskoi literatury* has contained his articles and his manuscript discoveries. See, for example, his "Dva neizvestnykh pis'ma protopopa Avvakuma," *TODRL*, Vol. XIV (1958); "Tri neizvestnykh sochineniia protopopa Avvakuma i novye dokumenty o nem," *Doklady i soobshcheniia Filologicheskogo instituta Leningradskogo gosudarstvennogo universiteta*, Vol. III (1951). The manuscript collection of the Institute of Russian Literature (Pushkinskii Dom), which he heads, is unique. See also his *Ust'-Tsilemskie rukopisnye sborniki XVI–XX vv.* (Syktyvkar, 1960).

9. See, for example, L. E. Ankudinova, *Sotsial'no-politicheskaia sushchnost' religiozno-obshchestvennogo dvizheniia v russkom gosudarstve tret'ei chetverti XVII veka* (unpublished dissertation, Leningrad, 1951) and "Sotsial'nyi sostav pervykh raskol'nikov," *Vestnik Leningradskogo universiteta, Seriia istorii, iazyka i literatury*, Vol. III, No. 14 (1956); A. I. Klibanov, "K kharakteristike novykh iavlenii v russkoi obshchestvennoi mysli vtoroi poloviny XVII—nachala XVIII vv.," *Istoriia SSSR*, No. 6, 1963; A. N. Robinson, "Avvakum i Epifanii (K istorii obshcheniia dvukh pisatelei)" *TODRL*, Vol. XV (1958), "Tvorchestvo Avvakuma i obshchestvennye dvizheniia v kontse XVII veka," *ibid.*, Vol. XVIII (1962), and *Zhizneopisaniia Avvakuma i Epifaniia* (Moscow, 1963); and N. S. Sarafanova, "Ideia ravenstva liudei v sochineniiakh protopopa Avvakuma," *TODRL*, Vol. XIV (1958).

10. The schismatics "clung persistently to the old ways" according to Jesse D. Clarkson, *A History of Russia* (New York, 1961), p. 157. The problem was in the ignorance and illiteracy of the "tradition-bound Muscovite clergy," states Herbert J. Ellison in his *History of Russia* (New York, 1964), pp. 77, 79. "To many of the Russian Orthodox the slightest alteration in

religious practices . . . appeared to be the work of the devil" (Sidney Harcave, *Russia: A History* [3d ed.; New York, 1956], pp. 39–40). "Attention to the form rather than the substance of Christianity, which had long characterized Russian Orthodoxy, brought stubborn support for the strange practices even when they were shown to be without scholarly foundation" (Michael C. Wren, *The Course of Russian History* [New York, 1958], p. 237). "First and foremost was Muscovy's traditional attachment to external observances . . . no question of principle or dogma was involved" (Michael T. Florinsky, *Russia: A Short History* [New York, 1964], p. 150). "Over a long period of time, errors in translation from the Greek and other mistakes had crept into some Muscovite religious texts and rituals . . . But in the face of general ignorance, inertia, and opposition little was done until Nikon became patriarch" (Nicholas V. Riasanovsky, *A History of Russia* [New York, 1963], p. 219; see also pp. 220 ff.). The only accurate and also detailed account is by Serge A. Zenkovsky, "The Russian Church Schism: Its Background and Repercussions," *The Russian Review*, Vol. XVI, No. 4 (1957). His interpretation follows those of pre-Soviet historians such as Kapterev and Mel'gunov.

11. On this whole issue, on the symbolism of the two and the three, and on the fact that, in the course of Christian history, the number of fingers used has ranged from one to all five, see, for example, P. S. Smirnov, *O perstoslozhenii* (St. Petersburg, 1904).

12. Florinsky, p. 154.

13. We have no statistics for the Old Believers until 1852, when a secret government expedition came to the conclusion that the official figures represented about one tenth the real number. Subsequently, both the government and the liberal scholars agreed on the figure of about 20 percent. See the government estimates made by the expedition of 1852, by Nadezhdin, and by Liprandi in Kel'siev; and, for an example of liberal calculations, I. Iuzov (I. I. Kablits), *Russkie dissidenty, starovery i dukhovnye khristiane* (St. Petersburg, 1881), Chap. 3. More convincing than all the statistics is the fact that, in his rebellion, Pugachev offered the peasants their "old faith" again, and, as far as we know, none of the great mass that he reached turned him down.

14. Partly, of course, because the Old Believers fled to the peripheries but also because their propaganda was particularly successful in those areas.

15. Except for the times of Catherine II and Alexander I; see *Sbornik Postanovlenii po chasti raskola* for the periods of those reigns. In general, legislation on the *Raskol* can serve as a touchstone for the evolution of government policy in Russia as a whole.

16. The civil wars of the Time of Troubles, the peasant unrest in the 1630s, the town rebellions in the 1640s and 1650s, the Cossack uprisings in the 1660s and 1670s (which usually involved the peasants), the *strel'tsy fronde* in the 1680s and 1690s. The *strel'tsy* were the infantry regiments created by Ivan the Terrible and armed with muskets.

17. As was the case in the religious conflicts of the sixteenth and seventeenth centuries in western Europe. On this problem see the very interesting suggestions of Ia. S. Lur'e, "K izucheniiu klassovogo kharaktera drevnerusskoi literatury," *TODRL*, XX (1964), 100–120.

18. See note 5 above. For example, opposing Nikonian reforms, the Old Believers also had to oppose the Nikonian clergy. This could only be done by denying the validity of clerical ordination performed by a heretical church. But then, if there were no priests, there could be no valid sacrament; and if no sacraments, then what about communion, absolution, or marriage in a theological or even social sense? Once every man became his own priest, there was no limit to how far one could go, and the *Raskol* suffered a constant splintering off of small and large sects pushed ever further by the logic of religious language.

19. D. S. Likhachev, *Kul'tura Rusi vremeni Andreia Rubleva i Epifaniia Premudrogo* (Moscow and Leningrad, 1962), pp. 48 ff.

20. *Polnoe sobranie russkikh letopisei* (St. Petersburg, 1834—), VI, 221 ff.

21. *Stoglav*, ed. D. E. Kozhanchikov (St. Petersburg, 1863), *passim*. See also A. A. Zimin, *Reformy Ivana Groznogo* (Moscow, 1960), pp. 375 ff.

22. N. F. Kapterev, *Patriarkh Nikon i ego protivniki* (2nd ed.; Sergeiev Posad, 1913 [first published in 1887]); hereafter cited as *Nikon i protivniki*.

23. *PSZ*, Vol. I, "Ulozhenie," Chap. 13; see also M. Arkhangel'skii, *O sobornom Ulozhenii v otnoshenii k pravoslavnoi tserkvi* (St. Petersburg, 1881). The Code also registered legislation which was clearly formulated at the council of 1666–67, by which parish priests, formerly chosen by their parishioners, were henceforth appointed by the bishops, under whose total control they passed.

24. See N. F. Kapterev, *Patriarkh Nikon i Tsar Aleksei Mikhailovich* (Sergeiev Posad, 1909) I, 71 ff.; hereafter cited as *Nikon i Aleksei*.

25. See Kapterev, *Nikon i protivniki*, pp. 105 ff. The makeup of the Zealots reflected the traditional split in the Eastern Church, between the white clergy—priests required to marry—and the black, who were monks. Again traditionally, only monks could become bishops and hence control both the monastic and the episcopal hierarchy.

26. The issue was *edinoglasie* (single voice), i.e., the conduct of the service with each litany recited separately, in sequence, versus *mnogoglasie* (many voices), an arrangement in which, to save time, several deacons would recite a number of litanies and psalms simultaneously while standing in different parts of the church. On this problem and its history, including the *Stoglav* legislation concerning it, see Kapterev, *Nikon i protivniki*, pp. 133 ff.

27. *Ibid.* Some of these priests, beginning with Avvakum himself, were such fiery preachers that they had to flee to Moscow from infuriated provincial parishioners whose sins they castigated.

28. See the formulation of P. Pascal, *Avvakum et les débuts du raskol* (Paris, 1938), pp. xvii ff.; he, in effect, rejects both the Orthodox and the liberal interpretations and suggests that the controversy originated from a clash between two conceptions of Christianity, spiritualized and secularized, that existed in Russia.

29. For a highly detailed account see Kapterev, *Nikon i Aleksei*, I, 106 ff.

30. Nikon failed to get any active support from Constantinople but managed to get the official adherence of Patriarch Macarios of Antioch, who was in Moscow in 1655. See the account of Macarios' son, Paul of Aleppo, in *Patrologia orientalis*, Vol. XXII, Part 1; Vol. XXIV, Part 4. The Russian translation, "Puteshestvie Antiokhskago patriarkha Makariia v Rossiiu," was published by G. Murkos in *Chteniia*, No. 4, 1896; No. 4, 1897; and No. 4, 1898.

31. This lack of interest continued during all the long years after his abdication, until his death two decades later.

32. To avoid confusion I call the council of Russian bishops which opened in April 1666 the "Church Council of 1666"; and the council presided over by the Eastern patriarchs, which opened in December 1666, the "Patriarchal Council of 1666–67." Kapterev's argument, in *Nikon i Aleksei*, II, 360 ff., was that the decisions of the second of these councils were the result of the cleverness of the Greeks—filled as they were with contempt for the Russians—in bringing pressure on the council to condemn all things Russian. But the argument does not hold, for Kapterev himself showed how totally dependent the Greek prelates were (particularly while in Russia) on the Russian government and how careful they were to anticipate every wish of Tsar Alexis (and then impose it on the Russian prelates).

33. See Pascal (p. 545, note 158), who points out correctly that we have no definitive evidence for the burning. The details of the execution are known to us only via Old Believer tradition.

34. This is, of course, an exaggeration; a number of priests shared the views of the prisoners, though they behaved with more circumspection. And then there was the active and fanatic adherence of the famous Sokovnin sisters—Feodos'ia, married to the boyar Morozov, and the younger Evdokiia, married to Prince Urusov. Both sisters were eventually imprisoned for their continued participation in the schism. See Pascal, esp. pp. 34 ff.

35. Nearly all their writings are published in Subbotin; Barsov, *Novye materialy*; and Ia. L. Barskov, *Pamiatniki istorii staroobriadchestva XVII veka* (St. Petersburg, 1907; "Russkaia Istoricheskaia Biblioteka," Vol. XXXIX).

36. Subbotin, IV, 90 ff.; see also Kapterev, *Nikon i Aleksei*, I, 451 ff.

37. Subbotin, III, 264.

38. I.e., plans for hegemony amongst the South Slavs and in Constantinople. Robinson, *Zhizneopisaniia*, adheres to this view but gives no reasons for doing so; he gives the literature on this problem on p. 17, note 58.

39. See Kapterev, *Nikon i Aleksei*, I, 151 ff.

40. Subbotin, II, 220 ff.

41. See Avvakum's reminders, in all his letters to Tsar Alexis, of the latter's "pious ancestors." For a highly dramatic and very late illustration of this tension, see the statement of Ivan Ermakov during his interrogation in 1855: "The civil laws are created not by the tsar but by the authorities (*nachal'stvom*) . . . Therefore I find these laws false and illegal, and I recognize [only] the *Stoglav* law of Ivan Grozny" (Kel'siev, I, 221). Ermakov rejected not only ecclesiastical but all laws passed after Ivan IV.

42. See Subbotin, III, 247, esp. 158–59; V, 227 (Avvakum). It is interesting that in one of these references to Moscow the Third Rome (Subbotin, VII, 86–87) the monk Filofei of Pskov

who first enunciated the doctrine, is called Saint Filofei; see Kapterev, *Nikon i protivniki*, 153–54, note 1.

43. Kapterev, *Nikon i Aleksei*, II, esp. 216 ff. Nikon's statements and opinions were published in *Zapiski Otdeleniia russkoi i slavianskoi arkheologii Russkogo arkheologicheskogo obshchestva*, Vol. II (1861); hereafter cited as *ZRAO*.

44. See Kapterev, *Nikon i Aleksei*, II, 465 ff.; in addition, Metropolitan Paisios Ligarid of Gaza, so instrumental in pushing through the Tsar's objectives, had actually been deprived of his episcopal status.

45. For the writings of Filofei, see V. Malinin, *Starets Eleasarova monastyria Filofei i ego poslaniia* (Kiev, 1901), Appendix.

46. For details, see my *Tsar and People* (New Haven, 1961), pp. 44 ff.

47. See *ibid.* for the references to the impressions of Paul of Aleppo; see also I. E. Zabelin, *Domashnii byt russkikh tsarei v XVI i XVII stoletiakh* (Moscow, 1872), for a most detailed description of the daily life of the Russian tsars.

48. *PSZ*, Vol. I, "Ulozhenie," Chap. 2.

49. See N. B. Golikova, "Organy politicheskogo syska i ikh razvitie v XVII–XVIII vv.," in *Absoliutizm v Rossii (XVII–XVIII vv.)* (Moscow, 1964), pp. 244 ff.

50. For the medieval theological origins of these terms in the West, see E. H. Kantorowicz, "Mysteries of State: An Absolutist Concept and Its Late Mediaeval Origins," *Harvard Theological Review*, XLVIII (1955), 65–91.

51. See, for example, Ia. L. Barskov, *Pamiatniki istorii staroobriadchestva XVII veka*, cols. 771–85, where the point is that though the spirit of Antichrist is present, he himself has not yet come.

52. See, for example, Pascal, p. 209, note 66; P. S. Smirnov, *Vnutrennie voprosy v raskole v XVII veke* (St. Petersburg, 1898), pp. 16 ff.

53. There were few attacks on Nikon after his abdication, and the emphasis shifted to the Tsar. For numerous expressions of this, see Pascal, *passim.*

54. See Smirnov, *Vnutrennie voprosy*, pp. 31 ff. Antichrist, like angels—or Moses—had the two horns of divinity. See Avvakum on this in Subbotin, IV, esp. 230.

55. Biblioteka Akademii nauk, Leningrad (BAN), ms 33–5–10, p. 151$^r$.

56. This identification was suggested by V. I. Sreznevskii, in Sreznevskii and F. I. Pokrovskii, *Opisanie Rukopisnogo Otdela Biblioteki Imperatorskoi Akademii Nauk* (St. Petersburg, 1910), I, 54.

57. The portraits are from the *Tituliarnik* of 1672, ordered by Alexis, containing the images of all the Russian rulers, as reproduced in *Portrety, gerby i pechati Bol'shoi Gosudarstvennoi Knigi 1672 goda* (St. Petersburg, 1903), plates 32 and 31 respectively. The Russian tsars in general were portrayed sufficiently alike (compare the portraits of Ivan IV and Vasilii Shuiskii), except for the moustache of Michael with its upward sweep (which leads me to suggest Michael as the prototype for the Antichrist) that a mistake would be natural. And by the early eighteenth century Old Believers would not have cared enough to distinguish between the two Romanov tsars.

58. Publichnaia Biblioteka imeni Saltykova-Shchedrina (PB), Leningrad, ms. Q.I. 1076, p. 66$^{ob}$.

59. Unnumbered portrait from the collection of the Muzei Istorii Religii i Ateizma (MIRA), Leningrad.

60. See S. A. Belokurov, *Arsenii Sukhanov* (Moscow, 1891).

61. Institut Russkoi Literatury (IRLI) (Pushkinskii Dom), Leningrad, ms 625 of the Peretts ollection, pp. 26$^v$–27$^{ob}$.

62. Ia. L. Barskov, *Pamiatniki pervykh let russkogo staroobriadchestva* (St. Petersburg, 1912), p. 333.

63. See, for example, Pascal, p. 250.

64. These calculations can be found in virtually every one of the Old Believer apocalyptic lracts, which number in the thousands. One theorem holds that Antichrist was to lie bound for the first 1000 years; released, he then obviously waited for his number, 666, to come up. The other theorem—more historical—is that the year 1000 marked the first appearance of the beast, with the fall of Rome from orthodoxy (the reference is clearly to the split between the Eastern and Roman churches—1054). Another 600 years pass before his second appearance (the Union of Brest, 1591), and then 66 years before his final appearance. On this last step, there are variations, with the third appearance coming 60 years after the second, or in 1660,

marked by the beginning of heresy, famine, and unrest; and then, 6 years later, the final coming. The variation provides a nice symmetry—600, 60, and then 6.

65. Ia. L. Barskov, *Pamiatniki istorii staroobriadchestva XVII veka*, col. 464. See also Robinson, *Zhizneopisaniia*, p. 29, where he argues that the glorification of the ruler grew greater between 1651 and 1657, that where the service book (*sluzhebnik*) of 1651 commemorates the tsar quite casually, among the other Christians, the service book of 1657 published by Nikon commemorates "Our Most Pious Tsar and Grand Prince," etc. There is no doubt that the reign of Alexis was the triumph of theocratic ritual and practices, but in this instance Robinson made a mistake. He is correct about the 1651 text (edition of July 18, p. 146), but he checked only one of the liturgies, and not a prominent one. The liturgy of St. John Chrysostom has the usual glorification of the pious ruler (p. 161), and the liturgy of St. Basil the Great included the real memorial, the prayer for the "well-being and salvation of our pious and Christloving Sovereign" (p. 112). This formula is repeated, word for word, in the St. Basil liturgy of the edition of April 4, 1657. In fact, in checking all the printed service books published in Russia between 1602 and 1676, I was unable to find any significant changes or variants in the memorial prayers for the tsar.

66. Ia. L. Barskov, *Pamiatniki istorii staroobriadchestva XVII veka*, col. 464; Subbotin, V, 229 ff.

67. For Avvakum's arguments, and also for his violent personal attacks against Alexis, see the references gathered in Robinson, *Zhizneopisaniia*, pp. 28 ff. On the identity of person and office in Russian theocratic rulership, see *Tsar and People*, Chap. 2.

68. Ia. L. Barskov, *Pamiatniki istorii staroobriadchestva XVII veka*, cols. 467, 477.

69. *Ibid.*, col. 477.

70. See, for example, N. A. Kazakova and Ia. S. Lur'e, *Antifeodal'nye ereticheskie dvizheniia na Rusi, XIV—nachala XVI vekov* (Moscow, 1955), for the apocalyptic thought of the late fifteenth century, which accompanied the emergence of the centralized state under Ivan III.

71. S. A. Belokurov, *Iz dukhovnoi zhizni Moskovskogo obshchestva XVII v.* (Moscow, 1902), pp. 152 ff. The role of the printing press in forming public concerns or mood deserves study, though it would be most difficult to do for Russia. One can hypothesize, however, that the mass production of a book would at least create a situation in which an enormous number of people (by medieval standards) would be concerned with the same problem at the same moment. And this, in turn, could generate a sort of dynamic spontaneity on a scale unthinkable for a society dependent on manuscripts.

72. For the literature on Kapiton, see Pascal, p. 62 and notes.

73. *Ibid.*, pp. 35 ff.; Barskov, *Pamiatniki pervykh let russkogo staroobriadchestva*, pp. xiv ff.

74. See p. 149 above and note 62.

75. The best account of the Nikon-Alexis controversy and the most complete sources for it are the studies of Kapterev cited above.

76. *ZRAO*, II, 543.

77. See *ibid., passim*; Kapterev, *Nikon i Aleksei*, II, 178 ff. The sources of Nikon's Hildebrandine doctrines (Ukrainian scholars, a Muscovite tradition?), however, have not been sufficiently explored.

78. Kapterev, *Nikon i Aleksei*, II, 196–97, notes.

79. *Ibid.*, p. 201, notes. Nikon wrote this in a letter to his friend, the boyar Ziuzin, who paid heavily for this friendship. See *Delo o Patriarkhe Nikone* (St. Petersburg, 1897), pp. 190 ff. (a publication of the Arkheograficheskaia Komissiia).

80. BAN, Druzhinin ms 134 ("Knizhitsa o Antikhriste"), pp. 16–17.

81. For sources on the Solovetskii rebellion, see the works by Barskov cited above (notes 35 and 62) and, in particular, Barsov, *Novye materialy*, and *Akty istoricheskie* (St. Petersburg, 1841–42), Vol. IV, *passim*.

82. See Andrei Denisov (one of the founders of the great Vyg community of Old Believers), *Istoriia o otsekh i stradal'tsakh solovetskikh*, ed. V. T. Usov (Moscow, 1907), pp. 20–21.

83. See Pascal, p. 443 and note 12, for the legend that Razin, in his rebellion, was accompanied by Patriarch Nikon. In popular tradition, therefore, everything got mixed up—Nikon, Avvakum, Razin, the Tsar—and the one clear fact that remained was rebellion itself.

84. See Barsov, *Novye materialy*, esp. p. 122.

85. See *ibid.*, "Akty otnosiashchiesia k istorii Solovetskogo bunta," for the reports of the local governor on the interrogations of prisoners.

86. See Pascal, pp. 435 ff.

87. On the role and problem of the *strel'tsy*, see S. M. Solov'ev, *Istoriia Rossii* (Moscow, 1959–), Vol. XIV; *Ocherki istorii SSSR: Period feodalizma, XVII v.* (Moscow 1955).

88. The full account of this affair is to be found in the *Istoriia o vere i chelobitnaia o strel'tsakh* of the ex-priest Savva Romanov, who wrote it in 1682. A nineteenth-century manuscript of this work was used for the edition by Nikolai S. Tikhonravov, in *Letopisi russkoi literatury i drevnostei*, V, Sec. II, 111–48.

89. Tikhonravov, p. 139.

90. *PSZ*, Vol. I, item 1102.

91. For the whole problem, see D. I. Sapozhnikov, *Samosozhzhenie v russkom raskole* (Moscow, 1891); also published in *Chteniia*, 1891, No. 3 (subsequent citations refer to the publication in book form).

92. Sapozhnikov, p. 144. See also E. V. Barsov, "Samosozhigatel'stvo raskol'nikov v Olonetskoi gubernii," in *Pamiatnaia Knizhka Olonetskoi Gubernii za 1868–69 god*, II, 194–96; "Samosozhzheniia staroverov," *Olonetskiia Gubernskiia Vedomosti*, No. 57, 1878, pp. 698–700.

93. Sapozhnikov, p. 126.

94. N. Kostomarov, "Istoriia raskola u raskol'nikov," *Vestnik Evropy*, No. 4, 1871, p. 493; in general, see V. G. Druzhinin, *Raskol na Donu v XVII veke* (St. Petersburg, 1889).

95. On the origins and history of this community, see the excellent study by R. O. Crummey, "The Old Believers and the World of Antichrist: The Social and Economic Development of the Raskol in the Olonets Region, 1654–1744" (unpublished Ph.D. dissertation, University of Chicago, 1964).

96. *Ibid.*, pp. 165 ff.

97. See S. G. S., "Otnoshenie raskol'nikov k gosudarstvu," *Vera i Razum* (Kharkov), No. 16, 1892, pp. 252 ff.; and E. V. Barsov, "Semen Denisov Vtorushin," *Trudy Imperatorskoi Kievskoi Dukhovnoi Akademii*, 1866, p. 222. On the subject of the Vyg community in general, see Ivan Filippov, *Istoriia Vygovskoi Pustyni*, ed. D. E. Koshanchikov (St. Petersburg, 1862).

98. On the *Filippovtsy*, see Kel'siev, IV, 236–41.

99. The *Stranniki* would have nothing to do with any aspect of Antichrist; they would not touch money, which bore the ruler's portrait and the state coat of arms; they would not obtain a passport, pay taxes, etc. To survive, the sect created the institution of shelter-givers; these people would live in the world, and, in effect, sacrifice, or pollute themselves, by worldly success. Their function was to provide shelter, food, and safety for the true *Stranniki*. Frequently a shelter-giver would be initiated as a true *Strannik* on his deathbed, so that he too might be saved completely. See S. G. S., in *Vera i Razum*, No. 23, 1892, pp. 642 ff.

100. For the argument that the forty-two months must be understood symbolically and that they could actually last many years, see P. S. Smirnov, *Spory i razdeleniia v russkom raskole v pervoi chetverti XVIII veka* (St. Petersburg, 1909), p. 173.

101. Kel'siev, IV, 252 ff.

102. *Ibid.*, p. 279; see also I. Iuzov (I. I. Kablits), "Politicheskiia vozzreniia Staroveriia," *Russkaia Mysl'*, No. 5, 1882, p. 190. That the merchants prayed, although reluctantly, is well illustrated by the famous Gnusin case. The Preobrazhensk Cemetery in Moscow was the richest and most powerful Old Believer community in Russia, for years under the patronage of the Moscow governors general and, during the reign of Alexander I, in effect under imperial protection. In 1820, however, the government learned that everything was not quite ideal in the community. Police officers who came to search the buildings and the chapel found, in fact, a portrait of Alexander I, with horns and tail, the number 666 on the imperial forehead. The painter, named Gnusin, managed to flee in time, and the portrait (unfortunately for us) was destroyed. See Kel'siev, I, 43; *Trudy Imperatorskoi Kievskoi Dukhovnoi Akademii*, No. 1, 1876, p. 115.

103. For instance, PB, ms Q.I. 1141, an illustrated apocalypse in which there are empty frames wherever the image of Antichrist or of his demons should appear. In contrast, an example from the year 1691, is an apocalypse borrowed by Old Believers who then drew in four-pointed "Latin" crosses and the "reformed" episcopal staffs in "indecent places;" see Barsov, *Novye materialy*, p. 17.

104. *PSZ*, item 4053.

105. On the evolution of the Preobrazhenskii Prikaz into a political police, see Golikova, pp. 243–80.

106. In his eagerness to suffer martyrdom Talitskii is a striking example of that category referred to by Peter in the law quoted above; he and others like him (see the Levin case below) were more than eager to talk and explain their theories. This did not exempt them, of course,

from the classic Preobrazhenskii Prikaz routine: interrogation with torture, confrontations, interrogation with torture until the same testimony was obtained three times running—then on to the next witness. No difference in procedure obtained between the accused and the witnesses.

107. The case is published in G. Esipov, *Raskol'nichii dela XVIII stoletiia* (St. Petersburg, 1861), I, 59–87.

108. Tsarevich Alexis was condemned and died under mysterious circumstances in 1718.

109. The case is published in Esipov, pp. 3–55.

110. Of course Sysoev had to make the tsars match the symbols of the prophecy, but it is interesting that he included the half-witted half brother of Peter, Ivan V, and omitted Feodor (II), son of Alexis and oldest brother of Peter, as well as Boris Godunov and Vasilii Shuiskii—tsars who were not members of the Riurik or Romanov dynasty.

111. Tsentral'nyi Gosudarstvennyi Arkhiv Drevnikh Aktov (TsGADA), *fond* 7, *Raskol'nichii dela, delo* 359.

112. See Esipov, *Raskol'nichii dela, passim*; M. I. Semevskii, *Slovo i Delo!* (St. Petersburg, 1885); Esipov, *Liudi starogo veka* (St. Petersburg, 1880); Solov'ev, *Istoriia Rossii*, Vol. XV; *Chteniia*, from 1863, *passim*; and the TsGADA folders of the Preobrazhenskii Prikaz and the Secret Chancellery (*Tainaia Kantseliariia*).

113. The records show, time and again, how many were punished in these investigations for hearing talk like this and not reporting it. According to the law, this made them guilty of the same crime, that is, in matters of state crime, misprision of treason was equivalent to treason.

114. For example, in the early 1730s an astonishing number of priests used any dodge, fair or silly, to avoid swearing allegiance to or praying for Empress Anna–excuses of illness, absence, ignorance of the requirement, or lack of opportunity. See the cases before the Most Holy Synod in the year 1773 alone, in Tsentral'nyi Gosudarstvennyi Istoricheskii Arkhiv (TsGIAL), Leningrad, *fond* 796, 1733, cases no. 14, 156, 185, 226, 233, 240, 268.

115. Gosudarstvennyi Istoricheskii Musei (GIM), *Museinoe Sobranie*, No. 156 ("Tolkovyi Apokalipsis"). See V. N. Shchepkin, "Dva litsevykh sbornika Istoricheskogo Museia," *Arkheologicheskie Izvestiia i Zametki*, V, No. 4 (1897), 97–102. The manuscript was written in the Far North, in the Pomor'e (Arctic Ocean coastal area), and is, apparently, unique in the boldness of its iconography.

116. 350[r]. If the baby is the Tsarevich Alexis, he was obviously associated (correctly) with his father's policies, rather than seen as a symbol of opposition to Petrine reforms and as the defender of ancient Orthodoxy.

117. 354[r].

118. Because the State Historical Museum manuscript was being readied for publication, I was allowed photographs of only the two miniatures which had been published by Shchepkin in 1897.

119. This arithmetic conjunction is emphasized in BAN, Druzhinin ms 171, p. 106.[r] The usual count was from Ivan III. Avvakum got Tsar Alexis as the eighth tsar by counting Vasilii III and including all the tsars. See Subbotin, IV, 247.

120. For the numerous expressions of this conviction, see the literature listed in note 112.

121. On the nature of the true and legitimate tsar, see my *Tsar and People*, pp. 55 ff.

122. At this point it is impossible for me to resist a personal anecdote. While working in June 1965 on the frescoes of the Arkhangel'sk Cathedral in Moscow, I was engaged in conversation by a guard from the Kremlin Museum, assigned that day to the Cathedral. In asking me about my work, he displayed great interest in the question of balance between church and state power. He said that only under Peter did the state win complete domination over the Church. I pointed out, casually, that Alexis seemed to have had little trouble handling Nikon (we were standing next to Alexis' tomb). But that was quite different, he argued. The clash was a personal one. Alexis was away at war quite often, and the patriarchal and imperial palaces were connected by a passage. So, Nikon used to stroll over and . . . anyway . . . Peter was really Nikon's son, and this was the reason for Alexis' enmity. (In fact, of course, Nikon abdicated in 1658, and Peter was born in 1672.) The man was not an Old Believer (I asked him about this). In fact, he was a professed atheist. Yet, in 1965, he believed in a legend which clearly belongs to the *Raskol* ethos.

123. See, for example, "Knizhitsa o Antikhriste" (BAN, Druzhinin ms 134), pp. 26 ff. In fact, according to a tradition dating back to the second century, Antichrist had to be a Jew (of the tribe of Dan), a requirement which presented some problems for Old Believer

historiography and was constantly emphasized by the Orthodox prelates, who argued that Peter could not be Antichrist.

124. "Sobranie ot Sviatogo Pisaniia o Antikhriste," in Kel'siev, II, 249. See also the variant "Istoriia pechatnaia o Petre Velikom: Sobranie ot Sviatogo Pisaniia o Antikhriste," *Chteniia*, No. 1, 1863. F. Eleonskii, *O sostoianii russkogo raskola pri Petre I-om* (St. Petersburg, 1864), p. 102 and note 1, shows convincingly that the work was originally composed immediately after 1725, though most of the available manuscripts are of a later date.

125. Kel'siev, IV, 252.

126. Library of the Ukrainian Academy of Sciences, Kiev, ms 97, p 10$^r$.

127. See, among many references, "Sobranie," in Kel'siev, II, 248. We have here, in the play on the words "patriarch" ~ "father," an example of the fitting in and utilization of all evidence. See below for the particular significance of the usurpation of a patriarchal, ecclesiastical title.

128. In the Old Russian system of designating numbers by letters, i = 10, n = 50, p = 80, and so forth. See, for example, Evfimii, in Kel'siev, IV, 253. The new title did puzzle many people, who neither pronounced it correctly nor understood it. Some of them paid a very high price for their illiteracy in the cellars of the Secret Chancellery; see Solov'ev, Vol. XV, *passim*.

129. See S. G. S., in *Vera i Razum*, No. 23, p. 646.

130. See, for example, the testimony of Ermakov in 1855, in Kel'siev, I, 220.

131. See, for example, the eighteenth-century manuscript "O napisanii dvoeglavogo orla," in Gosudarstvennaia Biblioteka SSSR imeni V. I. Lenina (GBL), Moscow, *fond* 238, ms 1307, pp. 371$^r$—391$^{ob}$. In contrast, the eighteenth-century manuscript PB, Q.I. 1075, p. 91, pushes the attribution of this symbol, actually adopted in the 1490s, back to Vladimir Monomakh in the twelfth century and hence exonerates it from all satanic implications.

132. GIM, Khliudov Collection, No. 361, a roll of 1841, entitled "Ob Antikhriste."

133. "Sobranie," in Kel'siev, II, 248–49.

134. BAN, Druzhin ms 134, p. 23$^{ob}$; for the same argument, see GBL, *fond* 98, ms 779 (end of the 18th century), p. 29$^{ob}$ and $^r$. See also the sermons of Iavorskii, *Propovedi blazhenyia pamiati Stefana Iavorskogo* (Moscow, 1804), III, esp. 112 ff.; and the law (*PSZ*, item 3891) in which the Most Holy Synod ordered that the Old Believers praise the emperor: *imeti by iako glavy svoia i otsa otechestva, i khrista gospodnia*.

135. See E. V. Barsov, "Drevne-russkie pamiatniki Sviashchennago Venchaniia tsarei na tsarstvo." *Chteniia*, No. 1, 1883, pp. 90 ff. and 105, for the coronation of Peter's older brother, Feodor Alekseevich, at which he was anointed on his head, his body, and his limbs, i.e., in an episcopal fashion.

136. These appellations were used constantly by the metropolitans Stefan Iavorskii and Feofan Prokopovich in their sermons, and they took special care to explain the meaning of the words. In medieval Russia, however, the term *pomazanik* was applied to the anointed clergy and to Biblical figures, particularly to King David; see Sreznevskii, *Materialy dlia slovaria drevnerusskogo iazyka*, s. v. *pomazanik*.

137. For example, the calendar reform of Peter, changing the beginning of the year from September 1 to January 1, and the year count from the creation of the world to the birth of Christ. Hence the apocalyptic prophecy that time and law would change under Antichrist was fulfilled by Peter, who, they said, introduced the "Janus count," two-faced, counting forward (from Christ) and backward (before Christ), and who picked January 1 in honor of Janus, a pagan deity and therefore Satan, See "Sobranie," in Kel'siev, II, 248; BAN, Druzhinin ms 134, p. 23$^r$.

138. See Kel'siev, IV, 265–66; *Chteniia*, No. 1, 1863, p. 7; Eleonskii, p. 108; S.G.S., in *Vera i Razum*, No. 23, p. 647.

139. An example of the awareness of Peter's brutality was the rumor that he was going to massacre two hundred soldier-deserters by lining them up and shooting cannon at them; see Esipov, *Raskol'nichii dela*, I, 564.

140. See Smirnov, *Spory i razdeleniia*, p. 161.

141. "Sobranie," in Kel'siev, II, 251.

142. The cases quoted in Solov'ev, Vol. XV, are full of references to the tax on souls and what it portended.

143. Kel'siev, IV, 254–65.

144. *Ibid.*, pp. 263–64.

145. Smirnov, *Vnutrennie voprosy*, p. 11; Subbotin, IV, 251.

146. For example, Evfimii always used the term *dukhovnaia vlast'* for ecclesiastical authority.

147. GBL, *fond* 98, ms 1668, p. 23ᵒᵇ.

148. "Chelobitnaia, ili Istoriia Petra Velikogo," in Shchapov, *Russkii raskol staroobriad-chestva*, pp. 106–9.

149. *PSZ*, item 1910.

150. *Ibid.*, item 2991.

151. *Polnoe sobranie postanovlenii i rasporiazhenii po vedomstvu pravoslavnogo ispovedaniia Rossiiskoi Imperii* (St. Petersburg, 1869–1916), II, 102, 410.

152. *Ibid.*, I, 27. For other discriminatory legislation see Smirnov, *Spory i razdeleniia*, pp. 3 ff.

153. *PSZ*, item 2877; see also item 3479.

154. See, for example, Prince I. Khovanskii's later confession to Talitskii that he had been appointed a "metropolitan" in the "council" and might have gained eternal life by refusing and undergoing martyrdom but that he lacked the courage. Esipov, *Raskol'nichii dela*, I, 68–69.

155. Ivan I. Golikov, *Deianiia Petra Velikogo, Dopolneniia* (Moscow, 1790–97), Vol. XVII: *Anekdoty*, pp. xciv, 354–56.

156. See Solov'ev, XIV, 570 and notes. See also *PSZ*, item 2874, Dec. 29, 1714; all these prescriptions were repeated over and over, with reminders of the heavy fines imposed for disobedience.

157. *PSZ*, item 1741; see also item 1887 (in the year 1701). Dummies dressed in such clothing were prominently displayed for the benefit of the public.

158. *Ibid.*, item 2874.

159. *Ibid.*, item 2929.

160. *Ibid.*, item 2991; see also item 3169 (in the year 1718).

161. *Ibid.*, item 3718, dated January 19, 1721.

162. *Ibid.*, item 3963.

163. *Ibid.*, item 4052. Birthdays and name days of the royal family and anniversaries of coronations were called *tsarskie dni* (tsar's days, or imperial holidays).

164. *Ibid.*, item 3893.

165. *Ibid.*, item 3223.

166. One striking expression of this can be seen in the amnesty proclaimed after the victorious peace with Sweden in 1721. It applied to most criminals, but Old Believers sentenced to hard labor were forgiven only if they renounced their "obstinate" beliefs (*PSZ*, item 3842). Another interesting aspect of this attitude was the welcome Peter extended to all foreigners, guaranteeing them full tolerance and protection, except for one group—the Jews (*ibid.*, item 1910). They, too, of course, were always "outside."

167. See the sermons of the Metropolitan Daniil during the reign of Vasilii III, in V. I. Zhmakin, "Mitropolit Daniil i ego sochineniia," Part 2 (texts), in *Chteniia*, No. 2, 1881.

168. See *PSZ*, item 1898, prescribing the parade dress proper for ceremonial days and holidays. On the significance of the uniform and its role in the religion of the state, see E. H. Kantorowicz, "Gods in Uniform," *Proceedings of the American Philosophical Society*, CV, No. 4 (1961), 368–93.

169. Eighteenth-century drawing on cardboard from MIRA, Druzhinin Collection (no acquisition number).

170. MIRA, ms B-607-IV, p. 12ʳ.

171. *Ibid.*, p. 80ᵒᵇ.

172. *Ibid.*, p. 50ᵒᵇ.

173. IRLI (Pushkinskii Dom), Kerzhenskoe Sobranie, ms 74, p. 82ʳ.

174. Alexander Herzen, with his usual insight, saw the *chinovniki* created by Peter's "revolution" as a civil clergy, "performing holy services in courts and police" (*Byloe i dumy* [Moscow, 1956], I, 252 [*Sobranie sochinenii v tridtsati tomakh*, Vol. VIII]).

175. For the Old Believers, "Peter I" was, in itself, proof of Peter-Antichrist, for the omission of the patronymic acknowledged what they suspected, that Peter was not the son of Alexis; as Antichrist, he had no father, and hence was the first of his name.

176. For a madly incongruous image of Catherine I, the servant-girl wife of Peter, as St. Olga (grandmother of St. Vladimir, who, according to historical legend, brought Christianity to Russia in the tenth century), see Address of the Most Holy Ruling Synod, July 5, 1725, in Barsov, *Novye materialy*, p. 159.

177. See the sermons of Iavorskii (*Propovedi blazhenyia pamiati Stefana Iavorskogo*) and of

Feofan Prokopovich (*Sochineniia* [Moscow and Leningrad, 1961]); and *Tsar and People*, p. 94 and note 47. On the Astraea imagery in general, see F. A. Yates, "Queen Elizabeth as Astrea," *Warburg Journal*, X (1947), 27–82.

178. For a typical variant, Peter as Augustus-like creator, see Prokopovich, esp. p. 45. For the ruler as creator, as the life-giving principle, in the West during this period, see E. H. Kantorowicz, "Oriens Augusti—Lever du Roi," *Dumbarton Oaks Papers*, XVII (1963), 165 ff.

179. "Kratkoe opisanie Blazhennykh Del Imperatora Petra Velikago, Samoderzhtsa Vserossiiskago," in *Zapiski russkikh liudei: Sobytiia Vremen Petra Velikago*, ed. N. Sakharov (St. Petersburg, 1841), p. 4. See also *Zapiski Ivana Ivanovicha Nepliueva* (St. Petersburg, 1893), pp. 120 ff.; *Razskazy Nartova o Petre Velikom*, ed. L. N. Maikov (St. Petersburg, 1891), pp. 60 ff.

180. See, for example, *Razskazy Nartova*, p. 69.

181. "Sobranie," in Kel'siev, II, 256.

182. V. Farmakovskii, "O protivo-gosudarstvennom elemente v raskole," *Otechestvennye zapiski*, CLXIX, No. 11–12 (1866), 633–34.

# Problems of the Russian Eighteenth Century: Gentry Monarchy and "Westernization"

# Continuity in Economic Activity and Policy During the Post-Petrine Period in Russia

## ARCADIUS KAHAN

To discuss economic activity in Russia of the eighteenth century is to deal with an economic and social order that antedates the age of industrialization. Industrial activity in Russia during the eighteenth century was carried on within the political framework of an autocratic state, with ill-defined norms of legal behavior, and against the background of a serf agriculture which reached its apogee during this very period. The state of the industrial arts was low in comparison with western European standards, and the use of waterpower as a motive force in manufactories was introduced in Russia by foreign entrepreneurs only in the seventeenth century. Against this background, the efforts by Peter the Great (reigned 1682–1725) to modernize Russia appear genuinely heroic. The demands of his policy forced the government to engage directly in a vast program of establishing new industries, of converting small handicraft workshops into large-scale manufactories, and of encouraging private entrepreneurs to follow the government's example.

The Petrine policy of what we would now describe as forced economic or industrial development was marked by a relentless race against time, dictated by political reasons. This haste and urgency led to major disproportions in the structure and production pattern of the "Petrine manufactories" and caused their mode of operation to differ from that of any other industrial complex built up elsewhere over a longer time span. It is the fate of the manufacturing sector in the Russian economy during the post-Petrine period that concerns us in the following discussion.

The early development of manufactures in eighteenth century Russia presents an interesting issue for the economic historian—namely, the problem of the continuity or discontinuity of the initial industrialization.

It will be argued that the economic process set in motion during the Petrine period continued during the post-Petrine period and that the policies that

FROM Arcadius Kahan, "Continuity in Economic Activity and Policy During the Post-Petrine Period in Russia," *The Journal of Economic History*, 25 (March 1965), 61–85. Reprinted by permission of the author and the publisher.

supported the early industrialization drive were not abandoned by Peter's successors. It will be assumed that the early development of a new branch of the economy is not necessarily marked by a smooth upward movement of its output curve. Such a development is in most instances a process by which the new branch asserts itself against various adverse social conditions, involving conflicts of economic interests and policies. However, when the general activity is being pursued and similar policies persist over a longer time span, the basic continuity is established.

The traditional concept of discontinuity in industrialization in Russia has given rise to two assertions voiced from diametrically opposed positions. The first concluded on the basis of this assumed experience that government intervention, so frequently undertaken during the period of early industrialization, is futile and unreliable as a factor in economic development. The second argued that this experience proves the dependence of continuing economic growth upon the continuity of an active governmental policy and hence that the government's direct involvement is the decisive element in the economic growth effort of a nation. Thus both the liberal school and the étatist school of Russian historians have assumed the discontinuity in economic growth during the post-Petrine period of the eighteenth century to be a fact and have used it as an historical example to lend added credibility to their respective positions.[1] The two outstanding authorities among the Russian historians who elaborated the concept of discontinuity and thereby helped to get their judgments and images of the post-Petrine period entrenched in the popular mind were V. O. Kliuchevskii and P. Miliukov, both representatives of the liberal school.

In the following essay, three problems are singled out for investigation: (1) How durable was the industrial development in Russia that occurred during the Petrine period? (2) How serious and of what nature was the slump in economic activity during the immediate post-Petrine period, and what was its impact upon the industrial sector of the Russian economy? (3) Could the post-Petrine period be considered as one of major discontinuity in the economic growth of Russia?

The theses of Miliukov and Kliuchevskii about economic discontinuity may be summarized as follows: The growth of manufactories under Peter the Great cannot be attributed to the increase of demand in the domestic market and is therefore not a "result of the organic development of the domestic industry";[2] it was created by an extra-economic factor—the government—to serve its political ends.[3] The existence of the manufactories depended upon government protection and special privileges, hence their instability.[4] Periods of government inactivity in the economic sphere are therefore correlated with slumps or declines in industrial activity. Miliukov supports his argument about the lack of durability of the manufactories created during the Petrine period by the fact that by 1780 only 22 of them were in existence.[5] Kliuchevskii reaches the sweeping but obviously erroneous conclusion for the whole period 1725–1762 that "industry after Peter did not make any noticeable progress."[6]

Although one might agree with some of these conclusions, I would question most of them as being irrelevant as explanatory factors and some of them as being simply erroneous. The general impression of a feeble state of manufactories in Russia and of a lack in indigenous entrepreneurship is largely built upon statements made by Peter the Great himself and upon the choice of methods used by him in his attempts to introduce and develop manufactories in Russia. Such a view ignores the historical experience of other countries at a similar stage in their economic development.

In discussing the nature of the post-Petrine period, one cannot ignore some features of the Petrine period that most impressed contemporaries and posterity (historians included). The features of Petrine economic policy that made the most lasting impression were: (1) the scope of public works and the creation of social overhead, and (2) the effort to supply the army and navy. Certainly in terms of employment (not in efficiency), the public works of the Petrine period remained unrivaled throughout the entire eighteenth century.

Thousands of forced laborers (drafted serfs) were employed in the construction of the Voronezh wharves and of the Black Sea navy during the turn of the century;[7] many thousands were employed in the digging of a Volga-Don canal; thousands were mobilized yearly for the construction of the Taganrog harbor[8] and for the erection of fortifications in Azov and Troitsk.[9] All these projects were later discontinued and abandoned. For years, resources (human and capital) were squandered in the construction of the Vyshnevolotskii canal system, in harbor construction in Rogervik, etc.[10] They all were monuments to the ability of the Petrine administration to mobilize the labor effort of the nation. Of course, the crown of Peter's domestic projects was the construction of the new capital, St. Petersburg. We now have some notion of the magnitude of its drain on labor resources.[11]

The government's public works programs do not account for all of the redistribution of resources or forced savings that were channeled into construction. Government pressure forced both the nobility and the merchants to channel a part of their savings or wealth into housing construction in St. Petersburg, in addition to substantial government expenditures.[12] Such investments might have turned out to be profitable for the individuals in the long run, but within the time horizon of the people involved they were considered as an inferior alternative to the ones existing elsewhere, as witnessed by the coercion applied by the government to enforce the investment in housing construction. Contemporaries regarded these involuntary investments as a form of additional taxation.

The channeling of labor and capital into construction and public works on such an unprecedented scale left its imprint both upon Peter's contemporaries and upon subsequent generations. None of the Russian historians has tried to find out what the real costs were, as though the mobilized labor force had zero opportunity costs. This is mentioned, not to question the economic rationale or political wisdom of the public works, but to call attention to the lack of elements of economic analysis in the works of the historians. Obviously, the awe and admiration of posterity for the labor mobilization policies of Peter were strengthened in view of the fact that they coincided with army recruitment carried out on an almost yearly basis.[13]

The volume of employment in manufactories is obviously dwarfed by the large numbers of the military draft and the forced labor mobilization in the Petrine period. Any increase in industrial employment in the post-Petrine period could not compensate, in terms of sheer numbers, for the decline in employment in public works.

The effort to supply the needs of the army and navy during the Petrine period was most impressive. Within fifteen to twenty years the newly established ironworks and munition factories were able to supply the needs of an army of about 220,000 men. In 1715, the Russian artillery already had about 13,000 domestically produced cannons of various sizes; by 1720, the yearly output of military rifles exceeded 20,000; a navy on the Baltic and Caspian seas was constructed and well equipped. The textile industries supplied an increasing portion of army cloth, all of the sailcloth, etc. This was the work of one generation.

Miliukov assumed the survival rate of manufacturing enterprises to be *the* criterion of the durability of entrepreneurial effort of a particular period. Leaving aside for the moment the validity of this assumption, it is necessary to point out certain pitfalls involved in Miliukov's procedure. The computation of a survival rate of enterprises that ignores the distribution of enterprises by size or by industry branches is a biased measure. Moreover, to ignore the distinction between one-owner firms, partnerships, and joint-stock companies tends to obscure a great deal of what we know about the various elements that determine the life structure of firms in general. These criticisms may be made without even raising considerations of the peculiar characteristics of turnover in ownership of enterprises or of the survival rate of firms in most European countries during the eighteenth century in general[14] and of the conditions of Russian manufactories in particular. But quite apart from all this, additional considerations make the survival rate a poor indicator of entrepreneurial activity.

Available evidence indicates that industrial plant and equipment were not the largest item in the total investment expenditures of particular firms;[15] hence, the continued existence of an industrial firm was only in part influenced by the desire to maintain the capital stock as a unit.[16] We have evidence that skilled labor frequently constituted a greater asset than the physical capital stock.[17] Therefore, transfers of capital stock and skilled labor from one firm to the other took place for entirely different reasons. Secondly, given the continuous engagement in domestic or foreign commerce, the occurrence of transfers, mergers, etc. might not necessarily reflect upon the viability of the manufacturing enterprises themselves.[18] In addition, partnerships and joint-stock companies, organized to remedy the scarcity of capital, were frequently broken up, transformed, and replaced, thus distorting the purely numerical relationship between the number of firms and the stock of capital with which the firms were identified. By tracing the history of individual enterprises and the transfers of labor and equipment, it is possible to ascertain a much greater real continuity than Miliukov was able to observe. An additional fallacy of Miliukov's approach in making the survival rate of the firms *the* criterion of entrepreneurial efficiency lies in his total disregard of both general and specific conditions that affected the operations of enterprises during this period. He disregards such phenomena as the transition from war to peace and its impact upon the product mix—a transition that not all modern enterprises could survive; the relative insecurity of life and property; forced relocations;[19] and the risks of fire and floods, to mention just some items of a rather extensive list.

The survival rate for private ironworks for the period 1725–1745 was 86 per cent.[20] A survival rate of 72 per cent for the same period for enterprises in all branches of the textile industry further weakens the validity of Miliukov's assertion.[21] A closer scrutiny of the older surviving enterprises reveals that they were of larger average size and of somewhat higher productivity than the ones that were liquidated or the ones established during the immediate post-Petrine period.[22] Under conditions of an almost stable technology, the size of plant, output, and capital endowment was apparently among the most important factors determining the survival of the enterprises. Some advantage from an earlier start on a larger-than-average scale, from superior knowledge of the market, and from possible preferential or privileged treatment by the government should obviously not be dismissed. In result, the survival capacity of the Petrine manufactories was as great as that of any manufactories established during the later periods and certainly contradicts Miliukov's assertions.[23]

The impressive achievements of Petrine policies were identified with the personality of Peter himself. His death could not but leave a mark upon the economic life of the country. From the many historical descriptions of the Petrine and immediate post-Petrine periods, the following general picture can be reconstructed about the immediate effect of Peter's death: Previously pushed and strained almost to the limit of endurance by the "Tsar-transformer," economic activity slowed down for a while. Entrepreneurs, hitherto conscious of a sense of direction, became uncertain whether the pressure in the same direction would be sustained by the new rulers before new directions were taken. The need for a reallocation of available resources, the accumulation and transfer of new resources, and the adjustment to a peace economy required time during which the pressures of the Petrine period had to abate. Consequently, some of the government projects were continued with diminished vigor (Ladoga canal), new projects were not embarked upon, and the conspicuous and massive government activity diminished markedly. The decrease in the scale of government economic activity, however, did not decrease the total activity of the various branches of the economy to the same degree. Not only was there a different effect upon various branches, but the slackening of government economic activity was rapidly compensated for by increased activity in the private sector of the economy.

Let us consider the extent to which the contraction of government activity in the area of public works was accompanied by a general contraction of foreign and domestic trade. With respect to foreign trade, the only continuous data available pertain to trade with England, which was Russia's main trading partner.[24]

A few comments are in order with respect to the degree to which the British data are indicative of the pattern of trade in general and for the years under consideration in particular. The chief characteristic of Russian foreign trade was its positive trade balance, the excess of exports over imports. Although the excess of total Russian exports over imports was proportionally not as high as in the case of Russian-British trade, that excess can be estimated for the year 1726 as against the years 1717–1719 (including 1718—the peak year for Russian exports to England during Peter's reign). Exports amounted to 4,238,810 rubles and imports to 2,125,543 rubles in 1726,[25] while for 1717–1719, exports of 2,613,000 rubles and imports of 816,000 rubles were recorded.[26] Consequently, there was a substantial increase in exports for 1726 as against 1717–1719, which can be explained in part by a rise in exports of manufactured goods, both iron and textiles.[27] Thus, the estimates for total trade as well as the British data testify to an unchanged pattern of Russian exports during the post-Petrine period.

The pattern of change of the imports of English goods into Russia during the immediate post-Petrine period can rather easily be explained in terms of the substitution of Prussian wool cloths for the English ones[28] and is in general not typical for the growing tendency exhibited by Russian imports. To the extent that the foreign trade data for 1726 or for Russian exports to England can be used as indirect evidence of the state of the Russian economy after Peter's death, at least they indicate neither an interruption in Russia's economic development nor a decline in the industrial output.

The sources of information about changes in the value or the volume of internal trade are even scarcer than those about the changes in foreign trade. The only available series pertains to the volume of trade on the Makarievska Trade Fair, which was an important trading institution but probably not representative of the volume or compositon of internal trade in general. But, since the Makarievska Trade Fair was the largest in Russia, it would be logical to expect that a serious economic disturbance would be reflected in the turnover at that fair. Although the figures suggest a general downward trend in the total taxes collected and show no evidence of growth in the custom-duty collections, which more directly reflect the turnover, on the whole the data do not point to a general stagnation in business after the death of Peter the Great.[29] Granted that there was a general slowdown in governmental economic activity, how strongly did it affect the industrial sector? Was there a slump in the output of Russian manufactories, following Peter's death?

The normal expectation would be that the cessation of war operations against Sweden (1721) and Persia (1724) should bring about a contraction of military output during the reign of Peter. The most affected branches of manufacturing would be iron and textiles, since their output level depended to a large extent upon the volume of governmental contracts. An examination of those industries ought to provide the clue to the nature of the post-Petrine slump in industrial output.

The change in the output pattern of the iron industry can be derived from the yearly data on total output and on the two sectors, state and private.[30] The temporary decrease in output for 1726 and 1727 registered in the data can in part be explained by factors outside the general impact of postwar contraction. The decline in output was most clearly marked in the state sector of iron manufacturing. Documents pertaining to this sector point to two causes: replacement of worn-out equipment, and labor unrest in the ironworks.[31] The decrease of iron output is not explained by any inherent deficiencies of the industry. Of course, an adjustment period was involved during which some markets were expanded (notably foreign markets for state-produced iron) to compensate for the decreased military demand, and adjustments of the output mix had to be made.[32] But there is ample evidence that even during the years of the "post-Petrine slump," there was net investment in the iron industry.[33]

Further supporting evidence for the contention that the "post-Petrine slump" had little effect upon manufacturing may be found in the data of copper output.[34] Not only had the output of copper almost doubled during 1725–1727, but by 1728 the rapid rise of private output had begun, a fact that indicates that private investments had been made during the preceding years, the "years of slump."[35]

The situation of the textile industry was not as clear-cut as that of the metal industry. A large part of the linen-hemp manufactories was geared to the production of sailcloth, and the sharp decrease in domestic naval construction forced the manufacturers to seek foreign markets for their output and to change the output mix of the industry. This accounts for the lack of new investment in this area during 1725–1727.

The wool industry, in turn, had to overcome an internal misallocation of resources with respect to the proportion of wool cloth to coarse wool lining material, previously established as a result of the demands of Peter's army quartermasters.[36] Nevertheless, new wool and silk manufactories were established during the years 1725–1728,[37] indicating that these branches of industry were not paralyzed by what has been called the post-Petrine slump.

Available evidence pertaining to other branches of manufacturing (chemical, leather, etc.) points to a similar conclusion. The years immediately following the death of Peter were years of adjustment for the newly established branches of manufacturing and for the manufacturing enterprises. They were not years of slackening of total demand that, according to some historians, caused far-reaching decreases in output and in investment in the manufacturing sector.

Data on the total volume and rate of capital investment would throw light upon the existence of a hypothetical downward trend in manufacturing. Unfortunately, estimates of the total capital investment in manufacturing are not available.[38] The closest approximations to such data are estimates of capital in the ironworks for certain years. Although a number of objections could be raised about the accuracy of the estimates, they can nevertheless be used in such conjectures.

The cumulative estimates supplied by S. G. Strumilin for the period under consideration are the following:

**Capital Investment in Ironworks**
**(in 1,000 silver rubles)**

| Year | Private | State | Total |
|------|---------|-------|-------|
| 1700 | 22 | n.a. | 22 |
| 1725 | 124 | 46 | 170 |
| 1735 | 288 | 83 | 371 |
| 1745 | 870 | 232 | 1,102 |

SOURCE: Strumilin (cited in n. 30), p. 240.

An approximate division of the total volume of capital investment in the private sector during the period 1725–1735 (1726–1729 and 1730–1735), using the number of furnaces and of forge-hammers installed as an approximate index of capital investment, would indicate about 40 per cent for the earlier and 60 per cent for the later period. An equal distribution of state investment between the two periods appears to be plausible on the basis of available evidence.[39] Consequently, the distribution of the total 201,000 rubles of capital investment between the two periods yields 85,000 rubles for 1726–1729 and 116,000 rubles for 1730–1735. If we allocate the capital investment outlays for the period 1700–1725 not to the whole period but to about ten years of the most intensive capital construction of ironworks, we end with a yearly average of about 15,000 rubles, while the yearly average for the period 1726–1729 (excluding the outlays for capital repair) would reach the sum of over 20,000 rubles. In iron manufacturing, therefore, there is no apparent evidence of a decrease in the volume of capital investment during the years following the death of Peter the Great.[40]

Among the basic elements of government policy with regard to industry that indicate continuity of the two periods, there can be no doubt that foreign-trade policy was of utmost importance. The need to obtain foreign markets for some raw materials and for industrial products led to a reexamination of the Petrine foreign-trade and tariff policies. This took place during 1727–1731 and resulted in a new tariff in 1731.[41] Most of the Soviet historians have condemned the 1731 tariff as a betrayal of Russian industrial interests to those of foreign countries and as a major deviation from the Petrine tariff policy of 1724. A more careful analysis of the two tariffs does not substantiate the charge of major liberalization of tariff policies. While the 1724 tariff was unabashedly protectionist, that of 1731 was much more selective in its discriminatory features. It was protective with respect to products manufactured within Russia, both by the new manufactories and by the craft or domestic industries. It was protective with regard to the export of manufactured goods and set high duties upon the export of raw materials used by domestic manufacturers. True, it deviated from the 1724 tariff with regard to the level of duties in a number of cases but was much more effective in enforcing them, whereas previous widespread smuggling had rendered many prohibitive duties of the Petrine tariff ineffective.[42] Built upon the reported market prices of Russian commodities, the new tariff resulted in continuous protection of the commodities produced for mass consumption and liberalized the import duties for so-called luxuries, the domestic production of which was clearly inadequate. The new tariff doubtless also resulted in more normal foreign-trade relations with other countries with which commercial treaties were subsequently concluded. While the desire to conclude long-run commercial treaties with some major partners was apparent, it must be realized that such an operation required concessions from both partners; therefore, commercial and tariff policies had to become more flexible. Although utterances were made about the desirability of Russian industries becoming more competitive in the domestic and world markets, the calculations upon which the tariff legislation rested tended to provide at least a 30 per cent margin for the Russian manufacturers (based upon the assumption that the transportation and other costs came up to 30 per cent of the price of the imports in the country of origin). Therefore, it seems safe to conclude that the tariff policy of Peter's successors was not less effective in its features protective of Russian industry. In fact, it introduced corrections into some of Peter's typical short-run measures which were designed to achieve high rates of growth in some chosen areas to the detriment of others.[43]

Needless to say, even during the latter part of Elizabeth's reign—when the gentry won the first round against the *posad* (urban population) in the fight over the trading rights of the peasants, the abolition of internal duties, and the increase of foreign trade duties—the manufacturers were little, if at all, affected by the increased foreign-trade duties. They certainly gained from the inclusion of the South in the domestic market by eliminating some foreign competition from it.

As far as fiscal policy is concerned, no additional burdens were put directly upon the manufacturers. It is difficult to assess the effect upon the demand for manufactured goods which resulted from an increased burden of direct and indirect taxation placed upon the agricultural producers.

There was, however, a turn in government policy that is of considerable significance for our problem. The policy change concerning the transfer of state-owned industrial enterprises to private ownership actually did not contradict the basic tenets of the Petrine period. However, prior to the change in policy it was necessary to test what could only be conjectured by some observers during Peter's reign—namely, the question of the relative efficiency of state-owned and private enterprises. The discussion pertaining to this subject was intensified during the period 1732–1736.[44]

The policy accepted by the government may perhaps be summarized as follows: (1) The higher efficiency of the private enterprises was basically admitted. (2) The state interests, whenever involved in the form of volume of deliveries and prices for the output or tax revenues, ought to be safeguarded in any transaction involving the transfer of state-owned enterprises to private hands. (3) A major condition of such transfer remained the promise on the part of the entrepreneur to increase capital investment in, and the output of, the particular enterprises.[45]

While the private share in total output increased as a result of the various transfers of previously state-owned enterprises to private ownership, this result was accompanied by an increase in the degree of state control and regulation of the private enterprises. The more refined aspects of the mercantilist system replaced the crude mercantilist policies of the Petrine period. The policy makers apparently decided that state control might serve in lieu of state ownership and that state ownership in the absence of profits was more expensive than the administration of state controls. We can, therefore, observe the simultaneous development of two interrelated phenomena. A more firm establishment of private property rights, accepted as a basic precondition of private entrepreneurial activity, went hand in hand with a more rigid definition of the conditions of exercising ownership rights in the area of manufacturing.[46]

The major areas of government control over private enterprises (including information collection and interference) were defined as follows: (1) preservation of the system of licensing and control of entry into industry; (2) control of the size of operations and of some sources of raw materials and labor (principally when imports and serf labor were involved); (3) control to insure continuous operation of the enterprise; (4) control and stimulation of capital investment. These policies or controls constituted a step forward in the direction of perfecting the mercantilist system in Russia and thereby could be considered as a continuation of the Petrine policies.[47]

However, my main contention would be that the basic economic continuity between the Petrine and post-Petrine periods in the manufacturing sector was not so much provided by government policy as by the existence of a "natural" link of an emerging distinct group of Russian manufacturers.

It has already been pointed out that the prevailing notion (especially among Russian historians) about the lack of indigenous entrepreneurship and "entrepreneurial spirit" in Russia is based largely upon the views expressed by Peter the Great. In this connection four factors should be borne in mind. (1) Peter, in appraising the entrepreneurial capabilities of the industrialist and merchant group, made the comparison with contemporary western Europe. He underestimated the differences in property rights, risks, and investment returns in western Europe and in Russia. Therefore, regardless of the many limitations imposed upon private enterprise previously (limitations among which Peter's fiscal policies were not inconspicuous), Peter's characterization of the Russian entrepreneur ought not to be taken as an unbiased observation. (2) Peter's view of Russian entrepreneurs was part and parcel of his political thought and of his ideas regarding his own calling and obligation. He considered himself the guardian of the welfare of his subjects who, because of their ignorance, had to be propelled into new conditions. Possessing superior awareness of new horizons and opportunities, he believed himself entitled to force his subjects to a rude awakening by a ruler who, by his own definition, placed the interest of the community above the interests of individuals. The rudeness of the treatment was justified, in his view, by the urgency of national interests as defined by him. (3) Command and outright coercion in social relations were not yet replaced in Russia by compromise and persuasion; therefore, imposing investment decisions upon entrepreneurs was almost perfectly consistent with methods generally employed in administering other areas of national activity. The impression given by Peter the Great is therefore a blend of "new" Western ideas and "old" Russian methods. (4) The Petrine period of development of manufactories was a period of almost uninterrupted war, with economic policies geared and tailored to the war effort. The largest investments were in the armament industries or those that supplied the army. The general pattern of resource use and the allocation of investment within industry differed from what would be considered optimal during a period of peace; the attitudes of entrepreneurs and the behavior of firms differed also. To understand the challenge and to evaluate the impact of a war lasting a quarter century upon a newly emerging entrepreneurial group were above even the very substantial analytical abilities and intellectual faculties of Peter the Great.

During the Petrine as well as during the post-Petrine period, this was a group still *in statu nascendi*, open to both gentry and the lower strata of merchants and even peasants, within the limits of government licensing.[48] Its structure was in large measure determined by the serf society in which it found itself, and very little effort was exerted by the entrepreneurial group to defy the norms of that society. The main problem for the manufacturers was to be able to perform their economic tasks within the limits prescribed by the social framework. It would, therefore, be a mistake to attribute to the eighteenth-century Russian entrepreneurs and manufacturers attitudes and concepts of liberal capitalism. While struggling for broader rights (to consolidate their position and to make more independent business decisions) they were quite willing to operate under an umbrella of basically paternalistic and protectionist government policies. Under the prevailing institutional arrangement, freedom of choice and decision for the entrepreneurs was limited. It was only through negotiations and pressures that the extension of freedom and greater independence from the government could be won, and at that the government was not always willing or able to understand the manufacturers' point of view. Peter seldom got involved in dialogues; his was the style of command. During the post-Petrine period, dialogues between the entrepreneurs and the government became more frequent. It is possible, therefore, to reconstruct some of the opinions and attitudes of the entrepreneurs and representatives of the government and to delineate and distinguish meaningful differences between their respective positions.

While the state officials would elevate the principles of output maximization and growth of investment as the chief criteria of success of manufacturing enterprises, the entrepreneurs would have the profit motive as their chief criterion. Therefore, once established in a particular branch of manufacturing, the owners of the enterprises would favor greater restrictions upon entry than the government would allow (in view of the slow growth in demand, the possibility to benefit from quasi-monopoly profits would rapidly disappear with free entry).[49]

The demands for exclusive monopoly privileges were perhaps less frequent during the post-Petrine period than during the preceding one.

The manufacturers were against government attempts to determine the product mix and to set quality standards of production. In the latter case the manufacturers exhibited a more intimate knowledge of the potentialities of the domestic market and the consumer demand.

The manufacturers resisted government measures that would impose upon them the financial responsibility of providing both social overhead (school buildings, roads, churches) and welfare measures for their labor force (accident and unemployment compensation, education, etc.).

They also resisted government price setting, both because of the principle involved and because of their anticipation that the price would be below the market level. Another source of this resistance was the suspicion that price setting ultimately leads to wage setting, which they wanted to avoid. The latter attitude does not imply that the private manufacturers were necessarily paying lower wages than the state enterprises but only that they guarded their rights to set wage rates in a manner that would maximize profits for the enterprise and would establish wage scales more flexible and geared to the effectiveness of the labor performance.

Needless to say, one of the major aspirations of the manufacturers was to gain a share in the opportunity to employ serf labor wherever that was profitable. Therefore, the actual extent to which manufacturers were able to acquire serf labor for the manufactories might be used as a tentative test of their economic and political influence.

We ought to begin with the assumption that, prior to the decrees of March 21, 1762, and August 8, 1762, resistance to purchases of serfs by manufacturers was widespread among the landed gentry, as they had been urging for forty years that such purchases be prohibited or limited. Clearly, since it was not until 1762 that such pressures took the form of law, it might be assumed that the existence both of counter pressures on the part of the manufacturers and of some reasons of policy led the government during the reigns of Anna and Elizabeth to steer a middle course. That the government did in fact pursue such a middle course, even going back to Peter's reign, may be learned from an examination of relevant legislation and from the record of actual purchases of serfs by manufacturers. First, about the evidence in terms of legislation: the Petrine policy expressed by the decree of January 18, 1721, was a typical compromise policy. It allowed merchants to buy villages by permission of the Berg and Manufacture Collegiums under the condition that they remain forever attached to the plants. A similar compromise policy prevailed under Peter's successors.[50]

Second, about the record of purchases: although the data may be inaccurate and somewhat confusing, they point to permission given for purchases of more than 60,000 serfs.[51]

Thus the policies of the state, prior to 1762, allowed the owners of the manufactories to invest in serf labor, thereby enabling them to continue the operations of their enterprises in the absence of free labor. This measure lessened the dependency of the manufactories' owners upon the gentry serf owners and resulted in greater stability for the activities of the industrial entrepreneurs.

The data and observations presented above would indicate two general conclusions: first, that the process of development of manufactures, started in the pre-Petrine period and gaining momentum under Peter, continued—at least in the private sector—into the post-Petrine period; second, that during the post-Petrine period the tendencies toward a strengthening of the entrepreneurial group were developing within a framework of government policy that was rather favorably inclined toward cooperation with this particular group. Thereby, continuity in policy and economic activity between the Petrine and the post-Petrine periods was essentially maintained.

## NOTES

1. The most widely known members of the liberal school were V. O. Kliuchevskii and P. Miliukov; of the étatist school, M. N. Pokrovskii.
2. "Die russische Manufaktur und Fabrik ist nicht organisch aus der Hausindustrie und nicht unter dem Einfluss des gesteigerten inneren Bedürfnisses der Bevölkerung heraus-gewachsen." Paul Miliukow, *Skizzen Russischer Kulturgeschichte* ("Essays in Russian Cultural History," [Leipzig, 1898]), p. 67.
3. "Sie wurde vielmehr ziemlich spät von der Regierung ins Leben Gerufen, die dabei einerseits ihre eigenen praktischen Bedürfnisse (Z. B. Tuchlieferungen für die Armee) im Auge hatte, anderseits aber auch die Unentbehrlichkeit einer nationalen Industrie erkannte." *Ibid.*
4. "Wie gering die Früchte der ersten Bermühungen waren, auf dem Wege des Schutzzoll-systems eine nationale Industrie zu schaffen, kann man aus den Ergebnissen der amtlichen Fabrikbesichtigungen etwa um 1730 sehen." *Ibid.*, p. 68.
5. *Ibid.*, pp. 68–69.
6. V. O. Kliuchevskii, *Sochinenia*, ("Collected Works"), IV (Moscow: Sotsekgiz, 1958), 335, "Industry after Peter did not make any noticeable progress; foreign trade remained, as it was, in the hands of foreigners."
The error in Kliuchevskii's judgment becomes obvious as soon as one compares the available data for the two major industries: iron and textiles. From 1725 to 1760, the number of enter-prises engaged in wool, linen, and silk manufacturing increased from 39 to 145; the number of machines from 2,070 to 11,666; and the number of workers from about 10,000 to 33,687. The output of pig iron increased from 13,350 tons in 1725 to 60,050 tons in 1760. The number of private iron and copper works increased from 28 to 138 in 1760, of which ironworks rose from 22 to 95. See E. I. Zaozerskaia, *Rabochaia Sila i Klassovaia Bor'ba na Tekstilnykh Manu-fakturakh v 20–60 gg. XVIII v.* ("Labor Force and Class Struggle in the Textile Manufactories" [Moscow: Akademia Nauk SSSR, 1960]), pp. 48, 72, 73. S. G. Strumilin, *Istoria Chernoi Metallurgii v SSSR* ("The History of Ferrous Metallurgy in the USSR" [Moscow: Akademia Nauk SSSR, 1954]), I, 197, 204. We would therefore have to reject Kliuchevskii's thesis as lacking any substantive support from the economic data.
7. The number of peasant serfs drafted during the years 1699–1701 for work in the Voronezh wharves was about 20,000 yearly; for 1703–1705, the number is not available. See Miliukov, *Gosudarstevennoe Khoziaistvo Rossii v Pervoi Chetverti XVIII Stoletia* ("The State Economy of Russia in the first Quarter of the Eighteenth Century" [St. Petersburg, 1892]), p. 269.
8. The number of peasant serfs and skilled workers employed in the construction of the Taganrog harbor was reported as follows: 1701—8,886; 1702—5,449; 1703—2,844; 1704—5,920. *Ibid.*
9. For the employment of forced labor in Azov and Troitsk, we have two estimates—one for the officially drafted, the other for those actually employed. The estimates are the following:

### Employment of Forced Labor in Azov and Troitsk

| Year | Officially Drafted | Actually Employed |
|------|-------------------|-------------------|
| 1704 | 30,370 | 16,696 |
| 1705 | 32,288 | 16,466 |
| 1706 | 37,208 | 7,272 |
| 1707 | 26,266 | 8,215 |
| 1708 | 1,500 | 1,350 |
| 1709 | 18,100 | 405 |

SOURCE: *Ibid.*

10. The list would probably be incomplete, even if it included the very inefficient (and ineffective) use of resources in the work on the Ladoga canal prior to Münnich's appointment as construction head.

11. The approximate number of the mobilized serfs employed in the construction of St. Petersburg can be inferred from the following data for the years for which figures are available. The numbers exclude the labor employed in the massive construction works conducted by the Admiralty and in the erection of such objects as the neighboring Kronstadt, Schlüsselburg fortress, etc. The numbers also exclude the employment of prisoners of war and criminals.

### Draft Quota and Actual Number of Landlord Serfs Employed in the Construction Works in St. Petersburg, for Selected Years

| Year | Draft Quota | Actually Employed |
|------|-------------|-------------------|
| 1706 | 40,000 | 20,000 |
| 1709 | 40,000 | 10,374 |
| 1710 | 43,928 | n.a. |
| 1711 | 30,448 | 24,381 |
| 1712 | 28,800 | 18,532 |
| 1713 | 33,779 | n.a. |
| 1714 | 32,253 | 20,322 |
| 1715 | 32,253 | n.a. |
| 1719 | n.a. | 6,232 |
| 1720 | n.a. | 4,853 |

SOURCE: S. P. Luppov, *Istoria Stroitel'stva Peterburga v Pervoi Chetverti XVIII veka* ("The History of Construction of St. Petersburg in the First Quarter of the Eighteenth Century" [Moscow-Leningrad: Akademia Nauk SSSR, 1957]), pp. 80–81.

12. The yearly expenditures out of taxes for civilian construction in St. Petersburg (excluding the Admiralty) were fixed until 1717 at 242,700 rubles; between 1717 and 1721 at 266,700 rubles; and from 1721, when a tax was substituted for labor services of the peasants, at 300,000 rubles. However the actual expenditures from the budget were usually higher. The total expenditures from the budget in 1720 were 316,484 rubles, and during subsequent years the government was called upon to assign an additional 80,000 to 100,000 rubles over and above the tax receipts earmarked for the St. Petersburg construction work. *Ibid.*, pp. 168, 170, 171.

13. **Yearly Number of Draftees in the Army and Navy**

| Year | Number | Year | Number | Year | Number |
|------|--------|------|--------|------|--------|
| 1701 | 33,234 | 1713/14 | 16,342 | 1724 | 20,550 |
| 1705 | 44,539 | 1714 | 500 | 1726 | 22,795 |
| 1706 | 19,579 | 1715 | 10,895 | 1727 | 17,795 |
| 1707 | 12,450 | 1717 | 2,500 | 1729 | 15,662 |
| 1708 | 11,289 | 1718 | 15,389 | 1730 | 16,000 |
| 1709 | 15,072 | 1719 | 14,112 | 1732 | 18,654 |
| 1710 | 17,127 | 1720 | 4,000 | 1733 | 50,569 |
| 1712 | 51,912 | 1721 | 19,755 | 1734 | 35,100 |
| 1713 | 20,416 | 1722 | 25,483 | 1735 | 45,167 |

SOURCE: L. G. Beskrovnyi, *Russkaia Armia i Flot v XVIII veke* ("The Russian Army and Navy in the Eighteenth Century" [Moscow: Voennoe Izadatel'stvo Ministerstva Oborony Soiuza SSR, 1958]), pp. 23–29, 33–34.

14. The available data on manufactories in Prussia and Saxony support the general impression that the "life expectancy" of industrial firms during the eighteenth century was short. See Horst Krüger, *Zur Geschichte der Manufakturen und der Manufakturarbeiter in Preussen* ("On the History of Manufactories and the Manufactorie Labor in Prussia" [Berlin: Rütten and Loening, 1958]), pp. 306–57.

Rudolf Forberger, *Die Manufaktur in Sachsen vom Ende des 16. bis zum Anfang des 19. Jahrhunderts* ("The Manufactories in Saxony from the End of the Sixteenth until the Beginning of the Nineteenth Century" [Berlin: Akademie-Verlag, 1958]), pp. 306–57.

15. The inventory of one of the largest private enterprises in Russia, that of the ironworks of Akinfii Demidov (1747), reveals that, while the value of plant and equipment was about 400,000 rubles, the value of the serf peasants employed in his iron and copper works was between 400,000 and 420,000 rubles. Among the various manufactories existing in the eighteenth century, ironworks were the most capital intensive. See B. B. Kafengauz, *Istoria Khoziaistva Demidovykh v XVIII-vv.*, ("The History of the Demidovs' Enterprise in the Eighteenth and Nineteenth Centuries"), I (Moscow-Leningrad: Akademia Nauk SSSR, 1949), 224–30.

16. In some branches of manufacturing in the eighteenth century, the nature of the technological processes and the type of equipment made it easier to subdivide enterprises than is the case in modern industry, and each part of a divided enterprise could still exist as an economically viable unit. The state-owned linen factory in Moscow (Polotniany Zavod) was divided among five entrepreneurs in the 1720's. The large silk manufactory (of Apraksin, Tolstoi, and Shafirov) was soon taken over and divided into three parts by groups of merchant entrepreneurs. Zaozerskaia, *Razvitie Legkoi Promyshlennosti v Moskve v pervoi Chetverti XVIII v.* ("The Development of Light Industry in Moscow in the First Quarter of the Eighteenth Century" [Moscow: Akademia Nauk SSSR, 1953]), pp. 213–42, 308–11.

17. This was generally the case in the early silk manufactories and leather factories. The expenditures to import foreign specialists and to train the indigenous labor force exceeded the costs of even imported equipment. *Ibid.*, pp. 297–300.

18. An examination of the activities of 41 merchants engaged in industrial entrepreneurship during 1710–70 indicates that 36 continued their activities in domestic or foreign trade, in tax farming, in alcohol supply contracts, etc. Thus their involvement in manufacturing depended upon the various alternative opportunities to earn a return on their capital. Under such circumstances, their participation in manufactories depended upon the state of their total business activity. This would explain many transfers of their holdings in manufacturing to relatives and partners and the sales to other entrepreneurs. For sources describing the behavior of various entrepreneurial groups, see *ibid.*; also, Zaozerskaia, "Labor Force and Class Struggle" (cited in n. 6); N. I. Pavlenko, *Istoria Metallurgii v Rossii XVIII veka* ("The History of Metallurgy in Russia in the Eighteenth Century" [Moscow: Akademia Nauk SSSR, 1962]); I. V. Meshalin, *Tekstilnaia Promyshlennost Krestian Moskovskoi Gubernii* ("The Textile Industry of the Peasants in Moscow Gubernia" [Moscow, Leningrad: Akademia Nauk SSSR, 1950]); and Arcadius Kahan, "Entrepreneurship in the Early Development of Iron Manufacturing in Russia," *Economic Development and Cultural Change*, X, No. 4 (July 1962).

19. The major relocation was connected with the government's conservation policies of 1754, when most of the ironworks, glass factories, and distilleries within about a 130-mile radius of Moscow were closed. Miliukov's calculation included in the total the enterprises liquidated by the government decree of 1754.

20. Pavlenko, p. 462. The survival rate and life span of ironworks in Russia were remarkably great in comparison with other countries whose ironworks were also based upon charcoal fuel. This phenomenon of the Russian ironworks can be explained principally by the greater supply of timber in the proximity of the ironworks.

21. Available data for the textile industry (linen, wool, and silk) indicate that out of 39 manufactories existing in 1725 (the year of Peter's death), 28 enterprises were still functioning in 1745. The number of basic machines in those enterprises had increased from about 2,070 to 3,073. The number of workers had increased in the "old" woolcloth manufactories by about 8 per cent and the value of output by about 50 per cent. In the silk manufactories, the output had increased by about 40 per cent. Zaozerskaia, "Labor Force and Class Struggle," pp. 34, 46, 48, 50, 52, 53.

22. In 1745, the "old" textile manufactories (established during the Petrine period) constituted 39 per cent of the total number of textile manufactories and represented 66 per cent of the basic equipment, 68 per cent of the labor force, and 70 per cent of the output. *Ibid.*, pp. 48, 50–51.

23. For the disappearance of manufactories established during the 1740's and 1750's, see Dmitrii Baburin, *Ocherki po Istorii Manufaktur-Kollegii* ("Essays on the History of the Manufaktur Collegium" [Moscow: Glavnoe Arkhivnoe Upravlenie NKVD SSSR, 1939]), pp. 189, 296–98. For the later periods, see Pavlenko, pp. 458–68, and K. A. Pazhitnov, *Ocherki Tekstilnoi Promyshlennosti* of Prerevolutionary Russia" [Moscow: Akademia Nauk SSSR, 1958]), pp. 168–73, 308–13.

24. The following series, recorded in English sources, represent the pattern of Russian-English trade.

### Trade of Russia with Great Britain
### (in £)

| Year | Russian Exports | Russian Imports | Excess of Exports |
|------|-----------------|-----------------|-------------------|
| 1715 | 241,876 | 105,153 | 136,723 |
| 1716 | 197,270 | 113,154 | 84,116 |
| 1717 | 209,898 | 105,835 | 104,064 |
| 1718 | 284,485 | 79,626 | 204,869 |
| 1719 | 140,550 | 55,295 | 85,255 |
| 1720 | 169,932 | 92,229 | 77,704 |
| 1721 | 156,258 | 95,179 | 61,079 |
| 1722 | 112,467 | 54,733 | 57,734 |
| 1723 | 151,769 | 56,697 | 95,072 |
| 1724 | 212,230 | 35,564 | 176,666 |
| 1725 | 250,315 | 24,848 | 225,468 |
| 1726 | 235,869 | 29,512 | 206,357 |
| 1727 | 144,451 | 21,883 | 122,568 |
| 1728 | 232,703 | 25,868 | 206,835 |
| 1729 | 156,381 | 35,092 | 121,289 |
| 1730 | 258,802 | 46,275 | 212,527 |
| 1731 | 174,013 | 44,464 | 129,549 |
| 1732 | 291,898 | 49,657 | 242,241 |
| 1733 | 314,134 | 42,356 | 271,778 |
| 1734 | 298,970 | 36,532 | 262,438 |
| 1735 | 252,068 | 54,336 | 197,732 |

SOURCE: Sir Charles Whitworth, *State of the Trade of Great Britain in Its Imports and Exports, Progressively from the Year 1697* (London, 1776), Part II, p. 29.

25. A. Semenov, *Izuchenie Istoricheskikh Svedenii o Rossiiskoi Vneshniei Torgovle i Promysh-lennosti* ("Study of Historical Information on Russian Foreign Trade and Industry" [St. Petersburg, 1859]), Part 3, pp. 23–25.

26. S. A. Pokrovskii, *Vneshniia Torgovlia i Vneshniia Torgovaia Politika Rossii* ("Foreign Trade and Foreign Trade Policy of Russia" [Moscow: Mezhdunarodnaia Kniga, 1947]), p. 89.

27. Semenov, Part 3, pp. 23–25.

28. The break in Russian-English diplomatic relations, coupled with the deterioration of the quality of Yorkshire coarse ·wool cloth, made the Prussian woolens competitive in the Russian market. As a result, the following quantities of Prussian cloth were ordered by the Russian government.

| Year | Quantity (in arshin) | Value (Reichsthalers) | Year | Quantity (in arshin) | Value (Reichsthalers) |
|---|---|---|---|---|---|
| 1725 | 233,375 | 119,000 | 1728 | 9,878 | 5,500 |
| 1726 | 316,792 | 170,000 | 1729 | 211,140 | n.a. |
| 1727 | 365,474 | 196,000 | 1730 | 59,026 | 33,000 |

Between 1725 and 1727, cloth for 485,000 *thalers* was delivered, for which one-third was paid in specie. W. O. Henderson, "The Rise of the Metal and Armament Industries in Berlin and Brandenburg, 1712–1795," *Business History*, III (June 1961), pp. 65–66. Douglas K. Reading, *The Anglo-Russian Commercial Treaty of 1734* (New Haven: Yale University Press, 1938), p. 380.

29.

**Internal Taxes and Custom Duty Payments Collected on the Makarievska Trade Fair, 1718–28 (in rubles)**

| Year | Internal Custom Duties | Total Taxes Collected |
|---|---|---|
| 1718 | 15,374 | 32,579 |
| 1719 | 14,074 | 30,957 |
| 1720 | 13,719 | 29,742 |
| 1721 | 13,735 | 26,845 |
| 1722 | 13,651 | 28,416 |
| 1723 | 16,525 | 28,619 |
| 1724 | 14,704 | 27,441 |
| 1725 | 15,121 | 27,340 |
| 1726 | 14,457 | 23,656 |
| 1727 | 15,803 | 24,278 |
| 1728 | 10,784 | 21,982 |

SOURCE: B. B. Kafengauz, *Ocherki Vnut-rennogo Rynka Pervoi Poloviny XVIII v.* ("Essays on the Internal Market of Russia in the First Half of the Eighteenth Century" [Moscow: Akademia Nauk SSSR, 1958]), p. 119. The figures for the year 1728, being for a terminal year, are not reliable. In addition, they show a very substantial decrease in the custom-duties collection concurrent with a fifteen-fold increase in the salt-tax collection and therefore must be regarded as inconclusive.

30.

**Output of Pig Iron, 1718–35**
**(in metric tons)**

| Year | State | Private | Total |
|------|-------|---------|-------|
| 1718 | 3,636 | 5,635 | 9,271 |
| 1719 | 3,622 | 5,518 | 9,140 |
| 1720 | 2,539 | 7,435 | 9,992 |
| 1721 | 2,752 | 7,453 | 10,205 |
| 1722 | 3,125 | 9,831 | 12,957 |
| 1723 | 2,233 | 8,316 | 10,549 |
| 1724 | 5,012 | 7,699 | 12,711 |
| 1725 | 4,717 | 8,633 | 13,350 |
| 1726 | 3,586 | 8,634 | 12,220 |
| 1727 | 3,472 | 7,912 | 11,384 |
| 1728 | 5,025 | 9,390 | 14,415 |
| 1729 | 6,185 | 8,485 | 14,670 |
| 1730 | 5,307 | 10,369 | 15,676 |
| 1731 | 6,323 | 13,039 | 19,362 |
| 1732 | 6,387 | 10,780 | 17,167 |
| 1733 | 5,962 | 11,483 | 17,445 |
| 1734 | 6,421 | 13,530 | 19,951 |
| 1735 | 7,198 | 15,758 | 22,956 |

SOURCE: Strumilin, pp. 180, 193, 197.

31. During 1726, the furnaces of the large Kamenskii and Alapaievskii and, in 1726–1727, of the Uktuskii, ironworks were out of order. Serious unrest was reported among the peasant serfs employed in the state ironworks during 1726 and 1727. *Ibid.*, p. 194.

32. The increase in the number of forge hammers, in view of an unchanged number of furnaces, indicates the shift toward harder types of iron products. The number of forge hammers increased from 110 in 1725 to 139 in 1727, while the number of active furnaces remained the same. The shift toward a different product mix of ironworks is substantiated by the data on the output of flat bar-iron, which show an uninterrupted rise.

**Output of Flat Bar-Iron, 1725–1730**
**(in metric tons)**

| Year | State | Private | Total |
|------|-------|---------|-------|
| 1725 | 1,704 | 4,455 | 6,159 |
| 1726 | 2,604 | 4,570 | 7,174 |
| 1727 | 3,325 | 4,144 | 7,469 |
| 1728 | 3,096 | 5,242 | 8,338 |
| 1729 | 3,486 | 4,930 | 8,616 |
| 1730 | 3,440 | 5,618 | 9,058 |

SOURCE: *Ibid.*, pp. 181, 197.

33. During 1726 and 1727, four new ironworks were completed (Sivinskii, Nizhe-Sinia-chynskii, Verkhne-Isetskii, and Shaitanskii). Since another three ironworks were completed during 1728–29, this shows that the investment flow into iron manufacturing did not cease.

34.                      **Copper Output, 1725–35**
                              **(in tons)**

| Year | State | Private | Total |
|------|-------|---------|-------|
| 1725 | n.a.  | n.a.    | 90.6  |
| 1726 | 155.2 | 3.2     | 158.4 |
| 1727 | 164.6 | 3.0     | 167.6 |
| 1728 | 150.7 | 15.8    | 166.5 |
| 1729 | 176.6 | 27.9    | 204.5 |
| 1730 | 166.3 | 51.2    | 217.5 |
| 1731 | 168.7 | 84.0    | 252.7 |
| 1732 | 143.9 | 68.8    | 212.7 |
| 1733 | 134.3 | 74.7    | 209.0 |
| 1734 | 179.8 | 100.3   | 280.1 |
| 1735 | 145.0 | 114.2   | 259.2 |

SOURCE: N. I. Pavlenko, *Razvitie Metallurgicheskoi Promyshlennosti Rossii v Pervoi Polovine XVIII veka* ("The Development of Metallurgy in Russia in the First Half of the Eighteenth Century" [Moscow: Akademia Nauk SSSR, 1953]), pp. 56, 78.

35. The two main uses of copper were the military and the monetary. The expansion of copper output might have been the result of the increase in demand for money, which would contradict the notion of a general slump.

36. While Peter the Great imported most of the wool cloth needed for army uniforms, the lining (*karazeia*) was almost entirely produced domestically. Government prices also made it more profitable to manufacture the lining than the cloth.

37. We have records about one wool cloth plant (later divided into four enterprises) and two silk factories that were established during those years. See Zaozerskaia, "Labor Force and Class Struggle," pp. 50–51.

38. Incomplete data on yearly government expenditures in the area of manufacturing are available for a number of years, but they include operating expenditures and those connected with the importation of foreign specialists, an item that was declining over time. Hence capital expenditures are difficult to extract from those data.

39. Strumilin, pp. 459–61. N. N. Rubtsov, *Istoria Liteinogo Proizvodstva v Rossii* ("The History of Castings Production in Russia" [Moscow-Leningrad: Akademia Nauk SSSR, 1947]), pp. 69–70, gives the following figures for the establishment of ironworks in the Ural:

Peter (1699–1725): 14 (.5 yearly)       Anna (1731–41): 25 (2.5 yearly)
Catherine I (1726–27): 4 (2 yearly)     Elizabeth (1742–61): 57 (3 yearly)
Peter II (1729–30): 4 (2 yearly)

40. The data on internal factory consumption of iron (which constituted a sizable share of the gross investment outlays for replacement of equipment and construction of new capacity) by the state-owned Ural ironworks point to the following quantities used (in tons):

| 1722–25 | 1,875 | 1730–33 | 1,261 |
|---------|-------|---------|-------|
| 1726–29 | 2,105 | 1734–37 | 2,121 |

If we assume the costs of production at 14.64 rubles per ton (24 kopecks per *pud*), the average yearly investment outlays from this source alone would amount to:

| 1722–25 | 6,860 rubles | 1730–34 | 4,615 rubles |
|---------|--------------|---------|--------------|
| 1726–29 | 7,704 rubles | 1734–37 | 7,763 rubles |

The above data do not indicate a slackening in this area of investment outlays for the state ironworks during the immediate post-Petrine period. See Pavlenko, "Development of Metallurgy," Table 16, p. 72.

41. *Polnoe Sobranie Zakonov Rossiiskoi Imperii (PSZ)* ("Complete Collection of the Laws of the Russian Empire" [St. Petersburg, 1830]), Vol. VIII, No. 5,821.

42. There are two ways of supporting the assertion about a decrease in the volume of smuggling. One is to cite the diminishing number of official reports, complaints, etc. The other is to investigate the volume of imports to the ports of the Baltic provinces (excepting St. Petersburg) and the volume of overland trade through the customs from the provinces into Russia, making an allowance for the volume of goods consumed in the Baltic provinces. On both accounts the data for the 1740's and early 1750's, when compared with the 1720's, appear to support the above assertion. For the trade to the Baltic ports, see N. E. Bang, *Tabeller over Skibsfart og Varetransport gennem Oresund 1661–1783* ("Tables on Shipping and Merchandise Transportation Passing through the Sund, 1661–1783"), Vol. II (Copenhagen: Gyldendalske Boghandel Nordisk Forlag, 1930).

43. An interesting case in point was the duty differential established between the ports of St. Petersburg and Archangel, which resulted in almost completely diverting trade toward St. Petersburg. The 1731 tariff equalized the tariffs for both ports and revived Archangel and its vast hinterland. The decrease of some tariff rates led to the abolishment of a number of trade monopolies, thus enabling other producers and merchants to enter the field on a more competitive basis. See Pokrovskii (cited in n. 26), pp. 94–97.

44. The relative profitability of the private manufactories as compared with those owned by the state was pointed out in the report of the Monetary Committee (Monetarnaia Komissia) to the Senate in 1732, in the "Senate Reports" of 1733–34, etc.

45. The above policy directives are spelled out in detail in the "Berg-Reglament" of 1739. *PSZ*, Vol. X, No. 7,766, and in the analysis of the conditions of transfer of state enterprises to private individuals. See Pavlenko, pp. 131–33.

46. The last case of summary expropriation of private property (not involving punishment of any particular individual) is the decree of January 6, 1704. The Berg Collegium Privilege of December 10, 1719, was a major attempt to provide assurance of property rights in the area of mining and iron-producing. During the post-Petrine period, the property rights of industrial entrepreneurs were widened, safeguarding for them not only physical property (plant and equipment) but also serfs. *PSZ*, Vol. VII, No. 6,255; Vol. IX, No. 6,858, Vol. X, No. 7,766.

47. See Dmitrii Baburin, *Ocherki Po Istorii Manufaktur-Kollegii* (Moscow: People's Commissariat of Internal Affairs, 1939), pp. 194–99. Baburin presents the basic features of government economic policy prior to the decree of 1775.

48. As an illustration, the following data pertaining to the iron and copper works could be cited.

### Entrance of New Entrepreneurs in Iron and Copper Works, 1701–1760

| Years | Total | Merchants | Gentry |
|---|---|---|---|
| 1701–10 | 1 | 1 | — |
| 1711–20 | 7 | 7 | — |
| 1721–30 | 12 | 11 | 1 |
| 1731–40 | 17 | 17 | — |
| 1741–50 | 35 | 32 | 3 |
| 1751–60 | 32 | 16 | 16 |
| Total 1701–60 | 104 | 84 | 20 |

SOURCE: Pavlenko, p. 463.

49. The conclusions about the relative positions of the manufacturers and the government officials are based upon an analysis of documents published in the following sources: N. I. Pavlenko, "Nakaz Shikhtmeisteru V. N. Tatishcheva" ("V. N. Tatishchev's Instructions to the Iron Master"), in Akademia Nauk SSSR, *Istoricheskii Arkhiv*, Vol. VI (Moscow-Leningrad: author, 1951). M. A. Gorlovskii and N. I. Pavlenko, "Materialy Soveshchania Ural'skikh Promyshlennikov, 1734–1736 gg." ("The Proceedings of the Meetings of Ural Industrialists, 1734–36"), in *ibid.*, Vol. IX (1953).

50. V. N. Tatishchev in 1734 got an instruction from Anna that regulated for the private iron masters the number of peasant serf families per ironwork, depending upon the volume and type of equipment. Anna's decree of 1736, which permitted the enserfment of free skilled workers, nonetheless forbade the non-gentry from purchasing whole villages ("only few households at a time"), although one wonders whether this particular clause was operative or followed in practice.

The Elizabethan decree of July 27, 1744, permitted non-gentry to purchase whole villages and cited the 1742 precedent of the merchant Grebenshchikov's purchase of 50 households. A decree of the Senate of January 17, 1752, established norms of serf purchases for textile manufactures and was implemented by an instruction of October 5, 1753, which permitted the purchase of serfs without land.

51. For 1743–62, we have 38,480 "souls" (males of all ages) and 2,440 households with land, and 3,034 "souls" and 50 households without land.

For ironworks and mining, the figures are 36,860 prior to 1752 and 8,683 afterwards—together, the 45,543 souls.

The Manufacture Collegium reported purchases of serfs by manufacture owners of 10,328 prior to 1752 and 6,532 after 1752—together, actual purchases of 16,860 serfs (males).

The Soviet historian Zaozerskaia estimated the total number of serfs acquired by all types of private-manufacture owners as being about 22,000 during 1720–43 and about 85,000 during 1743–50, while Semevskii gives the total for 1700–60 as about 60,000. See E. Zaozerskaia, "Begstvo i Otkhod Krestian v Pervoi Polovine XVIII v" ("Flight and Seasonal Leave of Peasants during the First Half of the Eighteenth Century") in *O Pervonachal'nom Nakoplennii v Rossii XVII–XVIII v.* ("About Primary Accumulation in Russia of the Seventeenth to Eighteenth Centuries" [Moscow: Akademia Nauk SSSR, 1958]), pp. 156–57.

# Home, School, and Service in the Life of the Eighteenth-Century Russian Nobleman

## MARC RAEFF

The Russian nobility of the eighteenth century played a major rôle in their country's development not only as its leading class in the eighteenth century but also as the seedbed of its cultural élite and intelligentsia in the nineteenth century. The Danish sociologist, Theodor Geiger, has suggestively defined the intelligentsia as the group of men who engage in the fundamental critique of their culture and the social and ethical presuppositions of their society.[1] This was precisely the function which the first generation of the Russian intelligentsia was most eager to perform. As it is only the active members of a culture who can want and are able to analyze it critically and fundamentally, it is not surprising that Russia's dominant élite should have provided the first leaders and recruits of the Russian intelligentsia. This makes it of great interest and importance to gain as clear a picture as possible of its mental, psychological, and social condition as a means of understanding the point of departure, the unspoken assumptions, of its destructive criticism and of the alternatives which it conceived and proposed. It will therefore be useful to consider some of the basic social institutions which helped to shape the way of life and the emotional and intellectual predilections of the active members of the eighteenth-century Russian nobility, particularly in the second half of the century. The influence which these institutions had on them and their specific intellectual content helped Russian noblemen to make their choice among available European ideas, philosophies, political attitudes, and literary forms. To those which they selected they imparted a dynamic structure of their own, and it is this structure which explains the peculiarities and originality of the intelligentsia's thinking and feeling. But it is itself explained in turn by the "existential choice" made on the basis of experiences and needs which the institutional framework imparted.

Childhood experiences are always important in shaping certain basic attitudes which remain influential throughout life. As Philippe Ariès has pointed out, it is too often forgotten that the child was viewed differently in the past, and that its

FROM Marc Raeff, "Home, School, and Service in the Life of the Eighteenth-Century Russian Nobleman," *Slavonic and East European Review*, XL, 95 (June 1962), 295–307. Reprinted by permission of the author and the publisher.

rôle in the family and society was very different from that which is accepted now on the basis of the experiences of western society in the last hundred years or so.[2] The material available on some of the important aspects of childhood in eighteenth-century Russia is unfortunately limited. But it still reveals certain interesting facts. Most members of the Russian nobility born towards the middle of the eighteenth century were born on the estates of their fathers. Their early years would be spent in the rural environment of these estates, though the winter months would often be passed in the city. The family was still predominantly patriarchal. But most of the time the father would be away on service. Even after 1762 it was only the invalid or extremely poor nobles who failed to spend a good part of their active life in service. As countless memoirs show, a nobleman on service was unable to visit his estate and family very often, and sometimes he stayed away for years. His children and particularly his sons, thus grew up in an alternation of almost anarchical freedom and shorter periods of very strict discipline and control. It is true, as the examples of the families of Sergey Aksakov and Ivan Turgenev show, that the authority of a mother and grandmother might sometimes be greater than that of a father. But it was no adequate substitute for the father's authority, especially a father endowed with an officially and socially sanctioned authority as an officer or government official.

Not all the nobles on service left their families behind on the estate. Some would have their immediate family with them in the place where their service was carried out. But in spite of the father's presence there was little feeling of permanency even here. Service needs forced families to move frequently from one town or garrison to another.[3] Residence in a town also meant separation from the larger family and the estate, and attachment to family and estate was an important aspect of a nobleman's life both emotionally and economically. Except among the few members of the most "aristocratic" families of dignitaries, the feeling prevailed throughout the eighteenth century that residence in the city or town was only temporary, and that the nobleman's place was in the countryside, on an estate.

The legal and economic problems involved in the Russian *pomestiye* system in the eighteenth century have still to be fully investigated. But the nobleman's relationship to his estate had some interesting aspects which deserve attention. Estates might be acquired as a reward for service or as a dowry or they might be purchased. Consequently they were often scattered over several districts or even provinces. This was particularly true of the estates of nobles who had acquired or received land in the steppe provinces or the newly opened border areas of the Ukraine and the middle Volga. The more recent acquisitions were often the more valuable estates economically, and the owner preferred to live on them rather than on the ancestral estate. The practice of dividing the estate among all the children (at least all the sons) continued to flourish in spite of Peter the Great's efforts to change it in his decree of 1714 on single inheritance; and to the extent that the inheritance had to be divided as fairly as possible each heir would receive lots in several estates or possibly one of these several estates if this proved more convenient. As the original property was split up and the size of estates decreased, noblemen found it necessary, or at least desirable, to acquire new property. This could be done in a variety of ways such as purchase, marriage, and exchange. But as often as not the new property was not assembled around the nucleus of the old estate. Instead the old estate tended to be sold or exchanged, and the family moved to a new area. Resettlement of this kind was particularly dramatic in new areas like the Ukraine and the middle Volga, as Sergey Aksakov's unforgettable picture shows. Alternatively the separate bits of property would be retained, and the family would live on them in turn. This meant that it would move from one province or district to another every few years or possibly oftener.[4]

The general result was that the Russian nobleman of the eighteenth century normally lacked strong roots in any particular area and had no real feeling of attachment to a specific locality and to a family estate on which his ancestors had lived for generations. The estate was simply a piece of property; the value placed on it was limited by its economic worth; and it was easily interchangeable with another estate of equal economic worth. There is little evidence of the attachment to and the ties with the ancestral home which characterised the mentality of western noblemen.[5] On the contrary the Russian nobleman tended to feel "at home" whichever estate he moved to. This feeling was fostered by the country's geographical uniformity and the identity of basic social conditions such as serfdom, which also strengthened the idea that every estate in Russia was interchangeable with any other. When a nobleman settled on another estate he had no impression that he was moving into a different environment, all the more so if he followed the example of the Aksakovs and had his serf families move with him.

This lack of roots in any specific locality and the ease with which estates were sold, exchanged, and sometimes even abandoned, without so much as a visit from the owner emerge clearly from the memoirs of the time. As one of the earliest of the few students of the Russian nobility has correctly pointed out, it is striking that except for the old families of former independent or appanage princes like the Golitsyns and Odoyevskys the Russian nobleman very rarely took his family name from the name of his estate or neighbourhood, as was the usual practice in the west.[6] It is also not without significance that when dealing with nobility in particular the great Russian novelists paid relatively little attention to the geographical locality in which the lives and actions of their characters took place. How often do they merely say "on an estate in the central provinces" or "near the town N"?

The absence of deep local roots and the overwhelming feeling of the uniformity of the Russian land and of the universal sameness of the social environment were undoubtedly among the important and permanent experiences of the Russian nobleman. They were also experiences acquired from childhood onwards and may go far towards explaining the nobleman's detachment from the soil and easy adaptability to the capitals and to foreign lands. They may also help to explain why the Russian nobleman often thought of his country, his nation, Russia in short, as a sort of complete entity, a general category, even an abstraction. This did not prevent him from feeling a strong attachment to her and even worshipping her emotionally. But his attachment lacked the concreteness and specificness of the attachment which the nobleman in the west possessed to a well-defined environment, to his *terroir*. In other words, while the nation, the *patrie*, was seen in the west as a union of many local loyalties, the comprehensive all-Russian loyalty had primacy in Russia both in fact and in feeling and did not necessarily have local "sub-divisions."

Another very important element in the early experiences of the Russian nobleman which is too often overlooked is that as a child he was in the care and under the supervision of serf nursemaids, tutors, and servants. These serfs had no rights and very rarely any powers of discipline. When clashes and conflicts occurred it was always the young master who prevailed and the serf nurses or tutors who had to give way and see their authority undermined by parents who seldom sided against their children. These children must also have been quick to sense from the bad example which their parents set them that the serfs need not be much considered or respected and were a kind of second-rate adult who had to be guided and supervised and were obliged to comply with their own wishes and caprices. The young nobleman thus suffered little from authority and controls and had his whims easily gratified.[7] He was able to give orders to grown-ups who had him under their care and was able to make use of other human beings to gratify his wishes. This meant that he could exercise his will on others even from an early age. Evidence is available to show that once the young *barchuk* had acquired some western knowledge he would try to transform his serf nurse, tutor, or playmates according to the idea of human nature which he had formed for himself. The general results were well described by a contemporary in the following words: "[serf-nurses] accustom the child to believe that his will must be executed without question; he gets used to this, and when he grows up this passion increases and the consequence is that the child entrusted to their care often becomes a slave to his passions, for without the approval of the nurse he could not have let his passions manifest themselves so easily and with such success."[8]

After the carefree years on the estate came the time to go to school and learn. Education for nobles was made compulsory by Peter the Great, who needed men with at least a rudimentary education for his modernised armies and administration. The obligation to learn, go to school, and pass examinations in order to be considered legally of age did not at first suit the average nobleman who strongly resisted it. In some instances the resistance persisted until late in the eighteenth century, as witness Fon Vizin's *Nedorosl'* or the regulations enjoining the young nobles of Tambov to attend school which the poet Derzhavin issued when he was governor of Tambov province.[9] But education nevertheless took hold of the majority of noblemen as the century progressed. It became a matter of pride as well as a requirement for a satisfactory career in the state service to possess whatever was considered the minimum of education at the time. It was their higher level of education, greater degree of culture, and more sophisticated style of life, which distinguished the nobility from other classes of society. In the absence of a clear legal definition of nobility, which resulted from the confusion caused by the conflicting claims of service and birth as the basis of noble status, participation in a cultured way of life came to be regarded as the real criterion.[10] The very poor and uneducated nobleman (in the western provinces, for example) was hardly considered to belong to the nobility and became assimilated to the peasantry in the course of the century.[11]

The obligation to undertake education involved attendance at school. During the first three decades or so of the eighteenth century this was the general rule. Later on, the private tutor and foreign teacher invited to the estate became more usual in the wealthier households. But the memoirs of the time indicate that the most commonly accepted method of education still remained the school, even if it was only a little private school like that which Bolotov ran in his house for his own and his neighbours' children, or some small boarding school in the provincial capital.[12] Boys were sent to school at an early age, which might vary from about six or seven to twelve or thirteen. As schools were not very numerous, distances great, transport difficult, and families often on the move, the pupils lived and spent nearly all their time in school and remained separated from their families throughout the year and often for several years at a stretch. Special family circumstances might sometimes even keep a child at school and away from his home and family for the whole duration of his studies, and it was only when he finished school that he would revisit his family, almost as a stranger, on his way to his service appointment. Whatever the circumstances, the break with the previous way of life and environment was undoubtedly radical and often caused a psychological shock. Sergey Aksakov's experience was perhaps extreme. But countless memoirs and even nineteenth-century literary works have recorded the anguish, feeling of sudden isolation, uprooting, and difficulties which these children experienced when first entering school.

To appreciate the element of psychological shock it should be remembered that to go to school meant not only to leave home but also to come under discipline and into a new and almost artificial atmosphere after years of capricious and virtually anarchic freedom on the estate. Prevailing pedagogical practices and the need for preparing the boys for a state service which was primarily military meant that discipline in schools was strict and military in character. The nature of the education provided also added greatly to the feeling of isolation, bewilderment, and disorientation.[13] Since Peter the Great's time the main function of education in Russia had been to help in the country's modernisation and westernisation and in the creation of a new type of Russian who would be European-minded and modern and capable of actively serving a modern and power-directed state. The aim of all Russian educators from Feofan Prokopovich to Ivan Betskoy and of institutions like the Cadet Corps and the boarding schools connected with Moscow University and the Academy of Sciences was to remove and isolate the pupils from their traditional environment, from "barbarous" and uneducated serf tutors, and from insufficiently westernised families, in order to be better able to fashion them according to their own very different lights.[14] Hence the attempts to keep them in school as long as possible without allowing them to return to the family. Betskoy's projects, for example, advocated a period of twelve years.

It is not surprising in these circumstances that school took the place of home, and that fellow students and the more popular teachers became the real family. The boys developed a feeling of closeness and a strong spiritual bond with one another. Pushkin's famous line "Our homeland is Tsarskoye Selo" not only had a metaphorical meaning for his contemporaries but actually depicted a reality, as witness also the life of Radishchev and the biographies of the Decembrists. As most of the friendships made at school were continued within the framework of state service and social and intellectual contacts in the capitals, a group solidarity was formed which rested not on family relationships (though these often existed in some circles) or on regional connections, but rather on a common educational experience. Those involved had shared the important and powerful experiences of discovering the worlds of ideas and emotions during adolescence, while cut off from their families and childhood environment and kept apart from the outside world by the cold discipline of an impersonal institution. At the same time their experiences isolated them from the lives and problems of those who had never shared these experiences with them. It thus became easier for them to conceive the outside world and those belonging to it as objects to be acted upon in the light of their experience than to think of them as something of which they themselves were part and with which they would have to share the future. The strength of school influences may also account for the lack of real contacts and ties between the older and younger generations and for the rapid succession and brevity of the "generations" in Russian intellectual life. In the closed atmosphere of the Russian boarding school every "class" was virtually a generation to itself.

In school the young Russian nobleman received a completely western education which had practically submerged the Muscovite traditions of learning and education by the middle of the eighteenth century. As a contemporary journal put it: "Our *forefathers* called it *education* when they taught their children the Psalms and how to count on the abacus; after this they would give their enlightened son a book of hours printed in Kiev . . . . This *education* can hardly be called education, for the duties of the citizen and Natural Law were unknown to the youngsters. . . ."[15] The infatuation with foreign languages and the western content of Russian education in the eighteenth century are too well known from literature and the reports of foreign travellers to need elaboration. What is more important to remember is that the education had no ties with the traditional culture of pre-Petrine Russia. The schools barely mentioned old Russian literature and history, and the repeated calls for a better knowledge of the Russian language indicate that even this was a rather neglected subject.[16] Significantly enough, the salary of a teacher of Russian was at the bottom of the salary scale for teachers in the corps of naval cadets.[17] It is true that towards the end of the century greater interest in Russian history and culture began to develop. But even this was a result of western intellectual fashions,[18] and it seems to have remained superficial and an inert element in the Russian nobility's mental outlook until the appearance of Karamzin's "History of the Russian State" early in the nineteenth century. Even Tumanskiy's *Novyi detskiy mesyatseslov s kratkoyu istoriyey geografiyeyu i khronologiyeyu, vseobshcheyu i Rossiyskoyu*, which was published in St. Petersburg in 1787, devoted only 10 out of its 202 pages to Russian history; and in most contemporary journals and reviews Russian history took the form of either fictionalized morality tales or a dry listing of rulers and dynastic ties. Dmitriyev's assertion that Russian literature and history were still not taught at the beginning of the nineteenth century is obviously exaggerated. But it should not be dismissed out of hand.[19] School syllabuses and speeches by academics on festive occasions fully confirm that the realities of Russia both past and present occupied a very small place indeed in the nobility's education, which imparted instead the cultural riches and historical traditions of western Europe.[20] Schooling thus widened the gulf between the educated élite and the people, including even the uneducated "hobereaux de province" whom Prince I. M. Dolgorukov so graphically describes in his memoirs.[21] In an intellectual sense school experiences and the content of education reinforced some of the basic psychological elements first developed by the home and family environment.

It is also important to realise that the content of this western-oriented education gave it a special dynamic function in Russia. In the west itself education never isolated children from their natural environment and the realities of their country however strictly they may have been treated in institutions such as Jesuit establishments and the later English public schools. The reason why it had the opposite effect in Russia is not far to seek. Peter the Great's reforms had produced a sharp break in the historical continuity of the Russian nobility's consciousness, and the traditional values and ways of thought and action of the Muscovite boyars had all been pushed out and discarded within one or at the most two generations.[22] Among what was abandoned were prejudices and much that was antiquated and useless. But spiritual and moral traditions were rejected as well, and their place was taken by the western ideas and models acquired at school. These were not felt to be merely substitutes. On the contrary, like all newly acquired values they were regarded as absolutes. In the west they were counter-balanced by traditional customs and habits of conflicting norms. In Russia by contrast they became imperatives to be applied as closely and completely as possible.

Russian drama and the satirical journals of Novikov contain many illustrations of the absurd and ridiculous form which this "worship" of foreign ways and values could take. But it also had more serious and valid aspects. Educated Russians wished to make themselves worthy of the new, more modern and powerful Russian empire and accepted foreign cultural ideas, philosophic notions, and historical examples as a necessary part of the process and as values or goals to be emulated. This frame of mind is graphically illustrated by Bolotov. But it was also true on a more sophisticated level of Radishchev, Novikov, Fonvizin, the Vorontsovs, and Princess Dashkova, who all criticized Russian realities in the name of what they regarded as "higher" moral, philosophical, cultural, and political values absorbed from the west. The less sophisticated were undiscriminating and went further. They treated these western values as values to be followed absolutely and were anxious to see Russian reality adapted to them instead of taking them as an inspiration and guide for the creation of new Russian values. Ignorance of the realities of Russia and acceptance of western philosophical, aesthetic, social, and cultural norms as absolute imperatives for thought and action were thus the intellectual result of the educational process and school experience of the average young Russian nobleman in the second half of the eighteenth century.

After schooling came state service which bulked much too large in the life and political experience of the Russian nobility at the end of the eighteenth and the beginning of the nineteenth centuries to be dealt with fully here. But one important aspect of the nobility's service experience, which has so far been insufficiently appreciated, deserves special mention. For the majority of the nobility state service meant primarily military service. Many even of the civil administrators began their careers in the army and sometimes returned to it before they retired. The Russian military establishment in the eighteenth century was almost identical with those in western Europe, particularly with the military establishment created and developed by Prussia. In contrast to the armies of earlier times, the fighting forces of the absolute monarchies of the eighteenth century were highly bureaucratised institutions, organised according to the principles of rationality, efficiency, and uniformity. They paid considerable attention to such externals of military life as uniforms, drill, and parades and laid great stress on uniformity of organisation and performance and on strict hierarchical subordination. Regulations and orders were absolutely binding and were meant to be the same everywhere. This attention to detail and emphasis on external uniformity reached their extremes in the caprices of Peter III and Paul I and in the methodical pedantry of Alexander I and Nicholas I. But they were common to all the European armies of the time. The Russian military establishment, however, showed one significant difference which aggravated the effect of these common elements. This was that the ordinary Russian soldiers were drawn from among the serfs, which meant that they could be used and abused almost at will. One of the army's functions was supposed to be to transform these unfortunate serfs into automatons, capable of performing on the parade ground with absolute precision and concerned only with the details of their uniforms and with the prompt and unquestioning execution of all and any orders which they received, however absurd they might be. It was the officer's duty to implement and enforce these notions about military discipline and military life.

From his experiences of military service the Russian nobleman acquired what may be described as a "militaristic" outlook. "Militaristic" in this context should naturally not be interpreted in terms of the aggressive and expansionist goals often ascribed to the Prussian and German officer corps. It simply means a strongly held belief that orders and regulations have universal and uniform applicability, and that as many aspects of the national life as possible should be organised according to the pattern of hierarchical centralisation and authority which holds true in the military establishment. Life in and even outside the service should be determined by rules having the value of absolute impera-tives; and in the observance of them the stress should always be on externals, on the forms of behaviour, and on the process of administration (*obryadnost'*). This militaristic outlook also implied a strong sense of hierarchy, which was heightened by Russia's table of ranks, the absolute subordination of every inferior rank to the orders of any superior, and the absence of any right of initiative at the lower levels in the hierarchy. Everything was to be highly central-ised and dictated from above on the basis of supposedly absolute and universally valid rules and ideas. Hence the disarray among the officer corps when the entire orientation of Russia's military organisation was suddenly changed by the ca-prices of Peter III and Paul I. In a less extreme form these same general considera-tions applied to the civil administration of the Russian empire, which also put a premium on uniform rules, the absolute force of orders from above, centralisa-tion, and strict hierarchy.[23] Naturally, the reality often fell short of the ideal. But it is important to understand that the norms of the ideal were instilled into the young nobleman in the course of his service and undoubtedly helped to shape his outlook and attitudes.

The Russian nobleman served not only an individual, charismatic ruler but also the Russian state. In this he differed from the French noble who served only his king. In France the nobleman's whole loyalty went to the person of his sovereign and he had no feeling that he was also serving France or the French state. The Russian nobleman on the contrary was always keenly conscious of serving the Russian state. This was perhaps the most important revolution which Peter the Great's reign had wrought in the consciousness of the Russian *élite*. The nobleman, whom upbringing and training left rootless, isolated, and detached in relation to his people and country, now became a willing tool in the service of an abstract concept: the modern, power-oriented state. For the sake of this abstraction and the glory of the Russian empire men were organised, trained, fashioned, and ruled according to a general scheme and uniform, abstract principles. The officer or the official was the chosen instrument in the process. In performing his service he was helping to modernise his country and transform the primitive, ignorant, apathetic peasant into an obedient tool of the Russian state, capable of meeting the requirements set by the new institutions. But it was less a sense of responsibility and awe which he felt than joy and satis-faction that he could now shape the destinies of men according to general, modern principles in the aesthetically pleasing way of rational orderliness and uniformity.

The intoxicating power produced by these service conditions was so strong that it often outlasted the period of active service. On retirement many a Russian nobleman tried to apply what he had absorbed during service and reconstitute the "beauties" of military organisation on his own estate. Certain of them organised their serfs on the model of military units, drew up precise time-tables and work schedules, and arranged to have all the planned activities of their serfs signalled by trumpets and drums. Their domestic servants were even more "militarised" and were sometimes made to form small military units which were drilled according to army regulations and paraded for the greater entertainment and joy of their owner and his guests.[24] But even more important than these sadly ridiculous external manifestations were the attempts of many landowners to regulate and shape the lives of their serfs by means of regulations, rules, and sometimes full-scale "codes" of law. These were copied from army regulations and had the same meticulous concern for uniformity and hierarchical, orderly, centralised organisation. They were in no sense pastimes and amusements. On the contrary they were put into effect and caused great hardships to the peasants. It would not be too far-fetched to see in the military colonies of Alexander I and Arakcheyev an extreme, large-scale example of the same kind of regulatory mentality and of the will to reshape people's lives according to certain abstract notions.

The influence of western ideas, particularly the ideas of the enlightenment, has to be seen in the context of the Russian nobility's institutional experiences and the attitudes which they engendered. In spite of the important qualifications made by recent scholars, it is still generally accepted that the eighteenth century was exceptionally rationalistic, didactic, and abstract in its approach to social and political problems; and its major representatives had a strong component of "Utopian mentality" in their make-up.[25] When the Russian nobleman came into contact with these ideas and approaches he readily accepted them and tried to apply them in his daily life. The social and psychological experiences derived from his own institutions also predisposed him to believe in their applicability. The rationalistic and voluntaristic elements of eighteenth-century thought thus proved to be particularly congenial and fitted to Russian experience, and the combination of the two was to exert its full force and effect on the Russian intelligentsia of the nineteenth century.

The rôle played by the reception of natural law in Russia should be looked at from the same point of view. Natural law came to Russia primarily in its German form,[26] and the German professors who expounded it in the eighteenth century laid great stress on two elements which were particularly well suited and congenial to the Russian *élite*. First, they emphasised the idea of social service and social solidarity. Secondly, they insisted that the active will played a paramount rôle in creating the right conditions for the moral life. The idea of service and social solidarity was directly in line with the Russian nobleman's own service obligations, while the emphasis on will was specially welcome to an *élite* engaged in westernising and thus transforming their state and country through conscious political and cultural effort. The attitudes of the Russian *élite* towards history should also be considered from the same standpoint: not only its attitude towards Russia's pre-Petrine past but also its attitude towards the problem of the rôle of "organic" development and historical traditions. The reign of Peter the Great had produced a break in Russian historical consciousness, or more accurately in the feeling for historical continuity. The members of the Russian *élite* felt themselves to be new men (as many were in practice), dedicated to the task of radical transformation. In Max Weber's sense, their whole frame of mind was "rationalistic" rather than "traditionalistic." For this reason they were particularly receptive to the rationalist, geometric, absolutist, uniformity-oriented, and universal ideas and attitudes amounting to Utopianism which they were able to derive from the west. Their "rationalistic" frame of mind in its turn grew out of their psychological experiences within the framework of Russia's basic institutions of family, school, and service.

## NOTES

1. T. Geiger, *Aufgaben und Stellung der Intelligenz in der Gesellschaft*, Stuttgart, 1949.

2. P. Ariès, *L'enfant et la vie familiale sous l'Ancien Régime*, Paris, 1960.

3. See A. T. Bolotov, *Zhizn' i priklyucheniya Andreya Bolotova opisannyya samim im dlya svoikh potomkov 1738–1793*, four volumes, St. Petersburg, 1871–73, I, (1871); I. F. Lukin, "Zhizn' starinnogo russkogo dvoryanina" (*Russkiy arkhiv*, No. 8, 1865, Moscow, pp. 899–930).

4. Bolotov has graphically described these moves from one estate to another, not only of himself but also of his numerous neighbours. See A. T. Bolotov, *op. cit.*

5. O. Brunner, *Adeliges Landleben und europäischer Geist*, Salzburg, 1949; J. M. J. vicomte de Marsay, *De l'âge des privilèges au temps des vanités*, Paris, 1946.

6. E. P. Karnovich, *Rodovyye prozvaniya i tituly v Rossii i sliyaniye inorodtsev s russkimi*, St. Petersburg, 1886, pp. 28–29.

7. What excessive permissiveness could do to create a feeling of insecurity in the child we can only guess at owing to inadequate documentation; but perhaps it contributed to the formation of basic character traits of alternating insecurity and an aggressive will to dominate which are visible in some members of the intelligentsia in the nineteenth century.

8. V. N. Zinov'yev, "Zhurnal puteshestviy po Germanii, Italii, Frantsii i Anglii, 1784–1788" (*Russkaya Starina*, XXIII, October, 1878, St. Petersburg, p. 229).

9. I. N. Dubasov, "Tambovskiy kray v kontse XVIII v." (*Istoricheskiy vestnik*, XVIII, 1884, St. Petersburg, p. 134).

10. See for example *Zerkalo lyubopytstva . . . sobrannyye iz raznykh pisateley*, St. Petersburg, 1791, pp. 58–59; also G. Gukovsky, *Ocherki po istorii russkoy literatury XVIII v.—dvoryanskaya fronda v literature 1750kh—1760kh godov*, Moscow-Leningrad, 1936.

11. See the satiric description in Narezhnyi's *Rossiyskiy Zhil' Blas*; M. M. Bogoslovsky, "Smolenskoye shlyakhetstvo v XVIII v." (*Zhurnal Ministerstva Narodnogo Prosveshcheniya*, No. 322, March, 1899, St. Petersburg, pp. 25–61).

12. It should be remembered that even when education took place at home with a tutor—usually in a foreign language—the moment the process of learning started the young nobleman found himself cut off from his former playmates and even from those members of his family—sisters, mother, grandmother, aunts—who could not share in his new intellectual experience.

13. Herein lies one of the great differences in the impact of school on the young Russian boy and on a pupil in a Jesuit school or an English public school. In spite of the strictness of discipline and the isolation enforced by these latter schools, neither their atmosphere nor the contents of their education were as unrelated to ordinary experiences at home and in society as were those of schools in eighteenth-century Russia.

14. I. Betzkoy, *Les plans et les statuts des différents établissements ordonnés par S. M. I. Catherine II pour l'éducation de la jeunesse et l'utilité générale de son empire*. (Trad. par Monsieur N. Clerc), Amsterdam-Leipzig 1782, I, 114–115. See also S. V. Rozhdestvensky, *Ocherki po istorii sistem narodnogo prosveshcheniya v Rossii v XVIII–XIX vv*, St. Petersburg, 1912 (also *Zapiski Istoriko-filologicheskogo fakulteta I. Sanktpeterburgskogo universiteta*, No. 104, 1912); V. Ya. Stoyunin, "Razvitiye pedagogicheskikh idei v Rossii v XVIII st." (*Pedagogicheskiye Sochineniya*, 2nd ed., St. Petersburg, 1903, pp. 91–175); M. Vladimirsky-Budanov, *Gosudarstvo i narodnoye obrazovaniye v Rossii s XVII veka do uchrezhdeniya ministerstv*, St. Petersburg, 1874.

15. "O smysle slova *vospitaniye*" (*Sobesednik lyubiteley rossiyskogo slova*, I, part 2, St. Petersburg, 1783, pp. 12–13). Italics in the original.

16. As a volunteer contributor to a journal confesses: ". . . with the condition that I shall not be responsible for correct spelling, because in our age our teachers were not great grammarians. . ." *Rastushchiy Vinograd*, III, June, 1786, p. 1.

17. F. F. Veselago, *Ocherk istorii morskogo kadetskogo korpusa s prilozheniyem spiska vospitannikov za 100 let,* St. Petersburg, 1852, p. 121.

18. H. Rogger, *National Consciousness in Eighteenth-Century Russia*, Cambridge, Massachusetts, 1960.

19. M. A. Dmitriyev, *Melochi iz zapasa moyey pamyati* 2nd ed., Moscow, 1869, p. 18.

20. It seems plausible to suggest that the rôle played by travel in Russian literature, as well as its passion for realism, may have been means to counteract the "alienation" of the élite from its physical and social milieu. Russian reality had to be discovered consciously, with effort; it was not a datum of experience.

21. I. M. Dolgorukov, *Zapiski kn. I. M. Doigorukova—Povest' o rozhdenii moyom, proiskhozhdenii i vsey zhizni*, Petrograd, 1916, pp. 124-125.

22. The exceptions that are always cited deal with the poor and backward gentry of remote provincial nests; they do not affect the picture for the active, influential elements of the nobility from whose ranks the intelligentsia eventually developed. Incidentally, these *starosvetskiye pomeshchiki* were the objects of either scorn (eighteenth century) or indulgent irony (nineteenth century) and were always regarded as untypical.

23. See my article "L'état, le gouvernement et la tradition politique en Russie impériale" which will appear shortly in the *Revue d'Histoire Moderne et Contemporaine*.

24. A. T. Bolotov, *op. cit.*, II, pp. 722-724.

25. R. Ruyer, *L'Utopie et les utopies*, Paris, 1946; A. Cobban, *In Search of Humanity*, London, 1960; R. Mauzi, *L'Idée du bonheur dans la pensée et la littérature française du XVIIIe siècle*, Paris, 1960, p. 16.

26. The literature on this problem is very large and has not been fully systematised. Useful indications can be found in: A. Lappo-Danilevsky, *Sobraniye i svod zakonov Rossiyskoy imperii sostavlennyye v tsarstvovanii Yekateriny II*, St. Petersburg, 1898; A. Fateyev, "K istorii yuridicheskoy obrazovannosti v Rossii" (*Uchenyye zapiski osnovannye russkoy uchebnoy kollegiyey v Prage*, I, vyp. 3, 1924, 129-256).

# The Costs of "Westernization" in Russia: The Gentry and the Economy in the Eighteenth Century

## ARCADIUS KAHAN

*I leave my inheritors in extreme poverty, since my debts, most illustrious Madam, exceed half a million rubles—[they accumulated] during my thirty years of service in the Admiralty, where, particularly in the beginning, I was compelled to entertain many guests, to feed almost everybody, and to get them accustomed not only to high society but also to affluence.*

COUNT I. G. CHERNYSHEV to Catherine the Great (1794)

Historians have described the gentry as the most powerful and influential social group in eighteenth-century Russia. The gentry developed during the sixteenth and seventeenth centuries as a social class, or estate, from the fusion of the old feudal aristocracy with the younger military and administrative service class. The view that the gentry was the pillar of absolutism and of the Russian state was virtually unchallenged during the eighteenth century. The special status of the Russian gentry derived principally from the fact that its members constituted the first social group that could not be treated arbitrarily by the state. The Russian state recognized certain rules of conduct in respect to the gentry, and by and large observed those rules, at a time when other social groups possessed no safeguards, as individuals or collectively, in their dealings with the state.

The political role of the gentry was to some extent determined by statutory arrangements that reserved for its members key positions in the bureaucratic apparatus, political-administrative and military alike. The special privileges and prerogatives of the gentry rested on the implicit condition that the gentry assist the state in executing its over-all policy. It was this very fact that inevitably led to social change and transformation of the gentry.

"Westernization" has served as a catchword to describe Russian policies during the eighteenth century in the economic, political, and cultural spheres. It embraces the modernization of technology, the development of new institutions and efficient administration, and the cultivation of more refined tastes. It means education and conspicuous consumption. Furthermore, the term connotes the

FROM Arcadius Kahan, "The Costs of 'Westernization' in Russia: The Gentry and the Economy in the Eighteenth Century," *Slavic Review*, XXV, No. 1 (March 1966), 40–66. Reprinted by permission of the American Association for the Advancement of Slavic Studies.

firm commitment of the gentry to behave according to an accepted standard, however defined; failure to conform entailed the risk of losing a share in the social privileges of the group.

Despite the imprecision of the term "Westernization," then, in this paper it is preferred over "modernization," because it is in widespread use and because, in effect, the two terms are almost interchangeable in reference to the particular situation discussed here—for the cultural modernization of the Russian gentry consisted largely in imitating "Western" standards and values. Although "Westernization" affected the gentry in many ways, this essay is concerned with only certain features of the process, namely, the new consumption patterns (dress, cuisine, home furnishings, services, education, travel, and the like) and their economic impact on the relations of the gentry, the peasants, and the state.

The title "Costs of Westernization" requires a further caveat. Costs are treated as expenditures by a particular social group, the gentry, rather than as costs to society as a whole.

Historians have, with varying degrees of success and accuracy, described both the process and the cultural effects of "Westernization." There has been no satisfactory analysis of the economic response of the gentry to the government's challenge of "Westernization." It is to the economic preconditions for the fulfillment of the gentry's political, social, and cultural role within the general framework of "Westernization" that I shall address myself in the following pages. I shall assume that exogenous factors gradually imposed upon the gentry[1] a new pattern and rising level of consumption and thus treat the gentry's increasing demand for income as a primary factor in the gentry economy. I shall try to indicate the order of magnitude of the expenditures imposed upon the gentry as a result of the demands of "Westernization" and to show the ways in which the gentry tried to meet these expenses by improving its income position. In a review of those income-generating activities of the gentry and their impact upon general economic activity in Russia, it will, I hope, become clear that an intensification of "ordinary" economic activity was insufficient to meet the expenditures of the gentry and that state assistance had to be called for. What criteria were applied by the state in distributing its assistance among members of the gentry class? Did the distribution of economic "aid" follow the actual distribution of economic and political power? The raising of such questions may contribute not only to a clearer understanding of the Russian economic universe but also to a more accurate appraisal of the political realities in the eighteenth century and of the relation between the state and the gentry.

# I

The political power of the state rested upon its ability to mobilize the human and material resources of the country (for example, in army recruitment and the provisioning of the army and the state bureaucracy) for particular and general goals. The economic and political power of the gentry rested upon its ability to collect the rent from its estates and to secure the assistance of the government in doing so. Upon what basis did the symbiosis of state and gentry rest? For the state to function and the gentry to exist, some means had to be found of dividing between the two the chief economic asset of the country, the labor of the peasantry, to which each had some claim. In a general sense, the economic position of both the state and the gentry rested upon the rent collected from the peasant population. The role of the state in maintaining the extraeconomic conditions that enabled the gentry to collect its rent was indispensable for the gentry to maintain its income and status.

This is another way of saying that the wealth of the gentry consisted of serfs, while the wealth of the government consisted of the serfs owned by the government directly, plus the capitalized income that the government derived from taxing other groups of the population (the gentry's serfs included). I deliberately stress the importance of serfs, rather than land, as an asset. Until the eighteenth century most of the land, even that of the gentry (except for the *votchiny*, the manorial estates), belonged in title to the state (or tsar); the concept of private property in land was not well developed. The gentry was granted recognition of its landholdings as its private property early in the eighteenth century, but the market for land was still limited and most transactions were conducted in terms of the basic asset, serfs. The abundance of land on the periphery of the Empire made the serfs the more significant factor; they were both the fiscal and economic unit of account. It was principally in the second half of the century that rentals and sales of land without serfs occurred to any extent and that recording began. During this period wealth derived from timberland and mining lands was reckoned an addition to wealth in the form of agricultural land tilled by serf-peasants, but up to the end of the eighteenth century land as such (independent of serfs) was not recognized as the measure of the gentry's wealth. Thus, a convenient way of measuring the absolute and relative wealth of the members of the gentry is to consider the ownership of serfs. The data on the number of the members of the gentry and their serfs are

Table 1. Estimates of the Number of Gentry and Their Serfs in Russia in the Eighteenth Century (males only; exclusive of those in military service)

|  | Gentry | Serfs | Serfs per Gentry Member |
|---|---|---|---|
| 1744 | 37,326 | 3,443,293 | 92.2 |
| 1762 | 49,777 | 3,783,327 | 76.0 |
| 1783 | n. a. | 5,092,867 | n. a. |
| 1795 | 193,132 | 9,997,625 | 51.8 |
| 1795* | 77,199 | 5,700,465 | 73.8 |

* On the territory comparable to that of the second and third census (*reviziia*), in 1744 and 1762.

SOURCE: V. M. Kabuzan, *Narodonaselenie Rossii v XVIII—pervoi polovine XIX v.* (Moscow, 1963), p. 154.

incomplete, but nevertheless, within certain limits, they show us the general order of magnitudes involved.

Since we are interested not only in the average number of serfs per gentry household[2] but also in the distribution of serf-ownership, we must rely upon other evidence. There are available two sets of data based on the third census (*reviziia*) of 1762. It is possible, but not certain, that the two sets pertain to the same universe, and they are here presented separately, in Tables 2 and 3.

Since the average annual rent payments (*obrok*) during the 1770s were estimated at 2.5 rubles per male, the average for the 1780s at 4 rubles per male, and for the 1790s at 5 rubles per male,[3] it will be assumed that the rent payment for 1777 was 3.5 rubles per male and 5 rubles for 1795. This assumption enables us to use the data of Table 3 in order to estimate the distribution of landowners by money incomes from agricultural rents collected from their serfs.[4]

The data of Tables 1–4 indicate a wide dispersion of serf ownership, the predominance of small ownership of serfs at one extreme, and high concentration of serfs per owner at the other extreme. Thus the traditional sources of gentry income, serfholdings, make for a high degree of heterogeneity among the gentry, both in terms of wealth and income and of status and interest.

Thus it is appropriate to raise the question of the adequacy of the gentry's income to meet the demand of cultural Westernization. We shall use the costs of Western-style consumption tastes for comparison with gentry incomes derived from the traditional sources in order to answer the question.

We shall assume that most foreign "luxury" goods for the period were consumed by the gentry.[5] Of the imports received through the European boundaries for 1793–95, it is estimated that the gentry's annual share averaged 11,411,500 rubles (41 percent of the total imports); if we add 1,145,500 rubles for duty payments and a minimum trade margin for retail trade of 20 percent, the result is a rounded sum of 15,068,000 rubles.[6]

Table 2. Percentage Distribution of Landowners
according to the Number of Serfs in Their
Possession, Third *Reviziia* (1762)

| Number of Serfs per Gentry Household | Percentage of Landowners (Heads of Household) |
|---|---|
| Fewer than 21 | 51 |
| 21–100 | 31 |
| 101–500 | 15 |
| 501–1000 | 2 |
| Over 1000 | 1 |

SOURCE: P. V. Köppen, "Über die Vertheilung der Bewohner Russlands nach Ständen, in den Verschiedenen Provinzen," *Mémoires de l'Académie Impériale des Sciences de Saint-Pétersbourg*, Sixth Series, Vol. VII (St. Petersburg, 1847), p. 429.

Table 3. Percentage Distribution of Landowning Gentry by
Number of Serfs Held, 1777

| No. of Males Owned by Landlord | All Provinces* | Blacksoil Provinces** |
|---|---|---|
| Fewer than 10 | 32.0 | 33.6 |
| 10–30 | 30.7 | 31.5 |
| 30–60 | 13.4 | 13.0 |
| 60–100 | 7.7 | |
| 100–150 | 5.0 } 23.9 | } 21.9 |
| 150 and over | 11.2 | |
| including 500–1000*** | 2.6 | 1.7 |
| including 1000 and over*** | 1.5 | .6 |

\* The provinces (*provintsii*) included in the total belong for the most part to Great Russia: Pskov, Velikie Luki provinces; St. Petersburg Guberniia; Vologda, Ustiug, Arkhangel'sk, Galich, Kazan, Perm, Viatka, Nizhegorod, Simbirsk, Arzamass, Sviazhsk provinces; Astrakhan and Orenburg guberniias; Penza, Tambov, Shatsk, Eletsk, Orel, Voronezh, Sevsk, Belgorod, Tobol'sk, Udinsk, Irkutsk, and Iakut provinces. Missing is Moscow Guberniia (11 provinces) and part (3 provinces) of Novgorod Guberniia.

\*\* Included are the Shatsk, Penza, Tambov, Eletsk, Orel, Voronezh, Ostrogozhska, Sevsk, and Belgorod provinces.

\*\*\* Derived from data of the Semevskii Archives, quoted in N. L. Rubinshtein, *Sel'skoe khoziaistvo Rossii vo vtoroi polovine XVIII v.* (Moscow, 1957), p. 27.

SOURCE: V. I. Semevskii, *Krest'ianie v tsarstvovanie Imperatritsy Ekateriny II* (St. Petersburg, 1903), I, 31. Since the data are derived from landholding data of the "general land survey," the landless gentry is not included.

If for the year 1795 we assume the number of gentry to be 200,000 males, the expenditures would amount to 75.34 rubles per male gentry. Let us assume 3 male members per gentry household, and we will arrive at an expenditure of 225 rubles per household. Since the yearly average rent collected from a male peasant "soul" during the 1790s was reported to have been 5 rubles, 225 rubles per gentry household required the income from 45 serfs. This excluded from the average expenditure more than half of the gentry as shown in Table 4. There is no need to compare any further the distribution of landowners by size of serf-holdings with the estimated average of expenditures, since such expenditures presumably were not evenly distributed. Undoubtedly, either the expenditures were beyond reach of a sizable part of the gentry, or they constituted a substantial portion of the gentry's income.

The total number of serfs according to the fifth census (1795) was 9,997,625, which, at a yearly rent payment of 5 rubles per serf, provided the gentry with 50 million rubles yearly income from this source. We have estimated the gentry's consumer expenditures on imported goods at over 15 million rubles yearly, not including a number of other expenditures usually connected with "Westernization," such as education and travel. My preliminary estimates indicate yearly expenditures for these two items of over 3 million rubles.[7] Thus expenditures for "luxuries," education, and travel amounted to over 18 million rubles per year, or over 35 percent of the gentry's income from its serfs. Needless to say, the share of expenditures stimulated by "Western" tastes in the total expenditures of the gentry was substantially higher than indicated by the above estimates.

We may, therefore, conclude that "Westernization" of the gentry required a level and pattern of expenditures that necessitated a substantial increase in its real income. The gentry's pressure for higher incomes thus becomes one of the major features of its economic and political activity in the eighteenth century. The demands for higher incomes or new sources of income were intensified by the trend toward fewer serfs per gentry household (see note 2 above); this was probably not a threatening development, since no attempt was made by the gentry to revive the issue of primogeniture.[8] Let us examine some of the possibilities available to the gentry for increasing real income.

## II

The areas in which the gentry attempted to increase its incomes may be conveniently classified as agricultural and nonagricultural, as either private activity outside state regulation or activity involving direct state interference.

**Table 4. Income of Landowners in 1777 and 1795 Based Upon the 1777 Percentage Distribution of Landowners by Number of Serfs Held**

| Percentage of Landowners (Heads of Household) | Rent Income, 1777 | Rent Income, 1795 |
|---|---|---|
| 32.0 | Less than 35 rubles | Less than 50 rubles |
| 30.7 | 35–105 | 50–150 |
| 13.4 | 105–210 | 150–300 |
| 7.7 | 210–350 | 300–500 |
| 5.0 | 350–525 | 500–750 |
| 11.2 | 525 and over | 750 and over |

It would be logical to expect that the first attempts of the gentry to increase income to meet the extra expenditures of "Westernization" should take place in the area of agriculture, on the estates of the gentry. It is therefore of crucial importance to see the general picture of the development of agriculture during the eighteenth century. Here, as in so many other areas of Russian economic history, a number of general propositions must be reexamined, rethought, and redefined. Within the framework of an article it is possible to present only conclusions; the process of reasoning and all the underlying data cannot be presented in detail. Let us start with the pattern of the development of agriculture during the second half of the eighteenth century, from the 1750s to the 1790s, inclusive.

We will consider the developments in the second half of the century in part as a result of a cumulative process under way and in part as a response to special stimuli. That growth was involved in this process is beyond any doubt. Even if none of the agricultural records had survived and the following table pertaining to foreign trade were the only relevant document, we would have to conclude that Russian agriculture made substantial progress during the period. One may wonder whether this increase in trade might have been due to the territorial expansion of Russia (particularly the absorption of some formerly Polish territories). The answer is negative, for the increased output of flax and

**Table 5. Exports of Certain Agricultural Commodities (yearly averages in tons)**

|       | 1758–1762 | 1793–1795 |
|-------|-----------|-----------|
| Grain | 9,820     | 59,434    |
| Hemp  | 36,281    | 50,155    |
| Flax  | 11,335    | 20,655    |

SOURCES: Heinrich Storch, *Supplementband zum fünften, sechsten und siebenten Theil des historisch-statistischen Gemäldes des Russischen Reichs* (Leipzig, 1803), pp. 34, 35; V. I. Pokrovskii, ed., *Sbornik svedenii po istorii i statistike vneshnei torgovli Rossii* (St. Petersburg, 1902), I, 2.

hemp centered almost entirely on the old territory of Russia. Even though the grain export figures may not have been characteristic of other exports and though they fluctuated substantially, they do nevertheless point to an over-all growth of agricultural production and its marketable share.

In the absence of readily available unbroken series or estimates of sown area or crop production, one must proceed with a general description of the conditions in Russian agriculture. In the eighteenth century it was only in the non-blacksoil zone that the three-field system was consistently applied to all arable lands. In the blacksoil zone the three-field system was supported by a large area of potentially arable land, a long fallow reserve that would be brought under cultivation in large masses every fifteen to twenty years. Thus, in addition to the normal fallow in the three-field system there existed a substantial reserve of land that helped to maintain the fertility of the soil (or to recoup it) within the three-field system during most of the eighteenth century.[9] If we are to describe the subsequent process of expansion of the sown area in Russia, we would therefore have to distinguish the following steps: first, the plowing up of long fallow land; second, the plowing up of meadow lands; third, the clearing of new land to increase the arable land area. Moreover, at each successive step there was a choice to be made between the performance of the operation mentioned and the breaking of virgin land in the southern and eastern provinces of the Empire. There is no doubt that both processes, using up more of the potentially arable land in the old areas and breaking new land on the peripheries, took place simultaneously. What was going on in Russia was a rapid process of expansion, with greatest acceleration during the 1780s and 1790s.

The groundwork for this process was laid during the 1750s and 1760s. The increases in the price of grain and fibers, which reflected the increases in both foreign and domestic demand for food and agricultural raw materials, were the signals transmitted to the gentry producers. The search for opportunities and ways to earn additional income or to expand output required greater mobility on the part of the gentry than the various existing military and civilian service obligations allowed. Under the circumstances, it was a logical consequence of economic expediency that the gentry be freed from military service. Thus, in 1762, the obligatory military service of the gentry was abolished, and its members were freed for the "pursuit of happiness" in the various directions of their choice.

The most typical reaction of the gentry was to take a greater interest in their estates and to demand more land. The opportunity to acquire more was given during the period of the "general land survey" (*general'noe mezhevanie*).[10] The decrees of 1765 and 1766 provided the general framework for distribution of unoccupied steppe and forest lands among the gentry. What followed was a land fever that affected most of the gentry, and the orderly transfer of owner-ship rights that took place lasted in some regions up to twenty years.[11] There are no summary data for the total amount of land involved nor of its particular characteristics, but there can be no doubt that the "general land survey" policy, a serfdom version of the land grants familiar in the United States, was of tremendous significance for the survival of serfdom in Russia and for the development of agriculture. It provided the gentry with wealth and future in-comes during the subsequent period of rise in land prices. The "general land survey" resulted in an expansion of the sown area in the more densely populated sections, thus increasing the land-labor ratio and creating conditions for an increase in population. Moreover, the expansion of the sown area into new agricultural regions of relatively high yields stimulated population migration.

A few general data will illustrate the extent of this process. Within the pro-vinces of European Great Russia (excluding the Ukraine, Belorussia, the Baltic provinces, and the Caucasus) was found a total of 44,346,000 *desiatiny*[12] of arable land according to the general land survey. Of this total, 39,039,000 *desiatiny* were located in 26 provinces for which the reports of 1795–96 indicate 27,236,000 *desiatiny* as being the sown area.[13] This gives on the average 69.8 percent of the arable land under cultivation. In a three-field system, almost 70 percent of the arable land under cultivation is a good record of land utiliza-tion. Even more interesting and significant are the data indicating that from the mid-1780s to the mid-1790s in 15 provinces (including 6 provinces of the non-blacksoil zone) the sown area increased from 12,992,000 to 18,944,000 *desiatiny*.[14] Even if the data for the 1790s are somewhat exaggerated, or the data for the 1780s involve an underestimate, there can be no doubt that a very substantial increase took place. The increase in sown area was accompanied by an increase in the average yield. Thus the presumption is that not only was the long fallow land being brought under cultivation but that advantage was also being taken of the fertile and high yielding lands of the blacksoil zones.

One of the more important innovations was the northward movement of wheat planting and the growing importance of this crop in the blacksoil zone. The introduction of potatoes, originally as a garden crop, took place in the eighteenth century. Tobacco was introduced on a large scale and its varieties improved. In animal husbandry the development of sheep raising (fostered by state-sponsored sheep farms and imported Spanish merino sheep) was an attempt to supply wool for the domestic textile industry. There were also attempts to teach the peasants the operation of improved agricultural implements.[15] Relatively little was achieved in these areas, however. For one reason, work stock and agricultural equipment were supplied by the peasants themselves in performing their services to the estates, and the gentry was not very much concerned about these matters. Animal husbandry was considered an auxiliary to crop agriculture, with the peasant households producing and supplying most of the output, and was somewhat neglected by the gentry. In additon, it was a branch of agriculture that required much more personal supervision and involvement than the gentry probably cared to devote to it. Typical of the developments in Russian agronomy in the last third of the eighteenth century were such progressive experiments as multi-field crop rotation, grass planting, and special seed preparation. The search for new crops and feed grasses and the application of various types of fertilizer were also intensified.[16]

An interesting feature is the fact that both the growth of the sown area and the rise in yields took place to a large extent through increasing the area farmed by the landlords, or the gentry, rather than by increasing the area within the serfs' farms. Indeed, the areas of progress in agriculture during the eighteenth century were those primarily under the direct control of the gentry. The efforts by the Free Economic Society (founded in 1765) to spread more modern farming methods among its gentry members, coupled with the interest of some landowners in deriving a higher income from their estates, suggest that agriculture was probably not so unresponsive to new opportunities and stimuli as some of the older historians would have us believe.

The second measure to achieve an increase in gentry income, the one most frequently (and inaccurately) mentioned by historians, was to increase rent. It is an often repeated mistake to assume that landlords, even under the conditions of serfdom, were at liberty to increase rent. In fact, the available evidence for the eighteenth century, particularly for the post-Petrine period, is to the contrary. There is no doubt that attempts to raise rents were repeatedly made by serfowners, but the attempts were largely unsuccessful. One of the major obstacles was the availability of cheap land on the eastern and southern fringes of the Empire. The abundance of land tended to keep rents low and the price of labor relatively high. The existence of a "frontier" enabled the peasant-serfs to engage in a "pedestrian-protest"; thus, peasant flights also prevented rents from increasing. A few figures suffice to illustrate the enormity of the problem that both the gentry and the state (under an obligation to search out and return fugitives) were facing. During 1719–27, 198,800 fugitive male peasants were found;[17] during the period 1719–42 a total of 526,000 were returned, leaving for 1728–42 about 327,000.[18] The yearly average for the two periods does not point to major differences between the periods. However, it is very likely that, because of famine or increased pressure by landlords in particular localities, the number of fugitives varied substantially from year to year, and from period to period. Likewise, the percentage of peasants in flight must obviously have varied from one locality to another, and probably from one estate to another. The individual cases for which information is available may not be typical for the country as a whole,[19] but peasant flights remained a problem during the

**Table 6. The Level of Taxation and Rent Payments of Private Serfs, for Selected Decades of the Eighteenth Century**

| | Head Tax (kopeks) | Money Rent (kopeks per male) | Total Burden (kopeks) | Price of Rye (kopeks per chetvert') | Rye Price Index |
|---|---|---|---|---|---|
| 1730s | 70 | 60 | 130 | 63 | 100 |
| 1750s | 70 | 80 | 150 | 80 | 127 |
| 1760s | 70 | 150 | 220 | 126 | 200 |
| 1770s | 70 | 250 | 320 | 172 | 273 |
| 1780s | 70 | 400 | 470 | 285 | 452 |
| 1790s | 100 | 500 | 600 | 382 | 606 |

| | Head Tax Deflated by Price Index | Rent Deflated by Price Index | Total Burden Deflated by Price Index | Real Burden (1730s = 100) |
|---|---|---|---|---|
| 1730s | 70.0 | 60.0 | 130.0 | 100.0 |
| 1750s | 55.1 | 63.0 | 118.1 | 90.8 |
| 1960s | 35.0 | 75.0 | 110.0 | 84.6 |
| 1770s | 25.6 | 91.6 | 117.2 | 90.2 |
| 1780s | 15.5 | 88.5 | 104.0 | 80.0 |
| 1790s | 16.5 | 82.5 | 99.0 | 76.2 |

SOURCES: S. G. Strumilin, *Istoriia chernoi metallurgii* (Moscow, 1954), p. 273; V. I. Semevskii, *Krest'ianie v tsarstvovanie Imperatritsy Ekateriny II* (St. Petersburg, 1903), I, 53, 59, 60.

whole of the eighteenth century.[20] The inability of the gentry to raise rents, or rather the real value of rents, substantially during the immediate post-Petrine period is reflected in the approximate data of Table 6. The table, based upon Semevskii's rent data and Strumilin's price data, provides a general insight into the real value of the rent payments by the gentry's serf-peasants. In addition, it allows us to draw some conclusions concerning the state's policies with regard to taxation of the gentry's serf-peasants, a topic that will be discussed later. Perhaps further research in the area both of rents and prices might refine the data and produce more reliable conclusions.[21] It is very unlikely, however, that such research would invalidate the basic contention that the level of rent in real terms did not increase in the post-Petrine period until the 1760s and that the total burden of rent and taxes probably remained the same.

The situation that emerges from the estimates in Table 6 explains why the total burden upon peasant households did not increase; although an increase in rents paid to landlords occurred, direct government taxation (in real terms) decreased at the same time. Thus one can view this relationship as a form of competition between the gentry and the government for income from the serf-economy. Apparently both sides were aware of this relationship—the gentry in its demand that the head tax should not be increased, and the government in its frequent insistence that the landowners, in their attempts to raise rents by increasing the labor services of the peasants, deprived the latter of the possibility of earning income for tax payments. "Not from the burden of state taxes but because of continuous work for the landlords are the peasants being impoverished," says a decree of the Senate of January 24, 1738.

The argument so often advanced by Russian historians that the increasing arrears in head tax reflected the impoverishment of the peasants overlooks other, possibly important, factors: first, the famines and other natural calamities that severely affected agriculture might have caused most of the accumulated tax debts; and, second, the gentry (which was responsible for collection of the tax from the peasants) at a time when its own demand for money was increasing, might have been giving preference to the collection of rents over the collection of taxes and hoping to make up its arrears sometime in the future, since neither severe punishment nor additional costs would legally be imposed upon tardy gentry tax collectors. In fact, the tax indebtedness on account of the peasants' head tax was so widely distributed among the Russian gentry that it cannot be attributed solely to the inability of their serf-peasants to pay or to the insolvency of landlords who would advance payment and subsequently collect it from their serfs. This contention is supported by Table 7, which gives a distribution of a part of the tax debt owed by tardy taxpayers. The list, from a document compiled in 1737, is not complete; it apparently includes only the major debtors.

Apart from some years during the latter part of Peter's reign and occasional years of droughts and natural calamities that simultaneously affected large parts of the territory of Russia, when an accumulation of tax arrears resulted, there is virtually no proof that the serfs in the eighteenth century were unable to pay the decreasing (in real terms) head tax. The tax-arrears data cannot be used convincingly in support of a hypothesis of general impoverishment of the peasants. Nor is there much substance to the other frequent contention that the gentry's serfs were either much worse off than the serfs owned by the state or were impoverished as a result of the burden imposed by the gentry. In fact, while the state-owned peasants' total burden (defined as the sum of the head tax and the rent payments) fluctuated in comparison with the burden on the gentry's serfs,[22] the ratio of the respective burdens at the end of the period was about what it had been at the beginning.

The preceding discussion has been directed toward establishing the premise that the attempts on the part of the gentry to increase its income from agriculture

**Table 7. 1737 List of Tax Arrears of the Peasant Head Tax**

| Serfowners | Number | Sum of Arrears (in rubles) | Rubles per Owner |
|---|---|---|---|
| *Individuals* | | | |
| Member of Cabinet | 1 | 16,029 | 16,029 |
| Senators | 11 | 7,900 | 718 |
| Supreme Procurator of the Senate ⎫ | | | |
| Head of Heraldry Office ⎬ | 3 | 3,956 | 1,319 |
| Head of Petition Office ⎭ | | | |
| Presidents and members of collegia and chancelleries | 53 | 16,207 | 306 |
| Court officials | 7 | 4,458 | 637 |
| Generals and admirals | 51 | 11,188 | 219 |
| Aristocracy | 111 | 455,088 | 4,010 |
| Elizabeth, daughter of Peter | 1 | 8,351 | 8,351 |
| Total listed above | 238 | 513,177 | 2,156 |
| Other gentry landowners | n.a. | 1,192,105 | |
| Total for individuals | | 1,705,282 | |
| *Institutions* | | | |
| Palace villages | | 154,872 | |
| Holy Synod villages | | 4,182 | |
| Prelate villages | | 9,201 | |
| Monastery villages | | 66,161 | |
| Commerce Collegium payment for state peasants attached to state-owned factories | | 31,578 | |
| Total for institutions | | 265,994 | |
| Total | | 1,971,276 | |

SOURCE: Akademiia Nauk SSSR, *Voprosy sotsial'no-ekonomicheskoi istorii i istochnikovedeniia perioda feodalizma v Rossii* (Moscow, 1961), p. 130.

had to overcome a natural barrier in the existing resources, physical and human, and the technological level of the serf-peasant economy. To overcome the barrier, the gentry would not break the existing social structure, but they were quite flexible in the application of various devices to increase their income.

Russian historians and students of Russian agriculture have in the past been particularly concerned with the two different forms of rent—money rent (*obrok*) and labor services (*barshchina*) on the estates—and with measuring their relative weight. In broad terms it would probably not be inaccurate to state that at the middle of the eighteenth century, in part as a result of the demand for cash and the growing share of very large estates in the total landholdings of the gentry, money rent was, or was becoming, the prevailing form of rent payment, but that by the end of the century a discernible switch toward labor services had taken place in many regions. This switch may be explained by several factors. Among the smaller gentry the 1762 decree affording them freedom from government service enabled them to devote most of their time to the management of their estates. But the overriding reason on all estates was that the total farmed area directly occupied by the estates was increasing. Given rising grain prices, serfowners favored labor services in expectation of higher income from the sales of output than from money rents with their probably slower rate of increase. The increase of the estate lands, which occurred at a higher rate than the increase of the cultivated area of the serf-peasants' lands, made the estate more flexible and more capable of reaping short-term gains from changing market situations than the serf-peasant economy. Thus, the relative success of the gentry in improving its wealth and income position by the end of the eighteenth century through both the land grants of the government and its own involvement in the market was, in part at least, the result of its management of the estate economy. In addition, typical of the gentry's economic behavior were ability to take advantage of the relative decrease of prices of manufactured goods and a steady increase in the consumption of manufactured goods. All these factors combined to strengthen among the gentry what we would now call the propensity to consume and the preference for present income over future income. As the wants of the Russian gentry increased with the degree of cultural Westernization, so did their expenditures for the goods and services that symbolized their "Westernization."

## III

The gentry, in order to derive a higher income from the available resources of the estates, could either allow or actively support the diversification of the peasant economy. They attempted to introduce more division of labor in the peasant economy and to develop higher and more complex skills than those used in ordinary agricultural work. The return on skills was relatively high, and the income or wage differential between skilled labor and unskilled very wide. The development of cottage industries or of specialized village crafts was very remunerative to both peasants and landlords. Interesting examples of such development were the villages Ivanovo and Pavlovo, nuclei of the subsequent centers of the textile and metalworking industries. The income derived by the owner of the two villages exceeded many times the income of agricultural settlements of the same size.[23] Wherever agricultural specialization had not yet entered into the village economy, the gentry often tried to derive additional income by employing peasant families in processing agricultural raw materials, in nonspecialized work like spinning of yarn, and in various other such tasks. Moreover, members of the gentry were involved in industrial entrepreneurship. Although there were gentry ventures, both successful and unsuccessful, as early as the 1720s and 1730s,[24] I would date the beginning of entrepreneurship among the gentry in the decade of the 1740s. The most successful and most atypical noble family, the Stroganovs, had gone into iron and copper works in the 1720s and 1730s, but industrial entrepreneurship for the gentry, either as a source of substantial auxiliary income or as a substitute form of utilization of the estate serfs, was more common in the next decade.

Given the wealth and income distribution of the gentry and the relative scarcity of cash in most gentry households, entrepreneurship promised to be a workable solution in the following cases: (1) if an individual had entrepreneurial qualities and no risk aversion—even to the point of willingness to borrow cash in the expectation of high returns under conditions of uncertainty; (2) if the cash and other resources were available and there was an established management of the estate that could handle the extended activities in the area of manufacturing; and (3) if the estate owner entered into partnership with either merchants or peasants who would supply the factors his economy lacked, namely, cash and business experience.

Among the gentry entrepreneurs of the eighteenth century the number of the daring was apparently very small indeed.[25] We find more entrepreneurs in the two other situations just mentioned. Let us consider first entrepreneurial and manufacturing activity based upon the existing managerial organization of a large estate. The first two examples—the Naryshkins' operation of the Kashir Iron Works and deposits (whose ores were exhausted as early as the 1720s) and the Stroganovs' managerial organization (originally involved in salt production) —were quite successful within the boundaries of the owners' own estates but were inconclusive precedents. Nevertheless, in the 1750s the government decided, not without pressure by the petitioners, to give a large part of the state-owned iron and copper works to a group of highly placed noblemen, serfowners, and bureaucrats. Altogether 27 such establishments were turned over to a handful of court nobles during the 1750s. In eight cases, the local ore or fuel supply was exhausted. The remaining 19 works did not long remain in the hands of their owners,[26] for none of them was able to integrate the industrial enterprises in the administration of their estates as a perpetual income-providing asset. Thus ended an unsuccessful experiment which tested the entrepreneurial ability of the top gentry—able statesmen and administrators who were unable, however, to readjust their estate management to cope with the intricate production and distribution problems of an industry that was relatively competitive. The gentry did much better in a less competitive industry, for example, woolen manufacture, where the government contracted for a share of the output for the needs of the army. After 1756, when the Army Quartermaster started to pay in advance for a part of the contracted cloth, the number of gentry entering this branch of textiles increased sharply—apparently attracted by the absence of competition, the availability of credits by the Manufacture Collegium, and the assured demand at favorable prices.

Many gentry entrepreneurs followed the third pattern, namely, that of enlisting the cooperation of either merchants or peasants and relying upon a mixed labor force, serf and hired, in their enterprises. It is difficult to establish how successful such partnerships or associations were as a general rule; a need for much more research and study of the topic is indicated. In some cases one of the parties remained for a long time a silent partner; in some cases the partnership was broken up, or one of the partners withdrew. In any event, the experience of cooperation was a useful one for the economy at large. Most of the gentry enterprises were located outside the cities, on the estates, and were producing for the national rather than the local or nearby urban market. The merchants gained some knowledge of, and insight into, the workings of serf-agriculture. The members of the gentry learned to take advantage of the use of free, hired labor, to meet members of other social groups on a more nearly equal footing, to understand the world of business, and perhaps also to acquire (in Pavlenko's phrase) "the experience of making the rounds of government offices as a petitioner."[27] In any case, the lessons learned by the gentry from the association with merchants and peasants served as groundwork for future successful activity.

The search for additional income on the part of the gentry brought them into conflict with two groups in society who, although lower in social status, were gaining in economic power and political influence and who, by and large, were winning the favor of the government in their economic pursuits. These two groups were the industrial entrepreneurs and the merchants.

Up until about the middle of the eighteenth century the industrial entrepreneurs, a socially mixed group, had been able to count on strong support from the government whenever they came into conflict with individual or local gentry interests. The main source of contention was the problem of serfownership by the nongentry industrialists. The gentry was unwilling to admit another group into the area of serfownership, in which it shared its privileges with two older institutions, the state and the Church. Nevertheless, for over forty years, until 1762, the government resisted the gentry's pressure to prohibit nongentry industrialists from acquiring serfs. It was a sign of the political influence of the industrial entrepreneurs that they were able to obtain government permission to purchase serfs whenever the state felt that it was absolutely necessary for the development of particular branches of industry. The acquisition of over sixty thousand serfs by the manufacturing establishments and a similar number to supply labor for ore mining and iron and copper works bears witness both to the wealth of the entrepreneurial group and to the willingness of the state to transfer to them some of the serf-labor resources of the nation. Under obvious pressure from the gentry, government policies gradually narrowed the opportunities for industrialists to acquire serfs;[28] limits of serf acquisition per unit of industrial equipment were established, and periodic inspection of manufacturing plants was instituted to detect violations by entrepreneurs who were using their industrial license as an excuse for acquiring serfs. Periodic "striking from the rolls" of licensed industrialists were carried out to dissuade such individuals from acquiring serfs. Similarly because of gentry opposition, in conferring nobility on successful industrialists the government as a rule appointed them to the civil or military bureaucracy rather than using the gentry offices or gentry assemblies. It is difficult to ascertain whether the opposition of the gentry was primarily motivated by "estate jealousy" or by the fear that the price of labor might increase. The gentry finally succeeded in having an end put to serf acquisition by industrial entrepreneurs (in 1762),[29] thus gaining a short-run advantage in using serf labor in manufacturing enterprises whenever it decided to enter this field of activity—and in the long run probably doing a service to the nongentry industrialists in forcing them to develop their enterprises on the basis of freely hired and more productive labor.

In the meantime some gentry landowners found it profitable to supply the existing nongentry factories with labor by hiring out their serfs to them under contract. The available records for the years 1738–79, for Moscow alone, indicate cases of 3432 serfs being hired out directly by their private owners.[30] Such arrangements encompassed both skilled and unskilled workers (of the latter category there are records including 637 youngsters of the ages 9–16). For present purposes we must consider this practice an already existing opportunity for the serfowners to earn additional income by exercising their ownership rights more effectively.

The conflict of the gentry with the merchants centered around two problems: the competition between them in alcohol distillery production, and the trade by serf-peasants.

Alcohol distilling under government contracts and farming of the alcohol taxes were among the most important sources of capital accumulation for the merchants and industrial entrepreneurs during the eighteenth and nineteenth centuries. Alcohol distilling was also one of the most widespread forms of processing agricultural products in which the gentry was engaged. In a certain sense the distillery business was the school of gentry entrepreneurship. It required relatively low fixed investment, the basically unskilled labor could be provided by the estate, and the raw material (rye, barley, and malt) could be supplied either entirely by the estates or in part by the peasants in surplus grain-producing regions. In addition, the system of contracts awarded by the government provided a guaranteed market where either advance payments or prompt payment by the alcohol tax-farmers eliminated the need for credits and made it relatively easy to engage in this activity. The competition between the gentry and the merchants became fierce in the late 1740s and beginning of the 1750s. While the gentry had the advantage of owning raw materials and serf labor, the merchants were perhaps more efficient, better organized, and more flexible. Around 1750 the capacity of the industry exceeded by more than two times the actual marketed output.[31] The merchants alone, having an estimated output capacity of over 1.7 million *vedra* of alcohol, were able to satisfy the total demand. The combined capacity of the commercial suppliers among the gentry[32] (over a million *vedra*) could also nearly satisfy the demand. Under pressure of the gentry the real opportunity that competition between the gentry and merchants would have offered was not accepted, and the gentry was given a monopoly on alcohol production (except in areas where gentry-owned distilleries did not exist). Thus a monopoly profit which ran into millions of rubles was awarded the gentry. On July 19, 1754, a government decree ordered the dismantling of the merchant distilleries and established the gentry monopoly. By 1765 a total of 157 gentry producers supplied 1,859,857 *vedra* of alcohol.[33]

As compared with the total number of gentry (approximately 16,600 gentry households),[34] the number of commercial suppliers—and therefore the number of the real beneficiaries of the monopoly—is strikingly small. On the other hand, as matters stood in the gentry economy of this period, few estates produced a very sizable grain surplus that could be converted either into exportable grain or into alcohol. During the subsequent two decades both the number of gentry producers and the volume of alcohol deliveries increased slowly, reaching during 1779–83 a yearly average of 211 suppliers and 2,153,159 *vedra*.[35] It was not until the 1790s that the increase in demand, technological improvement (which resulted in doubling alcohol output per unit of grain), and probably accumulated savings on the part of a larger group of gentry resulted in substantial growth of the number of commercial distilleries and suppliers. In fact, in 1795–96 on the territory of Great Russia there were 567 commercial gentry distilleries supplying 3,348,278 *vedra* of alcohol.[36] Thus the gentry was able to create for itself in commercial alcohol distilling a steady source of income through increase in grain output, on the one hand, and elimination of merchant competition, on the other.

The second, simultaneous victory of the gentry over the merchants concerned the trade of the serf-peasants. Curiously enough, in the case of the distilleries the government supported the gentry in establishing a virtual monopoly and in the second case supported gentry demands on grounds of "monopoly busting." The gentry was interested in increasing the serfs' money income through their participation in retail trade, in abolishing the internal duty system, and in putting an end to the exclusive privileges of the merchant class which were against gentry interests. Quite apart from the arguments employed in the debate on the reform of internal trade, the real hope of the gentry was for a "sponge" effect—to squeeze out more from a more prosperous serf economy. The Customs Statute (*Tamozhennyi Ustav*) of 1755[37] to a large extent undermined the trading privileges of the merchant class. The gentry gained the unlimited right of wholesale and retail trade in "products of their estates or peasants" and of wholesale trade in the ports. Formally the peasants were restricted to trade in a limited number of commodities, but lack of control made the restriction ineffective. The restrictions upon the volume of trade of the peasants were abolished, and they were allowed to trade in all rural areas beyond a 5-verst radius from the cities.[38] This specification enabled peasants and gentry to set up trading establishments and fairs in many more localities than before and to capture a much larger share of domestic trade. The gentry, under the provisions of the new trading laws, very often would enter into arrangements with some of their peasants for purposes of trading. The serf-peasants were encouraged by the gentry to enter trade and earn higher incomes, in order to share some of their profits with their owners.

## IV

Throughout our discussion of the economic conditions of the gentry's "Westernization" the basic premise has been that substantial money costs were involved in this process of cultural change. To meet the increasing expenses, it was essential that agriculture become more commercialized or that new sources of money income be developed. Our short survey indicates that some progress was achieved in both directions. On the one hand, during the later decades of the century agriculture was yielding a larger marketable share, and some not insignificant income was being earned by more effective utilization of the serf-labor force in agriculture, as well as in the processing of agricultural products and in operation of industrial enterprises.

These conclusions raise further questions. First, how was the increment of income distributed to meet the requirements of "Westernization," and, second, was the total increment from these sources adequate to meet the costs? In the attempt to determine how the costs of "Westernization" of the gentry were distributed among the members of this class, it would be convenient to assume that the distribution of costs was correlated to the distribution of income or wealth within the gentry class. Our data are insufficient, however, to derive the income or wealth distribution of the gentry in the eighteenth century with any precision. The information contained in Tables 2 and 3 makes it possible to present the distribution of the gentry by the size of their serf-holdings in very broad categories. Those two tables are summarized in Table 8.

It is the indeterminable serf population owned by the upper gentry group (over 1000 serfs) that makes any estimate of the number of serfs per owner in the other groups highly problematic. As an educated guess, it might be estimated that the upper 1 or 1.5 percent of the gentry (owners of more than 1000 serfs) held from 40 to 55 percent of all the serfs during the 1760s and 1770s.[39] This underscores the impression of extreme inequality in the serf-holdings among the members of the gentry. It would probably be correct to assume that for the gentry possessing fewer than 100 serfs "Westernization" meant a real strain on their resources. The costs of "Westernization" for the lower-income strata of the gentry were probably "subsidized" by the state in the form of compensation for particular services rendered to the state by individuals belonging to these strata.

Table 8. Distribution of Gentry Serfowners by Size
of Holdings (in percentage)

| Number of Serfs per Gentry Household | 1762 | 1777 |
| --- | --- | --- |
| Fewer than 100 serfs | 82.0 | 83.8 |
| 101–500 serfs | 15.0 | 12.1 |
| 501–1000 serfs | 2.0 | 2.6 |
| Over 1000 serfs | 1.0 | 1.5 |

This leaves us with the middle- and higher-income strata of the gentry, who, it is assumed, were bearing the major share of the costs of "Westernization." Although one would expect that the percentage of the total serf-population held by the top serfholding group would decline over time (in part through distribution of holdings among heirs), the percentage held by the middle groups ought to remain more or less stable. This pattern is in fact borne out by the much more detailed distribution of serfownership by the gentry which is available for 1834.[40] This distribution is amazingly similar to the 1762 distribution (Table 8) and at the same time indicates some decline in the share of serfs held by the top serfowners. The data for serfownership in 1834 for roughly the same territory as the estimates for the eighteenth century are summarized in Table 9.

Table 9. Distribution of Gentry Serfowners (Heads of Household) by Size of Holdings in Great Russia, 1834*

| Number of Serfs per Gentry Household | Percentage of Owners | Percentage of Serfs |
|---|---|---|
| Fewer than 100 | 81.5 | 19.6 |
| 101–500 | 15.1 | 35.2 |
| 501–1000 | 2.1 | 14.9 |
| Over 1000 | 1.3 | 30.3 |

* Derived from data in footnote 40, household serfs excluded.

Faced with the fact that the share of the major serfowners in the total serf-holdings of the gentry was declining (as was the number of serfs per landowner of this group), we would expect this particular group to be most vocal in demanding, or most active in seeking, new sources of income. It is not, therefore, surprising to find that, when the gentry were given a monopoly on alcohol distilling, the awarding of contracts followed to a large extent the wealth or income distribution of the gentry (as was the case, too, with recipients of iron and copper works). To be sure, it was the group of large serfowners whose estates produced a readily marketable grain surplus that could be used in alcohol distilling. Still, one is also tempted to view the awarding of alcohol supply contracts as an additional means of meeting the demands of those whose costs of "Westernization" were highest.[41]

Given the existing income distribution of the gentry, one cannot but raise the question of the relation between the distribution of economic power and the distribution of political power. Is there, in other words, any reason to suspect that, despite the existence of an economic oligarchy of major serfowners, political power in the state was distributed any differently than the economic power within the gentry? Is there any reason to believe that the state was pursuing a policy that deviated from the interests of this oligarchy and represented the interests of *all* gentry, or even interests different from those of the gentry?

In treating the institution of the state I shall not assume that the state was above society, independent of the existing social groups. I would, however, argue that the Russian state and the Russian absolute ruler should not be treated simply as an "executive committee" of the gentry to administer the affairs of Russia as a country for the exclusive benefit of this social class. The real situation was obviously much more complex. For most of the eighteenth century we can establish the virtual identity of the serfowning oligarchy and the ruling elite.[42] It is much more difficult to establish an identity between the state or government and the gentry class at large.[43]

The identification of the gentry with the state could not have been perfect, since the relationships between the government and the gentry class at large were not frictionless. Friction arose when Peter the Great attempted to make the gentry more "functional," to merge it with the upper echelons of the bureaucracy, and to introduce some elements of upward mobility based upon merit and "usefulness to the state." The very concept of "usefulness to the state" introduced an alternative yardstick as against that of hereditary nobility and served simultaneously as a guideline for gentry behavior. The gentry accepted the right of the state to set standards for gentry behavior and gentry support but demanded, and received, something in return—a *de facto* and later *de jure* change in its status. As individuals and as a class the gentry were treated in accordance with certain rules (the distinction between laws and rules is important) which restrained the absolutist nature of the government or ruler.

Thus during the post-Petrine period, with regard to the gentry a modified version of "L'état c'est moi" came into being. The extreme practices of the earlier centuries could no longer be repeated. A mode of bargaining between the government and the gentry class was established in which it was tacitly assumed that the gentry, as the pillar of absolutism and the foundation on which the state rested, would meet the basic demands of the state and help execute its policies. But since policies of the state did not necessarily coincide with the current interests of the gentry, the terms of cooperation arrived at had to be mutually advantageous and provide room for bargaining and maneuvering. "Westernization" of the gentry was, during the post-Petrine period, one of the demands of the state; the terms of, and conditions for, its accomplishment had to be worked out between the state and the gentry.

The area of common economic interest most important for both the state and the gentry was obviously the serf-labor force. In fact, ideological elements aside, this probably was the element most effective in keeping the gentry tied to the state. (Serfdom was the material base not only of the gentry but also of the state. Therefore the defense of the institution of serfdom by the state was the defense not only of the gentry but also of institutions on which the Russian absolutist state itself rested.) By tracing the changing relative shares of the state and gentry in serfownership and by measuring the relative shares of revenue from the serfs, it is possible to indicate the pattern of the relationship between the gentry as a class and the government. It was clearly in the interests of the gentry that the head tax on private serfs was not raised, although the burden of that tax was steadily declining in real terms.

Although the government was made up largely of upper-class gentry, its actions were often independent of short-run gentry interests.

One of the most obvious examples of the general proposition that in relation to the gentry the Russian state was able to preserve substantial independence and freedom of action is provided in the secularization of the Church estates in 1764. The Church estates included (according to the data of the third *reviziia*, quoted by Semevskii) 991,761 male serfs, compared with 3,783,327 gentry serfs.[44] Needless to say, the pious gentry of Russia was not adverse to the idea that the serfs owned by the Church institutions should be turned over to it.[45] The action of the government, which first extended a form of "receivership" over the former Church estates and subsequently brought the estates and the serfs into state ownership, indicates that reasons of state policy and state revenue prevailed over the demands of the gentry when these interests were in conflict. At least here we have a clear case in which the government denied the gentry an opportunity to earn additional income.

Disappointed by the government action with regard to the former Church estates, the gentry did not relax its demands for additional sources of income. The government chose the forms of direct subsidies and loans partly to placate the gentry[46] but basically to reserve for itself the full right of making decisions and to use its economic power to its political advantage. The preference for subsidies over other forms of income transfers that might endanger the fiscal interests of the state (and impair the success of its policies) is typical of the relation between the government and the gentry during the last third of the eighteenth century. Subsidies to the gentry, either in the form of direct government grants or bank loans made at a nominal rate of interest or on insufficient security, were by no means a purely Russian phenomenon. They were common in most countries on the Continent. It was also the arrangement and policy of most governments that they reserved to themselves the discretion to decide who among the gentry ought to be the recipients of the subsidies.

The Russian state (as represented by the ruler and government) was manifestly not indifferent to the aspirations of the gentry to increase its income. To the extent that the state was interested in the "Westernization" of the upper class of Russian society, it lent its support to the demands of the gentry, reserving for itself the final decisions with regard to both the extent and the distribution of the actual aid given. It was the coincidence of the essential interests of Russian absolutism and of the gentry that determined to a large extent the success of the gentry in achieving its economic goals.


V


In this very general review of the costs of "Westernization" to the Russian gentry in the eighteenth century conclusions concerning the social and moral features of the institution of serfdom have no place. To say that the burden of the serfs might not have increased over a certain period is not equivalent to saying that the burden was light or to justifying the existence of any burden whatsoever. To say that the gentry behaved with economic rationality does not contradict the belief that the institution of serfdom is morally abhorrent and humanly debasing. To say that the Russian government or state was not at all times a captive of the gentry does not imply that it represented the interests or opinions of the Russian people as a whole.

The conclusions that may properly be drawn from the discussion pertain to the economic and political sphere of the gentry's operations. Conformity by the gentry to the state's demands for "Westernization" involved some heavy expenditures by that class. By the end of the eighteenth century the total annual income of the gentry from their serfs may be estimated at approximately 50 million rubles, and the expenditures for "Western" amenities ran well over 18 million rubles yearly. To meet the rising expenditures, the quest for additional income on the part of the gentry became an important economic feature of the period and increased the gentry's participation in various areas of the economy. Apparently the increment was insufficient, for the state was solicited to supplement the income. This put the state in a stronger position in respect to the gentry. The distribution of state "aid" to the gentry by and large followed the pattern of the existing distribution of wealth and thereby supported the disparity of income within the gentry class. As a result of both government interference and the economic activities of the gentry, economic and political power in Russia remained concentrated in the hands of a few. Throughout the eighteenth century the Russian state was basically ruled by and in the interests of an oligarchy, and the "Westernization" process, which supposedly encompassed the large mass of the gentry, was not sufficiently advanced to have a leveling effect upon the distribution of economic and political power.

## NOTES

1. The assumption of pressure applied in imposing "Westernization" is realistic in terms of the historical record. It does not exclude the likelihood that a taste for "Westernization" was subsequently developed and that some features of it (conspicuous consumption, for example) grew at a rate that exceeded the original intentions of the state.

2. This can be estimated on the assumption of, let us say, three males per gentry household, which would give us the following results, derived from Table 1:

| Year | Gentry Households | Serfs per Household |
| --- | --- | --- |
| 1744 | 12,442 | 276.7 |
| 1762 | 16,592 | 228.0 |
| 1783 | 21,000 (est.) | 242.5 |
| 1795 | 25,733 | 221.5 |

(The rate of population growth of the gentry in the eighteenth century given in Table 1 indicates a family size of two to three males per family. The use of three males per gentry household does not determine the results of our analysis.)

3. S. G. Strumilin, *Istoriia chernoi metallurgii v SSSR*, I (Moscow, 1954) 273; E. I. Indova, *Krepostnoe khoziaistvo v nachale XIX veka* (Moscow, 1955), pp. 30, 186–87; K. V. Sivkov, *Ocherki po istorii krepostnogo khoziaistva i krest'ianskogo dvizheniia v Rossii v pervoi polovine XIX veka* (Moscow, 1951), p. 146.

4. Not all serfs paid money rent; many rendered labor services on the estate or paid rent in kind or were liable for a combination of the two. For our calculations we use the money rent as an approximation of the value of the other types of service. Depending upon the period, locality, and other conditions, the value of other types of rent fluctuated above or below the level of money rents.

5. For the portion of imported goods consumed by gentry and by nongentry we must rely on indirect evidence. The group closest to the gentry in terms of income was the upper merchant class, which presumably participated in the consumption of foreign goods if only for the status symbol thus provided. Some contemporary documents, however, clearly indicate a lag of the "import tastes" of merchants behind those of the upper gentry. In 1793 a government committee appointed to investigate the causes of the depreciation of the ruble on foreign exchanges and to recommend remedies included representatives of the Russian merchant class among those invited to testify. The merchants regarded most of the imported wines and food-stuffs, textiles, and leather goods as "luxuries" either totally superfluous or replaceable by satisfactory domestic products. Two merchants—Nikolai Rezvoi, head of the St. Petersburg merchant guilds, and Mikhail Samoilov, member of the first merchant guild, consisting of the richest merchants—listed in detail the imported commodities which, in their view, ought to be forbidden or restricted. Most revealing as a reflection of the consumer attitudes of the upper group of Russian merchants are the reasons given.

The following is a composite selection from the catalogues submitted by the two men (the explanations were given by Samoilov): fine woolens (domestically produced, can do without them); beer and porter (a delicacy, a whim); fine linens; socks and stockings (some domestically produced, one can do without others); fresh fruit (a great deal domestically produced); wines and liquors (unnecessary); furs (domestic of good quality available); foreign tobacco (imported for fashion, not for quality and usefulness); cheeses (a delicacy, anyone can make it for himself); sweet vodkas (a whim); syrup (sufficient from domestic sugar refineries); coconuts, Greek nuts, etc. (a delicacy and bad for health); gloves (some domestically produced, one can do without others); exotic birds (for no good reason); blankets (can do without); macaroni (a delicacy); chocolate (a delicacy).

Apparently keeping in mind that one ought not to deprive the gentry and rich merchants of all "luxuries," Samoilov proposed "heavy import duties" for 33 additional commodities. See N. N. Firsov, *Pravitel'stvo i obshchestvo v ikh otnosheniiakh k vneshnei torgovle Rossii v tsarstvovanie Ekateriny II-oi* (Moscow, 1901–2), pp. 181–89.

6. In 1793–95 the "luxury" goods imported into Russia through the European border averaged annually (in rubles):

| Items | Declared Value | Duty Payments | Total |
|-------|---------------|---------------|-------|
| Sugar | 5,595,200 | 332,400 | 5,927,600 |
| Silk wares | 1,821,900 | 62,000 | 1,883,900 |
| Coffee | 1,315,300 | 141,500 | 1,456,800 |
| Wines | 1,137,300 | 204,700 | 1,342,000 |
| Fruit | 903,600 | — | 903,600 |
| Fur | 412,800 | 16,000 | 428,800 |
| Beer and porter | 386,900 | 131,500 | 518,400 |
| Spices | 284,500 | 26,300 | 310,800 |
| Fine linen | 188,800 | 44,500 | 233,300 |
| Stockings | 126,400 | 25,300 | 151,700 |
| Cheese | 121,300 | 9,800 | 131,100 |
| China and pottery | 98,500 | 39,400 | 137,900 |
| Haberdashery | 95,500 | 9,400 | 104,900 |
| Silk scarfs | 74,800 | 29,900 | 104,700 |
| Total listed | 12,562,800 | 1,072,700 | 13,635,500 |
| Total imports | 27,886,000 | | |

Not included in the list is the share of "luxury" items in the import of woolen and cotton goods, the value of which amounted to 6,585,400 rubles, and the duty assessment to 955,900 rubles. The gentry's expenditures which will be used in our calculations include all items listed in the table, except one half of the sugar. It includes also one quarter of the imported cotton and woolens. Altogether the declared value of luxury imports consumed annually by the gentry would be 11,411,500 rubles, the duty payments 1,145,500 rubles, or a total of 12,557,000 rubles. See Heinrich Storch, *Supplementband zum fünften, sechsten und siebenten Theil des Historisch-Statistischen Gemäldes des Russischen Reichs* (Leipzig, 1803), pp. 53–54.

7. The direct costs of tuition for gentry education in the later decades of the eighteenth century amounted to about 100 rubles per male pupil, or, including room and board, to about 150 rubles per year. However, a part of the expenditures was borne by state subsidies to various educational institutions. Costs of educating gentry females—salaries to governesses, tutors, etc.—were smaller. Obviously, estimates of the costs of education to the gentry involve a substantial margin of error, and ought not to be undertaken in this essay. For our purposes, it is sufficient to realize that even a cost of 100 rubles for educating a gentry male imposed upon the gentry household an expense equal to the rent derived from 20 serf-peasants.

8. Primogeniture provisions were decreed by Peter the Great in 1714; see *Polnoe Sobranie Zakonov Rossiiskoi Imperii*, Vol. V, item 2789 (St. Petersburg, 1830). They were, however, repealed in 1730 (*PSZ*, Vol. VIII, item 5653) on the overwhelming demand of the gentry itself. In addition, primogeniture provisions could be effective only if many opportunities existed for gentry activity outside agriculture.

9. The Soviet agricultural historian L. V. Milov recently called attention to the existence of this reserve of long fallow land outside the three-field system. By using primary sources he was able to correct the errors of Rubinshtein and other historians and provide the explanation for the operation of the three-field system in Russia. See L. V. Milov, "O roli perelozhnykh zemel' v russkom zemledelii vtoroi poloviny XVIII v.," in *Ezhegodnik po agrarnoi istorii vostochnoi Evropy 1961 g.* (Riga, 1963), pp. 279–88.

10. The earlier land survey during 1754–55 had actually provided the gentry with ownership titles to state lands previously held and occupied by the gentry without title. *PSZ*, Vol. XIV, item 10,406.

11. *PSZ*, Vol. XVII, items 12,474, 12,570, 12,659.

·12. A *desiatina* equals 1.0925 ha.

13. Derived from N. L. Rubinshtein, *Sel'skoe khoziaistvo Rossii vo vtoroi polovine XVIII v.* (Moscow, 1957), pp. 323–24, 444–52.

14. *Ibid.*

15. An interesting case in point was the recruitment of 92 peasants in Livonia and Kurland to teach the use of the scythe instead of the sickle in grain harvesting to peasants in ten provinces in Russia proper. In five years (1721–26) they trained 13,299 peasants, and 16,210 scythes were introduced in four of the ten provinces. *PSZ*, Vol. VII, item 4,912.

16. K. V. Sivkov, "Voprosy sel'skogo khoziaistva v russkikh zhurnalakh XVIII v.," in *Materialy po istorii zemledeliia SSSR*, I (Moscow, 1952), 613.

17. *PSZ*, Vol. XI, item 8,619.

18. L. P. Rukovskii, *Istoriko-statisticheskie svedeniia o podushnykh podat'iakh* (St. Petersburg, 1862), p. 193.

19. According to data for the estates of Prince A. M. Cherkasskii, during the 1730s 11,467 fugitive peasants, or 16.4 percent of his male serfs, were recovered in the eastern and southern regions. *Istoriia SSSR*, No. 6, 1963, pp. 127–29.

20. Peasant flights also occurred frequently as a result of army recruitment by the government.

21. The price index used is particularly ill-suited. During periods of rising prices grain prices tend to rise faster than other prices. Therefore, the reader is cautioned with regard to the results of the real burden of taxation that emerge in Table 6.

22. According to the same procedure as that used in Table 6, the burden upon the state-owned peasants, in comparison with that of the gentry's peasants, was as follows: 1730s—85 percent; 1750s—83 percent; 1760s—77 percent; 1770s—84 percent; 1780s—78 percent; 1790s—91.7 percent.

### Rent and Tax Burden of the State-owned Serfs

| | Rent (in kopeks) | Rent Deflated by Price Index | Tax (in kopeks) | Tax (Deflated by Price Index) | Total Burden | | Index of Real Total Burden |
|---|---|---|---|---|---|---|---|
| | | | | | Nominal | Real | |
| 1730s | 40 | 40 | 70 | 70 | 110 | 110 | 100 |
| 1750s | 55 | 43.3 | 70 | 55.1 | 125 | 98.4 | 89.5 |
| 1760s | 100 | 50.0 | 70 | 35.0 | 170 | 85.0 | 77.3 |
| 1770s | 200 | 73.3 | 70 | 25.6 | 270 | 98.9 | 89.9 |
| 1780s | 300 | 66.4 | 70 | 15.5 | 370 | 81.9 | 74.5 |
| 1790s | 450 | 74.3 | 100 | 16.5 | 550 | 90.8 | 82.5 |

SOURCE: See Table 6.

23. Count Sheremetev, the owner of the villages, derived from them a very large share of the income from his total estates, which included up to 80,000 male serfs by the end of the eighteenth century.

24. I have omitted the attempts of Aleksandr Menshikov (not of gentry origin, but one of the richest land- and serfowners and the favorite of Peter the Great) to set up industrial enterprises in the 1710s. The joint-stock silk manufacturing company of the Counts Apraksin and Tolstoi and Baron Shafirov, established in 1717, was a clear example not of gentry entrepreneurship and initiative but of government action to set up gentry in the field of industrial activity (see E. I. Zaozerskaia, *Razvitie legkoi promyshlennosti v Moskve v pervoi chetverti XVIII v.* [Moscow, 1953], pp. 297–306). This case, too, is therefore omitted from the general discussion.

25. There is the interesting, though little explored, case of Prince Khovanskii, who tried to create a huge woolen mill based solely upon serf labor, expanding output and scale of operations in a daring fashion (Strumilin, I, 278). Needless to say, risk-taking without knowledge of the market ended in financial disaster for the noble knight-errant striving to master the dragon of industry with antiquated weapons.

26. The recipients of the iron and copper works were A. I. and P. I. Shuvalov, R. I. and M. I. Vorontsov, I. G. Chernyshev, S. P. Iaguzhinskii, A. G. Gur'ev, and P. I. Repnin. Of these the Shuvalovs owned the enterprises for nine years, Gur'ev ten years, Chernyshev thirteen, Repnin fifteen, and the Vorontsovs and Iaguzhinskii over twenty years. Eventually they all either returned the enterprises to the state or sold them at a profit to other entrepreneurs. N. I. Pavlenko, *Istoriia metallurgii v Rossii XVIII veka* (Moscow, 1962), pp. 327–86.

27. "Opyt khozhdeniia po prisutstvennym mestam." *Ibid.*, p. 435.

28. Peter the Great for a short while even allowed the owners of iron works to keep fugitive serfs and to pay a nominal price to the owner for a serf who was already trained in the iron works. Later on the acquisition was made more difficult. N. I. Pavlenko, *Razvitie metallurgicheskoi promyshlennosti Rossii v pervoi polovine XVIII veka* (Moscow, 1953), p. 353; and *PSZ*, Vol. VII, item 4533.

29. *PSZ*, Vol. XV, 11,490; Vol. XVI, item 11,638.

30. M. N. Artamenkov, "Naemnye rabochie moskovskikh manufaktur v 40–70kh godakh XVIII v.," *Istoriia SSSR*, No. 2, 1964, p. 142.

31. The Revenue Collegium estimated in 1753 an existing over-all output capacity of 3,962,471 *vedra* of alcohol, while the actually purchased and delivered output in 1752 was 1,534,818 *vedra* (a *vedro* contained about 12.3 liters). See the article by N. I. Pavlenko in *Voprosy genezisa kapitalizma v Rossii* (Leningrad, 1960), p. 63.

32. According to the estimates of the Revenue Collegium, the gentry owned 1295 distilleries, of which 264 were classified as commercial suppliers. The rest were producing alcohol for their own household needs. *Ibid.*, note 33.

33. Pavlenko, *Istoriia metallurgii*, p. 446.

34. See note 2, above.

35. Pavlenko, *Istoriia metallurgii*, p. 446; *Svedeniia o piteinykh sborakh v Rossii* (St. Petersburg, 1860), I, 38.

36. Pavlenko, *Istoriia metallurgii*, p. 446.

37. *PSZ*, Vol. XIV, item 10,486.

38. The decree of 1754 (*PSZ*, Vol. XII, item 9401) had not specified the distance from the cities, and the urban merchants were able to impose restrictions upon peasant trade even at a distance of 20 versts and more from the cities. See M. I. Volkov, "Tamozhennaia reforma 1753–1757 gg.," in *Istoricheskie zapiski*, LXXI (Moscow, 1963), 152.

39. If we nevertheless engage in the exercise of estimating (on the basis of the information provided in Tables 2 and 3), assuming the highest possible number of serfs for the lowest group (i.e., 9 serfs for the "below 10" category), continuing at the same proportion for the other categories (for example, 27 for the "10–30" category, etc.), and distributing the estimated number of 16,592 gentry households in the 1760s among the various categories, we arrive at the following curious percentage distribution of serfs among the various household groups of Table 8:

| Size of Serfholdings (per household) | Gentry Serfs Held by Various Household Groups (as percentage of total number of gentry serfs) | |
|---|---|---|
| | *1762* | *1777* |
| Less than 100 serfs | 16.2 | 11.1 |
| 101–500 serfs | 29.6 | 43.1 |
| 501–1000 serfs | 7.9 | 10.5 |
| Over 1000 serfs | 46.3 | 35.3 |

Obviously the above distribution is biased in favor of the lower groups and underestimates the share of the highest serfholding group.

The estimated number of serfs (male) held by the major serfowners during the eighteenth century in the Great Russian provinces were: P. B. Sheremetev 60,000–100,000; K. G. Razumovskii 45,000; A. S. Stroganov 33,870; D. G. Orlov 27,000; S. R. and A. R. Vorontsov together 27,605; A. A. and L. A. Naryshkin together 22,000; N. M., M. M., and D. M. Golitsyn 14,000 each; S. S. Gagarin 13,982; B. A. Kurakin 13,000; M. A., B. A., and A. A. Golitsyn together 13,000; B. G. Shakhovskoi and F. S. Bariatinskii 11,000 each; G. I. Golovkin, N. A. Golitsyn, Georgii Vakhtangeevich (Prince of Georgia), G. A. Potemkin, D. Iu. Trubetskoi, and E. A. Chernysheva 10,000 each. V. I. Semevskii, *Krest'ianie v tsarstvovanie Imperatritsy Ekateriny II* (St. Petersburg, 1903), I, 23–35.

40. Distribution of Gentry Serfs Owners by Size of Holdings in Great Russia, 1834*

| | Owners (heads of households) | | Serfs | | Serfs per Owner |
|---|---|---|---|---|---|
| | No. | Percentage | No. | Percentage | |
| Household serfs only | 10,583 | 12.9 | 30,506 | .5 | 2.9 |
| Up to 20 serfs | 37,857 | 46.3 | 314,310 | 4.6 | 8.3 |
| 21–100 serfs | 20,167 | 24.7 | 1,007,960 | 14.9 | 50.0 |
| 101–500 serfs | 10,854 | 13.2 | 2,360,217 | 35.0 | 217.4 |
| 501–1,000 serfs | 1,449 | 1.8 | 999,304 | 14.8 | 689.7 |
| Over 1,000 serfs | 870 | 1.1 | 2,037,947 | 30.2 | 2,342.5 |
| Total | 81,780 | | 6,750,244 | | 82.5 |
| Total landowning | 71,197 | | 6,719,738 | | 94.4 |

* Territory comparable to that of the third *reviziia* (as in Tables 2 and 3); data derived from table in P. V. Köppen, "Über die Vertheilung der Bewohner Russlands nach Ständen, in den Verschiedenen Provinzen," in *Mémoires de l'Académie Impériale des Sciences de Saint-Pétersbourg*, Sixth Series, Vol. VII (St. Petersburg, 1847), pp. 420–21 (table in source covers 45 guberniias of European Russia; data above, for Great Russia only, obtained by excluding 17 guberniias).

41. It is of interest to note that in 1765, of the 157 gentry suppliers of alcohol, only 8 delivered quantities of over 50,000 *vedra*, their combined contribution consisting of 44 percent of the total. The 1765 top eight suppliers were Andrei Petrovich Shuvalov (257,824 *vedra*), A. I. Glebov (179,421 *vedra*), Agrafena Leont'evna Apraksina (80,000), P. G. Chernyshev (70,215), Matvei and Sergei Kantemir (61,000), I. S. and Gavriil Ermolaev (59,106), N. A. Korf (58,778), and E. D. Golitsyn heirs (55,111). Among the major suppliers in 1779–83 we find Senator E. A. Shcherbinin (125,586 *vedra*), Senator N. B. Samoilov (110,000), Field Marshal K. G. Razumovskii (84,697), the widow of P. G. Chernyshev (70,000), and other representatives of the aristocracy and top bureaucracy. Pavlenko, *Istoriia metallurgii*, p. 440; *Svedeniia o piteinykh sborakh v Rossii*, I, 38.

42. The identity of the serfowning aristocracy and the ruling elite was established by this writer by examining the membership of the Senate and the Supreme Council, as well as the identity of the heads of collegia and the holders of court offices, during the eighteenth century, on the one hand, and the available lists (incomplete) of major serfowners (over 1000 serfs), on the other. What has so often been described by historians as favoritism on the part of the ruler in bestowing either power or wealth upon individuals was in essence a method used under absolutism to provide some mobility for the rich into the elite, or to provide wealth for the politically powerful, or to provide both mobility and wealth for the talented whose services were sought by the ruler.

43. A widespread view in Russian historiography is that the "king-making" capacity of the guards regiments demonstrated the decision-making role of the gentry (including the lower gentry) as a social class. This view is based upon the experience of 1741 and 1762. It is my impression that the guards regiments had as much voice in internal or foreign policy decisions as did the praetorian guards in ancient Rome: "king-making" and policy making are two separate categories. The actual pay-off of the guards regiments by the successful contenders for the throne indicates the "price" that the ruling oligarchy had to pay to the lower gentry for the support rendered on such occasions.

44. Semevskii, II, 254.

45. This point of view was represented even by such a conservative political thinker as Prince Shcherbatov. He argued that since most of the Church serfs had in the past been donated by the landowners, this would constitute a rightful and legitimate return of property previously owned by the landowning class.

46. The private debts of serf owners to the various government-established credit institutions (except private) were estimated for the year 1800 at 45.5 million rubles, which corresponded to 708,000 mortgaged serfs. See S. Ia. Borovoi, *Kredit i banki Rossii* (Moscow, 1958), pp. 76–78.

# Russia and the West:
# A Comparison and Contrast

HENRY L. ROBERTS

Comparisons of Russia with the "West" have been a staple of historians and of contemporary observers for a very long time, and no end is in sight. A recent appraisal of Soviet developments in the decade after the death of Stalin was devoted in part to a consideration of the prospects for "a gradual convergence of the social and/or political systems of the West and the Soviet Union."[1] The variety of the contributors' responses—"very likely," "necessarily uncertain," "unlikely any meaningful convergence," "highly improbable," "depends on what is meant by 'gradual' "—suggests an ample range of disagreement, both in expectations for the future and in the characterization of the contrasts under-lying these expectations.

The Russians themselves have, of course, been perennially preoccupied with this act of comparison. As Sir Isaiah Berlin has observed, in speaking of the nineteenth century: "Russian publicists, historians, political theorists, writers on social topics, literary critics, philosophers, theologians, poets, first and last, all without exception and at enormous length, discuss such issues as what it is to be a Russian; the virtues, vices and destiny of the Russian individual and society; but above all the historic role of Russia among the nations; or, in particular, whether its social structure—say, the relation of intellectuals to the masses, or of industry to agriculture—is *sui generis*, or whether, on the contrary, it is similar to that of other countries, or, perhaps, an anomalous, or stunted, or an abortive example of some superior Western model."[2]

Such concerns are not uniquely Russian. Americans and Canadians, colonial offspring of European culture, have spent a great deal of time meditating on their relations to the Old World; the inhabitants of the British Isles continue to have ambivalent feelings about the Continent; the Germans, though situated in Central Europe, have written at length about the significance of Germany's Eastern and Western "faces"; in Italy they say that Europe stops somewhere south of Rome; indeed, of the major European nations only the French seem

FROM Henry L. Roberts, "Russia and the West: A Comparison and Contrast," *Slavic Review*, XXIII, No. 1 (March 1964), 1–12. Reprinted by permission of the American Association for the Advancement of Slavic Studies.

not to have been much bothered by this particular problem of identification. Still, the relative intensity and persistence of the preoccupation in the Russian case, the fact that at times it has loomed as *the* question in discussions of Russian society and culture, would indicate a somewhat special problem.

It should be noted at the outset that what is involved here is not simply a nation-to-nation comparison but rather the relationship of one country, Russia,[3] to a more complex entity, the "West," by which is usually meant Western Europe. This latter entity, though comprising a number of nations, is assumed to have a degree of unity, the possession by its members of common features, against which Russia can be compared and contrasted. In other words, the question really means: does Russia belong to the West or not, is it a part of the West or is it somehow alien from that cluster of nations? Historically it is clear that the pathos and passion this question has aroused derive from the issue of participation or nonparticipation. And while, as we shall see presently, the historian might prefer to deal with it in different terms, this issue still lies at the heart of most discussions of Russia and the West.

We can take, as an example, two articles appearing recently in this journal. The one presented Russia as belonging to an East European cultural sphere quite sharply differentiated from, and opposed to, that of Western Europe: Eastern-Orthodox-Byzantine as against Western-Catholic-Roman. It urged, moreover, that the terms "East" and "West" in this setting "are so specific and meaningful that it would be unwise to introduce new concepts even as working hypotheses."[4] The second article, in contrast, was inclined to argue that while there have been periods, usually sterile ones, of Russian self-sufficiency and isolation, Russia and the West have "a common logic of development, a shared process of evolution. ... Russian culture has no vital existence of its own apart from Europe."[5] Although the authors are addressing different themes, the trend of their thought is clear: one sees Russia as essentially distinct from the West, the other as linked to and dependent on it.

The disconcerting feature of this divergence—and both positions have respectable ancestries—is not simply their apparent incompatibility but their plausibility and persuasiveness when presented in the course of the authors' argument. From these, and other examples, we must suppose that in considering Russia's relation to the West we are not dealing with a simple question of fact— otherwise it would have been settled long since—but with a more subtle and troubling problem.

In the face of conflicting interpretations which do not appear to arise from crude errors of fact, one can explore at least three possible avenues of explanation: (1) One may look for the warping presence of animus or prejudice as the source of trouble; (2) one may attempt to achieve a more satisfactory "perspective" that can somehow encompass or reconcile the conflicting interpretations; or (3) one may conclude that each interpretation is substantially correct in its own context but together they are not reconcilable because they are answering quite different questions and intentions and are, in fact, operating on different planes of thought. We shall look at each of these possibilities in turn.

That an enormous amount of passion and animus has entered into comparisons of Russia and the West is perfectly obvious. One thinks, for example, of Dostoevsky's painful encounter with Turgenev in Baden in 1867. According to Dostoevsky, Turgenev "abused Russia and the Russians vilely and terribly," and told him that the fundamental point of his (Turgenev's) book *Smoke* lay in the sentence, "If Russia were to perish it would cause neither loss nor distress to mankind."[6] In his account of the meeting, Turgenev, while denying that he would have expressed his intimate convictions to Dostoevsky, allowed that the latter had "relieved his feelings by violent abuse of the Germans, myself and my latest book."[7] We cannot go into the roots of this particular clash, but the passion evoked here by the Russia-West controversy is intense and unmistakable.

When Poles or Rumanians, despite the presence of linguistic or religious ties with the Russians and a fair measure of common if hardly joyful history, argue that Russia is not of the West, whereas their own nations most emphatically are, one feels that this is more than an academic classification, that it is an argument born of fear or desperation, and that the extrusion of Russia from the "West" is at the same time a call for support and assistance on the part of the Western nations. When a German author contends that the Russians, from the very beginning of their history, have been quite incapable of scientific and technological advance and have had to borrow and steal such knowledge from the West, which they hoped to overrun, one can agree with his enthusiastic translator that "this book is part of the Cold War."[8]

Undoubtedly the advent of the Soviet regime has greatly intensified passion and prejudice by placing Russia in the most violent possible antithesis to the rest of Europe: Communist Russia versus the Imperialist West. Moreover, the search for communism's Russian roots or antecedents, a natural and perfectly proper inquiry, has led to heightened and perhaps inappropriate emphasis on those features of the Russian past that would seem to mark it off most sharply from Western Europe: the prominence that has been given in recent years to Ivan the Terrible's *Oprichnina*, the Marquis de Custine's animadversions, and the murky character of Nechaev is surely in good part a reflection of present concerns.

And yet, while we may grant that when passions are strong the door is opened to the tendentious selection and misuse of evidence, we may doubt whether this can be defined as the major source of our difficulty. For one thing, the presence of passion or prejudice itself requires explanation, and that may lead us back, in circular fashion, to tensions inherent in the Russia-West comparison. For surely the fact that Dostoevsky and Turgenev, whatever their personal differences, should have clashed so violently on this subject does point to a peculiar quality in the Russian society of the time that should have made such great artists so painfully self-conscious about the national identity. One might have reservations about certain Polish or Rumanian views of Russian-Western relations, but it remains true that these nations have had long and intimate exposure to Russia: their fear of Russia as an alien intruder is at least derived from immediate experience. As a Rumanian writer remarked not long ago, with some acerbity: "There are some who feel that personal experience of the things described, or the fact that the writer has personally witnessed the events discussed, throws a suspicion of bias upon the author. A writer, in other words, is suspect precisely because he has too great and too close a knowledge of his subject. For our part, we feel that ignorance is not a guarantee of objectivity."[9]

So while we may strongly suspect that when we run across that tired phrase "Scratch a Russian and find a Tartar" we are not likely to get much enlightenment about either Russians or Tartars, it does not follow that no problem exists.[10] More than that, when we ask such a question as whether the 1917 Revolution brought Russian history closer to that of the West by placing it in the sequence of the other great "modernizing" revolutions of the last three centuries, or whether, on the contrary, it increased the distance by destroying, or disrupting, some potentially important convergent lines of development, we find ourselves faced with a real and quite intricate problem of historical interpretation, one that is not reducible to animus or partisanship.

Turning now from the role of animus, which while making the subject more prickly does seem to be marginal rather than central, we may consider some of the efforts that have been made to overcome, modulate, or get around the antithetical "either-or" of the Russian-Western relationship. It is my impression that these efforts have been quite fruitful in new insights, although, as we shall see, they tend to blur the Russia-West comparison or at least remove it from the center of the stage.

The most obvious approach is to replace the Russia-West polarity (with its overtones of an even more extreme Orient-Occident opposition) by the conception of a European "spectrum" ranging clear across the Continent, with changes occurring by degrees and shadings. This conception has the distinct advantage of calling in question the picture of the "West" as a homogeneous unit, which comparisons of Russia with the West so frequently posit. For example, the much vexed question of the existence of East European "feudalism" is cast in a rather different light when we are told that "the existence of a hierarchy is no longer thought to be a prerequisite to feudalism in the West, largely because the neat hierarchy assumed to have existed in the West is found to have been virtually a phantom."[11] Once this simple unity of the West is dissolved and the tremendous variety of its historical experience and its institutional and cultural forms is taken to heart, then the way is open to a much more flexible and subtle series of comparisons: within and between regions of Europe, and on different levels— religious, social, institutional, and the like. Moreover, if Europe is seen as a spectrum, one can then attempt to locate the smaller nations of Eastern Europe in a more relaxed fashion; when the West, or Western Europe, is presented as a sharply identifiable unit then there always is the painful scramble to determine who will be permitted to slip in under the tent.

I have the impression that there is much to gain through comparative studies in this vein—studies that would include Russia in the spectrum. For one example, recent investigations comparing the recruitment and social composition of the higher bureaucracy in the Habsburg and Hohenzollern monarchies[12] could profitably be extended to include imperial Russia. For another, I should like to see a close historical study of the correlation, if any, between certain patterns of landholding and leasing and peasant unrest from France and western Germany eastward to Russia.

It must be admitted, however, that this picture of Europe as a spectrum, with Russia, say, at the red end, does not take care of several important problems. It does not overcome the subjective sense of sharp contrast and opposition, which, as we have seen, has played such a significant role in the making of Russia-West comparisons. Moreover, the existence of sovereign states, of political boundaries, does mark real breaks in the spectrum, which is not a continuum, as anyone who has crossed a frontier post in Eastern Europe well knows. Finally, the fact that in the important realm of power politics Russia is usually set off, not against its immediate smaller neighbors, but against great powers farther to the West has certainly had a polarizing effect, of which the Iron Curtain division of Europe after 1945 is only the most recent and violent example. The impact of this effect upon other spheres of life and politics is very great indeed, as is illustrated by the sad history of countries and individuals that at times have sought to play the role of "bridge" between East and West. Still, for the student of history or comparative politics the "spectrum" approach does have real attractions, not least in helping do justice to the enormous richness and multiplicity of the European scene.

A second device for tackling the Russia-West comparison has been that of the "time lag." For those inclined to seek similarities rather than contrasts the time lag is very convenient: features in the Russian scene that seem different from the West are shown to be the same, but corresponding to an earlier date in the West; opposing trends turn out to be merely tangents drawn at different points along the same curve. Thus, it is thought enlightening to say that the style of Soviet life today is Victorian or at the latest Edwardian. (Such resemblances or echoes do not, of course, necessarily imply a time lag. On a fresco from the Palace of Knossos there is a charming Cretan lady whom the archaeologists call La Parisienne: presumably the parallel, though attractive, is fortuitous.) The use of the time lag is valid only if a more or less identifiable sequence of stages is occurring and if more than one nation or culture has come to participate in this sequence, usually by borrowing and adaptation. W. W. Rostow in his study of the stages of economic growth provides an analytical framework for the succession of stages and then places the different modernizing countries in their rank in this procession. Within such a defined setting he does show that Russia experienced a time lag vis-à-vis Western Europe in achieving the famous "take-off" and in reaching "maturity." At the same time the burden of his message is the general similarity of these stages: "In its broad shape and timing, then, there is nothing about the Russian sequence of preconditions, take-off, and drive to technological maturity that does not fall within the general pattern; although like all other national stories it has unique features."[13]

The time lag has its problems, however. As Thorstein Veblen pointed out some decades ago,[14] the latecomer to a historical sequence does not simply duplicate earlier performances; there is usually a foreshortening of the stages, a leaping over of certain steps, and a lumpy mingling of the old and the new. Among the

Russian Marxists Trotsky had perhaps the best sense of this feature of the time lag; indeed it underlay his thesis of permanent revolution. Despite the Marxist predilection for a unilinear view of history and its stages, Trotsky was able to observe: "The indubitable and irrefutable belatedness of Russia's development under influence and pressure of the higher culture from the West results not in a simple repetition of the West European historic process, but in the creation of profound *peculiarities* demanding independent study."[15] In other words, the conception of the time lag, although serving to increase the comparability of nations by putting them on the same track, may actually, when refined, reinforce the appearance of individuality and uniqueness.

A study of the mingling of the foreign and the indigenous, for which the term "symbiosis" can sometimes be used appropriately, affords a third approach to the comparative study of Russia and the West. In my judgment this is probably the most fruitful of all, since it corresponds to the common-sense observation that, in modern times at least, all nations are increasingly taking over or being bombarded by external influences which they must digest, naturalize, or otherwise cope with as best they can.

Two examples can illustrate the utility of this approach to a comparative study of Russia and the West. It is certainly to the Slavophiles that we owe part of our sense of Russia's difference and uniqueness. Not only were they intent upon stressing the differences, but the way they wrote and the features of the Russian scene they chose to emphasize strike the Western reader as peculiarly Russian. And yet, as we know from their education and the intellectual currents that influenced them, the conceptual apparatus of the Slavophiles was borrowed directly from German idealism and romanticism.[16] Paradoxically, increased access to "Western" ideas was to sharpen the picture of a Russia-West antithesis.

Or, to take an instance from the eighteenth century, a recent essay on the education and upbringing of the Russian nobleman[17] first brings out certain "Russian" features in his childhood experience: "The Russian nobleman of the eighteenth century normally lacked strong roots in any particular area and had no real feeling of attachment to a specific locality and to a family estate on which his ancestors had lived for generations. . . . There is little evidence of the attachment to and the ties with the ancestral home which characterised the mentality of the western noblemen." The child was under the supervision of serf nursemaids and tutors who had no rights and very rarely any powers of discipline. From this very "Russian" setting the young nobleman was sent to a school, where he received "a completely western education which had practically submerged the Muscovite traditions of learning and education by the middle of the eighteenth century." The author suggests that the effect of the somewhat abstract Enlightenment education upon children with this particular background was to produce a distinct cast of mind, exceptionally rationalistic and didactic, that was to have important consequences for Russia in the next century. For our present purposes the most interesting feature of this analysis is the way in which Russian and Western influences are seen to combine to produce a personality that is neither the traditional Muscovite nor the French man of the Enlightenment but rather the forerunner of the nineteenth-century *intelligent*.

Such an approach to the historical evidence can be extremely productive in dealing with a number of major problems of Russian institutional and social history: the impact of the Mongol conquest in Muscovy; the effects of Peter the Great's adoption of the goals and methods of contemporary German *Polizeiwissenschaft*; the consequences of taking a peasant, the son of a serf, and dropping him into the large factory of advanced Western industrialism; or the particular combination of Russian and Western Marxist elements that went into Bolshevism.

This approach is hardly an exciting discovery; it is the familiar province of the historian. But in the present connection two points need emphasis. First, such an approach, if it is to be fruitful, must be closely related to the material at hand; the results are illuminating to the degree that they lead to a concrete historical picture. It is not an approach that yields sweeping generalizations. Second, while such study does look beyond Russia's frontiers for some of its evidence and insights, its central purpose is to advance our understanding of Russia. Comparative study is a valuable tool to that end, but comparison *per se* is not the goal.

Indeed, all these approaches that I have mentioned as methods of looking at Russia and the West move away from direct comparison, either by blurring the comparison through reference to a "spectrum" or by becoming an analysis of the various factors, belatedness or foreign influences, that have contributed to the formation of Russia.

Would this suggest that such a comparison is a fruitless enterprise, that we may be engaged in an impossible endeavor to answer a pseudo problem? In one sense the answer must be yes. If we are asked whether two objects are alike or different, we are immediately impelled to counter: "With respect to what?" or "In terms of what standard?" If we ask whether two maple leaves are alike, we can answer affirmatively if it is a question of contrasting them to oak or elm leaves, or we can answer negatively if it is a question of their being congruent or having identical vein structures. We cannot make a comparison *sans phrase*, without reference to the setting and purpose of the question.

This rather simple but tricky ambiguity in the act of comparison was well analyzed by Kant in a section of his *Critique of Pure Reason*. As he observed, some scholars are interested in and attracted by the principle of "homogeneity," others by the principle of "specification." "Those who are more especially speculative are, we may almost say, hostile to heterogeneity, and are always on the watch for the unity of the genus; those, on the other hand, who are more especially empirical, are constantly endeavouring to differentiate nature in such manifold fashion as almost to extinguish the hope of ever being able to determine its appearances in accordance with universal principles."[18]

According to Kant these differences in attitude have nothing to do with questions of fact or with the nature of reality but with method. In his rather formidable vocabulary similarity and dissimilarity are "regulative principles"—working maxims, both of which are necessary and which describe diverse tendencies and interests of human thought. Difficulties occur when we mistake their function and take them to constitute reality. "When merely regulative principles are treated as constitutive, and are therefore employed as objective principles, they may come into conflict with one another. . . . The differences between the maxims of manifoldness and of unity in nature thus easily allow of reconciliation. So long, however, as the maxims are taken as yielding objective insight, and until a way has been discovered of adjusting their conflicting claims . . . they will not only give rise to disputes but will be a positive hindrance, and cause long delays in the discovery of truth."

My mention of maple, oak, and elm leaves suggests the possibility that we might bring the Russia-West comparison into more manageable shape by establishing the criterion of genus and species, of making our comparison within a hierarchy of classification. The terms of our comparison—Russia, a country, and the West, a group of countries—would point to just such a classification. In some restricted but relevant areas this kind of classification can be useful. If we wish to compare the Russian language with those of Western Europe, we do have a linguistic structure locating Russian in the Slavic branch of the Indo-European languages, to which French and German, through their respective branches, also belong. Even in the more elusive field of religion we can, by tracing the course of theological disputes and schisms, construct a reasonably workable classification of the branches of Christendom and place Russian Orthodoxy in its appropriate niche.

But these classifications extend only to such relatively well-defined subjects as language and religion; we are here concerned with such vast complexes as national entities, of which language and religion form only a part. How are we to establish classifications that can enable us to make comparisons on this larger scale?

Max Planck, the originator of the quantum theory, remarked that while the introduction of order and comparison is essential to scientific treatment and that order demands classification, "It is important at this point to state that there is no one definite principle available *a priori* and enabling a classification suitable for every purpose to be made. This applies equally to every science. Hence it is impossible in this connection to assert that any science possesses a structure evolving from its own nature inevitably and apart from any arbitrary presupposition. . . . Every kind of classification is inevitably vitiated by a certain element of caprice and hence of onesidedness."[19]

Such a cold douche from the austere natural sciences should make us cautious about the absoluteness of classifications in our rowdy and disheveled political and humanistic disciplines. I am entirely skeptical of any claims for a system of classification that purports to be inherent in the structure of history itself and free of arbitrary presuppositions. I find none of the principles of classification, whether based on geography or geopolitics, religion, ethnic-racial categories, social structure, or political system to be persuasive in providing an *objective* basis for ordering and comparing such complex congeries as nations. For example, to take the familiar Orthodox-Roman Catholic division of Christendom, while granting the enormous importance of this division as a historical influence, it would appear to me, after periods of residence in Moscow, Bucharest, and Athens—all Orthodox capitals—that this religious factor is, at least in the twentieth century, altogether inadequate as a principle of classification, though obviously of value in helping to explain many attitudes.

If we concede that we are not likely to find a purely objective order of classification that will enable us to compare Russia and the West, then we are driven back to the view that difference and similarity, homogeneity and heterogeneity, are tools to serve our diverse intellectual interests. As such they are necessarily tied to and get their meaning from our purposes and concerns in making the comparison. This is not to say that they conveniently produce answers we feed into them, but that, depending upon the questions which we bring to bear in our comparisons of Russia and the West, we will get a multitude of answers, indicating widely varying degrees of similarity and dissimilarity, each perhaps valid in its own setting, but only there. An anthropologist interested in the whole range of humanity's social organizations would probably regard the Russia-West contrast as relatively narrow. The political theorist, working within the framework of highly articulated and sophisticated political systems, would find the contrast, say, between autocracy and democracy very great indeed, perhaps representing the extreme ranges of his particular scale.

If we could be satisfied with such a modest and circumscribed role for comparisons of Russia and the West, there would be much less acrimony and controversy on this subject. But there's the rub; as we have seen, the motives that have impelled both Russians and Westerners into such endless debate and wrangling are powerful and urgent. Although we can hold, with Kant as our guide, that attempts to make absolute comparisons will produce intellectual confusion and error, I am afraid it is certain that efforts will continue to be made to find in a comparison of Russia and the West either support for normative positions on the *political* relations of the Soviet Union and the Western Powers or the basis for a prediction on the outcome of this relationship in the future.

With respect to the range of ideological, diplomatic, and moral issues that currently divide us from the Soviet Union, I should certainly not underestimate their reality and importance or question the need for us to defend our own positions. But while we have all become used to employing the term "West" as a kind of shorthand for "our side," it would be well if we based our policies on the preservation of values and principles because we believe in them and not because they are "Western."

As for the future, I do not believe that the outcome, whatever it may be, is prefigured in the comparison of Russia and the West. If we look back to the decade or two preceding the outbreak of the First World War, we have the impression that for a brief period the old debate over Russia's relationship to the West was losing its intensity and was perhaps beginning to appear irrelevant. These were the years of that profound intellectual and cultural eruption (Einstein, Freud, postimpressionism, etc.), the consequences of which are still jolting us and which, in a half century's retrospect, seems to have been one of the great historical watersheds. Russia in its "Silver Age" entered fully and immediately into that movement, its creative talents were at the forefront, there was no significant time lag. In this breakthrough, initially on a narrow front of thought and art, the traditional Russia-West debate seemed out of place, not resolved but overtaken by new challenges and horizons. The First World War and the Russian revolutions interrupted and in considerable measure obscured this development, and as we have seen, the old antithesis reappeared in the harsh form of communism versus "imperialism."

While this antagonism has by no means played out, it is becoming increasingly evident that the new world adumbrated at the beginning of the century is coming on apace, and whether we prefer to symbolize it by $E = mc^2$, or automation, or the return of the repressed, or abstract expressionism, it is a strange world. While Russia and the West will probably respond to it in different fashions, there is a distinct danger that by keeping our attention focused on Russian-Western relations and comparisons we may be quite unprepared to meet the challenge of novelty. If we think of the Western tradition as a kind of comfortable interest-bearing inheritance that we can bank on for the future, we are in for serious trouble.

## NOTES

1. *Survey: A Journal of Soviet and East European Studies*, No. 47 (Apr., 1963), pp. 37–42.

2. Isaiah Berlin, "The Silence in Russian Culture," in *The Soviet Union, 1922–1962: A Foreign Affairs Reader*, ed. Philip E. Mosely (New York: Praeger, for the Council on Foreign Relations, 1963), p. 337.

3. "Russia," of course, comprised numerous nationalities, and the term has occasioned much debate. In this piece, however, I shall not attempt to deal with this problem. By Russia I mean the Russian state or the culture and society of its Great Russian inhabitants only.

4. Omeljan Pritsak and John S. Reshetar, Jr., "The Ukraine and the Dialectics of Nation-Building," *Slavic Review*, XXII, No. 2 (June, 1963), 224–26.

5. Rufus W. Mathewson, Jr., "Russian Literature and the West," *Slavic Review*, XXI, No. 3 (Sept., 1962), 413 and 417.

6. Jessie Coulson, *Dostoevsky: A Self-Portrait* (London: Oxford University Press, 1962), p. 163.

7. *Ibid.*, p. 165.

8. Werner Keller, *East Minus West = Zero: Russia's Debt to the Western World, 862–1962*, trans. Constantine Fitzgibbon (New York: Putnam, 1962), p. 7.

9. Constantin Visoianu, in the introduction to *Captive Rumania*, ed. Alexandre Cretzianu (New York: Praeger, 1956), p. xvi.

10. Happily, the question of what the Russians *are* if they are not Western is beyond the scope of this paper. I am informed that a discussion of Russia and the East has been prepared for the preceding issue of this journal.

11. Oswald P. Backus III, "The Problem of Feudalism in Lithuania, 1506–1548," *Slavic Review*, XXI, No. 4 (Dec., 1962), 650.

12. For example, Nikolaus von Preradovich, *Die Führungsschichten in Österreich und Preussen (1804–1918)* (Wiesbaden: Steiner, 1955).

13. W. W. Rostow, *The Stages of Economic Growth* (London and New York: Cambridge University Press, 1960), p. 67.

14. In his *Imperial Germany and the Industrial Revolution*.

15. Leon Trotsky, *The History of the Russian Revolution*, trans. Max Eastman (3 vols.; Ann Arbor: University of Michigan Press, 1960), I, 464.

16. See Nicholas V. Riasanovsky, *Russia and the West in the Teaching of the Slavophiles* (Cambridge: Harvard University Press, 1952).

17. Marc Raeff, "Home, School, and Service in the Life of the 18th-Century Russian Nobleman," *The Slavonic and East European Review*, XL, No. 95 (June, 1962), 295–307.

18. See *Immanuel Kant's Critique of Pure Reason*, trans. Norman Kemp Smith (London: Macmillan, 1933), pp. 537–49.

19. Max Planck, *The Philosophy of Physics*, trans. W. H. Johnston (New York: Norton, 1936), pp. 13 and 14.

# Russia's Perception of Her Relationship with the West

## MARC RAEFF

The old French adage *comparaison n'est pas raison* indicates that comparison (contrast, too, for that matter) is never made for its own sake but only to lead to some conclusion. That is why the habit of comparing, or contrasting, the history of one country with that of another (or several others) gives rise to such vexing problems and generates such intense passions—and in turn feeds on them. We are dealing here not only with a "scientific" problem, whose solution would be an acquired truth, but with the attitudes of the participants and spectators of historical events as well. Unlike the scholar who is supposed to search only for truth, social and political thinkers and littérateurs engage in comparative analysis and reasoning in order to indulge whatever lies closest to their hearts at a given moment. In his paper Mr. Roberts has concentrated on the problems facing the scholar-scientist. His scientific similes and epistemological caveats are therefore neither mere literary embellishments nor a challenge to C. P. Snow's dichotomized view of the contemporary intellectual but quite deliberate and telling evidence that his main preoccupation is to clarify the methodological issues involved. In this very essential and laudable enterprise he has cut away much of the underbrush that all too often obscures comparative analysis and politically (or culturally or religiously) motivated contrasts. But in so doing he has perhaps allowed himself to lose sight of the reasons that made the question of Russia's relationship to the West an issue of such momentous concern for generations of Russians as well as Europeans—and now for Americans too. By taking up the discussion from the questions of method which Mr. Roberts has elucidated so well, we may be able to come to grips with the problem of attitudes and clarify a bit more the nature of the specific comparative issue with which we are concerned.

It may be worth recalling that the starting point of any judgment of comparison or contrast is a recognition, usually tacit, of identity. We do not compare or speak of the differences between two objects that have no elements in common.

FROM Marc Raeff, "Russia's Perception of Her Relationship with the West," *Slavic Review*, XXIII, No. 1 (March 1964), 13–19. Reprinted by permission of the American Association for the Advancement of Slavic Studies.

We do not compare pebbles and leaves. The question of the comparability of Russia and the West must perforce begin with a recognition—however unconscious—of some underlying identity that makes a comparison meaningful and possible, even if its result should be negative. Except for the obvious and unproductive awareness that both Russians and West Europeans are human beings, the question "Is Russia part of the West?" had no meaning, say, at the time of Ivan III.[1] Western travelers described Russia's condition and people in a detached way, much as modern anthropologists might describe some Samoan or Indian tribe, or—at most—with the incredulous indifference of Montesquieu's Parisian: "comment peut-on être persan?" The question of Russia's relationship to the West therefore arose only after some judgments of identity had been first made by either the Russians or the West Europeans.

For the Russians, no doubt, this recognition of some identity with the West took place in two steps. First, during the Times of Troubles, when in their political distress some Russians turned for succor to their Western neighbors, offering the throne to Władysław of Poland and identifying as much as they could with Polish cultural influence (e.g., Khvorostinin). The Western (mainly Polish-Catholic) answer was an attempt at incorporating Russia in such a way as to destroy its traditions and identity. Russia reacted by withdrawing and erecting a psychological wall between itself and the West. And yet it remained conscious of some identity with Western Europe, if only in contrast to its perception of Turkey or China as utterly alien.

The second step, of course, was taken by Peter the Great in his energetic and conscious efforts to make Russia into a Western state. How right he was and how well he succeeded need not be considered at this point. He obviously had more than a little success, as shown by the rapid westernization of the Russian elite and the fact that he enlisted the support of a fair number of persons in Russia for whom the underlying identity between Russia and the West, which had to be brought out, was axiomatic.[2] More significant in our context was the fact that Peter's reforms or transformation split Russian society and consciousness. In the first place, we see a break between the upper classes—the educated westernized elites—and the common people, who remained relatively untouched by the process of modernization. This phenomenon has been commented upon often enough not to bear repetition here. It does, however, point up one interesting aspect involved in the problem of comparison or contrast between Russia and the West: for *whom*, from *whose* point of view is, or is not, Russia part of the West? The Slavophiles (and some populists) were quite right when they stressed the existence of "two nations" in Russia and when they put the question of "Russia and the West" in terms of the relevance and differing meaning it had for each of these nations.[3]

The second split created by Peter the Great is even more important for our purpose. The Russian educated elite experienced a radical break with the nation's past (the experience was very likely shared by the people to some extent, though conclusive evidence is lacking). The educated nobleman of the eighteenth century found himself doubly cut off: from his own people's past, which he had learned to scorn and reject, and from Western Europe, which had not yet fully accepted him and of which he still did not feel the equal.[4] For the educated Russian the question of "Russia and the West" thus became the double problem of his sense of alienation and his need of identification. He felt alienated from Russia to the extent that its common people, its social system, its form of government were unlike those of France, England, and Germany. And the sense of alienation from that which, after all, was very close, in truth part of their very existence and being, produced the angry *ressentiment* and passionate rejection of Russia we find among many members of the intelligentsia. Is this not one of the reasons for Chaadaev's rejection of Russia's past and his denying that Russia had a civilization? And what other feelings could give rise to the unparalleled, nay shocking, admission of Pecherin that it is "sweet to hate one's fatherland"?[5] As to identification, the educated *intelligent* hoped to find it by becoming a West European and by feeling at one with all Western values. This proved difficult—if not impossible—for the more sophisticated. Conscious desire to identify with someone creates an idealized image of that which one aspires to be, an image which direct experience with reality tarnishes all too easily. The model proved to be a will-o'-the wisp; the "land of holy wonders" turned into a stench-filled cemetery. Herzen, Bakunin, and so many others experienced (to varying degrees) this shock of recognition, a shock that led them to reject and hate what they had worshiped from afar.

The very existence—and the anguished character—of the question whether Russia belonged to the West or not stemmed therefore from the double alienation experienced by the Russian elite in the eighteenth and nineteenth centuries (and *mutatis mutandis* perhaps still experienced by the Soviet intelligentsia of the twentieth). Alienated from both their own past and their people, they could not identify with a Western Europe that did not conform to their idealized image and failed to fulfill their hopes and aspirations.

The evolution of the West European (or American) view of the question offers a counterpart to the Russian picture. At first we can discern a growing sense of discovering an identity between Russia and the West. This was due either to a spreading belief that—in contrast to Asia, at any rate—Russia had been *basically* European for a long time or to the fact that, in appearance at least, Russia had become more Western with every generation since Peter had dramatically proven its European stature by his victory over Charles XII. The growth of the belief that Russia was becoming European and should participate in the affairs of the world as part of Europe is plainly evident in the dispatches of French diplomats and agents in Russia in the eighteenth century.[6] The change in Western opinion is well summarized in the latter part of the century in the words of a French diplomat: "Nous nous étions représentés les Russes comme des barbares [i.e., completely different and not subject to comparison—M.R.], nous les voyons aussi maniérés et aussi bien élevés que les hommes les plus policés."[7] A factor in the rapid acceptance of Russia as a *nation policée* (and of members of its elite in Western European intellectual circles) was the eighteenth-century belief in the uniformity of human nature (and process of civilization), on one hand, and the discovery of the radically different cultures of China and India, on the other. By virtue of being men, the Russians were obviously part and parcel of humanity, while as a country and as a culture Russia was quite clearly closer to Europe than to China or India, hence it was European. The problem of "Russia and the West" (Russia versus the West, rather) did not exist therefore in the eighteenth century, except as an occasional by-product of war propaganda.[8] On the contrary, the *philosophes* looked to Russia as potentially outdoing Western Europe in bringing solutions and values that would enrich the future of mankind.[9]

Whether Russia belonged to the West became a serious question only in the middle of the nineteenth century for both Russians and Europeans. That it remained a live issue throughout the nineteenth and into the twentieth century was mainly due, I think, to the fact that the cultural values which the Russian elite had absorbed from Western Europe (and by which it judged the West) were those of the eighteenth and early nineteenth centuries; and having been raised in Russia to the status of absolutes, they could not be made to fit into the changing reality of a Western Europe that was becoming increasingly industrialized, materialistic, and ugly. To be sure, many West Europeans—and some Americans —felt the same way (from the Romantics through Carlyle to Nietzsche), and their anti-Western "cultural despair" frequently echoed the cries of anguish and anger of Herzen, Dostoevsky, or Leontiev. Obviously what distinguished the "Europeans" from the latter was that they did not (except in a few extreme cases) have the experience of alienation from their own people and country that was so characteristic of the Russians. Hence the more traumatic, more immediately relevant, more easily politicized aspect of the debate on Russia's relationship to the West in Russia.

In the West the debate was usually provoked and carried by waves of Russophobia (Russia is not part of Europe and should be treated as a dangerous barbarian intruder), which were the by-products of developments in foreign policy. As a great power Russia was the adversary of many European states; its threat was heightened in the minds of those who recognized in it aspects of Europe's political structure that stood condemned and that, it was hoped, would soon disappear, for example, serfdom and political tyranny in an age of liberalization. This was the notorious message of the Marquis de Custine, for example. The twentieth-century fear of Russia in the West derives largely from the realization that Russia may be showing up the very essence of modern industrial society and the latter's inherent threat to Western traditions and values.

An essential element of historical comparability, therefore, is the question: who experiences the identity or difference, and for what purposes is this experience used? The preceding pages have dealt with the experiences of the Russian elite and of West European intellectuals. Naturally, if the question of Russia's belonging to the West were put to peasants in the eighteenth or nineteenth century, it either would be meaningless or produce reactions quite at variance with those we have been discussing and with which we are all familiar from our readings. Furthermore, the question may be meaningful to different groups at different times. It is most likely that a factory worker in France, Italy, or England today would feel that Russia is quite part of "his" world, by whatever adjective we may choose to describe this world; the Russian worker probably feels the same way with respect to the West. But this may not be true at all if we could put the question to a French or Italian peasant, on the one hand, and a Russian or Ukrainian collective farmer, on the other. In the nineteenth century, the question of Russia's relationship to the West was given different answers by the intelligentsia and by members of the "establishment." Many members of the intelligentsia doubted that Russia belonged to the West, but it never entered the mind of an official to think and act on this idea. To my knowledge, businessmen in both Russia and the West were quite indifferent to the problem around, say, 1900, and felt that both belonged to the same progressive, technologically oriented European civilization.

Mr. Roberts has quite rightly stressed that for purposes of analyzing and understanding the relations between two events or processes of development, one has to isolate specific institutions, factors, and trends. In analyzing them one discovers that their homogeneity is more apparent than real and that their variety permits a high degree of discrimination and differentiation; the result may be an ordering of national manifestations as if on a continuum. This type of historical analysis (which has been begun with reference to feudalism, serfdom, industrialization, etc.) has been—and will be in the future—very fruitful in insights and meaningful results.[10] The fault of so many alleged comparative analyses has been that one of these categories has been taken as an unchanging and rigidly definable concept and then used rather mechanically in differing historical contexts: if phenomenon X is present in both A and B, the latter must be similar, if it is absent, they cannot be the same. Besides making for very sterile (as well as questionable) results, such an approach flattens our perspective of the past. It fails to take into account the obvious fact that no human institution or activity remains the same for any period of time and that it may play quite different roles depending on its relation to other elements of the culture or polity.

Men do not accept passively and obey blindly institutions, cultural values, aesthetic preferences, or mental attitudes—all the elements we make use of when we compare or contrast historical processes and realities. Men live in them and make use of them, and thereby constantly transform them and their functions. The mechanical and static comparison of institutions, for example, fails to do justice to their dynamic functional relationships. For instance, a "progressive" economic technique or practice may—in the context of serfdom—acquire a most "reactionary" effect and even hamper the modernization of the country's economy.[11] It is the task of the comparative historian to detect and interpret the variety of functions and relationships which an institution, a style of thought or art, an administrative or economic structure, or a political system may have had in the context of the periods and cultures studied. The elements may have been the same in Russia and Western Europe (or Asia for that matter), but did they play the same role, did they belong to a pattern that made for similar effects? Could it not be that similar elements would have opposite historical effects on different contexts?

All of this brings me back to the final and essential point so forcefully made by Mr. Roberts. The quest for comparisons and contrasts without well-defined and historically meaningful questions in mind is a sterile occupation, fraught with many methodological pitfalls. To sharpen our understanding of the past, to shed light on the interplay of forces, on the pulls and stresses to which people have been subjected in a given situation, comparative historical analysis must deal with elements that are comparable and selected according to criteria that are relevant to the times and conditions studied. It must further be kept in mind that the contemporaries' perception of reality is a basic constituent element of the picture and that it rarely remains the same for long, either in space or in time. Only by being constantly aware of the complexity of reality, the delicacy of his tools of analysis, as well as the ever-changing nature of his subject matter can the comparative historian arrive at results that are historically true and intellectually meaningful.

## NOTES

1. Even if a consensus on what is the "West" could have been reached by contemporaries (a task that would not have been much easier then than it is today).

2. N. Pavlov-Sil'vansky, *Proekty reform v zapiskakh sovremennikov Petra Velikago* (St. Petersburg, 1897).

3. I am, of course, well aware that the dichotomy between the two parts of the Russian nation was not quite as sharp and fixed as the Slavophiles and others believed; otherwise it would be difficult to account, for example, for the popularity and assimilation of the great Russian classic writers of the nineteenth century by the common people as soon as the latter had learned to read.

4. We only need to recall the satirist's description of the young fop in Catherine II's time whose body belonged to Russia but whose soul was French, or that other *petit-maître* who bewailed the fact that under Russian conditions it was impossible to reach the exalted level of cultural sophistication of his dear Parisian models. And even the fad for Russian history at the end of the eighteenth century was but a form of westernization. Cf. Hans Rogger, *National Consciousness in Eighteenth Century Russia* (Cambridge, Mass., 1960).

5. "Kak sladostno otchiznu nenavidet'! / I zhadno zhdat' eia unichtozhen'ia! / I v razrushenii otchizny videt' / Vsemirnogo desnitsu vozrozhden'ia!" Cited by M. O. Gershenzon, *Istoria molodoi Rossii* (Moscow, 1908), p. 105.

6. Basile G. Spiridonakis, *Mémoires et documents du Ministère des Affaires Etrangères de France sur la Russie* (Quebec: Faculté des Arts, Université de Sherbrooke, n.d.).

7. Sabatier de Cabre, memoir of July 31, 1772, Archives du Ministère des Affaires Etrangères, *Mémoires et Documents, Russie*, Vol. LXXXV, Supplement No. 6 (1769–1772), p. 227.

8. It is interesting to note that the problem did not even arise during the Napoleonic wars and Russia's occupation of France in 1814–15.

9. Cf. Albert Lortholary, *Les "Philosophes" du XVIIIe siècle et la Russie: Le mirage russe en France au XVIIIe s.* (Paris, 1951); Dieter Groh, *Russland und das Selbstverständnis Europas: Ein Beitrag zur europäischen Geistesgeschichte* (Neuwied, 1961) and supporting documentation in Dmitrij Tschižewskij and Dieter Groh, eds., *Europa und Russland: Texte zum Problem des westeuropäischen und russischen Selbstverständnisses* (Darmstadt, 1959).

10. See Dietrich Gerhard, *Alte und neue Welt in vergleichender Geschichtsbetrachtung* (Göttingen, 1962); Otto Brunner, *Neue Wege der Sozialgeschichte* (Göttingen, 1956).

11. See Michael Confino, *Domaines et seigneurs en Russie vers la fin du XVIIIe siècle: Étude de structures agraires et de mentalités économiques* (Paris, 1963), pp. 136 ff.

# Aspects of Imperial Nineteenth-Century Russia

# Bureaucracy in Russia Under Nicholas I

## SIDNEY MONAS

The bureaucratization of Russia took place largely between the reigns of Peter I and Nicholas I, though its origins go back much further, and in a sense it is a process not yet over. I use the term "bureaucratization" somewhat as Max Weber used *Rationalisierung*, a synonym for modernization—the creation of an intensely specialized, functionally organized, hierarchically subordinated administration, with control over the levers of decision in the hands of (in this case) the Emperor. It implies "Westernization," with an attendant depersonalization of administration—uniformity, standardization, abstraction, a rationalized subordination and discipline. It implies as well a certain attendant isolation, in the interests of efficiency and what might paradoxically be called the interests of disinterestedness, from the normal ebb and flow, the uses of the traditional world where "thieves break through and steal, and moth and rust do corrupt." To make the best use of its own energies it excludes the energies of the uninitiated and unspecialized. It implies a separation, sometimes an extreme separation, of skill from affect, duty from emotion.[1]

In tone, temper, style and personnel, Peter's bureaucracy was dominated by what had been the ruling class, the gentry, the *shliakhetstvo*, later called the *dvorianstvo*. Whether Peter acted instinctively as the agent for the more vital segments of this class, or whether they simply followed or concurred in his lead makes relatively little difference. Peter did not create the Table of Ranks out of whole cloth, but out of the logic of the aspirations of a significant portion of the ruling class. By the time of Nicholas, however, although the personnel of the upper reaches of the bureaucracy were still predominantly gentry, neither their economic nor their social position within the gentry corresponded on the same scale as during the reign of Peter to their position within the bureaucracy.[2]

Peter used the bureaucracy with great energy and confusion. Many of his edicts ring with a missionary zeal, none more so than his instructions to the Chief Magistrate of St. Petersburg, the rhetoric of which, in expounding the good of order, regularity and regulation, is suffused with the secular mysticism of the police state. Under Nicholas, on the other hand, the bureaucracy greatly increased in numbers, and almost correspondingly in regularity and order. If it was Peter who shaved the beards, it was Nicholas who introduced the uniform, and in general the standards of the military parade-ground, to the civil service.[3] Yet what seemed an opportunity to Peter, to Nicholas seemed a burden and a cross. To all major state projects, Nicholas' gloomy response was that nothing could be done. It was not that Nicholas failed to see the need for change or that he did not probe the possibilities for major new developments in the realm of education, in the building of railroads, or in the modification and eventual abolition of the system of serfdom. To all such enterprises, however, Nicholas' Minister of Finance, the somber Count Kankrin, invariably replied that it could not be done, and Nicholas, although he disagreed with and overruled Kankrin on a number of particular projects, in the long run, and basically, acquiesced. Although much of significance that was put into effect in the following reign was to some degree *prepared* during the reign of Nicholas, the fact remains that during a thirty-year period, for all the enormous expansion of the bureaucratic apparatus, that apparatus in itself accomplished virtually nothing of significance. In this negative accomplishment, the preservation intact of the apparatus would seem to have been the major objective.[4]

Given the energy of the reign of Peter and the inertia of that of Nicholas, it seems odd that American and English scholars of Russia have devoted so much learned attention to Nicholas and so little to Peter.[5] Is it because inertia attracts inertia? To be sure, the reign of Nicholas offers a relative simplicity, integrity and stability of government policy. And the glamor of the golden age of Russian culture is there to draw upon. At the same time, there is no significant organized opposition to complicate matters with its own inner policies. Yet it is not entirely these attractions that have drawn us, or mere scholarly prudence. Although little changed socially, politically or economically, the reign of Nicholas I was nevertheless a turning point. A number of significant possibilities *failed* to happen, and this failure was crucial in determining the significance of the past and committing the nation to its future. In attempting to grasp the essence of modern Russia up to the time of the revolution one can hardly do better than starting with Nicholas.

I propose here to deal with the subject of the Russian bureaucracy under Nicholas I through the career of a single prominent bureaucrat, Pavel Dmitrievich Kiselev (1788–1872), and to try to reveal from such an examination something of the nature of the bureaucracy as a whole. Kiselev directed what was certainly the most ambitious and significant administrative enterprise undertaken during the reign of Nicholas. He, and his proposed reforms, offer the additional advantage of having been the subject of two extremely impressive, detailed and extensive monographs—one by his "disciple" and fellow bureaucrat, A. P. Zablotsky-Desiatovsky, the other by a former landowner turned Marxist historian, the extraordinarily patient, thorough and meticulous N. M. Druzhinin.[6]

Kiselev was a man of outstanding intelligence, ability, energy, and devotion to his work. During the reign of Nicholas, Speransky alone could outclass him in these matters, and only a few prominent officials were anywhere near his equals. In almost all other significant details, however, except perhaps for a certain personal tolerance and liberality of outlook, Kiselev was a typical high official of the time of Nicholas.

Born in 1788, Kiselev's childhood coincided with the years of the French Revolution, adolescence and early youth with the Napoleonic campaigns, and young manhood with the Restoration and nationalist unrest in Western Europe. Like the future Decembrists, among whom were not a few of his friends, he came easily to European culture from the background of the more enlightened eighteenth century Russian *dvorianstvo*. Like them, he was educated by events and the most intensive reading, inspired by events. Like them—only more so than most—he had a meteoric career in the army, entering the Cavalry Guards Regiment as ensign at the age of eighteen, and emerging from the Napoleonic wars and the occupation of France a general before he was thirty.

During the period immediately following the Peace of Tilsit, Kiselev, returned from Europe to St. Petersburg, participated like many young men of his class in the "frondeur" criticism of the regime then prevalent. Kiselev was barely turned twenty. In the sentimental, high-flown language of the time he expressed his loyalty to autocracy and his faith in "the personal qualities of the monarch," but complained of his neglect of the *dvorianstvo*, the ruinous economic effects of the Continental System, the "influence of foreigners," and the Emperor's use of a bureaucracy staffed by "men of base origin." The future Decembrists, Sergei Volkonsky and Mikhail Orlov, his good friends, joined him in these sentiments. Their criticisms were soon to take a more radical turn. But Kiselev, who denounced Speransky in 1810—the "base" bureaucrat who had tried to deny the *dvorianstvo* its traditional right of state service by introducing a rudimentary civil service examination!—was to wind up twenty-five years later as Speransky's closest collaborator in a bureaucratically administered attempt at agrarian reform.[7]

In 1812, Kiselev was appointed Wing Adjutant to Alexander I. In this capacity he served as courier, adjutant, staff officer, adviser. From that time on he was a "made" man, and promotion followed promotion. It was this particular kind of military career that Nicholas later was to prefer as background training for his high officials. In Kiselev's case it was reinforced later by distinguished service in the Turkish war of 1828 and his appointment as plenipotentiary to the Danubian provinces. Nevertheless, Kiselev, in addition to his brilliance and his experience in Moldavia-Wallachia, had the added virtue for Nicholas of twenty-six years of military service, during most of which he had not been a commander of field forces, but rather an adjutant and a staff officer, ready to give good advice when asked, but schooled in discipline and obedience, without any politically dangerous patriotic legend having gathered about him.

As chief of staff of the Second Army during the formative years of the secret Decembrist societies, Kiselev lived in Tulchin, and Pestel, Burtsev, Basargin and others were among his close friends. It was Kiselev who recommended Pestel for promotion to colonel. Like these young radicals, Kiselev had been appalled, on his return from Europe, at the corruption of Russian officialdom, the brutality of the Arakcheev regime in the army and military colonies, and above all by the plight of the serfs, caught between the debt-ridden nobility's need to exploit them and their own incapacity to wring a living from a scanty, backwardly cultivated soil. Kiselev admired Pestel's boldness and originality and tended to agree with his formulation of the problems facing Russia; he did not, however, sympathize with the proposed revolutionary solution.

Kiselev's background, in spite of its resemblance to the Decembrists', was not that of a revolutionary. He was, for example, solidly Orthodox in religion. Neither the pietism of Alexander I nor the atheism of Pestel nor the patriotic mysticism of Muraviev-Apostol nor the free-thought of Paris touched him very deeply. He was devoted to his parents, and through them to the whole *dvorianstvo* tradition. He never doubted the principle that in Russia the land belonged, and properly so, to the landowner, whether the landowner happened to be a *dvorianin* or the state. All his later plans for endowing the state peasants with civil rights and eventually emancipating the serfs were firmly anchored to this principle, and he conceived of "liberation" as a contractual arrangement between landowner and peasant that took this fully into account. Kiselev knew, of course, that the peasants often believed otherwise; but to him that was a pernicious myth leading inevitably to the chaos of a *Pugachevshchina*. He believed also in that special, familial, patriarchal, relationship between autocrat and *dvorianstvo* of which the most eloquent exponent was Karamzin, and which Nicholas I, the parade-ground atmosphere he imposed notwithstanding, also professed to believe in. Like Karamzin, Kiselev believed that if men were perfect a republic would be the ideal form of government, but that under Russian conditions autocracy was indispensable. That either the state service or the economy of the countryside in Russia could dispense with a specially privileged *dvorianstvo* in the foreseeable future Kiselev could not bring himself to believe. And however much he disliked the brutality of Arakcheev's regime in the army, military discipline as such was not uncongenial to him.

Without implying any gross kind of economic determinism, Kiselev's economic position must also be taken into account. His family was more than moderately prosperous and owned about twelve thousand acres of land and 600 male "souls" in two provinces, all of which he inherited in due time and to which he added two villages. His wife was the daughter of an extremely wealthy landowner and brought with her to their marriage in 1821 an enormous estate in Kiev province, which in 1830 numbered over four thousand "souls," a cloth factory, a wine press, and numerous mills and smithies. The Kiselevs' combined annual income during the 1830's was something close to 200,000 rubles. It should be added, however, that the Decembrists Volkonsky, Mikhail Orlov, and Trubetskoy were also wealthy men, even if the majority of the Decembrists came from more impoverished *dvorianstvo* families.

Kiselev was always an exceptionally able manager of his and his wife's estates. His successes were due, however, for the most part to very close accounting, tight organization, and efficient exploitation of traditional methods. He introduced few even purely technological innovations. With the peasants he prided himself on being "strict but just." A brutal or corrupt overseer received short shrift from him; but he did not abolish corporal punishment on his estates. He never attempted to take advantage of the law of 1803 which permitted a landowner to "liberate" his serfs.

In all fairness to Kiselev, with his attachment to autocracy and *dvorianstvo*, his passion for administrative control and strict bookkeeping, it should be pointed out that Pestel, the most radical and thoroughly informed of the Decembrists, however different his ultimate conceptions, foresaw, even for his "revolutionized" Russia, a transitional period of dictatorship, rule by a dedicated elite, and control by very "tight" administration.[8]

In February 1822, Vladimir Raevsky was arrested for seditious teaching in the military colonies and a membership list of the secret Decembrist society found among his papers was transmitted to Kiselev. Tactfully, Kiselev allowed Burtsev to destroy this list. Untactfully, Burtsev later testified to this effect before Nicholas' investigating commission. Kiselev, nevertheless, survived this "taint" on his loyalty. Later, he more than vindicated himself by his performance in the Turkish war. Such acts of friendship, however he might discourage them, were not considered by Nicholas entirely unbecoming to a nobleman. Ties of blood or friendship connected at least a substantial part of the *dvorianstvo* with the Decembrists. Nicholas always investigated such ties, but never regarded them in themselves as evidence of subversion.[9]

Before the investigating commission the captured Decembrists had testified concerning their plans for the amelioration of Russia—the introduction of legality, civil rights, and a social and economic transformation of the countryside through the abolition of serfdom. They had believed the autocracy incapable of carrying out such plans. Nicholas studied them carefully, and in some odd measure actually proposed to execute them—but, of course, in his own way.

Nicholas drastically, if not fundamentally, reorganized the bureaucracy. He did not abolish the Ministries, but rather put the finishing touches to their organization by abolishing the last remnants of collegiality and by subordinating their entire structure in strict heirarchical fashion. Nicholas assigned every office a definite rank. Promotion in rank was strictly associated with a superior office. The military atmosphere Nicholas imposed, even the uniforms he designed personally, served to emphasize the hierarchical structure of the bureaucracy. The last vestiges of local self-government dating back to Catherine's time were undermined and all but destroyed. The representative institutions in town and district that Catherine had founded on a class basis were strictly subordinated to the central administration and their always quite limited range of initiative drastically reduced. The provincial governments were subordinated to the Ministry of the Interior, and though this arrangement was complicated by the installation of governors-general and gendarme districts, these latter two institutions intended to, and did, increase centralization. The Senate and the State Council, those traditional centers of aristocratic opposition to the autocracy, were curtailed in their activity. Nicholas feared the establishment of constitutional precedents that might serve eventually to limit the monarch's power, and he reduced the Senate to a court of appeals and the State Council to recording sessions in which policy already decided was merely registered.

To discuss policy and draft legislation, Nicholas turned from the State Council to special *ad hoc* secret committees. To these committees Nicholas could appoint whom he wished without being traditionally obliged thereby to find a more or less permanent place for him in the government. These committees could also be kept small and secret—indeed, their sessions were sometimes so secret as to seem almost conspiratorial—and thus, disquieting rumors concerning impending changes could be minimized.[10]

In addition to the secret committees, Nicholas frequently issued personal commissions to draft legislation and more frequently to inspect the bureaucracy or gather information. He did not, like his older brother, appoint foreigners to high office. The foreign names in his entourage belonged to Baltic Germans who had been born in Russian cities. Men "of base origin" were few: Kankrin came of the petty German nobility and Speransky was a priest's son, but both had been ennobled in the previous reign.[11] On the whole, entry into the *dvorianstvo* became more difficult during Nicholas' reign. Even access to higher education—scarce and needed as the trained professions were—was, after 1848, almost entirely restricted to the *dvorianstvo*. While he went through the motions of once again offering the state service to the *dvorianstvo* as their preserve, Nicholas regimented, subordinated and controlled that preserve in a more systematic way than had ever been done in Russia before.

As a counterweight to the ministries, with an enormous total staff, which grew piece-meal, Nicholas founded an institution highly reminiscent of those private "cabinets" by means of which the absolute monarchs of the seventeenth and eighteenth centuries had enforced their powers against a recalcitrant nobility—His Majesty's Own Private Imperial Chancery. To this institution he assigned tasks which were either particularly close to him personally, or which he did not envisage as part of the permanent state order, or which deliberately overlapped with and might serve to control the functions of the ministries.[12]

These tasks were divergent, and by no means all of the same order of importance. The first section of the chancery had to do with the court, not merely with protocol, but with the management of the Imperial family's estates. The second section, under Speransky, was entrusted with the codification of Russian laws. The third section, the political police, overlapped all other existing institutions and concerned itself with public opinion, censorship, religious sectarians, factory inspection, charity, procedure in the law courts, and almost anything else one can think of. The fourth section, relatively innocuous, managed the Imperial charities. The fifth section, founded in 1835 under Kiselev, planned the emancipation of the serfs, and in 1837 was converted into the Ministry of State Properties. A sixth section was formed to administer new territories in the Caucasus.

The financial means available to Nicholas for supporting this much expanded bureaucratic network were not great. His Minister of Finances, Kankrin, was one of the most expert fiscal manipulators of his time, but the fact remained that the *dvoriantsvo* as a whole was heavily in debt to the state and had by no means recovered from its losses in the Napoleonic wars. Although he took a dour view of them as a class, Kankrin nevertheless turned the Commercial Bank into a bank for cushy loans to *dvoriane*, and their indebtedness to the state greatly increased.[13] The state peasants were chronically in arrears on their dues as well as their taxes. Because of fear of peasant unrest, these arrears had periodically to be cancelled by the Emperor.

The pay of a top bureaucrat was fairly high, and frequently supplemented by Imperial rewards. Nevertheless, life in St. Petersburg, especially in the court circle, was extremely expensive. Benckendorff, the head of the third section, allowed himself to be elected to the boards of a number of commercial corporations doing business in the capital and anxious to maintain good relations with the chief of the political police even if he did no work. Even so, his estate near Riga had to be sold after his death to pay off his debts. Kiselev's private fortune was a great asset to him. Indeed, it was all but indispensable.

On the lower levels of the bureaucracy salaries were chronically inadequate. Few of the officials under the provincial governor, for example, could live off their pay. On the provincial level bribe taking was generally accepted as a matter of course, part of the old tradition of *kormlenie*, living off the land. It was the peasant who could least afford to pay who paid most; sometimes voluntarily, sometimes not. Provincial service was considered to be such a corrupting experience even on middle grade officials that the third section requested the Emperor's exemption from the normal requirement that such officials appointed to St. Petersburg have served three years in the provinces first.[14]

Yet training through experience was in most cases the only training available for state servants. Nicholas founded a number of technical schools and expanded the staffs of the universities; yet total enrollment at institutions of higher learning remained absurdly small, never more than 4,000 at any time during the reign of Nicholas. Would-be doctors, lawyers, and engineers were sent abroad for training, but rarely more than thirty in any one year. The entire annual budget of the Ministry of Education was less than a million rubles. Furthermore, much time and staff work in the universities was taken with supervisory functions— part of Nicholas' intensive campaign to prevent current European political and philosophical ideas from being absorbed along with technological knowledge.

Thus, in order to maintain control of a process of social and economic change that Nicholas recognized as inevitable and even desirable, he released upon Russia a vast horde of ignorant and impoverished officials hardly likely to encourage the active cooperation of the population. Assuming, however, that widespread social initiative on the part of the population posed a threat to the foundations of order—and it was by no means insane to assume this—there was no choice but to work for change through the bureaucracy, however inadequate that might be.

In January 1835, Nicholas was much alarmed by the third section's annual "Survey of Public Opinion." The political police reported widespread unrest among the peasantry, revolts, a deepening of indebtedness. Even the political police suggested that serfdom was becoming a threat. To avoid arousing the *dvorianstvo*, Nicholas formed one of his secret committees, under the chairmanship of General Vasil'chikov. To it were invited Kankrin, Speransky and Kiselev.

Kiselev was fresh from his experience as the Emperor's plenipotentiary in Moldavia and Wallachia, where he had instituted a spectacular agrarian reform which, while remaining true to his principle that the land belonged to the landowner and maintaining the division of society into legally distinct social classes, had nevertheless reduced peasant indebtedness by regularizing dues and obligations assessed on the basis of payability, and had granted former serfs certain basic civil rights, such as the right to own and dispose of property and the right to trial in a court of law.

Kiselev and Speransky between them suggested a plan for the gradual emancipation of the serfs that met with Nicholas' approval against other more conservative proposals submitted. They projected a reform that would lead to the gradual abolition of serfdom, solve the problem of the shrinkage of peasant landholdings, liquidate peasant indebtedness to the state, facilitate trade and movement to the towns, and thereby eliminate the major causes of peasant unrest as well as provide the state with greater financial means.

It was proposed to begin with the state peasants and to proceed in slow stages, beginning with four provinces and then extending the reform to state lands throughout the Empire. A census, inventory and land survey were to be made. Illegal encroachments of private landowners on state-owned lands were to be rectified. Where peasants were landless, or where their holdings had shrunk to a size which could no longer support their families, resettlement projects were to be undertaken, making use of unpopulated state lands on the southern and eastern borderlands. Both Kiselev and Speransky were aware of the seriousness and dimension of peasant land-hunger and stressed the necessity of reapportionment. Special schools, law courts, and something like a primitive network of what we could call "county agents" were to be established. The peasants were to be allowed to own and dispose of property, and movement to the towns was to be less severely restricted. Entry into the "townsman" and merchant class was to be facilitated. Actually, it became one of the peculiar features of Nicholas' reign that while entry into the *dvorianstvo* was extremely restricted, entry into the middle classes became relatively free.

The central feature of the reform followed from the census, survey and inventory. On the basis of these, the "payability" of a peasant household was to be assessed. The per-capita "soul" tax was to be abolished, and taxes as well as dues calculated on the basis of the capacity of the land to produce. Dues in kind were also to be "normalized" and wherever possible converted into monetary payments; for *barshchina*, legal limits were to be set. Kiselev's central principle that the state and not the peasant was the landowner did not waver; he wished merely to endow the peasant with civil rights, and to make the burden of his rents and taxes both calculable and related to his capacity to produce. He also wished to encourage the growth of a more prosperous class of peasant entrepreneurs, who could rent and even buy land, use hired labor, set up mills and factories and trade in the towns. Unlike Stolypin four generations later, Kiselev believed it would be politically dangerous and fiscally unsound to undermine the village commune; nevertheless, he clearly saw the future economic and political advantage to the state inherent in the "strong and sober."

Kiselev's plan did not stop with the state peasantry. After the inventory of the state lands had been completed, he proposed a similar survey of the private estates, with a view, eventually, to introducing the reform into these as well, and thereby abolishing serfdom.

Unlike Kankrin, Kiselev and Speransky understood very well the necessity of transforming the entire economic and social structure of the Empire before the related problems of peasant unrest and chronic indebtedness—those manacles on the state's freedom of action—could be solved. What they did not understand were the difficulties involved in effecting such a transformation by means of the bureaucratic apparatus alone.

Kiselev, encouraged and advised by the aging Speransky, concentrated his energies and talents on this matter of peasant reform. Nicholas was impressed. Later, he was to assure Kiselev, "Our views on the peasant problem have always coincided." Kiselev knew that if he were to succeed he must have the full and enthusiastic support of the Emperor at every point. He was careful to avoid the "mistake" Count Uvarov, the Minister of Education, would make in 1848. Then, in order to forestall the rumored closing of the universities, Uvarov appealed directly to public opinion. He arranged for the newspaper publication of an article praising the Russian universities, distinguishing their loyalty to the crown from the turbulent atmosphere of universities in the West. That was enough for Nicholas. Uvarov was dismissed. Kiselev, on the other hand, scrupulously avoided responding to difficulties by making an appeal outside the chain of command.

In April 1835, Nicholas founded the fifth section of his chancery and appointed Kiselev his, as he put it, "chief of staff in peasant affairs." Kiselev's first step as head of the section was to prepare a compilation of existing legislation on the peasant question, going back to Peter the Great, and attempting to demonstrate that the proposed reform followed logically from, and was entirely in harmony with, previous legislation and intent.

Kiselev knew, of course, that he was faced with opposition from what was probably the majority of the *dvorianstvo*. He knew that representatives of this opposition—like A. S. Men'shikov, for example—were close to the throne. He also knew the volatile nature of the backward peasantry, and how easily the rumor of impending liberation could be converted into a call for the axe. He proceeded, therefore, with extreme caution and great skill. The inventories and subsequent legislation were worked out and carried through piecemeal, bit by bit, but in such a way that each step seemed to follow necessarily and inevitably from the one that preceded it.

In 1837, Nicholas converted the fifth section into the ministry of State Properties, with Kiselev as Minister. As annual budget, over Kankrin's objections, he appropriated a million two hundred thousand rubles. This was a greater sum than that at the disposal of any other ministry except War. Considering the magnitude of the ministry's tasks, however, it was not a great sum. Kiselev had in his trust, after all, the entire state peasantry, almost 40 per cent of the total population, about eighteen million people. We need only to recall that the total budget of the ministry was only six or seven times as great as the annual family income of the Kiselevs.

Kiselev's immediate staff consisted of outstandingly able men. One, Karneev, had been his secretary in the Danubian provinces. Another, Klokov, of merchant origin, had served under Speransky in the second section. Still others, like Insarsky and Zablotsky-Desiatovsky (Kiselev's future biographer) were "liberals" devoted to the cause of peasant reform and to the Minister personally as its outstanding proponent. Below this level, however, problems arose. The Ministry of State Properties inherited the provincial and district Treasure Offices, previously under the Ministry of Finances. These were riddled with corruption, inefficiency and incompetence. It is doubtful whether Kiselev had more than a few dozen really well trained men at his disposal at any one time.

From outside the Ministry, Kiselev received reports, suggestions, criticisms, from all classes of the population. He studied them carefully, and some proved quite useful. But they were unsolicited, random, and haphazard. Kiselev also wrote to Russian embassies abroad and requested information concerning the conditions of peasantry, especially in Austria and Prussia. The fact remains, however, that his resources (informational as well as financial) were never adequate.

Kiselev's first major failure occurred in 1839. The cadastral survey of the private estates which he undertook in that year had to be abandoned. It aroused the intense hostility of the *dvorianstvo* and provoked a number of peasant insurrections. From 1837, Count Benckendorff, the head of the third section, perhaps because of his commercial activities, became less and less accessible to Nicholas, until he died in 1844 and was replaced by A. F. Orlov, an opponent of Kiselev's. As early as 1839, however, the police Surveys of Public Opinion began to place Kiselev's activities in a negative light. Whether this was due to the calculated insinuations of a high police official or whether the surveys honestly reported the current state of mind among the *dvorianstvo* hardly matters. In 1843, Nicholas felt obliged to issue an assurance to the *dvorianstvo* that no change in the status of privately owned serfs was contemplated. This seemed to spell the defeat of Kiselev's final goal.

The cadastral survey of state lands was carried through. Peasant dues were normalized. Depradations by private landowners on the state lands were at least partly checked. Land-hungry peasants were resettled on the southern and eastern borderlands and new territory brought under cultivation. Elementary schools, loan and saving banks, fire insurance, veterinary stations, experimental farms, technical advice to the peasants, medical outposts—few in number and on the whole poor in quality—were nevertheless introduced, though far from uniformly, by the Ministry. Trade turnover doubled at the fairs and markets on state lands. The number of manufacturing establishments (mostly very small scale) and the number of workers employed by them almost doubled. Peasant mobility, both in a territorial and in a social sense significantly increased. With all this, however, peasant revolts did not cease.

On the contrary, they increased—in scope, in violence and in frequency. On private estates, it was often the proximity of relatively freer and more prosperous state peasants that fostered unrest. During the Crimean War, state peasants were chosen by lot, while the serfs were still subject to the caprice of commune and landowner. In some mysterious way this encouraged the prevalent rumor that army service guaranteed either emancipation or ascription to the state lands. Many attempts to disabuse volunteers and recruits of this notion were answered with mutiny and riot. On many of the state lands, however, especially in the east, it was the all-embracing tutelage of Kiselev's administrative system that provoked peasant outbreaks.

In attempting to bestow civil rights upon the peasantry, Kiselev in many cases actually undermined the freedom and independence the state peasants had previously enjoyed relative to privately owned serfs. The hated *chinovnik*— whether in the form of rural police, inspector, tax collector on the one hand, or doctor, veterinarian, agronomist, on the other (peasants did not always make subtle distinctions)—was far more ubiquitous in the villages than he had been formerly. Often, he was dishonest, incompetent and brutal, took bribes and inflicted cruel punishments. Even if he were honest and competent, his intentions were often misunderstood, as were the innovations he attempted to introduce. One of the unintended consequences of Kiselev's reform was that it went a long way towards destroying the last vestiges of independence enjoyed by the village commune, and made the elected representatives of the peasantry the mere agents of the central bureaucracy.

The shrinkage of peasant landholdings was checked but not stopped. Neither resettlement on the borderlands nor migration to the towns—both still on a limited scale—solved the problem of rural overpopulation. In spite of the effort at technological improvement, the productivity of the soil actually began to decline. Livestock was scarce, meagerly nourished, and frequently decimated by disastrous epidemics. Scarcity of manure compounded technological backwardness in exhausting the earth. Peasant arrears in dues and taxes, instead of declining, continued to increase, and once again in 1843, Nicholas had to issue an Imperial reprieve.

Such results were not likely to impress the *dvorianstvo* with the economic benefits of emancipation. Actually, many began to take the reform less seriously. There were jokes about Kiselev's "castles in the air." In 1848, A. S. Men'shikov coined the epigram: "Russia has nothing to fear from communism; only Kiselism."

Scarcely a year after Nicholas' death, Alexander II, destined ironically enough to become the "Tsar-Liberator," dismissed Kiselev from office. It was handled tactfully enough. A. F. Orlov, an old opponent, recently returned from negotiating the Peace of Paris, suggested that Kiselev might be useful as Ambassador to France. Within two years, the Ministry was placed under the direction of M. N. Muraviev, later known as "the hangman," for his exploits in Poland.

Nevertheless, Kiselev's work was not entirely lost. Not merely his inventories and cadastral surveys, but the entire carefully documented experience of his administration proved invaluable to the emancipation of 1861. N. A. Miliutin, the prime mover of Alexander's emancipation, was Kiselev's nephew and greatly influenced by him. Many of his co-workers had been trained in Kiselev's ministry. Furthermore, even before 1861, the hopelessness of a purely administrative solution to the peasant problem was grasped, even by the reluctant Emperor. Local self-government and a many-sided initiative from outside the government apparatus, as well as relatively free and open discussion, were viewed as logical components of emancipation. They seemed logical, however, only insofar as they did not seem to breach the integral fortress of the bureaucracy, but merely provide it with impetus and information. Both local self-government and the encouragement of spontaneous public intitiative were cautiously circumscribed, highly restricted, and constantly reminded to the tune of the scratching of the bureaucratic goose-quill of the precariousness of their tenure. In a way, the system that was formed under Nicholas persisted, with considerable modification, it is true, until 1905. The lesson posed by Kiselev's experience, although it was finally learned, was not so quickly nor so thoroughly learned as it should have been. Both autocracy and bureaucracy had enjoyed too long and too successful a career in Russia to submit themselves easily to dissolution.

## NOTES

1. For Max Weber on *Ratsionalisierung* and bureaucratization, see especially, *Wirtschaft und Gesellschaft*, 2nd ed., 2 vols., Cologne, 1964–65, Vol. I, pp. 185 f., 252; Vol. II, pp. 735 ff., 712 ff., 836, 1059 ff.; although Weber thought bureaucracy an inevitable consequence of modernity and democracy, he felt rather ambiguously about its virtues. See also Max Rheinstein (editor), *Max Weber on Law in Economy and Society*, Cambridge, Mass., 1954; H. H. Gerth and C. Wright Mills, *From Max Weber: Essays in Sociology*, N.Y., 1946, pp. 196–244; Max Weber, *Gesammelte politische Schriften*, 2nd ed., Tuebingen, 1958. Of the greatest interest in this connection also are, Otto Hintze, *Soziologie und Geschichte*, 2nd ed., Goettingen, 1964, pp. 66–125; *Staat und Verfassung*, 2nd ed., Goettingen, 1965, pp. 275–320; and Michel Crozier, *Le phénomène bureaucratique*, Paris, 1963. Without drawing an explicit parallel, Hans Rosenberg nevertheless cannot but impress on the attentive reader the many strong analogies between the Prussian and the Russian situation vis-a-vis bureaucracy in the eighteenth and early nineteenth centuries; see Hans Rosenberg, *Bureaucracy, Aristocracy and Autocracy: the Prussian Experience, 1660–1815*, Cambridge, Mass., 1958.

2. That Peter did not simply surround himself with "new men" and adventurers, but that representatives of the old noble families occupied the highest positions of power both in the nascent bureaucracy and in Peter's immediate entourage, has been a commonplace of every serious historical study since Kliuchevsky (See V. Kliuchevsky, *Peter the Great*, Vintage Books, N.Y., 1958). Nevertheless, the legend dies hard. A detailed study of the middle ranks of officialdom in addition to the very highest ranks emphasized by Kliuchevsky has yet to be done. A doctoral dissertation on this subject by Brenda Waters is now under way at the University of Rochester, under the direction of Professor Michael Cherniavsky. Professor Pintner is engaged on an archival study of the bureaucracy under Nicholas.

3. See especially the opening chapter of my book, *The Third Section: Police and Society in Russia under Nicholas I*, Cambridge, Mass., 1961.

4. Walter M. Pintner, *Russian Economic Policy under Nicholas I*, Ithaca, N.Y., 1967, pp. 10–26.

5. In addition to the work of Professor Pintner and my own book cited above, the following should be noted: N. V. Riasanovsky, *Nicholas I and Official Nationality in Russia, 1825–1855*, Berkeley, 1959; J. S. Curtiss, *The Russian Army under Nicholas I*, Durham, N.C., 1965; W. L. Blackwell, *The Beginnings of Russian Industrialization, 1800–1860*, Vol. I, Princeton, N.J., 1968; I should add also, the forthcoming study of the political police by P. S. Squire, *The Third Department* (Cambridge University Press) and the very interesting unpublished doctoral dissertation by Helma Repczuk, "Nicholas Mordvinov (1754–1845)," Ph.D. dissertation, Columbia University, 1962, which deals with the man who was a kind of Admiral Rickover of the time of Nicholas. Whatever their excellence, these works have by no means rendered obsolete the classic monographs on the reign of Nicholas: Theodor Schiemann, *Geschichte Russlands unter Kaiser Nikolaus I*, 4 Vols., Berlin, 1904–1919; M. A. Polievktov, *Nikolai I, biografiia i obzor tsarstvovaniia*, Moscow, 1918.

6. A. P. Zablotsky-Desiatovsky, *Graf P.D. Kiselev i ego vremia*, St. Petersburg, 1882; N. M. Druzhinin, *Gosudarstvennye krestiane i Reforma P. D. Kiseleva*, 2 vols., Moscow-Leningrad, 1946–1958. Except where noted, the data for what follows derive from one or the other source or both. See also, Olga Crisp, "The State Peasants under Nicholas I," *Slavonic and East European Review*, XXXVII (1959).

7. Marc Raeff, *Michael Speransky, Statesman of Imperial Russia, 1772–1839*, The Hague, 1957, pp. 303, 304, 349. See also the edition of Speransky's notes and projects published after the appearance of Raeff's volume. S. N. Valk (editor), *M. M. Speranskii: proekty i zapiski*, Moscow-Leningrad, 1961.

8. M. V. Nechkina (editor), *Dokumenty po istorii vosstaniia Dekabristov*, 12 vols., Moscow, 1923–1958; Vol. VII, 1958, is an edition of Pestel's *Russkaia Pravda*, with its variants and the documents that were later incorporated into it.

9. For a considerably more courtly image of Nicholas I than the one usually presented, see Constantin de Grunwald, *Tsar Nicholas I*, N.Y. 1955 (translated from the French Edition of 1946).

10. Monas, *op. cit.*, pp. 58, 88, 133–196.

11. For a tabulation of their careers through the ranks, as well as a similar tabulation for many of the top civil and military grades of the bureaucracy from the time of Peter the Great to 1917, see the incomplete but remarkable and indeed indispensable work of Erik Amburger, *Geschichte der Behoerdenorganisation Russlands von Peter dem Grossen bis 1917*, Leiden, 1966.

12. See, in addition to my own book, the forthcoming work of P. S. Squire cited above.

13. Pintner, *op. cit.*, pp. 35–38.

14. Monas, *op. cit.*, pp. 84–132.

# Problems and Patterns of Russian Economic Development

## ALEXANDER GERSCHENKRON

### I

The emancipation of the peasantry stands at the threshold of the period under review. The question of whether, on the eve of the reform, the system of serfdom was disintegrating for economic reasons or whether its vitality and viability were still essentially unimpaired has been the subject of much controversy. But even those who, like the present writer, tend toward the latter view must admit that the development of the nonagrarian sectors of the economy was virtually premised upon the abolition of serfdom.

To say this, however, does not at all imply that promotion of economic development was a paramount objective of the emancipation. As was true of most of the agrarian reforms in nineteenth-century Europe, the authors of the Russian reform either considered industrialization undesirable or, at best, were indifferent to it. The actual procedures chosen reflected these attitudes. In many ways they were bound to hamper rather than facilitate economic growth. The emancipation involved, first of all, a determination of the land area to be given over by the landowner to peasants for permanent use. There is no question that over wide parts of the country (and particularly in the black-earth belt) the peasants received a good deal less land than had been customarily assigned to them prior to the reform. Second, there was the question of the magnitude of the quitrents (*obrok*) to be paid by the peasants as compensation for land allotments. It is true that once those rents were set, subsequent acquisition of land by the peasants (the so-called redemption procedure, by which the right of use was changed to the right of ownership) was rendered very easy and as often as not did not entail any *additional* burdens upon the peasantry. But the original rents were set far above the contemporaneous market prices of the land. The example of the immediately preceding agrarian reform in Europe—that of

FROM Alexander Gerschenkron, "Problems and Patterns of Russian Economic Development." Reprinted by permission of the publishers from Alexander Gerschenkron (ed.), *Economic Backwardness in Historical Perspective* (Cambridge, Mass.: The Belknap Press of Harvard University Press), Copyright, 1962, by the President and Fellows of Harvard College.

Austria in 1848—where peasants' obligations were mostly determined on the basis of "equity," or cadastral values (much *below* their market prices), was not followed in Russia.

It might be argued that the two features of the Russian reform just mentioned should have provided a favorable climate for subsequent industrialization; the inadequacy of the peasants' landholdings in conjunction with the considerable financial obligations imposed upon the peasants' households could have been expected to favor the flight from the country and thus to provide a large reservoir of labor supply to the nascent industry. Such might have been the consequences indeed, if the reform and the later legislative measures had not erected considerable barriers to land flight by strengthening the *obshchina*, the village commune, wherever it existed.

An English yeoman who found the cost of enclosing the land excessive could sell his farm and use the funds so obtained for business ventures outside agriculture or, at worst, for covering his transfer cost. A Russian peasant who wished to leave the village commune not only had to relinquish his rights in the land, but in addition had to pay, under the terms of the redemption procedures, what often were very sizable sums before he could receive his release. A member of the household, rather than the head thereof, wishing to leave the village permanently also had to secure the consent of the head of the household. Where the periodic repartitions of land by the village commune were conducted on the basis of manpower at the disposal of the household, permanent departure of a family member was bound to reduce the extent of land to be made available to the household at the next repartition. In conditions of relative scarcity of land, the willingness of the head of the household to permit such departures could not be, and in general never was, very great. Nothing was more revealing of the irrational way in which the village commune functioned than the fact that the individual household had to retain the abundant factor (labor) as a precondition for obtaining the scarce factor (land). On the other hand, the readiness of the member of the household to sever for good his connection with the land and become firmly committed to non-agricultural pursuits naturally was adversely affected by these arrangements.

It is often claimed that the Russian emancipation procedure followed the "Prussian model." It seems that Lenin was the first to give currency to the thought. The analogy is hardly felicitous. The outstanding feature of the Russian reform was that instead of a class of landless laborers, it had firmly established the landowning peasantry and had taken special precautions to keep the peasants attached to their land. To be sure, this was done *inter alia* in order to satisfy the gentry's need for cheap labor. But here again the similarity with the Prussian reform is rather superficial and deceptive. Unlike the Prussian Junkers, the Russian gentry seldom showed much interest in technological innovations on their estates. The traditions of serfdom may partly account for that. Under these circumstances, the cheap labor assured the estates by the Reform Act may have been a very undesirable gift, inasmuch as it discouraged rather than encouraged them to introduce those improvements in the mode of cultivation which tended to have labor-saving effects and to increase the capital intensity of agricultural output.

While permanent migration to the city was rendered difficult, temporary moves on the part of the members of peasant households were much less so. Yet even in such cases, the permissive rights vested in the heads of the village administration and the heads of the household created various opportunities for impounding some portion of the earnings made in the city. The right to demand and to enforce the return to the village of the departed member certainly left much room for pressures and extortions of all kinds. If it is considered that age-long tradition and inveterate inertia would have hindered migration to industry under any circumstances, the Russian government by assigning to the *obshchina* and the *mir* such a strong role in the emancipation procedure and in the life of the post-emancipation village had created a considerable obstacle to the formation of a permanent industrial labor force in Russia.

If the double pressure to which the peasant economy was exposed—the inadequacy of land and the magnitude of the financial burdens—was prevented from causing a steady and considerable migration from the land, then that pressure itself was bound to assume the role of a retarding factor in the economic evolution of the country. The peasant economy was unable to increase its productivity because its income net of taxation and redemption payments did not permit sufficient investment; at times the low level of income even led to capital depletion. In addition, the prospect of repartitions militated against land improvements, even if and where they were financially possible; and the egalitarian nature of such repartitions prevented consolidation of landholdings assigned to individual households and precluded changes in cultivation methods and crop-rotation systems even where ignorance and inertia of the peasantry did not constitute an effective obstacle to such improvements.

In the long run, the scarcity of land available to the peasants in conjunction with the increase in population implied a steady deterioration in the economic position of the peasantry, despite purchases by village communes and individual peasants of gentry land and despite the formation, in the 1880's, of special institutions designed to finance such transactions.

It is true that the position of state peasants was more favorable than that of the former serfs in that their land allotments were somewhat larger and their financial burdens somewhat lighter, while the so-called imperial peasants were in between the two groups. Yet these differences, particularly in the long run, were not sufficiently large to warrant a different appraisal of the state and imperial peasantry. They too experienced the restrictive effects of the village commune, and the economic development of their farms also was restrained by the action of the government whose deliberate policy it was to bring their burdens in line with those imposed upon the former serfs.

It should be added that it would be a mistake to interpret the secular rise in land prices which characterized the period between the emancipation and the First World War as providing relief to the peasantry in the sense of reducing the real burden of their obligations. Over large areas of Europe market values of peasant land tended to be a good deal above the capitalized yield values. But in Russia that tendency was particularly strong. Land values moved upward even when prices of agricultural products were falling. The land hunger of the peasantry, stimulated by population growth, largely accounted for this discrepancy. Thus, the rise in land values, far from relieving the peasant economy, was an expression of its precarious position.

There is little doubt that the inhibitions upon the growth of output of the peasants' economy and the consequent limitations upon the peasants' purchasing power for industrial products were a serious obstacle to the industrialization of the country. They made it improbable from the outset that peasant demand for industrial goods could exercise a strong pull on industrial growth. This was clearly seen by a large number of Populist writers. Their conclusion was that industrial development in Russia was unlikely to start and, if started, was bound to founder in the shallowness of the "internal market."

This prospect left the Populists undismayed because of their aversion to industrialization and their fears of its social consequences. Yet the predictions did not come true. By 1914, Russia had taken very long strides along the road of industrial development. What had vitiated the Populists' predictions was their failure to see the manifold flexibilities and adjustabilities which are inherent in processes of economic development. The growing purchasing power of the peasant economy can be indeed important as a motive force of industrialization. Yet it is but one among a number of possible alternatives.

Economic development in a backward country such as Russia can be viewed as a series of attempts to find—or to create—substitutes for those factors which in more advanced countries had substantially facilitated economic development, but were lacking in conditions of Russian backwardness. Such "substitutions" are the key to an understanding of the way in which the original disabilities were overcome and a process of sustained industrial growth was started in Russia. It is these acts of substitution that came to determine the specific pattern of industrial development.

But the process of industrialization is also a process of diminishing backwardness. In its course, factors that were lacking formerly tend to become evident and acquire increasing importance within the body economic. What was once in vain looked for to serve as a "prerequisite" or a "cause" of industrial development came into being as its effect. It is a fascinating pursuit in the history of modern industrializations to see to what extent the original "substitutes" were thereby rendered obsolete and disappeared after having fulfilled their function; and to what extent they were preserved and continued to dominate the pattern of industrial development in its subsequent stages, even though the special need for them no longer existed.

The present assignment requires this writer to supply, within the scope of a few pages, a background chapter on the last hundred years of Russian economic history—a period of unprecedented economic change. Obviously, no more can be done than to select for discussion some significant aspects of that change. Perhaps the processes touched upon in the preceding paragraph may serve this purpose.

Over long stretches of the period under review, in manifold ways, in ever-changing forms, and at different levels, innovation and anachronism seem to coalesce and to separate, to follow and to displace each other. The remainder of this chapter will be devoted to an attempt to see the peculiarities of Russian industrialization in terms of these relationships.

## II

The great spurt of Russian industrialization in the prerevolutionary period largely coincided with the decade of the 1890's. Thus, almost thirty years had passed over the land before the great effort could come about. This is not surprising. The peasant reform would have had to be very different if a direct and immediate impact upon industrial growth could have been expected from it. Moreover, even if the reform had been deliberately designed to favor industrialization rather than to obstruct it, a certain preparatory period of slow growth was almost inevitable. The judicial and administrative reforms which came in the wake of the emancipation were essential in creating a framework for modern business activity. But other changes, at least equally significant, were much slower in coming. Certainly a radical improvement in communications was crucial. One does not have to conjure up the dramatic and pathetic vision of a huge boiler being dragged by teams of oxen through the deep mud of the Ukrainian steppes on its way to the construction site of the first blast furnace in the *Donbas* in order to understand that some railroad building had to antedate the period of rapid industrialization. Railroads were indispensable to sustain a level of exports consonant with the needs of an industrializing economy. Railroad materials had to be imported from abroad, which in turn meant pursuit of a liberal foreign-trade policy with but a modicum of encouragement to domestic industry. Besides, a period of rapid growth does not materialize overnight simply because an institutional barrier to industrialization has disappeared. Such a period requires a simultaneous development of complementary efforts in many directions. The component elements of growth in the individual industrial branches must be adjusted to each other, and only when a number of such "development blocks," to use Erik Dahmén's felicitous phrase, has been created is the stage set for the initiation of the great spurt.

There is little doubt that the decades following the emancipation can be conceived as such a period of preparation. And yet it is only in retrospect that they can be so viewed. The deficiency of the internal market, so untiringly stressed by the Populist writers, might have postponed the period of rapid growth until a far and indefinite future. The strategic factor in the great industrial upsurge of the 1890's must be seen in the changed policy of the government. The fear of industrialization, so much in evidence in the 1860's, was gone. Industrial development became an accepted and in fact the central goal. Once this happened, the problem of the peasant demand lost its previous significance, and its relation to industrialization was thoroughly reversed. It was as though a rotating stage had moved, revealing an entirely new scenery. The growth of peasant demand for industrial goods no longer was a prerequisite of successful industrialization. On the contrary, its curtailment became the objective. To reduce peasant consumption meant increasing the share of national output available for investment. It meant increased exports, stability of the currency, chances for larger and cheaper loans from abroad, and the availability of foreign exchange needed to service foreign loans.

The Russian state under Vyshnegradsky and Witte put the peasantry under very considerable fiscal pressure. It left the agricultural economy of the country to its own devices, satisfied that conversion of pastures into grain lands and some modest rise in productivity on those estates which were cultivated as such rather than leased to the peasants were sufficient to support the process of industrialization. Population of course was growing rapidly. In the closing years of the 1890's Russian agriculture produced less breadgrains per capita of the population than had been the case three decades earlier. If the increased exports are taken into consideration, the domestic availabilities were still smaller. A central principle of governmental policy was to impound a larger share of the peasants' output rather than to take active steps to raise that output.

Thus, the government's budgetary policy was effectively *substituted* for the deficiency of an internal market. The continuation of railroad construction on a large scale throughout the 1890's provided the government with convenient machinery for the maintenance of demand for industrial products. At the same time, in multifarious ways the government either supplied investment funds to industry directly or encouraged and facilitated investment in industry. Government action took the place of what in other countries was achieved by the pull of a growing free market, or by forced savings generated either by credit creation or by the impact upon current income of previously accumulated claims.

Those, however, were not the only processes of substitution that were taking place during the period of the great spurt of Russian industrialization. The Russian government, far from favoring all branches of industrial endeavor indiscriminately, concentrated its primary attention on the output of iron and steel and the machinery industries. The strategic interest in railroads and general political considerations certainly prompted the government in that direction. But as may be deduced from comparisons with other countries, this cannot be more than a part of the story. In a sense, this concentration upon certain branches of industry also was an emanation of substitutive processes.

Russia on the eve of its great industrial spurt suffered from many disabilities. Its entrepreneurs were far too few; their time horizon often limited, their commercial customs backward, and their standards of honesty none too high. The influx of labor to industry was inadequate because of the institutional framework that had been imposed upon agriculture. Such labor as was available was uneducated, restless and fitful in its habits, often trying to submerge the sense of frustration and loneliness in alcoholic excesses with consequent absenteeism, low productivity, and rebellion against the rules of the factory discipline. One of the few advantages that Russia, as many other backward countries in similar conditions, possessed was the possibility of borrowing technology from more advanced and more experienced industrial countries. In this field alone, Russia could equal, if not excel, them. It could concentrate on modern technology so that its factory equipment, though much smaller in the aggregate, could be much more up-to-date in its average composition. But the introduction on a large scale of technology from advanced countries, in its very nature, also meant a substitution of capital for labor. Far from being irrational in conditions of a backward country, it was the modern Western technology which enabled the Russian entrepreneurs to overcome the disability of an inadequate labor supply and very frequently also the inferior quality of that labor.

This is not to say that lack of suitable industrial labor in itself was not a hindrance to Russian industrialization. Introduction of a labor-saving process may mean lower cost per unit of the product; and still the entrepreneur may find the resulting saving insufficient to justify the effort of reorganization and modernization of the plant. His decision may be positive only if he feels that cost reductions will lead to a great expansion of output, thus increasing the total profits very considerably. But a sizable expansion of output, even though the innovation is labor saving, will require a large increase in the labor force; accordingly, the decision may still fall against the innovation, unless the labor needed may be expected to come forth without too great a rise in wage rates. The point, therefore, is not that the difficulties which Russia experienced with the formation of an industrial proletariat were not a bothersome obstacle. The point rather is that the assurance of government demand for a considerable portion of the growing output in conjunction with the introduction of modern technology created a situation in which the quantitative and the qualitative inadequacy of the labor supply could be neutralized to an extent that still permitted a relatively high rate of industrial growth.

A historian of the period cannot fail to be impressed with two aspects of this process of assimilation of foreign technology. It may be taken for granted that throughout the nineteenth century technology tended to become more and more labor saving. This was true of the individual industrial branches, and even more so of industrial economies as a whole, because of the increasing share of those industries where technological progress led to particularly rapid increases in the capital-labor ratios. It is true of course that, broadly speaking, the Russian entrepreneurs had to accept Western technology such as it was. But if they had wanted to keep down the capital-labor ratios, they might well have tried to obtain secondhand equipment built in earlier phases of Western industrialization. The least they could do was to try to import technology from those countries where technological progress had been less rapid. In fact, the opposite was true. In the period of the great spurt of the nineties, it was no longer the English technology, but the more progressive German technology that came to dominate Russian imports; and increasingly, the eyes of engineers and factory managers turned toward the United States whence even more capital-intensive equipment was brought into the country. Thus alternatives were available, and there is no reason to assume that the choices made were not the rational ones.

On the other hand, it would be wrong to see the process of technological acquisition as one of mere imitation. True, in the last decade of the nineteenth century, the Russians had as yet very little opportunity for producing equipment which combined certain features of, say, American and German machinery (as began to happen several decades later). But they exercised discretion in the processes that were modernized and those that were left unchanged, often within the same plant. While the Russian blast furnaces were rapidly becoming bigger and technically more advanced, the processes of introducing the charge into the furnaces remained untouched by this development, and workers equipped with wheelbarrows still carried out the job. Where industrial work was still similar to that used in agriculture and capable of being performed by an unskilled and fluctuating labor force, it was allowed to continue to do so.

Finally, there is the problem of bigness. Bigness, in a broad sense, is of course inherent in the concept of a great spurt. But the industrialization in Russia, as in so many other backward countries in the nineteenth century, was also characterized by bigness both of individual plant and individual enterprise. There were many reasons for this. For one, the technology of the nineteenth century typically favored the large plants, and to accept the most advanced technology also meant accepting larger and larger plants. The state promoting industrial establishments, for good and not so good reasons, showed remarkably little interest in small businesses. Large enterprises were a much more lucrative source of graft; and the corruption of the bureaucracy tended to reinforce a tendency that was already present for weighty economic reasons. Similarly, the Russian government did little to check the strong cartelization movement within Russian industry which acquired momentum after the great spurt of the nineties. But what is of interest here is that the bigness of plant and enterprise, too, must be viewed as a specific substitution process. The lack of managerial and entrepreneurial personnel was compensated for by a scale of plants which made it possible to spread the thin layer of available talent over a large part of the industrial economy.

But what were the results and the aftermath of these developments? In purely quantitative terms, in terms of growth of industrial output, the spurt was truly a great one. The average annual rate of industrial growth during the nineties was around 8 per cent, and it was even better than that in the last years of the decade. None of the major countries in Western Europe had experienced a comparably high rate of change. The very rapidity of the transformation, however, was making for maladjustments of various kinds. The discrepancy between the industrial segment of the economy which was forging ahead and the relatively stagnant agricultural segment perhaps was the most crucial among those lags and tensions. But others were by no means unimportant.

The specific processes of substitution, which have been referred to above, tended to reinforce the heterogeneous character of the resulting economic structure.

Contrasts between the new and the old appeared within the industrial group itself and within the individual plants and enterprises. Technology as a strategic factor in the industrial spurt implied modernization of some industrial branches and not of others. Within an industrial plant age-old processes based on tools used in the construction of the Pyramids were carried on side by side with methods representing the last word of the inventive genius of the nineteenth century. This inevitably was reflected in human contrasts within the labor force.

But the contrasts obviously transcended labor; they extended into the managerial group. The technical director, as the chief engineer frequently was called in a Russian factory, may have been indistinguishable from his Western counterpart. The commercial manager or the entrepreneur as likely as not was a much more complex phenomenon. He was able to understand and willing to exploit the economic advantages of the new technology, but at the same time he carried on attitudes and displayed forms of behavior which differed little, if at all, from those of preindustrial entrepreneurs in Russia. This was true of his relations to consumers, suppliers, credit institutions, and competitiors. In addition, his relations with the governmental bureaucracy called for special, often very devious, actions. He had to be a different man in his way of dealing with a German firm which supplied his business firm with machinery and know-how, and in dealing with an official in the Ministry of Finance whence he obtained both subsidies and orders for deliveries. The great spurt in conditions of Russian backwardness could not fail to give rise to manifold stresses, tensions, and incongruities. Sociological research which would view those tensions against the economic background of the mechanics of backwardness should discover a rich field for empirical findings and analytical comprehension.

All these disparities, created almost inevitably in the course of the great spurt, can be seen as problems for the succeeding phase of Russian industrial development that followed. However, overriding all of them in importance was the problem which the emancipation of the peasantry did not solve and the gravity of which was greatly enhanced precisely by the policy of rapid industrialization. Industrialization required political stability, but industrialization, the cost of which was largely defrayed by the peasantry, was in itself a threat to political stability and hence to the continuation of the policy of industrialization. The immediate effect of the basic substitution of the government's budgetary policies for the deficiency of the internal market was growth of industrial output. In the longer run, the effects were more complex.

## III

What happened in Russia in the nineties of the last century was the great upsurge of modern industrialization. Nevertheless, certain aspects of it were not modern at all. Several times before in the course of Russian history, economic development seemed to follow a curious pattern: the military interests of the state induced the government to bring about a rapid spurt of economic growth.

In the course of the process, heavy burdens were imposed upon the peasant population of the country, the enserfment of the Russian peasantry having been inextricably connected with the policies of economic development. So great were the burdens, and so heavy the pressure, that after a number of years the spurt tended to peter out, leaving an exhausted population to recover slowly from the stress and the strain that had been imposed upon it.

There is little doubt that military considerations had a good deal to do with the Russian government's conversion to a policy of rapid industrialization. True, no immediate military discomfiture preceded the initiation of the new policy. But the war of 1877 against the Turks was won on the battlefields in the Danube Valley and the Balkan Mountains, only to be lost in Berlin against the British and probably the Germans as well. In the course of the Berlin Congress, particularly during its dramatic moments, the Russian government had much opportunity and reason to reflect that it was not much better prepared for any military conflict with a Western power than it had been a quarter of a century earlier on the eve of the Crimean War. In the short run, Russian reaction consisted in shifting the direction of its expansionist policy away from Europe to Central Asia and the Far East. Taking a somewhat longer view and further prompted by the formation of military alliances in Central Europe, the government turned toward the goal of a drastic increase in the economic potential of the country.

In the 1890's, a renewed enserfment of the peasantry was, of course, not in the realm of practical politics. Nor was there any need for such a measure. The reforms of rural administration which had been introduced with the advent of reaction under Alexander III gave the central bureaucracy sufficient tax-exacting power over the peasantry; at least for some time it was possible to keep the peasantry in the state of docile compliance. The joint responsibility of the village commune for tax payments was helpful, though far from indispensable. The considerable shift to indirect taxation further increased the government's ability to pay for the industrialization in conditions of a relative price and currency stability. The fiscal policy of the government was able to perform the function which at an earlier age had been performed by the institution of serfdom.

The great spurt of the 1890's came to an end in 1900. The depression of that year was variously interpreted as an overproduction crisis, a financial crash, or a response to economic setbacks abroad, particularly in Central Europe. It is fairly clear, however, that below the surface phenomena lay the exhaustion of the tax-paying powers of the rural population. The patience of the peasantry was at its end. The following years were characterized by growing unrest in the villages until the folly of the war with Japan fanned the isolated fires into the flame of a widespread peasant rebellion in the course of the 1905 Revolution. All this was very much like the consummation of the traditional pattern of Russian economic development: a quick upsurge compressed within a relatively short period ending in years of stagnation. And yet there was a great deal more to the industrial spurt of the 1890's than simply a repetition of previous sequences of economic development. It would seem more plausible to view those similarities as the last emanations, in prerevolutionary Russia, of the traditional pattern. For the differences were fully as important as the similarities. Also in this broad sense, the new and the old appeared curiously commingled. Along with the resurrection of a specifically Russian past, there was also the assimilation of Russian economic development into a graduated but still general pattern of European industrialization.

Two, and perhaps three, factors stand out in distinguishing the upswing of the 1890's from similar episodes in the more remote past. One of them has just been mentioned. During the decade of the 1890's, the Russian government abstained from introducing for the sake of the industrialization any far-reaching institutional change which, while aiding the process in the short run, would have become a serious obstacle to its continuation in the long run. Neither the institution of the *zemskii nachal'nik* nor the additional steps taken in the 1890's to preserve and protect the village commune could of course compare in any way with the enserfment of the peasantry. That a government firmly committed to the policy of industrialization went out of its way to safeguard the *obshchina* seemed paradoxical. But apart from the fiscal value of the arrangement, it was felt that its existence contributed to political stability within the country. Neither reason was persuasive. Satisfactory substitutes for joint responsibility for tax payments could easily have been found; and the events of the subsequent years showed clearly that the village commune nursed rebellious rather than conservative sentiments. The abolition of the commune still remained a problem of industrial policies in Russia, but it was one which antedated the period of rapid industrialization.

The other factor was positive. A modern industrialization based on the creation of fixed capital of considerable durability was not followed by periods of protracted stagnation as easily as had been the earlier, much more labor-intensive spurts of economic development ("stagnation" of course is to be understood simply in terms of a very low or even negative rate of growth). The recuperative power of a capital-intensive economy was greatly superior to that of its historical predecessors. And, finally, a modern industrialization is characterized also by a more substantial investment in human capital. In particular, it tends to bring about, over a relatively short period, a considerable change in entrepreneurial and managerial attitudes as well as, though to a lesser extent, in those of skilled labor. All this means that the effects of the great spurt reached out strongly into the future; that the process of industrialization could be resumed at diminished *faux frais* and in a form more efficient and less dependent upon the support of the state.

Such were the characteristic features of Russian industrial growth in the years between the 1905 Revolution and the outbreak of World War I. This, too, was a period of rather rapid growth (some 6 per cent per year), even though the rate of change remained below that of the 1890's. During those years industrialization could no longer be the primary concern of the government. War and revolution had greatly strained budgetary capabilities. The redemption payments (as well as the institution of joint responsibility) had disappeared under the impact of the revolution. Kokovtsev, first as Minister of Finance and later as head of the

Cabinet, pursued a cautious policy of thrift. Railroad building continued, but on a much reduced scale. The execution of such armament plans as were conceived was being postponed from year to year. In the eighteenth century, the death of Peter the Great and the withdrawal of the state from active economic policy spelled the doom of the contemporaneous economic development. But in Russia of the twentieth century, Count Witte's fall and the abandonment of his policies did not prevent a renewed outburst of industrial activity.

Nothing underscores more clearly the changed attitude of the government than the fact that its most important action in the field of economic policy was Stolypin's legislation against the *obshchina*. In a radical reversal of the agrarian policies pursued only a few years earlier, Stolypin's reforms of 1906 and 1910 made it possible for the peasants to sever their connection with the *obshchina* through a simple and advantageous procedure, to acquire personal ownership of the land, and in the process often to swap the numerous strips of their former allotment for a single consolidated holding.

There is no question that many aspects of the reform were harsh and unfair to the less prosperous members of the village communes. There is also every evidence that the government's *volte-face* was caused by political considerations, that is to say, by the impressive lesson learned from peasant uprisings during the preceding revolution. The consequences of the reform for the process of industrial development were accidental from the government's point of view, despite some liberal phraseology ("liberal" in the European sense of the term) used in defending the reforms.

Nevertheless, the potential positive effects of the reform on industrial development were indisputable. The authors of the reform, despite considerable opposition within the government, refused to accept the concept of family or household ownership; the ownership of peasants leaving the village commune was vested in the head of the household. For the first time, the road was open for an unimpaired movement to the city of peasant family members; for the first time large groups of Russian peasants could, like their counterparts in the West, sell the land and use the proceeds for establishing themselves outside agriculture. The war of 1914 necessarily cut short the implementation of the reform, but its initial effect was considerable. Both those peasants who had felt that leaving the commune would enable them to increase the productivity of their farms and those peasants who had been anxious to leave the village hastened to avail themselves of the separation procedure. It was a considerable step on the road of Russia's westernization.

And this is the aspect of the reform that is of primary importance from the point of view of the present discussion. The economic stagnation that followed the reign of Peter the Great was burdened by the legacy of serfdom. The very modernization of the state machinery under Peter meant that the government was much better equipped to enforce the serfdom condition upon the peasantry and to deal effectively with fugitives from serf status. At the same time, the territorial expansion of Russia kept reducing and making more remote the frontier regions which formerly had been the sanctuary of so many peasants in their flight from oppression. It was under these conditions that the edict granting the nobility and the gentry freedom from service obligations marked the acme of the state's retirement from active guidance of the country's economic life. That act finally severed the original connection between serfdom and economic development and sealed the perpetuation of serfdom as a main obstacle to economic progress. With regard to both its historical locus and its "liberalizing" character, the Imperial Edict of Peter III (1762) bears a certain resemblance to Stolypin's reform. And yet, despite these similarities, it is the difference between the two measures which may be taken as a gauge of the contrast in historical situations. The great spurt under Peter the Great had not led to sustained growth. The traditional pattern of Russian economic development was allowed to work itself out fully. By contrast, the withdrawal of the state after the upswing of the 1890's was marked by a measure which was designed to further rather than thwart industrial progress.

The westernization of Russian industrialization between 1906 and 1914 expressed itself in a large variety of ways. To use the previously adopted terminology, one could say that the pattern of substitutions was changing rapidly. To some extent banks stepped into the vacuum left by the state. In this way, credit-creation policies and some entrepreneurial guidance by the banks continued to substitute for the scarcity of both capital and entrepreneurship in Russia. But this mode of substitution tended to approximate the pattern of Russian development to that prevailing in Central Europe. The credit policies of the banks were still a substitute for an autonomous internal market, but there is little doubt that one of the consequences of the industrial creations of the nineties was the gradual emergence of such a market.

It may be quite tempting to view again the change between the period under review and that of the 1890's in terms of Erik Dahmén's dichotomy between development blocks in the state of full completion and development blocks in the beginning stage. The years 1906–1914 were characterized by the relative scarcities of coal, oil, and metals, in conjunction with the rapid forging ahead of metal-processing industries. There is a persistent and very much exaggerated tendency in present Russian historiography to present those scarcities as consequences of monopolistic policies in the basic-materials industries. It is probably more reasonable, still following Dahmén, to say that during the years preceding the First World War the structure of Russian industry was distinguished by specific disproportionalities and that once again, though on a much higher level, industry may have been passing through a period of dynamic preparation for another great spurt. Such a spurt, of course, never materialized. The point, however, is that considering the years 1906–1914 as a period of formation of new development blocks may help to explain why the rate of growth during those years was not higher than it was. It cannot explain the high growth that was actually attained in a situation where the outside aid to industry had manifestly declined to a fraction of its previous volume. It is more helpful, therefore, to regard this period as governed by the effects of diminished backwardness, and in this sense to view the whole stretch between the end of the 1880's and the outbreak of the war as consisting of two disparate and yet connected parts: the great spurt of the 1890's had prepared for the subsequent continuation of growth under changed conditions.

Many of the tensions and frictions that could be so strikingly observed during the 1890's reappeared in the second period, if at all, in a considerably modified and tempered form. There is no question that great progress had taken place with regard to entrepreneurial attitudes. Without such progress and, in particular, without the general rise in trustworthiness of Russian businessmen, the banks could never have come to play a powerful role as suppliers of long-term credit to industrial firms. The general modernization of entrepreneurial attitudes no doubt made the complex of actions and relations of the individual entrepreneurs less heterogeneous. The decline in the importance of the government as an economic agent pointed in the same direction.

The years that had passed since the second half of the 1880's considerably increased the stock of permanent industrial labor in the country. At the same time, after 1905, more tangible improvements both in real wages and in working conditions became noticeable. The reduction in the importance of foreign engineers and foremen in factories and mines also tended to diminish friction. At the same time, the great pressure upon the peasantry had subsided. In contrast to the last decades of the nineteenth century, the quantity of breadgrain available for domestic consumption rose faster than did the population. The industrialization between 1906 and 1914 no longer offers a picture of a race against time and of progressive exhaustion, physically and mentally, of the population's power to suffer and to endure.

Those elements of relaxation and "normalization" in the industrial process should not, however, disguise the fact that in other respects the great spurt of the 1890's, the industrial upsurge under conditions of extreme backwardness, still dominated the course of the development in the later period. The composition of the growing industry continued to favor the same branches as before. As in the earlier period, the stress on bigness was characteristic of both the productive and the organizational structure. The movement toward cartelization, which was mentioned before, must be regarded as a part of this continued emphasis on bigness. As was true in countries west of Russia, the policies of the banks tended to accelerate the process. In this sense they were the true heirs to the policies previously pursued by the bureaucracy. And like the latter, they tended to exaggerate and accelerate the process both for good and bad reasons. Interest in small enterprises would have strained the organizational and supervisory powers of the banks as it had proved unmanageable for the bureaucracy. On the other hand, just as many a civil servant had found opportunities for personal enrichment in his official connection with large enterprises, similarly increases in capital, mergers, and mediation of monopolistic agreements, also when not required by the process of growth, proved a considerable source of profit for the banks. Still, when everything is said and done, it was of utmost importance that the stress on large-scale business, the very essence of industrialization in conditions of backwardness and the basis for its successful implementation, could be preserved after the withdrawal of the state.

Russia before the First World War was still a relatively backward country by any quantitative criterion. The large weight of the agrarian sector of the economy and the low level of the nation per capita output placed her far below and behind neighboring Germany. Nevertheless, as far as the general pattern of its industrialization in the second period was concerned, Russia seemed to duplicate what had happened in Germany in the last decades of the nineteenth century. One might surmise that in the absence of the war Russia would have continued on the road of progressive westernization.

It is not entirely pointless to speculate on what might have happened in the course of such a development. Diminution of backwardness is a complex process. As has already been noted, certain paraphernalia of backwardness are shed fairly soon after the beginning of the process. Other elements are more resistant to change. Thus, the great school of industrialization tends to educate the entrepreneurs before it educates the workers; and it takes still longer before the influence of the industrial sector of the economy penetrates into the countryside and begins to affect the attitudes of the peasantry. In the latter respect, prerevolutionary Russia saw no more than the first modest traces of such an influence. Yet the likelihood that the transformation in agriculture would have gone on at an accelerated speed is very great.

In addition to the age-long attitudes which are more or less rapidly modified under the impact of economic development, there are specific institutional and economic factors which are created in the very process of industrialization, and which often appear strange and incomprehensible from the point of view of an advanced country. But they are the stuff that industrialization in backward areas is made of. Some of them disappear after they have fulfilled their mission, teleologically speaking. Thus did the Russian government leave the economic scene after the upswing of the 1890's. It is again extremely likely that the banks would not have been able to keep their ascendancy over Russian industry for a very long time to come. Diminishing scarcity of capital, further improvements in the quality of entrepreneurship, and the sheer growth of industrial enterprises in all probability would have in due time enhanced the position of industrial firms to a point where they no longer needed the banks' guidance. This is what happened in Germany after 1900, and the natural course of events might well have moved Russian industry in the same direction. Even so, if the German example had predictive value, the banks would not have necessarily been transformed into the English type of commercial bank. They would have retained their interest in long-term investments, and in this sense the Russian economy would have remained characterized by a peculiarity created in the earlier stages of its development. Even more important, the stress of bigness, the specific composition of industrial output, and the significance of cartels and trusts within the industrial structure are likely to have increased rather than diminished over the years. One of the curious aspects of the European development was that the process of assimilation of backward countries to advanced countries was by no means a one-sided affair. To some extent, as the degree of backwardness was reduced, the backward country tended to become more like the advanced country. Yet precisely because in the process of its industrialization the backward country had been forced to make use of very modern technological and economic instruments, in the long run it was the advanced country that in some respects assimilated its economy to that of the backward country. A comparison of the structure of, say, the German and the English economy in 1900 and some decades later would serve to illustrate this point.

Russian industrial development around the turn of the century was frequently decried as "artificial." Count Witte used to reject the accusation with considerable vehemence as meaningless and irrelevant (probably with justice). For what matters is both the degree and the direction of "artificiality" or "spontaneity" in the process seen over an appropriately long time. Taking into consideration the economic conditions that prevailed in Russia prior to its great spurt of industrialization, it is difficult to deny that the Russian development fitted well into the general pattern of European industrialization, conceived, as it properly should be, in terms of a graduated rather than a uniform pattern.

The only purpose in speculating about the probable course of Russian economic development as it might have been, if not interrupted by war and revolution, is to try to cast more light on the general industrial trends that dominated the last period of industrialization in prerevolutionary Russia. Still the question remains whether war and revolution cannot be interpreted as the result of the preceding industrial development. Some Soviet historians certainly incline in that direction. If the Russian bourgeoisie could be saddled with the main responsibility for the outbreak of the war and if, in addition, it could be shown that in bringing about the war it had acted in response to the pressure of its economic interests—if, in short, the process of Russian industrialization carried in itself the seeds of the coming military conflict—then to abstract the war from the process in order to elucidate the course and prospects of Russian industrialization would mean to abstract the process as well. Some Russian manufacturers indeed may have welcomed the wartime orders for their products. Yet the precise mechanism through which such interests of the bourgeoisie were in fact translated into the decisions reached by the emperor and his government has remained altogether obscure.

The view just described seems to magnify the political significance of the Russian bourgeoisie out of all proportion and to substitute suppositions of various degrees of plausibility for historical evidence. It might be more persuasive to argue that the government saw a relatively short and victorious war as a chance to solidify the regime and to avert the danger of revolution. And the question then would be to what extent the preceding industrial development may be said to have been leading to another revolutionary cataclysm.

It is true, of course, that the social and political structure of the empire was shot through with manifold serious weaknesses. Opposition to the regime was nearly universal among the intelligentsia and certainly widespread among the industrial and mercantile groups. Since 1912, the year of the famous massacre in the Lena gold fields, the strike movement of the workers was again gaining momentum. And at the bottom of the social edifice there was the old resentment of the peasants who had never accepted the rightfulness of the gentry's ownership rights over the land. The peasantry's land hunger was a steady source of ferment. The sentiment in the villages was no doubt further exacerbated by the blows struck against the village commune and the threat of its dissolution. A new outbreak of revolutionary violence at some point was far from being altogether improbable.

And yet, as one compares the situation in the years before 1914 with that of the nineties, striking differences are obvious. In the earlier period the very process of industrialization with its powerful confiscatory pressures upon the peasantry kept adding, year in and year out, to the feelings of resentment and discontent until the outbreak of large-scale disorders became almost inevitable. The industrial prosperity of the following period had no comparable effects, however. Modest as the improvements in the situation of peasants were, they were undeniable and widely diffused. Those improvements followed rather than preceded a revolution and accordingly tended to contribute to a relaxation of tension. Stolypin's reforms certainly were an irritant, but after the initial upsurge their implementation was bound to proceed in a much more gradual fashion.

Similarly, the economic position of labor was clearly improving. In the resurgence of the strike movement economic problems seemed to predominate. It is true, of course, that in the specific conditions of the period any wage conflict tended to assume a political character because of the ready interventions of police and military forces on behalf of management. But this did not mean that the climate of opinion and emotion within the labor movement was becoming more revolutionary; as shown by the history of European countries (such as Austria or Belgium), sharp political struggles marked the period of formation of labor movements that in actual fact, though not always in the language used, were committed to reformism. There is little doubt that the Russian labor movement of those years was slowly turning toward revision and trade-unionist lines. As was true in the West, the struggles for general and equal franchise to the Duma and for a cabinet responsible to the Duma, which probably would have occurred sooner or later, may well have further accentuated this development. To repeat, I do not mean to deny that there was much political instability in the country. There clearly was. What matters here is that from the point of view of the industrial development of the country, war, revolution, or the threat thereof may reasonably be seen as extraneous phenomena. In this sense, it seems plausible to say that Russia on the eve of the war was well on the way toward a westernization or, perhaps more precisely, a Germanization of its industrial growth. The "old" in the Russian economic system was definitely giving way to the "new." It was left to the regime that finally emerged from the 1917 Revolution, generated in the misery of the war and the shame of defeats, to create a different set of novelties and to mix them with old ingredients of Russian economic history in the strange and powerful infusion of Soviet industrialism.

## IV

The 1917 Revolution redeemed the ancient hopes of the Russian peasantry by letting them seize the lands of the gentry. In addition, after the end of the Civil War, when the NEP compromise was put into operation, the peasants found themselves greatly relieved of obligations toward the state as compared with the prewar years. At length, the "internal market" of the Populists seemed to have become a reality.

If the revolution had effected nothing else but a change in the position of the peasantry, one might perhaps have envisaged a slow but steady growth in agricultural output and a rate of growth in industry perhaps slightly exceeding that of agriculture, if for no other reason because of a sustained shift of many industrial activities from the farms to urban industries. The increased strength of peasant demand was bound to effect a change in the composition of Russian industry in the direction of greater stress upon "light" industries. Presumably, the rate of investment would have been lowered and the over-all rate of growth of industrial output slowed down thereby. It was apparently in these terms that Stalin, during the twenties, envisaged the course of the country's industrial development.

Yet, in addition to the new role of the peasantry, the revolution also established a dictatorial government controlling the large-scale industry. Instead of asserting itself through a market mechanism, the peasant demand, if it was effectively to change the structure of relative prices and the composition of industry, had to be reflected in government decisions. These decisions, however, might or might not be the appropriate ones. During the NEP period, the problem expressed itself largely in the so-called scissor crisis: in the fact that the government-dominated industry had insisted upon terms of trade that were infavorable to agriculture. Nor was any shift toward greater stress on consumer-goods industries visible. If anything, toward the end of the NEP the share of heavy industries in total output was somewhat larger than before the war.

It is true that through most of the NEP period the high rate of industrial growth overshadowed the difficulties and prevented them from becoming overpowering. As long as the problem was to rebuild the prewar industry, largely using prewar equipment and prewar labor and technicians, the incremental capital-output ratios were very low and the rapid increases in the supply of consumer goods kept discontent at bay. The situation was bound to change as the prewar capacity of Russian factories was being reached and further increases in output began to require much more sizeable investment funds.

This, no doubt, was a crucial and critical moment in the economic history of Soviet Russia. The adjustment to a lower rate of industrial growth would have been difficult under any circumstances. In the specific Soviet conditions of the later twenties it was aggravated by political factors. To prevent too deep and too sudden a fall in the rate of industrial growth, either voluntary or politically enforced savings were necessary. But the savings of the peasant economy were small, since, despite all improvements, the absolute levels of peasant incomes still were very low. To increase the rate of taxation carried the threat of peasant resistance; and a rise in industrial prices charged to the peasants after the experience of the scissor crisis, when such prices had to be *lowered* in relation to farm prices, was hardly within the range of practical politics. The legacy of the NEP policies, with their low taxes, downward pressure upon the industrial terms of trade, and the failure to provide in time for a shift in the composition of industrial output in favor of consumer goods, expressed itself in a situation of inflationary pressures where too large a volume of purchasing power of the peasantry pressed upon too small a volume of available consumer goods.

The "internal market" supported by the peasantry had been regarded for decades as the natural and spontaneous form of industrialization. After what has been said above, it may be doubtful whether in conditions of still considerable backwardness the peasant demand alone would have sustained any reasonable rate of increase in industrial output. Too low a rate of increase in demand may have proved insufficient to solve the problem of indivisibilities and complementarities inherent in the process of development. Without a strong flow of external economies (in the broad sense of the word), the nascent industrial enterprises might have found themselves burdened with costs of production that were too high for successful operation. Paradoxical as it may sound, industry might have been better able to satisfy a strong rather than a weak increase in demand.

The immediate problem, however, was different. The change in the economic position of the peasantry greatly increased the flexibility of Russian agriculture. Under certain circumstances, higher outputs per farming household will lead to an increase in the peasants' demand for industrial goods—whether adequate or not from the industry's point of view. Under different and less favorable circumstances, the peasant economy can reduce the extent of its connections with outside markets by diverting cereals to production of converted products for its own consumption; and by assigning a larger portion of the land to fibrous crops for home spinning and weaving. For the Russian peasantry with its weak marketing tradition the escape into greater self-sufficiency suggested itself as an easy and natural response to the economic conditions which prevailed in the second half of the 1920's. As the marketings of grain began to fall off, the inevitable adjustment to a lower rate of industrial growth seemed to turn into the threat of a negative rate of growth, of de-urbanization and agrarianization of the country.

The economic crisis that thus marked the end of the NEP period was at the same time a political crisis of first magnitude. Inability to maintain the food supplies to the cities and the growing resistance of the millions of peasants, strong in their intangible diffusion, seemed to spell the doom of the Soviet dictatorship. To be sure, a change in the political system of Russia would not have in itself solved the economic problem. The inflationary pressures still would have called for a solution. It is possible that a government truly representing the peasants might have been able to raise taxes and by so doing to establish the equilibrium between rural purchasing power and the volume of industrial consumer goods available, and at the same time to reverse the declining trend in agricultural marketings. Such a government might have sought and found foreign credits and used the proceeds for importation of consumer goods from abroad—thereby making the increases in taxation less unpalatable. The immediate problem might have been solved in this fashion. The question of industrial growth would have been another matter. Barring further fundamental changes in the economic structure of the country, the conditions for resumption of industrial growth would seem to have been rather unfavorable under such circumstances.

In retrospect, the threat to the continuation in power of the Soviet regime appears blurred by the indubitable successes achieved subsequently. But it was real indeed. It was under the pressure of that threat that Stalin underwent a radical change of mind and embarked upon the gamble of the First Five Year Plan. Viewed as a short-run measure, the purpose of the First Five Year Plan was to break the disequilibrium through increase in consumer-goods output based on increase in plant capacity. It was a daring scheme if one considers that its coming to fruition presupposed a further though temporary deterioration in the situation as a result of deflecting a larger share of national income into investment and away from consumption. Again, in the best Russian tradition, it was to be a race against time. If the Soviet government could keep peasant resistance within bounds for the relatively short period of a few years, it might be able to offer sufficient quantities of consumer goods to the peasants at terms of trade not too unfavorable to them, and thus it could eliminate the dangers and place the relations between the villages and the city on a sounder basis.

Not unlike the imperial government after the revolution of 1905, the Soviet government was keenly aware of the peasants' hostility to it. In a very similar fashion it was anxious to find or to create at least some points of support in the villages which might facilitate its task during the difficult years to come. Stolypin had gambled on the "strong and the sober," expecting the prosperous peasant outside the village commune to neutralize in some measure the antagonism of the majority. After certain adjustments, the collective farms were originally supposed to perform the same function. They were conceived as limited injections of communal vaccine into the individualistic climate of the villages. As long as the number of collective farms was kept small, it would be possible to provide them with sufficient state aid, so that membership in the collective farms would carry real advantages.

The plans, however, did not succeed; alternatively, they succeeded only too well. The resistance of the peasantry proved much greater than had been expected. The peasantry which had emerged victorious from the revolution and the civil war was very different from the docile masses of the imperial period. The bitter struggles that followed developed a logic of their own. In the course of the "revolution from above," as Stalin termed it and which more justly might be called a "counterrevolution from above," the original plans of the Soviet government were quickly rendered obsolete. The dogged defense by the peasants of the revolutionary land seizures evoked an all-out offensive by the government. The

peasants went down in defeat and a complete, or nearly complete, collectivization was the result.

The collectivization supplied an unexpected solution to the besetting problem
of disequilibrium, the actual starting point of the great change in Soviet economic
policies. But it also affected profoundly the character of the government's plans
with regard to industrialization. Once the peasantry had been successfully forced
into the machinery of collective farms, once it became possible to extract a large
share of agricultural output in the form of "compulsory deliveries" without
bothering much about the *quid pro quo* in the form of industrial consumer goods,
the difficulties of the late twenties were overcome. The hands of the government
were untied. There was no longer any reason to regard the First Five Year Plan
as a self-contained brief period of rapid industrialization, and the purpose of the
industrialization no longer was to relieve the shortage of consumer goods. A
program of perpetual industrialization through a series of five-year plans was
now on the agenda. What was originally conceived as a brief spell became the
initial stage to a new great spurt of industrialization, the greatest and the longest
in the history of the country's industrial development.

Any historical contemplation of Soviet industrial history must begin with a
description of the proximate chain of causations which connects the period of the
NEP with that of super-industrialization under the five-year plans. Such a
description brings out and explains the precise timing of the change that took
place. The discussion must be in terms of the answers found by the Soviet government to the pressures and exigencies of a given situation. Yet to place the whole
weight of emphasis upon those aspects of the evolution may not be sufficient.
Other forces, perhaps less clearly visible may have been at work determining the
course of development and its outcome. Much of what happened at the turn of
the third and fourth decades of the century was the product of that specific
historical moment; however great the change, and however drastic the momentary discontinuity in the process, the deep historical roots and its broad historical
continuity must not elude the historian.

If Peter the Great had been called back to life and asked to take a good look
at Russia, say, in the second half of the thirties, he might have had some initial
difficulties because of changes in language and technology; he might have found
the purge trials unnecessarily cumbersome and verbose; and he might have upbraided Stalin for the unmanly refusal to participate physically in the act of
conveying the modern *Strel'tsy* from life to death. Yet it should not have taken
him long to understand the essentials of the situation. For the resemblance
between Soviet and Petrine Russia was striking indeed.

Nothing has been said so far about the role of foreign policy in molding Soviet
economic decisions. Yet it must not be forgotten that the smashing defeat of the
country by Germany stood at the very cradle of the Soviet regime. Foreign intervention in the Civil War, however halfhearted, certainly left memories that were
long in fading. The 1920's witnessed a gradual improvement in Soviet diplomatic
and commercial relations with foreign countries. But tensions were ever-
recurring, and in 1927 there was much talk of military dangers in the course of

the diplomatic conflict with England. Germany, despite the Russian aid to the *Reichswehr*, was still the military vacuum of Europe. After 1930, with the beginning disintegration of the Weimar Republic both Russian fears and Russian ambitions were increasingly concentrated on Germany; until after Hitler's advent to power the ambitions were frustrated and the threat of a military attack began to loom larger and larger each year. There is very little doubt that, as so often before, Russian industrialization in the Soviet period was a function of the country's foreign and military policies. If this is so, however, one might argue that there was more instability in the second half of the NEP period than that stemming from inflationary pressures alone. If, as has been indicated above, the continuation of NEP policies even after a successful removal of monetary disequilibriums was unlikely to lead to a period of rapid industrialization, pressures for a revision of those policies might well have materialized in any case.

A resurrected Peter the Great would have found sufficient operational resemblance between Charles XII and Adolf Hitler, however much he might have preferred his civilized contemporary to the twentieth-century barbarian. Nor would the great transformation in rural Russia cause him much trouble. He would have quickly recognized the functional resemblance between collectivization and the serfdom of his days, and he would have praised collectivization as the much more efficient and effective system to achieve the same goals—to feed gratis the nonagricultural segments of the economy and at the same time provide a flow of labor for the public works of the government, which the Soviet regime accomplished by the institution of special contracts between the factories and the collective farms. He would no doubt have acquiesced in the tremendous human cost of the collectivization struggles, once it had been explained to him that the quantitative difference between the Soviet period and his own time in this respect was largely the result of the colossal growth in population in the two intervening centuries. And while regretting the loss of animal draft power in Russian agriculture, he may have even understood that the reduction in cattle herds in the course of the "great slaughter" actually facilitated the task of industrialization inasmuch as the amount of calories per unit of land available for the feeding of the population was greatly increased as a result. Neither the formidable stress on technology in the earlier portions of the period of industrialization nor the resolute concentration upon heavy industries would have evoked the visitor's astonishment. True, at times Peter the Great was given to flights of fancy and attempted to launch in Russia production of Venetian mirrors and French Gobelins, but the great line of his policy, so different from that of French mercantilism, was essentially devoted to the increase of the country's military potential.

Thus a pattern of economic development which before the First World War seemed to have been relegated to the role of a historical museum piece was re-enacted in Soviet Russia. The anachronistic—or rather parachronistic—character of the Soviet experiment in rapid industrialization did not, however, prevent it from attaining a very high measure of success. On the contrary, the combination of ancient measures of oppression with modern technology and organization proved immensely effective. All the advantages of industrialization in conditions of backwardness were utilized to the hilt: adoption of the fruits of Western technological progress and concentration on those branches of industrial activity where foreign technology had the most to offer; huge size of plant and the simultaneity of industrialization along a broad front assuring large flows of external economies.

To be sure, the tendency to exaggerate and to overdo was ever-present. In many cases, smaller plant size would have been more rational. In addition, the very breadth of the effort kept creating and recreating bottlenecks; and the excessive bureaucratization of the economy absorbed an undue share of the available manpower. Yet when everything is said and done, the result in terms of growth of industrial output was unprecedented in the history of modern industrialization in Russia. True, the Soviet official index exaggerated the speed of growth. The rates of 20 and more per cent a year that were claimed never materialized in reality. It is, however, possible now on the basis of the computations performed by American economists and statisticians to conclude that the average annual rate of industrial growth in Russia throughout the first ten years after the initiation of the First Five Year Plan was somewhere between 12 and 14 per cent; the rate fell in the years immediately preceding the outbreak of the Second World War, but rose again after 1945. Its high level was maintained far beyond the period of reconstruction from war damages. In the first half of the fifties, industrial output still kept increasing at some 13 per cent a year. And it was only in the second half of the decade that the rate of growth began to decline, though very gradually. One has only to compare these rates with the high rate attained during Witte's great spurt of the nineties (8 per cent) in order to gauge the magnitude of the Soviet industrialization effort.

The success of the Soviet experiment is frequently described as a proof of the efficiency of a "socialist" system. That is how the leaders of Soviet Russia like to refer to their achievements. On the other hand, there is a good deal of unwillingness to accept the fact of rapid growth of Soviet industry because of the prevailing assumption of the fundamental inefficiency of socialism. Much of it is a question of semantics. It is at the least doubtful, for instance, whether Stalin's Russia could be described as a socialist country in terms of Anatole France's definition of socialism: *Le socialisme c'est la bonté et la justice.* A historian has little reason to get enmeshed in these discussions since he may find himself discussing the problem as to whether or not Peter the Great was a socialist. Nor is this the place to explain why in the opinion of the present writer Marxian ideology, or any socialist ideology for that matter, has had a very remote, if any, relation to the great industrial transformation engineered by the Soviet government.

What matters much more is the specific nature of the Soviet spurt and the economic mechanism which sustained it. The essential juxtaposition is between an approximate sixfold increase in the volume of industrial output, on the one hand, and, on the other, the level of real wages which in the fifties was still substantially below that of 1928, with the peasants' real income probably registering an even greater decline in comparison to 1928. By holding down forcibly the consumption of the population and by letting the area of consumer-goods output take the brunt of errors and miscalculations that occurred in the process of planning, the Soviet government succeeded in channeling capital and human resources into capital formation, thus assuring the rapid growth of the only segment of the economy in which it was interested. The Soviet leaders have kept asserting, and the Soviet economists have kept repeating after them, that according to Marx the rate of growth of producer-goods output must necessarily be higher than that of consumer-goods output. The reference to Marx is hardly meaningful within the context of the Soviet economy, which has no specific marketing problems with regard to consumer goods. Nevertheless, the assertion is quite correct as a description of the actual policy pursued by the Soviet government, pursued not by force of economic necessity but by virtue of *political choice*. It means implicitly that as the volume of output grows, so does the rate of investment in expanding output; in other words, a larger and larger portion of national output is allocated to the production of nonconsumable goods. It is these relationships that contain the essence of Soviet industrial development. This has been the strategic lever that permitted the Soviet government to make use of every advantage of backwardness to a degree unknown to all its predecessors.

V

As suggested above, the effects of industrialization begun in conditions of backwardness may continue for a long time to come. But the specific advantages of backwardness by their very nature must disappear in the course of a successful industrialization. Even if no restrictions on trade were imposed by the West, Russia today would stand to gain much less from imports than was the case a quarter of a century ago. What is true of foreign technology is also true of many other factors of growth. The exhaustion or at least the diminution of readily available labor surpluses in rural areas and the depletion of the reserves in high grade minerals, conveniently located, point in the same direction. There is no question that after the war Russia experienced the drag of all these vanishing advantages or growing disabilities. If she was still able to maintain the rate of industrial growth at a level fairly close to that of the thirties, the reason must be sought partly in the government's ability to keep consumption down so that the growing disadvantages were successfully offset by increasing supply of capital; and partly in the great effort to increase the quality of the labor force by an ambitious program of training and education.

It is too early to judge whether the recent declines in the rate of growth will be transitory or whether they will have marked the end of the great spurt of economic development. It cannot be my purpose to indulge in prophecies. Rather, the contingency that the great spurt of industrial growth in Russia may be nearing its end may be used here to cast some additional light upon the recent economic history of the country. In discussing the origins of Soviet industrialization, some emphasis was laid upon military dangers with which the Soviet government had to reckon. It is, however, a frequent though natural pitfall in histor ica writings to assume that a genetic appoach provides full explanation of a given phenomenon. If the policy of super-industrialization in Soviet Russia had been dictated exclusively by the needs of defense against foreign aggression, one might have expected a radical change in Soviet economic policy to follow the end of the war. This, however, did not happen. The stress on heavy industry and high-speed industrialization continued unabated.

Many reasons can be advanced to explain the fact. Perhaps not the least important among them lies in the peculiarities of the country's political system. It is a truism that a policy of high and rising investment rates could not be pursued in Russia unless by a ruthless and all-powerful dictatorship. But the obverse may also be true: the dictatorial system could not exist without an economic policy which provides it with a social function and a justification for its existence. If this is true, the prolongation if not the perpetuation of the economic spurt would be inseparably connected with the fate of the dictatorial regime. This is the point at which comparisons with the era of Peter the Great break down. The dynastic ruler of those days could stop and relax with impunity, but a modern dictatorial system is propelled by a specific dynamism which it can abandon only at the penalty of grave perils.

After the death of Stalin the problem of succession has proved a very difficult one. Concessions to the peasantry, Malenkov's attempt to shift Russian industry toward increased production of consumer goods, Malenkov's fall, Khrushchev's decentralization of the industrial organization and renewed promises of greater supplies of consumer goods, to say nothing of the two recent purges following each other in quick succession—all these seem to reveal a deep crisis in the Soviet dictatorship. Khrushchev's original effort to dissociate himself from his predecessor has unleashed a series of effects the consequences of which apparently have just begun to unfold. An entirely open situation has been created in which everything seems possible except perhaps one thing: continuation for any length of time of the present confusion. The road may lead back to a revival of Stalinist policies, including an undoing of the inchoate measures of relaxation taken in recent years. It may lead to a period of progressive resistance to the regime, culminating in a definite abandonment of the policy of high-speed industrialization, thus concluding the Soviet industrial upsurge in a way not unlike that at the end of the nineties. If, however, the former alternative were to prevail, it is a moot question as to what extent the rate of industrial growth could be maintained at levels comparable to those of the thirties and early fifties. The continuation of a steady increase in the rate of investment would be the most important single factor the Soviet government could rely upon to counteract the growing effect of the many retarding factors, including, it might be added, the increasing difficulty of agricultural output in keeping pace with the increase in population. This means that, in matters of economic policies, Stalinist policies would have to be pursued with a vengeance and consumption standards would have to be held down severely. Yet even in such a case one might assume that eventually the retarding factors would assert themselves and that a gradual fall of the rate of growth to much lower levels would be very difficult to resist.

## VI

At the time of the emancipation, Russia was an agrarian country with a sprinkling of inefficient industry. Russia of today is a big industrial power. In terms of aggregate levels of industrial output it has overtaken and surpassed the advanced countries of Western Europe. A profound transformation has occurred with regard to technology, organizational methods, and labor skills. The last century of Russian economic history has resulted in a far-reaching westernization of the country's economy. And yet the old curse, so clearly perceived by Plekhanov, remains on Russia's economic development: the processes of Russian westernization are un-Western. It still seems to be true, as it was several centuries ago, that for every step which Russia takes along the road of westernization in one respect, it must pay, and pay dearly, by taking steps which, in other respects, lead it away from the West.

The process of industrialization in a backward country inevitably involves a certain period during which consumption is being reduced in favor of capital formation. After the initial phase is over, consumption begins to rise, reaches again the level at which it was curtailed previously, and then continues to increase more or less *pari passu* with the increase in national income. The extent to which this generalized sequence is reproduced in reality varies from case to case. The depth of the decline in consumers' real incomes, the length of the time that elapsed before consumption could return to its "ante-spurt" level, the speed at which further increases in consumption were diffused throughout the various groups of the community, all depended on many factors: the country's degree of backwardness, the course of the international cycle at the time of the great spurt, the role of foreign trade and capital imports in the process, the strength of the labor movement, the institutional framework in agriculture, and so on. By and large, however, the sequence is a simplified but correct description of the story of the nineteenth-century industrialization in a number of major European countries.

As has been stressed in the foregoing pages, Russian economic history tells a different story or, more precisely, it tells only the first half of that story. Except for a brief and uncertain glimmer of coming improvements in the years preceding the outbreak of the war in 1914—and except for the period of return to prewar levels (or somewhat better than that) from the ravages of the Civil War—the Russian population has failed to derive any perceptible advantages from the long period of industrialization.

The reason for this lies in the existence of the dictatorship which no doubt has contributed to the course of industrialization more than any other single factor and which at the same time has prevented the consummation of the process on patterns observed in the West. The westernization achieved under the aegis of an Oriental despot has had to remain unfinished.

Again, it is possible and indeed likely that in the future the Soviet dictatorship may have to acquiesce in a gradual fall of the rate of industrial growth to levels considerably below those attained in the past. This could result from a growing scarcity of several ingredients of which industrial growth is made. But this decline in the rate of growth need not be caused or accompanied by larger shares of consumption in national income. There is no *economic* reason why the Soviet system could not go on, more or less indefinitely, channeling most of the annual accretions to national output into investment and keeping the levels of per capita consumption fairly stable. In other words, there is no economic force compelling the Soviet government to complete the process of industrialization.

And that is as far as an economic historian can go. It is with a certain sense of frustration therefore that he turns away from his contemplation of a century of Russia's economic history. It always was a "political" economic history and it is that now to an extent never witnessed before, at least in its modern periods.

The keys to an understanding of the nature of past economic change, let alone to its probable future course, lie outside the narrow purview of economic factors and relations. They must be sought in a sociology-of-power exercise by dictatorial governments, in a sociology of popular discontent. So far, students of Russian economic development have been compelled to work with rough and ready generalizations. It has not been difficult for them to see, with Bertrand Russell, power as the fundamental concept in social science. They know that much in Soviet industrialization makes sense in terms of a "power for power's sake" assumption. They realize that the Soviet identification with socialist ideology, though the latter has been thoroughly revised and denaturalized, has wrested from the Russian people the weapon of socialist protest which, along with other factors, has contributed so much to the humanization and consummation of industrial processes in Western Europe. They are aware that the policy of perpetual foreign tensions has been an effective tool in the hands of the dictators for eliciting a modicum of allegiance from an unwilling and sullen population. Yet more is needed than impressionistic insights and *ad hoc* hypotheses. An economist concerned with the process of Russian economic growth has every reason to hope that this volume [i.e., *Economic Backwardness in Historical Perspective*] will make a serious contribution to a searching and systematic exploration of these problems.

# The Parties and the State:
# The Evolution of Political Attitudes

LEOPOLD H. HAIMSON

## I

The common observation that the concept of political parties developed in the West in the context of representative institutions—and of the struggle for control of these institutions—and that in Russia, on the contrary, it was shaped in the absence of such institutions is substantially correct, of course. It really raises more questions than it answers, however; for underlying the problem of the emergence of both political parties and representative institutions is the broader question of the evolution of relations between state and society as expressed in the changing attitudes that social groups entertain toward one another and toward political authority.

What broad continuities appear to distinguish these underlying political and social tendencies in Russia before 1855, before the reign of Alexander II and the Great Reforms? However broad and controversial the problem, it seems to me that, aside from the Marxist school, most Russian historians, from Solov'ev to Miliukov and Presniakov, have tended to agree on three general propositions concerning it.

The first is that through most of its history—in the sixteenth- and seventeenth-century Russian state and society of service groups, as in the late eighteenth- and early nineteenth-century gentry-dominated state and society of estates—state power played a central role in the organization, indeed in the very definition, of large social groups, in the delineation of the rights and duties, privileges and "burdens," that constituted the basis of individual and group position in Russian society. The second generally held proposition is that through these centuries the relations among large social groups were marked by very sharp cleavages, by almost insuperable differences and conflicts of outlook, interests, and experience, reflected in and strengthened by the caste character of the administrative organs that governed their lives. Finally, most Russian historians would generally agree that, as a result of these two factors, individuals and social groups throughout this period did not generally seek to extend their privileges or to ease their burdens by collaborating with each other in order to impose their joint will on the existing political order. Instead they turned directly and individually to the state power as the only real and legitimate source of rights and duties in the Russian land, to favor or assist them against all other groups in society.[1]

For groups that felt themselves to be oppressed by the existing political authority there appeared to exist, by the middle of the seventeenth century, only two real alternatives to this political orientation. The first was to seek a change in the person of the supreme arbiter, a change of tsar or dynasty which, while leaving the existing framework of political and social organization completely intact, might bring about a redirection of the favors and benefits extended by the throne. The other was a *bunt*, an "elemental" revolt against the whole political and social order—elemental in that it involved a wholesale rejection of the existing framework of national life, without any conception of an alternative political and social order.

To state that these broad continuities may legitimately be found in the history of Russian political attitudes from the seventeenth to the early nineteenth centuries is not to deny that relations among individual social groups, or between them and the state power, changed in many significant respects during this long historical period. To mention only the aspect of these changes that is closest to our interests here: these three centuries saw an evolution in attitudes toward state power by a shift from the highly personal image of the tsar—as an arbiter between relatively fragmented and still relatively balanced service classes—which prevailed in the seventeenth century. The attitude shifted to the Petrine and post-Petrine conception of the state power as a dynamic, revolutionary, westernizing agency in social life; and finally to the disillusioned image held by advanced opinion in the mid-nineteenth century of a conservative, obscurantist autocracy, the willing prisoner and ally of gentry caste interests.

Yet, despite the obvious significance of these and other political and social changes, the broad continuities that we have detected in Russian attitudes toward state and society seem to persist throughout the seventeenth and eighteenth centuries, and to make their imprint on the early nineteenth-century political scene. Even the oppressive years of the reign of Nicholas I, and the general sense of political and social bankruptcy that they were ultimately to arouse in society, would not destroy the antagonism among the estates and the consequent centrality of state power. Indeed, it is during Nicholas's reign that we observe the articulation of the three strands of opinion which would challenge the validity of modern representative institutions (and of a party system operating within their framework) in the early decades of post-Reform Russia.

We may observe at this time, in the thought and activities of Kiselev and his disciples in the state bureaucracy as well as in the more abstract formulations of the "state" school of history and jurisprudence, the emergence of a revitalized conception of the autocratic power as the dominant force in Russia's development—the only one capable of upholding the national interest against the selfish claims of factions and of leading the way to the realization of social justice.

It is also during this period, in the late 1830's and 1840's, to be exact, that we witness the spread of utopian socialist views among the intelligentsia, views that would impel its members to reject the "futile" struggle for constitutional limitations and representative institutions, in the name of utopias in which not only social and economic differences but also the very existence of the state on which they rested would be eliminated.

And, finally, in the writing of the small Slavophile circle we observe, beneath the elaborate edifice of historical and philosophical fantasy, the more sensible, or at least the more influential, notion that the proper task for men of good will was not to struggle for control of a political structure which already exercised too pervasive an influence in Russian life, but rather to strive for the development of cultural and social forms free from the evil embrace of the political process.

All sharing the sense of the inextricable interdependence of the dominant forms of political authority and socioeconomic organization, these three strands of Russian opinion, though sharply divided during the post-Reform period on many issues of political and social life, persistently were to manifest a common and fatal reluctance to invest their energies in the "narrow" and "futile" work of political reform.

## II

There is a general note of awe in the reports of contemporary observers in the first years of Alexander II's reign about the metamorphosis that Russian society had suddenly undergone. "I can no longer recognize the old caravanserai of soldiery, the baton, and obscurantism," the historian Kavelin wrote in 1857, the year of the Nazimov decrees and of the opening of problems of reform to public discussion. "Everyone is talking, everyone is studying, including people who never before read anything in their lives."

Underlying the general aura of excitement, there appeared to exist at this moment a remarkable consensus in Russian society that the "old order" was doomed and that Russia was in need of "comprehensive" reforms, including the abolition of serfdom. There was even a general recognition that the elimination of serfdom would necessarily require a whole series of peripheral changes—changes in the administrative framework, in the judiciary, in military organization, in the whole structure of state and society.[2]

On these points the most diverse strands of opinion appeared in agreement. Under the shock of Russia's humiliating defeat in the Crimean War, the web of common interests and common fears that had kept state and privileged society so long paralyzed had finally come undone. Consequently, to the clamor of advanced opinion—to the shouts of Westerners, Slavophiles, and budding young Realists—were now joined the more sedate, and influential, voices of articulate spokesmen for gentry interests, and those of champions of the "state principle," in and out of the bureaucracy. But what was to replace the old congealed autocracy and society of estates? On this question, following the original call for "reforms," "modernization," and "rule of law," fissures were soon to appear in public opinion.

The conflict first broke out over the issue of "public participation" in the work of reform. To most of the deputies of the first and second calling, just as to later elected spokesmen of the gentry, the rule of law—the elimination of arbitrariness in Russian life—meant first and foremost that the range of bureaucratic control and interference should at all costs be restricted, and that the great work of reform should be taken out of the stranglehold of secretive bureaucratic agencies and largely placed in the hands of elected representatives of the public. This claim of the "gentry liberals" for public participation in the reform movement, a claim which was extended by some gentry spokesmen to a demand for a permanent national representation, appeared to most of the officials entrusted with the reforms (as indeed to other spokesmen for the "state principle") as suspect and premature, at the very least.

Some of the champions of state interest were opposed to the idea in principle. They too favored a "rule of law," indeed civic equality before the law, but under the cloak of these legal principles they visualized the emergence of a rejuvenated, yet unhindered, autocracy—freed from the pressure of gentry interests and from the limitations of gentry *votchina* rights—governing a now united nation on the basis of uniform legal procedures with the assistance of a modernized, disciplined, noncaste bureaucracy. This was essentially the viewpoint of Pobedonostsev, a firm opponent of serfdom, an enthusiastic advocate of the legal reforms (in the early sixties), but then, as in later life, a resolute defender of the integrity of autocratic power.[3]

However, opposition to gentry liberalism among the *gosudarstvenniki* (as the advocates of the state principle were called) was not confined to such firm champions of autocratic and bureaucratic rule. The defeat of the constitutional movement was ensured at this time by the fact that many of the more progressive figures who were responsible for the "democratic" features of the reforms discerned in the pressure for public participation and representation the reflection of antipopular, antinational, gentry caste interests. It was due to the chasm that they detected between the interests of the gentry and those of the peasant masses that an enlightened bureaucrat such as Nicholas Miliutin, a progressive public figure such as Kavelin, and even Slavophile sympathizers such as Iuri Samarin or Cherkassky so firmly opposed in 1858–1859 any large-scale participation by the elected deputies of the provincial nobility in emancipation legislation. Considering an unimpeded state power the only current representative of the national interest, these leaders of the reforms repeatedly expressed their concern lest the various deputies of the gentry reconcile their views and join in "party" pressures, which would inevitably be directed against the best interests of the people and of the state. When public clamor rose once again for the establishment of national representation in 1864–1865, Kavelin, Miliutin, and Samarin once more opposed the demands of the constitutional movement on the ground that any national legislature would necessarily be dominated at this time by gentry interests and by a gentry party.[4]

To add to the weakness of the movement for representative government, the *gosudarstvenniki* were joined in their opposition to national representation by the spokesmen of two other strands of Russian contemporary opinion: the Slavophile elements in the older generation of the liberal gentry and intelligentsia, and the radical spokesmen of the younger generation of Realists, Nihilists, and Populists.

The Slavophiles' abstract formulations of their hostility to Western constitutionalism and "legalism" need not detain us here. But it is important to note that underlying their arguments there was a general diagnosis of Russian conditions which, then as later, influenced much wider circles of Russian opinion, if only because it unquestionably incorporated some accurate perceptions of existing realities. Just as the *gosudarstvenniki* did, the Slavophiles recognized the centrality of the state power in Russia's historical development and in contemporary Russian life. However, it was precisely to this preponderant role of the state that they attributed all the social, economic, and spiritual evils in Russian society: the chasms separating the various estates, particularly "society" and the "people," the tendency of Russian social groups to look to the state for the definition of their rights and duties, and indeed for the delineation of the very course of their lives. The way out of these fundamental distortions in Russian life, the Slavophiles argued, was clearly not greater public participation in the political process, which in a different form would merely involve a perpetuation of the fundamental evil—the one-sided, altogether excessive orientation of individuals and groups toward the center, toward the state power. The only real remedy was to encourage the autonomous development of social, economic, and moral life, the emergence of organs of "self-administration," and class collaboration *outside* the prehensile arms of state institutions. Hence the Slavophiles were animated by a bitter hostility to the very idea of the party system. They viewed political parties as organizations of factional interests, feverishly seeking by servile maneuvers or by intimidation the favors which the state itself was not legitimately entitled to bestow upon them.[5]

The Slavophiles' ideal of a relationship of noninterference between the state and the land was reflected at this time, however diluted or distorted, in the political attitudes of broader strata of Russian opinion. Indeed it was subtly expressed in the image of government entertained by some of the firmest Russian constitutionalists, who considered the appurtenances of constitutional government that they advocated (such as a national legislature or an independent judiciary) not as functions or organs of the state, not as aspects of public involvement or participation in state affairs, but rather as agencies of society rooted outside the state framework and intended to contain or limit its influence. It is perhaps not surprising that such a viewpoint should have been entertained by the numerous advocates of decentralization among the Russian constitutionalists, but we find it upheld at this time by as firm a centralist and advocate of the "state principle" as B. N. Chicherin.[6]

More significant for the subsequent history of political attitudes and parties in Russia, however, was the reflection of the Slavophile diagnosis of the existing relationship between state and society in the outlook of the post-Reform radicals, the Realists and Populists of the 1860's and 1870's. Two broad continuities characterize the political and social attitudes of the various strands of the radical movement in this period.

The first is a sense of almost total estrangement from the values, mores, and institutional forms discerned in the prevailing political and social order. We find this common note of alienation in the writings of almost all the Realists and Populists of the 1860's and 1870's. We detect it in Pisarev's praise of the "thinking individual" who "recognizes no regulation, no moral law, no principle over and outside himself," as well as in his famous plea to his followers to "hit out boldly left and right," since whatever did not stand up to their blows was clearly "trash" and "not worth preserving."[7] We discern it in a quite different and more conventional Populist form in the pleas of Lavrov and Mikhailovsky to the student youth of the early 1870's to give up their "tainted" privileged stations, "born out of the sufferings of millions," and to pay their *dolg*, their duty and debt, to the oppressed masses of the people. We find it in the savage stories and essays of Saltykov Shchedrin, with their descriptions of the hopeless struggle between the *malchiki*, the young utopian advocates of a better world, and the *Tashkentsy*, the selfish, cruel, and corrupt representatives of property and privilege in the existing order. And finally, of course, we observe it in the insistence of the *buntarei* of the 1870's that the intelligentsia give up its distinctive social identity and fuse with the elemental masses of the people—to blow the whole existing order to bits and replace it with a new world of liberty, equality, and justice.

The second broad continuity is an acute sense of the interdependence, and ultimate concordance, of the various institutions and dominant groups of the existing political and social order. It is among the radicals of the 1860's and 1870's that we find the most absolute formulation of the belief in the close interrelationship between the political and socioeconomic structures that we have already found in other strands of Russian contemporary opinion. To the Russian radicals of the period any effort aimed at partial political, social, or economic reform within the existing framework seemed bound to fail—precisely because all the traditional aspects of the existing order, and all the modernizing forces then active beneath its surface, appeared mutually supportive, or at least by radical standards equally antagonistic to the intelligentsia's ideals of social harmony and individual moral and intellectual liberation. And for this reason, with the possible exception of the handful of Pisarev's followers in the middle 1860's, all strata of radical opinion were convinced that any useful political or social action would have to be based on forces estranged from both the traditional caste system and the emerging "capitalist elements" in national life.

In their search for supporters, the radicals of the 1860's and 1870's were consequently impelled to concentrate their attention on those groups that seemed to them estranged, or at least potentially estranged, from the ruling political and social order. Three such groups were singled out in the radicals' programs and appeals: the youth, particularly the student youth, the intelligentsia, and the communal peasantry. These three groups were the common targets, or at least the common objects of attention, of most of the radical appeals of·the 1860's and 1870's. But the nature of the respective roles assigned to each of them within the framework of a people's party differed, in substance or in detail, from one party program to another. If we put these party and factional programs of the 1860's and 1870's side by side, from M. I. Mikhailov's "To the Younger Generation" of 1861 and Zaichnevsky's "Young Russia" of 1862, to the programs of the far more substantial "Land and Freedom" (1876–77) and "People's Will" (1879) parties,[8] we can find, under the many differences in shadings, two major variants.

The first of these is the relative importance attached by the authors of these programs to the "political" as against the "economic" struggle. The most significant point to note about the difference between these two orientations is that, during those two decades, they did not involve broad differences in programmatic conceptions or objectives: the advocates of both the "political" and the "economic" struggle still tended to view the existing political structure and the dominant socioeconomic forces, old and new, as inextricably intermeshed. Both were aiming, in theory at least, at the complete destruction of the whole framework of national life; both proclaimed as their ultimate objectives—as the only legitimate objective of a people's party—the establishment of an anarchic federation of free, "self-administering" communes and *artels.*

Actually the conflict between *politiki* and *ekonomiki* was a purely technical one: it revolved solely on the question of how the mutually supportive political and socioeconomic structures could successfully be overthrown. To most advocates of the "political" struggle it appeared that the path to success lay in the organization of a revolutionary element in society—all those who appeared ready to join the proletariat in the struggle for political freedom—as the actual or potential dictatorship that would "eliminate" or neutralize the sources of support for the existing order. Then, and only then, could the way be cleared for the calling of a Constituent Assembly or People's Duma to carry out the establishment of the new social and economic utopia.[9]

The advocates of the "economic" struggle, on the other hand, believed that even if such a revolutionary *coup de main* were actually carried off, it would merely pave the way for the replacement of one arbitrary government by another, equally contrary to the people's interest. A "political" movement was necessarily condemned to futility for lack of any adequate social base. All of the ruling estates and emerging new privileged classes in contemporary society were the more or less willing allies of the existing order. The only possible path to the desired transformation was the organization of a wide popular movement, based on the cultivation of the people's own demands and needs.[10]

A second major variant in the radical programs of the 1860's and 1870's was the relative emphasis placed on the "readiness" of the peasant masses for revolution, and therefore on the intelligentsia's role in the preparation and execution of a revolutionary overturn. Naturally it was the advocates of the "political" struggle who, as a group, tended to stress the role of the intelligentsia conspirators instead of the people's. But even within their camp there were notable differences of emphasis—from the ruthless, elitist tone of self-affirmation characteristic of "Young Russia," and to a slighter degree of Tkachev's *Nabat*, to the more sober notes struck by the People's Will group. Similarly, we find among the advocates of the "economic" struggle varying degrees of idealization of the existing foundations of popular life and of the readiness of the people to revolt— from the Lavrovists' stress on the need for intensive socialist propaganda by the intelligentsia, to the Bakuninists' insistence that all the people needed was stimulation and the harnessing of their rage.

In the last analysis, from the range of attitudes represented one may draw two alternative images of the role and organization of a people's party, which the various radical programs approached with differing degrees of fidelity. At one end of the continuum was the image of a centralized, largely conspiratorial, intelligentsia-dominated party, aiming to destroy the whole existing social and political order by striking at its apex, the central state authority; a party intent on the establishment in the people's interest of a provisional revolutionary dictatorship as the most reliable instrument for the elimination of all forms of political, social, and economic oppression. At the other end of the continuum was the image of an infinitely broader and looser revolutionary movement, aiming to destroy the political and socioeconomic structure at its base, by mobilizing against it the instincts and aspirations of all those inchoate elements of Russian society which were "humiliated and insulted." But note that in both variants one can discern the outline of only one party—of one people's party acting as the spokesman or catalyst for all the groups estranged from the existing framework of national life.

In the preceding pages I have attempted to describe the confluence of anti-constitutionalist tendencies in Russian opinion which sapped the vitality of the liberal movement and influenced attitudes toward the party system during the two decades following the beginning of the Great Reforms. Underlying these various tendencies—the different programmatic stands of conservative and "democratic" *gosudarstvenniki*, Slavophile anti-*gosudarstvenniki*, and "political" as well as "economic" radicals—one finds certain common, or at least related, assessments of Russia's contemporary position, which reflected current Russian realities as well as the political and social traditions of the past: the sense of the centrality of the role of the state power in the general framework of social organization; or, conversely, the sense of the inextricable reflection by the state power of the existing organization of classes and estates; the sense of the chasms separating individual classes and estates, and of the lack of free, politically unmediated, interaction or collaboration between them.

Not only did these pervasive sentiments cause the constitutionalist movement to lose potential recruits to both conservative and radical opinion, but they also influenced attitudes within its own thin ranks. Among the older, and more moderate, of its members, this heritage from the past would periodically tend to confirm the views and, at crucial moments (1864–1865, 1881–1882), strengthen the influence of those who considered any large-scale political movement, any wholesale pressure for a national representation, premature—it would lead under existing conditions to complete anarchy, or to the hegemony of a selfish, gentry-dominated representation. Among the more idealistic and radical members of the constitutionalist movement, the same heritage would often be reflected in the feeling that to struggle for political reforms, to press for their *own* participation in the political process, was not enough—that nothing would do but a radical transformation of social and political forms by a truly national representative assembly with broad constituent powers.[11]

In a study of Russian liberalism, written in 1889, the publicist Dragomanov discerned in the weakness of the Russian liberal movement up to that moment, and particularly in the *zemstvo* liberals, an underlying "lack of determination."[12] This failure of nerve Dragomanov attributed in part to the difficult conditions of illegality under which any struggle for political freedom had to proceed in contemporary Russia. But underlying this timidity, I think, there was a more basic deficiency, characteristic of moderate and radical constitutionalists alike: this is the ultimate absence, in their confrontation of the redoubtable and omnipresent state power, of the sense—so pervasive among English country gentlemen in the eighteenth-century House of Commons and among the deputies of the French Third Estate in 1789—that they constituted in their own right the adequate representatives of country and nation. That the Russian constitutionalists still lacked such a sense of legitimacy in the 1860's and 1870's was in large measure due to certain persistent facts of Russian contemporary experience: the role of the state power in upholding the framework of national life was still too great; the mutual antagonisms of the various estates were still too sharp; the new noncaste organs of self-administration to which the Great Reforms had given birth were still too recent and imperfect to enable any organized social group to feel confidently that it could oppose the pretensions of the central political authority in the name of an already existent, let alone united, nation.

## III

In the history of Russian political attitudes, the decade of the 1890's may be viewed as the opening of a new chapter, marked by a range of dramatic developments: the attraction in the early and middle 1890's of varied strands of intelligentsia opinion to Marxism; the appearance, with the strikes of 1895–1896, of the industrial proletariat as a dynamic and potentially revolutionary force on the Russian scene; the emergence at the turn of the century of the ideological and organizational nuclei of potent liberal and neo-Populist movements. This confluence of events would lead by 1905 to the confrontation of the Russian autocracy with a seemingly irresistible coalition of opposition and revolutionary forces. But when viewed in the broad perspective of the evolution of Russian attitudes toward political action and political parties, the overriding significance of the decade is that it marks the time when significant strands of Russian opinion became persuaded of the need, and possibility, of mobilizing a broad political movement to gain political freedom and establish representative government in Russia.

To be sure, there had appeared some veiled and timid previsions of this point of view in earlier decades, particularly at the end of the 1870's and the beginning of the 1880's, but it was only in the 1890's that the spokesmen for significant strata of Russian opinion began to argue openly and unashamedly that political freedom was in and of itself a worthy and significant objective—for the attainment of which a wide combination of social forces, cutting across ideological and class lines, could legitimately and profitably be mobilized. Perhaps the best indication of the depth of this change in the public temper is that the new orientation toward "politics" made simultaneous inroads into the otherwise sharply divided Marxist and Populist camps.

It was the change within the Populist fold that appeared at the time more worthy of notice, if only because the adoption of the new point of view meant to its Populist converts nothing less than a dramatic renunciation of the basic assumptions of the past, of the deeply inrooted Populist prejudice against constitutionalism and liberalism, of the long-held axiom that the only objective worthy of a people's movement was a "basic" social and economic overturn. Yet these were the traditions that many of the most orthodox spokesmen of the Narodnichestvo—Stepniak, Mikhailovsky, Annensky, Korolenko—now repudiated in the most unequivocal terms.

"There are moments in the life of a state when one question assumes the leading place, relegating all other interests, however basic, to the background. Russia is confronting such a question at the present time, the question of political freedom." Thus stated the manifesto of the People's Rights Party (Narodnago prava), drafted by some of the editors of the Populist journal Russkoe bogatstvo in 1894. The only way to achieve this objective was to oppose to the government "the organized force of public opinion." This would be the main task of the projected party, the manifesto concluded: "to unite all the opposition forces in the country" in order to win for one and all "the rights of man and citizen."[13]

Two years earlier, Stepniak-Kravchinsky, hitherto one of the most dogmatic exponents of the "economic" struggle, had argued more heretically that the only practical path to political freedom was the establishment of a constitutional monarchy. Socialists would have to shed earlier prejudices and say right out that their immediate objective was the conquest of a constitution for Russia. Even more, they would need to give up their "utopian belief" that in the struggle against autocracy "an independent, let alone a leading, role" could be assumed by either the working class or the peasant masses. Political freedom would have to be won by the joint efforts of the only two significant progressive forces on the contemporary scene: the socialist intelligentsia and the educated liberal elements of "society."[14]

To be sure, neither Stepniak nor the editors of Russkoe bogatstvo were intent on cutting off completely their ideological ties to the Populist tradition. They did not demand that the Russian radicals give up their ultimate socialist objectives for the sake of the political struggle. Indeed, they argued that the attainment of political freedom was a "prerequisite" for the solution of broader social problems. But even in these arguments they displayed little willingness to appease old Populist prejudices: "We vigorously protest against the habit prevalent among many of us to subordinate the objective of political freedom exclusively to the resolution of the social question," Stepniak belligerently asserted in 1892. "We cannot view freedom solely as an instrument for this or that, as if the feelings and needs of a free people were foreign to us, as if, for the sake of our obligations to the People, we did not understand our obligations to ourselves, to human dignity."[15]

For the Russian Marxists, such an awareness of the need for a nationwide movement to win political freedom did not, of course, represent quite so radical a break with ideological tradition. After all, Plekhanov and Akselrod had been stressing the point ever since the organization, in 1883, of *Osvobozhdenie truda.*[16] Yet it is nonetheless symptomatic of the new mood of Russian radical circles in the early 1890's that, despite the intoxication with the discovery of "irresistible economic laws" and the consequent quietism which then temporarily possessed most of the younger generation of Russian Marxists, the one practical plank, the one call to action, to which many of them responded was Plekhanov's and Akselrod's statement of the political tasks of Social Democracy.[17] This was the call to lead the movement for the overthrow of absolutism, duly enlisting in the process the support of the "less politically mature" bourgeois-liberal elements in society; to mobilize the Russian workers to fight for the "bourgeois revolution" that would win them their civic and political rights.

We should note that both the Marxist and the new Populist programs of the early 1890's provided for a staggering of tasks which Russian radicals had once viewed as inextricably joined: both now drew a line (at least in timing) between the gaining of political freedom and the eventual social overturn. In the Marxist program this staggering of objectives was articulated in the conception of a two-stage revolutionary process, whose first stage (the bourgeois revolution) was to be separated from the glorious socialist revolution by a proper, largely historically determined, interval. In the Populists' case, this differentiation was reflected in the more imprecise vision of a political revolution which would enable Russian public opinion to effect, in due course, broad social and economic reforms.

What basic changes in the radicals' image of the existing political and social order did this new orientation toward political action ultimately reflect? The first was the disappearance of the sense of the inextricable interconnection between political and social-economic organization that had characterized the radicals' view of the framework of national life. Beyond the long arm of the state power, both Populists and Marxists were now able to discern the independent shape of an already existent—or fast emerging—society, animated at least for the moment by a certain community of values or interests transcending the barriers of caste and class differences. The second and related change in this image of national life was that in the chief constituent groups of the new society the Populists and Marxists now detected the emergence of a "public opinion" in *radical conflict* with the values and policies of state power, and in accord with the immediate interests, if not the ultimate objectives, of the socialist cause.

Both of these dimensions had been absent from the radicals' world view in the 1860's and 1870's. Both were prerequisites for the appearance of a favorable attitude toward the struggle for representative institutions. For a struggle confined to winning political freedom to appear practical, indeed conceivable, to the Russian radicals, it was necessary for them to perceive in national life a body of public opinion seeking political self-expression, and therefore to discern a society, a nation, distinct from the state. For such a struggle to appear useful in their eyes, it was equally necessary for them to see this public opinion as favoring objectives similar to their own.

The sources of this new image of society and public opinion must be traced ultimately to the Great Reforms which had created the legal setting for greater social mobility and closer contacts among classes in national life. But it was really only in the 1890's that the Russian radicals began to perceive at all clearly the shape of this new society and to discern in it a growing opposition to the state. The Populists and Marxists derived their discovery of the tension, the "dialectical conflict," between state and society from a common source: the process of rapid industrialization that Russia had begun to undergo in the late 1880's under the direction and sponsorship of the state. Both camps now diagnosed this process as a growth of capitalism at the expense of Russia's "natural" or "popular" economy, and they derived their belief in the inescapable conflict between state power and society from their sense of the contradictions attendant to this growth. Yet, in the last analysis, the two groups viewed this development of "capitalism" in sharply contrasting lights and held quite different pictures of the chief protagonists in the conflicts to which it was giving rise.

It naturally appeared to the Marxists that the growth of capitalism, in Russia as everywhere else, was merely a reflection of the unfolding of irresistible, "objective," economic laws. Whatever its social cost, whatever sufferings it was now producing, this process was to be welcomed by all enlightened elements in society, partly because it was giving birth to a conscious proletariat, the future agent of the socialist transformation, and partly because—in the more immediate perspective—it was giving rise to a modern, "bourgeois," westernized class society, whose interests strongly demanded the conquest of the civic and political rights that would so greatly benefit the development of the proletariat's consciousness.

Possessed, as most of them were, by this vision of a budding capitalistic society struggling for political self-expression against an out-dated "feudal" state order, the Russian Marxists naturally looked to its two "objective" class representatives—the proletariat and the bourgeoisie—to provide the chief impetus in the struggle for political freedom. It was the industrial proletariat that now showed "the most certain signs of political awakening." The bourgeoisie was still "politically inert"—but there was no doubt that this "other new class," even if more backward, would "be forced under the threat of ruin to become conscious of its own interests."[18] In the meantime, the Marxists were prepared to identify all "liberal" elements in society—all those who appeared ready to join the proletariat in the struggle for political freedom—as the actual or political spokesmen for a would-be politically mature, class-conscious bourgeoisie.

The Populist constitutionalists readily succumbed to precisely an opposite temptation. Ever since the 1880's they had viewed "capitalistic development" in Russia as merely the reflection of arbitrary, "unnatural" governmental policies which were driving the people's communal and *artel* existence, and indeed the nation's economy as a whole, to bankruptcy.[19] It was their conviction that the governmental policies were, or would be, widely opposed, not only by the peasantry and the intelligentsia but also by enlightened members of "privileged society," which drew the Populists of the 1890's to the idea of political freedom, to the vision of an aroused and mobilized public opinion replacing the existing regime by one more sympathetic to popular interests. Hence, the Populists were now tempted to consider all their actual or potential allies in "society" as spokesmen for antibourgeois, anticapitalistic tendencies, struggling against a procapitalistic state.[20]

By the turn of the century, the Populists had good reason to feel that the anticapitalistic, antibourgeois, antibureaucratic tendencies that they had discerned in contemporary society were now beginning to coalesce into a "public opinion" opposed to the policies of the state. Their chief cause for continued anxiety was that most "academic" and gentry liberals were still persuading themselves, as the 1890's drew to a close, that legality, self-administration, and concern for the popular welfare could be introduced into—or at least temporarily reconciled with—the political structure of autocracy. Some of the gentry liberals, such as D. N. Shipov and N. Khomiakov, the future leaders of the liberal right, still held on to the hopeful Slavophile vision of a benevolent, antibureaucratic tsar, peacefully consulting with the enlightened representatives of the Russian land.[21] Others of a more Western outlook, such as B. N. Maklakov, still looked forward to a gradual introduction, from the bottom up, of legal and eventually of constitutional principles into the machinery of government.[22] But only a handful of liberal spokesmen appeared prepared for an open militant struggle to secure these civic and political rights from the clutching hands of autocracy.

## IV

If the Populists still suffered from a relatively thin diet as the 1890's drew to a close, they were to be surfeited at the opening of the new century by an embarrassment of riches. Not only did the years leading up to 1905 see the appearance of the coalition between liberals and democratic intelligentsia for which the Populist constitutionalists had been calling since the early 1890's, but they also witnessed the emergence of an impressive neo-Populist movement, built along somewhat more traditional lines. In the ideological and organizational definition of both these movements, the Populist constitutionalists were to play a major, if not central, role.

In remarkable contrast to the travails of the past, the creation of the "all-nation" coalition against absolutism proceeded during these triumphant years with remarkable rapidity, comprehensiveness, and ease—and in a relative spirit of sweet reasonableness without parallel in the earlier or later history of Russian political attitudes. By the beginning of 1905, an imposing front was to be systematically mobilized against the autocracy, ranging all the way from the zemstvo congresses (or at least their dominant wing, the zemstvo constitutionalists) at the right, the professional unions, organized under the aegis of the Union of Unions at the center, to the Social Democrats and Socialist Revolutionaries at the left. All these more or less independent political groups were determined, ostensibly at least, to maintain their distinct programs and tactics; yet most of their leaders and followers asserted themselves to be equally intent on "striking together" against absolutism for the attainment of common, immediate political objectives.

I have deliberately omitted from this already impressive list the most influential, most remarkable, and most symptomatic political organization of the period, the Union of Liberation (*Soiuz osvobozhdeniia*). I have done so simply because the Union of Liberation did not at any time represent a particular political grouping or tendency in any conventional sense. What we actually find represented in the councils of the movement is nothing less than an array of ideological tendencies and attitudes, embracing almost the whole spectrum of contemporary revolutionary and opposition attitudes: the moderate gentry constitutionalism of Nikolai L'vov and Kokoshkin, the more fiery and uncompromising liberalism of Petrunkevich and Miliukov, the modern "scientific" liberalism of Struve, the reformist Western Social Democratic outlook of Prokopovich, as well as the Populist ethos of Peshekhonov and Annensky. Indeed, these capsule descriptions are but bare, unsatisfactory approximations, for what was truly characteristic of the individual components of the movement, as well as of the whole complex, was an amorphousness and fluidity, reflecting a common desire to absorb, or at least to comprehend, the whole swirling flow of oppositional and revolutionary opinion.

But the truly remarkable feature of the Osvobozhdentsy is that they saw it as their role not merely to unite or reconcile the variety of tendencies that they represented under a common platform or organization, but rather to take a hand in the actual creation, ideological delineation, and "independent" organization of a whole spectrum of political groupings and tendencies. In this fashion, between 1903 and 1905, the Osvobozhdentsy played a more or less central and public role in the organization of the Group of Zemstvo Constitutionalists—and through it, in the political mobilization of the whole zemstvo movement (on the basis of a carefully delimited, "political," constitutional platform) and in the political organization of the city intelligentsia into professional unions (in this case, in support of an appropriately more radical program of political and social reforms). Through the personal agency of Peshekhonov and Annensky, they even took a hand in the ideological and organizational development of the radical Socialist Revolutionary Party and, most astonishing of all (if true), in the formulation—in properly "folksy" style—of the platform of Father Gapon's Assembly of Russian Workers.[23]

What was the Osvobozhdentsy's purpose in performing this juggling act, and what was the basis of their success? Only in the most limited sense was it intended to impose on the various groups a single, definite political purpose and direction. Zemstvo groups, intelligentsia liberals and radicals, rebellious workers and peasants, all were to be persuaded of the need to win political freedom. But aside from this, there was not the slightest attempt to prevent, indeed there was many an effort to encourage, these various groupings to develop distinct and even conflicting political physiognomies—if only in the interest of a truly broad and successful mobilization of a national movement.

What did the Osvobozhdentsy expect from the society that they were helping to bring to life? What was the theoretical basis for their confidence that the different pieces, which they had helped shape, would somehow fall together in a reasonably coherent pattern? To be sure, a similar confidence is already to be found in the theoretical formulations of intelligentsia leaders during the 1890's. We find it in the orthodox Marxists' conception of the bourgeois revolution that was to be followed, after a proper interval, by the glorious socialist overturn, as well as in the Populist constitutionalists' more flexible vision of a political revolution that would give Russian citizens their civic and political rights—and create the political setting for eventual social reforms. But in both of these earlier conceptions, the hope to enlist "all-nation" support for the struggle against autocracy had rested entirely on the assumption that this struggle was to be confined to the conquest of political freedom. Under the exhilarating stimulus that the Osvobozhdentsy and their SR allies drew from the rising momentum and articulateness of the opposition movement, the distinction that the radicals of the 1880's had drawn between impending "political" changes and the eventual social transformation was to be largely swept away, or at least significantly blurred.

The "Westerner" elements among the Osvobozhdentsy—for the most part, the men of Struve's stripe who had matriculated earlier in the school of legal Marxism—were perhaps the least affected by the intoxicating mood of the moment, if only because their own long-range objectives for Russian society were no longer particularly radical. Yet even they now looked forward with remarkable sanguineness to the emergence at one stroke of a modern social and political order, to the appearance full-blown on Russian soil of the most advanced and progressive form of Western society. If they were so little concerned about the need to impose certain common, moderate, political objectives on the various elements of the opposition to absolutism, if they were in fact prepared to assist these groups, however disparate or radical they might currently appear, to organize independently, it was because they saw the end result of their efforts as largely predetermined. The new enlightened social and political order that was about to be born would necessarily bring in short order the domestication of all radical elements, the transformation of Russian revolutionary extremists into social reformers of the Western type. If this was now happening in Germany, Struve could well argue, why should it not also happen in Russia?[24]

As for the representatives of the school of Populist constitutionalism now active in the councils of the Osvobozhdentsy and their friends among the Socialist Revolutionaries, they looked forward to an equally hopeful, but quite different, perspective. It now seemed to them increasingly apparent that no insurmountable "objective" ideological differences really separated the vast majority of the opposition movement: the SDs, the SRs, and the advanced (that is, "real") liberals. All of these groups were, potentially at least, equally radical; all of them were "instinctively" opposed to both "feudalism" and "capitalism."

As early as 1898, Peshekhonov had insisted on the identity of the economic interests of industrial workers and toiling peasants and, almost from the very first, he and his disciple, Victor Chernov, expressed and elaborated this view in the pages of the official SR organ, *Revoliutsionnaia rosiia*. Of course, they conceded, capitalism was now spreading in the countryside and giving birth to a new kulak class—but all this meant politically was that the toiling peasants' traditional instincts for economic equality and cooperation would now be largely directed against capitalistic, rather than feudal, exploitation.[25] As we turn over the pages of *Revoliutsionnaia rossiia*, between 1902 and 1905, we observe the neo-Populist image of the nation-wide front against capitalism being extended (with increasing confidence) to include most of the members of the liberal opposition. From the original conception of a careful, rather distant, and wholly provisional collaboration, lasting only up to the moment when the autocracy would be overthrown,[26] the emphasis of the journal gradually but unmistakably shifts to an optimistic vision of the core of the liberal movement as the expression not of gentry, let alone bourgeois, interests but rather of the social conscience, however confused, of a nonclass, noncaste intelligentsia.[27] From 1903 to the outbreak of the 1905 Revolution, the neo-Populist leaders would feel increasingly certain, if only on the basis of their own experience with the Osvobozhdenie movement, that most of the liberal leaders were "antibourgeois" and "antigentry" in their instincts, if only "vulgarly so," and that they were not "hostile to socialism, but simply believe in it badly."[28]

These particular distortions in the neo-Populists' vision of the character and composition of the coalition against absolutism impelled them, far more seriously than their Westerner collaborators among the Osvobozhdentsy, to stretch the limits that had originally been assigned to the struggle for political freedom. The "democratic" revolution that they saw in the offing was no longer to be confined to mere "superficial" political reforms; it was to encompass radical social and economic changes (such as the socialization of the land) which would pave the way for the socialist transformation. Nor was this revolution any longer to depend in any significant degree on the support of an established group in privileged society; the broad social and economic changes that it would effect would be imposed by a "firm democratic regime" against the resistance of both gentry and bourgeoisie.[29]

These were the two ideologically different, yet equally optimistic and almost equally elastic, conceptions that animated the neo-Populist, neo-Marxist, and ex-Marxist figures who, in the years immediately preceding 1905, largely led and manipulated the growing forces in the opposition to absolutism. Both conceptions presented a challenge to the Menshevik and Bolshevik leaders of Russian Social Democracy who, however divided on other issues, were still in ostensible agreement on the need for "Social Democratic hegemony" in the "bourgeois" revolution.

To the Mensheviks, particularly to Plekhanov and Akselrod, it was the Western, liberal vision that seemed by far the less objectionable of the two, since it corresponded fairly closely to their own minimum program for the first, the "bourgeois," revolution. By contrast, the SR platform—with its "hopeless confusion" between the tasks of the impending bourgeois revolution and the objectives of the eventual socialist overturn—appeared to them calculated to produce dangerous divisions within the ranks of the opposition to the regime.[30]

But Lenin and his Bolsheviks would have been hard put to decide which of the two views was the more harmful. To be sure, it was the SRs who, in their long-range program and especially in their definition of immediate objectives (in their program minimum), were coming closer—disturbingly close—to the conception of the "democratic revolution" for which Lenin himself was groping. Like the SRs, Lenin now looked forward to a democratic revolution that would encompass broad social and economic changes to facilitate the transition to socialism. Like the SRs, he foresaw that these reforms would be resisted not only by the gentry but also by the bourgeoisie—which would try for compromises and some sort of reconciliation with the autocracy. And like the SRs, he foresaw that this resistance would have to be overcome by a "firm democratic regime," truly reflective of the interests of the toiling masses.[31]

We should note that both conceptions were directed equally against the "feudal" gentry and the "capitalist" bourgeoisie—in fact, if not in theory, against all dominant groups and existing social forms in Russian life. Both views contained (though for quite different reasons, as we shall see) the implicit assumption of the legitimacy of only one party as the suitable voice for the toiling masses. But there the similarity ended. Although the SRs envisaged the overturn as the culmination of a natural, and hence irresistible, process—faithfully expressing the clear aspirations of a crushing majority of the Russian people—Lenin visualized it merely as one of two, almost equally possible, historical alternatives. The bourgeoisie might well patch up its differences with the autocracy and succeed in denying the fuzzy, instinctive desires of the popular masses, since its influence was infinitely more pervasive—and the masses infinitely less prepared to resist it—than the SRs chose to assume.

There is no need to summarize here the two revolutionary perspectives that Lenin was now to develop, and which he would later summarize in his "Two Tactics," but we should recognize the rationale that this theory offered for the legitimacy of a single-party center: the relative isolation of "conscious" revolutionary elements in existing society and the enormity of the tasks confronting them. They had to extricate the "spontaneous" peasant masses, and even the working-class movement, from the shackles of feudalism and from the more insidious and potent influence of the capitalist bourgeoisie; to place these masses under conscious socialist leadership and control; to expose ruthlessly the perfidious bourgeois influence, the "dressed-up liberals," hidden even in the most revolutionary parties.[32] The SRs, on the contrary, drew their instinctive sense of the legitimacy of a single party, at least at this moment, from the optimistic, exuberant image of a broad popular movement of peasants, workers, and intelligentsia, all equally intent on the overthrow of autocracy and the eventual establishment of socialism.[33]

On the eve of 1905, the programs of the Bolsheviks and the SRs were the most extreme manifestations of the general tendency in the opposition movement to stretch the careful, deliberate schedule that the Marxists and Populists of the 1890's had drawn of their political and social tasks. This blurring of vision was in most cases to be quickly dispelled by political realities. Yet it should be amply clear that it was precisely that confusion of political and social tasks, precisely this melange of visions and objectives, which—compounded by the blindness and ineptness of the autocracy—permitted the triumphant build-up of the opposition and revolutionary forces. It was this very confusion that facilitated the mobilization of the remarkably checkered coalition of antiautocratic, antibureaucratic, antifeudal, and anticapitalistic forces which, by October 1905, the autocracy was unable to curb. And, by the same token, it was this confusion that reflected most clearly the internal weaknesses to which this majestic movement would eventually succumb.

In 1889, the liberal publicist Dragomanov had argued hopefully that a nationwide movement for political freedom could not be thwarted by a lack of brute strength, by a monopoly of armed force in the hands of its opponents. "If a political regime is deprived of a surrounding atmosphere of support, or at least of neutrality," he wrote, "it will fall—just as the French monarchy did in 1789, and Prussian absolutism, in 1848. These events transpired, not because the governments [in question] lacked physical strength, but because the moral atmosphere surrounding them prevented its use. . . . The Bonapartists found the strength to shoot up Paris, and the Hapsburgs, Vienna; the Hohenzollerns returned their army to Berlin [only] after divisions in public opinion were exposed."[34] The course of the 1905 Revolution was to confirm Dragomanov's diagnosis.

## V

The "all-nation" movement against autocracy, which the leaders of the Osvobozhdenie had so deliberately and energetically mobilized, reached its majestic peak with the general strike of October 13–17, 1905. Confronted by the almost unanimous opposition of society, into which even the faithful business and industrial bourgeoisie had been swept in the summer and fall of 1905, the demoralized autocracy was forced to follow the course predicted by Dragomanov sixteen years earlier. Despite its continued monopoly of the instruments of violence—with all its talk of an armed uprising, the Bolshevik-dominated

Central Committee of the RSDRP had at this moment fifty-odd Browning revolvers[35]—it was compelled to promise, in the October Manifesto, the civic and political rights demanded by Russian society.

The October Manifesto marked the high point of the nation-wide opposition movement. It also marked the beginning of its downfall. From this moment on, momentarily deceptive indications to the contrary—such as the working-class strikes of November and December 1905, the Moscow uprising and the origin-ally enthusiastic popular reception of the First Duma—the power and cohesion of the revolutionary forces slowly but surely began to decline, to the rising chorus of the mutual recriminations of the various opposition and revolutionary parties.

During the ensuing twenty months of political struggle, culminating in the dismal finale of the Stolypin *coup d'état* of June 3, 1907, each of the opposition parties would be guilty of more or less serious tactical errors. And since the errors of each party were based in part on a failure to predict accurately the course followed by its political rivals and allies, each felt justified in blaming the fiasco on other parties' inability, or unwillingness, to follow their "proper" political course. To weigh the relative merits of this long series of mutual recriminations would be futile: each of them, at least in part, was but a rationaliza-tion for failure; yet in the limited sense that each party's prospects had been adversely affected by the political course of the other parties in the political spectrum, each was partially justified. More important for our purpose is to try to understand the precise character of the trials that the broad conceptions of political dynamics now underwent in the turmoil of the revolutionary storm.

The first of these conceptions, we must recall, one already elaborated by the orthodox Marxists in the 1890's, was that the coming revolution would be in the last analysis a bourgeois revolution which would bring to Russia the advanced Western, democratic political institutions corresponding to the interests and aspirations of the industrial proletariat and of the "capitalistic" bourgeoisie, the two class representatives of the new society. The Osvobozh-dentsy liberals and the orthodox Marxists—the future Kadet leaders and the future Mensheviks—had been equally insistent that the coming revolution should not go beyond the objective limits assigned to it by history, by the current level of Russia's socioeconomic development, and by the aspirations or level of consciousness reached by the majority of Russian society. Both had forseen, and would continue to foresee, that if the revolutionary movement swept beyond its historical limits, if it should seek through unwise political action to overturn its "objective" base, it would be condemned to defeat by an inexorable "Thermidorian" reaction. It is probably fair to say that, both before and after 1905, the Kadet and Menshevik leaders were as conscious of this danger as any revolutionary leaders in history. Yet despite this, their vision of the revolution and the political diagnoses that they drew from it were soon to be shattered on the reefs of political reality.

Why was the Kadet-Menshevik picture of the revolution so confounded by the course of events after October 1905? In the following period the two parties unveiled some serious tactical differences, and each consequently accused the other of having "deviated" from the original true vision. These differences gave rise to periodic practical conflicts between the two groups which in some degree hindered the effectiveness of their alliance. But it is the degree to which the leaders of both parties succeeded, through the vicissitudes of these revolutionary years, in remaining true to their common vision and to each other that is truly remarkable. And it is in the very character of this common vision that the ultimate sources of their defeat must be sought.

In the years leading up to 1905 the Mensheviks and the Kadets had predicted repeatedly, and quite accurately as it turned out, that—to misuse a Marxist adage of the 1890's—either the bourgeois revolution would be achieved with the aid of the bourgeoisie or it would not be achieved at all. The ultimate cause of their defeat was that, unknown to them, the 1905 Revolution was not a bourgeois revolution. To be precise, it was a bourgeois revolution during the short period from the summer of 1905 to the October Manifesto when certain elements of big business and the industrial bourgeoisie actually joined in the nation-wide movement against the autocracy. But then there had come the momentous, unsettling events of October, November, and December 1905—the issuance of the October Manifesto itself with its sweeping promise of political reform, the November economic strikes of the Petersburg workers, the bloody Moscow uprising—and as precipitously as they had been swept into the opposition movement, the business and industrial elements had withdrawn to join with frightened "gentry liberals" and representatives of the bureaucracy in the formation of new parties. In the programs of these new parties, such as the Commercial-Industrial Party and the larger Union of the 17th of October (the two would merge after the dissolution of the First Duma), the Mensheviks and their Kadet allies might have discerned the emergence of a far more up-to-date, more explicitly bourgeois ideology than the constituent elements of these parties had ever before manifested. In the face of the revolutionary threat of the expropriation of their landed estates, the gentry supporters of the Octobrists now abandoned all traces of their earlier paternalistic attitudes toward the village commune and firmly supported Stolypin's program of agricultural reorganization as the proper basis for the development of a spirit of "individual enterprise" and "respect for property" among the peasant masses. As for the businessmen and industrialists who had now allied themselves with the gentry, many of them now displayed a new appreciation for the importance of legality in the functioning of the Russian state. And most significant of all, those new "moderate" parties of the right supported, in the name of these very principles of "order," "legality," and "respect for property," the government's suppression of revolutionary disorders and its eventual dissolution of the first two Dumas.[36]

The significance of the appearance of the Octobrists was not only that it indicated where the sympathies of the bourgeoisie really lay, but also that it provided the demoralized government with a new basis of support in "society," freeing it from the paralysis of the October days. From this point on, the government felt able to strike back at the opposition and revolutionary forces.

Since both Kadets and Mensheviks had been so emphatic about the danger of transcending the objective limits of political action, and since the Mensheviks in particular had been so insistent on the need for bourgeois participation in the bourgeois revolution, why did neither group call a halt to the "assault on autocracy" in the light of these symptomatic signs after the issuance of the October Manifesto, or at least after the opening of the First Duma? Why did they not accept the new legal and political framework that had been established, as one truly corresponding to the existing equilibrium of forces, and rest their hopes for Russia's political future in the further natural development of social, economic, and cultural forms? This was the kind of self-restraint for which Struve now desperately called but the Kadet and Menshevik leaders failed to display it, due (so Struve insisted) to their traditional intelligentsia revolutionary psychology.[37]

I think that we can ascertain two main assumptions underlying the two groups' head-on pursuit of the "bourgeois revolution" well after the bourgeoisie had actually deserted from their camp. The first of these, to which the Kadets held with particular devotion, was that the development of the modern, advanced, industrialized society that they saw irresistibly emerging in Russia would necessarily entail the progressive realization in political and social life of the principles of freedom and social justice. One may find touching expressions of this faith in the writings of most Russian liberals of the period—from the naive and inflated sociological demonstrations of Maxim Kovalevsky to the far more sophisticated historical analysis of Paul Miliukov.[38] It was this instinctive belief in the golden laws of progress which made the Kadets so confident of the objective basis in Russian life for the realization of their "advanced" social and political objectives (all immediate evidence to the contrary), and which blinded them to the possibility that an excessive radical course might involve permanent political setbacks.

The second of these deluding assumptions, which was especially important for the Mensheviks, was that the Kadets represented a "bourgeois" party. Even though the Kadets occasionally attracted bourgeois voters, this was an erroneous, or at best a meaningless, assumption: for the Kadets were, first and foremost, a party of the intelligentsia, a quite distinctive social and political category even if it happened to be missing in the Marxist scheme of things. The assumption that the Kadets were a bourgeois party helped the Menshevik leaders to rationalize, indeed impelled them to believe in, the "objective" validity of the political course that after October they were all too inclined to pursue. For, as long as the Kadets stood with them in the opposition, as long as this "bourgeois" party had not fully assumed the reigns of political power, they felt justified in believing that the historically prescribed course of the bourgeois revolution had not yet been completed—and that they had, therefore, every right to push on.

Underlying the readiness of these two groups to hold on to these assumptions in the face of adverse political circumstances, there was undoubtedly the large dose of the traditional intelligentsia prejudice to which Struve had pointed: a persistent—if now less overt—sense of estrangement from the whole fabric of the existing order; a consequent impatience for broad social, as well as political, reforms; a readiness to use the instrumentalities of the state power to enforce changes rather than waiting for "objective processes" to bring them about.

But to what extent could Kadet and Menshevik leaders have changed the course of the opposition and revolutionary movement had they more sternly contained these "fatal inclinations" of their intelligentsia natures? Very little, I think, for the simple reason that once again 1905 was not an orderly "bourgeois" revolution, but rather a spontaneous upsurge of heterogeneous elements seeking to overturn the whole existing order. The seemingly irresistible character of the revolutionary wave in the initial stages of the revolution was due to the fact that it mobilized not only the long-standing protests against the crumbling traditional order but also the resentments against the pains and dislocation of the early stages of the "capitalistic," and specifically industrial, development that the autocracy had attempted to push at so rapid and forceful a tempo. Thus, to use the language of the intelligentsia left, 1905 was the compressed expression of outbursts of revolt against "capitalism" as well as "feudalism," against "bourgeois" as well as "gentry" rule.

# VI

During the politically torpid and often demoralizing years that immediately followed the *coup d'état* of June 1907, a number of prominent intelligentsia figures issued a series of powerful appeals for a fundamental reassessment of the intelligentsia's traditional attitudes and values. They urged the intelligentsia—now that a modern society perfectly capable of deciding its own fate had come to political life—to give up their "out-dated" wholesale involvement in politics and instead to follow the rules, to enjoy the fruits of a normal civilized existence.[39]

Of these appeals, perhaps the sharpest and the most pointed were those issued by that remarkable figure, Peter Struve. In his contribution to the *Vekhi* symposium (1909),[40] and in his articles in *Russkai mysl'*,[41] Struve urged the intelligentsia to alter their ways in two important and largely complementary respects. First he called on them to give up their obsession with revolutionary politics, their tendency to evaluate all problems—all areas of life—on the basis of rigid, usually completely misplaced, ideological criteria. He urged them to lead stable and fruitful lives, to invest their energies, in an orderly way, in suitable social and cultural activities, and to enjoy these activities for their own sake. His second major point was that the intelligentsia should develop at long last what he termed a sense of *gosudarstvennost'*. By this word, Struve now meant to denote a sense of the continuity of institutions, a respect for, or at least a certain restraint in the face of, historical traditions, a sense of law—in substance, an understanding of the slow, halting, and painful character of the process that had been involved in the growth of Russian civilization and of the social and the political forms in which it was now enclosed. Only such an understanding, Struve firmly believed, only an awareness of the "elemental" conditions of cruelty and savagery from which existing institutions had ultimately emerged and to which their destruction might bring a return, could impose on desires for radical political changes the restraining influence of a sense of reality.

In this appeal for a more acute and realistic sense of the public interest, and in his more specific political pleas of the period, Struve was attempting to convince his readers that only by agreeing to operate under the existing social and political order—by dedicating themselves within its framework to professional pursuits, helpful to the development of Russian society and culture—could they expect to exercise a genuinely creative and transforming influence on the evolution of the state order itself.

But most of Struve's critics chose to interpret his appeal as a complete repudiation of the intelligentsia's glorious revolutionary tradition, a slur on its saintly succession of heroes and martyrs. Those who felt compelled to answer the substance of his arguments concentrated on one major debating point: the alleged contradiction between Struve's plea for the repudiation of the intelligentsia's tradition of *sotsialnost'* (the almost compulsive absorption that it had displayed throughout its history in political and social problems) and his appeal, on the other hand, for a new sense of *gosudarstvennost'*, for a new statesmanlike concern for the national interest.[42] In Struve's eyes such a sense of political responsibility required above all a display of political moderation and realism. But to his traditionally minded intelligentsia critics a call to "public duty" could only mean one thing: a demand for an even more intensive effort to mold Russia's fate "directly" by destroying, reforming, or assuming control of the state power—the organizational center of the whole complex of Russia's economic, social, and cultural institutions. Hence they discovered in Struve's pleas a contradiction which was not really there, a misunderstanding which mirrored only too clearly the persistent hold of their own "intelligentsia" prejudices.

Actually, in the years following the dissolution of the Second Duma, the leadership of the Kadet Party, and indeed much of the intelligentsia at large, heeded Struve's conception of duty in practice if not in theory. Many in the intelligentsia, deserting their traditional allegiance to the revolutionary cause, were now absorbed into the normal, humdrum, and useful professional existence that they had formerly despised and had undergone as a result an inevitable mellowing of outlook. The Kadet deputies in the Third Duma, their numbers now drastically reduced by changes in the electoral law, as well as by the un-questionable, if temporary, swing of public opinion to the right, began to follow cautious, businesslike, "constructive" parliamentary tactics, of which even a Maklakov could feel proud.

This Kadet sagacity—compounded by the Octobrists' subservience to the arbitrary and often illegal turns in government policy—was to be rewarded in the elections to the Fourth Duma by a sharp rise in the Kadet vote, particularly in the pre-eminently bourgeois First and Second Curiae of the cities.[43] And most helpful of all, the sessions of the Fourth Duma saw the emergence of a growing collaboration between Kadets and now disillusioned Octobrists which promised the eventual ascendancy of a moderate, yet liberal, center. This almost came about, but only during the First World War with the organization in the summer of 1915 of the Progressive Bloc.

Did the gravitation of so many in the intelligentsia toward the new semi-parliamentary institutions, the already established organs of self-government, and the normal cares of professional roles that occurred in the wake of 1905 indicate that Russia had now entered an era of growing social and political stability? Most historians of the period would say that it did and would argue that only the added strains and dislocations of the First World War kept the bright promise of the years leading up to 1914 from being fulfilled.

Indeed, there were many further signs of progress in Russian national life during those years: evidence of a new flowering in the cultural life of the intelligentsia, now largely freed from the obsession of radical politics; indications that, beginning in 1909, Russia's industrial growth had not merely resumed much of its earlier pace but had become more self-sustaining and independent of the artificial stimulus of state subsidies; evidence that the communal institutions which had so greatly hindered the development of Russian agriculture were rapidly disintegrating, and that a new class of ambitious, property-minded peasant proprietors had emerged in the Russian countryside. Yet by the light of historical hindsight at least, one might have discerned certain disquieting features in this bucolic scene, or raised a number of disturbing questions.

One might even have questioned the optimistic inferences that were now being drawn from the evident disintegration of the sectarian dogmas and ethos that had hitherto kept so many in the intelligentsia together, and apart from existing society. To be sure, for a large and vocal element in the intelligentsia, this disintegration of traditional values and loyalties opened the way for a genuine reabsorption into the framework of national life. But to what degree did this breakdown of traditional bonds also contribute to the embitterment, the "hardening," of those irreconcilable factions of the intelligentsia "left" which, in 1917, would help sweep away both the existing order and the traces of old intelligentsia culture? And perhaps most important of all, how many of those in the intelligentsia who joined in the flight from radical politics, and indeed from any political involvement, after 1905 found themselves unable in succeeding years to gain new values to replace those that they had lost? How many were there who shared, however inarticulately, Alexander Blok's sense of the continued thinness of Russia's civilized layers and his readiness to capitulate, as one of the privileged few, before a new revolutionary holocaust?[44]

Blok's pessimism about the thinness of contemporary Russian culture brings to mind perhaps the most important and the most difficult issue to be raised about the developments of this period. To what extent did the contemporary mood of the Russian masses correspond to the sentiments of those in the intelligentsia who were now reabsorbed into existing society? The industrial workers and, to a lesser degree, the peasantry had risen in 1905 in a largely instinctive burst of revolt against the conditions of their existence. Were their varied, amorphous resentments against the crumbling traditional order and the painful dislocations attendant to the rise of a modern world now being assuaged, or were they slowly building up toward a new—more general and more violent —outburst? If the latter was the case, the new mood of political moderation and, in some cases, political indifference which was now being displayed by many intelligentsia circles could well have meant that the few connecting links between these intelligentsia groups (and the society that they had rejoined) and the masses were now gradually being cut, leaving the latter completely exposed to the embittered pleas of the intelligentsia extreme left.

Even the greatest governmental achievement of the period, the measures that Stolypin so forcefully initiated for the dissolution of communal agriculture, opened some disturbing immediate perspectives in this connection. For these policies meant the introduction of new dislocations in village life, largely imposed in practice if not in theory by governmental fiat. How would the masses of the peasantry respond to these dislocations? Would their grievances mount up against the more prosperous individual farmers and, combined with their never wholly suppressed desire to obtain the remaining gentry lands, give rise to new and more potent revolutionary outbreaks? To be sure, the peasants were quiet in the years leading up to 1914, but how might they respond to new revolutionary disorders in the cities, particularly among the industrial workers? The question is not entirely academic since we do witness a new upsurge of opposition sentiments in 1913–1914 and, particularly, a dramatic rise in the curve of industrial strikes which, even according to official governmental statistics, were now assuming an increasingly "political" character.[45]

## VII

A student of 1917 finds it hard to escape the impression that Lenin and his followers won their victory largely by default—largely as a result of the failure of the other parties of the left to grasp the opportunities that had once been theirs. The burden of responsibility for the defeat that the concept of multi-party representative government now underwent lay most heavily on the leaders of the Menshevik and Socialist Revolutionary parties; for, unlike the Kadets, these parties were not lacking in popular support at the moment when the breakdown of the old regime called them to the center of the political stage.

Yet the failure of the leaders of the moderate left in 1917 is by no means easy to specify. Indeed, the first impression that one might draw from a comparison between the political attitudes that they now expressed and the sentiments which had been voiced by the earlier generation of Russian radicals would be the realization of how close they had finally come to the spirit of representative government. In practice, if not in theory, the Mensheviks and SRs of 1917 were no longer animated by the sense of radical estrangement from society which had traditionally impelled Russian radical circles to dismiss any but the most drastic changes in existing political and social institutions. Unlike the Radicals of the 1860's and the Bolsheviks of 1917, they were possessed by no burning desire to seize the levers of political power to destroy the old, or to install a new, framework of national life. Indeed, they were now, all too eagerly, prepared to recognize the legitimacy of the current demands and interests of other groups in Russian society, and the claims to political authority of the parties through which these groups purportedly spoke. On almost every major issue that arose in 1917—the question of peace or war, the settlement of the land question, the timing of the election to the Constituent Assembly—the majority leaders of the Mensheviks and the SRs compromised with the wishes of the rightist parties, at the price of denying the clear aspirations of their own popular following.[46]

Paradoxically, in the visage of political moderation that the Mensheviks and the SRs maintained through 1917, in the exaggerated degree to which they consistently made concessions to parties which, by a more natural logic, they might have viewed as their rivals for power, we might find the reflection of the traditional intelligentsia prejudices still present in attitudes toward representative government.

To understand the Mensheviks' and the SRs' reluctance to assume the responsibilities of power at this time, one must recall the terms under which the Russian radicals had been converted to the view that something useful could be achieved by winning a decisive voice in the political process for the constituent groups of Russian society. In the radicals' theoretical tenets at least, the conversion to the cause of political freedom had not been based on any wholehearted reconciliation to the legitimacy of the existing framework of national life. Rather, it had been justified by the historical forecast that once the existing social order was liberated from the shackles of autocracy, it would more quickly destroy itself and give birth to the socialist utopia.

To be sure, the adoption of a more dynamic view of the interplay between politics and social life had given rise among the Russian radicals to more positive attitudes toward the role of representative institutions. It had awakened in many of them a new sense of the legitimacy, or at least of the inevitability, of the presence of the variety of social and political tendencies that were now emerging in Russian life. Yet this recognition of the legitimacy of a multiparty system had been, and continued to be, phrased by most of the Russian radicals in wholly provisional terms. Until 1917 it remained an almost axiomatic article of their faith that "basic class conflicts," and therefore the legitimate existence of basic political differences, would come to an end with the establishment of socialism.

It was in part this dogma—that the legitimacy of a genuine multiparty system was not rooted in any natural order of things and was justified only for a limited historical period—which crippled the effectiveness of the right-wing Mensheviks, and even of the moderate SRs, in 1917. From this dogma the Mensheviks concluded, and taught their followers (including many of their SR allies), that they should not assume any of the prerogatives of power until "objective conditions" had finally put an end to the legitimacy of "bourgeois" rule. From this they also drew the inference that their assumption of power would coincide with the end of the legitimate tenure of bourgeois interests and bourgeois parties in Russian life. In the last analysis, it was these two beliefs which, more decisively than the political immaturity of the masses or the wiles of the Bolsheviks or even the war, trapped the parties of the moderate left and brought on the decisive defeat of representative government in 1917.

The realities of political life now confronted the moderate socialist parties with an insoluble dilemma. To refuse to assume any of the responsibilities of power would have meant, so they thought, to surrender the country to anarchy, to an eventual counterrevolution of the right or, as events actually demonstrated, to their eager Bolshevik rivals on the left. To assume all the prerogatives of power, on the other hand, would have amounted to a declaraton that the legitimate presence in Russian society of bourgeois interests and bourgeois parties had once and forever come to an end.

It may well be that at this moment of truth the Mensheviks and the majority of the SRs hesitated to assume power because they had finally come to realize the inherent falseness of the view that freedom could be maintained without a permanent recognition of the legitimate presence in political life of basic differences of values and interests. In practice, however, they strove to straddle the issue. Confronted by the evident inability of the bourgeois parties to mobilize adequate social support, they entered a coalition government to prolong the life of the democratic political order that had come into being. But, obsessed as they were by the illegitimacy of assuming political authority in such a pluralistic political context, they failed to assume the prerogatives of power, and thus failed in their duty to represent with sufficient vigor the aspirations of their own following, the majority of the Russian people.

After all, what did the mass followers of the parties of the left desire in 1917? Clearly they wanted peace and land, at virtually any price. But even more, from the opening days of the revolution, most of the workers, in Petrograd at least, appeared to feel that they were arrayed against "bourgeois society" and a "bourgeois state," as well as against the crumbling autocracy. From the first they recognized only the authority of their "own" leading organ, the Petrograd Soviet, and pressed their reluctant "representatives" in the Soviet to check the menace of "bourgeois reaction"—to take more and more of the "power" into their own hands.[47]

Such a sense of isolation from "society" had already arisen among the Petrograd workers in the closing days of 1905. But in this earlier episode, this feeling had come to them as an unwelcome discovery, as the bitter fruit of their defeats after the exhilarating days of the October general strike. Twelve years later, it assumed from the very start the character of a more belligerent, more articulate, and more generalized opposition to the whole existing political, social, and economic order.

It was the sense of the chasm that had now opened between "society," including the liberal intelligentsia, and the masses which impelled Miliukov, in the first days of 1917, to plead—in the tones of a Struve or a Maklakov—for the rights of the youthful Alexis to succeed to the throne. Much to the surprise of some of his colleagues, the leader of the Kadets now argued that it was imperative to maintain some continuity in the state power, if the country was not to descend into anarchy.[48] It was this same sense that the Provisional Government and his own party were operating in an almost complete vacuum that also impelled Miliukov to insist from the very beginning on the formal support of the Petrograd Soviet and of the moderate socialist parties.[49] The most prominent figure of the liberal intelligentsia had now been transformed in the eyes of the Petrograd workers into one of the "Messieurs, the bourgeois Ministers," and he knew it.

By July 1917 the unrest among the Petrograd workers (skillfully exploited by the Bolsheviks, to be sure) would explode into a rebellious insistence that *their* socialist representatives, *their* Soviet, take all the "power" away from the "bourgeoisie." "Take the power, you son of a bitch, since it is being offered to you," an irate worker told the frightened Chernov (then already Minister of Agriculture) during the July demonstrations.[50] In the face of such popular feelings, the more moderate socialist leaders had already felt compelled, some months earlier, to take some of the power for fear that otherwise they would shortly have to take it all.

Such problems did not embarrass a man like Lenin. He, alone among the socialist leaders, was from the first moment of his return to Russia not only prepared but eager to take all of the power—even at the price of exploiting the blind, "spontaneous" instincts of the masses. Indeed it may be argued that, in part, Lenin's image of the revolution and the revolutionary instincts of the workers had now temporarily merged. The mood of the workers in 1917 was clearly to destroy the whole existing political and social structure—the "capitalistic" as well as the autocratic state, "bourgeois" as well as "gentry" rule. And this was precisely what Lenin was now urging them to do. The task of the socialist proletariat, he argued in *State and Revolution*, was not merely to conquer the existing state structure, but to destroy it. The working class had to "shatter," "break up," "blow up," the whole existing "state machine" until "not a single stone" would be left standing.[51] This vision—along with Lenin's demagogic appeals—put him temporarily in accord with the mood of the popular masses.

To be sure, we find even in *State and Revolution* a more ambivalent view of the state than most of Lenin's rank-and-file followers were able to discern. Almost every page in this curious document reflects, under the thin coating of Marxist phraseology, an emphasis on the centrality of the role of state power in organizing, controlling, propping up (for the time being at least) the whole structure of Russian social and economic life. In terms reminiscent of the revolutionary appeals of the 1860's, *State and Revolution* repeatedly stresses the proposition that it is only after the proletarian dictatorship is consolidated that it will begin to wither away.[52]

This belief in the centrality of the role of state power was perhaps the key element in Lenin's image of the revolution. If from the very first he was so eager to wrest the "power" away from the bourgeoisie—and from any parties willing to compromise with it—it was not because he was less aware than any other socialist leader that, by all the conventional Marxist yardsticks, Russia was "still a peasant country, one of the most backward in Europe."[53] Rather it was because he assigned less significance than they to "objective" social and economic criteria, and more to the role of political power, in the overthrow of bourgeois society and in the building of socialism. Similarly, if, before and after the Bolshevik seizure of power, Lenin was so unwilling to abide by democratic electoral procedures, if he was so reluctant to let the Bolsheviks share the power with other parties, it was not simply because he was more driven than other socialist leaders by personal ambition. It was also because he was animated by a far more "generous" view of the uses to which he and his party could put the political authority imbedded in the state.[54]

Political action always represented for Lenin a crucial, and quite independent, dimension in human affairs. Throughout his career he was never willing to concede that his party should constitute merely the passive expression of the level of consciousness and organization attained by the working class which it purported to represent. Almost as consistently he tended to discern in the political authority of the state not simply the reflection of an independently developing society but perhaps the chief mold in which the attitudes and institutions of this society were shaped. And, largely for this reason, the Western view of political representation, as an instrument of control over the state by social groups in some way independent of its influence, always remained in his eyes a meaningless or at best a highly deceptive conception.

After the dissolution of the Constituent Assembly and the elimination of the representatives of all other socialist parties from any significant share in the "Soviet power," Lenin wrote, in answer to his critics:

Now it is this dialectic which the traitors, numbskulls, and pedants of the Second International could never grasp: the proletariat cannot conquer without winning a majority of the population over to its side. But to limit this winning over of the population, or to make it conditional, on "acquiring" a majority of votes in an election, *while the bourgeoisie is in power*, is an impracticable imbecility or simply cheating the workers. In order to win a majority of the population over to its side, the proletariat must first overthrow the bourgeoisie, and seize the state power into its own hands; secondly, having smashed to bits the old state apparatus, it must introduce the Soviet power, by which action it immediately undermines the dominion, authority, and influence of the bourgeoisie, and the petty-bourgeois compromisers among the majority of the nonproletarian laboring masses, through the revolutionary fulfillment of their economic needs at the expense of the exploiters.[55]

In this statement, written well before the authoritarian tendencies in Soviet life had reached their full bloom, one can already see the degree to which the Bolsheviks would feel free—by the "natural" and "logical" order of things— to use the power of their party and state to shape the conditions of "representation" in the society over which they ruled.

To be sure, the picture of the proletarian dictatorship during the "transition to socialism" that Lenin drew in 1917 was almost anarchistic in its simplicity and mildness: no independent administrative class would be needed to govern it, no special police would be needed to guard it, since it would constitute, in the most literal sense, the rule of the majority of the people.[56] In this measured, almost miserly, image of authority no specific role was even assigned to the party, the molder and guardian of the workers' consciousness which had been given such sweeping powers in the struggle to overthrow the old order.

It is at least possible that in the days before October Lenin actually visualized the role of his party—following the destruction of the autocratic and bourgeois state—as one of relatively gentle leadership and guidance rather than heavy-handed control. But the modest image of the future role of the party that he may have held at the time hinged on a false assumption which, along with so many other aspects of his outlook, he had inherited from the radicals of the 1860's: a belief that the more radical the destruction of the existing state order and of the whole complex of social and economic relations that it supported, the easier it would be eventually to establish a stateless, truly free, and harmonious society. Little, probably, did Lenin realize that, before destroying all other, independent, social and administrative forms, in a society born in a vacuum, resting solely on the ruins of the past, individuals would necessarily be compelled to look, more than ever before, for the definition of their rights and duties, for the pattern of their lives, for their very identity—not to themselves or to each other—to his new party and state.

## NOTES

1. For reasoned, if not wholly persuasive, Marxist critiques of this dominant view in Russian historical writing, see: M. S. Aleksandrov, *Gosudarstvo, biurokratiia, i absoliutizm v istorii Rossii* (St. Petersburg, 1910); M. N. Pokrovsky, *Russkaia istoriia s drevneishikh vremen* (4 vols.; Moscow, 1922–1923); M. N. Pokrovsky, ed., *Russkaia istoricheskaia literatura v klassovom osveshchenii* (Moscow, 1927); and N. L. Rubinshtein, *Russkaia istoriografiia* (Moscow, 1941).

2. For a brilliant tableau of the movement of opinion during the reign of Alexander II, see A. A. Kornilov, *Obshchestvennoe dvizhenie pri Aleksandre II* (Moscow, 1909). For briefer sketches, see A. A. Kornilov, "Istoricheskii ocherk epokhi 60-kh godov," in D. N. Ovsianiko-Kulikovsky, ed., *Istoriia russkoi literatury XIX veka* (5 vols.; Moscow, 1908–1911), III, 9–41; and L. Martov, "Obshchestvennyia i umstvennyia techeniia 70-kh godov," *ibid.*, IV, 1–52.

3. For a lucid summary of Pobedonostsev's conception of the state, see Robert F. Byrnes, "Pobedonostsev on the Instruments of Russian Government," in Ernest J. Simmons, ed., *Continuity and Change in Russian and Soviet Thought* (Cambridge, Mass., 1955), 114–128.

4. See B. E. Nolde, *Iurii Samarin i ego vremia* (Paris, 1926), 119–121, 188–189; and B. B. Veselovsky, *Istoriia zemstva za sorok let* (St. Petersburg, 1911). III, 14–22.

5. For a summary of Slavophile views about the zemstvo institutions, see Veselovsky, III, 19–32.

6. For Chicherin's contemporary views on the proper functioning of the state, see B. N. Chicherin, *O narodnom predstavitel'stve* (Moscow, 1866); and *Vospominaniia Borisa Nikolaevicha Chicherina. Moskva sorokovykh godov* (Moscow, 1929), 283 ff.

7. See especially "Bazarov," in *Sochineniia D. N. Pisareva* (St. Petersburg, 1894), II, 377–378.

8. For the texts of these programs, see V. L. Burtsev, *Za sto let, 1800–1896* (2 vols.; London, 1897), I, 25–152.

9. See, for example, "Molodaia Rossiia" (1862), *Nabat*, no. 1 (1875), and "Narodnaia volia" (Program of Executive Committee, 1879), in Burtsev, I, 44, 134–135, 150–152.

10. See, for example, "Nasha programma," *Vpered*, no. 1 (1873), *Zemlia i volia*, no. 1 (1878), and "Pismo k byvshim tovarishcham," *Chernyi peredel*, no. 1 (1880), in Burtsev, I, 106–112, 136–138, and 203–208.

11. For surveys of the trends of opinion within the liberal movement during this period, see I. P. Belokonsky, *Zemskoe dvizhenie* (2nd ed., Moscow, 1914), chs. 1–2; and Veselovsky, III, chs. 1–12.

12. M. P. Dragomanov, *Liberalizm i zemstvo v Rossii, 1858–1883* (Geneva, 1889), 43.

13. The full text of this manifesto may be found in Burtsev, I, 200–202. See also "Nasushchnyi vopros" (1894), a fuller statement of the party's credo drawn up by Bogdanovich; and the background article by Aptekman, "Partii 'Narodnago Prava' po lichnym vospominaniiam," in *Byloe* (St. Petersburg, July 1907).

14. "Chego nam nuzhno" and "Nachalo Kontsa" (1892), in Burtsev, I, 251–256.

15. Burtsev, I, 255.

16. See, for example, G. V. Plekhanov, *Sotsializm i politicheskaia borba* (Geneva, 1883), and his *Nashi raznoglasiia* (Geneva, 1885).

17. Cf. the organization in the winter of 1893 of the *Peterburgskaia Gruppa Osvobozhdenii Truda*. For fuller discussion, see Leopold H. Haimson, *The Russian Marxists and the Origins of Bolshevism* (Cambridge, Mass., 1955), chs. 3–4.

18. G. V. Plekhanov, *O zadachakh sotsialistov v borbe s golodom v Rossii* (1893), in *Sochineniia*, (Moscow, 1923–1927), III, 405. See also P. B. Akselrod, "K voprosu o sovremennykh zadachakh i taktike russkikh sotsial demokratov," and "Istoricheskoe polozhenie i vzaimnoe otnoshenie liberal'noi i sotsialisticheskoi demokratii" (Geneva, 1898).

19. See, for example, V. V. (V. P. Vorontsov), *Sud'by kapitalizma v Rossii* (St. Petersburg, 1882), and Nikolai-on (N. F. Danielson), *Ocherki nashego poreformennago obshchesvennago khoziaistva* (St. Petersburg, 1893).

20. See, for example, Nikolai-on, "Apologii vlasti deneg," *Russkoe bogatstvo*, I (1895), and V. V., "Proizvoditel'nye klassy i intelligentsia v Rossii," *Novoe slovo*, (March 1896).

21. See D. N. Shipov, *Vospominaniia i dumy o perezhitom* (Moscow, 1918), 145 ff.

22. See V. A. Maklakov, *Vlast' i obshchestvennost' na zakate staroi Rossii* (Paris, 1936), and *Iz vospominaniia* (New York, 1954); also Michael Karpovich, "Two Types of Russian Liberalism: Maklakov and Miliukov," in Simmons, 129–143.

23. For a convenient summary of the activities of the Osvobozhdenie, see George Fischer, *Russian Liberalism* (Cambridge, Mass., 1958), chs. 5, 6.

24. See "Germanskie vybory," *Osvobozhdenie*, no. 25 (June 1903).

25. See especially "Krest'ianskoe dvizhenie," *Revoliutsionnaia rossiia*, no. 8 (June 1902), and "Programnye voprosy," I and III, in *Rev. ros.*, nos. 11, 13 (September, November, 1902).

26. See "Novoe vystuplenie russkikh liberalov," *Rev. ros.*, no. 9 (July 1902), and "Oppozitsiia ego Velichestva i g. von-Plehve," *Rev. ros.*, no. 13 (November 1902).

27. See N. Novobrantsev (A. V. Peshekhonov), "Osnovnye voprosy rev. programmy," *Rev. ros.*, nos. 32, 33 (September, October 1903).

28. See "Sostav liberal'noi partii," *Rev. ros.* (October 1903), and "Sotsialisty-revoliutsionery i nesotsialisticheskaia demokratiia," *Rev. ros.* no. 56 (December 1904).

29. See Novobrantsev, and "Proekt programmy partii S-Rev," *Rev. ros.*, no. 46 (May 1904).

30. A more comprehensive discussion may be found in Haimson, ch. 8.

31. Haimson, ch. 8.

32. Haimson, ch. 8.

33. See "Otvet Zare," *Rev. ros.*, no. 4 (February 1902).

34. Dragomanov, 51.

35. V. S. Voitinsky, *Gody pobed i porazhenii* (2 vols.; Berlin, St. Petersburg, Moscow, 1923–1924), I, 162. Voitinsky's memoirs constitute perhaps the most dispassionate and revealing single account of 1905.

36. See the remarkably dispassionate account in F. Dan and N. Cherevanin, "Soiuz 17 Oktiabria," in Y. O. Martov, D. Maslov, A. Potresov, eds., *Obshchestvennoe dvizhenie v Rossii v nachale XX — go veka* (3 vols.; St. Petersburg, 1909–1914), III.

37. See especially, "Iz razmyshlenii o russkoi revoliutsii," in P. B. Struve, *Patriotica* (St. Petersburg, 1911), 20–43.

38. See, for example, Kovalevsky's "Vzaimootnoshenie svobody i obshchestvennoi

solidarnosti," in K. Arsenev, ed., *Intelligentsiia v Rossii* (Moscow, 1910); and Miliukov's *Russia and Its Crisis* (Chicago, 1906).

39. See contributions by N. A. Berdiaev, S. N. Bulgakov, M. O. Gershenzon, A. S. Ozgoev, B. A. Kistiakovsky, and P. B. Struve, in M. O. Gershenzon, ed., *Vekhi* (Moscow, 1909). Also N. A. Berdiaev, *Dukhovnyi krizis intelligentsii* (Moscow, 1910); B. A. Kistiakovsky, *Stranitsy proshlago. K istorii konstitutsionnago dvizheniia v Rossii* (Moscow, 1912); A. S. Izgoev, *Russkoe obshchestvo i revoliutsiia* (Moscow, 1910); and P. B. Struve, *Patriotica* (St. Petersburg, 1911).

40. Entitled "Intelligentsiia i revoliutsiia."

41. See particularly "Velikaia Rossiia," *Rus. mysl'*, I (1908), and "Otryvki o gosudarstve," *Rus. mysl'*, V (1908), in *Patriotica*, 73–108.

42. See N. Avksentev and others, *Vekhi kak znamenie nashego vremeni* (Moscow, 1910), especially the contributions by L. Shishko and N. Gardenin (V. M. Chernov).

43. See A. Martynov, "Istoriia konstitutsionno-demokraticheskoi partii," and Cherevanin in *Obshchestvennoe dvizhenie*, III.

44. See A. Blok, *Intelligentsiia i revoliutsiia* (St. Petersburg, 1918), a collection of articles written between 1905 and 1917.

45. The statistical data published by the Ministry of Trade and Industry list 466 strikes involving 105,110 workers in 1911, 2,032 strikes involving 725,491 workers in 1912, 2,404 strikes involving 887,096 workers in 1913, and 3,466 strikes involving roughly 1,300,000 workers during the first seven months of 1914 (the highest figure since 1906). Of these totals the following percentages are listed as "political": 5.1 per cent of the strikes, 8 per cent of the strikers in 1911, 64 per cent of the strikes and 75 per cent of the strikers in 1912, 54 per cent of the strikes and 56 per cent of the strikers in 1913, and 70 per cent of the strikes (2,565) and 75 per cent of the strikers (1,059,111) in 1914. These figures only cover strikes in factories under governmental inspection. See Ministerstvo torgovli i promyshlennosti, *Svod otchetov fabrichnykh inspektorov* for the years 1911, 1912, 1913, and 1914 (St. Petersburg, 1912, 1913, 1914, 1915).

46. The literature on 1917 is, of course, enormous. The accounts that I have found most useful are P. N. Miliukov, *Istoriia vtoroi russkoi revoliutsii* (Sofia, 1921–1924), I, pts. 1–3; and *Vospominaniia* (New York, 1955), II; Oliver H. Radkey, *The Agrarian Foes of Bolshevism* (New York, 1958), a splendid study of the SR's in 1917; and N. Sukhanov (N. N. Gimmer) *Zapiski o revoliutsii* (7 vols.; Berlin, St. Petersburg, Moscow, 1922–1923).

47. There is substantial agreement on this general point between Miliukov and Sukhanov, two observers of quite different political views, but equal political acumen. See Miliukov, *Istoriia*, I, pt. 1, chs. 2–4, and Sukhanov, I, chs. 1–6.

48. See Miliukov, *Istoriia*, I, pt. 1, 53–56, and *Vospominaniia*, II, 316–318.

49. Miliukov, *Istoriia*, I, pt. 1, 46–49.

50. Miliukov, *Istoriia*, I, pt. 1, 244.

51. See *State and Revolution*, Vanguard Press edition (New York, 1929), 135, 138, 144, 146–147, 218–219.

52. Lenin repeatedly denounces the view of the Marxist "opportunists" that capitalism can be eliminated without the complete ovethrow of the bourgeois state, without the most ruthless elimination of its political and administrative institutions and relations (pages 125–126, 128–129, 210–211, 213, 220). But he is equally impelled to point out to his opponents on the left, the Anarchists, that during the transition to Communism, the power of the state will be an indispensable lever for the class transformation — for the suppression of the evil minority by the majority (pages 166–170, 216–217, 220–221).

53. "Farewell Letter to the Swiss Workers" (April 8, 1917), in *Sochineniia* (3rd ed., Moscow, 1935–1937), XXIX, 343.

54. See Leonard Schapiro, *The Origin of Communist Autocracy* (Cambridge, Mass., 1955), part 1, for a splendid account of the evolution of Lenin's attitude toward the seizure of power and collaboration with other socialist parties in 1917.

55. In *Sochineniia* (3rd ed.), XXIV, 641.

56. See *State and Revolution*, 149–151, 155–156, 165, 195, 205–206.

# The Problem of Social Stability in Urban Russia, 1905-1917

## LEOPOLD HAIMSON

### I

When a student of the origins of 1917 looks back through the literature that appeared on the subject during the 1920's and early 1930's, he is likely to be struck by the degree of consensus in Soviet and Western treatments of the problem on two major assumptions. The first of these, then almost as widely entertained by Western as by Soviet historians, was that, just like other "classical" revolutions, the Revolution of 1917 had to be viewed, not as a historical accident or even as the product of immediate historical circumstances, but as the culmination of a long historical process—stretching back to the abolition of serfdom, if not to the appearance at the beginning of the nineteenth century of the Russian revolutionary intelligentsia. The second, balancing, assumption, which even Soviet historians were then still usually prepared to accept, was that, notwithstanding its deep historical roots, this revolutionary process had been substantially accelerated by the additional strains imposed on the Russian body politic by the First World War.

To be sure, even the sharing of these two assumptions allowed for a range of conflicting interpretations and evaluations of the Revolution and its background. Yet it made, however tenuously, for a common universe of discourse, transcending the insuperable values that were already supposed to separate "Marxist" and "bourgeois" historians. The years of the Stalin era and the Cold War have seen the disappearance of this common universe of discourse, and the emergence in its stead—particularly in Soviet and Western representations of the decade immediately leading up to the Revolution of 1917—of two almost completely incongruent, and almost equally monolithic, points of view.

The first of these, which Soviet historians have advanced to demonstrate the *zakonomernost'*, the historical logic (and therefore the historical legitimacy) of October, distinguishes in the years immediately preceding the First World War

FROM Leopold Haimson, "The Problem of Social Stability in Urban Russia, 1905–1917," *Slavic Review*, Part One: XXIII, No. 4 (December 1964), 619–642; Part Two: XXIV, No. 1 (March 1965), 1–22. Reprinted by permission of the American Association for the Advancement of Slavic Studies.

the shape of a new, rapidly mounting "revolutionary upsurge." According to the periodization that has become established for this stereotype, the first modest signs that the period of "reaction" that had descended on Russian society with the Stolypin coup d'état had come to an end appeared as early as 1910–11. At first, the new revolutionary upsurge built up only very slowly, and it was only in April-May, 1912, in the wake of the Lena goldfields massacre, that it really began to gather momentum. From this moment on, however, the revolutionary wave is seen as mounting with such dramatic swiftness that by the summer of 1914 the country was ripe for the decisive revolutionary overturn for which the Bolsheviks had been prepating since the summer of 1913. In this scheme, obviously, the war is not viewed as contributing decisively to the unleashing of the revolutionary storm. On the contrary, it is held that by facilitating the suppression of Bolshevik Party organizations and arousing, however briefly, "chauvinistic" sentiments among the still unconscious elements in the laboring masses, its outbreak temporarily retarded the inevitable outcome. It was only in late 1915 that the revolutionary movement resumed the surge which two years later finally overwhelmed the old order.

Partly as a response to this Soviet stereotype and to the gross distortions of evidence that its presentation often involves, we have witnessed during the past quarter of a century the crystallization in many Western representations of the origins of 1917 of a diametrically different, and equally sweeping, point of view. It is that between the Revolution of 1905 and the outbreak of the First World War a process of political and social stabilization was under way in every major sphere of Russian life which, but for the extraneous stresses that the war imposed, would have saved the Russian body politic from revolution—or at least from the radical overturn that Russia eventually experienced with the Bolshevik conquest of power.

It is important to note that not all the data on which these conflicting Western and Soviet conceptions rest are as radically different as their composite effects suggest. Indeed, as far as the period stretching from the Stolypin coup d'état to 1909–10 is concerned ("the years of repression and reaction," as Soviet historians describe them), it is possible to find in Soviet and Western accounts a rough consensus *on what actually happened*, however different the explanations and evaluations that these accounts offer of the events may be.

For example, even Soviet historians are prepared to recognize the disintegration that the revolutionary movement underwent during these years: the success, even against the Bolshevik underground, of the government's repressive measures; the "desertion" of the revolutionary cause by so many of the hitherto radical members of the intelligentsia; the sense of apathy that temporarily engulfed the masses of the working class. Soviet historians also recognize the new rationale inherent in the Regime of the Third of June—the government's attempt to widen its basis of support by winning the loyalties of the well-to-do sector of the city bourgeoisie. And they emphasize, even more than is warranted, the willingness of these elements of the "counterrevolutionary" bourgeoisie to seek, within the framework of the new institutions, an accommodation with the old regime and its gentry supporters. To be sure, Soviet historians are less prepared than their Western confrères to concede the progress that was actually achieved during the Stolypin period in the modernization of Russian life. But the basic trends that they detect during these years—in both government policy and public opinion—are not, for all that, so drastically different.

Where the minimal concensus I have just outlined completely breaks down is in the interpretation of the period stretching from 1910–11 to the outbreak of the First World War. What is basically at stake, as we have seen, is that while Soviet historiography discerns, beginning in the waning days of the Third Duma, the onset of a new, rapidly mounting, revolutionary upsurge, most Western historians are not prepared to concede the validity of any such periodization. On the contrary, with the growing impact of the Stolypin reforms in the Russian countryside and the increasing vitality displayed by the zemstvo and other institutions of local self-government, they find the processes of modernization and westernization which they see at work in the earlier period now sweeping even more decisively into the rural and provincial corners of national life. To be sure, many Western historians do recognize the alarming note introduced on the eve of the war by the growing clash between the reactionary attitudes of government circles and the liberal expectations of society (a crisis often excessively personalized in their accounts as a consequence of Stolypin's assassination). But most of them are drawn to the conclusion that in the absence of war this crisis could and would have been resolved without deep convulsions, through the more or less peaceful realization by the liberal elements of Russian society of their long-standing demand for genuine Western parliamentary institutions.

Oddly enough, the completely different representations entertained by Western and Soviet historians of the immediate prewar years rest, in part, on inferences drawn from a phenomenon on which both schools of thought concur —the fact that beginning in 1910–11, the industrial sector of the Russian economy recovered from the doldrums into which it had fallen at the turn of the century and underwent a new major upsurge. Soviet historians are less apt to emphasize the more self-sustained and balanced character that this new industrial upsurge assumes in comparison with the great spurt of the 1890's, and they are less sanguine about its long-range prospects, but they do not deny the fact of the spurt itself. On the contrary, they consider it the major "objective factor" underlying the revival of the Russian labor movement and the recovery of the Bolshevik Party that they distinguish during these years.

It is here that we come to the root of the disagreement between Western and Soviet historians on the dynamics of the prewar period and, more broadly, on the origins of the Russian Revolution. Even as cautious and sophisticated a historian as Alexander Gerschenkron sees in Russia's economic development on the eve of the war, in contrast to the admittedly socially onerous industrial growth of the 1890's, a factor making for social and political stabilization. And what is really the crux of the issue—if only because it involves the core of the Soviet historians' case—Gerschenkron and other Western commentators find this stabilizing effect of Russia's economic progress on the eve of the war reflected in a perceptible lessening of social and political tensions in both the countryside and the working class districts of the cities. "To be sure," he concedes, "the strike movement of the workers was again gaining momentum" since April, 1912. But the economic position of labor was clearly improving, and "in the resurgence of the strike movement, economic problems seemed to predominate." Gerschenkron recognizes that "in the specific conditions of the period any wage conflict tended to assume a political character because of the ready interventions of police and military forces on behalf of management. . . . But this did not mean that the climate of opinion and emotion within the labor movement was becoming more revolutionary. As shown by the history of European countries (such as Austria and Belgium), sharp political struggles marked the period of formation of labor movements that in actual fact, though not always in the language used, were committed to reformism. There is little doubt that the Russian labor movement of those years was slowly turning toward revision and trade unionist lines."[1]

Against this alleged background of the growing moderation of the Russian labor movement, the picture that Western accounts usually draw of the fortunes of the Bolshevik Party during the immediate pre-war years is a dismal one. Thus, for example, Leonard Schapiro's treatment of this period lays primary stress on the state of political paralysis to which Lenin and his followers appear to have driven thenselves by July, 1914; on the isolation of the Bolshevik faction within the political spectrum of the RSDRP, as demonstrated by the line-up at the conclusion of the Brussels Conference called in July, 1914, by the International, at which the representatives of all other factions and nationality parties in the RSDRP with the single exception of the Latvians sided against the Bolsheviks; on the havoc wrought in Bolshevik Party cadres by periodic police arrests, guided by Okhrana agents successively hidden at all levels of the party apparatus; on the alleged permanent loss of popularity that the Bolsheviks suffered among the workers beginning in the fall of 1913 as a result of their schismatic activity, particularly in the Duma; on the ultimate blow to the Bolsheviks' prestige inflicted by the exposure of their most popular spokesman in Russia, Roman Malinovsky, as just another *agent provocateur*. "There was more unity now [at the close of the Brussels Conference] on the non-bolshevik side than ever before," Schapiro concludes:

With the weight of the International behind them there was more likelihood than there had been in 1910 that the menshevik leaders would find the necessary courage to break with Lenin for good if he persisted in his policy of disunity at all costs. If Lenin were isolated in his intransigence, there was every chance that many of his "conciliator" followers, who had rejoined him in 1912, would break away again. The bolshevik organization was, moreover, in a poor state in 1914, as compared with 1912. The underground committees were disrupted. There were no funds, and the circulation of *Pravda* had fallen drastically under the impact of the split in the Duma "fraction."[2]

In substance, like many other Western historians, Schapiro considers that by July, 1914, a death sentence had been pronounced against the Bolshevik Party, which but for the outbreak of war would shortly have been carried out.

The contrast between this picture and the accounts of Soviet historians is, of course, quite startling. It is not only that their conception of the twenty-seven months leading up to the war is dominated by the image of a majestically rising strike movement which month by month, day by day, became more political in character and revolutionary in temper. It is also that they see this movement as one dominated, in the main, by a now mature, "class conscious," hereditary proletariat, hardened by the experience of the Revolution of 1905 and the years of reaction, and directed by a revived Bolshevik Party to whose flag, at the beginning of 1914, "four-fifths of all the workers of Russia" had rallied. To be sure, the party was faced in its unswerving drive toward revolution by the opposition of various factions of Russian Social Democracy. But according to the Soviet view, these factions represented by the summer of 1914 little more than empty shells resting mainly on the support of "bourgeois opportunist" *intelligenty* in Russia and the emigration. The correctness of the party's course since the Prague Conference of January, 1912, and the Krakow and Poronin Conferences of 1913—of rejecting any compromise with these "bourgeois opportunist" elements, of combining economic and political strikes and mass demonstrations in a single-minded drive toward an "all-nation political strike leading to an armed uprising"—is considered amply confirmed by the evidence that in July, 1914, such an all-nation strike was already "under way" and an armed uprising "in the offing."[3] Indeed, Soviet historians allege, the revolutionary upsurge had reached such a level by the beginning of 1914 that even the leading circles of the "counterrevolutionary" bourgeoisie had come to realize the irreparable "crash" of the Regime of the Third of June.[4]

What are the realities submerged beneath these harshly conflicting representations? Any careful examination of the evidence in contemporary primary sources suggests, it seems to me, that the vision advanced by some Western historians of the growing moderation of the Russian labor movement can be even partially upheld only for the period stretching from the Stolypin coup d'état to the spring and summer of 1912. This, almost up to its conclusion, was a period of relative labor tranquillity, as in a context of economic stagnation the masses of the Russian working class relapsed into apathy, after the defeat of their great expectations of 1905.

It was in this ultimately deceptive setting of labor peace, and of the futile and increasingly degrading spectacle of the Bolsheviks' collapsing underground struggle (this was the classic period of Bolshevik "expropriations"), that the leaders of the Menshevik faction began to articulate the philosophy and programs of an open labor party and labor movement. The current task of Social Democracy, they insisted, was not to pursue in the undergound, under the leadership of a handful of intelligentsia conspirators, now clearly unattainable maximalist objectives. It was to outline for the labor movement goals, tactics, and organizational forms which, even within the narrow confines of the existing political framework, would enable the masses of the working class to struggle, day by day, for tangible improvements in their lives and to become through the experience of this struggle "conscious" and responsible actors—capable of making their own independent contribution to the vision of a free and equitable society. Not only did the Menshevik "Liquidators"[5] articulate this vision of an open labor party and labor movement during these years but they appeared to be making progress in erecting the scaffolding of the institutions through which the vision was to be realized. They were seeking to organize open trade unions, cooperatives, workers' societies of self-improvement and self-education, and workers' insurance funds: organs intended not only to help the worker but also to enable him to take his life into his own hands. Even more significantly, the Menshevik "Liquidators" appeared to be succeeding during this period in developing, really for the first time in the history of the Russian labor movement, a genuine workers' intelligentsia animated by their own democratic values, which, it seems, would have been far more capable than any self-appointed intelligentsia leadership of eventually providing an effective bridge between educated society and the masses of the workers, thus fulfilling at long last Akselrod's and Martov's dream of "breaking down the walls that separate the life of the proletariat from the rest of the life of this country."

To be sure, in 1910–11, the Mensheviks' workers' intelligentsia still appeared very thin, and the number and size of their open labor unions pitifully small in comparison with the size of the labor force, or indeed with the level that the organization of the working class had reached on the eve of the Stolypin coup d'état. And even these puny shoots were being periodically cut down by the authorities, with only the feeblest echoes of protest from the still somnolent labor masses.

Thus even in this early (and in certain respects most successful) period of the Mensheviks' struggle for a Europeanized labor movement one must distinguish a considerable gap between vision and tangible achievement. The private correspondence of Menshevik leaders during 1909, 1910, and 1911 is replete with despondent statements about the "depression" and "fatigue" prevailing among the older generation of the Menshevik movement at home and in the emigration, about the failure to draw new members into the movement, about the negligible number of "praktiki" actively engaged on the new arena of the open labor movement—in substance, about the wholesale withdrawal from political and social concerns that seemed to have accompanied the radical intelligentsia's recoil from the underground struggle. Most party members, these letters suggest, had in fact withdrawn from party activities and were wholly absorbed in the prosaic if arduous struggle to resume a normal, day-to-day, existence.[6]

Beginning in the winter of 1909–10 the gloom in these letters was occasionally lifted by reports of the travails that Lenin and his followers were experiencing, now that they had split with Bogdanov and his followers. Such consoling news about the difficulties of their political opponents continued to appear in the correspondence of Menshevik leaders up to the end of 1911, but what chiefly kept up their spirits during these lean years was the expectation that things were bound to improve, once Russian society emerged, as it necessarily would, from its current state of political apathy.

After all, could not the contrast between reality and dreams be attributed not only to the immaturity of the labor movement but also to the obstacles thrown in its path by the repressive measures of the authorities? Once the expected political revival occurred, was it not to be expected that a more progressive Duma, supported by an aroused public, would legislate the necessary legal safeguards for the open labor organizations from which a massive and yet self-conscious and self-disciplined workers' movement would at long last emerge? In his correspondence with Potresov, Martov discerned the approach of such a turning point in the movement of opinion as early as November, 1909: "The signs are multiplying " that "the counterrevolution is ending," he then wrote hopefully to his somewhat more bearish colleague. "And if the course of events is not artificially forced, and if, as is almost unquestionable, two to three years of industrial upsurge lie before us, the time of the elections [to the Fourth Duma] can provide the occasion for the turning point [*perelom*]."[7]

Martov's forecast actually proved too conservative. It was not in the fall but in the spring of 1912 that the break he awaited occurred, under the immediate impact of the Lena goldfields massacre. The news of the massacre provoked a great outburst of public protest and, what was more important, a veritable explosion in the Russian working class. Between April 14 and 22, close to 100,000 workers struck in Petersburg alone, and the total number of strikers in the country as a whole probably reached about 250,000. This wave of protest strikes and demonstrations persisted almost without interruption through mid-May. May Day, 1912, saw nearly half a million workers out on the streets, the highest number since 1905, and this was a correct augury of the incidence and scope of political strikes and demonstrations during the balance of the year. Even the official statistics compiled by the Factory Inspectors of the Ministry of Trade and Industry, which undoubtedly were seriously underestimated, recorded that close to 550,000 workers had participated in political strikes during 1912, a level well below that of the revolutionary years 1905–6 but much higher than that of any other previous years in the history of the Russian labor movement.[8]

In the light of these awesome developments the labor commentator of the Kadet newspaper *Riech'* observed in his yearly review of the Russian labor scene:

One must recognize that the peculiarity of the movement of 1912 was the great rise in the number of political strikes. . . . The general picture of the labor movement for the past year allows one to say with assurance that if the industrial revival continues, and it would appear that it will the year 1913 may bring such an upsurge of labor energy that it may vividly remind one of 1905. The general results of 1912 are unquestionably extremely notable, and filled with implications for the immediate future.[9]

The strike statistics for 1913 would in fact reveal a further upsurge of the labor movement, though not one of quite the dimensions envisaged by the *Riech'* commentator. The yearly compilations of the Factory Inspectors showed but a relatively modest rise in the total number of strikes and strikers, and indeed indicated a small drop in the number of those listed as political. However, the monthly breakdowns of these figures registered such a drop only in April and

May, for which a much smaller number of political strikes and strikers were listed than for the corresponding months of 1912—the exceptionally agitated aftermath of the Lena goldfields massacre.[10] Thus it would be questionable to infer that there occurred in the course of 1913 a general decline of political unrest among the Russian working class. The prevailing opinion among contemporary observers was that the year had instead been marked by a rise in the intensity of both political and economic strikes.[11]

The correctness of this diagnosis was to be confirmed by developments in the following year. The first half of 1914 would witness an unprecedented swell of both political and economic strikes. Even the overconservative estimates of the Factory Inspectors reported for this period a total of 1,254,441 strikers. Of these, 982,810 were listed as political—a figure almost as high as that for 1905, the previous peak year, even though the calculations for 1914 covered only the first six months of the year, and excluded for the first time the highly industrialized Warsaw gubernia.[12]

What realities do these statistical aggregates actually reflect? To justify their belief in the increasingly reformist character of the Russian labor movement on the eve of the war, some Western writers have argued that the very distinction drawn in the reports of the Factory Inspectors between political and economic strikes is artificial: Economic strikes were quick to assume a political character when they ran up against brutal police interference, and were often listed as such in the reports of the Factory Inspectors. This is a correct observation, often noted in contemporary reports of the labor scene. But as Menshevik commentators continuously emphasized, the opposite was just as often the case. Strikes ostensibly economic in character often demonstrated by the unrealistic character of their objectives and the impatience and violence of the tactics with which they were conducted that they merely provided an excuse for the expression of political unrest. This appears to have been true even in 1913, the one year of the "upsurge" in which, according to official statistics, economic motifs were predominant in the strike movement. The *Russian Review* noted in its yearly review of the labor scene:

> Since early spring, an irregular and chaotic strike movement has been in progress. The strikes, sometimes without any reason at all [sic], have rarely benefited the workers directly. Most are manifestations of extreme dissatisfaction with the conditions of public life rather than an expression of clearly formulated economic grievances. A conference of manufacturers in Moscow decided that preventive measures were impossible as the strikes were political. The Mensheviki pointed out the harmfulness of mere disorderly and inconsiderate striking, but the movement continued its plunging, incalculable way.[13]

Indeed, it appears that from the Lena massacre to the outbreak of war, the progress of the strike movement was characterized by an almost continuous flow in which political and economic currents were inextricably mixed: quite often, even the ostensible objectives of individual strikes combined political and economic demands; and even more notably, the individual waves of "economic" strikes and "political" strikes and demonstrations proved mutually reinforcing, each seemingly giving the next additional impetus, additional momentum. By the beginning of the summer of 1914, contemporary descriptions of the labor scene forcibly suggest, the workers, especially in Petersburg, were displaying a growing spirit of *buntarstvo*—of violent if still diffuse opposition to all authority—and an instinctive sense of class solidarity,[14] as they encountered the repressive measures of state power and what appeared to them the indifference of privileged society.

However, the most telling evidence against the thesis that beneath the surface the Russian labor movement was actually developing a reformist and trade unionist orientation, is the reception that the workers gave, as the war approached, to Bolshevik as against Menshevik appeals.

In the first months of the new upsurge, Menshevik commentators had naturally been heartened by the impressive revival of the labor movement. Writing shortly after the "grandiose political strikes" of April and May, 1912, Fedor Dan called them not only a "turning point in the Russian labor movement" but also "the beginning of the liquidation of the Regime of the Third of June." Dan even quoted approvingly the observation of a correspondent of *Riech'* (in its issue of May 11, 1912) to the effect that the workers were now opposing themselves to the rest of society and that the working class movement was generally assuming "a much more sharply defined class character" than it had had in 1905. This, Dan observed, was merely a reflection of the growing maturity and organization of the proletariat and an indication of the successful work that the Menshevik "Liquidators" had conducted during the years of reaction. Besides, *Riech'* was being expediently silent about the other half of the picture. If the workers were now opposing themselves to society, so society was now opposing itself to the workers:

To the growing class maturity of the proletariat corresponds a similar growing class maturity of the bourgeoisie. And the "support" that now surrounds the labor movement has little in common with the foggy romantic support which in 1905 impelled *Osvobozhdenie* to exclaim: "How enchanting the workers are" and Mr. Struve to declare triumphantly: "We have no enemies to the left." . . . The proletariat has ceased to be "enchanting" in the eyes of bourgeois society, and the "support" of this society is confined to those minutes in which the proletarian movement constitutes a necessary factor in its own emancipation.[15]

In this passage Dan was describing approvingly what would indeed become one of the major conditioning factors in the development of the labor movement during the new upsurge—the break in the fragile and tenuous psychological ties that had been so painfully built up between the workers and the opposition circles of educated society during the decade leading up to the Revolution of 1905. But if the Mensheviks were originally inclined to consider this mutual confrontation of workers and society a positive indication of the growing class maturity of both, they were soon to change their minds.

The first signs of alarm were sounded within a few months, with the returns, in the fall of 1912, of the elections to the Fourth Duma. In these elections, as Lenin and his followers untiringly emphasized thereafter, Bolshevik candidates won in six of the nine labor curiae in Russia, including all six of the labor curiae in the major industrial provinces. In their published commentaries on the election returns the Menshevik leaders pointed out (most often quite accurately) the major flaws in the Bolshevik claims to a sweeping victory,[16] but in their private correspondence, they conceded more readily that, whatever the extenuating circumstances, the results of the elections in the labor curiae had been a definite setback. Martov observed in a letter to Potresov: "The failure of the Mensheviks in the labor curiae (partially compensated by [their] moral victory in Petersburg) shows once more that Menshevism caught on too late to the reviving danger of Leninism and overestimated the significance of its temporary wholesale disappearance."[17]

The developments on the labor scene in 1913, and especially during the first six months of 1914, would amply confirm Martov's estimate of the significance of these election returns. Not only were these eighteen months generally characterized by a stready rise in the spirit of *buntarstvo*, of the elemental, revolutionary explosiveness of the strike movement, particularly in the capital. Not only were they marked by a growing responsiveness on the part of the amorphous and largely anonymous committees in charge of the strikes, as well as of the workers' rank and file, to the reckless tactics of the Bolsheviks and to their "unmutilated" slogans of a "democratic republic," "eight-hour day," and "confiscation of gentry lands." They also saw the Mensheviks lose control of the open labor organizations they had struggled so hard to build. From the spring and summer of 1913, when the Bolsheviks, heeding the resolutions of the Krakow and Poronin Conferences, began to concentrate their energies on the conquest of the open labor organizations, the pages of the Mensheviks' journals and their private correspondence were filled with the melancholy news of the loss of one position after another—by the very Menshevik-oriented workers' intelligentsia in which the wave of the future had once been discerned.

To note but a few of the major landmarks:

In late August, 1913, the Mensheviks were routed by their Bolshevik opponents from the governing board of the strongest union in Petersburg, the Union of Metalworkers (*Soiuz metallistov*). In January, 1914, an even more bitter pill for the Menshevik initiators of the labor insurance movement, the Bolsheviks won, by an equally decisive vote, control of the labor representation on both the All Russian Insurance Council and the Petersburg Insurance Office (*Stolichnoe strakhovoe prisutstvie*). Even more surprising, by late April, 1914, they could claim the support of half the members of the newly re-elected governing board of that traditional citadel of Menshevism in the Petersburg labor movement, the Printers' Union (*Soiuz pechatnikov*). In July, 1914, when the Bolsheviks laid their case before the Bureau of the Socialist Internationale for being the only genuine representatives of the Russian working class, they claimed control of $14\frac{1}{2}$ out of 18 of the governing boards of the trade unions in St. Petersburg and to 10 out of the 13 in Moscow.[18]

To be sure, the Mensheviks' situation in the two capitals was far bleaker, and the Bolsheviks' far brighter, than anywhere else in the country. But even with this reservation, their position gave the Mensheviks little ground for comfort. As early as September, 1913, upon receiving the news of the Bolshevik victory in the elections to the Union of Metalworkers, Martov foresaw the further catastrophes that were likely to befall the Menshevik cause. "I am dejected by the story of the Unions of Metalworkers which exposes our weakness even more than we are used to," he then wrote to Potresov. "It is altogether likely that in the course of this season our positions in Petersburg will be squeezed back even further. But that is not what is awful [*skverno*]. What is worse is that from an organizational point of view, Menshevism—despite the newspaper [the Mensheviks' Petersburg organ, *Luch'*, launched in late 1912], despite everything that has been done during the past two years—remains a weak little circle [*slaben'kii kruzhok*]."[19] And at a meeting of the Menshevik faction in the Duma, in late January, 1914, the Georgian deputy, Chkhenkeli, observed in an equally catastrophic vein that the Mensheviks appeared to be losing all of their influence, all of their ties, among the workers.

Bitterest and most desperate of all were the complaints of the Menshevik trade unionists, the representatives of their now defeated workers' intelligentsia. In March, 1914, Fedor Bulkin, one of the Menshevik *praktiki* driven out of the governing board of the Union of Metalworkers six months earlier, exclaimed in the pages of *Nasha zaria*:

The masses which have recently been drawn into the trade union movement are incapable of appreciating its great significance for the proletariat. Led by the Bolsheviks, they have chased the *Likvidatory*, these valuable workers, out of all leading institutions. . . . The experienced pilots of the labor movement have been replaced by ones who are inexperienced, but close in spirit to the masses . . . for the time being, the *Likvidatory* are suffering and, in all likelihood, will continue to suffer, defeat. Bolshevism—*intelligentskii*, narrowly fractional, jacobin—has found its support in the masses' state of mind.[20]

In the concluding passage of this statement, Bulkin was reiterating the thesis (which he had already spelled out in an earlier article) that the Bolsheviks' victories had been largely attributable to the sway that the Social Democratic intelligentsia—with its narrow dogmatism, its intolerance, its factional spirit—still continued to hold over the workers' minds. Once the proletariat freed itself from this pernicious influence of the intelligentsia and grew to affirm its own independent spirit, its own self-consciousness, the Bolsheviks' strength would evaporate into thin air.[21]

Naturally, the editors of *Nasha zaria* could not allow this argument, so reeking of the old "economist" heresies, to appear without an answer. His old Iskraist spirit aroused, Martov, in the same issue of the journal, wrote a fulgurant reply. It was all too easy for Bulkin to assert that Bolshevism was an intelligentsia influence grafted onto the body of the hapless Russian working class. Even if it had had any merit in the past, his argument was ten years out of date. Where was the Bolshevik intelligentsia which supposedly still "stood on the shoulders of the proletariat?" It simply was no longer there. All of the major figures in the Bolshevik intelligentsia—Bogdanov, Lunacharsky, Rozhkov, Pokrovsky, Bazarov, and so many others had deserted Leninism. All that was left was "a handful of people with literally no names, or names it would be inexpedient to mention."[22]

If the culprit was not the pernicious influence of the intelligentsia, to whaι source was the new mood of the labor movement to be traced? The Bolsheviks had a simple explanation: The workers' new mood was merely a reflection of the growth to consciousness of a now mature hereditary Russian proletariat— recovered from the defeats of 1905, hardened by the years of reaction, and rallied solidly behind the Bolshevik Party. Needless to say, Menshevik commentators found this explanation wanting. Indeed, in their writings of the period we find them groping for precisely an opposite answer: The laboring masses which had crowded into the new labor movement during the years of the new industrial upsurge—and of the new explosive strike wave—were in the main no longer the class-conscious, mature proletariat of 1905. Some of the most acute Menshevik observers (Martov, Levitsky, Gorev, Sher) pointed specifically to the social and political effects of the influx into the industrial working class of two new strata.[23]

The first of these was the younger generation of the working class of the cities, the urban youths who had grown to working age since the Revolution of 1905— without the chastening experience of the defeats of the Revolution, or the sober- ing influence of participating in the trade unions and other labor organizations during the years of reaction. It was these youths, "hot-headed and impulsive," "untempered by the lessons of the class struggle," who now constituted the intermediary link between the leading circles of the Bolshevik Party and the laboring masses. It was they who now provided, in the main, the correspondents and distributors of Bolshevik newspapers, who instigated the workers' resolu- tions and petitions in support of Bolshevik stands, and who dominated the amorphous, *ad hoc* strike committees which were providing whatever leadership still characterized the elemental strike wave. More recently, in the spring and summer of 1913, it had been these green youths who had begun to flow from the strike committees into the open trade unions and had seized their leadership from the older generation of Menshevik trade unionists. "Here," noted one observer, "the representatives of two different periods, [men] of different habits, different practical schools—two forces of workers, "young" and "old"—have encountered one another for the first time . . . [the takeover] which occurred extremely quickly, for many almost unexpectedly, took place in an atmosphere of patricidal conflict."[24]

Of course, the cadres of the new generations of the hereditary working class of the cities would have remained leaders without followers had it not been for the influx into the labor force of a second, much more massive, new stratum. These were the recruits, usually completely unskilled, who, from 1910 on—the year of the "take-off" of the new industrial upsurge and of the turning point in the Stolypin agrarian reforms—had begun to pour into the labor armies of the cities from the countryside. It was these many thousands of ex-peasants, as yet completely unadapted to their new factory environment, "driven by instincts and feelings rather than consciousness and calculation," who gave the mass movement "its disorganized, primitive, elemental character," noted Martov's younger brother, Levitsky. Naturally, these "unconscious" masses proved most responsive to the extremist objectives and tactics advocated by the Bolsheviks: to their demands for "basic" as against "partial" reforms, to their readiness to support any strikes, regardless of their purpose and degree of organization. Above all, the Bolshevik "unmutilated" slogans of an eight-hour day, "complete democratization," "confiscation of gentry lands"—and the basic vision underlying these slogans of a grand union of workers and peasants arrayed against all of society, "from Purishkevich to Miliukov"—were calculated to sound a deep echo among these new elements of the working class, which combined with their current resentments about factory life the still fresh grievances and aspirations that they had brought from the countryside.[25]

Indeed, by the early months of 1914, the influx of these ex-peasant masses into the cities had led not only to a striking rise in the Bolshevik fortunes but also to a still relatively modest and yet notable revival among the workers of Left Populist tendencies. Commenting on this revival of Left Populism, which now threatened to replace Menshevism as the chief opposition to the Bolsheviks, Martov emphasized in a series of articles "the swilling mixture of anarchist and syndicalist tendencies with remnants of peasant urges and utopias" which appeared to animate the Left Populists' adherents. These workers might have physically left the village, he observed, but they had by no means broken their psychological ties with it: "As they face the hardships, the darkness of city life, they hold onto their dream of returning to a patch of land with their own cow and chickens . . . and they respond to the slogans of those who promised them the fulfilment of this dream."[26]

To what extent can one support with statistical evidence the emphasis that the more discerning Menshevik observers of the labor scene laid on the role played in the industrial unrest of the period by the younger generation of urban industrial workers and the recruits to the labor force from the countryside? We know, of course, that the increasingly explosive strike wave broadly coincided with an industrial upsurge which saw the Russian industrial labor force grow from some 1,793,000 in January, 1910, to approximately 2,400,000 in July, 1914, a rise of over 30 per cent. And obviously this sharp and sudden increase in the labor force could be achieved only if to the recruitment of a new generation of urban workers was added the massive inswell into the urban labor market of landless and land-poor peasants, freed of their ties to the land by the Stolypin legislation—particularly by the arbitrary provisions of the statutes of 1910 and 1911. The literature of this period is replete with reports of the influx of these raw recruits into the industrial army. But let us refine the analysis, and focus our attention on those sectors of the Russian labor force which appear to lead the contemporary strike movement, and especially those strikes which bear a distinctly political character. One can easily distinguish two such sectors. The first of these may be defined geographically: it is the labor force of the province and particularly the city of Petersburg and suburbs, which in the first six months of 1914 contributed close to 50 percent of the total of 1,254,000 strikers estimated for the country as a whole, and almost two-thirds of the 982,000 strikers listed as political. Secondly, when one compares strike statistics for different industries (as against different regions) it becomes apparent that by far the heaviest in-cidence of strikers, particularly of political strikers—in Petersburg just as in the country as a whole—is to be found among the workers in the metalworking industry.

It is notable, and undoubtedly significant, that these two sectors of the labor force—which we have singled out because of their exceptional revolutionary explosiveness—underwent during the years of the new industrial upsurge an expansion well above that of the Russian labor force as a whole: they grew by an average of roughly 50 per cent as against the national average of less than 30 per cent. If we consider the necessity of allowing for replacement as well as increases in the labor force, we may assume that by 1914 well over half of the workers in Petersburg, as well as in the metalworking industry in the country as a whole, were persons who at best had undergone a very brief industrial experience. It has already been noted that while some of these recruits were urban youths who reached working age during these years, most had to be drawn from outside the cities. In this connection, one further observation appears relevant: It is that since the beginning of the century a marked shift in the pattern of labor recruitment from the countryside into the Petersburg labor force had been taking place. As the labor supply available in Petersburg province and in other provinces with relatively developed manufacturing or handicraft industries declined, a growing percentage of the recruits into the Petersburg labor force had to be drawn from the almost purely agricultural, overpopulated, central provinces of European Russia[27]—the very provinces in which the dis-solution of repartitional tenure, achieved as often as not under irresistible administrative and economic pressure, was making itself most heavily and pain-fully felt.[28]

A vast mass of workers who combined with their resentments about the painful and disorienting conditions of their new industrial experience a still fresh sense of grievance about the circumstances under which they had been compelled to leave the village. A new generation of young workers of urban origin to lead them—impatient, romantic, singularly responsive to maximalist appeals. Our puzzle would appear to be resolved if it were not for a disconcerting fact. The conditions I have so far described, except perhaps for the presence of a somewhat lower percentage of young workers of urban origin, also largely ob-tained in other areas and sectors of the Russian labor force, which remained, however, less animated than the ones we have singled out by the spirit of *buntarst-vo* of which we have been seeking the roots. These conditions probably obtained, for example, almost as much in the Donbas as in Petersburg; and for workers in chemicals as much as for those in the metalworking industry. This is why we necessarily have to add one further element which, for obvious reasons, was gen-erally absent in most contemporary Menshevik analyses: the role exercised by Bolshevik party cadres—workers and *intelligenty* alike. If the Petersburg workers displayed greater revolutionary explosiveness, and especially greater responsive-ness to Bolshevik appeals, than the workers of the Donbas, it was undoubtedly in part because of the Petersburg workers' greater exposure to Bolshevik propaganda and agitation. Similarly, if the workers in the metalworking industry were so much more agitated politically than the workers in other industries, it was partly because the labor force in the metalworking industry consisted of a peculiar combination of skilled and unskilled, experienced and inexperienced, workers—the older and more skilled workers contributing in their contacts with the young and unskilled a long-standing exposure to revolutionary, and specifically Bolshevik, indoctrination. It is not accidental that so many of the major figures in the Bolshevik Party cadres of the period—Voroshilov, Kalinin, Kiselev, Shotman, to cite but a few—had been workers with a long *stazh* in the metalworking industry.

This is not to say that during these years the Bolshevik Party cadres in Petersburg, and especially their underground organizations, bore even a faint resemblance to the depictions of them currently offered by some Soviet historians. Penetrated from top to bottom by agents of the secret police (no less than three of the seven members of the Petersburg City Party Committee in July, 1914, were on the payroll of the Okhrana),[29] they were experiencing serious difficulties in replenishing their ranks, depleted periodically by arrests: between January and July, 1914, the Petersburg City Party Committee was riddled no less than five times by such arrests.

Yet even under these conditions the Bolshevik Party apparatus managed to survive, to retain some old and recruit some new members: younger workers, but also older workers, with a background of participation in the revolutionary underground, who in many cases had left the party during the years of reaction but were now returning to the fold; survivors of the older generation of the Bolshevik intelligentsia, but also fresh recruits from those elements in the intelligentsia youth who for temperamental reasons or because of adverse material circumstances were now attracted by the Bolsheviks' maximalist appeals. These recruits were, to be sure, not very numerous, nor was their mood representative of that of the intelligentsia as a whole. Indeed, many of them were animated by a new kind of anger and bitterness—as Berdiaev put it, the bitterness of a new incarnation of the Raznochintsy of the 1860's—whose strident quality often appeared to reflect not merely outrage about the betrayal of the revolutionary cause by the "opportunist" majority of the intelligentsia, but also a sharp sense of social antagonism: the antagonism of the young for the older and more established, of the less favored for the more fortunate members of society.[30]

And all this anger and bitterness now struck a responsive chord in the masses of the working class. Given this correspondence of mood, given the even more precise correspondence between the image of state and society that the Bolsheviks advanced and the instinctive outlook of the laboring masses, the Bolshevik Party cadres were now able to play a significant catalytic role. They succeeded, as we have seen, in chasing the Menshevik "Liquidators" out of the existing open labor organizations. They transformed these organizations into "fronts" through which they managed to absorb, if not to control, the younger workers who headed the Petersburg strike movement. Through the pages of *Pravda*, through the verbal appeals of their deputies in the Duma, by leaflet and by word of mouth, they managed to stir up and exploit the workers' embittered mood. Thus, it seems fair to say that by the outbreak of war the Bolshevik center in Petersburg, and particularly its open organizations, had developed into an organism whose arms, while still very slender and vulnerable, were beginning to extend into many corners of the life of the working class.

In January, 1914, in the reply to Bulkin from which we already quoted, the Menshevik leader Martov, dismissing the argument that all the difficulties of the "Liquidators" stemmed from the continued influence exercised by intelligentsia elements, with their accursed sectarian psychology, over the labor movement, gloomily noted the correspondence between the Bolsheviks' appeals and the workers' contemporary state of mind. The threat presented by Bolshevism, he argued, lay not in the handful of *intelligenty* and semi-*intelligenty* that it still managed to attract, but rather in the response that it had evoked, the roots that it had unquestionably sunk, among the masses of the workers themselves. Against whom had the workers struck in their spirit of *buntarstvo*? Martov harried his opponent. Against the "Liquidators," against the scaffold of the open European-type party that had been erected between 1907 and 1911 by those proletarian elements that had been genuinely indoctrinated with Marxism— in substance, against their own workers' intelligentsia, Comrade Bulkin among them. And if the workers had done so under the "*lumpen* circles of the Pravdisty," Martov concluded, it was because of all the demagogical groups in Russian society, this one, at least for the time being, was best attuned to the workers' own mood.[31]

If I might summarize my own, and to some degree, Martov's argument, it is that by 1914 a dangerous process of polarization appeared to be taking place in Russia's major urban centers between an *obshchestvo* that had now reabsorbed the vast majority of the once alienated elements of its intelligentsia (and which was even beginning to draw to itself many of the workers' own intelligentsia) and a growing discontented and disaffected mass of industrial workers, now left largely exposed to the pleas of an embittered revolutionary minority.

This is not to suggest that by the outbreak of war the Bolshevik Party had succeeded in developing a secure following among the masses of the working class. The first year of the war would show only too clearly how fragile its bonds to the supposedly conscious Russian proletariat still were. Indeed, it bears repeating that the political threat of Bolshevism in 1914 stemmed primarily not from the solidity of its organizations nor from the success of its efforts at ideological indoctrination, but from the workers' own elemental mood of revolt. That even Lenin was acutely aware of this is suggested by an Okhrana report of his instructions to the Bolshevik deputy Petrovsky in April, 1914. This report stated:

Defining the state of affairs at the present moment, Lenin expressed himself as follows:
Our victory, i.e., the victory of revolutionary Marxism, is great. The press, the insurance campaign, the trade unions, and the societies of the enlightenment, all this is ours. But this victory has its limits. . . . If we want to hold our positions and not allow the strengthening labor

movement to escape the party's sway and strike out in an archaic, diffuse movement, of which there are some signs, we must strengthen, come what may, our underground organizations. [We] can give up a portion of the work in the State Duma which we have conducted so successfully to date, but it is imperative that we put to right the work outside the Duma.[32]

Thus, two and a half months before the outbreak of the war, Lenin already detected the chief immediate threat to his party's fortunes not to his "right" but to his "left"—in the possibility of premature, diffuse, revolutionary outbreaks by the Russian working class.

The elements of strength and weakness in the Bolshevik leadership of the labor movement on the eve of war and the relative significance of this movement as a revolutionary force are graphically illustrated by the contrast between the general strike which broke out in the working class districts of Petersburg in the early days of July, 1914, and the nature of the mutual confrontation of the workers and educated society that had characterized the high tide of the Revolution of 1905. On the earlier historical occasion—in September and October, 1905—the workers of Petersburg and Moscow had rejoined, however briefly, the world of Russian educated and privileged society. Flocking out of their tawdry factory districts, they had descended into the hearts of the two capitals to join in society's demonstrations, to shout its slogans, to listen in the amphitheaters of universities and institutes to the impassioned speeches of youthful intelligentsia agitators. This had been the background of the awesome spectacle of the truly general strikes which paralyzed Petersburg and other cities of European Russia during the October days, driving the frightened autocracy to its knees.

In July, 1914, in protest against the brutal suppression by police detachments of a meeting of the Putilov workers called in support of the strike in the Baku oil fields, a strike as massive and explosive as any that had erupted among the workers in 1905 swept the outlying working class districts of Petersburg. (A call for such a general strike had been issued by the Bolsheviks' Petersburg Party Committee on the evening of July 3.) On July 7, three days after the opening of the strike, Poincaré arrived in Petersburg on a state visit to dramatize the solidity of the Franco-Russian alliance against the Central Powers. By this time, according to official estimates, over 110,000 workers had joined in the strikes. Almost all the factories and commercial establishments in the working class districts of the city were now closed, and many thousands of workers were clashing in pitched battles with Cossacks and police detachments. The news of the growing international crisis and the accounts of Poincaré's visit had crowded the reports of labor unrest out of the front pages. But even during the two days of Poincaré's stay, newspaper readers were told in the inside columns that workers were demonstrating in the factory districts, throwing rocks at the police and being fired upon in return, tearing down telegraph and telephone poles, attacking street cars, stoning their passengers, ripping out their controls, and in some cases dragging them off the rails to serve as street barricades.[33]

It was also during the two days of Poincaré's visit that some workers' demonstrations, brandishing red flags and singing revolutionary songs, sought to smash their way out of the factory districts into the center of the capital. But Cossacks and mounted police blocked their access to the bridges of the Neva as well as on the Petersburg side, and the heart of the capital remained largely still.

By the morning of July 9, the Bolsheviks' Petersburg Party Committee, sensing that the strike was doomed "due to inadequate party organizations" and "lack of weapons," decided to call on the Petersburg proletariat to go back to work. But it quickly discovered that it could not control the strike movement. The workers had now "gone berserk," according to police reports, and were "not even willing to listen" to those orators who asked them to call off the strike. Whatever element of leadership the strike still maintained would now be assumed by younger and more impatient hands. On the night of July 9, at a meeting held at Nauka i Zhizn', one of the societies of cultural enlightenment of the capital, a group of rebels against the line adopted by the Petersburg Party Committee, described in police reports as "green and immature youths" (most of them were in their early twenties), issued a resolution arguing that the current street disorders showed that "the proletariat [had gone] over to an active and spontaneous struggle" and did "not contemplate to subordinate itself in the future to any directive whatsoever." "It is imperative to assist the proletariat to organize, finally and without delay," the young party workers concluded, "to issue a call to go over to an armed uprising, and for this purpose to hurry to print leaflets and appeals with a suitable content." The Bolshevik insurgents did not actually succeed in mimeographing such an incendiary manifesto until July 12, when the strike was already drawing its last gasp and conflicting leaflets calling on the strikers to return to work were being circulated by the now desperate Party Committee.[34] In the meantime, despite the ever more massive intervention of Cossacks and police detachments, despite the dispatch to the working class districts of the capital on July 11 of a whole cavalry brigade from Tsarkoe Selo, the strike movement lurched forward, in an atmosphere of increasingly violent conflict and despair.

In a two-page review of the strike, published on July 12, the reporters whom *Riech'* had sent out to the factory districts described some of the scenes they had witnessed during the preceding three days. The biggest clashes, they agreed, had occurred on the night of July 9 and during the succeeding day. Many thousands of workers had then clashed with the police—at times fighting them with clubs, or hailing them with rocks from behind improvised barricades. Women and children had joined in building these barricades—out of telephone and telegraph poles, overturned wagons, boxes and armoires. No sooner was a demonstration dispersed, or a barricade destroyed, than the workers, after evacuating their wounded, would regroup, and clashes would start all over again. Whole districts were without light, their gas and kerosene lamps having been destroyed. Most commercial establishments were closed, particularly the wine shops and taverns which the workers themselves had shut to maintain and demonstrate the discipline in their ranks. By the evening of the twelfth, the peak of the violence was over, as army and police detachments, with drawn bayonets, patrolled the now largely deserted streets. One of the *Riech'* reporters recorded these sights (the likes of which he said he hadn't seen since 1905), and noted the

general background of devastation: the shattered street lights, the uptorn telegraph poles, the deserted barricades, the trolley cars abandoned or overturned,
the closed factories and stores. "And on the Petersburg side, the usual traffic,
the usual life, and the trolleys are moving about as usual."[35]

It was not until July 15, four days before the outbreak of the war, that order
in the factory districts of Petersburg was fully restored.

## II

The four-day interval between the last gasps of the Petersburg strike and the
outbreak of war may not altogether dispose of the thesis of Soviet historians
that only the war prevented the strike movement of July, 1914, from turning into
a decisive attack against the autocracy: after all, it may be argued that even
before the war actually broke out the rapidly gathering international crisis
acted as a brake on the revolutionary wave. Yet surely much of the conviction
of this argument pales in the light of the two glaring sources of political weakness
that the strike revealed from its very inception—weaknesses that had caused its
original Bolshevik leadership to seek to bring it to an end at least five days
before it at last petered out.

One of these sources of impotence had been the failure of the clashes in
Petersburg to set off anything like the all-national political strike which even the
Bolshevik leaders had considered (probably excessively) a necessary condition
for the armed assault against the autocracy. The unfolding of the Petersburg
strike had given rise to sympathy strikes and demonstrations in other industrial
centers: in Moscow and Warsaw, Revel, Riga, and Tallin, Kiev, Odessa, even
Tiflis. But nowhere, not even in Warsaw and Moscow, had these strikes displayed
a degree of massiveness and revolutionary intensity comparable to that of the
Petersburg movement.

Yet another factor was even more crucial: the inability of the Petersburg
workers to mobilize, in time, active support among other groups in society. To
be sure, by July 12–14 shocked editorials had begun to appear, not only in
liberal organs such as *Riech'* and *Russkiia viedomosti* but even in the conservative
*Novoe vremia*, attacking the government for its last-minute declaration of a
state of siege, condemning its labor policies as calculated only to exacerbate
further the workers' already "monstrous anger and despair," arguing that only
complete legalization of the open labor organizations could possibly restore
domestic tranquillity. But perhaps partly because of the gathering international
crisis, these appear to have been the only articulate expressions of the concern
of educated society. No demonstrations, no public meetings, no collective
petitions—no expressions of solidarity even barely comparable to those that
Bloody Sunday had evoked were now aroused. Thus, in the last analysis, the
most important source of the political impotence revealed by the Petersburg
strike was precisely the one that made for its "monstrous" revolutionary
explosiveness: the sense of isolation, of psychological distance, that separated
the Petersburg workers from educated, privileged society.

Where does this analysis leave us with respect to the general problem of political and social stability in Russian national life on the eve of the war that we posed at the beginning of this discussion? Clearly, it seems to me, the crude representations to be found in recent Soviet writings of the "revolutionary situation" already at hand in July, 1914, can hardly be sustained. Yet when one views the political and social tensions evident in Russian society in 1914 in a wider framework and in broader perspective, any flat-footed statement of the case for stabilization appears at least equally shaky.

It isn't so much, as some of the soberer Soviet accounts suggest, that the Bolshevik Party Congress scheduled for the summer of 1914 was likely to stimulate at long last the broad organization and coordination of party activities required for the conduct of a successful all-nation political strike. Or even, as Lenin firmly expected, that the continuation of the new industrial upsurge was calculated to bring workers in other industrial centers, in fairly short order, to the same pitch of revolutionary unrest as their Petersburg "vanguard." The first development was conceivable; the second, even likely. But it is probable that Lenin and his followers assigned to both somewhat exaggerated importance. If the February revolution revealed what could be achieved with a minimum degree of organization, the October seizure of power would show how decisively an overturn in Petersburg could affect the rest of the country.

A far more important source of the explosiveness of the revolutionary tendencies at work in Imperial Russia on the eve of war lay, rather, I believe, in a phenomenon which has been substantially underestimated by many Soviet and Western commentators. It is that by July, 1914, along with the polarization between workers and educated, privileged society that we outlined in the first part of this essay, a second process of polarization—this one between the vast bulk of privileged society, and the tsarist regime—appeared almost equally advanced. Unfolding largely detached from the rising wave of the labor movement, this second process could not affect its character and temper but was calculated to add a probably decisive weight to the pressure against the dikes of existing authority. By 1914 this second polarization had progressed to the point where even the most moderate spokesmen of liberal opinion were stating publicly, in the Duma and in the press, that an impasse had been reached between the state power and public opinion, which some argued could be resolved only by a revolution of the left or of the right.

Perhaps the most dramatic symptom of this growing political crisis was the progressive disintegration of existing intra- and inter-party alignments, particularly on the political spectrum of the liberal center. This political *bouleversement*, which finally came to general public notice in late 1913 and early 1914 as "the crisis of the parties," actually appears to have been developing, largely behind the scenes, from the opening days of the Fourth Duma.

As will be recalled,[36] the Menshevik leader Martov had deduced from the returns, especially in provincial cities, of the elections of the Fourth Duma the imminence of a split between what he termed the "bourgeois" and "*raznochintsy-radical*" wings of the Kadet Party. According to still unpublished testimony given by Paul Miliukov in 1927,[37] such a split did in fact develop at this time: from the fall of 1912 onward the joint meetings of the Kadet Party's Central Committee and the Kadet deputies in the Fourth Duma began to witness increasingly bitter clashes between the representatives of the now coalescing center and right wings of the party, headed by Miliukov, and the Left Kadets, usually led by Nekrasov.

The very fact that the Center and Right Kadets, who had been so bitterly divided since the first two Dumas, should now have been impelled to combine forces suggests that a completely new issue, overshadowing their old personal and political differences, had become paramount. According to Miliukov, the new issue that, even at this early stage, had come so dramatically to the fore was whether the Kadet Party should now adopt a "revolutionary" or an "evolutionary" orientation, whether (to use the Aesopian language of the times) it should direct its tactics inside and outside the Duma to an "organic" or a "nonorganic" resolution of the conflict between the tsarist regime and the liberal majority of educated society. From the revolutionary orientation advocated by Nekrasov and the "evolutionary" one supported by Miliukov flowed a whole series of more specific tactical differences. Nekrasov, Kolubakin, and their supporters advocated, for example, the formation of a "bloc" with the Trudovik and Social Democratic deputies in the Duma. Miliukov, while willing to entertain informal contacts with these groups, opposed any closer and more formal alignment, on the ostensible ground that the parties these groups represented, particularly the Social Democrats, had been the Kadets' chief competitors in the Second Curiae of the cities during the just-concluded elections to the Duma. Of course, this argument failed to impress Nekrasov and his supporters, weary as they now were of the search for "parliamentary solutions."

The conflict came to a head, according to Miliukov, over the issue whether the Kadet deputies should be permitted to contribute to the quota of signatures that the deputies of the leftist parties needed to raise their usually incendiary parliamentary questions. Nekrasov, himself a frequent signer, strongly supported this practice. Miliukov opposed it with equal vehemence on the ground that it seriously strained the Kadets' relations with their more conservative Octobrist allies, and on this issue he formally won a majority of the party to his side. But this was a hollow victory. In defiance of party discipline, Kadet deputies continued to endorse the requests for parliamentary questions of their Trudovik and Social Democratic colleagues (thereby making possible many a parliamentary *skandal*), and as time progressed a growing number of deputies of the Progressist Party joined them in this practice.

The Progressist Party, recruited in the waning days of the Third Duma from a combination of the old *Partiia mirnogo obnovleniia* and dissatisfied Octobrist and Right Kadet deputies, was, at least in its leadership, preeminently a party of big businessmen and industrialists. That representatives of this party, theoretically well to the right of those moderate elements in the Kadet ranks that were making such an issue of the matter, should now be prepared to endorse the requests for parliamentary questions of Socialist deputies clearly suggested that a major political realignment was in the making. This realignment saw the leadership of the Progressist Party move so sharply to the left *in its tactical course* that by early 1914 it had established close contact with representatives of the major parties of the radical left, including the Bolsheviks. Indeed, letters and police reports published in recent years in Soviet historical journals indicate that in late February, 1914, at the initiative of the Moscow industrial magnate and leader of the Progressisty, A. I. Konovalov, a so-called Informatsionnyi Komitet, consisting of Progressisty and Left Kadets, was organized in Moscow to develop "liaison" with left-wing groups and entered into active negotiations with Bolshevik representatives.[38] The first report that Lenin ostensibly received of these overtures was a long agitated letter from the old Moscow Bolshevik, I. Skvortsov-Stepanov. This letter gives such a remarkable picture of the attitudes of liberal circles in Moscow in early 1914, and particularly of the state of mind of a figure who, internal evidence indicates, was clearly A. I. Konovalov, that it deserves to be quoted at some length:

> In *liberal* circles one can observe a notable phenomenon. Everyone is beginning to affirm that they have lost hope in, let us say, an organic outcome and way out [*organicheskii iskhod i vykhod*]. And everyone is beginning to say more and more stubbornly that one must be prepared for an "over-organic" [*nad-organicheskoe*] or let us say "super-organic" solution. Some individuals are endowed with a good "temperament," and feel badly among their liberal friends who lack any "temperament." . . .
>
> *In a conversation with me one of the most notable* [such] "individuals with temperament" [Konovalov (L. H.)] *expressed his minimal desires* as follows. In the past, when a super-organic solution had been advanced, he said, his social acquaintances had committed a major error. Frightened of active force, with which they were completely unacquainted, they had convinced themselves that the "super-organic solution" had already been accomplished, and had dropped off and turned their backs. Let not this happen a second time. And to prevent this, it is imperative that there take place some kind of mutual acquaintance, if only on a personal basis. [Lenin's comment in the margin: "Ha! Ha!"] It is imperative that my friends understand what an active force represents, and not leave the arena so quickly (or more precisely not change camps). It is imperative that elements of different types meet from time to time in order to inform one another of what is happening in different social strata.[39]

"Note that the person who said all this," added Skvortsov, "is one whose social weight and influence is to be measured *in many millions of rubles* (I am employing the standard of measure appropriate for contemporary society), and who together with his closest acquaintances represents many more millions of rubles":

> And so to this *ekzempliar* [Skvortsov's term of reference for Konovalov throughout the letter] the Kadets came with the proposal: *to call together 50 to 70 public figures, Kadets and Progressisty*, to listen to *a speech* by one of the most eminent Kadets in the Duma about Duma affairs, and by an eminent university-affiliated Kadet about university affairs, and perhaps still another speech by a Progressist on whatever subject he might want to discuss. [His] reply was: this would mean to stew in our our own juice and not to understand the sense of the oncoming events.

"There is no doubt that underlying this reply there was *a personal element* [*nechto lichnoe*]," Skvortsov shrewdly observed. "My *ekzempliar cannot stand* the Kadets for bragging that they are more left-wing than he. And given his 'temperament' he is right to feel insulted. It is understandable that he wants *to break up the Kadets' enterprise.* Yet if he is to depend on his soft-hearted friends, he cannot accomplish anything. Hence the following course: rather than stew in our own juice *let us invite the left!*"

In righteous tones, Skvortsov wrote Lenin, he had judiciously replied to Konovalov's proposal by stressing that the time for combinations of the order of the Union of Liberation had passed. Agreements could now be concluded even in principle "only among already consolidated political organizations with definite political orientations, and these only in specific instances as they came along [*ot sluchaia k sluchaiu*]." Skvortsov would feel free to participate in the meetings that Konovalov had in mind only if it were made clear that he was doing so for informational purposes only, reserving for himself complete freedom of action.

All this Skvortsov explained to Lenin with evident trepidation, fearing a reprimand even for the limited initiative he had taken. Yet in the same breath, he sought to communicate to his leader some of his excitement:

I should like you to be able to feel what *great interest all this presents: to observe the process* [of growth] *of a new unrest* [*budoraga*] from its very inception. I do not doubt in the least that in all likelihood the character that the encounters will quickly assume will make their continuation impossible for me. . . . But while one can observe, without compromising oneself and one's friends—*why not observe?* I would like very much that you give me such an answer. But I repeat: if you react negatively to all this "dirty business," the first encounter (*it will probably take place earlier than your answer reaches me*) will also be the last.

To Skvortsov's probable surprise, Lenin responded to his letter with great interest and enthusiasm. Skvortsov's "remarks about the great interest and usefulness of observing the process of growth of the new unrest" were "absolutely correct." His fears that his participation in these meetings might cast a shadow on his own loyalty to the party were "without foundation, absolutely without foundation [*naprasno, sovsem naprasno*]." Then turning to business: "Could one not get money out of *Ekzempliar*?" "It [was] badly needed." "But it wouldn't be worth taking less than 10,000 rubles." And, further, could Skvortsov let him know to what extent he could talk frankly: (a) with *Ekzempliar*, (b) with his friends and acquaintances, and (c) with all the participants in the "meetings"?

In my view one must single out those with whom one can talk frankly, and frankly put to them questions of the following order: (a) we are going to the following means of struggle: can you not inform us how far you are going? Unofficially, privately!! (b) we are contributing such and such in the sense of force, means, etc.: can you not inform us what you are capable of bringing into the "non-Duma" struggle? You say: *Ekzempliar* finds that liberals changed camps too early in 1905—well, "inform us": does everyone view things in the same way and *for how long, for example, are they contemplating delaying a change of camps* (of course, the question is not one of time, of interval, but of [the scope of] political changes)? (c) are they capable of giving money? (d) are they capable of establishing an illegal organ? etc.

"Our goal," Lenin concluded, "is to inform ourselves and to respond to every active support of the revolution by raising—as directly and frankly as possible (with *a*, or with *b*, or even with *c*; this will be apparent to you)—precisely the issue of a revolution. If possible, it would be good for you to make a speech [at one of the meetings] concerning the theses of which, if need be, I would gladly give you my opinion."[40]

What followed can be gathered substantially from the reports of the chief of the Moscow Division of the Okhrana, A. Martynov, to the director of the Department of Police. A report dated April 27 (May 10), 1914, indicated that at a meeting on April 19 the Moscow Informatsionnyi Komitet had issued some kind of promise to give the Bolsheviks 20,000 rubles to assist the convocation of the Party Congress which Lenin considered so imperative to lay the organizational basis for a successful all-nation political strike. To collect this money, the report continued, Lenin had instructed the Bolshevik deputies Petrovsky and Malinovsky to deal directly wih three members of the Informatsionnyi Komitet: Konovalov, his fellow tycoon Morozov, and Riabushinsky, the editor of *Utro Rossii*, organ of the Progressisty. But this was to be the extent of the Bolsheviks' involvement. As of this moment Lenin suggested that the Bolsheviks take no further part in what he termed "Konovalov's enterprise," that is, in the deliberations of Informatsionnyi Komitet.[41] It seems that Konovalov responded in kind to the Bolsheviks' new hands-off policy. For on May 13 (26), the chief of the Moscow Okhrana reported to the Department of Police that when Petrovsky had approached Konovalov about the promised financial subsidy, "Konovalov declared that the question was not settled as yet, noting in passing that the Progressisty had already given money to the Bolsheviks: through Roman Malinovsky 2,000 rubles for the legal labor press a year ago and this year 3,000 to Lenin via Elena Razmirovich."[42] The available evidence does not definitely indicate whether the Bolsheviks did or did not finally obtain the promised subsidy for their Party Congress. One is entitled to doubt it, however, if only because of the complaint in a letter of Krupskaia in early June about "the complete lack of money" in the Bolshevik treasury for the congress, which was then scheduled to open two months later.[43]

Even if, largely due to Lenin's reticence, the Bolsheviks ultimately failed to cash in on the Progressisty's promissory note, the episode we have just recounted gives a notable indication of the progress of the crisis of the parties by 1914 and of the risks that responsible figures in Russian liberal circles were now prepared to take in their search for a revolutionary solution to the current political deadlock. For the pages of the Bolshevik press all too clearly suggested that Lenin and his followers had now set their sights on the emergence from the expected revolutionary overtures of nothing short of a "genuine," Bolshevik-led, "democratic regime of the working class and peasantry."

Indeed, by the beginning of 1914 any hope of avoiding a revolutionary crisis appeared to be evaporating even among the more moderate representatives of liberal opinion. Under the impact of the blind suicidal course pursued by the government and its handful of supporters, the Octobrist Party had split at the seams. Commenting on the decision of the sixteen Left Octobrist deputies to revolt against their party leadership and to oppose any suggestion of reconciliation with the existing regime, A. S. Izgoev, himself a proponent of political moderation since the days of Ve*khi*, now trumpeted in the pages of *Russkaia mysl'*:

The failure of the "Left Octobrists" is not their personal failure. It has marked the crash of a whole conception. Russia's renovation cannot be accomplished by the forces of the gentry class. Its best people are helpless. 1861 will not be repeated. The resolution of society's tasks is being turned over to other hands. "Democracy is on the march."[44]

In a long wail of despair, Peter Struve, the most eloquent spokesman in Russian liberalism for an "evolutionary orientation," described in the same issue of *Russkaia mysl'* the course of collision with society which the government and its fanatic supporters appeared to be setting. Ever since the failure of the Stolypin experiment, he recalled, the state power had been engaged in an increasingly bitter struggle against the very legal order that it had sanctioned with the October Manifesto. The state power recognized the legal existence of the Duma; yet with every weapon at their command its agents sought to stifle the existence of the majority of the parties represented in it. It purportedly recognized society's right to representation; yet its bureaucracy zealously struggled to suppress society's organs of local self-government. Given these basic contradictions in the Russian body politic, there was a superficial logic to the "shameless propaganda" now circulating in higher official circles about the need for new violations of the Fundamental Laws, for a counterrevolution of the right which at a minimum should reduce the Duma to a purely consultative organ. But the pursuit of such a course, Struve desperately argued, would inevitably lead in short order to a radical revolutionary overturn. The only real salvation for the state power lay in its own restoration to health, a restoration which could be achieved only through the abandonment of its suicidal struggle against society. "Never was the country so much in need of what one calls a healthy *vlast'*, and never was the real state of affairs so distant from the realization of such a healthy, or normal, *vlast'*." Yet one way or another, Struve concluded, on a new militant note, the country would have its way:

If we see in the cure of the state power the standing task for Russia's political progress, it is not because otherwise we would despair for Russia's fate. We simply desire that our country's political development be achieved wisely and firmly, without the "great upheavals" which are always as painful as they are inevitable when from "upheavals" no [appropriate] lessons are drawn concerning "tranquillization."[45]

The willingness that Struve displayed in this concluding statement at least to contemplate the unleashing of the very revolutionary Antaeus against which he had warned so eloquently but five years earlier was perhaps the most dramatic indication of how far by 1914 the polarization between state and educated society had actually progressed.

To be sure, one could still encounter in the *publitsistika* of the day the observation, so frequently repeated in later émigré memoirs, that "the frustrating atmosphere" that enveloped one in Petersburg evaporated when one got but "100 *versty* from the large centers." "There everything is quiet," observed the moderate Kadet commentator Gessen in his annual review for *Riech'* in

January, 1914. "There nonetheless a complex process of adjustment is taking place; the wall between city and country is breaking down."

Indeed, many signs of economic and social progress could be found in the Russian province of the year 1914—the introduction of new crops, new techniques and forms of organization in agriculture, and the industrialization of the countryside; the growing literacy among the lower strata and invigorated cultural life among the upper strata of provincial society. But no more than in the major cities were these signs of progress and change in the localities to be viewed as evidence of the achievement or indeed the promise of greater political stability. Even Gessen, generally a professional optimist, felt compelled to note the all-pervasive and increasingly acute conflict in provincial life between "society," seeking to organize, to strengthen its bonds, and local bureaucratic administrative organs. Under the immediate stimulus of the Beilis affair, the fissure in provincial circles between officialdom and educated society had been revealed to be as deep and as unbridgeable as in the two capitals. An article published by S. Elpatevsky in *Russkoe bogatstvo* in January, 1914, strikingly described the two almost hermetically separated worlds that were now apparent in most provincial towns:

There is taking place a kind of gathering on the opposing sides of the wall which is dividing Russia. On one side have gathered the united *dvorianstvo*, the united bureaucracy, office-holders—generally the people who, in one way or another, "are feeding at the public trough." On the other side have gathered the plain citizens [*obyvateli*], the crowd of provincial society.[46]

To be sure, Elpatevsky recognized, the division between "official" and "unofficial" Russia was of long standing, but in the years since the 1905 Revolution, it had become far sharper than ever before. "Twenty-five years ago, provincial liberal or cultured society was [still] a mixed society. It included office-holders who were considered to have the liberalism or enlightenment required for membership in cultivated society." But most of the middle and small gentry had now given up their distinctive gentry traditions and had been incorporated into educated society. And by the same token, "the ranks of the office-holders [had] long since been purged of anyone endowed with a civic sense."

Thus it was that "official" and "unofficial" Russia had now turned into two worlds completely sealed off one from the other. The inhabitants of these two worlds still met more or less peacefully—at the theater, on the boulevard, in the public park. But they now belonged to different clubs, attended different public lectures, were no longer welcome at each other's soirées. The Beilis case had contributed an ultimate element of exacerbation to this process of mutual estrangement. It had removed the grounds for any possible effort at conciliation between the two camps; it had laid bare, and provided a focus for, their sense of irrevocable conflict: "In the camp of official Russia," there now prevailed "a mood of hostility against those who recognize[d] the October Manifesto, against those of other nationalities and faiths, against those who believe[d] differently and worship[ed] differently." On the other side, "desires [had] become clearer and more definite," and "thoughts, more agitated and intense." "Official Russia

[had] learned nothing and forgotten nothing"; it had "outgrown nothing," and "become adjusted to nothing." And, for its own part, society "had long since ceased to expect the realization of its aspirations from above."

Thus, Elpatevsky discerned in Russian provincial life, by the beginning of 1914, the same signs of the polarization of opinion as in the center of the political arena where "the government, after seeking to reach an understanding with the Kadets, then with the Octobrists, [had] now moved over to the right-wing parties," while on the other side of the fence "all expectations within the Duma of any [possible] legislative work with the government [were] steadily declining." The crisis had now become so acute that revolution or counterrevolution appeared the only way out: "Even some of the Octobrists [were] now being heard to say that there was no longer any sense in trying to safeguard the Duma," while the right-wing factions, which for a year now had been loudly warning of "impending conflict," "revolution," and "repetition of 1905," had managed to persuade themselves of the inevitability of a "catastrophic confrontation." From all this Elpatevsky concluded, in scarcely disguised Aesopian language, that the tensions in national life were rapidly approaching the breaking point: "The government is leaving society, just as society is leaving it. It makes the conflict all the graver, and reconciliation all the more difficult. The ditch is widening; the wall is rising. . . . But some sort of readjustment is imperative and inevitable. . . . Life is moving on! [*Zhizn' idét!*]"[47]

One paradoxical aspect of the polarization between state and society under these gathering clouds of revolution and counterrevolution deserves to be considered further, for its examination will lead us to some of the distinctive and essential dimensions of the historical situation that has been discussed throughout this essay. It is clear that in many respects the Russian state—on the eve of the First World War just as in February, 1917—was ripe, indeed overripe, for a takeover by a new *pays réel:* by new would-be ruling groups and institutions ready to assume formal control of national life.

The fumes of the Beilis case, the brewing scandal of the Rasputinshchina, the striking absence in official circles of men capable of governing provided dramatic evidence of the advanced state of decomposition of the tsarist regime: of the disintegration of its intellectual and moral resources and of its loss of support among any of the viable social elements in the country at large. At the same time, it appeared that in the proliferating organs of self-expression and independent activity of educated society—in the political and journalistic circles surrounding the State Duma and the local organs of self-government, in the cooperative societies of city and country, in the various societies of public enlightenment and the now more militant associations of big business and industry—a whole organized structure of order and potential authority had now crystallized, far better prepared to take and effectively exercise power than had been the case, say, of any of their institutional counterparts on the eve of the French Revolution.

Yet, when a reader pores over the various commentaries in the Russian *publitsistika* of late 1913 and early 1914, he is likely to be struck by the frequent note of despondency, sounded even by temperamentally sanguine observers, about the sense of confusion and malaise pervading the political and social scene. The note is to be found even in Gessen's *tour d'horizon* in the yearly review of *Riech'* of 1914. The current confrontation between an agitated public and an obstinately intransigent state power bore a superficial resemblance to Russia's situation in 1904–1905, Gessen noted in this review. "But here the similarity ends":

Much of [society's] activism is expected in tensions between groups and within groups . . . [on] useless conversations about the formation of blocs, about [the conclusion of] agreements. The same is true of intra-party relations. The most striking example in this respect is Social Democracy, in which the conflict between Bolsheviks and Mensheviks has consumed everything else. [But] the same is generally true of other parties.[48]

Seeking an explanation for "this unhealthy situation," and for "the exacerbated reactions" of the public "to all phenomena" which this situation allegedly reflected, Gessen found it in "the general decline of morals," and "the unappeasable hunger for sensations" in contemporary society—the standard reaction of an *intelligent* of the old school to all of the untoward, novel phenomena of the day.

It is likely that the political and social *anomie* that Gessen myopically discerned had more to do with the impact on public opinion of the deadlock between the state power and educated society than with any of Sanin's sexual orgies. As we have already noted, the essence of the "crisis of the parties" was that every responsible political figure now had to decide for himself whether to abandon the frustrating path of reform and risk the unleashing of a new revolution. Not only was the confrontation of this issue calculated to cause a reshuffle in all existing political alignments; it also brought the realization that the very organisms of the more moderate parties were not suitably organized for, or adaptable to, the pursuit and exploitation of a revolutionary situation.

Yet even this does not appear an adequate explanation for the sense of frustration and futility that Gessen detected among the leaders of the parties of the center and moderate left. Its chief source, I believe, lay in an often inarticulate but widely shared feeling that these parties were not sufficiently broadly gauged, that they were representative at best of the *tsenzovye elementy*, the privileged sector of society, and were woefully lacking support among its lower strata— most emphatically, of course, among its now politically aroused industrial workers. This feeling, so acutely reflected in Alexander Blok's apocalyptic sense of the thinness and fragility of contemporary Russian culture, made for the realization in circles of "advanced opinion" that existing political combinations were no longer adequate to turn the corner successfully: to carry off a revolution and yet keep under control the "elemental" instincts that such a revolution was likely to unleash among the urban and rural masses. It is in this light, it seems to me, that we need to view the vain attempts of a Konovalov to strike some sort of accord, some sort of understanding, with the Bolsheviks. Konovalov's attitude was but one manifestation of the yearning, so widely expressed by representatives of "advanced opinion" on the eve of the war, to recapture somehow the spirit and the thrust of the old, pre-1905 Liberation movement—to establish anew a broad political combination, capable of mobilizing the support of all politically significant and potentially significant sectors of Russian society, through the medium of new personal contacts and associations, through the thread of new informal links between the representatives of the liberal center and the radical left.

It is in this same perspective, I believe, that we should interpret and weigh the character of that still shadowy phenomenon of Russian political and social life in the immediate prewar period, the contemporary revival of Masonry. The role of Masonry in the prehistory of the Russian Revolution has remained to this day so shrouded in obscurity and so wrapped in controversy as to defy precise historical description. Yet the evidence at hand[49] forcibly suggests a number of general observations. It suggests, in the first place, that, beginning in the waning days of the Third Duma, a significant effort developed to revive and activate the Russian Masonic movement, while substantially altering its character. In the minds of at least some of its initiators, the purpose of this effort was, from the very start, to mobilize an effective "democratic" coalition against the existing regime by bringing into close contact representatives of "advanced opinion," from all the parties of the center and left (from the Progressisty to the Bolsheviks) and from all "progressive" organs of education, public discussion, and independent activity of "society." "In this form," one of the leaders of this effort, the old Osvobozhdenets Kuskova, recalls, "it was hoped to restore the Souiz Osvobozhdeniia and to work underground for the liberation of Russia."[50]

Kuskova and other participants indicate that in the effort to achieve this broad political objective the old Masonic rituals were abandoned, although the ritual of initiation still included an oath of secrecy, "of absolute silence." We should hasten to note that behind this wall of silence the leaders of the Masonic movement did not generally manage, or in fact seriously attempt, during the prewar period at least, to work out any specific plans of political action (with the possible exception, as we shall see, of the Moscow Masonic Lodge). Indeed, much of the superficial success of the new Masonry in attracting recruits from various circles of opinion lay precisely in the vagueness of the ideological commitments and the looseness of the political allegiance that it actually required of its members.

Under these conditions, the new Masonic movement underwent between 1911 and 1914 a quite rapid and seemingly impressive organizational growth. By the outbreak of the war, it had established a number of lodges not only in the two capitals but also in such widely separated provincial centers as Kiev, Samara, Saratov, Tiflis, and Kutais. And by the summer of 1912, these lodges were loosely united in a *Velikii Sovet narodov Rossii*, a national organization headed by an executive council and periodically elected executive secretaries, which in the period leading up to the Revolution of 1917 actually held three national conventions (in 1912, 1914, and 1916).

Indeed, the Masonic movement managed, on paper, to fulfill Kuskova's dream of "filling the existing political vacuum" by creating a broad new political network, overlapping the now "bankrupt" party divisions, and "taking in hand' through its "own people" existing organs of public opinion and activity.[51] By the outbreak of war Masonry recruited into its ranks prominent representatives of a broad range of political groupings of the center and left, from A. I. Konovalov and I. I. Efremov of the Progressisty, and Nekrasov and Tereshchenko of the Left Kadets, to Kerensky of the Trudoviki, and Galpern, Skobelev, Chkheidze, Chkhenkeli, and Gegechkori of the Menshevik faction of the RSDRP (the Georgian Social Democratic deputies in the Duma found Masonry particularly attractive). And it managed with equal success to attract prominent figures from the various organs, old and new, of the independent activity of "society"—from the traditional recruiting grounds of the zemstva, city dumas, and Free Economic and Technical Societies of Liberation days, to the more recently organized teachers' and cooperative organizations.

Indeed, although any conspiratorial theory of the origins of the Russian Revolution can hardly seriously be entertained, it would be equally hard to assert that the personal contacts, the informal political bonds, cutting across party lines, that the lodges made possible, were altogether devoid of political significance, in the prehistory of 1917 and its eventual unfolding. As far as the prewar period is concerned, it may be sufficient to note that most of the prominent Progressisty and Left Kadets active in 1914 in the Moscow Informatsionnyi Komitet (whose negotiations with the Bolsheviks we described earlier in this discussion)—Konovalov, Morozov, Nekrasov, Stepanov, Volkov—were Masons, and that in all probability this committee was itself a front organization (an "auxiliary organ," to use the language of the time) of the Moscow Masonic Lodge, politically the most activist of the lodges then operating in Russia.

And to take a more long-range perspective, it would appear difficult to deny that the personal bonds forged in the Masonic lodges actually exercised some influence on the selection of the members of the Provisional Government in 1917, and on the nature of the alignments within it. As Miliukov, who considered himself the victim of their intrigues, broadly hints in his memoirs, all four members of the central quadrumvirate in the Provisional Government during the early phase of the Revolution of 1917—Kerensky, Nekrasov, Tereshchenko, and Konovalov—were Masons of long standing. And it may even be argued that the informal political concord that Masonry had fostered over the years between the likes of Nekrasov and Tereshchenko—the permanent fixtures among the "bourgeois ministers" of the Provisional Government—and leading figures in the Petersburg Soviet substantially eased the way for the precarious experiment of the *dvoevlastie* and of the eventual coalition ministries.[52]

Yet, even when all this is conceded, what seems most notable about Russian Masonry throughout these years is its political weakness rather than its strength. This weakness of the new Masonic movement lay not so much in its failure to bind its members to common political goals and tactics. Or even in the inability of its fuzzy vision of a human family, transcending class and national boundaries, to provide an adequate substitute for a viable, relevant ideology for the Russian society of the day. After all, it may well be argued that neither the *sociétés de pensée* of the eighteenth century nor, to come closer to earth, the Osvobozhdentsy and their political allies of the early twentieth ever displayed the capacity, or indeed the need, to formulate such a clear programmatic or tactical course. In fact, throughout its history Osvobozhdenie deliberately remained a broad, amorphous "loose organization" seeking to comprehend rather than to unite and control groups of often quite different social attitudes and doctrinal views. Rather, what the Osvobozhdentsy succeeded in articulating was a vision of Russia's *immediate*, although not distant, future, which proved broadly acceptable, at least for a while, to the variegated elements over which they held sway. And the secret of this success lay, in the last analysis, in the fact that beneath the surface of doctrinal differences a common ethos—certain common attitudes and values, however diffuse or submerged—still held together at the beginning of the century *the more articulate and politically significant* groups in Russian national life.

This was the nature of the achievement that a decade later the Russian Masons and other like-minded groups could not manage to duplicate. To be sure, they did draw into their ranks prominent representatives of the Trudoviki and of the Menshevik faction of Social Democracy, and continued to do so during the war years. But the bonds that were thereby forged between the liberal and radical sectors of Russian society were from the start more apparent than real, and proved under the stress of any significant political crisis more ephemeral than had been the case even in 1905. This time, the fault did not substantially lie as it had in 1905 in the fickleness of the spokesmen of the moderate left. On the contrary, the majority of these leaders of the left would now seek even under stress to remain faithful to their liberal allies, but at these moments of crisis they found themselves leaders without an army, deserted by the very laboring masses which they purported to represent. This of course was to be the eventual destiny of the moderate leaders of the soviets in 1917. But it was already the fate in 1914 of those Mensheviks who, unlike their Bolshevik rivals, continued to participate in the meetings of the Moscow Informatsionnyi Komitet, and other like-minded efforts.

In substance, I am trying to suggest that almost from the start Masonry was unable to bridge the chasm that now separated, at least in Russia's urban centers, the more privileged, educated strata of Russian society from its vocally dissatisfied and restless industrial working class. The network of the Masonic lodges could do little more than paper over this chasm: as we have seen, it could do no more not so much because of the magic of the Bolsheviks' appeals to the workers as because of the workers' own spirit of *buntarstvo*, their own elemental mood of revolt.

In this perspective, the chief historical significance of Masonry lay in the degree to which it reflected the nature and progress of the revolutionary crisis in Russia by the eve of the war and the character of the efforts to which this crisis gave rise. In this same perspective, it may perhaps not be difficult to outline a set of hypothetical circumstances under which Russia might have undergone—even in the absence of the specific additional strains induced by the war, though maybe under the immediate stimulus of some other, purely domestic crisis—the kind of radical overturn on which Lenin was already gambling by late 1913–early 1914 and which Russia actually experienced with the October Revolution.

However, I would rest my case on somewhat more modest, and more solid, grounds: on the prosaic, but often ignored, proposition that *the character, although not necessarily the gravity*, of the political and social crisis evident in urban Russia by the eve of the war is more reminiscent of the revolutionary processes that we shall see at work during Russia's second revolution than of those that had unfolded in Russia's first. Or to put the matter in the form of a "vérité de La Palisse," that, as we knew all along, 1914 is, if only approximately, a half-way station between 1905 and 1917. What the war years would do was not to conceive, but to accelerate substantially, the two broad processes of polarization that had already been at work in Russian national life during the immediate prewar period.

On the one hand, these years would witness not only a sharpening of the dissatisfaction of educated society with the inept, helpless tsarist regime but also the further crystallization—in the State Duma, the Zemskii Soiuz, the Soiuz Gorodov, the War-Industrial Committees, and other central and local organs of public expression and activity—of a seemingly effective network of new organization, new order, new authority, fully prepared to take over and hold the reins of power as soon as the old state power fell.

But these same years witnessed as well the further progress of the other process of polarization that we have already observed in the prewar period—the division between the educated, privileged society and the urban masses—a process which would sap the new regime of much of its potential effectiveness, its authority, its legitimacy, even before it actually took over. Underlying the progress of this second polarization were not only the specific economic deprivations caused by the war but also the substantial acceleration of the changes in the character and temper of the industrial working class that we already noted in the immediate prewar years: the influx at an even more rapid tempo of new elements into the industrial army under the impact of the war boom and of the army's drafts.[53]

Some of these new workers were women, some were adolescent or under-age boys, some (in the metalworking industry, for example) were older industrial workers shifted from nonstrategic to strategic industries, but most, we presume continued to be drawn to the industrial army from the countryside—in the first order, from the overpopulated agricultural provinces of Central European Russia, which in 1913–14 had already provided such suitable recruits for Bolshevik agitation. The experience of 1917 would show only too clearly, if admittedly under the stresses of war, what a few more months of this agitation could do.

To be sure, the experience of the first eighteen months of the war temporarily obscured the workings of these disruptive processes. These months witnessed an indubitable crack-up of the Bolshevik Party under the combined blows of police arrests and of the draft of Bolshevik Party workers. Indeed, they saw a brief rally of public opinion under the spell of the national emergency which unquestionably affected not only educated society but also substantial elements of the "laboring masses." Even more notably, this period saw an accentuation, or at least a sharper articulation, of the desire already displayed in the prewar period by the older, Menshevik-oriented, labor intelligentsia to rejoin the framework of national life. Left momentarily at the center of the Russian labor scene, many of the most prominent figures in this workers' intelligentsia now joined the Labor Groups of the War-Industrial Committees. Some did so with the undivided purpose of supporting the war effort; others, admittedly, with a more complex mixture of "defensist" sympathies and revolutionary hopes—both elements, however, articulating and solidifying by their participation in these organs of "society" more conciliatory attitudes toward the liberal elements represented in them.

But the political and social significance of these phenomena was proven, all too quickly, to be ephemeral. By late 1915–early 1916, some of the leaders of "advanced opinion" already resumed, this time in earnest, plots for the overthrow of the tsarist regime. By 1916, the wave of labor unrest once again began to swell. And within another year, the Menshevik workers' intelligentsia, whose stature had been so suddenly and dramatically magnified by the special conditions of war, would demonstrate an equally dramatic inability to influence, even minimally, the course of events. One of the most notable phenomena of 1917, which became evident almost from the very first days of the Revolution, was the failure of any of the leaders of the Workers' Group in the Central War-Industrial Committee to strike any responsive chord among the rank and file of their own working class, and to play a political role even comparable to that of their nonproletarian, but more radically inclined, confrères in the Menshevik Party. By this time the wall of mutual incomprehension that had come to separate this workers' intelligentsia from the rank and file of the laboring masses rose almost as high as the wall that these masses perceived between themselves and "bourgeois" society. This was to be one of the most startling features of 1917, the sorry outcome of the Mensheviks' long effort in the aftermath of 1905 to build in Russia a genuinely Europeanized labor movement.

As a historian's eyes follow the unfolding of the revolutionary processes that have been outlined in this essay, they may well search for the illumination to be derived from comparative historical perspectives—from the comparisons that we have already implicitly drawn of the revolutionary situations in Russia in 1905, 1914, and 1917; from comparisons between the character of the labor disorders in Petersburg on the eve of the First World War and that of contemporary labor unrest in other European capitals; from the even bolder and broader comparisons that might be drawn between the prehistory of the great Revolution of 1917 and that of the great Revolution of 1789. Yet, it seems to me, the differences that any of these comparisons might bring out would loom far larger than the similarities.

There is an obvious singularity about the decade leading up to 1917 in the perspective of contemporary Western experience. This singularity lies, at least in part, in the fact that these years incorporate and compress to such an extraordinary degree the two sharply distinct revolutionary processes that I have discussed—processes which in the history of other European countries are not to be found coinciding, with such intensity, in any single phase of historical development. The nearest equivalent to the political and social attitudes displayed by the Russian workers in 1914 is probably to be found on the prewar European scene among elements of the French working class, which manifested at least a comparable sense of alienation from the existing political order and the prospering world of other strata of French society. But even if this state of affairs had led by the eve of the war to a serious crisis in the system of the Third Republic, the crisis was not further complicated and aggravated by the remaining presence on the stage of substantial vestiges of an old order and an Old Regime. By the same token, if vestiges of an Old Regime may be argued to be far more visible on the German political and social scene of 1914, and to have contributed to an unresolved deadlock between the Imperial Government and the Reichstag, it surely would be difficult to claim that the social attitudes that the German working class contributed to this crisis are even barely comparable to those of the stormy Russian proletariat.

If we view the prehistory of 1917 in the perspective of the decade in Russia's development leading up to 1905, its singularity does not lie so much in the range of groups and attitudes represented among the opposition and revolutionary forces. After all, the all-nation movement which finally emerged in October, 1905—only to distintegrate even more quickly than it had come together—was marked by an even greater heterogeneity of constituent elements: gentry, professional men, and belatedly aroused big businessmen and industrialists; workers and peasants, or, more precisely, would-be representatives of a peasant movement; Bolsheviks, Mensheviks, Socialist Revolutionaries, and that grab bag of political tendencies gathered under the umbrella of the Soiuz Osvobozhdeniia.

And all these groups and tendencies were animated by quite different underlying attitudes toward the economic and social processes that were at work in national life. Some were driven to revolutionary opposition by their impatience for a clearer and fuller articulation in Russian life of the values and institutional forms attendant on their vision of a modern world. Others were filled with resentment largely by the very forces that were at work in this modernization, or at least by the forms that this modernization had assumed during the Witte experiment: by the sufferings and deprivations that weighed on the countryside, the darkness and strangeness of life in the barracks and hovels of the industrial slums, the gross and offensive sight of the new rule of money. And even the members of the intelligentsia, who had contributed so much to patching this coalition together, had temporarily succeeded in doing so precisely because so many of them —drawn as they were from many of these sharply separated corners of Russian society—actually combined in themselves, beneath the flimsy logical constructions of ideologies, the maelstrom of chaotic and conflicting attitudes represented in national life.

While this heterogeneity of the constituent groups in the all-nation opposition to absolutism at the beginning of the century, and of the underlying attitudes of the members of the intelligentsia who led them (Liberals, Marxists, and Populists alike), ultimately accounts for the rapidity of the disintegration that this coalition underwent in the crucible of 1905, it also explains, of course, the irresistible power that it briefly manifested. If only for a flickering historical moment, the autocracy was confronted by the outline of a new and seemingly united nation. For this flickering moment, the intelligentsia, which had emerged as the prototype— the microcosm—of this united nation, managed to induce the groups under its sway to bury the long-standing differences of interests, outlook, and values that had separated them and to agree to a common set of discrete political objectives, to a common vision, however partial and abstracted, of Russia's immediate future if not of her ultimate destiny.

The potential significance of this achievement of getting different groups to agree on a limited set of political objectives—of finding a common denominator for some interests and suspending, postponing the clash of others—should not be underestimated, since it constituted the essential prerequisite for the successful launching of that great French Revolution of 1789 whose image possessed the political imagination of so much of Russia's intelligentsia in 1905: for in the prerevolutionary years 1787–88 the opposition to the *ancien régime* drew much of its strength not only from the "progressive" aspirations of the Third Estate but also from the resentments of nobles and churchmen rebelling, in the name of thinly disguised feudal liberties, against the administrative innovations of a haltingly modernizing state. To be sure, in the France of 1789, the balance between "progressive" and "reactionary" forces had been far more heavily weighted in favor of the former than turned out to be the case in the Russia of 1905. Still, if any even partially valid historical analogy is to be sought between the French and Russian prerevolutionary experiences, it should be drawn, it seems to me, between the French prerevolution and the years in Russian life leading up to 1905, not to 1917.

Indeed, it is difficult to escape the conclusion that the failure of Russia's first revolution, and the repudiation that it induced among so many in the intelligentsia of their traditional revolutionary ethos, substantially contributed to the character and pattern of the second. For if the intelligentsia's sense of messianic mission, which its *Vekhi* critics so bitterly deplored, had unquestionably contributed to the growth of revolutionary tendencies and thus to the instability of the existing political order, it had also made—particularly from the 1890's, when both Populists and Marxists had been converted to the cause of political freedom —for the translation of the new feeling of mobility in national life into a somewhat greater sense of social cohesion; for the bridging, however slow and precarious, of the psychological chasms that had hitherto divided Russia's society of estates.

By the same token, it may well be argued that the failure of the intelligentsia to secure these bridges in 1905—even in the minimal form of a political and social framework temporarily acceptable to a broad spectrum of Russian society—and the decline in subsequent years of its sense of messianic mission substantially contributed to the character and gravity of the divisions in Russian life that we have examined in this essay. For, as it turned out, a brief historical interval, the partially reformed political order gained a new lease on life. But this brief measure of *political stability* was achieved in part at the price of the promise of greater *social cohesion*, greater *social stability*, which, for urban Russia at least, had been contained in the turbulent years leading up to 1905. The tensions and strains which earlier had been largely contained in the channels of common political objectives would eventually be polarized into separate revolutionary processes, each adding to the pressures against the tsarist regime but also contributing—by their separation—to the eventual disintegration of the whole fabric of national life.

Thus it was that 1917 would witness the collapse of an ancient old order at the same time that it would see an industrial working class and eventually a peasant mass, impelled by an amalgam of old and new grievances, combine against a stillborn bourgeois society and state. Thus it was, finally, that in the throes of these two separate revolutions, Russia would not manage for many years to recover a new historical equilibrium—to find its own Thermidor.

## NOTES

1. Alexander Gerschenkron, "Problems and Patterns of Russian Economic Development," in Cyril E. Black, ed., *The Transformation of Russian Society* (Cambridge, Mass.: Harvard University Press, 1960), p. 60.

2. Leonard Schapiro, *The Communist Party of the Soviet Union* (New York, 1959), pp. 139–40.

3. In the words of the standard Soviet text of this period: "The revolutionary upsurge in Russia had reached such a level that an armed uprising already appeared in the offing . . . the onset of the revolution was broken off by the World War in which the tsarist government, just like the imperialists of other countries, sought salvation from revolution." *Ocherki po istorii SSSR, 1907–Mart 1917,* ed. A. L. Sodorova (Moscow, 1954), pp. 239–40. The new *Istoriia Kommunisticheskoi partii Sovetskogo Soiuza* (Moscow, 1959) uses substantially the same language. For far more cautious, and historically more faithful earlier Soviet analyses of the St. Petersburg general strike of July, 1914, and of the sympathy strikes to which it gave rise, see *Proletarskaia revoliutsiia,* No. 7 (30), July, 1924; and No. 8–9 (31–32), Aug.–Sept., 1924.

4. *Ocherki po istorii SSSR,* Chap. 3, *passim.*

5. The term of opprobium that the Bolsheviks applied to those whom they accused of advocating the "liquidation" of the revolutionary underground.

6. The most valuable source on the private reactions of Menshevik leaders to developments on the Russian scene for the period 1908–13 is the still unpublished correspondence between A. N. Potresov, who was residing in Petersburg during these years, and Iu. O. Martov, who remained in emigration until after the amnesty of 1913. This correspondence, consisting of some two hundred letters, is now in the Nicolaevsky Archives, Hoover Institution, hereafter referred to as NA.

7. Martov to Potresov, letter 133, Nov. 17, 1909 (NA).

8. The compilations published by the Ministry of Trade and Industry offer the following statistical aggregates about strikes in factories covered by factory inspection for the period 1905–14:

| Year | Strikes | Strikers | Number of Strikes Listed as Political | Number of Strikers Listed as Political |
|------|---------|----------|------------------|------------------|
| 1905 | 13,995 | 2,863,173 | 6,024 | 1,082,576 |
| 1906 | 6,114 | 1,108,406 | 2,950 | 514,854 |
| 1907 | 3,573 | 740,074 | 2,558 | 521,573 |
| 1908 | 892 | 176,101 | 464 | 92,694 |
| 1909 | 340 | 64,166 | 50 | 8,863 |
| 1910 | 222 | 46,623 | 8 | 3,777 |
| 1911 | 466 | 105,110 | 24 | 8,380 |
| 1912 | 2,032 | 725,491 | 1,300 | 549,812 |
| 1913 | 2,404 | 887,096 | 1,034 | 502,442 |
| 1914 | 3,534 | 1,337,458 | 2,401 | 985,655 |

See Ministerstvo torgovli i promyshlennosti, *Svod otchetov fabrichnykh inspektorov za 1913 god,* and *Svod . . . za 1914, passim* (St. Petersburg, 1914; Petrograd, 1915).

The accuracy of these and other, unofficial estimates of the strike movement, particularly for the period 1912–14, is almost as widely in dispute as is the actual significance of the labor disturbances that these estimates reflect. For example, while the Factory Inspectors' reports estimate 549,812 political strikers for 1912, the calculation of the Menshevik labor observer, A. Mikhailov, is 1,065,000, including over 950,000 in factories under Factory Inspection. (See A. Mikhailov, "K kharakteristike sovremennago rabochago dvizheniia v Rossii," *Nasha zaria,* No. 12, 1912.) The contemporary estimates of *Pravda* are even higher. It is probably safe to assume that while the figures listed in the contemporary Social Democratic press are undoubtedly overblown, official estimates seriously err in the opposite direction (by an order of at least 20 per cent). This at least was the view expressed by more neutral contemporary observers of the labor scene. (See, for example, the articles by A. Chuzhennikov on the labor movement in the annual reviews of *Riech'* for 1913 and 1914.)

9. A. Chuzhennikov, "Russkoe rabochee dvizhenie," *Riech' za 1913 god.*

10. The Factory Inspectors' reports estimate the number of political strikers in April and May, 1912, as 231,459 and 170,897, respectively; for April and May, 1913, the figures listed are 170,897 and 116,276. This discrepancy more than accounts for the difference between the total aggregates for political strikers estimated for these two years (549,812 for 1912 and 502,442 for 1913).

11. See, for example, A. S. Izgoev, "Nasha obshchestvennaia zhizn'," and A. Chuzhennikov, "Russkoe rabochee dvizhenie," in *Riech' za 1914.*

12. See *Svod . . . za 1914, passim.*

13. *Russian Review,* II, No. 3 (1913), 176.

14. This phenomenon is noted in the *publitsistika* of the day even by some of the Bolsheviks' most severe critics. In an article published in June, 1913, for example, A. S. Izgoev emphasized the great political importance of the current "transformation of the chaotic Russian labor masses into a working class . . . under the ideological sway of Social Democracy." The article cited the evidence of the Petersburg workers' steadily increasing involvement in elections, political strikes, and demonstrations, the "most impressive sight" of the impact exercised by *Pravda* on the working class of the capital during its first year of publication, and especially the indications in the daily life of the Petersburg workers of their growing class solidarity: workers' willingness to make financial sacrifices on behalf of fellow workers in other factories, the "devastating moral effect" of the boycotts enforced on strikebreakers. Clearly, Izgoev concluded, Russia's current "social crisis" was giving way to an extremely significant process of "social crystallization." See A. S. Izgoev, "Rabochii klass i sotsial-demokratiia," *Russkaia mysl',* June, 1913, *passim.*

15. F. Dan, "Politicheskoe obozrenie: Posle 'Leny'," *Nasha zaria,* No. 5, 1912.

16. The Bolshevik candidate in Petersburg, Badaev, had won, they argued, only thanks to the votes that he had received at the last stage of the elections from anti-Semitic Octobrist *vyborshchiki* (the Menshevik candidate in the Petersburg labor curiae had been Jewish); the

Bolshevik deputies Petrovsky (in Ekaterinoslav gubernia) and Muranov (in Kharkov gubernia) had run on electoral platforms actually drawn up by the Mensheviks; and even that stormy petrel, the Moscow deputy Malinovsky, had been elected with Menshevik support.

For such Menshevik interpretations of the returns in the elections to the Fourth Duma, see L. Martov, "Vybornye zametki" and M. Oskarov, "Itogi vyborov po rabochei kurii," in *Nasha zaria*, No. 9–10, 1912; and especially L. Martov, "Raskol vo sotsial-demokraticheskoi fraktsii," *Nasha zaria*, No. 10–11, 1913. For contrasting Bolshevik interpretations, see V. Il'in, "Itogi vyborov," *Prosveshchenie*, No. 1, Jan., 1913 (in Lenin, *Sochineniia*, 4th ed., XVIII, 462–85); and "Materialy k voprosu o bor'be vnutri S. D. dumskoi fraktsii," *Za pravdu*, No. 22, Oct. 29, 1913 (in Lenin, *Soch.*, XIX, 414–29).

17. Whatever consolation was to be sought, added Martov, could be found in the election returns in the First and Second Curiae of the cities, which had revealed, as the Mensheviks had forecast (in contrast to their Bolshevik opponents), a significant shift of the liberal elements in society to the left. Indeed, this shift had been so pronounced in some of the provincial centers, Martov observed, as to hold forth the promise of the division of the Kadet Party into "bourgeois" and "raznochinets radical" factions. Martov to Potresov, letter no. 178, Nov. 11, 1912 (NA).

18. For detailed presentations of the Bolsheviks' claim of support by the Russian working class on the eve of the war, see "Ob'ektivnye dannye o sile raznykh techenii v rabochem dvizhenii" (in Lenin, *Soch.*, 4th ed., XX, 355–60), and "Doklad Ts. K. RSDRP i instruktivnye ukazaniia delegatsii Ts. K. na Briussel'skom soveshchanii" (*ibid.*, pp. 463–502). My own reading of the contemporary Menshevik press suggests that the specific statistical data cited in these two statements, *although by no means the conclusions drawn from them*, are not grossly exaggerated.

19. Martov to Potresov, letter no. 188, Sept. 15, 1913 (NA). This is the last letter that has been preserved of the Martov-Potresov correspondence of the prewar period (as noted earlier, Martov returned to Petersburg shortly after the amnesty).

20. F. Bulkin, "Raskol fraktsii i zadachi rabochikh," *Nasha zaria*, No. 6, 1914.

21. For Bulkin's first, and most radical statement of this thesis, see his "Rabochaia samodeiatel'nost' i rabochaia demokratiia," *Nasha zaria*, No. 3, 1914.

22. L. M., "Otvet Bulkinu," *Nasha zaria*, No. 3, 1914.

23. For such Menshevik analyses of the new tendencies in the labor movement during the immediate prewar period, see G. Rakitin [Levitsky], "Rabochaia massa i rabochaia intelligentsia," *Nasha zaria*, No. 9, 1913; L. M., "Otvet Bulkinu," *op. cit.,* B. I. Gorev, "Demagogiia ili marksism," *Nasha zaria*, No. 6, 1914; and especially V. Sh–r' [Sher'], "Nashe professional'noe dvishenie za poslednie dva goda," *Bor'ba*, Nos. 1, 2, 3, and 4, 1914.

24. V. Sh-r', *op. cit.*, Nos. 3 and 4, 1914.

25. Pakitin, "Rabochaia massa . . .," *op. cit.*

26. L. M., "Narodniki i peterburskoe rabochee dvizhenie," *Severnaia rabochaia gazeta*, Nos. 21, 24, 28, Mar., 1914; and "Tak i est'," Apr. 12, 1914.

27. See A. G. Rashin, *Formirovanie rabochego klassa Rossii* (Moscow, 1958), pp. 438–39.

28. As Geroid Robinson notes, the Stolypin legislation effectively enabled individual householders in the repartitional communes to obtain under certain conditions "a permanent and more or less unified holding against the unanimous opposition of the communal assembly." Similar conditions obtained for those repartitional communes which were converted to hereditary tenure under the arbitrary Dissolution Law of 1910. See G. T. Robinson, *Rural Russia under the Old Regime* (New York, 1932), p. 219; also note 28 on p. 305.

29. The Petersburg Party City Committee consisted at that time of the following members: Schmidt, Fedorov, Antipov, Shurkanov, Ignatiev, Sesitsky, and Ionov. Of these, Shurkanov, Ignatiev, and Sesitsky were agents of the Okhrana. For further details, see A. Kiselev, "V iule 1914 goda," *Proletarskaia revoliutsiia*, No. 7 (30), July, 1924.

30. It is suggestive, in this connection, that so many of the student recruits into this "second generation" of the Bolshevik faction were *externy,* who were not sufficiently prepared, or well to do, to enroll as regular students in the gymnasia and higher schools.

31. L. M., "Otvet Bulkinu," *op. cit.*

32. "Agenturnye svedeniia nachal'nika Moskovskogo okhrannogo otdeleniia A. Martynova," *Istoricheskii arkhiv*, No. 6, 1958, p. 11.

33. *Russkiia vedomosti*, July 8, 1914, p. 3, July 9, p. 2; *Novoe vremia*, July 8, p. 5; *Riech'*, July 8, p. 3. The Petersburg newspapers did not appear between July 9 and 11, owing to a strike of the typographical workers.

34. This ungrammatically written appeal is worthy of quotation, for it vividly expressed the feelings that animated at this stage of the strike the Bolsheviks' rebellious following: "Comrades! The government headed by the capitalists has not declared merciless war on the laboring masses in jest; everywhere, in political as in economic strikes, bloodthirsty police heroes have appeared. They are committing acts of violence with impunity, carrying out mass arrests, sometimes shooting, closing trade unions as well as organizations of cultural enlightment, but all this is of no avail to them. Every day, Russia's jails are growing like mushrooms; every day, the newspapers carry mentions of the deportations of our comrades to the most desolate places! [Yet] everywhere we see that the strikes are assuming the most colossal scope. The peasants are not paying their quit-rent, they are cutting down the woods of the crown and the gentry, burning down their manors; the soldiers are not taking the oath, they are insulting their officers, reading subversive newspapers. The government is trembling, worrying because around it the army of labor is growing not by the day but by the hour, and preparing for a decisive clash with its century-old foe. But your attempts to hold the people in chains are in vain; you are showing only for the n-th time that you are helpless, and the more you inflict violence on the people, the deeper you are digging your own pit. It is in vain, you bloodthirsty tribe, that you have taken up arms against the laboring masses. The government is fighting with bayonets, the capitalists—with no money, and the clergy—with sermons; but the people have taken this into account, they no longer believe in fairy tales, and in answer to you, instigators of police repressions, the whole laboring class is declaring that your song is over. We are on the eve of great events, if not today then tomorrow your luxurious palaces will be turned into people's clubs and unions. . . . The factories and plants will work only for the laboring masses. The jails will be overflowing with the likes of you. . . . Your woods, meadows, fields, everything you have, will fall into the hands of those you humiliated. Comrades! Lend your ears and prepare yourselves for anything. To wait and endure—enough with these words! Our motto is—hail the relentless struggle against the government and the capitalists! Down with capital! Comrades, get ready! Hail socialism!" This document was originally printed in *Pamiatniki agitatsionnoi literatury RSDRP.* VI, Part I (Petrograd and Moscow, 1923), 79. It is reprinted in "Iul'skie volneniia 1914 g. v Peterburge," *Proletarskaia revoliutsiia,* No. 8–9 (31–32), Aug.–Sept., 1924, p. 318.

35. Dispatch of correspondent S., *Riech',* July 12 (25), 1914, p. 5.

36. Martov-Potresov, letter No. 178, Nov. 11, 1912 (NA). See note 17.

37. Interviews of Miliukov by B. N. Nicolaevsky recorded in 1927, now in the latter's personal archives.

38. These negotiations between the Moscow Informatsionnyi Komitet and the Bolsheviks are discussed in the following published documents: "Pis'mo I. I. Skvortsova-Stepanova, V. I. Leninu" [received by Lenin on Mar. 9 (22), 1914], and "Pisv'mo V. I. Lenina I. I. Skvortsovu-Stepanovu" [Mar. 11 (24), 1914], published in *Istoricheskii arkhiv,* No. 2, 1959, pp. 13–17; "Agenturnye svedeniia nachal'nika Moskovskogo okhrannogo otdeleniia A. Martynova . . . ob ukazanniiakh Ts. K. RSDRP po sozyvu s'iezda partii" [Apr. 27 (May 10), 1914], "Donesenie A. Martynova v Departament politsii ob obeshchannoi progressistami denezhnoi subsidii sotsialdemokratam po ustroistvu s'iezda" [May 13 (26), 1914], and "Iz zapiski nachal'nika Moskovskogo okhrannogo otdeleniia v Departament politsii o podgotovke bol'shevikami partiinogo s'iezda" [May 16 (29), 1914], in *Istoricheskii arkhiv,* No. 6, 1958, pp. 8–10, 12–13.

39. "Pis'mo I. I. Skvortsova-Stepanova V. I. Leninu."

40. "Pis'mo V. I. Lenina I. I. Skvortsovu-Stepanovu," p. 13.

41. "Agenturnye svedeniia nachal'nika Moskovskogo okhrannogo otdeleniia . . .," *Istoricheskii arkhiv,* No. 6, 1958, pp. 8–10.

42. "Donesenie A. Martynova . . .," *ibid.,* pp. 12–13.

43. "Pis'mo N. K. Krupskoi Ural'skomu oblastnomu komitetu RSDRP" [June 4 (17), 1914], *ibid.,* p. 20.

44. A. S. Izgoev, "Na perevale," *Russkaia mysl',* No. 1 (Jan.), 1914, p. 147.

45. Peter Struve, "Ozdorovlenie vlasti," *ibid.,* p. 159.

46. S. El'patevsky, "Zhizn' idet," *Russkoe bogatstvo,* No. 1 (Jan.), 1914.

47. *Ibid.,* pp. 288, 299.

48. I. V. Gessen, "Vnutrenniaia zhizn'," *Ezhegodnik gazety "Riech'"* na *1914,* p. 75.

49. The data on which the following discussion of the role of Russian Masonry during the last years of the empire is based have been drawn from the following sources: I. V. Gessen, *V dvukh vekakh* (Berlin, 1937); S. Mel'gunov, *Na putiakh k dvortsovomu perevorotu* (Paris,

1931); P. N. Miliukov, *Vospominaniia*, Vol. II (New York, 1955); "Pis'mo E. D. Kuskovoi k N. V. Vol'skomu ot 15 noiabria 1955g." and "Iz pis'ma E. D. Kuskovoi k L. O. Dan ot 12 fevralia 1957g.," in Grigorii Aronson, *Rossiia nakanune revoliutsii* (New York, 1962), pp. 138–42; and especially the unpublished interviews on the subject conducted by B. N. Nicolaevsky in the 1920's with N. S. Chkheidze and A. Ia. Galpern (records in the personal archives of B. N. Nicolaevsky).

50. "Pis'mo E. D. Kuskovoi k N. V. Vol'skomu. . . ."

51. See "Iz pis'ma E. D. Kuskovoi k L. O. Dan. . . ." This letter, written when Kuskova was in her eighties, is indeed permeated with the conviction that all this was in fact "brilliantly accomplished."

52. Miliukov writes: "I should like to stress in addition the tie between Kerensky and Nekrasov—and the two ministers I have not mentioned, Tereshchenko and Konovalov. All four are very different in their personalities, backgrounds, and political roles; but they are united by more than just radical political views. Besides this, they are connected by some kind of personal tie, not only of a purely political, but also in its way of a politico-moral, character. It would seem that they are even united by mutual obligations, stemming from one and the same source. . . . Their friendship goes beyond the general realm of politics. From the remarks made here one can infer precisely what tie unites the central group of the four. . . . If I don't speak more clearly about it here it is because, while observing the fact, I did not make out its origin at the time and learned of it from an accidental source." And in an earlier, even more revealing, passage, discussing the selection of the Ministers of the Provisional Government at the onset of the February Revolution: "It was most difficult of all to recommend the generally unknown novice in our ranks, Tereshchenko, the sole 'capitalist minister' among us. From what 'list' had he 'emerged' in the Ministry of Finance? I didn't know then that the source was the same as that from which Kerensky had intruded himself, from which stemmed the republicanism of our Nekrasov, and from which originated the unexpected radicalism of the 'Progressisty,' Konovalov and Efremov. I learned of this source much after the event." Miliukov, *Vospominaniia*, II, 332–33 and 311–12.

As a matter of fact, according to reliable testimony, both Nekrasov and Kerensky served as secretaries of the Executive Committee of the *Velikii Sovet narodov Rossii*, the new Masonry's national organization, during the years leading up to 1917: Nekrasov in 1912–13 and again, following Kolubakin's early death at the front, from the summer of 1914 to the summer of 1916; Kerensky, after the summer of 1916. This information is drawn from interviews recorded by B. N. Nicolaevsky in the 1920's with A. Ia. Galpern, a prominent Menshevik and at the time a member of the Executive Committee of the *Velikii Sovet narodov Rossii*; it is partially confirmed by the less complete testimony of N. Chkheidze. (Records in the archives of B. N. Nicolaevsky.)

53. Again we should note that these changes in the composition of the labor force were most dramatic precisely among those strata of the industrial working class which eventually displayed in 1917 the greatest revolutionary explosives: thus, while the total size of the Russian industrial labor force rose, during the war years, by only 6.5 per cent (although its composition, of course, was much more substantially affected), the size of the stormy Petersburg industrial labor force rose by 58.5 per cent; that of the metalworking industry as a whole, by 69 per cent; and, to use an even more precise yardstick, that of the "vanguard of the Russian revolutionary working class" of Bolshevik fame, the workers in the Petersburg metalworking industry, by 134 per cent. See A. G. Rashin, *Formirovanie rabochego klassa v Rossii* (Moscow, 1958), pp. 72–83.

# The Dissidence of Russian Painting (1860-1922)

## ALAIN BESANÇON

Today, beyond the differences in painting styles among schools, one can readily speak of a world-wide painting style. However, a sizable enough exception maintains and affirms itself: Russian and Soviet painting.[1] Russia is a unique civilization, with its own values and its own museum: a world isolated from us by a frequent lack of understanding and a rarity of contacts. In a recent article, M. M. Alpatov complains, and rightly so, about the overly circumspect attitude toward Russian art in France; and he points out several obvious cases of injustice.[2] In the spring of 1960 how many Parisians saw, in an almost deserted gallery, the first Paris exhibition of Russian canvases, which are the pride of Russia and her sincerest message and which detain the crowds at the Tret'iakov Gallery? Similarly, the magnificent Matisses of the Hermitage of Leningrad see only a thinly scattered, perplexed public pass by.

Here, emotion and throng; there, silence and mockery. This is what deserves the attention of the historian: not only painting is involved when a phenomena capable of orienting the entire décor of a civilization, and perhaps more than its décor, is in question.

We do not claim, after forty years, to redo in a few pages the very useful book of Louis Réau.[3] Our purpose is to search for the historical origins of this dissidence within Russian art, to measure the action of the social forces that, throughout their evolution, were able to perpetuate it. We shall not seek to follow all the movements of an evolution of sixty years, which was never unilinear. We shall keep our eyes set on the branch from which Soviet painting has sprung and which constitutes almost by itself the contemporary museum of the Soviet world. Is it the principal branch? On the historical plane, we believe that it is the most vigorous, the one most in harmony with the cultural movement that prevailed over the others. On the esthetic plane, we shall avoid formulating any judgments. Desiring to penetrate a sensibility so remote from that of the West, it is wise not to introduce our own. The essential task is to understand the intentions of the painters and, even more, the reactions of the

FROM Alain Besançon, "La dissidense de la peinture russe (1860–1922)," *Annales*, 2 (March-April 1962), pp. 252–282. Reprinted by permission of the publisher.

public. The crowd at the Tret'iakov Gallery: this, in truth, is the problem that has been posed for us.

## Origins of the Crisis of Subject Matter

Born in France at the end of the eighteenth century, the crisis of subject matter, which attained its paroxysm under the Second Empire, seized Russia in the years immediately preceding and following the Reforms of 1861. In France, this crisis rapidly led to the issue of expression.[4] In Russia, on the contrary, despite several digressions, the pictorial formulas developed during 1860–1880 have been maintained until today. It was therefore after 1860 that Western painting and Russian painting separated. What conditions did the "subject crisis" encounter in Russia for it to be resolved in an exceptionally solid stabilization of pictorial expression, whereas elsewhere it inaugurated a permanent revolution?[5]

In the mid-nineteenth century the originality of Russian painting is not so much in its plastic expression as in its social situation, so to speak. The great religious works of Bruni and the military parades of Chernetsov are neither better nor worse than their neoclassical French, Italian, and German models. But what is properly Russian is the "Colbertian" role still played by the Academy of Fine Arts, which promulgated the commands of the Ministry of the Court on which it depended, quartered young talent, dictated subjects, conferred on paintings grades within the hierarchy of ranks—in short, administered painting. There was no counterbalance to this monopoly—neither a private market, be it ever so small, nor an independent public.

The forerunners remain marginal: Ivanov embodies—on the shores of the Tiber—the virtues of Russian painting: national faith, sincerity[6] and personal involvement, the taste for noble subjects extracted from national history, "treated with all the archaeological exactitude so necessary for our times."[7] Fedotov, an officer, paints, in the manner of Teniers and Wouwerman, everyday scenes but adds a moralistic and satirical note. Thus there are premonitions of the great movement of 1860–1880. However, and this is essential, the initiative for the revival comes not so much from the painters themselves as from the critics. In France, Baudelaire comments on the experiences of painters; in Russia, Chernyshevsky precedes them. The emancipation of literature precedes by forty years the emancipation of painting, which develops in its wake, as if in its shadow. Whence the immense, overwhelming influence, comparable to that of a Proudhon, which Chernyshevsky exerted on painting. In France the great pictorial events are "The Stone Breakers," "Luncheon on the Grass." In Russia, it is a book: *Esthetic Rapports Between Art and Reality.*[8]

This is a remarkable book both in ideas and attitudes. For Chernyshevsky the source of all beauty is in nature, in reality; and art gives but an impoverished reflection of it. This inferiority of art in comparison with reality leads Cherny-shevsky to devalue the successes of the past: "Neither in painting, nor in music, nor in architecture will one find a single work, or hardly so, created 100 or 150 years ago, which does not appear tasteless or ridiculous today, despite the imprint of genius on it."[9] After having settled, with a dash of the pen, the scores of Homer (incoherent), Aeschylus and Sophocles (too austere and dry), and Shakespeare (oratorical and bombastic), Chernyshevsky passes to painting: "We must acknowledge the same thing; Raphael is the only one against whom voices are rarely raised. As for all of the other painters, a multitude of weak points were discovered in them a long time ago. But even Raphael is to be reproached for ignoring anatomy."[10] This joyful destruction of the classical heritage[11] aids Russian painting in ridding itself of the oppressive feeling of inferiority to Western art and in breaking with academic values.

These limits posed, what the utility of art might be remains to be learned. A substitute for reality, art may serve to provide pleasure. However, art should not remain a means for enjoyment and nothing more. The dignity that it does not possess in itself can be found in its humanist aims. Reality, which it reproduces, interests man: "The works of man should have their purpose in the needs of man and not in themselves. This is why useless imitation provokes a disgust which is the greater when the exterior resemblance is perfect."[12]

The reproduction of reality is to be explanatory. "The force of art is that of a commentary."[13] "It is much easier and much more attractive for man to become familiar with works of art than to become familiar with the formulas and the strict analysis of science."[14] It will be partisan: "An artist, unable to stop being a man, cannot, even if he wants to, refuse to pass judgment on the phenomena represented. This judgment is expressed in his work; here is a new meaning for works of art by virtue of which art is placed among man's moral activities."[15] The privileged ground of the artist will be social life: "His paintings . . . will pose and resolve the problems which surge from life for a thinking man; his works of art will be, as it were, suggested by life. . . . Thus the artist becomes a thinker, and the work of art, while remaining in the domain of art, acquires scientific value."[16]

That in 1857 Chernyshevsky implicitly shares the conception of an art "competing" with nature—the painting providing an optical illusion with respect to reality—is not at all astonishing. He does not question either Renaissance perspective or space, seeing in them, like all his contemporaries, facts in accord once and for all with the nature of human vision. What he—as a literary man, in Russia, in 1860—demands in the end is essentially a change of subject. But Chernyshevsky's tremendous importance lies in the fact that he commits an entire generation to consider this thematic displacement as a whole esthetic revolution. The valorization of art as a social activity and its simultaneous depreciation as an absolute value (or an independent reality) can lead, in this period, only to the maintenance of the most generally used pictorial language, since the urgent problem is to spread it among the masses, instead of insignificant anecdotes and moral truths, progressive and liberal though they may be. Russian painting is pointed toward militant activism. And this is the great movement of the *Peredvizhniki*.

## The *Peredvizhniki*: Three Works

On November 9, 1863, fourteen students of the Academy, competing for the gold medal, presented a petition for the right to choose their subject of competition. Refused, they left the Academy in an uproar, which resulted in their being classed as suspicious and subjected to police surveillance.[17] The hostility of official society on the one hand and the narrowness of the public on the other, compelled the dissenters to form a group in order to survive. The *"Artel'* (Association) of Free Painters" was formed, centered around the extremely strong personality of Kramskoy and following the example proposed in *What Is to Be Done?* Every Wednesday, artists and writers met for discussion and debated the current problems and the ideas of Chernyshevsky.[18] Young artists outside the Association, such as Repin and Iaroshenko, came to learn.

When the Association was dissolved in 1870 a more flexible, more extensive organization replaced it: the Society of Traveling Exhibitions, whose purpose was to unite all the artists on their side in an annual traveling exhibition.[19] Warmly upheld by the democratic press of the *Sovremennik* and the *Annals of the Fatherland*, based on the School of Painting and Sculpture of Moscow,[20] the society of the *Peredvizhniki* (Wanderers) gathered together or profoundly influenced for at least thirty years all that counts in Russian painting.[21] There are but two poles, the Academy and the Society of Wanderers, the latter much more attractive than the former. For the Soviet critic, this is the golden age of Russian painting, and even of all modern painting.[22]

Here we shall present only three works from an enormous output. Illustrious in the U.S.S.R., they molded the sensibility of several generations. In them we shall look for the germ of a divergent evolution, the source of the schism of Russian art. We shall also try to see them through the eyes of the Russian spectator.

### Kramskoy: "Nekrassov at the Time of His Last Poems" (1877–1879)

The poet-citizen is in bed, leaning against a pile of pillows.[23] His bloodless face announces approaching death. Several flasks of medicine, the cup and spoon, the little bell for calling the servants, the large slippers at the foot of the bed: everything symbolizes sickness, the defeat of the body. But here also are the symbols of the triumphant spirit: the dreamy gaze, lost in the future; the sheet of paper that the poet holds in his hand, on which he is writing one of his last patriotic poems;[24] books and newspapers that cover the bolster; portraits on the wall, among them one of Dobroliubov, the collaborator and friend of Chernyshevsky.

The painter and the public had the feeling that this was an audacious work. It is, in the sense of Courbet, "a genuine allegory" that claimed to sweep away the academic traditions. The mythological apparatus is replaced by the

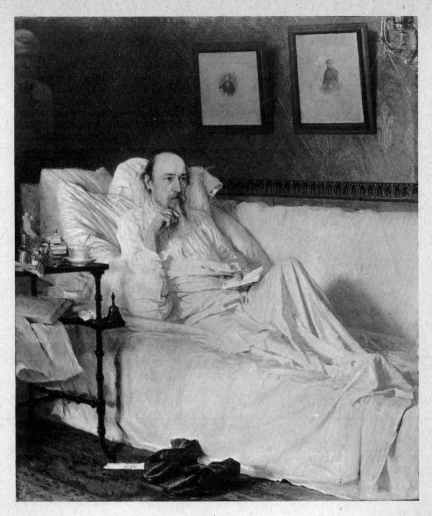

**FIGURE 1**
I. N. Kramskoy: Nekrassov at the Time of His Last Poems (1877–1879).

contemporary symbolism of medicines, slippers, and Dobroliubov. This leaves the traditional plastic language intact. The dominant lines converge about the face, the golden cross section cuts and recuts the design of the painting, the design does not trifle about either with perspective or with the draping of the night shirt; everything bears witness to an irreproachable finish.

The primary characteristic of the *Peredvizhniki* is clear: it associates the process of expression of traditional painting with a new theme.

The explanation must be sought in the hostility of official society, much more serious in the Russia of Alexander II than in the France of MacMahon. Since the painter uses his painting for the diffusion of ideals divergent from the ethical and political norms of established society, his art can be tolerated only if it alleges its conformity with the esthetic norms of society, which it defies with its painting but on a different level from that of painting. The *Peredvizhniki* rebels are proud of having been the best students of the Academy. When the police take down their works from the stands, they protest in the name of art. A struggle on both the esthetic and political fronts is less possible in Russia than anywhere else.

Another explanation, and a more general one, is the "populist" conception of the artist: "Let art be content with its high and magnificent destination: in default of reality, to be a reliable substitute and to be manual of life for man."[25] A manual, to be understood, must use a language understood by all, the one adopted by Russia almost two centuries earlier and spread for a century by the Academy. The artist is not an explorer of reality but an educator. Formal refinement inevitably becomes a withdrawal from the public, which does not understand at all. As Repin said: "Today it is the *moujik* who is the judge, and that is why it is necessary to rouse his interest."[26]

**FIGURE 2**
I. E. Repin: They Were Not Expecting Him (1884).

*Repin: "They Were Not Expecting Him" (1884)*[27]

A clandestine militant revolutionary, dressed as a peasant, returns home unexpectedly. Pale, appealing, intelligent, worried, he wonders how they are going to greet him? The servant has opened the door. The aging mother has already recognized her son; and with a trembling hand she seeks support from the back of a large, ugly armchair. Beaming, the wife gets ready to rise. The little girl is frightened, but the son, in the tunic of a high-school student, greets his father with a joyful smile. On the walls are the portraits of Nekrasov and of Shevchenko, the great persecuted Ukrainian poet.[28]

This is surely a painting that lends itself to stylistic analysis. The lateral illumination, the play of perspective with the doors and the doorframes evoke —from afar—certain Dutch Intimists whose tradition was maintained with honor in Russia by Venetsianov, Fedotov, and Tolstoy.[29] The colors are very triturated; the blues are mixed with green, the browns with grey and violet, the reds are purplish-blue.

But for the Russian spectator the interest resides above all in the scenario produced by Repin. The collaboration of painting with literature is obvious: both are united with the *subject*, which nourishes the work. Repin's skill consists in compressing, on the stage suggested by classical perspective, the elements of a drama which, on a real theatrical stage or in a novel, are advanced successively and which, here, are presented simultaneously. The eye has leisure to run through these messages transcribed in the conventional writing of classical painting: the peasant clothing of the revolutionary, the unsteady pose of the old woman, the "expressions" on the faces, the mute participation of Nekrasov and Shevchenko.

One sees why Repin is considered the *bogatyr* (epic hero) of Russian painting and of what is called its temperament: the giant and jovial fellows of the "Zaporogians," the blood that streams in "Ivan the Terrible and his Son," the political audacity of the "Refusal of the Confession" and of "The Arrest of the Propagandist"—in a word, the emotional quality of the subject. In France, at the same time, the temperament of Manet bursts forth in "The Lemon."

*Surikov: "Boyarina Morozova" (1887)*[30]

The disciple of Avvakum is displayed on a sleigh in the streets of Moscow, thronged with people, some pitying, others hostile; her extended hand, with the two joined fingers, attests to the Old Belief. This canvas, so famous and so rich, reveals the attitude of the *Peredvizhniki* toward the Western artistic heritage and the problem of the creation of a national school. Before painting this great work, Surikov wanted to go abroad. He saw nothing interesting in Paris and left at the end of eight days. In Venice, in contrast, he became enthusiastic about Veronese. Since Surikov refused the facility of academic pastiche, he used transposition. His characters are not Venetian gentlemen, but figures of

**FIGURE 3**
V. I. Surikov: Boyarina Morozova (1887).

Muscovite society: these include the Innocent, symbol of the people (as in *Boris Godunov*), who repeats, alone among everyone, the schismatic sign of the cross with two fingers. To the sparkling light, to the brocades and silks, to the beauty of the women of Italy correspond the snow, the blue skies of winter, the sable, the bedizened cloths, the Russian type of feminine beauty. The need for a national painting was satisfied by a translation into Russian, word for word, of the Western pictorial vocabulary.[31] On the whole, the valorization of the national past in *Peredvizhnik* painting of history is not accompanied by a rehabilitation of the old formulas of Russian art. The old icons are beginning to be collected, but for religious motives, by Old Believers. There is no trace in Repin's painting of his apprenticeship in an atelier of icon paintings. In the decorations of Vasnetsov at Saint Vladimir of Kiev, there is a romantic sympathy for the Middle Ages, as in our troubador painting (Slavophile art, as Benois noted), but no thought on the art of Rublev or of Feofan the Greek.[32] The *Peredvizhnik* movement does not result in an enlargement of the museum.

### The Esthetic Education of Russia: *Peredvizhniki* and Populism

"Realism" was a brief moment in French painting; in Russia it is the dominant stream. The adoption by a society of one esthetic formula from among several is a complex problem: history furnishes several reference points.

First let us take into account the peculiarities of the *Peredvizhnik* group itself, its dynamism, its monopoly of the art scene. Here is a group of more than twenty painters—larger, more united, more durable than any other group in Europe—whose style is uniform and whose purpose is the conquest and education of the common people. Everything had to be done. Since the decline of icon painting in the seventeenth century, "great art" was intended, in the Westernized form disseminated by the Academy, for the very small class of *pomeshchiki* (gentry estate-owners) and bureaucrats. The principal collection, the Hermitage, did not have the status of a museum open to all comers. Except for St. Petersburg, and to a smaller extent Moscow, easel-painting was not very widespread. Then, for fifty-three years, the exhibitions of the society traveled the length and breadth of Russia and came to more than twenty provincial cities.[33] Satellite groups broke off: the Society of Artists of Southern Russia, launched in Odessa in 1890, sent its exhibitions to Ekaterinoslav, Nikolaev, Sebastopol, Kishinev. At the end of the century the Society of Traveling Exhibitions of Siberia appeared.[34] In Moscow, Tret'iakov, a merchant, dedicated his whole life to assembling a collection worthy of forming the core of a national museum of painting.[35] For forty years (1856–1898) he visited studios, bought canvases, "carried on his shoulders," as Repin says, "the very existence of the whole Russian school of painting,"[36] and presented in the end a homogeneous ensemble whose pedagogical influence was exerted principally in favor of the *Peredvizhniki*. Young Gorky found, in 1900, that along with the Art Theater the Tret'iakov Gallery was the best thing there was in Moscow.[37]

The *Peredvizhniki* performed the pictorial education of Russia. They succeeded because they were supported by a larger movement. Chernyshevsky is, in fact, only the initiator of a fundamental tendency in Russian culture of the sixties and seventies. Even Tolstoy, so remote from revolutionary materialism, is not an exception. Ge, Kramskoy, and Repin are his friends and paint his portrait. He borrows from them several traits for the character of the painter Mikhailov in *Anna Karenina*.[38] In 1898, while the esthetics of the Wanderers is in its decline, Tolstoy pronounces a total condemnation of modern art, Impressionism in particular.[39] The reasons for this severity are not very different from those of Chernyshevsky: "One will not understand the real meaning of art until one ceases to look for the purpose of art in beauty, that is, in pleasure."[40] It is not a diversion, but a means of reuniting men. And Tolstoy stigmatizes the "Art of the Elite," the "quest for obscurity," the "corruption of art." Basically, the utilitarian point of view is preserved.

In truth, despite Tolstoy's moral authority, this awakening—in 1898—of the old iconoclasm of Chernyshevsky and Pisarev is anachronistic and rouses the protest of Chekhov.[41] But it is anachronistic for only part of the intelligentsia.

First populists, then, as we shall see, social democrats remained faithful, in effect, to the spirit of Chernyshevsky. The great opportunity for the *Peredvizhnechestvo* was to profit from its association with the revolutionary movement in all the phases of the latter.

First of all there is the illustration of populist themes: indictments against oppression and superstition (Repin's "The Boat Haulers," Perov's "Easter Procession to the Village," Iaroshenko's "The Stoker"); the religious sublimation of suffering in Ge; pacifist humanism (Vereshchagin's "Apotheosis of War"); and even direct representation of the revolutionary militants (V. E. Makovsky's "The Soirée," Repin's "The Arrest of the Propagandist," Iaroshenko's "The Prisoner").

There is still a populist conscience about the responsibilities of the artist: "He must himself give a humanitarian character to his works . . . he must be imbued with progressive thinking when beginning his work," wrote Lavrov.[42]

This idea of responsibility is identified with the Lavrovist idea of the debt contracted by the "thinking personality" to the people, and it results in an amalgam of a single condemnation of the search for form and of art for art's sake. A short story by Garshin, inspired by Iaroshenko's "The Stoker," admirably illuminates this relation of painting to its public—"The Painters," published in 1879.[43] Dedov paints "for pleasure"; he personifies art for art's sake. Riabinin, on the contrary, torments himself: What is the purpose of art? "When I visit an exhibition, what do I see? Canvases in which colors are disposed in such a way as to reproduce impressions analogous to different objects. The public marvels at these ingenious arrangements, and that is all. I have come to doubt the importance of art. I have never seen a painting make a man better." He is disgusted "to serve the stupid curiosity of the crowd . . . or the vanity of the potbellied nouveau riche." One day the two friends are walking along the docks when they see a horrible sight: copper riveters at work, eardrums punctured, chests ravaged. Riabinin, fascinated, wants to paint one of these riveters. His friend, who sees in art a means to escape from this inhuman world, protests against "this plebeian movement in art. . . . What is the good of Repin's 'The Boat Haulers'? They have been done by the hand of a master, that is incontestable; but that is all their worth. Where is beauty, harmony, elegance?"

Riabinin has finished his painting. He speaks to his character: "Come, you whom I have chained to the canvas, come and contemplate these frock-coats and these dress trains, and cry to them: 'I am a gnawing ulcer'. . . . Destroy their peace as you have destroyed mine." But what is the use? "The public will pass by, indifferent, or with a disagreeable pout; the ladies will do nothing but murmur in French: 'Ah comme il est laid ce bonhomme' (Ah, how ugly this fellow is), and they will glide to the next painting, 'The Little Girl with the Cat' . . . only one young man or one young girl will stop to read in the martyr's eyes the clamor with which I have filled them." Several days later, when his friend, who dreams only of honors, wins the academic gold medal, Riabinin enters the Normal School for teachers.

One sees that Garshin, like Chernyshevsky twenty years earlier, questions not the traditional system of representation, but its use: individual pleasure or collective liberation. Garshin goes even further and leans toward iconoclasm, since, as an instrument of emancipation, art does not have the effectiveness of direct militant action.

*Peredvizhnik* painting is thus found at the heart of an even larger cultural movement than populism, since it goes from Gogol to Tolstoy and to Gorky, who distrusts pure art and demands that art be above all an instrument of redemption.

This further explains its emotional power. The real public of the *Peredvizhniki* is the plebeian (*raznochinets*) intelligentsia of the sixties and eighties, alienated (*otchuzhdennyi*) from Russian society and seeking at all costs to break its isolation, to find an access to the people. The "people" are only the actual public; the moujik—Garshin states it clearly—does not frequent the wandering exhibitions. This painting functions, therefore, not only as a reflection of the real world but as a screen onto which the intelligentsia's aspirations and conception of the world are projected. The little hunchback of the "Peasant Procession in Kursk Province" embodies the moral beauty of the peasant seen through populist mythology.[44] This art gives the intelligentsia access to an imaginary, nonalienated world, and is also a mirror for the intelligentsia.

Vera Figner, after a quarter of a century spent in the casemates of Schlusselburg, sees a reproduction of "Boyarina Morozova": "Reclining in a low sleigh, bound in chains, the Boyarina was leaving for exile, for the prison in which she was to die. She had a handsome face, emaciated, hard, marked by the resolution to go to the end. The chained hand, raised in a gesture of defiance, still made the sign of the cross. . . . This painting was alive. It spoke of a struggle for beliefs, of persecution, of the loss of the strongest ones, those who remain faithful to themselves. It resuscitated a page of life . . . April 3, 1881, the carts of the regicides, Sophia Perovskaia. . . ."[45] Because it is an affective projection, *Peredvizhnik* painting is a living art.

The union of the *Peredvizhniki* with the revolutionary movement is, in the end, the principal factor that assures their formula for long life. The imagery they propose, in the Russia of Alexander II and Alexander III, is charged with enough emotional power so that the painter is tempted neither to go further in the analysis of reality nor to examine the conditions of his vision. The transfer of subject matter does not result, as in France, in "open airism," in the breakup of light, in the destruction of cubic space.[46] It is sufficient to arouse emotion. This is why the old system of forms is taken over by those who are the future of Russia and who place it in the service of the Revolution and identify it as revolutionary art.

One of the ambitions of the Association of Free Painters is to create a national school. *Peredvizhnik* production is extremely abundant in all domains: portraits, landscapes, genre paintings, history, battles. But does this powerful flourishing result in the emergence of a properly Russian style? At first glance, the Russian school looks like a province of a European style rarely displayed today: subject painting, national and social painting, abundantly represented in France itself by Bastien-Lepage, Regnault, and many others. In Eastern Europe, historical conditions further valorize it. In Poland, Matejko exhibits, for example, "King Stephen Batory at the Siege of Pskov"; in Bohemia, Brozik shows "The Condemnation of John Huss," Grigoresco, the "Convoy of Turkish Prisoners." But what is specifically Russian is the dominant power of this movement. For if there is not, in our sense, the affirmation of a *style* (we have seen that the pre-Petrine tradition was almost unknown), there is the affirmation of a coherent esthetics, "theorized" by doctrinaires, supported by the great novelists, and illustrated by twenty painters: "subject esthetics," let us say, rather than "realism," which is too comprehensive. By basing themselves on it the *Peredvizhniki* utilize the plastic language of Western classical painting, while at the same time isolating themselves from the West. Not that they are deprived of contacts with the West, they deliberately refuse them, thus manifesting an astonishing resistance to French influence.

In Rome in 1873, Repin is impressed only by Michelangelo's "Moses." "The rest, especially Raphael, is so old, so childish, that one would prefer not to look at it. There is so much filth (*gadost'*) in the museums here." And in Paris, in 1874, the year of the birth of Impressionism, he complains, "Nowadays the painting of the French is so empty, so stupid, that there is nothing to be said about it. The painting technique may show talent, but only the technique; there is no content. . . ."[47] Perov becomes so bored in Paris that he begs the Academy for an end to his leave: "Rather than consecrate several years of my life to the study of a foreign country, it would be better to exploit the invaluable treasure of subjects furnished by the city and rural life of our country."[48] A particularly important opinion is that of Stasov, who is the most eminent critic (and friend) of the *Peredvizhniki*. In 1873, in an account of the international exhibition of Vienna, he gives French painting first place in Europe: but it is Regnault, Ronnat, Delaroche, and Breton whom he honors, and, above all, two masterpieces: "The Gladiators" of Gérôme, and the "1807" of Meissonier. He is also impressed by Courbet, although this painter is "extremely uneven and has produced insignificant and mediocre works."[49]

Some thirty years later, neither Repin nor Stasov has changed his mind. In an open letter to the *Mir Iskusstva*, Repin complains that snobs buy Degas at a tremendous cost, while Meissoniers and Fortunys can be acquired at prices far below their value. "If Monet succeeded once with his yellows and lilacs in achieving the effect of Ajvasovsky's "The Deluge," you would lift him up on a shield."[50] Repin prefers Stuck, Klimt, and Boecklin.

Stasov sketches a panorama of European art in 1901.[51] He holds the Barbizon school in esteem, he praises Millet, Courbet, Regnault, and after them, Bastien-Lepage and Rosa Bonheur. He expresses himself with clarity on the new art: "Impressionism has touched only exterior forms, exterior ways of representation and artistic expression; it has not touched the profound content of art, or rather, it has completely forgotten this content and has left it aside; even more, it has disfigured and belittled it. . . . To claim that Impressionism has changed the frontiers of art, opened new horizons, extended its influence over new domains of sensibility, of thought, of poetry, as the flatterers and defenders of Impressionism are striving to make us believe—that is false, and Impressionism itself never cared about all this."[52]

Manet dissociates himself from man and abandons the psychological portrait. In "The Bar of the Folies Bergères" attention is held by the reflections of the mirrors and decanters, while the psychology of the "principal characters of the painting," the girl and the man in evening dress, remains sketchy.[53] Stasov finally formulates the fundamental grievances: the gratuitousness of this art which "aspires to amuse the spectator independently of all ideas."[54] Flight from life: "All the tasks of history, all that concerns man and all the events of our existence have been declared outdated, boring, and useless by them (the Impressionists)." Stasov therefore concludes about the decadence of French art that the twentieth century will certainly not repeat the errors of the closing nineteenth century.[55]

All of this holds together and not only because of nationalism. The rejection of French art is a logical development of the coherent esthetics that, about 1890, again dominated Russian culture and that, in the pictorial domain, based itself on a full ensemble of works that fully realized it. The nationalist reaction was aggravated by the incompatibility of two esthetics, which asserted themselves concurrently and arranged their values in different hierarchies.

## The *Peredvizhnik* Tradition and Modern Art

From about 1890 onward, the movement of the Wandering Exhibitions became winded.[56] Surikov, Vasnetsov, Levitan made their styles flexible and became interested in Western experiments.[57] Then the evolution speeded up. In 1899, an open rupture with the old *Peredvizhnik* program occurred; this was the movement of the *Mir Iskusstva*, from the name of the journal (*The World of Art*) launched by Serge Diagilev (Diaghilev). From 1906 onward, there was a rapid multiplication of small schools: Blue Rose,[58] Jack of Diamonds,[59] Rayonism,[60] Suprematism,[61] Constructivism. In a few years it would be said that Russia had assimilated Impressionism, Symbolism, Cézanne, Cubism, and had invented Abstractionism. Matisse was famous in Moscow sooner than in Paris. Apparently the separateness of Russian painting had ended.

For the West, it was the golden age of Russian art, Russia's first and major contribution to modern art. For Soviet criticism it was decadence. We shall not argue about this. We know that the avant-garde did not, at least in Russia, long survive the Revolution and that it was a passing episode in a temporal evolution. What will occupy us is its defeat. We shall limit ourselves to two points: the fragility of the social foundations of the new painting and, in its choice of methods of expression, the direct or indirect repercussions of the long reign of subject matter esthetics.

### New Painting and the Bougeoisie

At the time of Alexander II, painting represented both the projection of the aspirations of an intelligentsia without a grasp on reality and an attempt to get hold of this reality, to break its isolation by conquering and educating a still existing public. The atrophy of this body led, in compensation, to an attempt to appeal to all of Russia. Thirty years later, an important part of the intelligentsia dissolved itself by integrating into the framework of bourgeois society; and it abandoned its revolutionary perspectives.[62] (The France of the Second Empire had known this kind of evolution.) The relation between the Russian artist and his public was thus upset and now resembled those of European artists in bourgeois society.

This Russian bourgeoisie, relatively small, but very vigorous, was certainly more cultivated and refined than the landowner and the bureaucrat of former years. It was impatient to live in Western style. The new Maecenases—Diaghilev, Mamontov, Shchukin, Morozov—did not care to perform, like Tret'iakov, a national, educational function. Art no longer blushed for being an ornament and a pleasure. The main activity of the *Mir Iskusstva* was not easel-painting but theater and ballet decoration (Bakst, Benois, Kórovin) and illustration of the luxurious, classical, and even erotic book (Benois, Lansere, Somov).

There appeared a new type of painting, worldly, and of good family and good company.[63] The era of the *raznochintsy* and the militants was finished. Like literature, painting dissociated itself from the revolution in proportion as the latter approached.[64]

This new bourgeois Russian public engendered, as in the West, both a worldly movement in painting and the appearance (from 1908 onward) of avant-gardist phenomena in rebellion against this public. As a Marxist, Trotsky thought that literary symbolism (but also pictorial: for example, Vrubel) corresponded to the age in which the intelligentsia, having set up its distances vis-à-vis the people—submissive, in fact, to the bourgeoisie—was striving psychologically and esthetically not to be merged with the latter.

Whatever it may be, the correlation between the bourgeois phase of Russian history and the introduction of modern art wrought disastrous consequences upon the latter—first of all, because it remained confined in brilliant but narrow circles. The *Mir Iskusstva's* liveliest center was in St. Petersburg and did not extend beyond it. Futurism, according to Trotsky's remark, proclaimed the Revolution in Muscovite cafés but not in factories. Provincial torpor was not disturbed. As an individualistic art without a collective framework and with groups only at the level of luxury journals, Maecenian salons, and galleries, it could not have the force of persuasion and diffusion that the solid *Peredvizhnik* phalanx had; moreover, it sought neither to persuade nor to spread. Painting did not escape the general condition of Russian culture at the beginning of the twentieth century. "Many gifts were bestowed upon Russia in those years," wrote Berdiaev. "But all of this happened in a closed circle isolated from the rest of the social movement. . . . It was as though one were breathing a hothouse atmosphere; fresh air was lacking."[65]

Modern art remained apart; worse, it became suspect in a decisive environment—the social-democratic one. Marxist esthetics probably did not imply the upholding of any particular type of pictorial expression. Certain Russian Marxists, such as Trotsky, who outlined a sociology of Impressionism and Futurism, had a certain (critical) sympathy for modern art. Lunacharsky always seemed attentive and understanding toward it. A certain ambiguity can be noted in the prewar chronicles of the future Commissar of Public Instruction,[66] the key to which, as C. Frioux states it very well, "is perhaps a slight divergence between his tastes and his rigorous theoretical convictions."[67] While speaking with a predilection for it, he in effect acknowledges and explains as a Marxist "the generally recognized decadence of the French school."[68] Cézanne, for example, was a courageous seeker, betrayed, however, by an insufficient amount of artistic talent—in short, like the character of Zola's *Work*. Chagall "does not know how to draw," "his taste is doubtful," he ought to have learned his trade. But the painter is forgiven, Lunacharsky hurried to add, because he is sincere.[69] Like all social democrats, he rose up against art, which was decadent and "without ideas," attacked Benois and his "sempiternal Versailles studies," but at the same time he liked very much the studies of Dobrizinsky, London, and Maliavin.[70] In its totality Russian social democracy appears to have inherited the populist sensitivity and then to have interpreted in Marxist terms the latter's antipathy toward an art in collusion with the imperialist decomposition of capitalism. The mark of *Peredvizhnik* education on Plekhanov and Lenin is particularly clear.

Plekhanov did not doubt that modern art was decadent; the decline was in the triumph of Formalism: "It is always expressed, among other things, by this fact, that one begins to appraise form more than content. But content is so intrinsically linked to form that the disdain of content entails first the end of beauty and then the ugliness of form. I will cite Futurism in literature and, no doubt, Cubism in painting as examples."[71]

Form and content: the terms of the problem have not varied nor has the identification of content and subject. Reproaching the Impressionists for "their complete indifference to ideological content," Plekhanov gave as proof of it their almost exclusive taste for light, for landscape—beautiful but "without soul"—and their disdain for the portrait and the grand subjects upon which great painting is founded. "The painter who limits his attention to the domain of sensations is indifferent to feeling and thought."[72] Very curiously, Plekhanov contrasted da Vinci's "The Last Supper" with Impressionist painting. The passage is worth quoting because of the unconscious attitudes it reveals: "The task of Leonardo da Vinci was to represent the spiritual state of Jesus, Himself profoundly distressed by that terrible revelation (of Judas' betrayal), and the state of His disciples, who cannot believe that a traitor has crept into their little group. If the artist had deemed that the principal character of the painting ought to have been the light, he would not have dreamed of painting this drama. And if he had executed this fresco in spite of everything, the great artistic interest in it would no longer have resided in the inner state of Jesus and of his disciples; but it would have been dispersed onto the walls of the room in which they met, to the table at which they were seated, and even to their skin, that is, onto the various effects of light. We would have before us not a poignant internal drama, but a whole series of perfectly rendered spots of light; one, for example, on the wall of the room, another on the carpet, a third on Judas' crooked nose, a fourth on Jesus' cheek, and so forth. The impression produced by the fresco would have been much weaker; Leonardo da Vinci's work would have been much less valuable."[73]

As we see, what affected Plekhanov in 1912 in "The Last Supper" were the scenario, the "expressions," the gestures of the actors; everything else—light, décor, subject matter—were but accessories to the dramatic action. These unconscious attitudes were the only ones he consolidated and integrated into the coherent system of Marxist sociology. The *Peredvizhniki* thus profited from their participation in the great populist impetus, while the artists of *Mir Iskusstva* were compromised in the general condemnation of the bourgeois decadence of counterrevolutionary Russia. That Plekhanov looked upon the pioneers of contemporary art as the expression, despite their declared intention, of a decomposition that had arrived at its term was of great importance in the future.[74]

As for Lenin, we know his preferences, principles, and taste, lacking, as we do, any theory, which he was careful not to express and which he never did formulate. These tastes were still those of the generation of populism.[75] He esteemed the *Peredvizhniki* "to the highest degree,"[76] and he did not like modern art. After the revolution, he confided to Clara Zetkin: "We are good revolutionaries, but we believe ourselves to be held, I do not know why, to prove that we are also 'at the height of modern culture.' I cannot consider Expressionist, Futurist, Cubist, and other 'ist' works as supreme manifestations of artistic genius. I do not understand them. They do not bring me any pleasure."[77] The Leninist conception of art is probably very close to that of Chernyshevsky in that it is a relativization of the value of art to its social role. "It matters little what art gives to hundreds, indeed to thousands, of people in a population that numbers in the millions. Art belongs to the people. It should penetrate with its roots to the depths of the working masses. It should be accessible to these masses and loved by them. . . . Is it necessary to offer superfine biscuits to a small minority while the working masses and peasants lack black bread?"[78]

Thus the social bases of modern art were fragile in Russia, and they rendered art vulnerable to a mass revolution, especially since the *Peredvizhnik* tradition was kept alive, as if in reserve, and secretly influenced modern art.

### The Esthetics of Subject Matter and Modern Art

In the beginning of the twentieth century the *Peredvizhnechestvo* no longer had a monopoly on painting. But it continued and assured its hold on art. Almost all artistic teaching was in its hands; it controlled the Academy, which Repin, Shishkin, V. Makovsky, and Kuindzhi entered and in which they taught,[79] and the School of Painting, Sculpture, and Architecture of Moscow. The Wanderers' influence was also very strong on the Union of Russian Artists, a Muscovite association founded in 1903, in which the old and young generations mingled: Nesterov, Vasnetsov, Surikov and Arkhipov, Juon, the two Korovins, and others.

At the sides of the old masters, such as Repin and Surikov, who were still full of life, appeared Kasatkin, who took his subjects from the young proletariat; Maliavin, the painter of peasants; Ivanov, Korovin, Riabushkin, Arkhipov, and others. Also remaining under the influence of the same esthetic trend were Nesterov, the painter of Holy Russia, and Serov, who linked the social sensitivity of the Wanderers (he resigned from the Academy the day after Bloody Sunday) with the worldly elegance of the *Mir Iskusstva* ("The Tsar's Hunts," "Ida Rubinstein," "Portrait of O. K. Orlova"). The striking formal relationship between contemporary Soviet painting and the painting of the noble *Peredvizhnik* epoch is explained by this transmission without hiatus of technique and manner.

The influence of the *Peredvizhniki* can be seen even in the movements that were most opposed to them. It seems to us, in effect, that the *Mir Iskusstva* is still within the esthetics of subject matter, and that Abstractionism no doubt also developed within this same context. Let us consider a typical work of the *Mir Iskusstva*, "The King's Promenade" by Alexander Benua (Benois, 1906). It is part of a Versailles series that is important in the work of Benois, who, as codirector of the *Mir Iskusstva*, editor of the *Zolotoe Runo*, and a historian of Russian art, was a central figure of the group as well as its theoretician. "The King's Promenade" is a representative canvas also because there was a veritable obsession with the Ancien Régime and with the eighteenth century, apparent in a number of the movement's paintings. Somov, and particularly Lansere, multiplied the "Views of Peterhof," of Tsarskoe Selo, carnivals, and masquerades.

In the foreground of the painting is a pond. A mythological group is reflected in the tranquil water. In the middle distance there is a well-raked avenue along which three couples parade ceremoniously; small pageboys hold the ladies' dresses. Beyond the railing are hedges of young hornbeams stripped of their leaves, and a row of linden trees that disappear in the haze of a winter sky.

It is a studio landscape;[80] a refinement of style is recognized in the simplified design, in the flatness of coloring, in the perspective with planes graded in depth, as in a stage setting. It was not, however, this rather art nouveau decorativism that created the scandal. What this "retrospectivist" (that is the name of the tendency) canvas proclaims is the rejection of *sovremennost'* (contemporaneity); the artist keeps his distance, dissociates himself. But the type of pictorial language was so fixed at that time that in order to manifest the rights of subjectivity, the independence of art, the painter quite naturally employed the most tried means—change of subject. In fact, a rupture with the traditional mode of expression was useless: the Russian public was educated in such a way that a complex of emotions was released at the sight of Benois' "The King's Promenade," as earlier with Repin's "Boat Haulers," so that the public was not mistaken about the meaning of this nostalgia for a great century, displayed the day after the Revolution of 1905. The significance of the painting is in what it represents.

With the exception of the astonishing Vrubel (Wroubel), so like Gustave Moreau, but perfectly original and greater, the *Mir Iskusstva* participated in the modern art adventure only in its minor aspects—those of modern-style decorativism, in which it always excelled, by the way. If it was interested in the Russian past,[81] if it encouraged the peasant art of the *Kustari* (artisans), it took nothing from the style of the icons and the *lubki*:[82] all this was antiquarian or ethnographic curiosity and nothing more. The *Mir Iskusstva* was less revolutionary than it thought, and it might even have contributed to the aggravation of the confusion over the problem of modern art. The emotional value of the subject, the sentimental, but not esthetic, valorization of the Russian past, in which Tsarinas and wigged courtiers simply replaced Cossacks and *Bogatyrs*, a tight connection with literature (symbolist and no longer realist),[83] all this prolonged in effect the tradition that the movement was combating. It did this so well that the real avant-garde did not succeed the *Mir Iskusstva* until very late, about 1907. For everyone—symbolists of the Blue Rose, Cézannians of the Jack of Diamonds, and especially Abstractionists—the rupture with the subject tradition was radical from then on. But the fact that the latter was maintained so late gave this rupture a sudden and extreme nature, which led to the isolation of the avant-garde groups. The Abstractionists in particular

**FIGURE 4**
A. N. Benois: The King's Promenade (1906).

broke simultaneously from figuratism and with the public. It is from this narrow angle that we arrive at the problem of Abstractionism.

The first astonishing aspect was the way in which French experience was included. One of the innovations of great significance by the *Mir Iskusstva* was to have systematically introduced Western and French painting into Russia. From 1899 onward it organized international exhibitions. The choice of works showed an eclectic sympathy rather than a true understanding of the main stream of European art. Neither Cézanne, Seurat, Gauguin, nor Redon was represented; instead, and abundantly, Daghan-Bouveret, Aman-Jean, Casin, Menard, and La Touche.[84] In 1908 the exhibition of *Zolotoe Runo* centered on new art and Fauvism.[85] The great masters began to occupy the place that was due them. A Rouault ("Girls"), several Matisses, several Braque Fauves (the "Estaque") were seen there. Articles by Charles Morice and Voloshin introduced and commented on the new tendencies. In 1912 there was an exhibition from David through the Impressionists, organized by the French Institute.[86] At the same time, two collections without equal in the world were formed in Moscow: the Shchukin collection, started in 1897, and Morozov's, founded in 1903.[87] French art was henceforth present.

This produced a shock effect on the public that nothing in its pictorial past had prepared it to understand. "These paintings are never understood at once and demand considerable familiarization of the eye," wrote Voloshin in 1908.[88] The critic tells how, at the Luxembourg, upon seeing the canvases of the Caillebote collection, his eyes were "revolted" at first and that afterwards, with familiarization, it was the external world that appeared different to him; he understood that a new way of seeing the world had just been born. Not all were so discerning. The sudden invasion of Russia by French art, with all its successive tendencies coming simultaneously, in a falsified historical perspective, gave the impression of an anarchical explosion and of an arbitrary treatment of form—whence surprising misinterpretations.[89]

The most significant reaction was that of the Abstractionists, or, as they were called, the Cubo-Futurists. Here is the precious testimony of Kandinsky, who was affected, he says, to the depths of his soul by Monet's "Haystack":[90] "I knew only naturalistic art, and in truth, exclusively the Russians. I would sometimes remain for a very long time before the hand of Franz Liszt, in Repin's portrait among others, and suddenly, for the first time I found myself before a painting which represented a haystack, as the catalogue indicated, but which I did not recognize. My incomprehension greatly troubled and tormented me. I felt that the painter did not have the right to paint in such an imprecise fashion. I secretly felt that the object (the subject) was missing in this work. But I realized with astonishment and confusion that it did more than surprise, that it imprinted itself indelibly in my memory and that it re-created itself before my eyes in its smallest details. I remained confused by all this, and I could not foresee the natural consequences of this discovery. But what became clear was the incredible power of a palette that surpassed all my dreams. The painting appeared to me as though it were endowed with a fabulous power. But, unconsciously, the 'object' (the subject) as an indispensable element lost its importance for me."[91]

Thus Monet's effort to depict reality more exactly, more in conformity with his vision, was interpreted by Kandinsky as an unreality, as a poem in autonomous colors. In the same way, Cubism, that end point of French realism, that ambition to sieze the object completely, was interpreted by the Rayonist Larinov, and the Suprematist Malevich, as a pure play of forms; and it served as a pledge to their a-realism. It is only by taking this misunderstanding into account that one may speak of a filiation of French Cubism with Russian Cubo-Futurism.

But why this misconception, and why this sudden need for a brutal rupture with figurative art? The influence of Symbolism, of Marinetti, as well as the desire to render a pictorial equivalent of music have been proposed.[92] "Painting teaches us childhood. . . . It teaches us simply to recognize red, green, white," wrote Blok.[93] All that is true. But it is also necessary to take into account the long fidelity of the public and of Russian painting to subject esthetics. A number of painters—in contact with Western painting, in contact also, it must be stressed, with icons, with *lubki*, with the popular signboards that finally enter the imaginary Museum of Modern Art[94]—became conscious of a need for a purely plastic expression of their sensibility. But to arrive at that expression through a dialogue with nature, letting whatever might be recognizable be born on the canvas, would have been risky: the inveterate nature of the painting-subject bond would have confused the public and led it to demand the anecdote, that kind of emotion which painting for the first time was not charged with communicating. When in 1911 Kandinsky painted his "Battle," in which horses' heads and lances could vaguely be recognized, he preferred to change its title to "Composition IV." The spectator was no longer tempted, in this way, to become lost in a search for figurative elements. And he explained: "The principal motive of the painting is this passage from the clear-soft-cold to the animated-sharp (war)."[95]

In 1913, Malevich of the Jack of Diamonds exhibited his famous square carefully crayoned in black on a white background—"Supreme." Later he justified it in this way: "The object in itself means nothing for the artist. Sensibility is the only thing that counts, and it is along that path that art, in Suprematism, attains pure expression without representation. Art reaches a desert where there is no longer anything that is recognizable, only sensibility itself."[96]

In France, at the time Malevich was writing, a notable part of the public had learned to read in even a figurative painting the plastic signs through which the subjective message of the painter was expressed. The Cubist experiment had not led to Abstractionism, but, on the contrary, to a durable return to figurative painting:[97] Matisse, Picasso, Braque, and Léger were admired first, and not Herbin, Delaunay, or Arp. If the hypothesis that we are venturing is well-founded, the precocious success of Abstractionism in Russia, and its tardy success in France, can, without prejudice to other explanations, be related to

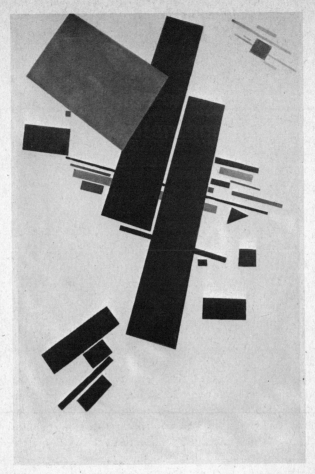

**FIGURE 5**
Malevich: Dynamic Suprematism (1914).

the moment and the style which gave rise to the ambiguity of subject-matter gradually and very early in France, very late and in a revolutionary manner in Russia.

This staggering of the rhythms of evolution produced also a very serious consequence: a break between the new painting and the public came about in Russia at the very moment at which it was in the process of ending in France. The career of the *Peredvizhniki* was difficult, but glorious and, in the end, fulfilled; that of the *Mir Iskusstva* was brilliant; the Futurists were the first "cursed" painters of Russia, copiously insulted from all sides. In bourgeois Russia, where the *Peredvizhniki* themselves ended by occupying the academic armchairs, the Futurists were among the few artists to declare themselves revolutionaries. But while they dreamed of an art of the masses, they were locked in the stifling schools of prerevolutionary Russia, so that they were the first to greet the Revolution.

## The Soviet Choice

We shall not plunge into the still hazardous study of postrevolutionary Russian painting. In its broad outlines it presented movements of flux and reflux—a sudden soaring of the avant-garde, then, after 1921, an impetuous return to the *Peredvizhnik* tradition, which submerged the former very quickly.[98] The rapport between the two tendencies made such an evolution possible, although improbable. The Revolution precipitated successively the triumph of the avant-garde, then of subject painting. The new public and the new power played the principal role in this story. Let us recall the main facts.

We have seen the reticence of the social democratic circles concerning modern art. But for several years, political revolution and pictorial revolution marched together. Some transitory circumstances brought about the reversal of alliances. The Revolution needed allies. The largest part of artistic society, including the *Peredvizhnik* followers (The Union of Russian Artists, etc.), was opposed to the October Revolution, remained silent, or emigrated.[99] The Futurists, on the contrary, thoroughly committed themselves to the Soviets. "The Futurists were the first to come to the aid of the Revolution, and of all the members of the intelligentsia, they showed themselves to be the closest to it, those who sympathized with it the most," wrote the Commissar of Public Instruction, A. Lunacharsky, in December 1918.[100] The Futurists, in fact, believed that they had everything to gain from the Revolution. "Rejected as we were by establishment criticism and by the bourgeois public, when the Revolution came it seemed to us that it was going to open all paths for us."[101] There was an affinity between the Futurist impulse and the overworked, overly tense utopian atmosphere of war communism. "To uproot, destroy, and sweep from the surface of the earth the old artistic modes; how could the new artist, the proletarian artist, not dream of that?"[102] There are several points of contact between Marxism and the program of one of the Futurist tendencies, Constructivism. Tatlin and his friends became interested in the industrial production of the work of art, condemned easel-painting, attempted experiments in liaison with factories, and arranged free-standing structures that were semisculptural, semiarchitectural, and that directly heralded Calder and Schöffer. "The art of the new world will be an industrial art, or it will not exist."[103]

In this way a handful of young people, born to art just before the war, succeeded in occupying, provisionally, a dominant position in the new organs of state. Sterenberg directed the Department of Fine Arts of the Narkompros; Tatlin headed the Advanced School of Technique and Art of Moscow. Kandinsky dominated the Institute of Fine Arts of Moscow, nucleus of the future Academy. They arranged the décor of the Firsts of May, the Sevenths of November, the anniversaries of the Red Army. Alt'man used the Alexander column as a support for a rhythmic design of triangles and circles. Finally the Constructivists managed, if not to implant a style, at least to launch a fashion.

In Moscow, cafés, billboards, and printed fabrics were part of the décor of the "great Suprematist celebration."[104]

And yet, after 1921 initiative escaped them more and more. Let us note their defeat with some dates. On February 20, 1922, after four years of interruption, the forty-seventh exhibition of the Society of Traveling Exhibitions opened. It was a great success. The old masters were returned to honor. Kasatkin received the distinction of Artist of the People, which soon came also to Polenov and to Arkhipov. A delegation went to Finland to beg Repin to renounce his voluntary exile. Several months later, the Association of Painters of Revolutionary Russia, or the AKhRR, emerged from the exhibition.

Insignificant at first, the AKhRR very quickly obtained the adherence of fresh young painters shaped by the schools as well as experienced artists united against Futurist painting. Three years later the AKhRR was the largest group; it had branches in all of Russia, as well as its own ateliers, library, and publishing house; and it even controlled an artistic association for youth.

In 1926 the Union of Painters of Moscow, which included in particular the former Cubist Lentulov, the Cézannians Konchalovsky and Kuprin, and Igor Grabar', joined as a bloc. There were to be new splits, other kernels of adhesion (Ost, Onkh, Makovets, Zhar-Tsvet, Rapkh), and personal quarrels; this did not hinder the fact that everything was going toward the consolidation of the principles of "heroic realism" proclaimed by the AKhRR in its beginnings.

At the same time, Futurism continued to decline. The "discussion exhibition" of 1924 did not help. Some, such as Kandinsky and Annenkov, emigrated; others such as Malevich, as bourgeois individualists, found themselves isolated in Soviet society just as they had been, as revolutionaries, in bourgeois society. In 1932, the birth date of the Union of Soviet Artists, and certainly in 1934, the date of the definition of socialist realism, it was evident that Abstractionism had been dead for a long time in Russia.

The reasons for the inflexible return to tradition are found at a much deeper level than that of the political decisions on which they are sometimes based. Let us first note the blatant contrast between the totalitarian ambitions of an avant-garde that wanted to make a new world and the creations that the misery of the times allowed it. Its monuments were of staff, cardboard, and plaster, and they did not last the winter.[105] Tatlin planned a monument to the Third International that was to be several hundred meters high and animated with a tremendous amount of gyratory movements; but he could make no more than a wooden model, four to five meters high, which did not move.[106] Trotsky had remarked that Futurism, which intended to be the art of industrial society, had developed in Italy and in underdeveloped Russia in the same way that the French Revolution had found its philosophical expression in Germany.[107] The realization of such a program in a Russia drained of blood, with its factories in ruins and its cities deserted, was a dream as utopian as that of war communism.

It would have needed the adherence, at the very least, of a large public; but the public refused. When Lentulov remodeled (in painted canvas) the

Theater Square in Moscow, a worker's journal protested: "It is an idea of decadent Futurism and it should not have a place at a festival of the proletariat."[108] The "leftists" themselves recognized with melancholy that "the Soviet public is not yet ready to appreciate nonobjective art."[109] Public pressure continued to grow. While the state of general mobilization lasted, a mass debate could not begin; after the end of the civil war, with the NEP, the public intervened. A placard or a décor did not need general approval, but the frescoes of a club of the Red Army or of a House of the Public could not do without the assent of those who were to enjoy them. No longer was art nothing more than an auxiliary to agitation; it now had to insert itself into the new society that was being built, and it had to be accepted by this society at each stage. The problem did not escape the leftists who, in 1921, became divided over the interpretation of the social role of art.[110] But by this time the public had already turned away from the leftists. As Tugenkhold noted,[111] with the coming of peace the Soviet public wanted illustrations of the heroic epoch that it had just been through, an iconography of the heroes, a representation of Soviet life, but a representation conforming to the old canons; in short, it wanted a return to the subject. The public immediately agreed with declarations like this one: "Our civic duty before humanity is to capture artistically and in a documentary manner the greatest moment of history in its revolutionary élan. We represent the life of today, the existence of the Red Army, of the workers, of the peasantry, and of work heroes. We will produce a truthful painting of what is and not abstract lucubrations that discredit our Revolution before the proletariat of the world."[112] They were lucubrations which upset the great values that the young public revered. The public reacted like Lenin who, upon seeing the model of a monument to Karl Marx, said to Lunacharsky: "Anatoli Vassilevich, please tell the artist to modify the hair so that we may receive the same impression of Marx that comes from the portraits, for I think that there is little resemblance here."[113] A Cubist bust of Sophia Perovskaia had to be withdrawn.

Chagall, the commissar of Fine Arts in Vitebsk for a short period, had undertaken to decorate the city; that is, instead of Marx and Lenin the visitors would be able to see cows and horses hovering in the air: even his friends protested, and he had to leave town.[114] The day after Lenin's death, there was a blossoming of portraits: none strayed from a respectful resemblance to the traits of the great man, and all were realistic.[115]

The continuity of style was assured by the amalgam of the old and new generations. Not only, as is natural, did the old men of the Union of Russian Painters and of the Wandering Exhibitions join the AKhRR, but also the Cézannian Sarian, Konchalovsky of the Blue Rose, and Igor Grabar' became great masters of the young school of Realism. Nesterov, painter of hermits, nuns, and Holy Russia, pursued a career as a portraitist and was loaded with honors. The AKhRR was also an outlet for artists of the provinces, who had remained rebellious to avant-gardism. Thus, the first masters of Soviet art belonged either to the generation of already famous painters (Nesterov, Grabar',

**FIGURE 6**
M. Grekov: The Clarions of the First Cavalry Army (1934).

Konchalovsky) or to the generation of their pupils—Grekov, a student of Repin; Gerasimov, a student of Korovin and Arkhipov, as well as Joganson.[116] But there were almost none who became known only after the Revolution. In France also, Davidism, which had preceded the Revolution, was adopted by the Revolution as its own style. Finally the Communist party, benevolent toward Futurism while the confusion between artistic leftism and political leftism had not been cleared up, did not delay in giving all its support to the tendency represented by the AKhRR.

The party had always refused Futurism the stamp of an official art. "Futurists absolutely must not profit from the eminent position that they acquired in the machinery of the artistic administration to consider themselves a school of the state or to dictate from above even a revolutionary art form," wrote Lunacharsky.[117] The party no longer partook of their taste for the *tabula rasa*. Its principal concern was the conservation of all the riches of the past—the Bolshevik Revolution was the least vandalistic of all revolutions—and the founding of generalized instruction upon them. No important Bolshevik believed in a laboratory development of proletarian culture, such as the *Proletkult*[118] desired, nor in a rupture with bourgeois culture. "Instruct yourselves, take up bourgeois culture,"[119] said Lenin. Marxism wanted to integrate the past; in that sense it was conservative.

Futurism could have triumphed only with the unconditional support of the party. This was refused on questions of principle. The influx of new cadres very quickly eliminated the most Westernized men and those most open to avant-gardist experiments—Trotsky, Rakovsky, Lunacharsky, and Bogdanov. The old Bolshevik core thought like Lenin; and the new generation of militants, issued from the peasant and workers' depths of Russia, actively supported the "Realists." The Red Army, a direct expression of the new public, was prompt to take a side. It supported the AKhRR financially on the occasion of the exhibition on its fifth anniversary, which formed the core of the Museum of the Revolution. The *Peredvizhnik* tradition finally benefited from the massive diffusion of classical Russian culture, to which it was so tightly linked. Each edition of Chernyshevsky and Tolstoy, widely distributed throughout a population that only yesterday did not know how to read, brought new crowds of admirers to the canvases of "Heroic Realism." Thus, when in 1922 the party declared itself more and more vigorously in favor of this interpretation of realism, it was in complete agreement with the general attitudes of the Soviet public. Party pressure, then, only hastened a spontaneous process.

Such was the misfortune of avant-garde painting. Unlike the French school, it did not have the opportunity for a prolonged gestation in the shelter of narrow and protective schools. Born too late, it had to confront the light of day prematurely. The revolutionary crowd into which it was plunged, and upon which it hoped to act although it did not have the means, either possessed no culture and could not understand its intentions or remained under the influence of a culture that was directly opposed to it. It is necessary to add that in France the battle for the new art was conducted against the bourgeois public in the Flaubertian sense of the word and against the people of the salons and in the fine arts, who could be made to look ridiculous, whereas in Russia the arbitrator was the popular public, represented in fact by the militants. By definition—that is, in the logic of the Soviet system—those judges were unimpeachable; more than elsewhere, in addition, they possessed the means to impose their views.

In these few pages we cannot claim to have revealed the entire complexity of an evolution that extended over more than sixty years. We have wished only to show how, because of social pressures, the historical setting, and chronological displacements, Russian painting, in developing from positions initially very close to those of Western painting, was able to diverge so much that its creations appear to us today almost as aberrant and incomprehensible as ours do to the Soviet public. We are very poorly acquainted with this style of painting; we should study it, however, for it constitutes, if nothing else, an extraordinary witness-experience in comparison to our style.

A comparative study ought to carry over terms: for example the antique specializations in the painting trade have been conserved—in Russia an artist is still a portraitist, a landscapist, and even, to recapture the Russian words, a "genrist" or a "batailliste."[120] It might compare values: does the Soviet public have, as we do, a pluralistic vision of art history, or does it have a monistic vision of it that leaves outside the museum all that entered it in the twentieth century after modern art—the Primitive, and the African and American arts, and so forth; does it arrange the art of the three centuries that preceded ours in a different hierarchy than we do?

We might again delimit the frontiers, follow the advances and setbacks of socialist realism in Eastern Europe, in China, indeed in France; confront post-revolutionary Soviet painting with postrevolutionary Mexican painting; measure the influence of painting on the creation of an industrial society technically analogous to ours but of a totally different décor. We might determine the path of evolution: will it follow the present line or become ruptured from it?[121]

Although difficult to carry out, these inquiries would surely be profitable. Our more modest purpose has been to attract attention to the gravity of this *raskol* (schism) of European painting, a symptom among others of a schism of sensibility.

## NOTES

1. "Henceforth and for the first time since the prehistoric period there exists a type of universal art," P. Francastel, *Art et Technique* (1956), p. 241. Francastel saw the Soviet exception as a break in evolution.
2. M. M. Alpatov, "L'art russe vu par la critique française," *Cahiers du monde russe et soviétique*, No. 2 (1960).
3. L. Réau, *L'Art russe de Pierre le Grand à nos jours* (Paris, 1922), hereafter cited as Réau.
4. Shown by P. Francastel in his *Peinture et Société* (Lyon, 1951), pp. 143 ff.
5. The most complete and detailed general work on Russian painting of the *Peredvizhnik* period is that by N. G. Mashkovtsev, *Istoriia Russkogo Iskusstva*, Vol. II (Moscow, 1960). The 381 plates are a magnificent research tool. Some of the other general works are: Réau, *op. cit.*, and his *L'Art russe*, (Paris, Lausanne, 1945); A. Benois, *The Russian School of Painting* (London, 1916) where (p. 199) we get the viewpoint of the theoretician of *Mir Iskusstva*; the color plates of the *Gosudarstvennaia Tretiakovskaia Gallereia* (Moscow, 1953), part of the series *Khudozhestvennye Sokrovishcha SSSR*.
6. "To paint, without faith, a religious painting is immoral, it is a sin." Cited in Réau, p. 151.
7. *Ibid.*, p. 146.
8. It was his doctoral thesis, defended in 1855. The second edition came out in 1865, with Chernyshevsky in exile, and aroused immense interest. I cite from the edition of N. Tcherny-chevski, *Textes philosophiques choisis* (Moscow, 1957).
9. Tchernychevski *op. cit.*, p. 377.
10. *Ibid.*, p. 378.
11. Which Pisarev pushed toward total destruction around 1865.
12. Tchernychevski, *op. cit.*, p. 413.
13. *Ibid.*, p. 408.
14. *Ibid.*, p. 458.
15. *Ibid.*, pp. 420–421.
16. *Ibid.*, p. 421.
17. Mashkovtsev, *op. cit.*, p. 9.
18. *Ibid.*, p. 13.
19. *Ibid.*, p. 83.
20. Which was not under the Ministry of the Imperial Court. The school offered an atmosphere favorable to the development of new ideas. Smel'kov, Savrasov, famous for his "The Rooks Have Arrived," Pukirev, the landscapist Shishkin, Perov, and others studied there. Cf. Mashkovtsev, *op. cit.*, p. 11.

21. To name only the more famous of the painters who participated regularly in the traveling exhibitions: Perov, Kramskoy, Ge, Savrasov, Shishkin, Iacobi, Iaroshenko, joined later by Repin, Surikov, Vasnetsov, and, by 1890, by Levitan and Serov; the last two were more on the periphery of the movement. Mashkovtsev, *op. cit.*, pp. 83–84.

22. Mashkovtsev, *op. cit.*, pp. 13, 87; since 1850 Russian painting is "the most progressive" in the world.

23. This commentary and those that follow are based on the analysis of Mashkovtsev, *op. cit.* On Nekrasov, cf. p. 109.

24. According to the statements of Kramskoy.

25. Tchernychevski, *op. cit.*, p. 425.

26. Cited by Mashkovtsev, *op. cit.*, p. 81.

27. *Ibid.*, p. 177.

28. Repin was from the South.

29. Réau, *L'Art Russe* (Paris, 1945), pp. 95–96.

30. This canvas has always been greatly admired. A. Benois admired it as much as contemporary Soviet critics. Cf. Mashkovtsev, *op. cit.*, p. 203.

31. M. Alpatov writes, with good reason, of Surikov's knowledge of icons. However, these have influenced, in my opinion, only the bearing, the posture, the expression of Surikov's personnages but not the plastic expression, not the painting as a whole. M. Alpatov, *op. cit.*, p. 301.

32. I am thinking of his Saint Vladimir, his Saint Olga, his Nestor the Chronicler. Cf. Alpatov, *op. cit.* p. 218.

33. Until 1923, with only the interruption of 1919–1923.

34. Mashkovtsev, *op. cit.*, p. 84.

35. A. P. Botkina, *Pavel Mikhailovich Tretiakov v zhizni i iskusstve* (Moscow, 1951). These are the memoirs of his daughter. His authority was such that his choices immediately determined the "stock" value of any artist.

36. Mashkovtsev, *op. cit.*, p. 87.

37. *Ibid.*

38. *Anna Karenina*, Part 5, chap. X ff.

39. *Qu'est-ce que l'art?* (Paris, 1918), chap. IV.

40. *Qu'est-ce que l'art? op. cit.*, p. 50.

41. His letter to Souvorin in 1898. Cf. Sophie Lafitte, *Léon Tolstoi* (Paris, 1960), p. 206.

42. Lavrov, *Lettres historiques*, Goldsmith (tr.) (Paris, 1903), p. 91.

43. Garshin, *Sochineniia*, "Khudozhniki" (Moscow, Leningrad, 1960) pp. 71–96.

44. There is a whole gallery of *moujiks* in *Peredvizhnik* painting: cf. Perov, "The Funeral Procession" (1865), "Fomusyhka-sych" (1869), "The Pilgrim" (1870); Kramskoy, "The Forrester" (1874), "The Peasant Holding the Bridle" (1883); also Miasoedov, Repin— "The Moujik with the Evil Eyes" (1877), "The Frightened Peasant" (1877), etc.

45. V. Figner, *Mémoires d'une révolutionnaire*, V. Serge (tr.) (Paris, 1930), pp. 177–178.

46. In France reality lost its allegorical meaning. "Les joueurs de cartes ne sont plus des hommes 'du peuple,' les témoins d'une revendication plus ou moins aiguë et romanesque; ils sont considérés en eux-memês comme constituant la matière indiscutable de l'art." Francastel, *Peinture et Société*, p. 183. The word "narod" (people) still had in Russian an affective resonance, an allegorical value lost in France since the days of Michelet.

47. Cited in V. V. Stasov, *Izbrannye sochineniia*, Vol. I (Moscow, 1952) p. 266. We should note that Repin was not bothered by his contradictions. Some of his canvases, such as "Parisian Café" (1875) or "On a grass bench" (1876) show traces of his stay in Paris. M. Annenkov had a letter of his in which he wrote sympathetically about Impressionism. But this does not seem to me to be within the mainstream of his development.

48. Cited by Réau, p. 219.

49. Stasov, "Nyneshnoe iskusstvo v Evrope," *op. cit.*, Vol. I, p. 557.

50. *Niva*, 1899, No. 15; cited by A. O. Grishchenko, *O Sviaziiakh russkoi zhivopisi s vizantieii zapadom, XIII–XX v. v.* (Moscow, 1913), p. 50.

51. Stasov, *op. cit.*, Vol. III, "Iskusstvo v XIX veke."

52. *Ibid.*, p. 553.

53. *Ibid.*, p. 555.

54. *Ibid.*, p. 556.

55. *Ibid.*, p. 558.

56. There are no good studies for the period 1899–1917. Soviet works go on at great length

about the survivals of the *Peredvizhniki* but are brief about the *Mir Iskusstva*. Fortunately, one can make up for this gap by using the three great journals: *Mir Iskusstva*, 1899–1904; *Zolotoe Runo*, 1906–1909, a very luxurious journal; and *Apollon*, 1909–1914, more academic. As for avant-garde trends—Suprematism, Constructivism, Rayonism—the sources are widely scattered. This is why I am so very grateful to Mr. Larionov and to Mrs. Goncharova who were kind enough to answer my questions, and to Mr. G. Annenkov who took the trouble to give me the viewpoint of an eyewitness and even to show me articles as yet unpublished. Certainly no one is in a better position than Mr. Annenkov to give us the history of the Russian avant-garde. Let us hope he will do so one day.

57. In 1889 Levitan develops an enthusiasm for Monet, Casin, and Besnard. Cf. Réau, p. 221. The technique of this melancholy landscapist, friend of Chekhov, rests close to that of Daubigny or of Constable, but this does not diminish the quality of his emotion.

58. Founded in 1907; Symbolist.

59. Founded in 1911; Cézannist.

60. The first Rayonist canvases—1911.

61. The "Supreme" of Malevich, 1913. Cf. G. Habasque, "Malevich," *L'Oeil* No. 7 (1960).

62. Cf. Vekhi, *Sbornik statei o russkoi intelligensii* (Moscow, 1909); M. Malia, "The Russian Intelligentsia," *Daedalus* (1960), pp. 441–458; Kanchalovski, "L'Intelligentsia avant la Révolution," *Revue des études slaves* (1960).

63. The painters of the *Peredvizhnik* generation were often of lowly origin; Perov was a foundling. Those of the prewar generation are from comfortable families: Benois, son of a well-known architect; Serov, son of a famous musician; Prince Trubetskoi, and so forth.

64. The formulation is that of C. Corbet, *La Littérature russe* (Paris, 1951), p. 179. The three major successive reviews of art—*Mir Iskusstva*, *Zolotoe Runo*, *Apollon*—established an intimate collaboration between painters and writers. Here, for example, are the collaborators of the *Zolotoe Runo*: the painters Benois, Bakst, Vrubel, Grabar', Dobuzhinsky, Kuznetsov, Krovin, Lansere, Rerikh, Serov, Somov; the writers Leonid Andreev, Balmont, Blok, Belyi, Merezhkovsky, Remizov, Sologub, and so forth—all the great names of Symbolism.

65. N. Berdiaev, *Essais d'autobiographie spirituelle* (Paris, 1958), pp. 177–178.

66. Collected in the volume Lunacharsky, *Stat'i ob iskusstve* (Moscow, Leningrad, 1941).

67. C. Frioux, "Lunacharskij et le futurisme russe," *Cahiers du monde russe et soviétique*, No. 2, (1960).

68. *Ibid.*, p. 241.

69. *Ibid.*, pp. 437–440.

70. *Ibid.*, pp. 408–427.

71. In his *Histoire de la pensée sociale en Russie* (Oeuvres, Vol. XXI), pp. 208–209. Cited in G. Plekhanov, *L'Art et la vie sociale* (Paris, 1949), p. 74.

72. *Ibid.*, p. 136.

73. *Ibid.*, pp. 136–137; he wrote this in 1912.

74. *Ibid.*, pp. 136 ff.

75. On the very profound influence that Chernyshevsky had on Lenin, see Valentinov, "N. Černyševskij et Lénine," *Contrat social* (May–July 1957).

76. Lunacharsky, "Lénine et l'Art," in *Lénine tel qu'il fut. Souvenirs de contemporains*, Vol. II (Moscow, 1959), 426.

77. Clara Zetkin, "Mes souvenirs de Lénine" in *Lénine tel qu'il fut, op. cit.*, II, 598.

78. *Ibid.*

79. Mashkovtsev, *op. cit.*, pp. 302 ff.

80. The Russian school for a long time opposed abandoning the studio setting. Cf. Mashkovtsev, *op. cit.*, p. 333.

81. Cf. the journal published by the group, *Starye Gody*.

82. Except, perhaps, for the excellent engraver Bilibin and for Kustodiev.

83. "Art is eternal, for it rests on the immutable, on that which cannot be destroyed. Art is one, for it has a single source: the soul. Art is symbolical because it encloses a symbol, the reflection of the immutable in time. Art is free, for it is the result of a spontaneous creative effort." The prefatory manifesto of the *Zolotoe Runo*, No. 1 (1906).

84. *Mir Iskusstva*, No. 4 (1899).

85. *Zolotoe Runo*, Nos. 7–8 (1908).

86. *Apollon*, No. 5 (1912).

87. Schukin had hung the "Dance" of Matisse in his stairwell. The collection of Morozov, less striking, included seventeen Cézannes and eleven Gaugins. *Apollon*, Nos. 3–4 (1912).

88. M. Voloshin, "Ustremleniia novoi frantsuzkoi zhivopisi," *Zolotoe Runo*, Nos. 7–8 (1908).

89. The *Mir Iskusstva* did not follow French experiments after Impressionism. Already Somov saw nothing in it (at least according to Strelkov, *Mir Iskusstva* [1923]). One of the very few Russian Impressionists and also among the most cultivated members of the group, Igor Grabar', on seeing a Cézanne in 1904, experienced "the greatest disappointment of my life" and condemned the ballyhoo of Vollard and the art dealers (*Mir Iskusstva*, Nos. 8–9 [1904]). But a new group, like the Jack of Diamonds (*Bubnovyi Valet*) forms, on the contrary, a Moscovite province of Cézannism.

90. I assume that the reference is to one canvas of the series "Meules" done in 1891.

91. Kandinsky, *Regards sur le passé*, Buffet-Picabia (tr.) (Paris, 1946); written in Munich in 1913.

92. According to Annenkov, this influence of music was at the root of the paintings of Tschiorlianis, a Lithuanian who, from 1910, worked in St. Petersburg in full abstractionist style. Scriabin, as a musician, had, at the same time, similar preoccupations.

93. A. Blok, "Kraski i slova," *Zolotoe Runo*, No. 1, p. 102.

94. The whole book of Grishchenko (cited above) is a brief to show the fidelity of Russian avant-gardists to the great tradition of Rublev. Larionov also told me of the interest that the Rayonists had in popular signboards.

95. *Les Sources du XXe siècle* (Paris, 1960–1961) (Catalogue de l'exposition), p. 106.

96. Malevitch, *Die gegenstandlose Welt* (Munich, 1927), pp. 65–72, cited in Seuphor, *Dictionnaire de la peinture abstraite* (Paris, 1957), pp. 97–98.

97. Cf. J. Golding, *Le Cubisme* (Paris, 1962).

98. The most detailed study is volume XI of the great academic history of Russian art which deals with the period 1917–1934, *Istoriia Russkogo Iskusstva*, I. Grabar' (ed.) (Moscow, 1957); the chapters on painting were written by S. A. Kaufman. Unfortunately the volume has little on the experiments of the avant-garde. One may add the subtle and thoughtful book of Tugenkhold, *Iskusstvo oktiabrskoi epokhi* (Leningrad, 1930). I have also used C. Grey, "Futurism, Suprematism, Constructivism", *Soviet Survey*, No. 1 (1959); K. A. Jelenski, "Avant-garde et Révolution," *Preuves* (May 1960); Shchekotov (*Iskusstvo SSSR* [1926]), who represents the point of view of the Association of Painters of Revolutionary Russia, known as *AKhRR*. Finally I should state that a number of important studies and collections of periodicals were inaccessible to me. I found only a few issues of the *Iskusstvo kommuny*, the journal of Punin, at the Bibliothèque de Documentation Internationale Contemporaine.

99. For instance Benois and Repin.

100. Lunacharsky, *Iskusstvo kommuny* (December 29, 1918).

101. Statement of G. Annenkov to Jelenski, *op. cit.*, p. 442.

102. Punin, *Iskusstvo kommuny*, No. 1, cited by Kaufman, *op. cit.*, p. 20.

103. Pletnev, *Pravda* (September 27, 1922).

104. Punin, *Iskusstvo kommuny* (February 9, 1919).

105. Lunacharsky, "Lénine et l'Art," in *Lénine tel qu'il fut, op. cit.*, II, 424.

106. Told me by G. Annenkov.

107. L. Trotsky, *Literature and Revolution*, (Ann Arbor, 1960), p. 127.

108. *Rabochii mir* No. 18 (1918).

109. Cited by Jelenski, *op. cit.*, p. 442.

110. Kandinsky, Malevich, and Gabo insisted on the spiritual and speculative character of a work of art, whereas Tatlin and his friends (Rodchenko, Stepanova, Popova, etc.) wished to devote art to the people and to participate in the construction of a new world. Cf. Grey, *op. cit.*

111. *Iskusstvo oktiabrskoi epokhi*, p. 276, note 4.

112. From the manifesto of the founders of *AKhRR* in 1922. Cited in *Istoriia russkogo iskusstva*, XI, 186.

113. Lunacharsky, "Lénine et l'art," *op. cit.*, p. 423

114. L. Venturi, *Chagall* (Geneva, Paris, New York, 1956), p. 58. There is little of relevance of Chagall to this study; he is totally original and stands apart—because of his provincial and "indigenous" origin, because he came too late to St. Petersburg (1907) not to be repelled by the teaching of Bakst and the *Mir Iskusstva* and left too early (1910) to be involved in the battles of the prewar period, and because, after the Revolution, he kept away from the various rival factions and soon returned to Western Europe. The painter of the Russian village, often so close to the poet Essenin, is not mentioned in the great academic history of Russian art.

115. Tugenkhol'd, *op. cit.*, pp. 30–32.

116. *Istoriia russkogo iskusstva*, XI, 344.

117. Lunacharsky, *Iskusstvo kommuny*, *op. cit.*,

118. "With the excuse of a purely proletarian art and a popular culture, they have presented something unimaginable and absurd." Lenin, First All-Russian Congress on nonschool Education, Opening Speech (May 6, 1919) (*Oeuvres* XXIX, 308). Quoted in V. Lénine, *Sur la littérature et l'art*, (Paris, 1957), p. 165.

119. Iakovlev's speech at the Conference on Literary Policy of the Russian Communist Party (May 9, 1924), quoted in Lénine, *Sur la littérature et l'art, op. cit.*, p. 214.

120. There is a studio of battle painters, the Grekov studio, where the young "bataillistes" learn their trade.

121. Rupture or continuity—I see no possibility of a "compromise." If circumstances allow, it is possible that one shall witness (like today in Poland) an "inflation" of abstract painting. The situation then will be similar to that in 1910. There are certain indications that the present, forty-year-old trend in Soviet painting may be coming to an end. The indications appear outside of painting—in architecture, for example, but that is a different problem. At the same time, no matter how dominant the main current has been, it has not shut out completely an underground element. Thus, under Stalin, the painter Falk (still unknown in the West), who died in 1958, has created profoundly original and admirable works of art. But we have only been concerned with mass phenomena; and these usually concern the history of art rather than the works themselves.

# The Revelation of St. Boris:
# Russian Literature and Individual Autonomy

SIDNEY MONAS

### Art and Society

In this paper I propose to discuss the extent and limits of the renewed concern for individual autonomy, privacy, and freedom in Russian literature, not in the light of official controls—these have been and are being widely discussed elsewhere—but rather in terms of certain currents and impulses I believe to be inherent in Russian literature itself. In some ways, these drive freedom on; in others, inhibit and limit it. I mean to suggest rather than to define the territory and the problems. I would like to begin by rehearsing some loose impressions of the relationship between art and society current in our own culture.

We do not regard art as altogether purposeless, but we do tend to regard its purpose as rather mysterious, and art and the artists as, to some degree, independent of moral claims that are exerted from elsewhere in the society. The relationship is an uneasy one, and the independence is at most never absolute. But art has shaken loose from the religious teleology of the Middle Ages and also from the moral didacticism of the eighteenth century. We no longer believe, like Alexander Pope, that the poet should be *representative*, should strive to represent the common opinions of his society, like a Congressman—"What oft was thought, but ne'er so well expressed"—yet we become a little restive, and eventually maybe even indifferent if he strays too far.

In the artist's commerce with his public, we expect a certain tension. Between them is the work of art. Implicit in the work of art is an *imaginary* audience different from the public as it actually exists. In the words of a contemporary American poet: "The poem is creating the audience for the poem."[1] Sometimes the distance between the real, bourgeois public and the imaginary audience the poet is trying to create is so enormous the mind spins and standards collapse, because there is no way of reaching the intention or bridging the gap. Autonomy becomes unintelligibility, and communication breaks down.

FROM Sidney Monas, "The Revelation of St. Boris: Russian Literature and Individual Autonomy," in D. W. Treadgold (ed.), *Soviet and Chinese Communism, Similarities and Differences*, University of Washington Press (1967), pp. 255–290. Reprinted by permission of the publisher.

Since the time of Napoleon, military metaphors have crept into talk about art. We speak of an *avant-garde* with which a "main body" will presumably someday catch up. We speak of the artist "conquering" new areas of experience. For Nietzsche, art, or at least tragedy, which he thought the highest form of art, is where "what is warlike in our soul celebrates its Saturnalia."[2] Sometimes it is experience that is conquered, sometimes the public, sometimes both audience and artist participate in a common conquest.

A number of metaphors are not directly military, but still imply struggle, tension, "wrestling with the angel." Some are passive and imply a kind of ravishment by, or self-sacrifice to, psychic forces. Keats spoke of "negative capability." Jung writes: "Art is a kind of innate drive that seizes a human being and makes him its instrument. The artist is not a person endowed with free will who seeks his own ends, but one who allows art to realize its purposes through him. . . . It is not Goethe who creates *Faust*, but *Faust* which creates Goethe."[3] Thus, in relation to society the artist may sometimes strut like a hero back from the wars; but in actual combat, he is helpless and merely endures the battle. In the crowd, Big Ego; home at his desk, he has between himself and the universe almost no skin at all.

Nietzsche and Jung are both very much part of what John Bayley has called in our literature "the romantic survival."[4] They do not altogether disregard society, but for them art is essentially something that takes place between the artist (the product of his culture and of his society, to be sure) and the dark forces of the unconscious. Not necessarily contradictory, but somewhat different emphases come from Marx and Engels on the one hand, Freud on the other.

Peter Demetz has recently written an extremely interesting book, *Marx, Engels und die Dichter,* in which he demonstrates at considerable length that Marxism does not necessarily lead to socialist realism. He points out also the vital connection between Marx and Engels and romantic literary figures like Gutzkow, Boerne, and Carlyle, whom Engels translated. Neither Marx nor Engels favored didacticism in literature; they did not advocate a positive hero or an insight into the unfolding of the rosy socialist future. In a number of works, both Marx and Engels, though they connected literature with the "superstructure" of society, took pains to give it a certain autonomy.[5] It is true, however, that both Marx and Engels logically and inevitably associate art with the division of labor, civilization, and civil society, so that in Marxist terms it has to be seen as an aspect of repression and alienation—a compensatory aspect perhaps but fatally connected. I quote from Engels' most profound, most poetic and touching work: "From its first day to this, sheer greed was the driving spirit of civilization; wealth and again wealth and once more wealth; wealth, not of society, but of the single scurvy individual—here was its one and final aim. If at the same time the progressive development of science and a repeated flowering of supreme art dropped into its lap, it was only because without them modern wealth could not have completely realized its achievements."[6] In the new society art will be replaced by the full flowering of the individual, whose very life will become a work of art, and who will therefore have no need of the estranged and alienated perspective of "civilized" art.

Freud's enormous respect for art is beyond dispute, as is the delicacy of his own artistic sensibility. While he shares their capacity for appreciation, he does not, as Marx and Engels do, consciously and deliberately, look forward to the future abolition or utter absorption of art. Nevertheless, like Marx and Engels, he tends to view art as a product of repression. Art is a form of sublimation, which is "successful" repression; yet it is inseparable from that "unsuccessful" repression which leads to neurosis, aggression, and war. For about thirty years now, a number of writers on art and literature have tried to combine the insights of Marx and Freud—from Christopher Caudwell to Edmund Wilson. Only recently, however, two of them, Herbert Marcuse and Norman O. Brown, have drawn the logical conclusion that in a society without repression—*if* Marx and Freud are correct—art would wither away.[7]

Within the arts themselves, we have seen something like an anti-art movement, beginning with Dadaism and extending to the "happenings" of our own day. There have always been dissident "Bohemian" movements in the arts, at least since modern times, which, in assaulting the conventions of established schools, assault the conventions of the established classes of society as well, tend to associate themselves with democratic, radical political movements, to undermine "sacred cows," attack sacrosanct traditions, and in general make the atmosphere of art less stuffy, exclusive, aristocratic. As they succeed, they tend to become absorbed into the society they began by attacking. One generation's rebels are the academicians of the next. The Dadaists set out to be extremely destructive; they wished to destroy the very notion of "art" as something set apart and on a pedestal or in a frame. Yet before long they were considered "artists." The "happenings" are intended to lead art back into daily life, to inspire audiences to participate in and look upon the life around them with the kind of energy and attention they have been devoting to works of art. Yet the overall effect has been—or at least so it seems to me—not to make art more democratic, but rather less so; and Rauschenberg is in the museums.

The Russians, though they participate with us in a common culture, are less advanced in these matters than we are. Except for a relatively brief, wildly experimental period in the arts between 1909 and 1921, Russia has tended to be slightly archaic, somewhat of the past, especially in literature. This may turn out to be, as it once was, what saves it from exhaustion.

## Pushkin's Two Muses

In the last chapter of Pushkin's novel *The Captain's Daughter*, there is a scene in which Maria Ivanovna confronts the Empress, Catherine II. She is on a self-imposed mission to plead for the life of her fiancé, unjustly condemned to lifetime exile in Siberia for his alleged participation in the Pugachev uprising, and she pretends not to know who the buxom lady is. Victor Shklovsky has pointed out that the Empress as she appears in this scene comes straight out of Utkin's engraving of one of her official portraits; her unseasonable attire emphasizes the artificiality of her pose and introduces a note of parody.[8] The entire scene and its sequel are highly stylized. They suggest the deliberately arranged pastoral dream of Arcadia in which Marie Antoinette (among others) used to play milkmaid.

Maria Ivanovna is no less stylized. If Catherine represents the muse of Empire playing at mercy and sentiment and spontaneity, at being a rococo shepherdess, Maria Ivanovna represents a real shepherdess—the daughter of a provincial garrison captain—playing at the same game. Behind her play, however, there is real earnestness of purpose: the life of her fiancé hangs in the balance.

In one of his very early poems, Pushkin writes of the private nature of his muse, his *tainaia devka*, and the rural place where she visits him secretly to give him lessons on "the seven-stopped flute" of pastoral. His most imposing heroines are associated with this muse, from the central figure of "Mistress into Maid" to Maria Ivanovna and Tatiana. In Stanza V, Canto VIII of *Onegin*, Pushkin tells of how he sought his muse literally among wild shepherd tribes only to find her on a provincial Russian landowner's estate, appearing as Tatiana: "She'd visited the quiet tents of nomad tribes in the depths of brooding Moldavia; among them, she grew wild, forgot godly speech, for those undeveloped, unfamiliar tongues, for the songs of the steppe dear to her. . . . Suddenly, everything around became transformed, and there she was in my garden, a provincial miss with a pensive look in her eye; a small paper-bound French book in her hand." Just as the provincial estate of Tatiana's parents is a place halfway between the stylized Arcadia of European pastoral (as Nabokov has pointed out) and the fields Tolstoy's Levin watered with his sweat—so Tatiana, with her pale broodiness and her bookish melancholy is part of the process of transformation from the stylized shepherdess of conventional sentiment to the Natasha who dominates the poetic atmosphere of the Rostov household and in whom, Tolstoy tells us, "body and soul are one."

For the moment, in the garden at Tsarskoe Selo, the "private muse" and the "muse of Empire" share a common convention, a common language. The real shepherdess, simple, faithful, modest, spontaneous, distinguished by her delicate but unobtrusive feelings, is nevertheless not without a touch of Machiavel. The Empress, for all of what Pushkin referred to elsewhere as "the cruel reality of her despotism," plays at delicacy of feeling, assumes the role of her own official portrait. She pardons the fiancé and spares him a life of Siberian exile. It should be pointed out that the fiancé is also the narrator, and hence the poet's surrogate; indeed, that is about the only character he has.[9]

Pushkin believed that good prose, unlike poetry, which he thought could afford to be somewhat more discursive, had to be "brief and precise" and loaded with "meanings" (*smysli*); and so I feel to some extent justified in expanding the meaning of this brief scene beyond the confines of the novel in which it occurs, in terms of Pushkin's associations, as expressed elsewhere.

Empire: for Pushkin, power and civilization together; Westernization, but on Russia's terms; *independent* civilization. All this is implied in the apostrophe to Petersburg that opens *The Bronze Horseman*, reminiscent, in its pomp and splendor, of the odes of Derzhavin. Poetry had been born at court, and the court poets sang full-throated praise of their Imperial mother. A brilliant Soviet ironist, Abram Tertz, and a scholar, Gukovsky, have called attention to the similarity between eighteenth-century patriotic and didactic verse and socialist realism.[10] Poetry praised Empire which had created the possibility of civilization in Russia. But civilization did not mean power alone: it meant also tradition, honor, welfare, privacy, family life, and a world of subtle and spontaneous human feelings.

This is the world of lyric and pastoral, the world of the private muse. The worlds have different muses, but the common symbol of their interdependence is Russian literature itself. Pushkin was the singer of Empire and freedom, as G. P. Fedotov once put it.[11] Yet as he grew older, Pushkin became aware of a tragic incompatibility between the two worlds. Evgenii of *The Bronze Horseman* aspired only to ". . . a table, two chairs, a pot of cabbage soup, and I my own master . . ." as did Pushkin himself. It is a dream that is denied Evgenii by the flood that drowns his sweetheart. He has a sudden insight into the cost of Empire and the arbitrariness of Imperial will. Yet he is himself so much the product of that will, his domestic dream and its poetry had been so utterly dependent on its benevolence, that his weak and momentary impulse to revolt dissolves in the very gesture and he goes mad. The statue of the horseman comes to life in his mind and seems to drive him into the Neva.

The private muse presided over Russian literature for decades to come, over prose as well as poetry; indeed, primarily over prose; over the greatest prose works of art produced in the nineteenth century. Her origins in pastoral should not be forgotten. The pastoral critique of urban ways is built into Russian literature at its very foundation.

The city is not only loud, gregarious, and corrupt; the specific quality of its corruption consists of a false rationality, based on the ego, the rationality of Economic Man and cost accounting, bourgeois rationality. The city is the place where careers are made and where military and police power are organized. Life is based on hard calculation, yet fundamentally it is irrational, divorced from the traditional, moral rationality of rural life. Those who try to bring to the world of the city the Edenic dream of the Russian countryside are defeated, disillusioned, and crushed as Pushkin's Evgenii was crushed by the monster within their own minds.

Oblomov cannot bring Oblomovka to St. Petersburg; in the upper reaches of the bureaucratic hierarchy, Kalinovich grows corrupt for all his good intentions; Raskol'nikov, standing on a bridge over the waters of the Neva which are the waters of death, feels encroaching upon him the depressing melancholy of the beautiful, artificial city that has replaced the idyll of his childhood; with the energy and thought he has amassed in the country, Prince Andrei plays out to the point of disillusion the brilliant game of his career under Speransky;

finally, in Biely's great hoax of a novel, *Peterburg*, the statue of the horseman pours itself in molten bronze down the throat of a double agent. The metropolitan city, symbol of power and civilization, paradigm of the intellectualized ego, the autonomous and alienated individual, paradoxically destroys the self that it asserts, breaks down the walls of individuality, undermines the authenticity of the individual, and drives him either to defeat, suicide, and destruction, or (literally or metaphorically) back to the Russian countryside, where, Antaeus-like, he may take fresh strength from the earth for a new beginning.

The Russian pastoral is not without its counterparts in Western Europe. There is a sense in which, for example, Flaubert's *Un coeur simple* might be considered a Russian novel. The pastoral critique of civil society is hardly limited to Russia! Even European sociology, let alone the novel, participated in this critique, as witness Engels' *Origins of the Family, etc.,* F. Toennies' *Gemeinschaft und Gesellschaft* and a number of other works. It is largely a question of emphasis and degree. The pastoral element is much stronger in Russian literature.

Unlike the American, the Russian literary landscape is essentially human. It is inhabited, settled, and its settlements have a close identity with the land itself, reaching far back into time. It is not "wild nature" from which man is alienated and to which he longs to return to be made whole. It is the landscape of poor villages, of Holy Russia.[12] When self-knowledge, self-fulfillment, self-revelation come to people in the European or the American novel, they come outside the scope of community, outside society, either in confrontation with wild nature, or with or against some other separate individual or individuals, in the teeth of a hostile society. In the Russian novel self-knowledge may come while separate from society, as to Prince Andrei under the sky at Austerlitz or to Ivan Il'ich on his deathbed, but self-fulfillment is always conceived in communal terms; in terms of the creation of a spontaneous human community, the model for which is the family, living in some kind of close connection with the landscape and the seasons. Even when family life (and life in the countryside, too) is depicted as horrible or terrifying—as it often is—the horror is seen against the implicit norm. I think this is true of even so seemingly "detached" a story as Chekhov's "Peasants." In Dostoevsky, the ruin of the family as an institution means that its relationships must be recreated among all men— "All men are brothers," as in the late parable of Tolstoy.

Throughout Russian literature of the classic period runs an opposing set of images, two chains of association. On the one hand: the city, the state bureaucracy, calculated self-interest, power, self-aggrandizement, ratiocination, stagnant air, stifling rooms, artificiality, high society, rank, social prestige, aggression, vanity, self-will, intellectual pride. On the other hand: fresh air, trees, earth, water, the seasons, the "folk," family, tradition, kinship, community, a love for created beings, poetry, the acceptance of suffering, and the free and spontaneous play of the emotions.[13] Individual autonomy and integrity are seen to consist of detaching oneself from the first chain of associations and attaching oneself to the second. The poeticized family is potentially extendable to all of Russia, or even all humanity. Without this poetic potentiality the family remains the realm of *poshlost';* without the familial strain, there can be no real poetry.

The realm least suitable for the private muse is the state, the chanceries of the state bureaucracy. Here men outwardly conform but are inwardly alone. The state is the opposite of the family, and hostile to it. It is the realm of ratiocination and self-will, illusion and death. Insofar as state figures appear in a sympathetic light (and there are few who do) they carry with them into the unfavorable atmosphere of the chanceries something of the Christian acceptingness of Platon Karataev, something at once priestlike, sacrificial, and familial, and rather foreign to the style of the world they inhabit. I refer primarily to Kutuzov in *War and Peace* and Porfiry Petrovich in *Crime and Punishment.* Kutuzov is almost a complete counter part of Karataev, and is reviled and mocked by those around him. Porfiry is respected, but has nevertheless about him something monkish and awkward. His relation with Raskol'nikov goes beyond the official and assumes something of the paternal. Above all, he keeps his role a modest and a secondary one, in spite of temptations to self-assertion.

In *War and Peace*, the opposition between state and family appears most starkly, most articulately and extensively. Curiously, the novel was conceived and written over a decade (1857–67) during which the power-state seemed to be demonstrating in the most drastic and spectacular manner that it was the determining historical force of the era. I refer not only to the cult of Napoleon in France, but to Bismarck and Cavour, the American Civil War, the Second Reform Act in England, the independence of Canada, the creation of the Hapsburg dual monarchy, and last but far from least, the whole complex of Russian legislative reforms that followed from the Emancipation of the serfs. To crown this decade, Tolstoy wrote a book that attempted to demonstrate the utter futility and illusoriness of acts of state and the intentions of statesmen. In the clearest, most commonsensical prose, Tolstoy tells us that history is unknowable.

History is unknowable, not because God chooses to obscure the functions of great men and state institutions, but because neither great men nor state institutions have anything to do with the course of events. God expresses himself not in affairs of state, with their difficulties, complications, and technicalities, but in the most ordinary, familiar, and commonplace events and patterns of everyday life. God's expression is by no means obscure—merely vast and far-reaching in space and time, orchestrated with such extraordinary nuances that no man can hope to understand it in its totality, though its fragments are the most ordinary yet most marvelous stuff of which our lives are made. What the discursive passages do for the narrative passages in *War and Peace* therefore is indirectly to imbue them with the force and magic of destiny. They show, as Hegel said it was the task of philosophy to show: "Here is the rose; dance here."

With its emphasis on community, the family, nature, acceptance of the world as God created it, yet with continually fresh and renewed responses,

Russian prose literature could be characterized by its comprehensiveness of form and spontaneity of style. Common colloquial speech is always the standard referred to and played upon, even by such baroque stylists as Gogol and Leskov. As Eric Auerbach has put it, the Russian novel on the whole represents a world view that is essentially Christian in its sense of creatural realism—that magic sense of the miraculous and the eternal about to burst into epiphany in the most ordinary and everyday circumstances: shepherds tending their flocks, or the birth of a child; the fateful junction of the divine with the commonplace—and hence all the more impressive for seeming, when it became known in Europe late in the nineteenth century, a little archaic, a little behind the times.[14]

If the didactic, civilization-affirming, power-sponsored muse of Empire tends to disappear as an important concern and inspiring presence in Russian literature, she bobs up again in a curious and unexpected place: in literary criticism. Of course, the politically radical critics, from Belinsky to Mikhailovsky, opposed the state-order, and in more cases than not were as "populist" in their attitude to the peasant and the village commune as the writers. Their hopes, however, were more rationalist, more affirmative of science and civilization and even of "civil society," though not of the particular form of civil society they perceived in Russia. They were less overtly religious in their outlook, though not in their tone or temper. For them, from Belinsky on, literature was primarily an occasion, an opportunity to speak out on what really mattered, which was not literature but morality. Moralizing critics in the century of Taine and Arnold, Sainte-Beuve and Ruskin, were plentiful elsewhere, too. Belinsky and his heirs were certainly not the only critics to tell writers how they should go about their business or who, like Belinsky in his letter to Gogol, bullied and threatened them with moral excommunication. But in Russia such critics had a special claim on the conscience of both public and writers. In the struggle against the repressive aspects of autocracy, the critics occupied a far more exposed and dangerous position, and they wielded the power of their impending martyrdom with a holy, self-righteous, and zealous flair. Of course, the radical critics were essentially partisan, and the great writers only incidentally and peripherally so. Both, however, addressed themselves to the *narod*— the vital audience they felt themselves in the process of creating out of the Russian reading public. It was Belinsky who first announced that Russian literature had created the possibilities for human self-awareness for free and meaningful and honest and spontaneous human intercourse that power politics in Russia had failed to create, that the private muse had created a nation, or was on its way to creating a nation where the Imperial muse had failed. The fact that literature was a tiny island of privileged freedom, where the values of individual autonomy, spontaneous and honest expression, and the sincere pursuit of a meaningful morality could enjoy a haven amidst the icy blasts of autocracy, the critics insisted, imposed a kind of *littérature oblige,* which writers found extremely difficult to resist, especially within themselves. The critics turned Oblomov into Oblomovism, superfluous men into *the* superfluous man,

Yaroslavna and Tatiana and Natasha and Grushenka into *the* strong woman, Bazarov into nihilism, and the writers protested, sometimes vigorously, but in some corner of their souls they capitulated, as even Gogol, I suspect, capitulated to Belinsky. In his youth, Tolstoy ridiculed Chernyshevsky and the critics of the *Contemporary* who tried to lionize him. In his sixties, the guilt-ridden nobleman wróte a long, brilliant essay on art that went far beyond Chernyshevsky in the extent to which it insisted on lacing art into a moral-utilitarian strait jacket. Art was community—a work was art to the degree it could "infect" others, could communicate the expression of a common experience; but it was "good" art only to the extent that it was moral, and it could hardly be moral, as some had it, "in spite of itself"; the artist's intentions must be clear as well as beneficent, and the moral folk tale became the standard for all written art. Not only Shakespeare and the earlier Tolstoy were tried and found wanting by this standard but even large parts of the Bible. Not long after Tolstoy finished *What is Art?* he began the task of clearing the Bible of its "priestly" excrescences, clearing away its obscurities so that "the people" could for the first time understand it in its "true," i.e. purely moral, sense.

By 1897, the year in which *What is Art?* appeared, Pushkin's two muses had inspired a long, complex, and extraordinarily brilliant development. The Imperial muse had left the court for the thick journals, and the private muse seemed affected and cliquish and showed circles of fashionable European weariness under the eyes. One could hardly imagine them sitting on a bench in the same garden. . . .

## Apocalypse

"All great art," writes Boris Pasternak in *Doctor Zhivago*, "resembles and continues the Revelation of St. John."[15]

St. John of Patmos wrote the Revelation in the second century, when Christian apocalyptic expectations were beginning to fade. The end had not come. In order to stave off disillusion and desiccation of the faith, John translated Christian expectations into a *symbolic* quest for the meaning of the end whenever it might come. In a prolonged and intense meditation on death, he dredged up Christian and pagan symbols, red and green dragons, beasts from the abyss, trumpets and seals, arranged them into the patterns of an esoteric number-symbolism, hoping to replace the expectation that certain events would take place in the external world with the notion that the expectation was its own meaning and bore a sign from God, though the actual "when" and "how" of the events might be a dark matter indeed. I think, at least, that this is what "St. Boris" had in mind: that literature is "a meditation on death in the hope of overcoming death."[16]

Most Russian writers, like the intelligentsia of which they were a part, opposed the Bolshevik revolution. A number, however, tried to come to terms with it, tried to see it in the perspective of a broader vision in which the specifically Bolshevik and Marxist features were assimilated to Russian destiny or to an unknown but dimly perceived human and cultural revolution which was not necessarily the revolution the Bolsheviks carried through, but of which the Bolshevik revolution might be the historic agency. There is something of this in Eurasianism, in the Scythian movement, in the Living Church, in Blok's *The Twelve*, Pilniak's *Naked Year*, and many years later in *Doctor Zhivago*. One of the most eloquent and elegant discussions of the apocalyptic cultural revolution occurs in the "Correspondence Between Two Corners," between M. O. Gershenzon and Viacheslav Ivanov in the summer of 1920.[17]

Both Ivanov and Gershenzon see as "the authentic vessel of reality" the individual. Both believe in some form of personal immortality, though both insist that the "immortal part" has nothing to do with what is conventionally known as "the self," which is a merely contingent social mask, a persona. Both try to find some relationship between culture and the "new rebellion that is shaking the earth . . . striving to free itself from age-old complications, from the monstrous fetters of social and abstract ideas. . . ." Ivanov affirms cultural continuity, "Memory, mother of the muses," insisting that a revolution which attempts to abolish inherited cultural forms and start anew will produce not something new but merely a deformed and monstrous version of the old. What prevents cultural forms from becoming stifling and deadening is the ever-present possibility of vertical transcendence, the individual's access to the godhead. His argument resembles at points that of T. S. Eliot in "Tradition and the Individual Talent," where Eliot argues that any tradition "to be inherited, must be made new"; freshness comes from the continuity of culture, not from its disruption.

Gershenzon starts from a personal experience of spiritual weariness and exhaustion. He feels trammeled by the enormous cultural apparatus he carries with him, trapped by the tyranny of logic, ensnared by hollow metaphysical systems. "For me," he writes, "there is prospect of happiness in a Lethean bath that would wash away the memory of all religious and philosophical systems; all scientific knowledge, arts, and poetry could be washed away from the soul without a trace; and then, to re-emerge on the shore, naked as the first man, naked, light, and joyful, stretching freely and lifting to the sky my naked arms, recalling from the past only one thing—how burdensome and stifling were those clothes, how light and free one is without them." Ivanov accuses him of Rousseauistic primitivism; he replies that, like Rousseau, he wants to unburden himself of a dead culture in the hope of being able to create a living one. What Ivanov fails to grasp, he argues, is that the "vertical transcendence" Ivanov relies on as an escape from culture is itself inhibited and actually debilitated and defeated by the desiccation of the religious forms through which, presumably, this transcendence takes place—religious forms which suffer the same creeping death as culture in general.

The further course of the revolution did little to nourish the hopes of either man. It is curious that Gershenzon, who wished to throw off the burden of the past, was a historian by profession; and Ivanov, who defended cultural continuity, had previously played an important role in bringing the cult of Nietzsche (with its anti-historicism) to Russia, and was best known as a difficult, experimental *avant-garde* poet.

In 1918, Alexander Blok urged the Russian intelligentsia to "listen to the music of the Revolution," which he interpreted as an elemental upsurge from the depths of the people and which he, like Gershenzon, hoped would re-energize a "weary, stale, and bookish literature." The revolution, like a storm, teemed with "the new and unexpected." The intelligentsia, unlike the bourgeoisie, was hindered by no worldly chattels or vested interests from affirming this new and unknown force. Blok urged it to "tune in" on the Revolution.

Three years later he struck a somewhat different note. Speaking on the anniversary of Pushkin's death and not long before his own death, Blok denounced those who were trying to harness the poet to tasks that were external to poetry. The poet's role, he insisted, was not to "instruct his brethren" but to bring rhythms from "primal chaos" and embody them in language. Those who tried to make out of the institutions of the state "one organ alone, the censorship," had been called by Pushkin "the high-society mob," Blok said. Then he went on, and he was no longer speaking of Pushkin: "Let them beware of a worse epithet, those officials who are trying to direct poetry into channels of their own, infringing on her inner freedom and preventing her from fulfilling her mysterious calling." The aims of art could not be known, and to attempt to interfere with the poet's "fancy" (*prikhot'*), his imagination, his *private* freedom, was worse than censorship.[18]

Gershenzon and Ivanov had been entirely private figures. Blok was a very influential poet but still essentially a private man. The literary concern that the apocalyptic mood seemed to foster was shared, however, by so prominent a public figure as Trotsky. In a book published three years after Blok's death, *Literature and Revolution*, Trotsky anticipated the official position on literature of the Central Committee of the Party, a position that would hold from 1925 to 1930, and the predominance of RAPP.

It is a remarkable book, brilliantly written, witty, self-assured (perhaps too much so), full of insights any literary critic or social historian might well envy. Deriding the notion that a socialist revolution should strive to produce a proletarian art, it seems antidoctrinaire. Proletarian art Trotsky views as an interesting and instructive but relatively weak sister beside older traditions. He sees the production of a great culture and a great art as the purpose of history, the purpose and hope of the October Revolution. Ultimately, he says, every society will be judged by the culture it creates. "Communist man . . . will develop all the vital elements of contemporary art to the highest point. . . . The forms of life will become dynamically dramatic. The average human type will rise to the heights of an Aristotle, a Goethe, or a Marx. And above this ridge new peaks will rise." One may criticize this as Marxism, but its messianic splendor is genuine and clear.

There were some more ominous notes. Although Trotsky mentions casually in passing that Freud and psychoanalysis might ultimately be reconcilable with Marxism, it is the party that "will have to look into it," and it is the party that will decide. Throughout, he celebrates consciousness at the expense of "blind, elemental forces," at the expense of the unconscious. He sees progress in history not in terms of the achievement of harmony between the conscious and unconscious in man, but rather in terms of the conquest of the unconscious, step by step, by reason and the will; he seeks not coexistence with the unconscious but total domination, the triumph of the will, a *fully* conscious and completely transparent art. If such a thing can be imagined, it is difficult to see how it would differ from socialist realism, or why it should. "The art of this epoch will be entirely under the influence of the revolution," he says. It requires "a new self-consciousness" and is incompatible with obscurity of any kind, mystical or romantic; "collective man must become sole master, and the limits of his power are determined only by his knowledge of natural forces and his capacity to use them."

What Trotsky most wholeheartedly admires in art belongs either to the past or the future, especially the latter. Of the present he is extremely skeptical. Many of his critical remarks on his contemporaries are shrewd and true, yet behind them lurks the assumption that the true poets of the time are the Bolsheviks, poets in revolution rather than verse, but much more creative than the literary variety and far more to be admired. A society must, according to Trotsky, ultimately be judged by the art it produces, yet society itself is the ultimate art form. The Bolsheviks are better poets than the poets, and the function of the latter must therefore be subordinate, a secondary one, "to haul away the rubbish and police the streets," as Blok would have put it. Trotsky's artistic insights and his own poetic flair went far beyond that of any "culture commissar" who was to succeed him; yet even he found little room for any conception of creative freedom that ran counter to his own.

## The Conspiracy of Feelings

Andrei Babichev, "the great sausage-maker," mutters over the sleeping figure of his foster son Volodia, the absolute technocrat and true man of the future. "If everyone were a technician, wickedness, vanity and other petty feelings would disappear. . . ." Kavalerov, whom Andrei has tossed out, has taken refuge with Andrei's brother, Ivan, and hears him talk in turn of "shaking the heart of a burned-out era." Ivan Babichev wants to muster "the representatives of what you call the old world. I mean feelings like jealousy, love for a woman, vanity. I want to find a blockhead so I can show you: look, comrades, here's an instance of that human state called stupidity. . . . To me has fallen the honor of conducting the last parade of the ancient human passions. . . ."

These are passages from Olesha's great forlorn novella of the twenties, *Envy*, the story of the futile and absurd "conspiracy of feelings" against the gleaming, entwining, sterile, collectively euphoric utopia that is leaping up about and around Kavalerov and Ivan Babichev, and against which they have no chance.

The sausage-maker is obviously right. He has everything but language on his side. Kavalerov and Ivan Babichev have nothing but language: wonderful, spinning, burning, gleaming words, out of which they make a secret weapon of malice and revenge—"Ophelia." But even Ophelia turns against them in the end and they lapse into indifference. The reader, however, is indifferent only to the other pair, for it remains painfully clear that the shining Volodia is nobody anyone would ever like to be.

So it was with the other great revolutionary writers of this time; with Mayakovsky and Babel', and even the grand old man, Gorky. They wanted wholeheartedly to affirm the revolution and the wholly rational world the revolution seemed to promise. They tried to kill the Kavalerov and the Ivan Babichev in themselves. It wasn't easy.

Mayakovsky didn't want to foster his private feelings, which were anyway, like his ego, "too big for him." He wanted to "turn himself inside out," make himself "all mouth." Not only did he write placards and posters and advertisements; he wanted to make poetry itself into a placard and a poster for the new world in which the torture of privacy would become definitely outmoded. He not only wanted to abolish those domestic parlors where stale, trite thoughts sat like lackeys on overstuffed couches; he wanted to abolish the privacy that had produced these monsters. The idea of poetry on a pedestal tormented him. Forgetting what happened to indiscreet poets who addressed monuments, he asked Pushkin to come off his pedestal but did not really know how to entertain the stone guest. He made his life into a public spectacle. The primping and pampering and rococo posturing of the Bayans and the Elsevera Renaissances of this world fascinated and revolted him. He did not want to be like that. He wanted above all to be ordinary, to be human, to be part of everyone else. His apotheosis to Lenin was based on the consideration that Lenin was "the most ordinary man." He wanted poetry to be a social, sociable task. "My job's like any other," he told his imaginary tax collector. Even his suicide note turned into a poem and began with self-mocking irony: "She loves me? She loves me not?" Identifying with Prisypkin-Skripkin, he wanted to eliminate this bedbug-self and turn into mankind. Yet in the end it was the future that became unreal, a never-never land of cold, sterile chrome and glass against which echoed a human bedbug's genuine cry of pain.

Gorky belonged to an older generation, but in his work too the conspiracy of feelings mustered arms against a self-willed and self-imposed utopianism. As Erik Erikson has pointed out, Gorky's autobiography is an account of how he liberated himself from that great-souled temptress, his grandmother, whose universal compassion and acceptance of her own suffering were so much in the tradition of the Russian heroine.[19] She was beautiful and attractive; but she accepted all the brutalities of her environment and seemed to call on him to accept them, too. It was not to be accepted, but overcome. Later, Tolstoy assumed for Gorky when he thought back on him the guise his grandmother had assumed in *Childhood*. From both he had learned beauty; both urged upon him a passivity he wanted to break. Gorky could not stomach the doctrine of

Christian acceptance, yet whenever he is not thinking about it, he slips naturally into an attitude of passive receptivity, alert but unassertive.

For Gorky, liberation came through book learning, and book learning so strenuously acquired that it almost *had* to seem useful to justify itself. Book learning that merely accentuated or deepened or framed suffering, or added to the bewilderment, could be a terrible and pathetic thing, as with Lyuba in *Foma Gordeev*. Gorky drew back instinctively from an aesthetic view of literature. If he could not *do* anything for people, he wanted to be able to inspire them to do something for themselves. At the turn of the century, when almost all important literature was a literature of despair, he tried to sound optimistic. Chekhov accused him of being "literary" and highfalutin. It was true, and he tried to become simpler; but the one thing he really could not stand was the notion he might be useless. Once during his youth when he had suspected this might be the case, he had tried to kill himself. Gorky regarded this as shameful, and mentions it only in passing in his autobiography.[20] Yet of all his literary creations the only ones that live and have resonance in the imagination are the "useless" ones, who suffer and are defeated by suffering and who struggle to be able to accept life as it is rather than to make life good. The grandmother, all those magnificent tormented women in *Foma Gordeev*, that other tormented woman, the Volga, Piotr Artamanov, or that surface-cold but deeply introspective *intelligent*, Klim Samgin, who in pursuit of an authentic personality finds himself unable to make a deep commitment to any of the significant historical movements of his time and whose failure to find integrity and autonomy is expressed in a nightmare in which he sees himself split into a wild number of disparate personalities.[21]

They did not approve of such characters, these writers. But as Olesha identified himself with Kavalerov, Mayakovsky with Prisypkin, so Gorky, too, identified himself with Klim Samgin and was unable to finish the long, fascinating "chronicle" of which Klim was the central figure. The case of Isaac Babel' is somewhat different.

In his masterpiece, *Red Cavalry*, Babel', or rather his narrator, has a threefold range of identities. First, the Jews of the Pale in their long-suffering and helpless pathos. Both sides in the war ride roughshod over them. It is to root out such human misery that the bespectacled narrator has joined the Cheka and the Red Cavalry. The Jews are his people; he feels a tender irony for them, but steels himself against solicitude. Their pathetic helplessness is almost more than he can bear. The starry-eyed, bookish idealism of Gedali, the rag-and-bone man who longs for an "international of good people" speaks to him, but he must guard against the Gedali within himself. To break the subtle bonds of passive suffering the narrator has committed himself to the present international with all its violence and imperfections.

His second identification is incomplete, but he strives to perfect it. He wants to make himself like the men of power and courage who are fighting the revolution, the Cossacks and the Red commanders. They are crude, savage, violent; but they are doing what needs to be done, and in an epic manner.

The narrator tries to make himself as they are, against the intellectual he still is. He tries to be violent and savage in a situation in which violence is more merciful than mercy.

There is yet a third identification. "The wise and beautiful life of Pan Apolek went to my head like an old wine," the narrator writes. Pan Apolek, the drunken artist of the Novograd-Volynsk churches, who sees the poor miserable sinners of these Polish towns and villages as eternal archetypes of good and evil and in his paintings and frescoes creates a powerful and disturbing relationship between the living inhabitants and the long dead of the Bible. He paints people as they are, with recognizable and living features, yet at the same time as archetypes. A local Jewish whore is seen as Mary Magdalene. In the Novograd church, his miraculous virgins break out in sexual sweat at the sight of the men of Savitsky's squadron. Pan Robacki assures the narrator that Pan Apolek will come to no good end. Surely, the Church—or *some* Church—will have him inquisitioned for heresy. Meanwhile, he is Apollo himself, and all that is left of the life of these poor towns is in his pictures.[22]

## The Sausage-Maker Capitulates

The sausage-maker had his wish and the reign of Volodia, the man of steel, settled on the land. Everyone became a technician. First, the production and publication of literature were organized; then, by means of socialist realism literature was inwardly organized. The private muse, like Pasternak's Larissa, became a number and disappeared in one of the innumerable "mixed or women's concentration camps in the far north." Love could be made only to tractors. The emblems, the signs, the symbols, the metaphors, the referents of love, and of nature, too, culled from the classics, combed "systematically" out of old songs and folklore, proverbs, expressions that had soaked in the air around the peasant's stove—vernalized, Lysenkoized, rendered purely emblematic—were worked into poetry and prose and produced on a mass basis. All the muses wore a solemn mustache, at which it was death to laugh.

"The growing strength of the positive hero," writes Abram Tertz, "is shown not only in his incredible multiplication—he has far surpassed other kinds of literary character in quantity, put them into the shade and sometimes replaced them altogether. . . . He . . . becomes more and more persuaded of his own dignity, especially when he compares himself to contemporary Western man and realizes his immeasurable superiority. 'But our Soviet man has left them far behind. He is close to the peak while they are still wandering in the foothills'—this is the way simple peasants talk in our novels."[23]

Then Stalin died, "Ah," wrote Tertz, "if only we had been intelligent enough to surround his death with miracles! We could have announced on the radio that he did not die but had risen to Heaven, from which he continued to watch us, in silence, no words emerging from beneath the mystic mustache. His relics would have cured men struck by paralysis or possessed by demons. And children, before going to bed, would have kneeled by the window and addressed their prayers to the cold and shining stars of the Celestial Kremlin."

The undermining had actually set in before Stalin died. Perhaps the first "new" writer was the inobtrusive, unspectacular, but quietly private Vera Panova. Controls remained; but after 1956, conviction drained from them. There was unease and bad conscience in the party hierarchy, before the popular disquiet on the one hand, and the disquiet of its own intellectual children on the other. The children were eager to break away from the stereotyped pseudo-culture of their fathers. Lierature seemed to offer once again the warmth of a true community, and in spite of many and frequent setbacks, everything seemed to conspire to increase its range.

Even the Sino-Soviet conflict helps loosen the literary bonds. Attacked in August, 1964, in the Chinese press, Voznesensky, Evtushenko, and Akhmadulina were defended in *Izvestia* in the same terms they had used themselves the previous spring against their present defenders.[24] Kochetov, praised by the Chinese as the one genuinely revolutionary writer in Russia, thereupon shook hands with Dudintsev and invited him to contribute his new novel to *Oktiabr'* rather than *Novy mir*.

From Pomerantsev's famous article in December, 1953, to Tvardovsky's recent editorials in *Novy mir*, the persistent concern with sincerity, honesty, authenticity in literature has set up as its all too vulnerable targets the *lakiro-vanie* (varnishing) and *retushirovanie* (retouching) of Stalinist rhetoric. Indeed, Georg Lukacs to the contrary notwithstanding, there is little left of socialist realism but its title. There are many bad books, as everywhere; but one does not judge the course or nature of a literature by them.

It is one thing to demolish a rhetoric, another to create a new literary language or even to revive an old one. Suddenly, the few grand old men (and one woman) who had survived the Stalin era emerged from obscurity. Voznesensky brought his poems to Pasternak at Peredelkino. Vinokurov visited Zabolotsky. Akhmadulina gave Akhmatova an absolutely symbolic "lift" in her *Pobeda*. Memoirs began to appear.

"History," Ilia Ehrenburg writes in *People, Years, Life,* "is full of gorges and abysses, and men have need of bridges, however fragile, to link one epoch with another." In spite of the great bulk of these memoirs, which he is still writing, Ehrenburg's style is terse and dramatic. He has obviously made some effort to pare away the fatty clichés he had cynically learned to manipulate over the years. He is talking, now, to the younger generation. In large measure, the memoirs are an apologia. "Many of my contemporaries have found themselves under the wheels of time. I have survived—not because I was stronger or more far-seeing, but because there are times when the fate of a man is not like a game of chess dependent on skill, but like a lottery." This is almost too modest. Throughout the memoirs, Ehrenburg attempts subtly to extricate himself from any close knowledge of or participation in what went on in the high places. It comes as a surprise to most of his readers that, as he notes in a recent installment, he never saw Stalin till late in his life, and then only at some distance. Extricating himself from the Kremlin *collective*, Ehrenburg takes great pains and makes vivid prose to identify himself with the *community* of art. Suddenly it means something positive to be a cosmopolitan. Ehrenburg's memoirs are peopled with exotic, fabulous figures, the denizens of the Cafe Rotonde and the lost Russian writers of three decades. Art as a way of life is, in places, marvelously dramatized. This may perhaps be an instance of an audience—those intense young men in the turtleneck sweaters, the shy, eager girls with the knit brows—creating a writer. Certainly the memoirs contain the best prose Ehrenburg has written.

Paustovsky's memoirs are different. They come in two sets. One is called *A Story About Life*. The other, *The Golden Rose*, might easily bear the subtitle, "A Story About Art." The first contains hardly a single famous person except the author. It is full of sights, sounds, smells, colors, tones, remembered with a precision of detail and a power of evocation that is truly astonishing, from the Ukrainian farm of his childhood to his life as a streetcar conductor in Moscow. It consists perhaps too exclusively of minutely wrought and knitted together sensual details. The second seems more spontaneous and more varied, containing notes on books, on the craft of writing, as well as reminiscences of writers, and the places and the very particular and peculiar landscapes and environments associated with particular writers—Odessa with Babel', Tarusa with Bunin and Blok and Prishvin. Paustovsky is also building bridges. "The grandsons do not understand," he writes, "and do not want to understand the poverty wept over in songs, adorned with legends and fairy tales, with the eyes of timid mute children, and with the lowered eyelashes of girls, and agitated by the tales of wanderers and cripples, by the constant feeling of an unbearable mystery living alongside one in the forests, in the lakes, in rotten logs, and in boarded-up peasants' houses, and the always present sense of a miracle. 'I slumber and behind my slumber is a mystery, and in the mystery you sleep, Russia.' "[25]

Even Evtushenko, when he was only thirty, felt compelled to write (he was later reprimanded) what he rightly called *A Precocious Autobiography*. It was written abroad and never published in the Soviet Union. Much of it is hasty, carelessly put together; much of it is hollow, and there is some false posturing. His "imaginary audience" is with him in places, though, and there are passages that have the ring of authentic statement. He is not so much concerned, like Ehrenburg and Paustovsky, with the gap between generations (on the contrary, he makes himself at home, though not altogether at ease, with the language, the poses, the attitudes, of writers as diverse as Mayakovsky, Pasternak, Hemingway) as with what he calls "that most dreadful menace in the history of any people—a split between their external and their inner lives."

In the first long poem that made him famous, "Winter Junction" (later, he wrote a sequel, "Again at Winter Junction," and he has made numerous references both to the poem and to the trip), Evtushenko described an Antaeus-like return to his Siberian home, where the strength of an integral family tradition of nonconformity and stubborn idealism refreshed his confidence that had suffered such a staggering blow from the first awareness of the "split" mentioned in the Autobiography. Evtushenko is lyrically most at home in the presence of someone of an older generation, preferably someone who isn't famous. His best poems are about old women and an old man. The sense of encroaching death, the pain and pathos of fading away, the sense of pain of personal loss make poems like "Our Mothers Are Leaving Us" (an emotion all but impossible to convey in English, in spite of the excellence and authenticity of the Russian original) and "The Windows Look Out on the Trees" (which Evtushenko reads aloud with such simple and astonishing drama) among the best now written. His father, with whom, one gathers, his relations are sometimes touchy, comes alive in a casually and incidentally inserted anecdote in the Autobiography, in which, as Evtushenko tells it, he and his father are refused admittance to a Moscow restaurant one evening for not wearing neckties, and his father tells him how at his age he was thrown out of the university because he wore a tie.

Evtushenko denounces the "lyrical hero" of Stalinist days. He wants to be his own lyrical hero, the "I" of his poems to be his own "I" "Even the simple words, 'I love' were sometimes spoken in so abstract, so oratorical a voice that they might have been 'we love.'" Yet in his attempt to speak for himself, to speak for his friends the young writers, to speak for the Jews, to speak for Cuba, and for Hemingway, to speak for communism, he defeats his own integrity. It is possible, as Pushkin did, to invoke the Imperial as well as the private muse. It is possible, like Mayakovsky and Gorky, to feel torn between them. But one cannot pretend they are one and remain the poet Evtushenko wants to be. Evtushenko is the prime victim of what, in a brilliantly perceptive article, Vera Dunham has called "spokesmanship."[26] A hollow, bragging sound slips into the "I." Without wishing to belittle the courage or the generosity that went into the famous poem "Babi Yar" one has only to compare it with Auden's "The Diaspora" to see at once how affected it is, how short of its subject. And if the following modest disclaimer did not sound just a little bit false there would be something pathetic in it: "My poetry is only the expression of moods and ideas already present in Soviet society but which had not so far been expressed in verse. Had I not been there, someone else would have expressed them."

The new Soviet literature has been much underrated in this country. It is fresh and vigorous, if not altogether new. Akhmadulina's long poem "The Rain" has a marvelous frisky animism; I know of nothing fresher, more alert, more personal. Voznesensky's poems range from the gay satire of "Fire in the Architectural" through the wistful nostalgia of "Moonlit Nerl" to the somber, dark-syllabled play of "I Am Goya." Kazakov writes little, but his short stories are among the best anywhere of the past ten years. True, he is not as good as Chekhov or Bunin, whom he resembles, but neither is anyone else. Nagibin and Aksionov are uneven, but vital and interesting. Nevertheless, for all the awakened interest in the private muse, in style and honesty, in the exploration of personal relations, private moods, in the problematics of everyday life, in the nuances of personal psychology, something is deeply lacking.

Here is a passage from a proletarian novel of the RAPP period around 1930, Libedinsky's *Birth of a Hero*. The central figure, a Bolshevik, finds himself torn between his assistant, a formalistic bureaucrat, and his wife, whose narrow domestic concerns have their counterpart in his own soul. ". . . a quiet new meat grinder glistening in the corner, and her comfortable worn slippers under the bed. And he looked upon all this, which had before been so sweet to him, as a new manifestation of the old enemy, as the elemental repetition of immemorial and hateful forms of life. He had fought with them all his life, all his life he had exposed them, tearing the hypocritical masks from them; and now he had even discovered them inside himself."[27]

Not great literature, certainly; but it has a certain dignity, an impressive thematic weight. Here is a parallel passage from a recent novel, Granin's *After the Wedding*. True, the household items are seen from the point of view of the bride, but she is meant to be altogether sympathetic. " 'All this is ours, mine. My window sill, my window. I'll wash it myself, and I'll seal it with paper, and between the frames I'll put heather. . . .' From work, she ran straight to the department store. . . . Tonia could look at the dinner sets for hours, price the vases, turn the meat grinders. She hadn't suspected there were so many wonderful things in the world and they were all absolutely necessary. Mentally, she decorated her room with them, disposed them about her kitchen. The number of things that were necessary depressed her. There was no chance of acquiring all this, even in the next few months. She railed at herself for her greediness, called herself a *meshchanka*, a bourgeois housewife; she and Igor didn't really need a thing. And she was really quite happy in their empty, unfinished room. She even exulted in her contempt for all 'trappings.' Yet when she dropped into the store, surrounded by things that flashed their newness, she forgot about everything, roused by the desire to possess all these pretty things. Not for herself—for the home. She was ready to deny herself food and clothes, to economize on everything. The enticement was too great; she could not restrain herself, and every single time, she bought some petty item. These unforeseen acquisitions ruined all her accounts and plans, but in return she experienced incomparable pleasure walking home along the streets with her heaps of parcels and most important, when she got home, unloading all this noisily on the table. 'Guess what I bought!' "[28]

The second passage is pleasant and humorous, if a little long. It hints at greater if less passionate complexities than the first, affirms domesticity, and is gay about privacy. But it has a touch of soap opera. It has a touch of *poshlost'*. One is tempted to ask: "So what?" It lacks dignity. It is bourgeois.

The very best stories and poems have been written about children, about love affairs, about old people, social outcasts, *otshchepentsy*, about nature. These are the themes that are furthest removed from the compromising rhetoric of Stalinism, and at the same time closest to the tradition of the private muse.

They concern present experience as opposed to the corrosive joy of the Happy Future, which is, however, a difficult monster to exclude.

But something is missing. Something is being avoided. It is not just the false genuflections to the Imperial muse, not just the incapacity to woo her with real flair. Even in the realm of privacy and private feelings, the ultimate concerns are being avoided, the strenuous attempt to break through beyond privacy into the world of Molly Bloom's night thoughts, some major effort to come to grips with, to discover, whether man is after all "the sum of his social relations" as Marx in one of his more extreme moments said, or whether, past all the entanglements, there is indeed something there that is more.

## St. Boris

"A voice from the grave," Isaac Deutscher called Pasternak's *Doctor Zhivago*.[29] Superstitious, he seems afraid to listen.

True, the novel reaches back into the past. Pasternak invokes Pushkin's private muse, the family theme, the traditional association of poetry-family-landscape, the Tolstoyan sense of the freshness of ordinary things, seen as though for the first time, as over and against abstract ideas and metaphysical systems which blear in retrospect. He invokes Chekhov's self-effacing inwardness. As in many of his poems, he attempts to build into the novel itself discussions, hints, suggestions of his *ars poetica*. He uses not only the tradition of the private muse but the creatural realism of the New Testament, in which the sense of miraculous destiny is transferred from the realm of enormous and public events like the plagues of Egypt or the opening of the Red Sea to the ordinary, the private, and the everyday—the vigil of shepherds, or the birth of a child. He refers to Flemish paintings of the nativity, in which the creatures of nature group themselves around a crib and the darkness organizes itself around the light.

As to its thrust into the future, it is still a difficult book for anyone to come to terms with. I believe that Edmund Wilson's allegorical exegesis, though valuable in many of its details, has done the book scant service, for what we need most to take in hand are not the book's (on the whole not very formidable) obscurities of reference but our own feelings about its major themes.

I have noticed that my very best students when they write about *Zhivago* tend to write badly; they become sentimental, vague and lax, and feel unduly called upon to make some great but amorphous gesture of affirmation. If great books create their own audiences, one can say that *Zhivago* has not yet created the one it needs. It has been treated not as a novel or a poem (and it is both) but as a moral treatise or an early Christian commentary, which in some sense at least it really does resemble. In the Soviet Union it will remain unpublished even with the forthcoming Collected Works of Pasternak. Yet is is unmistakably, uncomfortably, ineluctably *there*. Pasternak regarded it not only as the climax, but as the summing up of his entire poetic career, and as a Summa, a gloss, a commentary, a clarification of all his previous work in poetry and prose.

There is no mind, inside or outside the Soviet Union, at all concerned with Russian literature in a serious way, within which this bear does not cast a great shadow.

The Christian symbolism that runs throughout the book strikes me as token of a poet's Christianity, a poet so strong and sure in his sensibility that the religion seems rightly to derive from the poetry, not the other way round, yet without sacrilege. Uncle Nikolai Vedeniapin tells us that the meaning of Christianity consists on the one hand of "the mystery of the individual," and on the other of "the idea of life as sacrifice." Around these two seemingly contradictory but actually dialectical notions, the novel is built. The central figure, who bears the name of life itself, is a poet; in the course of the novel his life is used up and exhausted by his poetry, which, after his death, organizes a human community around itself in much the way Belinsky once described Russian literature as organizing a genuine Russian community based on freedom and a fresh conception of life. The novel is about the life of the poet, his personal death, and his resurrection in the species.

"The novel gives no real picture of the country or the people," the editors of *Novy mir*, rejecting *Zhivago*, wrote to Pasternak. "Nor consequently does it explain why revolution became inevitable in Russia. . . . Theoretically speaking, it would be hard to imagine a novel in which the scene was set to a large extent in 1917 that would not, in one way or another, give definitive appraisal of the difference between the February and the October revolutions."[30] Indeed, there is barely any mention of the most important historical events in Russia between 1917 and 1921; the Civil War is seen from the point of view of a minor backwater in Siberia, and the NEP summed up by Zhivago's heart attack in a stalled trolley. Deutscher joins the editors of *Novy mir* in emphasizing Pasternak's lack of concern for the major events and major issues of the time.

It is not, however, Pasternak who is unconcerned, but Zhivago who *makes* himself "unconcerned" at enormous effort and paying a great price—his family, his friends, his career, much of his own more active quality as a human being. During a partisan battle in the Siberian forest, he pities both sides and concentrates his attention on the tree of life. All the important events of his life are internal events. They are affected—indeed, the arena is prepared—by time and place and circumstances, yet they are in touch with a larger cosmic order in the grip of which time, place, and circumstances are also seen to play. "Art," writes Camus, "teaches us that man cannot be explained by history alone and that he also finds a reason for his existence in the order of nature."[31] On that reason, Zhivago concentrates. He is first and foremost a poet, and it is as a poet that he maintains his integrity. Late in the novel, he bewails his earlier commitment to the Revolution, not because he feels he did anything wrong (it would be difficult to discover that he did anything political at all) but because he has come to realize that such a commitment *if made inwardly* precludes, or at least infects, all others.

The book is not meant to justify an ivory-tower attitude or indifference to human beings who do, after all, take part in history; but rather to exalt intensity of purpose, the "safe-conduct" of destiny, the role of poet, a moral burden of the kind that Zhivago's "Hamlet" assumes in the first poem of his cycle—especially when "the time is out of joint" or "a play not to the taste" is actually on the boards. The poet must be an individual, not like those dominated by the "herd-instinct" (*stadnost'*) no matter whether the group they flock to bears the banner "of Kant or Soloviev or Marx." It is by the quality of his perceptions, not by what he does, that the inner Zhivago is made known to us.

Zhivago is extremely sensitive to light, which he sees in the whiteness of it; that is, not in the political significance of "white" but in the sense of wholeness, that which contains within itself the possibility of all colors. He is an expert medical diagnostician and an authority on sight. The way in which Zhivago "sees the light" characterizes him. He notices Lara's candle shining from behind a frozen window as he passes by on a Moscow street. "Consciousness," he says, "is like a locomotive headlight. Turned outward it lights up the track for miles; directed inwardly, it blinds." He is not, therefore, introspective, *self-conscious*, but, if one may switch metaphors, in *tune*, alert to the world around him. In contrast, Strel'nikov (who on occasion suggests the lonely pathos of Mayakovsky) is all self-consciousness. On his wedding night, the light he is most acutely and uncomfortably aware of is the street light shining *in*. He always feels the streets observing him instead of observing the streets. The quality of his sight is defined by the color "red"—only partly intended in its political sense, much more so as the color of blood, the color confronted when straining to stare at the world through closed eyelids.

Zhivago's perceptions are always his own and his opinions are related to his perceptions. Throughout the book there is a constant denigration of groupiness and "playing at people." Social relations are not altogether ignored, but downgraded, seen as somewhat incidental and secondary, if often mysterious and interesting and compelling. "National" or "folk" character is also seen as an interesting side effect, something already receding into the background. Lara, for all her associations with Mother Russia, has a Greek name and is of Belgian extraction. Evgraf has "narrow Kirghiz eyes." Russians, Jews, Europeans, and Orientals mingle among and amidst and within each other. Social position and material affluence are unimportant to Zhivago and most of his friends, nor do such matters seem to have much to do with which side of the revolutionary struggle the characters choose. Zhivago is certainly not a bourgeois individualist like Komarovsky; he is, indeed, starkly contrasted with him. Komarovsky's individuality depends on his property, on the things he owns and the routine he establishes around them: his apartment, landlady, friends, his English bulldog. Although he is moved by Lara, he cannot accommodate her into his routine, for she, classless and without property, will not be made into a fetish. Zhivago, on the contrary, sees her as life itself: "You cannot communicate directly with life, but she was its representative." He lives with her in a kind of perpetual present, devoid of routine, where there is neither time nor money. But it is Komarovsky who comes out on the right side of the revolution.

As a doctor, Zhivago resembles Chekhov in his modest urge to be useful. Chekhov also figures in Pasternak's *ars poetica*, along with Pushkin, as the unassuming kind of writer—unlike Dostoevsky or Tolstoy who thundered big panaceas at the world—minding his own business, and almost as if by accident, so to speak, allowing the world to discover that his business was also everybody's business: the artist who maintains the integrity of his sensibility in the face of loud moral imperatives. T. S. Eliot's mysterious remark about Henry James, that he had "a mind so fine, no idea could violate it," seems much more aptly applied to Chekhov or Pushkin or Zhivago.[32] In his work as a doctor, Zhivago displays the same qualities that he displays as a poet: perceptiveness, skill at diagnosis, imaginative contact with the world of organic nature. He has no sweeping theories and makes no grandiose self-assertions.

He is also a husband and a family man, not a very good one as it turns out. At first, Zhivago affirms the traditional Russian identification of poetry with domestic life: "This was what art aimed at—homecoming, return to one's family, to oneself, to true existence." And Zhivago often thinks, in connection with his family, of Nikolai's observation that "Christ speaks in parables taken from life, that He explains the truth in terms of everyday reality." Under the stress of cataclysmic events, however, as "the landscape assumed the form of modern art," distaccato, fragmented, wrenched awry from its normal positioning, poetry loses its old connection with the family and has to fall back on a more intimate relationship with life itself.

If Zhivago has, therefore, no unmitigated commitment to private property, the family, or the state, wherein (since, as the editors of *Novy mir* rightly point out, Pasternak's tone of irritation is unmistakable) lies his quarrel with Marxism?

In spite of the irritation, neither Zhivago's nor Pasternak's quarrel with Marxism implies a complete or absolute rejection. The first objection is that Marxism claims too much for itself. It is not a science, and in advancing the claim to be one, it tramples whatever may be left of a disinterested regard for the truth. Secondly, in exalting human consciousness and will not only above all else but literally without limits, it destroys man's connection with the source of his own energies. " 'Transformation of life' . . . can only be talked of by people who don't know life. . . . In them, existence is a lump of coarse material which has not been ennobled by their touch and which requires fashioning. But life has never been a material, a substance. . . . It is constantly refashioning and realizing itself and it is far beyond our boneheaded theories about it." Thirdly, Marxism is life-denying by its enormous emphasis on the future, which ends to displace a sense of the importance of experience in the present. "A man is born to live, not to prepare to live. And life as such—the phenomenon of life—the gift of life—is so thrilling and serious! Why then substitute for this a puerile farce of adolescent contrivances, these Chekhovian children's flights to America?" (The reference is to a story by Chekhov in which children, beguiled by the gadgetry of America, decide to run off there but get no further than the next town.) This seems to be the full extent of Pasternak's quarrel with Marxism.

Zhivago's individualism, then, is mainly a certain power of resistance to the grand encroachments of his time, his capacity to be himself under all circumstances, not to be violated by ideas, no matter how tempting, to keep his consciousness and his sensibility intact. It is not self-aggrandizement. At the highest point of his life, when he is living with Lara at Varykino and writing his best poems, the closest to Eden he ever comes, it is as though not he himself is writing but rather "the force of poetry in his time." This richly rewarding, almost selfless piety towards life also has, eventually, its price. It makes him perhaps too passive and yielding to circumstances, and in the end Zhivago deteriorates unnecessarily rapidly, to live again only in his poems.

Pasternak's novel sits like a great beast in the center of the new period of Soviet liberalization. The editors of *Novy mir* made no bones about rejecting it on ideological, not on aesthetic, grounds. Actually, their discussion of these ideological grounds, which was entirely serious and which included numerous quotations from the book (later published) revealed also a colossal aesthetic and philosophical misunderstanding of the book, a misunderstanding by no means based on lack of generosity but rather on the blighting principles of socialist realism, which, though no writer follows them, are the only official criticism there is. It is curious and striking that today, when asked why *Zhivago* has not been published, official Russians, if they are also clever, fall back on the diversion that it was "a bad novel." During the last year of his life, Pasternak exercised, and he still exercises, an overwhelming influence, both personal and poetic, on all the younger Soviet poets with any talent at all. "People," Evtushenko writes, "react to Pasternak not as to a man but as to a color, a smell, or a sound." He is a force. With that force Soviet literature will yet have to reckon.

## NOTES

1. Louis Simpson, "Confessions of an American Poet," *New York Times Magazine*, May 2, 1965, p. 110.

2. Friedrich Nietzsche, "Twilight of the Idols," trans. W. Kaufman, *The Viking Portable Nietzsche* (New York: Viking Press, 1954), p. 530.

3. Carl G. Jung, *Modern Man in Search of a Soul* (New York: Harvest Books, 1955), p. 169.

4. John Bayley, *The Romantic Survival* (London: Constable, 1957).

5. Peter Demetz, *Marx, Engels und die Dichter* (Stuttgart: Deutsche Verlags-Anstalt, 1959).

6. Friedrich Engels, *The Origins of the Family, Private Property and the State* (New York: New World Paperback, 1964), p. 161.

7. Norman O. Brown, *Life Against Death* (Middletown: Vintage Books, 1959); Herbert Marcuse, *Eros and Civilization* (Boston: Beacon Press, 1955).

8. Viktor Shklovsky, *Zametki o proze russkikh klassikov* (Moscow, 1955), pp. 47–53.

9. It would seem evident, as Shklovsky suggests, that Pushkin, consciously or unconsciously, invested his real feelings about the Imperial order—which had at least a touch of restless, threatening, frustrated rebelliousness—not in the utterly conventional and merely convenient narrator but in the much more interesting "villain" of the piece, the turncoat nobleman, Shvabrin.

10. Abram Tertz, *On Socialist Realism* (New York: Pantheon Books, 1960).

11. G. P. Fedotov, "Pushkin, pevets Imperii i svobody," in *Novyi grad* (New York, 1952).

12. On "Holy Russia," see Michael Cherniavsky, *Tsar and People* (New Haven: Yale University Press, 1960), pp. 101–27.

13. See the highly suggestive article by George Gibian, "Traditional Symbolism in *Crime and Punishment*," *PMLA*, LXX (1955), 979–96.

14. Erich Auerbach, *Mimesis* (Princeton: Princeton University Press, 1953), pp. 520–24.

15. This line began to reverberate in my mind and memory after I heard N. O. Brown one evening take off from it into a possible chapter of his forthcoming book. Of course, his use of the line was very different from my own.

16. For an interesting recent interpretation of the Book of Revelation, see Austin M. Farrer, *A Rebirth of Images: The Making of St. John's Apocalypse* (London: Dacre Press, 1949); see also D. H. Lawrence, *Apocalypse* (New York: Viking Press, 1932).

17. M. O. Gershenzon and V. Ivanov, *Perepiska iz dvukh uglov* (Petrograd, 1921); English translation, "A Correspondence Between Two Corners," *Partisan Review*, XV (1948), pp. 951–65, 1028–48.

18. The two pieces referred to may be found in Alexander Blok, *Sobranie Sochinenii* (Moscow-Leningrad, 1960–62), Vol. VI.

19. Erik Erikson, *Childhood and Society* (New York: Norton, 1963), pp. 359–402.

20. For a luminous understanding of this episode in Gorky's life, see Helen Muchnic, *From Gorky to Pasternak* (New York: Random House, 1961), pp. 79–90.

21. For an interesting interpretation of *Klim Samgin*, which (outside the Soviet Union) is generally regarded as the most elephantine of Gorky's white elephants, see Juergen Ruehle, *Literatur und Revolution* (Cologne: Kiepenheuer & Witsch, 1960), pp. 38–44; this book also contains chapters on the Chinese left-wing writers and those of other Asian countries.

22. If not Apollo, at least Orpheus, through whom Apollo spoke.

23. Abram Tertz, *op. cit.*, pp. 53–54.

24. M. Mikhailov, "Moskovskoe leto," *Novoe russkoe slovo*, March 27, 1965; in somewhat the same manner, I suppose, the visiting American businessman finds himself defending, when in Moscow, abstract art.

25. Quoted from *Pages from Tarusa*, ed. Andrew Field (Boston: Little, Brown, 1964), p. 361.

26. Vera S. Dunham, "Poems about Poems," *Slavic Review*, XXIV (1965), 57–76.

27. Quoted from Edward J. Brown, "The Year of Acquiescence," in *Literature and Revolution in Soviet Russia*, ed. Max Hayward and Leopold Labedz (London and New York: Oxford University Press, 1963), p. 54.

28. Daniil Granin, *Posle svad'by* (Moscow-Leningrad, 1964), p. 8.

29. Isaac Deutscher, "Pasternak and the Calendar of the Revolution," *Partisan Review*, XXVI (1959), 248–65; see also the reply by Irving Howe in the same issue.

30. The letter is translated in full in Robert Conquest, *The Pasternak Affair* (Philadelphia: Lippincott, 1962), pp. 139–63.

31. Albert Camus, *The Rebel* (New York: Vintage Books, 1958), p. 276.

32. And yet, it cannot be denied that, through Zhivago, Pasternak commits himself to "spokesmanship" of a kind.